Southern Black Leaders of the Reconstruction Era

BLACKS IN THE NEW WORLD: *August Meier, Series Editor*

(A list of books in the series appears at the end of this book.)

Southern Black Leaders
of the Reconstruction Era

Edited by Howard N. Rabinowitz

UNIVERSITY OF ILLINOIS PRESS
Urbana   Chicago   London

For my parents, Abe and Gertrude Rabinowitz, with love

LIBRARY OF CONGRESS CATALOGING IN PUBLICATION DATA

Main entry under title:

Southern Black leaders of the Reconstruction era.

(Blacks in the New World)
Includes bibliographical references and index.
1. Afro-American leadership—Southern States—History—19th
century—Addresses, essays, lectures. 2. Afro-Americans—Southern
States—History—19th century—Addresses, essays, lectures. 3.
Afro–Americans—Southern States—Biography—Addresses, essays,
lectures. 4. Reconstruction—Addresses, essays, lectures. 5. Southern
States—History—1865–1877—Addresses, essays, lectures. 6. Southern
States—Race relations—Addresses, essays, lectures. 7. Southern
States—Race relations—Addresses, essays, lectures. I. Rabinowitz, Howard
N., 1942–   . II. Series.
E185.92.S68   975'.0049607330922 [B]   81-11372
ISBN 0-252-00929-0 (cloth)   AACR2
ISBN 0-252-00972-X (paper)

Acknowledgments

It has been a delight to work with the excellent people at University of Illinois Press. Two of them have played an especially important role in the publication of this book. I therefore want to thank Richard L. Wentworth for his early and continued confidence in this project and Rita P. Zelewsky for the careful attention she gave the manuscript and the illustrations. I also want to thank August Meier and Peter Kolchin for their valuable comments on earlier versions of the introduction and chapter 10.

John Hope Franklin's contribution goes well beyond his own essay. His remarks in seminar fifteen years ago about the need to study black leaders at the local level served as the inspiration for my work on Holland Thompson out of which this anthology grew. Among his fellow contributors in this volume are four of his University of Chicago students—Loren Schweninger, Eric Anderson, Carl Moneyhon, and myself. As a scholar, teacher, and friend, he has enriched all our lives. Yet our debt is merely part of a much larger one all scholars in the fields of southern and black history owe this remarkable human being.

Thanks of a different kind go to my parents, my children—Lori and Deborah—and, especially, to Vesta. Together they helped make this past year the most gratifying and happiest in my life.

Howard N. Rabinowitz
Albuquerque, New Mexico
November 1981

Contents

INTRODUCTION: THE CHANGING IMAGE OF BLACK RECONSTRUCTIONISTS
  Howard N. Rabinowitz   xv

PART I: CONGRESSMEN

  1. BLANCHE K. BRUCE OF MISSISSIPPI: CONSERVATIVE
     ASSIMILATIONIST
       William C. Harris   3

  2. JOHN ROY LYNCH: REPUBLICAN STALWART FROM MISSISSIPPI
       John Hope Franklin   39

  3. RACE AND FACTION IN THE PUBLIC CAREER OF FLORIDA'S JOSIAH
     T. WALLS
       Peter D. Klingman   59

  4. JAMES T. RAPIER OF ALABAMA AND THE NOBLE CAUSE OF
     RECONSTRUCTION
       Loren Schweninger   79

  5. JAMES O'HARA OF NORTH CAROLINA: BLACK LEADERSHIP AND
     LOCAL GOVERNMENT
       Eric Anderson   101

PART II: COLLECTIVE BIOGRAPHY OF STATE AND LOCAL LEADERS

  6. NEGRO DELEGATES TO THE STATE CONSTITUTIONAL
     CONVENTIONS OF 1867–69
       Richard L. Hume   129

  7. THE ORIGINS OF NEGRO LEADERSHIP IN NEW ORLEANS DURING
     RECONSTRUCTION
       David C. Rankin   155

  8. RICHMOND'S BLACK COUNCILMEN, 1871–96
       Michael B. Chesson   191

9. NEGRO STATE LEGISLATORS IN SOUTH CAROLINA DURING
   RECONSTRUCTION
        Thomas C. Holt   223

PART III: INDIVIDUAL STATE AND LOCAL LEADERS

10. HOLLAND THOMPSON AND BLACK POLITICAL PARTICIPATION
    IN MONTGOMERY, ALABAMA
         Howard N. Rabinowitz   249

11. AARON A. BRADLEY: VOICE OF BLACK LABOR IN THE GEORGIA
    LOWCOUNTRY
         Joseph P. Reidy   281

12. WILLIAM FINCH OF ATLANTA: THE BLACK POLITICIAN AS CIVIC
    LEADER
         James M. Russell and Jerry Thornbery   309

13. DR. BENJAMIN A. BOSEMAN, JR.: CHARLESTON'S BLACK
    PHYSICIAN-POLITICIAN
         William C. Hine   335

14. GEORGE T. RUBY AND THE POLITICS OF EXPEDIENCY IN TEXAS
         Carl H. Moneyhon   363

AFTERWORD: NEW PERSPECTIVES ON THE NATURE OF BLACK POLITICAL
     LEADERSHIP DURING RECONSTRUCTION
         August Meier   393

THE CONTRIBUTORS   407

INDEX   411

Illustrations

Blanche K. Bruce   *5*

John Roy Lynch   *41*

Josiah T. Walls   *61*

James T. Rapier   *83*

James O'Hara   *105*

Alabama Constitutional Convention, 1867   *131*

Louisiana Officeholders, 1868   *159*

John P. Mitchell, Jr.   *195*

South Carolina Republican Legislators, 1868   *227*

First Colored Baptist Church   *251*

Electioneering at the South   *283*

William Finch—Advertisement, *Atlanta
City Directory*, 1892   *311*

Atlanta University   *320*

Dr. Benjamin A. Boseman, Jr.   *337*

George T. Ruby   *365*

Howard N. Rabinowitz

Introduction: The Changing Image of Black Reconstructionists

Between 1870 and 1901 the southern states sent twenty-two Negroes to Congress.[1] Countless other blacks served as state legislators, city councilmen, and other officials throughout the South, especially during Reconstruction. Even during the height of Reconstruction, however, no black was elected governor or mayor of a major city, and only in South Carolina did blacks constitute a majority in a state constitutional convention or legislative chamber. Nevertheless, the backgrounds, qualifications, and performance of Negro officeholders figure prominently in any assessment of Reconstruction; and conclusions about their ability have varied with changes in our understanding of Reconstruction in general. Not only does the study of southern blacks during the late nineteenth century have relevance for our understanding of Reconstruction and its aftermath, it also helps provide perspective for an appreciation of the nature of black political leadership throughout American history.

It is not surprising that the treatment of black officeholders has in most respects followed the changing perceptions of Reconstruction. Contemporaries and subsequent chroniclers critical of Reconstruction have had little positive to say about black leaders; those more sympathetic toward the goals and achievements of Reconstruction have been more favorable. Yet, until recently, black political leadership during this period has been treated only incidentally.

The negative image of Reconstruction still shared by most Americans today is largely the product of work done by Columbia University professor William Archibald Dunning and his students at the beginning of this century. Criticism of Reconstruction as corruption-ridden, divisive, and dominated by carpetbaggers, traitorous scalawags, and illiterate blacks, however, was already common in a number of accounts that were published during and soon after Reconstruction. These works appeared in the midst of rampant popular racism and longing to reunite the country; and, in each of them, black leadership was either condemned outright as venal and inexperienced or dismissed as under the total control of unprincipled whites.

Southern authors naturally led the way. In a popular textbook, for example, Woodrow Wilson, then a Princeton political scientist, drew heavily on James S. Pike's *The Prostrate State: South Carolina under Negro Government* and the essays on individual states in Hilary A. Herbert's *Why the Solid South?* Wilson concluded that during Reconstruction "Unscrupulous adventurers appeared, to act as the leaders of the inexperienced blacks in taking possession first of the conventions, and afterwards of the state governments; and in the States where the negroes were most numerous or their leaders most shrewd and unprincipled, an extraordinary carnival of public crime set in under the forms of law. Negro majorities gained complete control of state governments, or rather, negroes constituted the legislative majorities and submitted to the unrestrained authority of small and masterful groups of white men whom the instinct of plunder had drawn from the North."[2]

Northerners as well, distressed by the alleged abuses of Reconstruction, drew similar conclusions about black leaders. James Ford Rhodes, an Ohio businessman and influential historian, revealed his own belief in Negro racial inferiority by his use of Pike's phrases, such as *dregs of the population*, to describe black leaders. Although he acknowledged the presence of a handful of qualified black leaders, he concluded that most blacks were uneducated, without property, had achieved nothing of value, and were easily manipulated by whites.[3] To John W. Burgess, a political scientist at Columbia University, who shared Rhodes's racism and belief that Reconstruction had undermined the good the Civil War had achieved, black leaders were "trifling and corrupt politicians" brought to power by universal Negro suffrage, one of the " 'blunder-crimes' of the century."[4]

But it was the northerner Dunning and his students, most of whom were southerners, who provided the scholarly apparatus that seemed to raise Reconstruction history above the level of mere emotion and partisanship. In a series of doctoral dissertations, Dunning's students examined Reconstruction in individual states, and Dunning himself produced a synthesis based on his own research and that of his students. These books, which are commonly lumped together as part of the Dunning School or Dunningite interpretation of Reconstruction, shared an overall condemnation of Reconstruction; but they vary greatly in tone, emphasis, and objectivity.

Nowhere are these differences as great as in their treatment of black leaders. In the works by Mildred C. Thompson (Georgia), Charles William Ramsdell (Texas), and J. G. De Roulhac Hamilton (North Carolina), for example, comparatively little attention was given to black leaders.[5] Walter L. Fleming, however, went to great length to criticize the performance of Alabama's black leaders. Fleming's was the least objective and perhaps most racist of all the Dunning studies, though it did devote more space to blacks and especially to the role of local black leaders and their organizational activities. Typical of Fleming's approach was the unsupported claim that at the Constitutional Convention of 1868 "two [Negro] delegates could write a word, and the others had been taught to sign their names and that was all."[6]

Thomas S. Staples (Arkansas) and James W. Garner (Mississippi), on the other hand, offered relatively balanced assessments of black leadership, as befits their status as the most balanced of all Dunningite studies in general. Though critical of the overall quality of black leaders, Garner, for example, frequently used *alleged* to soften charges of widespread incompetence and corruption and, more than any other Dunning student, included references to intelligent and able blacks. After cataloging the unpreparedness of most blacks in Mississippi's first Reconstruction legislature, for example, he added, "There were, on the other hand, some very intelligent negroes in the legislature, this being particularly true of the ministers of the gospel, of whom there were about one dozen in the lower house." And in introducing Speaker of the House John R. Lynch, he observed that "It is not to be supposed, however, that all the colored speakers were men of ignorance and incompetency." Paying what was for the typical Dunningite the highest compliment, Garner found Lynch "distinctly caucasian in his habits" as well as conservative in his views.[7]

Burgess and Rhodes had used the earliest products of the Dunning School to supplement their heavy reliance on Pike and Herbert; but the complete work of Dunning and his students was given a much broader popular audience in 1929 with the publication of Claude G. Bowers's *The Tragic Era*, which has gone through numerous editions and is still in print. Bowers generally selected the most condemnatory sections of Dunningite works, ignoring most of the qualifications present in even the least balanced studies. For him blacks were lazy, ignorant, childlike, and controlled by carpetbaggers and scalawags, who preached hate and distrust of the former Confederates. The Mississippi legislature was "one of the most grotesque bodies that ever assembled. A mulatto was Speaker of the House, a darker man was Lieutenant-Governor, the negro Bruce had been sent to the Senate, a corrupt guardian was in charge of the public schools, a black, more fool than knave, was Commissioner of Immigration."[8]

A less strident approach was taken in the first full-length treatment of black political leaders, Samuel Denny Smith's *The Negro in Congress 1870–1901*. Smith was a grandstudent of Dunning, for this book began as a dissertation under Hamilton, who wrote the foreword. Smith, like most Dunning disciples, with the notable exception of Fleming, at least professed to be writing objective history, but it is clear that he shared the racism of his predecessors. After offering the first systematic, if often inaccurate, biographical profile of any segment of Negro leadership, Smith concluded that by education, previous political experience, and wealth, the black congressmen were "rather well-equipped for their job"; but of seemingly more importance to Smith is the fact that "most of them had considerable white blood in their veins and were frequently aided by white friends." In general he found that "the Negroes failed to accomplish much worthwhile in Congress"; and while quoting contemporary assessments pro and con, he clearly emphasized negative evaluations that charged incompetence, manipulation by white bosses, dishonesty, and demagoguery. Nevertheless, the congressmen were as a whole "superior to those of their race who, with unfortunate results, took a contemporary part in local, county and state government."[9]

The Dunningite view of Reconstruction, especially of the quality and role of black leaders, did not go unchallenged during these early years. Examples of what might be termed the Rehabilitation School were already present during the teens and twenties. There were occasional full-length accounts by self-interested parties, such as Reconstruction leader John R. Lynch or Maud Cuney Hare, the daughter of Texas black politician Norris Wright Cuney. More common were the articles about black leaders published by black scholars and laymen in the *Journal of Negro History,* the organ of the Association for the Study of Negro Life and History founded in 1915.

Consistent with the fledgling association's desire to encourage a more "scientific" appraisal of the Negro's place in history while also promoting the race's interests, the *Journal* authors sought to demonstrate that black leaders were more able and worthy of remembrance than critics of Reconstruction had acknowledged. Thus, in 1920, Monroe Work provided the names and backgrounds of selected local, state, and national Negro officeholders for scholars interested in exploring the positive aspects of Reconstruction. As in most subsequent accounts of Reconstruction leaders, Work's compilation dealt most extensively with South Carolina and challenged the biased Dunningite monograph by John S. Reynolds.

Two years later Alrutheus Ambush Taylor evaluated the Negroes who served in Congress between 1871 and 1901, along with those whom he believed had "good title" to office but were not seated. He concluded that, in terms of intelligence, capacity for public service, and chief interests, they had performed admirably and deserved to sit in Congress. The only reason they failed to accomplish more was because they were "the object of the suspicion of their party colleagues." Shortly afterward, David G. Houston examined the career of one of these congressmen, Mississippi senator Blanche K. Bruce. He concluded that Bruce's career "looms up as a monument to the American Negro's self-confidence, resolution, and persistency," and that Bruce himself deserves "a prominent place among the progressive and constructive statesmen of this country."

During the twenties Taylor also wrote monographs on Reconstruction in South Carolina and Virginia with the support of the Association for the Study of Negro Life and History. As in his article on congressmen, Taylor separated his evaluation of black officeholders from the study of Reconstruction per se because, he argued, that period's alleged abuses were the fault of whites rather than blacks, for "At no time in the history of South Carolina or any other State did the Negroes control the government altogether." Because black influence was most marginal in Virginia, Taylor devoted little space to black political leadership, but, almost as an afterthought, he observed that "Those Negroes who attained office, . . . were generally persons of intelligence or common sense and they gave a good account of themselves." In South Carolina, however, black leaders were accorded a central place, especially in a lengthy chapter assigned to "The Reconstructionists and Their Measures." Though Taylor appreciated the unpreparedness for office of "some few" blacks, he concluded that "Most of the leaders of the Negroes in politics were men of fair education and some were exceptionally well trained," and that they "labored for the progress of the State" with good results.[10]

Other favorable assessments of black leaders by blacks continued into the following decade. These were climaxed by W. E. B. Du Bois's *Black Reconstruction*, the first full-length revisionist analysis of the period. Though critical of black leaders for a lack of clarity in their economic thought—for being plagued by petty bourgeois ideas—and conscious of the many ignorant or unqualified officials, Du Bois emphasized the positive qualities of black leaders, particularly those in South Carolina and New Orleans. Typically, Du Bois, who based his study on secondary sources, used the Dunningite works; but he chose to emphasize the positive rather than negative material on Reconstruction and black leaders.[11]

By the 1940s and 1950s the rehabilitation of black leaders found expression in *Phylon, Negro History Bulletin*, other racially oriented journals, and additional monographs. But by then, though rehabilitation was still the prime aim, nonblacks and professional historians were discovering the virtues of some, if not all, black leaders.[12] The new trend had its roots in the 1930s. In 1932 Francis Butler Simkins and Robert Hilliard Woody published their revisionist account of Reconstruction in South Carolina. Though marred by a condescending tone and racial stereotyping, Simkins and Woody presented the most favorable assessment of Reconstruction yet published by white scholars. They did not treat Negro leadership systematically, but presented profiles of major leaders that emphasized competence and intelligence.[13]

The following year Woody published a study of Jonathan Jasper Wright, the black associate justice of the South Carolina supreme court. Another landmark effort, it was a dispassionate, scholarly account in which Wright is portrayed as competent, a moderate in politics, and a compromiser who wanted to attract experienced men to the Republican party regardless of race. He was respected even by Democratic opponents, and his judicial career "evidenced considerable ability." Woody did not explicitly present his essay as a challenge to earlier criticism of the quality of Negro leadership, but the intent was clear.[14]

The same was true of a study of P. B. S. Pinchback of Louisiana written almost ten years later by a white M.A. candidate. Even though Alice Grosz was less fond of her subject than Woody was of his and shared some of the traditional views of Pinchback, she concluded after a solid and perceptive account that "Although shadows hang over Pinchback's career, credit must be accorded his indomitable will and courage, his ability and personal magnetism."[15]

By then if the general public was not coming to reconsider the long accepted interpretation of Reconstruction, scholars were. A period of revisionism brought forth new state studies of Reconstruction; along with a smattering of general histories, these studies portrayed the contributions and qualifications of black leaders in a more favorable light. Vernon Lane Wharton led the way with his monograph on Mississippi blacks originally published in 1947. Wharton made a greater effort than any previous author to ascertain information about state and local officeholders, especially legislators and constitutional convention delegates. Like Simkins, Woody, and a few of the Dunningites, Wharton found some of the major black leaders to be quite able; but more tellingly, he noted that "Even more remarkable than the rise of Bruce, Lynch, and others to prominent positions in the state and nation was the amazingly rapid development of efficient local leaders among the Negroes."[16]

Joel Williamson's later assessment of South Carolina black leaders, conceived and written during the height of the Civil Rights Movement, was similar. Though more critical of the integrity of black leaders in his state, Williamson echoed Wharton in concluding that, "In view of the high degree of natural ability extant among leading Republicans of both races, it is hardly surprising that the higher offices were filled with men who were quite capable of executing their responsibilities."[17]

Building on this wave of revisionist works in addition to their own research, John Hope Franklin and Kenneth Stampp fashioned syntheses which asserted that, contrary to the Dunningite view, throughout the South, blacks did not control state government, were not vindictive toward their former masters, and when elected to office usually served ably and effectively. And though acknowledging the dominance of white politicians, they claimed that blacks developed their own leaders who, in Stampp's words, "were not always the mere tools of white Republicans."[18]

Nevertheless, discussions of black leadership in these new works formed only a small, indeed minor, part of the larger story, were generally still cut from the Rehabilitation mold, and were not done systematically. Some articles devoted entirely to individual leaders did continue to appear during the 1960s. Joe M. Richardson, for example, used Florida's black secretary of state, Jonathan Gibbs, to challenge explicitly the view that during Reconstruction that state was controlled by "incompetent, illiterate, and venal Negroes." Gibbs "was a man of intelligence, integrity, and dedication and in his time, one of the outstanding men in Florida." Richardson was soon to publish a general revisionist history of the Negro in Florida during Reconstruction, and it is clear that his study of Gibbs was a by-product of his interest in the broader topic.[19]

Since 1971, however, scholars have increasingly turned directly to biography, both collective and individual, as a way of reevaluating the role of blacks in Reconstruction Era politics. There have been monographs on the black state legislators in Louisiana and South Carolina and biographies of black congressmen Robert Elliott, Robert Smalls, Josiah Walls, and James T. Rapier.[20] Numerous journal articles have also sought to uncover the origins and contributions of local politicians.[21] As a result of these efforts we now have a greater appreciation of the sources and nature of southern black leadership.

It is worth noting, however, that, while recent studies of black political history in the South for the years between the Civil War and the Great Migration have been oriented toward biography, examinations of the political experience of blacks in the North have taken a different form. There the rule has been more comprehensive studies of the entire range of black life, of which politics is only a part. Like Lawrence Grossman's recent monograph on blacks and Northern Democrats, specific discussions of blacks in politics have been less interested in individual or even groups of blacks than in general attitudes and policies.[22]

The difference in emphasis is not startling, for with a few notable exceptions like Frederick Douglass, most significant black political figures of the post–Civil War years functioned in the South. The preoccupation with leaders among southern blacks, however, is also due to a strong desire on the part of more liberal members of a new historical generation to destroy the earlier stereotype of black leaders during Reconstruction as being illiterate, dishonest, and unqualified to hold public office.[23] Such a purpose is laudatory and in its time necessary, but we need to look at black politicians for other than mere purposes of rehabilitation. If we are to truly understand the role of black politicians and in the process obtain insight into the meaning of Reconstruction, we must pay more attention to the kinds of structural questions raised by students of black politics in the postbellum North.[24]

Though the emphasis in the essays in this book varies due to the availability of evidence, each seeks to do three things: (1) to provide basic biographical details for individuals or groups of black leaders; (2) to present the stands the leaders took on major issues; and (3) to examine how blacks gained, maintained, and finally lost power—in other words, how they *functioned* in Reconstruction politics and within the Republican party. The third aim is the most crucial, for it has been largely absent from recent works on southern politicians. The key question here is the extent to which blacks were able to develop their own base independent of white support. What difference did it make in terms of their policies and eventual position in the party whether they were the creation of a white sponsor or the product of a black constituency? Of critical importance will be an understanding of the recruitment pattern of black leaders, and the relationships between them and white leaders and among themselves. Though Dunningites and Rehabilitationists have noted in passing the importance of divisions within the Republican coalition, only rarely have such divisions, particularly among blacks, been examined closely or their importance accurately weighted.[25] Without such an examination, however, neither the nature of black leadership nor the course and direction of Reconstruction can be properly grasped.

A word about chronology and the selection of topics is in order. The focus of this collection is clearly on Reconstruction, commonly defined narrowly as the period from 1867 to 1877. But to assess the significance of what happened during these years, it is also necessary to examine their aftermath. Most of the essays therefore follow their subjects through their post-Reconstruction careers; and, indeed, some of the essays are more concerned with what happened during the years commonly thought of as post-Reconstruction. I believe that this chronological approach is useful, for it provides needed perspective on Reconstruction, helps to remind us that the impact of Reconstruction varied from state to state, and shows us the diversity of black response to actions taken by whites, be they allies or opponents.

I have divided the essays into three broad categories that reflect the kinds of research now underway—selected congressmen, collective biography of state and local figures, and individual state and local leaders. I sought to be as comprehensive as possible in the choice of specific subjects; but as is often the case in such collections, selection was somewhat arbitrary. In certain instances I chose subjects because the contributor had already dealt with them in full-length works, though often from a different approach, and they might reach a larger audience if combined with complementary material. In other cases, subjects either never before treated or treated inadequately were assigned to scholars who were working in parallel areas. At the same time, however, I tried to balance the topics in order to encompass the range of Negro leadership in terms of geography, background, and accomplishments. Some topics originally planned for inclusion had to be eliminated due to the unavailability of contributors able to meet the volume's time constraints. As a result, key states, such as Mississippi, South Carolina, and Alabama, receive more attention than others; but the ten states that underwent Congressional Reconstruction are all represented. The afterword by Professor August Meier summarizes the major themes and findings, provides suggestions for future study, and places late nineteenth-century southern black political leadership within a broader framework.

The purpose of this volume, then, is twofold. It seeks to make the

xix

fruits of the recent biographical work more readily available to the general public, students, and scholars unfamiliar with it. Yet I also hope these essays, by going beyond what has already been done, will be of interest to specialists in the fields of black and Reconstruction history and will point the way for future investigations.

Notes

1. Two were U.S. senators from Mississippi: Hiram Revels, who served a partial term, and Blanche K. Bruce, who served a full term. The other twenty served the following states in the House of Representatives: South Carolina— Joseph H. Rainey, Robert De Large, Robert Brown Elliott, Richard H. Cain, Alonzo J. Ransier, Robert Smalls, Thomas E. Miller, George W. Murray; North Carolina—John A. Hyman, James E. O'Hara, Henry P. Cheatham, George H. White; Alabama—Benjamin S. Turner, James T. Rapier, Jeremiah Haralson; Virginia—John Mercer Langston; Georgia—Jefferson F. Long; Florida—Josiah T. Walls; Louisiana—Charles E. Nash; Mississippi— John R. Lynch. Black congressmen served a total of twenty-four terms between 1869 and 1879, but only fourteen between 1879 and 1901.

2. James S. Pike, *The Prostrate State: South Carolina under Negro Government* (New York: D. Appleton & Co., 1874); Hilary A. Herbert, ed., *Why the Solid South? or, Reconstruction and Its Results* (Baltimore: R. H. Woodward & Co., 1890); Woodrow Wilson, *Division and Reunion 1829-1889* (1893; rev. 1894, 1898; reprint ed., New York: Longmans, Green & Co., 1908), p. 268. Wilson was a Virginian, Pike a South Carolinian, and Herbert an Alabamian. All essays in the latter's book were by southerners.

3. James Ford Rhodes, *History of the United States from the Compromise of 1850 to the Final Restoration of Home Rule in the South in 1877,* 7 vols. (New York: Macmillan Co., 1920), 6:89–90; 7:75–76, 92–93, 104–5, 152–55, 169–72; quote, 7:153.

4. John W. Burgess, *Reconstruction and the Constitution 1866–1876* (New York: Charles Schribner's Sons, 1911), pp. 134, 244–45. See also pp. 133, 245–46.

5. Mildred C. Thompson, *Reconstruction in Georgia, Economic, Social, Political 1865–1872* (New York: Columbia University Press, 1915); Charles William Ramsdell, *Reconstruction in Texas* (New York: Columbia University Press, 1910); J. G. De Roulhac Hamilton, *Reconstruction in North Carolina* (New York: Columbia University Press, 1914).

6. Walter L. Fleming, *Civil War and Reconstruction in Alabama* (New York: Columbia University Press, 1905), pp. 556–63, 711–12, 749, 772, 776–77; quote, p. 518.

7. James W. Garner, *Reconstruction in Mississippi* (New York: Macmillan Co., 1901), pp. 269, 305–11; quotes, pp. 269–70, 295–96. See also Thomas S. Staples, *Reconstruction in Arkansas 1862–1874* (New York: Columbia University Press, 1923), pp.124, 157, 166, 168, 179, 219–20, 229–31, 335, 342–43, 373–401. Dunning himself pictured blacks as controlled by white carpetbag-

gers; and unlike Fleming, Staples, and Gardner, he never evaluated the role or impact of Negro officeholders. See William Archibald Dunning, *Reconstruction, Political and Economic 1865–1877* (New York: Harper & Brothers, 1907), p. 116.

8. Claude G. Bowers, *The Tragic Era: The Revolution after Lincoln* (Cambridge, Mass.: Houghton Mifflin Co., 1929), pp. 294–95, 414, 453–54, 203; quote, p. 448.

9. Samuel Denny Smith, *The Negro in Congress 1870–1901* (Chapel Hill: University of North Carolina Press, 1940), pp. 143–44 and passim.

10. John R. Lynch, *The Facts of Reconstruction* (New York: Neale Publishing Co., 1913); Maud Cuney Hare, *Norris Wright Cuney: A Tribune of the Black People* (New York: Crisis Publishing Co., 1913); Monroe Work, comp., "Some Negro Members of Reconstruction Conventions and Legislatures and of Congress," *Journal of Negro History* 5 (Jan. 1920):63–119; Alrutheus A. Taylor, "Negro Congressmen a Generation After," ibid., 7 (Apr. 1922): 127–71; David G. Houston, "A Negro Senator," ibid., pp. 243–56, quotes, pp. 243, 255; Alrutheus Ambush Taylor, *The Negro in the Reconstruction of Virginia* (Washington, D.C.: Association for the Study of Negro Life and History, 1926), p. 285; id., *The Negro in South Carolina during the Reconstruction* (Washington, D.C.: Association for the Study of Negro Life and History, 1924), pp. 153–85, quotes pp. 311, 310. See also A. E. Perkins, "Some Negro Officers and Legislators in Louisiana," *Journal of Negro History* 14 (Oct. 1929):523–28.

11. W. E. B. Du Bois, *Black Reconstruction: An Essay toward a History of the Part Which Black Folk Played in the Attempt to Reconstruct Democracy in America, 1860–80* (New York: Harcourt Brace, 1935), especially pp. 350–52, 402–4, 470, 490–91, 498–99, 505–7. Du Bois earlier had made some of the same arguments in "Reconstruction and Its Benefits," *American Historical Review* 15 (July 1910):781–99. See also Horace Mann Bond, *Negro Education in Alabama: A Study in Cotton and Steel* (Washington, D.C.: Associated Publishers, 1939), pp. 26–27; Mason J. Brewer, *Negro Legislators of Texas and Their Descendants: A History of the Negro in Texas Politics from Reconstruction to Disfranchisement* (Dallas: Mathis Publishing Co., 1935); A. E. Perkins, "James Henri Burch and Oscar James Dunn in Louisiana," *Journal of Negro History* 22 (July 1937):321–34.

12. See, for example, A. E. Perkins, "Oscar James Dunn," *Phylon* ([Sum.] 1943):105–21; Luther Porter Jackson, *Negro Office-Holders in Virginia 1865–1895* (Norfolk: Guide Quality Press, 1945); Alrutheus Ambush Taylor, *The Negro in Tennessee, 1865–1880* (Washington, D.C.: Associated Publishers, 1941); Herbert Aptheker, "South Carolina Negro Conventions, 1865," *Journal of Negro History* 31 (Jan. 1946):91–97; id., "Mississippi Reconstruction and the Negro Leader Charles Caldwell," *Science and Society* 11 (Fall 1947):340–71; Leonard Bernstein, "The Participation of Negro Delegates in the Constitutional Convention of 1868 in North Carolina," *Journal of Negro History* 34 (Oct. 1949):391–409; Clarence A. Bacote, "William Finch, Negro Councilman and Political Activities in Atlanta during Early Reconstruction," ibid., 40 (Jan. 1955):341–64; Nerissa Long Milton, "Know Your Congressmen [Hiram Revels]," *Negro History Bulletin* 18 (Feb. 1955):

112–13; Arthur Z. Brown, "The Participation of Negroes in the Reconstruction Legislatures of Texas," *Negro History Bulletin* 20 (Jan. 1957):87–88; Eugene Feldman, "James T. Rapier, Negro Congressman from Alabama," *Phylon* 19 (Win. 1958):417–23; Martin Abbott, "County Officers in South Carolina in 1868," *South Carolina Historical Magazine* 60 (1959):30–40; the entire issue of *Negro History Bulletin* 5 (Mar. 1942) consisted of articles about southern black leaders from Reconstruction through the early twentieth century.

13. Francis Butler Simkins and Robert Hilliard Woody, *South Carolina during Reconstruction* (Chapel Hill: University of North Carolina Press, 1932), esp. pp. 74–80, 123–33, 360–61.

14. Robert H. Woody, "Jonathan Jasper Wright, Associate Justice of the Supreme Court of South Carolina, 1870–77," *Journal of Negro History* 18 (Apr. 1933):114–31; quote, p. 121.

15. Agnes Smith Grosz, "The Political Career of Pinckney Benton Stewart Pinchback," *Louisiana Historical Quarterly* 27 (Apri. 1944):527–612; quote, p. 607.

16. Vernon Lane Wharton, *The Negro in Mississippi 1865–1890* (Chapel Hill: University of North Carolina Press, 1947), pp. 147–49, 157–80; quote, p. 164.

17. Joel Williamson, *After Slavery: The Negro in South Carolina during Reconstruction, 1861–1877* (Chapel Hill: University of North Carolina Press, 1965), pp. 376–78, 389, 393; quote, p. 378.

18. John Hope Franklin, *Reconstruction after the Civil War* (Chicago: University of Chicago Press, 1961), pp. 88–91, 103, 105, 133, 133–38; Kenneth M. Stampp, *The Era of Reconstruction 1865–1877* (New York: Alfred A. Knopf, 1965), pp. 167–69; quote, p. 168. See also Charles E. Wynes, *Race Relations in Virginia 1870–1902* (Charlottesville: University of Virginia Press, 1961); Frenise A. Logan, *The Negro in North Carolina 1876–1894* (Chapel Hill: University of North Carolina Press, 1964); Peter Kolchin, *First Freedom: The Responses of Albama's Blacks to Emancipation and Reconstruction* (Westport, Conn.: Greenwood Press, 1972).

19. Joe M. Richardson, "Jonathan C. Gibbs: Florida's Only Negro Cabinet Member," *Florida Historical Quarterly* 42 (Apr. 1964):363–68; quotes, pp. 363, 368; id., *The Negro in the Reconstruction of Florida* (Tallahassee: Florida State University Press, 1965). See also Edward F. Sweat, "Francis L. Cardoza—Profile of Integrity in Reconstruction Politics," *Journal of Negro History* 46 (Oct. 1961):217–32; Norman W. Walton, "James T. Rapier: Congressman from Alabama," ibid., 30 (Nov. 1967):6–10.

20. Charles Vincent, *Black Legislators in Louisiana during Reconstruction* (Baton Rouge: Louisiana State University Press, 1976); Thomas Holt, *Black over White: Negro Political Leadership in South Carolina during Reconstruction* (Urbana: University of Illinois Press, 1977); Peggy Lamson, *The Glorious Failure: Black Congressman Robert Brown Elliott and the Reconstruction in South Carolina* (New York: W. W. Norton & Co., 1973); Okon Edet Uya, *From Slavery to Public Service: Robert Smalls 1839–1915* (New York: Oxford University Press, 1971); Peter D. Klingman, *Josiah Walls: Florida's Black Congressman of Reconstruction* (Gainesville: University Presses of Florida,

1976); Loren Schweninger, *James T. Rapier and Reconstruction* (Chicago: University of Chicago Press, 1978).

21. Many of these are cited in the following essays, but see esp. William C. Harris, "James Lynch: Black Leader in Southern Reconstruction," *The Historian* 34 (Nov. 1971):40–61; Elizabeth Balanoff, "Negro Legislators in the North Carolina General Assembly, July, 1868–February, 1872," *North Carolina Historical Review* 49 (Jan. 1972):22–55; Edward Magdol, "Local black leaders in the South, 1867–75: An essay toward the reconstruction of Reconstruction history," *Societas* 4 (Spr. 1974):81–110; David C. Rankin, "The Origins of Black Leadership in New Orleans during Reconstruction," *Journal of Southern History* 40 (Aug. 1974):417–40; Randall B. Woods, "George T. Ruby: A Black Militant in the White Business Community," *Red River Valley Historical Review* 1 (Aut. 1974): 269–80; Walter J. Fraser, Jr., "Black Reconstructionists in Tennessee," *Tennessee Historical Quarterly* 34 (Win. 1975):362–82; Barry A. Crouch, "Self-Determination and Local Black Leaders in Texas," *Phylon* 39 (Dec. 1978):344–55. Additional articles may be found in great numbers in recent issues of *Journal of Negro History, Phylon, Negro History Bulletin*, and to a lesser extent in southern state historical journals. But see also Euline W. Brock, "Black Political Leadership during Reconstruction" (Ph.D. diss., North Texas State University, 1974); and Lawrence Chesterfield Bryant, *South Carolina Negro Legislators: A Glorious Success: State and Local Officeholders: Biographies of Negro Representatives 1868–1902* (Orangeburg, S.C.: L. C. Bryant, 1974).

22. David M. Katzman, *Before the Ghetto: Black Detroit in the Nineteenth Century* (Urbana: University of Illinois Press, 1973); David A. Gerber, *Black Ohio and the Color Line 1860–1915* (Urbana: University of Illinois Press, 1976); Kenneth L. Kusmer, *A Ghetto Takes Shape: Black Cleveland, 1870–1930* (Urbana: University of Illinois Press, 1976); Lawrence Grossman, *The Democratic Party and the Negro: Northern and National Politics, 1868–92* (Urbana: University of Illinois Press, 1976).

23. An exception is E. Merton Coulter, *Negro Legislators in Georgia during the Reconstruction Period* (Athens: Georgia Historical Quarterly, 1968). A throwback to the Dunningites, Coulter examined the lives and careers of Henry M. Turner, A. A. Bradley, and Tunis Campbell. Extremely critical of Bradley and Campbell and only less so of Turner, Coulter seems to have turned to the biographical approach to sustain the traditional negative view of Reconstruction then under massive attack. Six of the seven chapters appeared in 1964, 1967, and 1968 in the *Georgia Historical Quarterly* and are reprinted with minor changes, together with a four-page conclusion.

24. For a promising beginning to such a structural approach, see Holt, *Black over White*. For evidence that other scholars are beginning to realize the need to move from rehabilitation to functional analysis, compare Euline W. Brock's "Thomas W. Cardozo: Fallible Black Reconstruction Leader, " *Journal of Southern History* 47(May 1981):183–206, with her more laudatory "Thomas W. Cardozo: Mississippi's Black Superintendent of Education during Reconstruction" (paper delivered at the Organization of American Historians convention, Apr. 1978). It is significant that Brock's is the first article the *Journal of Southern History* has published on a southern black Reconstruc-

tionist, further illustrating the growing impact of the biographical approach.

25. However, see Holt, *Black over White,* and Howard N. Rabinowitz, *Race Relations in the Urban South 1865–1890* (New York: Oxford University Press, 1978). For an unanswered earlier call to focus on how Negroes functioned in Reconstruction, see August Meier, "Comment on John Hope Franklin's Paper," in *New Frontiers of the American Reconstruction*, ed. Harold M. Hyman (Urbana: University of Illinois Press, 1966), pp. 77–86.

I

Congressmen

William C. Harris   **1**

Blanche K. Bruce of Mississippi:
Conservative Assimilationist

Aᴄᴛᴇʀ the Civil War the lower Mississippi Valley, where a large
black population lived, became a Mecca for many young, intelligent
border-state Negroes. Some, like James Lynch, Thomas W. Stringer,
and Hiram Rhoades Revels, came to the area as missionary-teachers
from northern churches and societies to evangelize the freedmen.
Others settled in the region in anticipation of political opportunities
after passage of the Reconstruction laws of 1867 establishing black political equality. Still others, like many white carpetbaggers, combined
political ambition with a strong desire to succeed in farming or business. Blanche Kelso Bruce fitted the latter mold.

Born in 1841 and raised in slavery, Blanche Bruce's early life had
provided him with some preparation for political leadership and economic success in the postwar South. His childhood as a slave, first in
Virginia, then briefly in Mississippi, and finally in Missouri did not
significantly differ, as he later recalled, from that of the sons of whites.
This benign experience in slavery perhaps owed a great deal to the fact
that he was a light-skinned mulatto and the servant of a benevolent
master and mistress.[1] When young Bruce left the friendly environment
of the plantation, his obviously white ancestry (he was either a quadroon or an octoroon) normally protected him from the taunts and
threats of unsympathetic whites.[2]

As a boy Bruce was the playmate of his master's only son and shared
a tutor with him. But after his master moved the family to an agricultural community near the Missouri River in central Missouri in 1850,
he enjoyed few of the amenities of the planter society that he had
known in his old home in Prince Edward County, Virginia. As he grew
into adolescence during the 1850s, he could not escape the stigma, the
feelings of personal insecurity, and the racial identification attached to
the institution of slavery. Nevertheless, Bruce's chores on his master's
tobacco farm were not time-consuming for most of the year, and he
had an opportunity to pursue his interest in books and learning.[3] Bruce
also was an acute observer of the commercial life around him; and although his master was a small planter, he gained a sound knowledge of
the workings of the diverse agricultural economy along the Missouri
River.

Living near Kansas, where the bitterest scenes of the slavery controversy were then enacted, young Bruce was intensely aware of the
growing sectional division. He might have escaped to freedom, but his
cautious nature—a product of his halfway existence between slavery
and freedom—which later would be an important influence on his political behavior, prevented him from taking the risk at this time. But
when the Civil War began, Bruce almost casually fled to Lawrence,
Kansas, the center for the antislavery forces, where he proclaimed his
freedom and founded a school for black refugees from slavery.[4] After
a narrow escape from William C. Quantrill's notorious Confederate
raiders, Bruce moved in 1864 to the security of Hannibal, Missouri.
Slavery having been abolished in the state, he established there the
first school for blacks in Missouri. He also became a printer's devil in a
local newspaper office, but his insatiable thirst for reading caused him
to neglect his training, and he soon abandoned the apprenticeship.[5]

After the war, in 1866, Bruce followed a friend to Oberlin College
with the intention of studying for the ministry, a popular avenue of advancement for ambitious black youths. Lacking funds, he sawed wood
and performed other arduous chores in an effort to remain in school.
Even so, he could not make ends meet, and he returned to Missouri in
1867. He became a porter on a steamboat that plied the river between
St. Louis and Council Bluffs, Iowa.[6] Soon opportunity beckoned him
south.

The reconstruction program Congress had imposed upon the former
Confederate states in 1867 included temporary military rule, black political equality, and the protection of loyal citizens. After some hesitation, perhaps to gauge the full implications of the dramatic change in
national reconstruction policy, Bruce cast his lot with the new order in
the South. First he visited Arkansas; then he went to Memphis, the
gateway to the Yazoo-Mississippi Delta, where he met Samuel J. Ireland, another young mulatto who was seeking the main chance in the
postwar South. In Mississippi the Republican party, supported by a
twenty-thousand black majority at the polls, was in the midst of the
campaign to ratify a progressive Reconstruction constitution and also
to win control of the new government under it. Bruce and Ireland journeyed into the Mississippi lowlands to attend a black political rally and
hear an address by James Lusk Alcorn, the Republican candidate for
governor.[7]

The trip persuaded Bruce to put down his roots in the Delta. He observed that a dearth of Republican leaders existed in this overwhelmingly black area of the state. The opportunity for local political power,

Blanche K. Bruce
Library of Congress

in addition to the golden prospect of participating in a crusade to give meaning to the freedom of a large number of poor, illiterate members of his race, must have fired his imagination and given him a new purpose in life. Economic opportunity also stirred his interest in the Mississippi bottom lands. Bruce learned that because of the instability of the labor system, the uncertainty of protection from floods, and the difficulty of clearing and improving the swampy areas, land in the fertile Delta could be purchased for as little as five dollars an acre.[8] Nevertheless, with only seventy-five cents in his pocket when he entered Mississippi in 1869, he had to bide his time before establishing residence and investing in land.

Meanwhile, at the age of twenty-eight, Bruce threw himself into the political contest of 1869, speaking with other Republicans to large crowds of blacks in the Delta. A few weeks before the election, after military commander Adelbert Ames ordered the wholesale replacement of conservative officials with Republicans, Bruce received an appointment to fill a vacancy as a voter registrar in Tallahatchie County. On election day the Republicans easily won control of the state government, and in January 1870 Bruce appeared in Jackson to see the new political order installed and to seek political preferment from state Republican leaders.

As a conservative contemporary remembered him, Bruce was a man of magnificent physique, handsome countenance and possessed of the manners of a Chesterfield. He soon came to the attention of the Republican hierarchy.[9] In the politically charged atmosphere of Jackson he demonstrated to Republican leaders like Governor-elect Alcorn that he possessed a quick grasp of the intricacies of Reconstruction politics and government. When the state senate organized, Bruce, with the support of Alcorn, was selected as sergeant-at-arms over several white aspirants, although blacks held only five seats in the chamber. The state Republican newspaper reported his election as "a simple recognition of distinguished service in the cause of Republicanism, and eminent fitness for the duties of the office." The carpetbag editor of this journal hailed Bruce as "one of the most promising young men in the State."[10]

When the legislature adjourned, the scalawag Alcorn appointed Bruce tax assessor of Bolivar County in the heart of the Delta. Because this official was charged with the first assessment of property under the new policy of having land pay a large share of the taxes, the position of assessor was an important one. In the hands of a vindictive Republican, the authority of the office could be used to punish conservative planters; and since the assessor received a commission of 7 percent for his work, the job could also be a source of considerable financial gain for the overzealous operator. Unlike the assessors in several river counties, Bruce performed his duties in an honest and efficient manner. He also plunged into local Republican politics, and his amicability quickly endeared him to young carpetbagger H. T. Florey, who had begun the organization of the Republican party in Bolivar, a county with 2,084 black and 590 white voters. When the first election for local offices under the Reconstruction constitution was held in fall 1871, Bruce ran for the combined position of sheriff and tax collector; and his ticket, consisting mainly of blacks, easily defeated the Conservative opposition.[11]

A few weeks later he gained still another important office in Bolivar County. The Republican state board of education appointed him county superintendent of education, replacing an official who had left school affairs in disarray. With this position and those of sheriff and tax collector, Bruce became the political master of Bolivar County. Only a handful of Mississippi blacks served as either superintendent of education or sheriff, the most important local offices; only Bruce held both posts. His influence soon extended beyond Bolivar, resulting in his selection in 1872 as a member of the board of levee commissioners for a three-county district.[12] In all three positions he gained the confidence of all classes in the lowlands. Bruce also succeeded, at least in his home county, in harmonizing all political elements and substantially reducing white-planter opposition to the new regime. In view of the political and racial hostilities in the postwar South and the continuation of the white-dominated plantation economy in the Delta, his success in allaying local planter fears was a remarkable achievement. Planters recognized that the fair and rigidly honest Bruce was no threat to them; and according to a eulogist years later his "infectious good humor disarmed prejudice." White landowners soon concluded that his control of local politics and government could significantly advance the cause of labor stability, an elusive objective of postwar Delta planters.[13] Their confidence in the mulatto leader soared when he became a landowner himself.

Bruce's first economic venture occurred in 1872 when he assisted in the founding of Floreyville, a small river town that the Republicans immediately established as the county seat of Bolivar. A thrifty and shrewd financial manager, Bruce invested $500 of his income from his three public offices to buy six town lots and parts of three others. On one of these lots he built a home, which he would continue to occupy

7

until he took a seat in the U.S. Senate in 1875. In 1874 he purchased 640 acres of swampy but fertile land for $950 and soon developed it into a plantation.[14] He later increased his agricultural domain, and by the 1880s he was a wealthy man, although his assets were at the mercy of the fluctuating farm economy and Mississippi River overflows. Records of the plantation's operations do not exist; but it is safe to assume that cotton, the staple crop of the Delta, was produced on most of Bruce's land, and that blacks supplied the labor to produce it.

Bruce's success in disarming planter-conservative opposition to local Republican control was clearly apparent in his administration of the new school system. Republicans, including Bruce, viewed public education as the cornerstone of their reform program in the South, believing that it would ensure the success of republican government and institutions, would ultimately end racial hostilities, and would ameliorate the condition of the black masses. In 1870 Mississippi Republicans had launched their experiment in comprehensive, racially separate schools for blacks and whites. At first whites refused to cooperate in a program that they felt would squander precious tax receipts on inferior blacks and indoctrinate them in the political catechism of the Republican party. But with the actual establishment of the schools in 1871–72, opposition to the system declined dramatically; and many whites, especially in the western plantation counties, joined in the work of organization.[15]

In December 1871, Bruce assumed control of the faltering school system in Bolivar County. He soon made it a model for biracial cooperation in the formation of free public schools. He immediately calmed planter fears that the county's school system would become a radical vehicle to oppress white taxpayers and to inculcate a partisan spirit among blacks. To placate whites and gain their support for the system, he instituted a rigid economy in the administration of the schools and promised to employ as teachers "industrious and ambitious" black youths in the Negro schools, which evidently were primarily staffed with northern whites. Bruce also promoted the notion, which a few planters had already considered, that "an educated peasantry" would increase labor stability and reduce crime.[16] State Republican policy dictated that the school system should be racially segregated, an arrangement that Bruce tacitly accepted.

After having achieved some success in gaining white support for public education, Bruce called on planters to provide land and buildings for the establishment of schools in several communities "that were destitute of educational privileges." Planters not only responded generously to Bruce's requests for aid, they also—he reported—paid the school tax "more promptly and cheerfully than any other, and in many instances [they] have advanced money to pay teachers and keep the schools in operation when my resources were utterly inadequate to meet the exigencies of the moment."[17]

By the end of 1872 twenty-one schools, though primitive by twentieth-century standards, were in operation and were teaching more than one thousand students. Most of the schools remained open for the six-month term desired by state administrators in Jackson. The black superintendent also had instituted litigation to recover Sixteenth Section lands, a prewar federal endowment for educational purposes that had been alienated from the public domain. He was only partially successful in this effort, and the problems of school finance continued to plague the system. Nevertheless, Bruce optimistically reported in early 1873 "that there are no longer difficulties besetting my progress in the future administration of the school system in this county, which energy and time will not remove."[18] A few months later he resigned as county superintendent to devote more time to his duties as sheriff and, more important for his career, to state politics.

When Bruce began to seek state political preferment in 1873, his fame had spread beyond the Delta. In 1871 he had attended the state Republican convention, and the following year he had served as secretary of the Mississippi delegation to the national convention that renominated Grant for president. But statewide, he faced formidable competition in his quest for political advancement. In addition to powerful carpetbaggers and scalawags who felt threatened by the rise of a popular Negro leader, other ambitious blacks, including some who had greater claims for patronage than Bruce, sought in 1873 to replace the deceased James Lynch as the most influential Negro leader in the state. Young Negro Republicans John R. Lynch (no relation to James), James Hill, and Ham Carter and older Reconstruction warriors Hiram R. Revels, Robert Gleed, and Thomas W. Stringer all had devoted followers who expected them to emerge victorious in the black community and secure the endorsement of the party for high public office.[19]

In a contest for influence and office, Bruce had one important advantage over his opponents: unlike them, he had not aligned himself with either Republican faction—the moderates or the radicals—in the bitter struggle to control the state. His pursuance of conciliatory policies toward whites in Bolivar County had earned him the friendship of the moderate Alcorn wing. At the same time he had done nothing to challenge the growing radical demand for legislation to end racial discrimination on public transportation and in public places.

The radicals, who were especially strong in the overwhelmingly black districts, saw no compelling reason to cultivate white voters, since they felt confident that the black vote, if protected—which seemed to be the case under the federal Enforcement Acts of 1870–71—would sustain Republican control of the state. Moderate Republicans, on the other hand, believed that the new political order could not survive without the support of a relatively large number of the "best citizens," despite a twenty-thousand majority of black voters in the state. They therefore advanced a platform built around a commitment to racial harmony and material progress that would placate whites and attract many of them, particularly Union Whigs, to the party.[20] The struggle between the radicals and the moderates climaxed in the state political campaign of 1873, precisely at the time when Bruce sought a more important role in Mississippi politics.

When the year began, the moderate wing, including carpetbag Governor Ridgley C. Powers, held the upper hand. But the politics of Powers and his predecessor, Alcorn (who was now in the Senate), had alienated many Republicans. In addition to its political blunders, the Alcorn-Powers faction had shown its indifference to Negro rights and interest at a time when black political assertiveness was growing in the state. Adelbert Ames returned to Mississippi during the summer to rally radical and dissident Republicans in a campaign to wrest the state party from the Alcorn-Powers moderates. The carpetbag senator and his friends were especially successful in winning control of river-county conventions and selecting Ames delegates for the state convention that would write a platform and nominate candidates for the fall election. Bruce, evidently fearful of committing himself to either faction at this stage, chose not to be a delegate from Bolivar County, though he planned to attend the state convention.[21]

Because of Bruce's political ambiguity and his influence with a large number of black voters in the Delta, he became a focus of intrigue when he arrived in Jackson in August to attend the Republican convention. In an effort to undercut the black support for Ames, moderates sought to hoist Bruce to the top of the Republican ticket, but he refused to cooperate, correctly believing that the Alcorn-Powers faction was acting out of desperation. Moreover, by this time Bruce could see that the moderate wing of the party, which had lost to the radicals in the black community, was becoming increasingly conservative in its efforts to snare white support.[22] Although unobtrusive in his advocacy

10

of black rights in public places, Bruce had no desire to sell out his race or party to a conservative coalition.

The Ames managers in the Republican convention were the next group to call at Bruce's room in Jackson. Black delegates, whose support of Ames was essential to his success, insisted on three places, including the office of lieutenant governor, for their race on the state ticket. Ames had intimated that he wanted to return to the U.S. Senate once he had won control of the governor's office for the radical wing. But the black demand for the lieutenant governorship, which he could not ignore, seriously complicated his plans. If he left the state in the hands of a black man, Ames knew that in order to still the racial passions that would be aroused by the sight of a former slave in the governor's chair, he would have to select someone whose reputation was impeccable. That man was Bruce.[23] But when Ames's managers laid out the plan to the mulatto leader, much to their surprise he declined second place on the ticket. It soon became apparent that Bruce had another office in mind—a seat in the U.S. Senate.[24] In rejecting the governor's office for the uncertainty of a legislative election to the Senate, Bruce was evidently guided by his disposition to avoid the kind of personal conflict and harassment that Republican governors in the South had been forced to endure. The Senate, with friendly northern Republicans in control, would be a much more congenial setting for a man of his sensibilities and talents.

Bruce's refusal to run for lieutenant governor produced a serious problem for the radicals. For the position they were forced to choose between two controversial blacks, Ham Carter and Alexander K. Davis. When they selected the nondescript Davis, Carter and his followers denounced the action, giving encouragement to Alcorn Republicans who formed their own party to challenge the radicals in the election. The radical ticket, however, was successful in November; but because of the controversy that swirled around Davis, Ames abandoned his plans to return to the Senate.[25]

When the new Republican legislature met in January 1874, Bruce's ambition to be elected to the U.S. Senate was close to realization. In the Republican legislative caucus at the beginning of the session, black members, who constituted a majority in the caucus and a large minority in the legislature, insisted that Bruce be selected for the full term of six years rather than the short term created by Ames's resignation from the Senate. Both Congressman George C. McKee, a carpetbagger, and U.S. District Attorney G. Wiley Wells, also a carpetbagger, sought the seat. But Governor Ames used his influence on behalf of

Bruce, and when the caucus nominated the black leader by a vote of fifty-two to thirty-six, his election to the full term was assured. On February 4 the legislature sent Bruce to the Senate by an almost unanimous vote, including a few Democrats. [26]

As had been the case with Revels's election to the Senate in 1870, hardly a voice was raised to protest the elevation of another mulatto to this prestigious body. A number of Republicans and even a few Conservatives expressed approval of the choice. The moderate carpetbag editor of the Vicksburg *Times* predicted that the new senator "will prove himself a man of mark, wining [sic] and retaining the respect of his associates."[27] The conservative Greenville *Weekly Times*, the leading newspaper in the Delta, believed that the important cause of levee improvements had been substantially advanced by Bruce's election to the Senate, where his experience as a levee commissioner would be applied to obtain federal aid for the work. [28]

While waiting until 1875 to take his seat in the Senate, Bruce returned to Floreyville to manage his properties. He wisely refrained from involvement in the bitter intraparty strife that, instead of abating with the triumph of the radicals, had reached into the Ames faction and threatened to destroy the party's control in Mississippi. The weakness of the Republican government became apparent when racial violence erupted in Vicksburg in late 1874, and Governor Ames stood helpless while White Leaguers vented their hostilities on country blacks. [29] Bruce, with a larger audience than before, might have spoken out against the terror, but he did not, perhaps because like other Republicans he believed that the Vicksburg violence was unique, having been created by local mismanagement. He probably also believed that President Grant's suppression of anti-Republican violence in Louisiana and his ultimate dispatch of troops to Vicksburg meant that in the future federal authority would be brought to bear to protect southern Republicans. If Bruce held such hopes, they would soon be dashed.

On March 5, 1875, thirteen months after his election, Bruce, at age thirty-four, appeared before the Senate to take the oath of office. [30] Customarily, the senior senator from the state escorted the new member to the front of the chamber for the swearing in ceremony. But when Bruce's name was called, Senator Alcorn, now Mississippi's senior senator, remained in his seat in a display of pique toward Bruce for having joined the Ames faction. Greatly embarrassed, the sensitive Bruce moved up the aisle without an escort. Halfway to the front he was met by Senator Roscoe Conkling, who linked his arm with the new senator's and accompanied him to the well where he was sworn in. Bruce never forgot Conkling for this courtesy, and during his term in the Senate he frequently followed the New York senator's lead despite his reputation as a political spoilsman.[31]

With the support of the powerful Conkling, Bruce received what he considered to be good committee assignments in the Senate. For most of his term he served on the standing committees for Pensions, Manufactures, and Education and Labor. He also served on Senate select committees on Mississippi River improvements and on the Freedmen's Bank; he temporarily chaired the former committee and was the only chairman of the latter.[32]

During Bruce's first two years in the Senate, he mainly concerned himself with the distressing political developments in the South that ended Republican rule there. At first, in the special session of early 1875, which met primarily to consider the Louisiana imbroglio, he maintained a low profile, believing, as he explained later, that he should not speak or assert himself until he "had acquired a larger acquaintance with [the Senate's] methods of business and a fuller experience in public affairs."[33] The Louisiana issue was postponed until the regular session. Meanwhile, Bruce's attention was turned to events in his home state, where a revolution or, more accurately, a counterrevolution was occurring.

After the Vicksburg "troubles" of late 1874, Mississippi Republicans were faced with a determined and united conservative campaign to rid the state of "the dirtiest despotism on Earth." The specific goal of the revived Democratic-Conservative party was to sweep the fall election that was to be held to choose a new legislature and a state treasurer. When Bruce returned home from Washington after his first session in Congress, he was stunned by the political excitement that had engulfed the state, even though the election was several months away. For the first time since the establishment of the Republican order, the Delta counties were affected by racial and political turmoil that caused severe divisions among local Republicans, who found themselves vulnerable and apprehensive about the future.[34] But in Bolivar County, Bruce and his lieutenants managed to retain a united party and keep out White Leaguers and other Democratic extremists.[35]

As the 1875 campaign in Mississippi entered its final phase, political and racial violence occurred, prompting Governor Ames to appeal to President Grant for troops. In his famous reply, Grant refused the carpetbag governor's request, explaining that "the whole public are tired out with these annual autumnal outbreaks in the South, and the great

13

majority are ready now to condemn any interference on the part of the Government."[36] With these remarks Grant sealed the fate of the Republican order in Mississippi.

Some Republicans, however, continued to campaign for party candidates, though not in the hotbeds of White League activity. Like most black leaders during the campaign, Bruce remained close to home, evidently confining his electioneering to Bolivar County.[37] He did join with thirteen other state black leaders in a printed address to "colored voters," warning them that their "civil rights and privileges as freemen" were at stake in the election and pleading with them to persevere in the face of White-League threats, to go to the polls on election day, and to vote Republican. The address prophetically predicted that if the Democrats succeeded in the fall, "the colored man will at once sink back to the status held in 1865—free in name, but not in fact—poor, ignorant and helpless, hedged in by unfriendly laws, which he will have no power to circumvent."[38]

Although thousands of black voters did brave White-League threats and vote Republican, the Democratic-Conservatives achieved an overwhelming victory in the November election. Then, in early 1876, the so-called Redeemers dismantled the Republican order, forcing Governor Ames and others to resign from office. The revolutionary events in Mississippi, however, shocked many national Republican leaders, especially in the Senate, the only chamber of Congress the party still controlled. Even President Grant was disturbed by the news from Mississippi, and he took steps, despite the political risk, which caused Republicans to hope that he might yet intervene to save the Reconstruction settlement.[39]

When Congress convened for its regular session five weeks after the Mississippi debacle, Senator Bruce, along with other Republicans, appealed to the Senate for an investigation of the fall election. Like Republican stalwarts Roscoe Conkling, Oliver P. Morton, and Benjamin F. Butler, Bruce hoped that such an investigation would lead to a federal reversal of the election results. On December 15, Senator Morton offered a resolution for the appointment of an investigation committee in the Senate, but the motion was tabled until March 29.[40] Congress's delay in acting on the issue, while Republicanism was being dismantled in Mississippi, dismayed Bruce, although he refrained from publicly criticizing his colleagues' reluctance to act. His distress, however, surfaced on February 10 in a supposedly secret executive session of the Senate called to discuss the question of seating P. B. S. Pinchback, a Louisiana black leader and new friend of Bruce. When it became clear

14

during the debate that a sufficient number of Republican senators might join with Democrats to block Pinchback's elevation to the Senate on the ground that he had been elected by a bogus legislature, Bruce obtained the floor and in a fifteen-minute speech upbraided the national Republican party for its failure to protect southern blacks. A second-hand account of Bruce's remarks, which the press eagerly reported and exploited, claimed that the mulatto senator had denounced President Grant as "untruthful, treacherous, and insincere," and had advised members of his race to make terms with southern whites.[41]

Since senators were bound to secrecy in the debate, neither Bruce nor his Senate friends would initially respond to this report of the speech. But two days later a Washington correspondent to the New York *Times*, after checking with unidentified senators, pronounced the account "very much exaggerated." The source of the original report was evidently a Democrat who saw an opportunity to create a division in the Republican party. The writer in the *Times* reported that actually the black senator's speech "was in the nature of a lamentation for the condition of his race," which Bruce "despondently regards as deserted by the President and by the Republican Party." He also was critical of the president's failure to consult with him on patronage matters, a subject that would increasingly concern him during the remainder of his Senate term.[42]

Ironically, a few days earlier Benjamin F. Butler complained to Governor Ames, his son-in-law, that Mississippi Republicans could not depend on Bruce for aid in Washington, since he "doesn't stand up like a man anywhere."[43] Actually, Butler had mistaken Bruce's silence for his attitude of deference to the national Republican leadership and his usual caution in dealing with inflammatory issues. Furthermore, the black senator was reluctant to defend Ames against impeachment charges, which was Butler's main concern. Like John R. Lynch and other Mississippi black leaders, Bruce evidently believed that the governor's mismanagement had contributed to the Republican collapse in the state.[44]

The Senate's apparent intention to reject Pinchback's claims for a seat when it again met in open session stirred Bruce to action. On March 3 "the silent senator" made his maiden speech in the Senate. His arguments at this time were more reasoned than those in his emotion-laden address to the executive session. He began by apologizing for his "limited experience in the consideration of such questions" as the seating issue, and he professed "a just appreciation of the learning and ability of the gentlemen who have already attempted to elucidate and determine the case." With this show of deference aside, Bruce asserted that the Senate would make a grave error if it turned its back on Pinchback. He pointed out that, in the bitter struggle in Louisiana over the state house, President Grant had ruled that the William Pitt Kellogg legislature—which elected Pinchback to the Senate—was the legitimate lawmaking body of the state. Bruce contended that if the Senate refused to seat Pinchback it would be "a great wrong to the people who sent him here" and would provoke hostile whites "to renewed and continued agitation and violence."[45] Despite the appeals of Bruce and other stalwart Republicans, the Senate by a three-vote margin rejected Pinchback.[46]

A few days later, when Morton's resolution calling for an investigation of the Mississippi election of 1875 finally came to the floor of the Senate, Bruce spoke at length in favor of it. He placed the matter in a broader context than the mere defeat of the state Republican party. The issue, he declared, was "the protection in all their purity and significance of the political rights of the people and the free institutions of the country." A violent upheaval had occurred in Mississippi, which was not caused by the normal desire to win political control but by a passionate Conservative purpose to destroy the rights of blacks and their white political allies. "Violence so unprovoked, inspired by such motives, and looking to such ends, is a spectacle not only discreditable to the country, but dangerous to the integrity of our free institutions." The use of such tactics, he reminded the Senate, was spreading throughout the South; and the congressional response to the political crisis in his state would determine whether or not such revolutionary activities could be suppressed.[47]

Bruce spent much of his lengthy March address defending black capacity to exercise political rights, a fundamental issue in the debate on federal intervention to protect the Reconstruction settlement. He pointed out that blacks began their "political careers under the disadvantages . . . that generations of enforced bondage had entailed upon [the] race." Citing economic and social data on Mississippi blacks, he said that since freedom they had made "commendable and hopeful advances in the qualities and acquisitions desirable" for citizenship and political equality with whites.[48]

The black senator felt compelled to answer critics who claimed that blacks, in voting solidly for the Republican party, proved they were incapable of overcoming their own racial prejudices and functioning independently in the American democratic system. "The unanimity with which the colored voters act with a party," Bruce informed the

Senate, "is not referable to any race prejudice on their part. On the contrary, they invite the political co-operation of their white brethren"; they only voted for the Republican party because white Democrats threatened to take away their rights. Blacks, he said "deprecate the establishment of the color line by the opposition, not only because the act is unwise and wrong in principle, but because it isolates them from the men of the South, and forces them, in sheer self-protection and against their inclination, to act seemingly upon the basis of a race principle that they neither respect nor entertain." Blacks "must be guaranteed in the unproscribed exercise of [their] honest convictions and be absolutely, from within or without, protected in the use of [the] ballot" before they "can either wisely or safely divide" their votes.[49] Pointedly reminding his Republican colleagues that he represented almost one million voters, Bruce affirmed that blacks "do not ask the enactment of new laws, but only the enforcement of those that already exist."[50]

Later, on the same day of Bruce's speech, the Republican majority in the Senate, probably influenced more by the forthcoming national political contest than by the black senator's rhetoric, passed the Morton resolution, creating a committee to investigate political conditions in Mississippi. After an extensive study, the Senate committee, in its report, confirmed the view of Bruce and other Mississippi Republicans regarding the election of 1875.[51] But with the House of Representatives in the hands of the Democrats and President Grant immobilized, no congressional action was taken to overturn the Democratic victory.

As Republicans gave way to white Conservatives in the South and the scope of black rights narrowed, Bruce became more attentive to intraparty politics. He chaired the Mississippi delegation to the Republican convention of 1876 that cast its votes for Rutherford B. Hayes for president. Although Bruce's first choice for president was Oliver Morton, after Hayes's nomination he served as a member of the committee to notify the Ohioan officially of the convention's action. Behind the scenes in the convention, blacks expressed their dismay with the decline of the Republican commitment to equal rights, despite the party's platform promises and public show of deference toward Bruce and other black delegates.[52]

After the convention Bruce wrote Hayes a warm letter of congratulations on behalf, he said, of the four million former slaves whom he represented. He also reminded Hayes of his commitment to the rights of all Americans.[53] Bruce later campaigned for the party in Louisiana and Mississippi, and experienced at first hand the fever of racial excitement in areas where blacks and their white Republican allies continued to challenge the Democrats for control. When conflict threatened in a rally he attended in his home county, to reduce tension the black senator laid aside his prepared speech and exhorted his friends not to provoke violence.[54] He realized, as well as other Republicans, that it was no longer safe to canvass even in the predominantly black river counties. Although Bruce continued to be a leader in the Mississippi Republican party, he rarely again campaigned for the party in the South.

When Hayes abandoned the southern Republican leadership as a part of the celebrated Compromise of 1877 that put him in the White House, a chorus of denunciation from party faithfuls in the South erupted. Bruce and a number of black leaders, however, were strangely silent. Some, including John R. Lynch, James T. Rapier of Alabama, Robert Smalls of South Carolina, and John Mercer Langston, acting president of Howard University, expressed the belief that Hayes's policy would bring peace to the post-Reconstruction South. Many black leaders, including Bruce, obviously realized they had nowhere to turn except to the national Republican leadership. They probably also felt that Hayes would soon see the error of his southern strategy and would abandon it as he had promised to do if the policy did not work.[55]

Bruce had an additional reason for not criticizing Hayes. With Alcorn's retirement from the Senate in early 1877, Bruce might control federal patronage in Mississippi if he maintained his support of the new president and deflected Hayes's interest in building a new base for the Republican party in the South. Three weeks after the inauguration Bruce met privately with Hayes at the White House.[56] The substance of their discussion is unknown, but it is clear that Hayes did not give the black senator much encouragement on the matter of patronage. Soon the president was asking "respectable" white Republicans of Mississippi for advice on appointments and was choosing some Democrats to federal positions in the state.[57]

Bruce hoped Hayes would soon realize that his patronage policies were undermining the Republican party and black rights in the South. To Bruce a wise federal patronage policy and security for southern blacks were inseparable. Unless patronage could be extended to true Republicans, no well-disciplined and viable party could exist in the South; and without a strong Republican party, able to challenge the Democrats for power, black rights could not be maintained short of military intervention, which, Bruce knew, northerners would no longer support. Eventually, however, the concern for patronage, which was concrete and immediate, became the absorbing issue for Bruce and for many other southern Republicans as well. Although he remained committed to the Reconstruction ideal of political equality for his race, he lost much of his zeal for the cause of black rights and gradually turned to the doctrine of self-help as the best policy for black success.

To strengthen his position at home, which in turn, he believed, would improve his standing in Washington, Bruce formed a political alliance with two other Mississippi mulattoes, John R. Lynch and James Hill, the young secretary of state in the Ames administration. Their purpose was to wrest control of the organization in Mississippi from a white-dominated moderate faction that had controlled the party since the revolution of 1875.[58] By 1878 this "triumvirate" had succeeded in their objective, mainly due to a remarkable blending of the political talents and influence of the three men. Hill, a tall, outgoing, and energetic young man, managed the everyday, nuts-and-bolts business of the organization, including the control of conventions in counties where blacks held a preponderance of votes.[59] These conventions selected friendly delegates to the Republican state convention, where Hill also provided able floor leadership for the black alliance. Lynch, an aggressive and effective organizer, chaired the state Republican executive committee from 1881 to 1892.[60] Meanwhile, Bruce represented the interests of the alliance in the national capital.

The success of Bruce and his colleagues was soon recognized in Washington. Disregarding his southern strategy, President Hayes in 1878 turned to the state's regular Republicans for appointments to federal office in Mississippi. Several of these appointees, including James Hill, who was selected for the important post of collector of internal revenue in the state, were recommended to him by Bruce. Bruce's rise in status with the Hayes administration was not missed by Republican machinators and office seekers in Mississippi who now appealed to him to use his influence in their behalf.[61]

Black control of the Mississippi Republican party and federal patronage could be sustained only as long as Bruce, Lynch, and Hill acted together. Some white Republicans bitterly resented the trio's domination of the party and waited for an opportunity to divide and conquer. Clashes, usually over patronage, between Lynch and Hill, both of whom were strong-willed individuals, did occur; but the shrewd and tactful Bruce intervened and worked out a satisfactory compromise that preserved the alliance.[62] Not until the 1890s did the black political coalition come unglued. With offices at stake, most white Republican

19

functionaries came to accept the black leadership. In seeking appointments to office, the triumvirate showed no preference for members of their race; indeed, they recommended only a handful of Negroes for federal positions. Several of the white Republicans favored by Bruce and his associates were "to the manner born."[63]

With his confidence buoyed by renewed political success during the last three years of his term in Congress, Bruce discarded the image of the "silent senator" and became more assertive as a national leader of his race. Nevertheless, like Revels, who was the first black to serve in the Senate, Bruce recognized the limits of his position in this august body as well as the need to exercise propriety in his relationships with the powerful. "The novelty of my position" not only as a black senator but also as a representative of the much maligned southern Republican party, he explained, compels me "to cultivate and exhibit to my honorable associates a courtesy that would inspire reciprocal courtesy, and manifest an unobtrusive manliness in my individual life that would command respect from those among whom I move."[64] But unlike Revels, who had unimpressively served a year in the Senate and soon afterward allied with Mississippi Conservatives, Bruce warmed to his responsibilities and continued to express confidence in the ultimate success of the political ideals of Reconstruction.[65]

Bruce's renewed commitment to his senatorial duties was evident in an increase in his committee work. He became an active member of Senate committees on pensions, education, and labor. He regularly reported minor bills from these committees to the floor, and sometimes spoke briefly in their favor.[66]

His most important assignments were to select committees on navigation improvements and flood control on the Mississippi River and its tributaries. In early 1877 Bruce temporarily replaced Alcorn, whose term had expired, as chairman of the Senate Committee on River Improvements. When a similar committee was organized a few months later, he was appointed to it but was not selected as its chairman. Along with other representatives of the lower Mississippi Valley, Bruce was anxious to obtain federal aid for flood control and a permanent system of levees to protect the fertile low country. In 1879 he introduced a bill to organize the Mississippi River Improvement Association, which, with federal aid, was designed to control the river and protect the alluvial lands. The measure failed to pass, but his prestige as a knowledgeable spokesman for Mississippi Valley interests had grown. His authority in levee affairs was apparent when his Democratic colleague L. Q. C. Lamar supported his reappointment to the

Committee on River Improvements after he had earlier resigned to devote more time to the chairmanship of another select committee. Despite the vigorous efforts of Lamar, Bruce, and other valley promoters, Congress, which had recently tightened the purse strings on appropriations for internal improvements, rejected all proposals for levee and river improvements.[67]

Bruce and Lamar, whose personal relationship was always friendly, also teamed up to advance other interests of their constituents. In 1880 the black senator introduced a bill to provide federal aid for construction of the long delayed Mississippi Valley and Ship Island Railroad, which would give the Mississippi interior access to a state harbor on the Gulf of Mexico. Lamar, as chairman of the Committee on Railroads, managed the bill on the floor, but again the Senate refused to recognize Mississippi's claims for federal largesse. Bruce and Lamar, along with other southerners in Congress, also unsuccessfully sought congressional approval for a refund of the cotton tax placed on the South immediately after the war.[68] However, Bruce did not always agree with Lamar on material issues. In 1878, when he followed the instructions of the Mississippi legislature and voted for the Bland-Allison Silver Purchase bill and Lamar did not, the state House of Representatives praised his stand and excoriated his white colleague.[69]

During his last two years in the Senate, Bruce became increasingly attentive to his role as a national leader of his race. When in 1879 he spoke out against a Chinese exclusion bill and for a more humane Indian policy, he did so mainly because of the harsh implications that such racist, exclusionist policies had for blacks. In the Senate debates on these issues, he expressed a "large confidence in the strength and the assimilative power of our [American] institutions" and the value of first-class citizenship for nonwhite residents. Blacks, Bruce claimed, had been "successfully introduced into the body-politic" and were enjoying its benefits.[70]

No issue, however, received more of his attention during his last two years in the Senate than the controversy surrounding the failure of the Freedmen's Savings Bank, an institution founded during Reconstruction for the purpose of encouraging industry and thrift among southern blacks. When it failed during the 1870s hundreds of blacks lost their life savings; and since it had a semipublic character, many injured depositors appealed to Bruce for relief. Suspecting mismanagement or worse in the administration of the bank, Bruce in 1879 secured the appointment of a Senate committee, with himself as chairman, to investigate all aspects of the bank.[71]

The so-called Bruce committee consisted of three southern Democrats, including the prominent John B. Gordon of Georgia, and two Republicans. From May 1879 to March 1880 the committee, with Bruce in the chair for every session, conducted an exhaustive inquiry into the affairs of the bank. The report of the committee, which covers more than six hundred pages of testimony and documents and provides the principal source for the bank's history, revealed that the institution had indeed been mismanaged; it especially pointed a condemning finger at the three federal commissioners who were charged with winding up the bank's affairs.[72] The New York *Tribune* hailed the report as "a straight forward statement of the fact . . . without any attempt to produce a sensational document, and it reflects great credit upon Senator Bruce."[73]

Nevertheless, the Bruce committee report had the effect of closing the gate after the horses had escaped. Congress did abolish the incompetent board of commissioners and place the comptroller of the currency in charge of closing the business of the Freedmen's Savings Bank. But a Bruce-sponsored Senate bill to obtain congressional reimbursement for black depositors in the bank failed, although the black senator had won considerable support for the measure. He was more successful in arranging the government's purchase of the bank building and adjacent property in Washington.[74]

With the enforcement of the Reconstruction amendments in shambles, Bruce during the latter part of his senatorial term only occasionally sought a revival of the national commitment to equal rights. In 1878 he spoke in support of a Senate bill to remove racial distinctions in army enlistments. At this time Bruce expressed the hope that America had passed the critical period in its history when such distinctions were viewed as necessary. He predicted that "under the influence of a healthy public sentiment" prejudice against blacks "will pass away," and they will receive the full benefits of American civilization. For their part, blacks "are beginning to appreciate the value of citizenship. . . . We are willing to stand upon our own merits and rest our fortunes upon the same forces that give success to other citizens."[75]

Bruce's commitment to racial progress through assimilation into white American culture received its greatest test in the debate over black migration during the late 1870s. The migration movement, principally to Kansas and Liberia, grew largely out of the black impulse toward self-help and racial solidarity after the crushing collapse of political Reconstruction in the South. Black leaders like Bruce and Frederick Douglass, whose lives had been consumed in the struggle for equality in the white world, found all their assimilationist assumptions challenged by the supporters of what quickly became an emotional crusade to separate from white America. A number of "representative colored men," who were disenchanted with politics and the American creed, succumbed to the fever of the movement, especially the Kansas "Exodus," although its pell-mell execution appalled them.[76]

Bruce, who represented in the Senate the state most affected by the Kansas Exodus, had to tread softly lest he become involved in a bitter controversy that was not to his liking. Furthermore, as a planter in the Mississippi lowlands, precisely where blacks were most discontented with the prevailing order, he had an economic interest in the matter, and he was wary of the effect the Kansas fever would have on agricultural production there. He coupled this concern with the argument that "Exodusters" would experience great property losses and personal hardships. He announced his approval of a convention convened by Conservatives in Vicksburg at the height of the Kansas movement for the purpose of adopting a plan to check black migration from the Mississippi Valley. But he warned white Conservatives against the adoption of a simple solution that would ignore the grievances of blacks. "The causes prompting this movement, " he wrote a Conservative leader at the Vicksburg convention, "are complex." The exodus occurred first because of a "feeling of uneasiness and insecurity among the colored classes, springing from the unfortunate race collisions and violence that have sometimes existed in certain localities, and . . . second from the fact that colored laborers have not, in many instances, received satisfactory returns for the products of their labor." Bruce lamented that smooth-talking promoters of the exodus, using the legitimate concerns of blacks as a springboard, had painted to prospective settlers "rose-colored pictures of the advantages of Western life and home. I hold, and have ever held," he said, "that the interests of the two races at the South are so blended that one cannot suffer without . . . materially affecting the other, and that there is no necessary conflict of interests between them which should render an exodus of the laboring classes expedient or desirable."[77] The remedy for black discontent, he declared, should be worked out in the Vicksburg convention by "the competent men of every class of our people, [and] should not only look to measures and actions that will remove all causes of uneasiness and insecurity from the minds of those contemplating emigration," but also "encourage the colored working class to

23

acquire property in the Southern States." The ownership of property would closely identify blacks with their southern communities and "thus lay the foundation for growth and contentment among them."

The Mississippi senator, although invited, did not attend the Vicksburg convention. He cited a busy schedule for his absence, but by remaining away he perhaps also wanted to avoid a close identification with the Conservative effort to check the exodus.[78] Nevertheless, concerned planters and merchants in the convention, following the advice of Bruce as well as the dictates of self-interest, adopted resolutions designed to placate discontented blacks in the Mississippi Valley and thus halt the flow of blacks to Kansas.[79]

Despite Bruce's opposition to the exodus, he did not turn a deaf ear to the pleas of black emigrants who suffered in Kansas. An attempt by conservatives in the Senate to prevent the passage of a bill that would admit duty-free charity goods from England for the relief of destitute Exodusters raised the black senator's ire, and he spoke out in favor of aid for the sufferers. "It is not now a question of how they came there or why they went there; it is not a question of whether they ought to have gone there or not; but they are there and they are in distress." He appealed to the Senate "in the name of the hundreds of colored people now starving in Kansas to pass the pending measure that they may receive the benefits of this charity."[80] One week after the black senator's appeal, Congress enacted the duty-free measure for the relief of the Kansas refugees. Actually, Bruce desired more federal aid for the Exodusters. A bill, which he supported, providing direct federal assistance for the destitute in Kansas, was introduced only to die in committee.[81]

The black senator expressed less sympathy for the Liberia movement of 1877–78. This colonization effort, another in a series of schemes to settle dispossessed blacks in Africa, was more noise than results, but at its height Negroes throughout the South were stirred by promises of its promoters and hope that financial support would be available for the voyage across the Atlantic. In the beginning Bruce saw no compelling reason to take a position on the movement, since he did not think anything would come of it. In late 1877, however, when 423 Mississippi blacks petitioned Congress through Bruce for $100,000 to aid their settlement in Liberia, he referred the request to the Senate Committee on Commerce with the comment that, though he did not support it, "the number and character of the signers" entitled them to a hearing.[82]

Three months later, after hundreds of blacks had converged on

Charleston anticipating emigration to Africa, Bruce could no longer ignore the Liberia fever. He selected the columns of the Cincinnati *Commercial* to announce his opposition to the movement because, as he indicated, this newspaper had a wide circulation and would reach the people most affected by the emigration propaganda.[83]

The assumption in the back-to-Africa movement, Bruce wrote, was that black "advancement could only be supplied in a land free from the dominating contact of the white race, and independent, in its institutions, of the American Republic." "The pregnant facts of history," he argued, had destroyed this assumption. Bruce explained that since the antebellum period the Negro "has attained to rights, personal, civil, and political, that are not only conventionally recognized, but covered by the sacred provisions of the fundamental law of the land." The black man, furthermore, according to Bruce, had become "so vital a factor in the production" of the South "and so potent a force in its political system, that the whole structure of the civilization of eleven states would not only be shocked if his rights should be generally denied, but its prosperity would be shattered if his varied forces and living presence were removed from the communities in which he lives." The Liberia enterprise, Bruce said, was not only incongruous, but also "antagonistic to the beneficent results that time and the free institutions of America have brought to the black race."[84]

Bruce warned that blacks who went to Liberia would be abandoning material security for an uncertain life in "the unenlightened wilds of Africa." Blacks had attained a livelihood in the South "by slow and painful processes," and they could not "afford to make an experiment that may be disastrous in its results." He admitted that southern blacks continued to be "the sufferers of exceptional and inexcusable violence." But, he said, "my estimate of American character and my hope of the outcome of American civilization forbid that I should believe that these evils will be continued, and this violence a permanent quality of the society of my country. The sober second thought of the people will supply a corrective, and the stern sense of justice and sentiment of humanity will apply it." The black man needed only to be patient, resolute, and true to himself and to his country, and "he will live to rejoice over a condition of society in the communities of the South in which he can entertain independent political opinions without prejudice, and to assert and exercise all the rights without hindrance and without danger."

In concluding his roseate analysis of the status of blacks in American society, Bruce declared: "The Negro of America is not African, but

25

American—in his physical qualities and aptitudes, in his mental development and biases, in his religious beliefs and hopes, and in his political conception and convictions. . . . His destiny—whether he fulfill it in the South or the North, in the East or the West—will be controlled by the same conditions that determine that of his white brother."[85]

Despite the warnings of Bruce and other black leaders, a ship carrying 206 emigrants to Liberia departed from Charleston one month after the senator's letter appeared in the Cincinnati *Commercial*. The emigrants experienced a disastrous crossing, which for a time checked black enthusiasm for migration to Liberia.[86]

Although Bruce had accurately predicted the hardships blacks would experience in the Kansas and Africa movements, his prestige in the Negro community suffered considerably because of his strong opposition to emigration. His optimistic view of the black man's future in the South ignored the realities of the post-Reconstruction world, causing critics to charge that he no longer represented the interests of his race in the national government. The light-skinned, distinguished-looking Bruce, who suffered few social indignities in Washington or even when he visited Mississippi, never seemed to understand that for many blacks the uncertainties of emigration were preferable to the political and economic oppressions of the "redeemed" South. Although a majority of the blacks remained in the South, most felt an emotional attachment to emigration and especially to the Kansas Exodus. They obviously resented efforts by Bruce, which appeared to coincide with those of their oppressors, to check the black search for real freedom. Ever the harmonizer, Bruce refused to admit, what the black masses and their local leaders knew, that the Reconstruction dream of black assimilation into white American society had died with the collapse of Reconstruction in the South and the abandonment of the Fourteenth and Fifteenth amendments to the Constitution.

Bruce's separation from the black masses went deeper than the differences over emigration. As a youth and, later, as a rising politician in Mississippi, he had not experienced the harsh realities of the life of a southern slave or freedman. He was caught up in the postwar crusade to elevate blacks in southern society, and he took justifiable pride in his rise as a leader in the movement. But, unlike many Negro leaders who either entered the deep South as missionaries or were old residents there, Bruce, who was neither, did not establish an intimate association with his black followers. As Thomas Holt has demonstrated for South Carolina, class distinctions among Negroes made an important difference in the black leadership's stand on issues affecting their

26

race.[87] This was especially true of Bruce, a successful landowner and politician, who saw black needs from a distance and largely in political terms.[88]

At some point during his senatorial career Bruce's separation from the black masses became virtually complete. His marriage in 1878 to Josephine B. Willson, the beautiful daughter of a prominent mulatto dentist of Cleveland, Ohio, and the couple's acceptance into white Washingtonian society, were probably the points that sealed Bruce's insulation from the black people. The Bruces spent a pleasant honeymoon in white European society; they also enjoyed the company of former President U.S. Grant, who was visiting in Paris.[89] After their return to Washington, the Bruce home at 909 M. Street, N.W., became a center of social life.[90] The majority of the guests were white, although leading Negro intellectuals and political leaders, like Frederick Douglass and John R. Lynch, attended receptions at the Bruce home. The Bruces also attended a white church, the First Congregational Church of Washington. Bruce's preference for white society angered many middle-class black Washingtonians, and they vented their displeasure with him in the black press.[91]

Despite black criticism, Bruce continued to view himself as a "representative man of his race." His conservatism inclined him more and more to the self-help doctrine, a formula for black progress that received considerable attention from Negro leaders after Reconstruction. Bruce's support of the Reconstruction ideal of public education for his race served as a bridge to the self-help position. Along with political rights, he came to believe that industrial training, financed in part by the federal government, was an important key to black success. In the Senate he routinely, as a member of the Committee on Education and Labor, supported bills that would extend federal aid to schools. Although these measures failed to pass, most of them contained a formula for distributing among the states the proceeds from public-land sales in proportion to the illiteracy in the population.[92] Such an arrangement favored the South and black education, which had suffered large reductions in state school appropriations at the hands of the Redeemer governments.

Bruce himself introduced a bill in 1879 that would have distributed to five Negro colleges in the South the interest on the unclaimed pay and bounty money of black soldiers. The publicity over the bill, however, led to a run on the fund by claimants, reducing it to such an extent that the Senate, with Bruce's concurrence, rejected the distribution plan. Bruce believed, however, that the debate on the issue had spurred interest in federal aid to education. This assistance, he predicted, would favor "technical education—education, industrial and mechanical, and for the ordinary business pursuits rather than for what are called the learned professions."[93]

After Bruce left the Senate in 1881, he continued to promote the cause of black education. In several public addresses he urged passage by Congress of the Blair bill, which would extend federal aid to public education based on the old formula of state illiteracy. Later, during the 1880s, he delivered a series of lectures in the North on "The Race Problem." In these speeches he stressed the importance of material and educational growth for blacks. As usual, he found cause for optimism in the progress along these lines that blacks had made since emancipation. Educational and economic improvements for both races in the South, he said, would also lessen racial antagonisms and draw blacks and whites into closer business, political, and social relationships.[94]

Bruce's commitment to the self-help doctrine of black advancement within the context of the larger American culture soared with his appointment as director of the black exhibits in the Industrial Cotton Centennial Exposition held in New Orleans in 1884–85. He took considerable pride in the black exhibits he put together with the aid of state directors. Bruce justified the separate displays for Negro wares on the ground that the arrangement would highlight the material progress the race had made. "This is the first, and doubtless will be the last time," the sanguine Bruce declared, "that the colored people will want or have such an opportunity to show their advancement and deny the assertion so often made that freedom has not developed in them the higher aims and better accomplishments all citizens should have."[95] He particularly pointed with pride to the displays of "great mechanical skill" by blacks in the exposition.

In 1890 Bruce visited Tuskegee and delivered the commencement address at Booker T. Washington's famed institute. He was so impressed by what he saw there that three years later he joined in an attempt to establish an industrial school for Mississippi and Arkansas blacks. The effort failed. For the remainder of his life, Bruce, a resident of Washington, focused his educational interest on nearby Howard University and on the public schools of the District of Columbia; he served on both boards of trustees.[96]

Politics, particularly the Republican variety, continued to be a consuming passion for Bruce. With the Democrats in the ascendancy in Mississippi, the likelihood of his winning a second term in the Senate was remote. Although he retained his Mississippi political base, where the black alliance of Bruce, Hill, and Lynch still held sway in the Republican party, he looked to the national administration for sustenance. On the eve of his retirement from the Senate, Bruce plunged into the presidential contest of 1880, perhaps motivated mainly by the need to improve his prospects for appointment to a federal position if the party succeeded in the election. First he went to Mississippi, where a bitter struggle had developed over the selection of delegates to the national Republican convention.[97] A few months before the state convention met, state Republican leaders had leaned toward U. S. Grant for the presidential nomination. But Grant's unexpected praise of President Hayes's discredited southern policy, in contrast to Secretary of Treasury John Sherman's denunciation of southern Democrats for using "midnight murder and masquerade" to maintain control, created confusion and conflict in the Mississippi party.[98] Bruce had earlier endorsed Grant for the presidency; but in 1880 he favored Sherman, not only because of the secretary's expression of support for southern Republicans, but also because he represented a national administration that now sought the black senator's advice on patronage matters. Collector of Internal Revenue Hill, who had emerged as the strongest member of the black alliance, also could not ignore the candidacy of Sherman. Nevertheless, most black delegates, including Lynch, favored Grant, who was still popular with the Negro masses.[99]

The black division over presidential candidates immediately created an opportunity for the opposition wing of the party. Its leaders, who were mainly white, hoped by their support of Grant to enter the breach and destroy the Bruce-Hill-Lynch ascendancy in the state organization. Bruce quickly recognized the strategy of the opposition and suggested that the three black leaders meet and arrange a compromise. When they met, an arrangement was made in which the state delegation to the national convention would be equally divided between the supporters of Grant and Sherman, with the understanding that the hero of Appomattox would be the second choice of the Bruce and Hill group. The compromise averted a serious division within the black leadership and preserved its control of the state Republican party.[100]

In the national Republican convention, when Sherman's candidacy collapsed, Bruce and other friends of the treasury secretary dutifully gave their support to Grant. The black senator's political intrigue, however, had gone for naught. James A. Garfield and not Grant won the Republican nomination, placing Bruce's hopes for political preferment in jeopardy and sending him on the campaign trail to canvass for the Ohioan. After Garfield won the presidency, Bruce received support from several quarters for a position in the cabinet. A few white Republicans and national leaders of his race, who probably felt closer to Bruce than did the black masses, urged his appointment. [101]

Surprisingly, the Mississippi Democratic delegation in Congress, except for one member, also endorsed Bruce for a cabinet seat. Senator Lamar, in recommending his black colleague for a cabinet position, reportedly declared: "Mr. Bruce's conduct in the Senate has been such as not to alienate himself from the Southern people. He has not joined in the abusive warfare upon the South that many of his Republican colleagues in the Senate Chamber have constantly pursued. He is an intelligent man, and the best representative of his race in public life." [102] Although Lamar and other Mississippi Democrats had received favors from Bruce and had been captivated by his good manners and strong sense of propriety, their main reason for advocating him for the cabinet was probably a political one. Faced with a white independent revolt at home, which was seeking Republican support, the Lamar Democrats, by supporting Bruce and posing as racial moderates, hoped to neutralize the state's black leadership in the forthcoming struggle for power. If this was their purpose, they succeeded both in dividing the Republicans in the crucial gubernatorial election of 1881 and in defeating the independent challenge. [103]

Bruce, however, failed to receive an appointment to Garfield's cabinet. Instead, the new president asked him to serve as minister to Brazil or as an assistant to the postmaster-general. He declined both positions and asked to be appointed register of the treasury. Because this official supervised the work of more than one hundred persons, including white women, Garfield, fearing an outburst of white racism, hesitated to honor Bruce's request; but after consulting with James Blaine, he made the appointment. No opposition to the choice developed; and with Lamar's active support, Bruce's former colleagues in the Senate confirmed his selection to the highest appointed position that a black man had ever received. *The Nation*, which was generally critical of black participation in government, observed upon his confirmation by the Senate: "The vote on Mr. Bruce showed that he had won the entire respect of his colleagues from both sections, and that his fitness for the position may be presumed." [104]

The office of register of the treasury, which Bruce described as "practically the official bookkeeper of the United States," did not tax his energies, though he by no means treated it as a spoils position. He found time to campaign for the Republican party, mainly in the North, to visit his property in Bolivar County, to patch up disputes between Lynch and Hill in the Mississippi party, and to serve as director of black exhibits at the New Orleans exposition. His tenure as register ended in 1885 with the inauguration of Democrat Grover Cleveland as president. One year later he moved to Indianapolis, where his father-in-law had settled; but he soon returned to Washington. Viewed as a leading spokesman of his race, Bruce received numerous invitations to lecture; and in late 1886 he embarked on a series of speaking engagements in which he appealed for racial harmony and fair treatment for all minority groups. [105]

After four years out of office, Bruce entered enthusiastically into the presidential campaign of 1888. He campaigned for Benjamin Harrison before large crowds in Michigan, Wisconsin, and Indiana; and after the Republican became president Bruce was appointed recorder of deeds for the District of Columbia. When complaints arose that Harrison was ignoring reports of violence against southern blacks, Bruce defended him, emphasizing that under existing laws the president had no authority to intervene in the South. In an uncharacteristically strong manner, he denounced the southern outrages against members of his race, and he predicted that the new Republican Congress would be sufficiently aroused to correct this "frightful condition of things." He bristled at a black editor's suggestion that Negroes would be better off under Democratic rule than under the Republicans. [106]

When the Lodge bill to enforce Fifteenth Amendment guarantees for blacks failed to pass in 1890, Bruce probably realized that the Republican party would not provide even minimal protection for southern blacks. Nevertheless, as a Republican officeholder, he continued to support the party; and in 1892 he campaigned for the reelection of Harrison. When Cleveland regained the presidency, Bruce again found himself out of public office. Now in his early fifties, Bruce did not need the emoluments of office for financial security, since he had accumulated a small fortune, consisting mainly of more than one thousand acres of fertile Delta land. [107] Almost by habit, however, he continued his political activity and his involvement in presidential politics. He was an early supporter of William McKinley's successful campaign for president in 1896, and after the election the Washington *Post* suggested that a black man, either Bruce or Booker T. Washington, should be appointed to the cabinet. [108]

The suggestion by a prominent white newspaper that blacks should have a place in the cabinet produced an outpouring of Negro support for the idea, with most of the attention focusing on Bruce. Declaring

31

that the former black senator "stands in the front rank of public men and is by odds the leading Afro-American in the United States," W. Calvin Chase of the Washington *Bee* led the campaign for Bruce's appointment.[109] In mid-December 1896 the *Bee* reported that the black press in America almost unanimously supported Bruce for the cabinet, constituting a demand "so universal that it can not be overlooked by" McKinley.[110]

But the demand to put Bruce in the cabinet was overlooked by the president. Even if McKinley had desired to make the appointment, rising antiblack feeling in the country made it politically unwise for him to select Bruce for a high position. Instead, after some hesitation in which he evaluated rival Negro claims to office, McKinley appointed the former black senator register of the treasury, an office that since Bruce had first held it under Garfield and Arthur had been reserved by Republicans for leading black politicians. Four months after he received this measure of satisfaction, on March 17, 1898, Blanche K. Bruce died of diabetes at the age of fifty-seven. A large crowd of both races attended his funeral at the Metropolitan African Methodist Episcopal Church in Washington. Republican congressmen acted as honorary pallbearers, and Senator William B. Allison of Iowa delivered the eulogy.[111]

After Bruce's death, numerous memorials and commentaries on his life appeared in the press. A New York *Times* writer acclaimed him, next to Frederick Douglass, "the foremost man of his race."[112] The Washington *Post* did not believe that "he was especially beloved by the masses of his colored fellow-citizens," but he "was admired by the judicious and respectable among the whites and blacks alike, and the example of his high character and his useful life was of . . . value" to all. Years later John R. Lynch remembered Bruce as "the strongest and most influential colored man that our country has produced—able, courteous, respectful, and dignified, yet bold, outspoken, and aggressive in the advocacy and defense of what he believed to be right."[113]

A historian's judgment would be less extravagant in its praise of Bruce. Nevertheless, any objective evaluation of this black leader's career would have to award him high marks for political skill and the ability to harmonize both black and white elements in the Mississippi Republican party and to achieve the respect of many white conservatives. As a leader of his race in Washington, he perhaps pursued too conservatively and too optimistically the Reconstruction objectives of political equality, fundamental civil rights, and education for blacks. Assimilation into American society and culture, he seems to have believed, could be achieved through the realization of these Reconstruction goals. He rarely spoke out and never agitated for so-called advanced rights for blacks, which to the late twentieth-century mind are indispensible to the success of racial assimilation.

Bruce characteristically chose to ignore, at least in his public statements, the hardening racial practices of late nineteenth-century America and the negation of the post–Civil War gains of blacks. However, in maintaining his faith in the Reconstruction ideology, he avoided the despair that drove many of his black contemporaries to accept the separate-but-equal dogma contained in Booker T. Washington's philosophy. Bruce never gave up the dream that black equality, however ambiguously expressed, would come true in republican America and blacks would enjoy the full benefits of a civilization that had once enslaved them.

Notes

1. New York *Times*, Mar. 18, 1898; Henry Clay Bruce, *The New Man: Twenty-Nine Years a Slave, Twenty-Nine Years a Free Man* (York, Pa: P. Anstadt & Sons, 1895), pp. 14, 26–27. Born with the surname Branch, he assumed the name Bruce, the last name of his mother's master, after he freed himself during the Civil War. The identity of his father is unknown.

2. For an excellent recent account of the special status of mulatto slaves in southern society, see Robert Brent Toplin "Between Black and White: Attitudes toward Southern Mulattoes, 1830–1861," *Journal of Southern History* 45 (May 1979):192.

3. For the life of the Branch (Bruce) family in Missouri, see Bruce, *The New Man*, chs. 7, 8.

4. "Washington Letter," Kansas City *Times*, Oct. 17, 1886.

5. Ibid.; Sadie Daniel St. Clair, "The National Career of Blanche Kelso Bruce" (Ph.D. diss. New York University, 1947), pp. 20–21.

6. New York *Times*, Mar. 18, 1898; Vicksburg *Times*, Feb. 15, 1874; St. Clair, "Bruce," p. 22.

7. St. Clair, "Bruce," pp. 23–24; Maurine Christopher, *America's Black Congressmen* (New York: Thomas Y. Crowell Co., 1971), p. 16.

8. For postwar conditions in the Delta, see William C. Harris, *The Day of the Carpetbagger: Republican Reconstruction in Mississippi* (Baton Rouge: Louisiana State University Press, 1979), pp. 486–87.

9. Frank A. Montgomery, *Reminiscences of a Mississippian in Peace and War* (Cincinnati: Robert Clarke Co. Press, 1901), p. 279.

10. Harris, *Day of the Carpetbagger*, pp. 297–98; John R. Lynch, *The Facts of Reconstruction*, ed. with intro. William C. Harris (Indianapolis: Bobbs-Merrill Co., 1970), p. 80; Vicksburg *Times*, Feb. 15, 1874; Jackson *Weekly Pilot*, Jan. 29, 1870 (quote).

11. Lynch, *Facts of Reconstruction*, p. 80; Montgomery, *Reminiscences,*

33

pp. 272, 279, 282–83; Election Returns, 1871–1900, Records of the Secretary of State of Mississippi, Mississippi Department of Archives and History (MDAH), Jackson.

12. Vicksburg *Times*, Feb. 15, 1874; Washington *New National Era,* June 12, 1873.

13. Works Progress Administration, Historical Research Project, Bolivar County, Mississippi, Records: Reconstruction, MDAH; Montgomery, *Reminiscences*, p. 279; Greenville *Weekly Times*, Sept. 12, 1874; Jackson *Weekly Clarion*, Jan. 27, 1881; New York *Times*, Mar. 18, 1898 (quotes). When Bruce became sheriff, friendly planters advanced $15,000 to cover the bond.

14. Melvin I. Urofsky, "Blanche K. Bruce: United States Senator, 1875–1881," *Journal of Mississippi History* 29 (May 1967):122; St. Clair, "Bruce," pp. 60–61.

15. Harris, *Day of the Carpetbagger,* pp. 323–29.

16. Supt. Bruce's report for 1872, in *Journal of the Senate of the State of Mississippi, at a Regular Session Thereof, Held in 1873* (Jackson: Kimball, Raymond, & Co., 1873), app., pp. 817–18; report of Supt. C. G. Smith, Bruce's successor, in *Journal of the House of Representatives of the State of Mississippi, at a Regular Session Thereof, Held in 1874* (Jackson: Kimball, Raymond, & Co., 1874), app., p. 841.

17. *Senate Journal*, 1873, app., pp. 816–17.

18. Ibid.

19. William C. Harris, "James Lynch: Black Leader in Southern Reconstruction," *Historian* 34 (Nov. 1971):57–59.

20. For a discussion of the radical-moderate Republican division in Mississippi, see Harris, *Day of the Carpetbagger,* pp. 459–61.

21. Adelbert Ames to his wife Blanche, June 28, 1873, in Blanche Butler Ames, comp., *Chronicles from the Nineteenth Century: Family Letters of Blanche Butler and Adelbert Ames,* 2 vols. (Clinton, Mass.: Colonial Press, 1957), 1:468; Vicksburg *Times and Republican*, July 29, Aug. 9, 28, 1873.

22. Ames to wife, Aug. 16, 1873, in Ames, *Chronicles,* 1:524; Vicksburg *Times and Republican,* Aug. 28, 30, 1873.

23. John Roy Lynch, *Reminiscences of an Active Life: The Autobiography of John Roy Lynch*, ed. with intro. John Hope Franklin (Chicago: University of Chicago Press,1970), p. 116.

24. Ibid., pp. 115–16; Ames to wife, Aug. 28, 1873, in Ames, *Chronicles,* 1:540.

25. Harris, *Day of the Carpetbagger*, pp. 466–67; Lynch, *Reminiscences*, p. 116. Although the Republican platform of 1873 took a strong stand against racially discriminatory practices, including the dual public-school system, when harassed radicals assumed control of the state, they ignored the state party's promises.

26. William M. Hancock to Adelbert Ames, Dec. 31, 1879, Blanche K. Bruce Papers, Rutherford B. Hayes Memorial Library, Fremont, O.; Urofsky, "Bruce," p. 124; Lynch, *Reminiscences*, pp. 118–19.

27. Vicksburg *Times*, Feb. 15, 1874.

28. Greenville *Weekly Times*, Sept. 12, 1874. On February 5, 1874, the Jackson *Weekly Clarion,* the bellwether of the Democratic press in Mississippi, said of Bruce upon his election: "He is well thought of by his political

opponents, as a man of moderation and integrity, without brilliance or force."

29. For an account of the "Vicksburg Troubles," see James W.Garner, *Reconstruction in Mississippi* (1901; reprint ed., Gloucester, Mass.: Peter Smith, 1964), pp. 332–37.

30. This was a special session of the new Congress, whose regular session was not scheduled to begin until December 1875. One week before Bruce took his seat in the Senate, the old Congress passed the Civil Rights bill of 1875.

31. Lynch, *Reminiscences,* pp. 119–21; John W. Cromwell, *The Negro in American History* (Washington, D.C.: American Negro Academy, 1914), pp. 167–68. Bruce also later named his only son Roscoe Conkling Bruce.

32. Cromwell, *Negro in American History,* p. 168; *Congressional Record,* 44th Cong., spec. sess., 1875, pp. 8–9; ibid., 46th Cong., 1st sess., 1879, pp. 286, 913; ibid., 46th Cong., 3d sess., 1880, pp. 14–15.

33. *Congressional Record,* 44th Cong., 1st sess., 1876, p. 2101.

34. Jackson *Weekly Pilot,* Sept. 4, 1875; Jackson *Times,* Sept. 30, Oct. 5, 1875.

35. The fall election returns indicate that Bruce was able to maintain peace in the county as well as a united party. Bolivar Republicans won 1,920 votes and Democrats only 348, which was a larger margin for Bruce's party than in 1873. *Mississippi in 1875, Report of the Select Committee to Inquire into the Mississippi Election of 1875, with the Testimony and Documentary Evidence,* 2 vols. (Washington, D.C.: Government Printing Office, 1876), 2:144–45.

36. Atty. Gen. Edwards Pierrepont to Gov. Adelbert Ames, Sept. 14, 1875, in *Appleton's Annual Cyclopaedia,* 1875, p. 516.

37. The conclusion that Bruce did not campaign outside of Bolivar County is based on a study of the Jackson *Weekly Pilot,* Sept.–Oct. 1875, which failed to mention him in its reports of the Republican canvass. Bruce did visit Jackson on one occasion and discussed political developments with Governor Ames. Ames, *Chronicles,* 1:150.

38. This address appeared for several issues in most of the state's Republican newspapers. It can be found in Jackson *Weekly Pilot,* Oct. 4, 1875, and Jackson *Times,* Oct. 4, 1875.

39. Harris, *Day of the Carpetbagger,* p. 693.

40. Garner, *Reconstruction in Mississippi,* pp. 408–9.

41. St. Clair, "Bruce," pp. 95–97; Jackson *Weekly Clarion,* Feb. 23, 1876; Natchez *Democrat,* Feb. 12, 1876.

42. New York *Times,* Feb. 12, 1876. Historians also have accepted the dubious first version of Bruce's speech. See St. Clair, "Bruce," pp. 95–97; Urofsky, "Bruce," p. 126; Samuel Denny Smith, *The Negro in Congress, 1870–1901* (Chapel Hill: University of North Carolina Press, 1940), p. 28.

43. Benjamin F. Butler to Adelbert Ames, Feb. 2, 1876, in Ames, *Chronicles,* 2:281.

44. Ibid.; *Mississippi in 1875,* 1:1020–21.

45. *Congressional Record,* 44th Cong., 1st sess., 1876, pp. 1444–45.

46. Edward McPherson, *Hand-Book of Politics, I, 1872–1876, Being a Record of Important Political Action, National and State, July 15, 1870–July 15, 1876* (New York: Da Capo Press, 1972), 1876, p. 139.

47. *Congressional Record,* 44th Cong., 1st sess., 1876, p. 2101.

48. Ibid., p. 2102.

49. Ibid., p. 2103.

50. Ibid., pp. 2103-4.

51. See the majority report in *Mississippi in 1875*, 1:ix–xxix.

52. Blanche K. Bruce to Rutherford B. Hayes, June 25, 1876, Rutherford B. Hayes Papers, Rutherford B. Hayes Memorial Library, Fremont, O.; *Nation* 22 (June 22, 1876):393; New York *Tribune*, June 15, 17, 1876.

53. Bruce to Hayes, June 25, 1876, Hayes Papers.

54. St. Clair, "Bruce," pp. 104–5; Smith, *Negro in Congress*, p. 30.

55. Vincent P. De Santis, *Republicans Face the Southern Question: The New Departure Years, 1877–1897* (Baltimore: Johns Hopkins Press, 1959), pp. 104, 130–31.

56. T. Harry Williams, ed., *Hayes: The Diary of a President, 1875–1881* (New York: David McKay Co., 1964), p. 86.

57. J. L. Morphis to Rutherford B. Hayes, July 17, 1877, Hayes Papers; De Santis, *Republicans Face the Southern Question*, pp. 92–93.

58. Harris, *Day of the Carpetbagger*, p. 713; Jackson *Weekly Clarion*, Apr. 5, 19, 1876.

59. For a description and biographical sketch of Hill, see Jackson *Weekly Pilot*, Sept. 22, 1875.

60. Lynch, *Facts of Reconstruction*, pp. 192–93.

61. Lynch, *Reminiscences,* pp. 210–11; Rutherford B Hayes, "Ploughing the Four Acres: Mississippi" (a memorandum book kept by him), Hayes Papers; id., list of nominations to office: Mississippi, ibid.; George M. Buchanan to Blanche K. Bruce, Nov. 24, 1877, Bruce Papers; William M. Hancock to Bruce, Oct. 8, 1879, ibid.; Hancock to Adelbert Ames, Dec. 3, 1879, ibid.

62. Lynch, *Reminiscences*, pp. 211–12, 236–38, 241–43.

63. Hayes, list of nominations to office, Hayes Papers. In the state Republican convention of 1880 a black observer from Louisiana (probably P. B. S. Pinchback) marveled at "the presence of a very large number of native whites—men of ability, character and influence in their respective localities." New Orleans *Weekly Louisianian*, May 8, 1880.

64. Quoted, ibid., Feb. 7, 1880.

65. For a recent sketch of Revels's career, see David C. Roller and Robert W. Twyman, eds., *The Encyclopedia of Southern History* (Baton Rouge: Louisiana State University Press, 1979), pp. 1051–52.

66. *Congressional Record*, 45th Cong., 2d sess., 1878, p. 4866; 46th Cong., 1st sess., 1879, pp. 836, 45, 71; New York *Times*, Apr, 4, 1879.

67. *Congressional Record*, 45th Cong., spec. sess., 1877, p. 39; 45th Cong., 1st sess., 1877, p. 245; ibid., 3d sess., 1879, pp. 1260, 1316; 46th Cong., 1st sess., 1879, pp. 2315, 913.

68. Ibid., 46th Cong., 2d sess., 1880, pp. 1920, 4508; 45th Cong., 2d sess., 1878, p. 2598.

69. Albert D. Kirwan, *Revolt of the Rednecks: Mississippi Politics, 1876–1925* (New York: Harper & Row, 1965), p. 50. For other matters of concern to his constituents that Bruce promoted, see *Congressional Record*, 44th Cong., 2d sess., 1877, p. 1547; 46th Cong., 3d sess., 1881, pp. 476–77.

70. *Congressional Record*, 45th Cong., 1st sess., 1879, p. 1314; 46th Cong., 2d sess., 1880, pp. 2195–96.

71. Ibid., 46th Cong., 1st sess., 1879, p. 286; Carl R. Osthaus, *Freedmen,*

Philanthropy, and Fraud: A History of the Freedman's Savings Bank (Urbana: University of Illinois Press, 1976), p. 217.

72. Osthaus, *Freedmen, Philanthropy, and Fraud*, p. 217; St. Clair, "Bruce," p. 150.

73. Quoted in Osthaus, *Freedmen, Philanthropy, and Fraud*, p. 217n.

74. St. Clair, "Bruce," p. 151; *Congressional Record,* 46th Cong., 2d sess., 1880, pp. 2053, 2303.

75. *Congressional Record,* 45th Cong., 2d sess., 1878, p. 2441.

76. August Meier, *Negro Thought in America, 1880–1915: Racial Ideologies in the Age of Booker T. Washington* (Ann Arbor: University of Michigan Press, 1963), pp. 59, 64–65; Nell Irvin Painter, *Exodusters: Black Migration to Kansas after Reconstruction* (New York: Alfred A. Knopf, 1977), p. 243.

77. Blanche K. Bruce to W. L. Nugent, Apr. 18, 1879, printed in New Orleans *Weekly Louisianian,* May 10, 1879.

78. Ibid.

79. For results of the Vicksburg convention, see Painter, *Exodusters,* p. 218.

80. *Congressional Record,* 46th Cong., 2d sess., 1880, pp. 1041–42.

81. Painter, *Exodusters,* p. 250n.

82. *Congressional Record,* 45th Cong., 1st sess., 1877, p. 414.

83. Cincinnati *Commercial,* Feb. 19, 1878.

84. Ibid.

85. Ibid.

86. Painter, *Exodusters,* pp. 139–40.

87. Thomas Holt, *Black over White: Negro Political Leadership in South Carolina during Reconstruction* (Urbana: University of Illinois Press, 1977).

88. Bruce also owned real estate in Cleveland, Ohio. New York *Times,* June 23, 1878.

89. New York *Times,* June 23, Dec. 7, 1878; Washington *Bee,* Nov. 21, 1896; Louis R. Harlan, *Booker T. Washington: The Making of a Black Leader,1856–1901* (London: Oxford University Press, 1972), p. 98.

90. St. Clair, "Bruce," p. 128.

91. New Orleans *Weekly Louisianian,* Aug. 9,1879.

92. Ibid., Mar. 13, Apr. 3, 1880; James M. McPherson, *The Abolitionist Legacy: From Reconstruction to the NAACP* (Princeton: Princeton University Press, 1975), pp. 72–73.

93. *Congressional Record,* 46th Cong., 2d sess., 1879, p. 124; 1880, p. 1495; New Orleans *Weekly Louisianian,* Apr. 3, 1880 (quote).

94. St. Clair, "Bruce," p. 197–98.

95. Quoted ibid., p. 191; Smith, *Negro in Congress,* p. 39.

96. St. Clair, "Bruce," p. 219; Washington *Bee,* Nov. 21, 1896.

97. New Orleans *Weekly Louisianian,* May 8, 1880; Lynch, *Reminiscences,* p. 211.

98. For a description of the changing posture of national Republican leaders on southern affairs in 1879–80, see Stanley P. Hirshon, *Farewell to the Bloody Shirt: Northern Republicans and the Southern Negro, 1877–1893* (Bloomington: Indiana University Press, 1962), pp. 58–61.

99. New Orleans *Weekly Louisianian,* May 8, 1880; Lynch, *Reminiscences,* p. 211.

100. Lynch, *Reminiscences*, pp. 212–13.

101. Ibid., p. 240; New Orleans *Weekly Louisianian*, Feb. 5, 1881.

102. Jackson *Weekly Clarion*, Jan. 27, 1881, quoting the Washington *Post*.

103. For the Republican division over the independent movement, see Lillian A. Pereyra, *James Lusk Alcorn, Persistent Whig* (Baton Rouge: Louisiana State University Press, 1966), pp. 188–89.

104. St. Clair, "Bruce," p. 173; *Nation* 32 (May 26, 1881):360.

105. Urofsky, "Bruce," pp. 138–39; St. Clair, "Bruce," pp. 194, 199.

106. St. Clair, "Bruce," pp. 204–5, quoting New York *Age*.

107. Ibid., pp. 214–15, 247.

108. Washington *Bee*, Dec. 5, 1896.

109. Ibid., March 6, 1897. During December 1896 and January 1897, the *Bee* carried numerous excerpts from black newspapers promoting the candidacy of Bruce for a position in the cabinet.

110. Ibid., Dec. 19, 1896; Jan. 30, Mar. 6, 1897. The New York *Age* was a notable exception to the black newspapers that supported Bruce. T. Thomas Fortune, editor of the *Age*, charged that Bruce was "a negative character on the race question."

111. New York *Times*, Mar. 18, 1898; Smith, *Negro in Congress*, p. 41.

112. New York *Times*, Mar. 18, 1898.

113. St. Clair, "Bruce," p. 251, quoting Washington *Post*; Lynch, *Reminiscences*, p. 402. See also, New York *Tribune*, Mar. 18, 1898, and Washington *Colored American*, Mar. 26, 1898, quoted in St. Clair, "Bruce," pp. 252–53.

2

John Roy Lynch: Republican Stalwart from Mississippi

J OHN ROY LYNCH'S LIFE encompassed a momentous era, and he was a part of much that occurred. Born on a Louisiana plantation in 1847, he knew slavery from experience and observation. He knew the heartbreak of a slave mother when an Irish father died before completing the planned emancipation of her and her children. He knew her bitter disappointment when the father's friend broke his promise and kept them all in slavery. He experienced the tragic breakup of the family, when he was sent to work on a plantation while the others remained in Natchez/ He knew hard work, the rewards for doing the "right thing and staying in his place," and the punishments for precocity and for "conduct unbecoming a slave."

Long before John Roy Lynch became paymaster in the United States army, he knew what war was like. As a teenager he saw Union forces invade the lower Mississippi River Valley, where he lived. This was, for him, a war of deliverance; and when Union forces approached the area, he joined other slaves in a general strike and in the enjoyment of freedom long before the cessation of hostilities. Perhaps this early contact with soldiers—as a camp employee and a waiter on a naval vessel—had something to do with his seizing the opportunity, some thirty-five years later, to become a major in the United States Army. In 1863 and 1864, however, so lofty a rank in so grand an army was beyond his wildest dreams.

For Lynch the postwar years were years of discovery. He picked up a few of the rudiments of education as he served his owner and the guests at meals. The most valuable lesson he learned was that education was important; his mistress, he observed, became outraged when he displayed any knowledge at all. When the whites of Mississippi began to establish schools in 1865, they made no provisions for educating blacks. Lynch had to wait until a group of northern teachers established an evening school for freedmen in 1866. Lynch attended for the four months that it remained open. After that his education was at best informal—reading books and newspapers and listening to the recitations in the white school across the alley from the photographic studio where he worked. Within a few years he had not only become quite literate but had also developed a capacity for expression that made a favorable impression on his listeners. He was developing talents and acquiring experience that would take him successively into politics, public service, the practice of law, and the pursuit of historical studies.

I

For Mississippi freedmen—indeed, for freedmen everywhere—the postwar years were exceedingly difficult. For more than two years after the Civil War, they had no economic opportunities that would set them on the road to real freedom and independence. The great fear was that the freedmen might actually become independent or dangerous in some other way, and everything was done to forestall any such grave eventuality. The black codes, especially those enacted by Mississippi in 1865, were in many respects reminiscent of the old slave codes. In the effort to prevent freedmen from becoming independent farmers, Mississippi went so far as to forbid the sale of land to Negroes, except in incorporated towns. Under the pretext of preserving the public peace, the state also restricted the activities of freedmen in a dozen different ways.

Meanwhile, Mississippi and the other states of the old Confederacy were governed at every level by whites, most of them native born and former Confederates. Political participation of blacks, however well qualified, was beyond the thought of any responsible white leader in the South and, indeed, of most citizens in the country. The suggestion that they should become voters was greeted with the same kind of amused incredulity that greeted the suggestion that schools should be provided for the freedmen.

Most southerners seemed to feel that it was difficult enough to go down to defeat in the Civil War and to lose their slaves as well. It was too much to expect them to go beyond the acceptance of defeat and emancipation to regard the freedmen as political and social equals. They had reached the limit in making concessions. They would stand firm against the Freedmen's Bureau, which proposed not only to educate the freedmen but to encourage them to seek economic independence. They would be even more firm, if that were possible, against such groups as the Union League, which catechized Negroes in politics and held before them the prospect of social equality. Southern whites did their best, through laws, economic sanctions, intimidation, and violence, to hold the line. But their intransigence ignored the implications of the very concrete results of the Civil War. The victors would

40

JOHN ROY LYNCH
Moorland-Spingarn Research Center, Howard University

not, at least in 1866 and 1867, permit the vanquished to turn the clock back. Consequently they insisted on a new dispensation in 1867, in which the freedmen were to enjoy political equality. Surely this was an indication that the old order was changing.

Lynch was scarcely twenty years old when new political opportunities came to him and the other freedmen with their enfranchisement in 1867. He made the most of his opportunities. He became active in one of the local Republican clubs in Natchez and wrote and spoke in support of the new state constitution. Soon he displayed the talents that were to take him far in the political world. One of the first to recognize them was Governor Adelbert Ames, who, in 1869, appointed him to the office of justice of the peace. His own account of his experiences as a neophyte judge is a rare documentation of the efforts of freedmen to understand the intricacies of the law and their obligations and rights under it. The picture Lynch gives of himself is that of a venerable sage, freely sharing his advice with the uninitiated who appeared before him. One almost forgets that at the time Lynch was only twenty-one.

Lynch was destined for higher public office, and before the end of his first year as justice of the peace he was elected to the House of Representatives of the Mississippi legislature, where he served until 1873. The journals of the legislature make it clear that he was a most active and even popular member. In his first term he became a member of two important standing committees: the Committee on Military Affairs and the Committee on Elections. Immediately he indicated a lively interest in the deliberations; and if he was not always successful in carrying the day for the measures he advocated, he succeeded in serving notice that he would not be ignored. He offered amendments to pending bills, presented riders to measures before the House, and dropped into the hopper his own bills covering a variety of matters.[1]

He was a much more important member in the next session of the legislature, which met in 1871. He even received one vote for the speakership. The new speaker, H.W. Warren of Leake County, made good use of his erstwhile rival. He appointed him to the special committee on resolutions to express sympathy in the death of members of the House and to the joint special committee on printing rules for the use of the House and the Senate. Warren also appointed Lynch to the standing committees on public education and the judiciary and to the chairmanship of the Committee on Elections.

Lynch soon established himself as one of the most important members of the legislature. Frequently he offered resolutions, motions, and bills. Apparently he assumed a responsibility that was tantamount to that of majority leader. Lynch frequently offered the motion to consider the business that lay on the Speaker's desk, and invariably his motion carried. He offered amendments to pending legislation, and the amendments were supported by a majority of the House. The member from Adams County had clearly achieved a status that was in marked contrast to his position as neophyte and outsider in the previous session.[2]

When the legislature met on January 2, 1872, few would dispute the claim that John R. Lynch could become the most important member of the House. On the first day he gained a seat on the Committee on Credentials; on the second day he was elected Speaker of the House. It is not difficult to believe that he had much to do with the election of his political ally, James Hill, as sergeant at arms of the House. As Speaker, Lynch generally voted with the majority and joined the efforts of the legislature to eliminate most of the laws of the pro-Confederate legislature of 1865–66. When the House was unable to agree on a plan for redistricting the state, the body placed the matter in the hands of the Speaker. Lynch then devised a plan that would make five districts safely and reliably Republican and one district Democratic. At the end of the session, in April 1872, the House considered a resolution to tender thanks to "Hon. J. R. Lynch, for the able, efficient, and impartial manner in which he presided over the deliberations of this body during the present session." John Calhoun of Marshall County moved to strike the word *impartial*, which was lost, and the resolution was adopted.[3]

Thus Lynch was clearly becoming one of the state's outstanding and influential young leaders. Although only twenty-four years of age in 1872, he was ready for bigger things. That year his party sent him as a delegate to the Republican National Convention, where he served on the Committee on Resolutions.[4] Upon his return to the state, he and his friends decided that he should run for the lower house of Congress against the white Republican incumbent, L. W. Perce. Lynch described Perce as a strong and able man who had made a creditable and satisfactory record. As a native New Yorker and a veteran of the Union Army, however, Perce was the object of bitter attacks in the Democratic press. When Lynch defeated him for the Republican nomination, one Mississippi newspaper called it "retributive justice." It gloated over Perce's defeat and said, "There is special satisfaction in the overthrow of Perce, whose malignant and slanderous accusations of the white people of Mississippi are familiar to the public."[5]

Lynch's campaign was conducted by three popular and resourceful

Negro Republicans, William McCary, Robert H. Wood, and Robert Fitzhugh. The contest was heated and exciting, but there were no bitterness and, apparently, no strong racial overtones. As far as can be ascertained, Lynch's principal reason for ousting Perce was not that Perce was white but that Lynch wanted the seat himself. In the general election, his white Democratic opponent was Judge Hiram Cassidy. Although the congressional district he sought to represent was safely Republican, Lynch would need the votes of white Republicans to defeat Cassidy. After his nomination, Lynch received the support of all or most of Perce's supporters. On several occasions he and Judge Cassidy engaged in joint debates before enthusiastic crowds. When the returns were in, Lynch, the victor by a majority of more than five thousand votes, became Mississippi's first black member of the U.S. House of Representatives.[6]

As congressman-elect Lynch presided over the 1873 session of the lower house of the Mississippi legislature. It was a busy and productive session, which dealt with matters from the changing of persons' names, to regulating the sale of liquor, and incorporating a large number of banks, industrial firms, and colleges. At the close of the session, the House unanimously adopted a resolution complimenting and thanking the Speaker for the manner in which he had presided, "with becoming dignity, with uniform courtesy and impartiality, and with marked ability."[7] Later J. H. Piles of Panola, the chairman of the Committee on Public Works, took the floor and made a presentation to Lynch. He said, in part:

> The members of the House over whom you have presided so long and so well, with so much impartiality and so much of the *debonair,* irrespective of party, have generously contributed, and complimentarily confided the agreeable task upon me of presenting to you the gold watch and chain, which I now send to your desk by the son of one of Mississippi's deceased Speakers.
>
> Believe me, sir, it is not for its intrinsic worth, nor for its extrinsic show, but rather as a memento of our high admiration and respect for you as a gentleman, citizen, and Speaker.
>
> Indeed, if it were possible to weld into one sentiment, and to emit by one impulse of the voice the sentiments of all, at this good hour, methinks it would be "God bless Hon. J. R. Lynch; he is an honest and fair man. . . . "
>
> Doubtless we shall not all meet again this side of the All Hail Hereafter. We will miss you, Mr. Speaker. Be it my privilege now, on behalf of the House of Representatives, to bid you a long, lingering and affectionate farewell.

44

Another member of the House, R. W. Houston of Washington County, spoke of the many questions of parliamentary law that had arisen during the session and observed that the Speaker's decisions on those questions had given "no cause to murmur on account of urbanity or impartiality. And I ask, Mr. Speaker, that you accept my profoundest gratitude for the dignified courtesy and distinguished manliness and marked ability which have characterized your entire conduct as the chief honored officer of this body." Lynch replied that his leaving was "more than an ordinary separation . . . wherein we expect soon to meet again." He remarked that all members had been uniformly courteous. "For your manifestations of confidence and respect, accept my earnest and sincere thanks. In regard to your token of admiration, language is inadequate to express my thanks. I shall ever preserve it in grateful remembrance of the generous hearts of those who contributed to it."[8]

When Lynch took his seat at the opening of the Forty-third Congress in December 1873, he was, at twenty-six years of age, the youngest member of that body. He drew two committee assignments, the Committee on Mines and Mining and the Committee on Expenditures in the Interior Department.[9] Despite his age, he had poise, self-confidence, and considerable legislative experience. On December 9, eight days after he took his seat, Lynch made his maiden speech. He offered an amendment to the bill to repeal the increase of salaries of members of Congress. He spoke with grace and good humor; and although his amendment did not pass, he made a favorable impression on the members of the House.[10]

During his first term in Congress, Lynch was careful to attend to the needs of his constituents. He introduced bills for the relief of private persons, to donate the marine hospital at Natchez to the state of Mississippi, and to provide for an additional term of the U.S. District Court for the southern district of Mississippi. He also offered a bill to fix the time for the election of representatives to the Forty-fourth Congress from the state of Mississippi.[11] He was successful in securing the passage of most of these bills; and throughout his tenure, his success with similar legislation continued.[12]

When the Civil Rights Bill was before the House in June 1874, Lynch plunged into the debate. He said that he had not been anxious to get into the fight but felt impelled to do so because of the extent of the discussion concerning the bill both in and out of Congress. He argued for the bill "not only because it is an act of simple justice, but because it will be instrumental in placing the colored people in a more independent position; because it will, in my judgment, be calculated to bring about a friendly feeling between the two races in all sections of the country, and will place the colored people in a position where their identification with any party will be a matter of choice and not of necessity."[13]

In succeeding months Lynch engaged in the debate on the Civil Rights Bill whenever it was before the House. He sought to deal with the canard that civil rights meant social equality. He pleaded for the retention of the provision that would open all public schools to children of all races. He chided all Republicans who had not supported the bill. In February 1875, less than a month before the bill became law, Lynch made an impassioned plea for its passage. He said:

> I appeal to all members of the House—republicans and democrats, conservatives and liberals—to join with us in the passage of this bill, which has for its object the protection of human rights. And when every man, woman, and child can feel and know that his, her, and their rights are fully protected by the strong arm of a generous and grateful Republic, then can all truthfully say that this beautiful land of ours, over which the Star Spangled Banner so triumphantly waves, is, in truth and in fact, the "land of the free and the home of the brave."[14]

Because of his vigorous support of the Civil Rights Act, many white citizens of Lynch's district were more determined than ever to unseat him. They were encouraged, moreover, by the national Democratic trend that had become clear in the elections of 1874. Their opportunity, they thought, would come in their own congressional elections—to be held in 1875 instead of 1874—and in the regular elections of 1876. While Lynch's renomination was assured, nomination was no longer tantamount to election. Many white Republicans in Mississippi were going into the Democratic camp, either because of intimidation or because they believed the Democratic party served their needs.[15]

Lynch was an active, even aggressive, candidate for reelection. His Democratic opponent was the popular Colonel Roderick Seal. Lynch stood by his record in Congress, pointing out how much he had done for his district and for the state. During September and October 1875, he campaigned vigorously throughout his district. When he spoke at Biloxi in early October, the local reporter said he had been "agreeably impressed" with him. "His deportment and bearing were respectful and polite. . . . He at some length alluded to his record in Congress and gave his reasons for voting for several obnoxious measures, but felt no regret for what he had done."[16] He may have been a victim of foul play during his appearance in Vicksburg. In the course of his speech the lights went out, and a "pell mell stampede of the audience took place which was frightful to behold."[17]

The race was close, but Lynch was victorious. The Democrats, however, made a clean sweep of the other offices. Each side accused the other of misconduct and even fraud. One Mississippi paper exulted over Lynch's victory. The writer said, "Notwithstanding the fraud and intimidation practiced in Claiborne County to defeat the Republican ticket and the determined opposition made against Mr. Lynch on the Sea Coast, we are happy to chronicle the fact that the Republicans of Mississippi will have at least one representative in the Forty-Fourth Congress in the person of Hon. John R. Lynch."[18]

One of the first items on the agenda of the new Democratic legislature was the redistricting of the state. Five districts were to be safely Democratic, and a sixth—taking in every county on the Mississippi River and dubbed the "shoestring district"—was Lynch's district. Although most of the voters were still Republican, there was little hope, even on Lynch's part, that he could win in 1876. His opponent was General James R. Chalmers of Fort Pillow fame, a likely candidate to keep black Republicans in their place.[19] During the campaign Lynch experienced numerous incidents of hostility, which he relates at length in his *Reminiscences.* When it was over, the Democrats claimed a majority of more than four thousand votes. Charging fraud, Lynch sought to contest the election in the House of Representatives. His attorney, T. Hewett of Natchez, served notice on General Chalmers to that effect. When Chalmers indicated that he had not received the notice, Hewett requested that he waive the "want of notice and let the contest proceed." Chalmers declined, insisting that the contest was "prompted by partisan motives and only intended to stimulate and prolong a political assault on the State of Mississippi through him."[20] In the circumstances, the Democratic-dominated House Committee on Elections, of which John R. Harris of Virginia was chairman, would not even consider the case.

Lynch would have another chance to even the score with General Chalmers. In 1880 he announced that he was again a candidate for Congress. The leading paper in his district greeted the announcement with the following rebuff: "Unless we read the times incorrectly she [Adams County] will not only give a majority to [the Democrats] but will also give John such a 'setting down' that he will abandon politics entirely."[21] But Lynch was not easily rebuffed. For more than two months he traveled throughout his district organizing Garfield-Arthur-

Lynch clubs and delivering speeches wherever he could find an audience. One hostile newspaper said his canvass was "tame and spiritless, and his speeches [were] received without applause by his meagre audiences."[22] However, another no less hostile paper reported that every meeting of the local Lynch club was "larger than the preceding one."[23] A Jackson paper recognized the formidable campaign by Lynch when it observed that Chalmers was making a "gallant fight against heavy odds."[24]

Lynch was not surprised to discover that the district, with the election machinery in the hands of the Democrats, gave Chalmers a majority of 1,468. In Warren County alone, more than two thousand Lynch votes were thrown out; and several hundred were thrown out in Adams County. It was estimated that of the 5,358 votes declared illegal, 4,641 were for Lynch and 717 for Chalmers.[25] During the campaign, Lynch had served notice that if he were defeated it would be by fraud and that he would contest the election. On December 21 he served notice that he would contest the election. The notice said:

Gen. James R. Chalmers: Please take notice that I intend to contest your pretended election on the second day of this present month as member from the sixth congressional district of Mississippi to the Forty-Seventh Congress of the United States, and to maintain and prove before that body that I was, and you are not, elected as representative to that Congress from said district; and I hereby specify to you the following named frauds and violations of the law of the land and of the purity of elections which I charge were committed on the day of said election, or with ballots cast on that day in the election for Congressman, by our Democratic friends and supporters with your connivance, and in your interest and behalf as Democratic candidate for Congress in that election.

Lynch made specific charges of fraud in Adams, Issaquena, Bolivar, Jefferson, Claiborne, Washington, Coahoma, and Warren counties.[26]

Then followed the long, dreary contest before the Committee on Elections, about which Lynch tells, in great detail, in his *Reminiscences*. Meanwhile the people of the Sixth District, who were without effective representation for a year, followed the developments in Washington with great interest. If Lynch had been pessimistic about the outcome of the election itself, some Mississippi Democrats were pessimistic about the outcome before the Committee on Elections. They were especially critical of the young Republicans in the House who made much of "rifled ballot boxes, stifled justice, the shot gun plan, etc." One paper complained that such comments forced the main points at issue into the background.[27] On April 27, 1882, the House of Representatives, by a vote of 125 to 83, adopted a resolution declaring that Lynch was entitled to the seat. Lynch, escorted by William H. Calkins of Indiana, then went to the bar of the House, where the Speaker administered the oath of office.[28]

If Lynch felt vindicated by the decision of the House to seat him, he also felt obliged to seek reelection to that seat a few months hence. General Chalmers, however, was so disillusioned by what he regarded as the unseemly control of the state Democratic party by U.S. Senator L. Q. C. Lamar that he announced he would withdraw from the party, become an independent, and support the Republican administration of President Chester A. Arthur.[29] In September the Republican convention at Magnolia conferred the congressional nomination on Lynch, who promised a hard fight to retain his seat.[30] As his opponent, the Democrats nominated Judge Henry S. Van Eaton, "a strong man, an excellent lawyer, [and] a forceful debater."[31]

During the campaign the newspaper attacks on Lynch were especially harsh. When he said he did not favor an early or active campaign, a Natchez editor refused to believe him. "Mr. Lynch," he said, "is a cunning politician, and it will do the Democratic party no harm if a close watch is kept upon him, notwithstanding his quiet professions. He knows very well that still hunting is sometimes better than the most noisy drive."[32] When Lynch visited Ellisville and, instead of speaking, inspected the registration rolls, the same editor pointed to this as an example of "still hunting."[33] The *Ellisville Eagle* said that Lynch's visit was not very productive, since he "found no material to become as clay in the hand of the potter. He said and did enough to give his little game dead away, and to put us on our guard."[34]

Lynch was not merely "still hunting." He spoke throughout the Sixth District during the campaign. At Williamsburg the judge of the Covington County circuit court adjourned the afternoon session of the court, and Lynch spoke for more than two hours.[35] In Natchez he spoke to a "tolerably fair audience" on November 4. He assured his listeners that as a Republican he could do more for them in Washington than a Democrat could.[36] If the Adams County voters believed Lynch, there were others who did not. He carried his home county by a comfortable majority but lost the election by some eight hundred votes. Complimenting Judge Van Eaton for conducting a fair and honest campaign and thanking him for his courtesies, Lynch announced that he would not contest the election.[37]

The loss of his seat in Congress did not lead to Lynch's retirement from politics. He had been the chairman of the Republican state executive committee since 1881, and he would continue to serve in that capacity until 1892. He had been a delegate to the Republican National Convention in 1872 and would be a delegate to four subsequent conventions—in 1884, 1888, 1892, and 1900. At the 1884 convention he received the highest recognition he would ever receive as a party man, even though the circumstances that brought the honor resulted from a factional dispute.

The two principal contenders for the Republican nomination in 1884 were President Chester A. Arthur and James G. Blaine. The followers of Blaine were supporting Powell Clayton of Arkansas for temporary chairman. The Arthur supporters were willing to concede that choice but were prepared to challenge the Blaine forces at some other point. Then young Henry Cabot Lodge and Theodore Roosevelt, who were supporting Arthur, learned that Clayton hoped to receive a cabinet post in return for delivering the votes of Texas and Arkansas to Blaine. Outraged, they decided to oppose Clayton's becoming temporary chairman.[38]

The two young easterners worked throughout the night to garner support for an opposing candidate. When Clayton's name was presented, Lodge got the floor and said he wanted to make a nomination. He assured the convention that he did not wish to introduce a personal contest or to make a test vote as to strength of candidates. He merely wanted to make a nomination for temporary chairman

> which shall have the best possible effect in strengthening the party throughout the country. . . . I therefore have the honor to move, as it is certainly most desirable that we should recognize, as you have done, Mr. Chairman, the Republicans of the South—I therefore desire to present the name of a gentleman well known throughout the South for his conspicuous parliamentary ability, for his courage and character. I move you, Mr. Chairman, to substitute the name of the Hon. John R. Lynch of Mississippi.

The motion was promptly seconded by C. A. Simpson of Mississippi and Silas P. Dutcher of New York.[39] There ensued a lengthy debate with many speeches from both sides. Then the roll of the states was called, and Lynch was elected by a vote of 414 to 384.[40]

Because Lynch was not aware of the possibility of becoming the temporary chairman until the convention opened, he had not prepared a keynote address. Upon taking the chair, he spoke briefly of the importance of unity in the convention and of supporting the nominees "whoever they may be." In condemning the Democrats for their fraud and intimidation in elections he concluded: "I am satisfied that the people of this country are too loyal ever to allow a man to be inaugurated President of the United States, whose title to the position may be brought forth by fraud, and whose garments may be saturated with the innocent blood of hundreds of his countrymen. I am satisfied that the American people will ratify our action"[41] It was the first time a Negro American had delivered the keynote address before a major national political convention, and there would not be another such occasion until 1968.

As a politician, Lynch had few peers in Mississippi or elsewhere. He was a loyal Republican, but he was also loyal to his own supporters within the party. He was a formidable and resourceful foe both within the Republican party and outside it. Much of the appraisal of him by a Mississippi newspaper in 1881 was accurate: "He made and unmade men, organized and disorganized rings and cliques, and directed and controlled legislatures like a very autocrat. He is yet a man of power and authority—yet a shining light in the Republican camp."[42]

II

From Lynch's retirement from Congress in 1883 to his death in 1939 he was engaged in a variety of activities of both a public and private nature. His strong partisanship prompted him to decline a position offered him in 1885 by Democratic President Grover Cleveland. He did, however, accept an appointment by President Harrison as fourth auditor of the treasury, a position he held from 1889 to 1893. We know almost nothing of the manner in which Lynch conducted that office or if, indeed, he was happy in his position in the bureaucracy. He continued his political activities, however; and one gets the impression that politics continued to be of greater interest to him than his position in the treasury.

Meanwhile Lynch had become very active in the plantation and city real-estate market in Adams County. He purchased his first parcel of land in Natchez in January 1869, when he was twenty-one years of age. Before the end of the year he had purchased another parcel of land in Natchez.[43] That was merely the beginning. Between 1870 and 1898 he purchased eleven tracts of land in Natchez, ranging from one to four lots, and four plantations in Adams County.[44] The property in Natchez was clustered in three areas, each on the outskirts of the city. Several of his lots were on Homochitto Street, in the southwestern part of Natchez. He also had several parcels on Saint Catherine Street, in east

Natchez, and several along Pine Ridge Road, in the northeastern part of the city.

None of his plantations were actually on the Mississippi River. Ingleside, which he purchased in 1885 and sold in 1893, was the smallest rural tract, with 84 acres.[45] It was located just south of the city. Providence, a few miles south of Ingleside, was purchased in 1875 and sold in 1898. It contained 189 acres at the time of the purchase, but Lynch purchased some adjoining acreage, so that at the time he sold it there were 221 acres in Providence.[46] In 1891 Lynch purchased 90 acres of the Saragossa plantation, presumably with a view to acquiring all of it later. He had not done so by the time he sold it in 1894.[47] His largest plantation was Grove, the farthest from Natchez, six miles from the city on the southwest side. In 1884 Lynch purchased a part of the plantation, amounting to 694 acres. Two years later he purchased the remainder, 840 acres "more or less."[48] He did not part with Grove until 1905, perhaps the last piece of property he had in Mississippi.[49] Lynch's brother William was involved in some of the transactions and perhaps served as his attorney and business manager.[50]

In the early 1890s Lynch began to study law.[51] In 1896 he passed the Mississippi bar on the second attempt. Shortly thereafter, he became a partner in the law firm of Robert H. Terrell in Washington, D.C. Terrell had been a clerk in Lynch's office when Lynch was fourth auditor of the treasury, and Lynch had developed a high regard for the young man. Lynch continued to practice law in Mississippi and the District of Columbia until he went into the army in 1898.

Surely it was not a strong interest in military life or a deep sense of patriotism that lured Lynch into the United States Army during the Spanish-American War. It was, rather, a high regard for President William McKinley, whom he had known during his years in Congress, and a keen sense of party responsibility when the president asked him to serve. To his surprise he was immensely pleased with the life of an army officer; and since he was at loose ends, he also found it a source of fulfillment. His marriage to Ella Somerville in 1884, by whom he had one daughter, had ended with a divorce in 1900. There was at least no family reason why he should not accept the regular-army commission that was offered him in 1901.

As paymaster, Lynch had the opportunity to travel to many parts of the world. He went to Haiti and to other islands in the Caribbean. For a time he was stationed at San Francisco, where he witnessed the earthquake and fire in 1906. He journeyed to the Philippines and visited other faraway places. Everywhere he showed that zest for life and healthy curiosity about people and places that had characterized his early years. During these travels he met Mrs. Cora Williamson, whom he married in 1911, the year he retired from the army.

In the following year Lynch and his wife moved to Chicago, where he entered the practice of law and engaged in real estate business. In 1915 they purchased a home at 4028 Grand Boulevard (later South Parkway and still later Dr. Martin Luther King, Jr., Drive) where they lived for the remainder of their lives. In Chicago Lynch lived a rather quiet life. He was not active in politics, and the records do not reveal a very active law practice or real estate business.[52] He saw clients in the late afternoon and evening. Most of his business dealt with real estate transactions. He took great care in explaining to his clients the meaning of all statements in the legal documents, and he made certain that their income was adequate to make the payments on the property they were purchasing.[53]

When Oscar DePriest was nominated for Congress in 1928, Lynch, who was referred to as a "patent expert," was asked to comment on his years in Congress and on what would be required of a Negro in Congress in the twentieth century. He said: "We need a man who will have the courage to attack not only his political opponents, but those within his own party who fail to fight unfair legislation directed toward people of color who helped to elect them. He should use every effort to force the hand of the man who says he is our friend while seeking support, but maneuvers just the opposite way when vital issues come up."[54] Doubtless the requirements he set up for DePriest were requirements that Lynch felt he had set up for himself some forty-five years earlier.

III

While Lynch's principal lifelong interests were centered in politics, business, and military affairs, he participated in the discussion of the general problem of the position of Negro Americans in the life of their country. To be sure, he frequently spoke on the subject during his years in Congress, but he also played a part with his fellow blacks as they searched for solutions to the critical problems they faced. As early as 1879 he participated in the National Conference of Colored Men held in Nashville. It was an important gathering to consider the implications of Negro migration. Among those in attendance were William H. Councill of Alabama, John W. Cromwell of Washington, Norris Wright Cuney of Texas, Richard R. Wright of Georgia, and William Still of Pennsylvania. Lynch presided over the meeting and may have had something to do with writing the address that commended Negroes for leaving their communities, viewing it as "evidence of healthy growth in manly independence."[55]

Several years later Lynch discussed the problem of Negro labor in an article entitled "Should Colored Men Join Labor Organizations?" He enthusiastically endorsed the proposition that Negroes should join a labor organization if it did not seek to accomplish its objectives "through a resort to lawlessness and violence. They should maintain their reputation of being a law-abiding and law-observing people, except so far as may be necessary for the protection of themselves and their families." Lynch believed that organizations were indeed the best way for laborers to secure the rights to which they were entitled without violating the law. He urged Negro parents to educate their sons and daughters who planned to enter the industrial field so that they could not be denied membership in labor organizations—which he did not seem to trust—because they lacked the training. "There ought not to be any discrimination in the interest of, or against, any class of persons on account of race, color or religion," he concluded.[56]

Lynch believed the history of Negroes in American life had a direct and important bearing on their current and future status. He was an avid reader, and although he did not mention specific titles of books, he doubtless read many works that impugned the ability and integrity of Negroes during Reconstruction. He stated in 1913 that "in nearly everything that has been written about Reconstruction during the last quarter of a century," the claim had been set forth that the enfranchisement of black men had been a mistake, that the Reconstruction governments in the South were a failure, and that the Fifteenth Amendment was premature and unwise.

The contemporary interpretations of the Reconstruction era greatly distressed Lynch, and in 1913 he published a book entitled *The Facts of Reconstruction* to "present the other side." His primary objective, he said, was "to bring to public notice those things that were commendable and meritorious, to prevent the publication of which seems to have been the primary purpose of nearly all who have thus far written upon that important subject." He insisted, however, that his work contained no extravagant or exaggerated statements and there had been no effort to "conceal, excuse, or justify any act that was questionable or wrong."[57] Lynch's work is the most extensive account of the post–Civil War years written by a Negro participant.

Lynch's efforts to write Reconstruction history had little or no immediate impact on the historical profession. The view that James W.

Garner had set forth in 1901 in his *Reconstruction in Mississippi* and that Lynch was seeking to refute was widely accepted. And although Lynch's volume went through three printings in two years, his *Facts* did not find its way into the histories that were written in the two decades following its appearance.[58] It received none of the attention that was lavished on Thomas Dixon's *Birth of a Nation*, which was filmed two years after *Facts* appeared, or Claude Bowers's *The Tragic Era*, which appeared in 1929. The film and Bowers's popular, journalistic version of Reconstruction merely made even more acceptable the interpretation that Lynch was attacking.

During his last years Lynch spent much time working on an autobiography, *Reminiscences of an Active Life*, in which he sought once more to set the record straight. Shortly after he completed the work, his health began to decline. On November 2, 1939, he died in his Chicago residence at the age of ninety-two. Two days later funeral services were held at Saint Thomas Episcopal Church, and he was buried with military rites at Arlington National Cemetery in Washington, D.C., on November 6.[59] The New York *Times* referred to him as "one of the most fluent and forceful speakers in the seventies and eighties."[60] The Chicago *Tribune* called him "the grand old man of Chicago's Negro citizenry."[61]

The political leadership that Lynch provided is an example of how it was possible for a person of remarkable talents to transcend race. As a member of the state legislature and Speaker of the lower house, he won the respect and even the admiration of members on both sides of the aisle. He was not so deferential to whites that he would not seek an office held by a white member of his own party. In successfully opposing an incumbent congressman Lynch argued the point that blacks had as much right to public office as whites. The vigor with which he contested elections, even when unsuccessful, demonstrated a resourcefulness and political acumen that were uncommon among politicians of any race.

Obviously Lynch was no mere party functionary. Whether in Jackson, Mississippi, or Washington, D.C., or at a national convention of the Republican party, he was more "his own man" than an uncritical servant of the party's biddings. His career as an active politician spanned an entire generation that saw the political fortunes of Negro Americans rise to a level of some respectability in some quarters and then descend to a level where they had virtually no respectability anywhere. Through it all Lynch stood for party allegiance but only if, through justice and fairness, the party deserved it.

Notes

An earlier version of this essay appeared as the introduction to John Hope Franklin, ed., *Reminiscences of an Active Life: The Autobiography of John Roy Lynch* (Chicago: University of Chicago Press, 1970), and parts are reprinted with the permission of the University of Chicago Press. Unless otherwise noted, references to Lynch's early life and political career are drawn from his *Reminiscences*.

1. See the *Journal of the House of Representatives of the State of Mississippi* (Jackson: Kimball, Raymond & Co., 1870), pp. 98–99, 155, 159, 415, 776–77.

2. *House Journal* (Jackson: Alcorn & Fisher, 1871), pp. 7, 12, 24, 25, 30, 34, 263, 756–57, 1042.

3. *House Journal* (Jackson: Kimball, Raymond & Co., 1872), pp. 3, 4, 9, 34, 333, 343, 863.

4. *Presidential Election, 1872: Proceedings of the National Union Republican Convention* (Washington, D.C.: Gibson Brothers, 1872), pp. 9, 33.

5. Jackson *Weekly Clarion*, Sept. 5, 1872.

6. John Hope Franklin, ed., *Reminiscences of an Active Life: The Autobiography of John Roy Lynch* (Chicago: University of Chicago Press, 1970), pp. 99–106.

7. *House Journal*, 1873 (Jackson: Kimball, Raymond & Co., 1873), p. 2055.

8. Ibid., pp. 2057–58.

9. U.S., Congress, House, *Congressional Record*, 43d Cong., 1st sess., 1873, p. 74.

10. Ibid., pp. 118–19; James G. Blaine, *Twenty Years of Congress: From Lincoln to Garfield with a Review of the Events Which Led to the Political Revolution of 1860*, 2 vols. (Norwich, Conn.: Henry Bill Publishing Co., 1884–86), 2:515.

11. *Congressional Record*, 43d Cong., 1st sess., 1873, pp. 370, 766, 1121, 3770, 3990-91, 4445-46.

12. See, for example, ibid., 44th Cong., 1st sess., 1875, pp. 206, 321, 1203; ibid., 47th Cong., 1st sess., 1882, pp. 3946, 4531.

13. Ibid., 43d Cong., 1st sess., 1873, p. 4955.

14. Ibid., 43d Cong., 2d sess., 1875, p. 947.

15. James W. Garner, *Reconstruction in Mississippi* (New York: Macmillan, 1901), p. 372.

16. *Hinds County Gazette*, Oct. 25, 1875.

17. Quoted ibid., Oct. 12, 1875.

18. Jackson *Weekly Mississippi Pilot*, Nov. 20, 1875.

19. During Reconstruction *black Republican* was an opprobrious term used by Conservatives to describe Republicans who supported equal rights for Negroes.

20. *Hinds County Gazette*, Jan. 31, 1877.

21. Natchez *Daily Democrat and Courier*, Sept. 12, 1880.

22. Greenville *Times*, Sept. 24, 1880; quote, ibid.

23. Natchez *Daily Democrat and Courier,* Sept. 30, 1880.

24. Jackson *Weekly Clarion*, Oct. 20, 1880.

25. *Hinds County Gazette*, Dec. 8, 1880.

26. Natchez *Daily Democrat and Courier*, Dec. 21, 1880.

27. Ibid., Apr. 29, 1882.

28. Ibid., Apr. 30, 1882.

29. Ibid., May 13, 1882.

30. Natchez *Daily Democrat,* Sept. 2, 1882.

31. Raymond *Gazette,* Nov. 1, 1882.

32. Natchez *Daily Democrat*, Sept. 26, 1882.

33. Ibid., Oct. 3, 1882.

34. Quoted ibid.

35. Ibid., Nov. 3, 1882.

36. Ibid., Nov. 5, 1882.

37. Ibid., Nov. 17, 1882.

38. John A. Garraty, *Henry Cabot Lodge: A Biography* (New York: Alfred A. Knopf, 1953), p. 78.

39. *Proceedings of the Eighth Republican National Convention Held at Chicago, Illinois, June 3, 4, 5, and 6, 1884* (Chicago: Republican National Committee, 1884), p. 6

40. Ibid., p. 22–23.

41. Ibid., p. 23

42. *Hinds County Gazette*, Oct. 19, 1881.

43. Adams County Indirect Index to Land Conveyances, from 1789, bk. PP., p. 298, Office of the Chancery Clerk, Adams County, Natchez, Miss.

44. Ibid., bk. QQ, p. 226; SS, pp. 435, 558; VV, p. 657; WW, p. 355; YY, pp. 36, 329, 569; ZZ, pp. 372, 638; 3-A, pp. 469, 757; 3-B, pp. 432, 547, 549, 679, 761; 3-C, pp. 580, 589, 661; 3-D, p. 260; 3-O, p. 657; 3-R, p. 215.

45. Ibid., bk. ZZ, p. 372; Adams County Land Deed Records, Office of the Chancery Clerk, bk. 3-K, p. 348.

46. Index to Land Conveyances, bk. UU, p. 444; YY, p. 36; 3-B, pp. 547, 549, 679, 761; Land Deed Records, bk. 3-P, p. 723.

47. Index to Land Conveyances, bk. 3-G, p. 495; Land Deed Records, bk. 3-K, p. 371.

48. Index to Land Conveyances, bk. YY, p. 569; 3-A, p. 469.

49. Land Deed Records, bk. 4-P, p. 19.

50. In several of the transactions William Lynch is the grantor, the agent and attorney for John R. Lynch, or the plantation lessor.

51. Lynch discusses his legal career in Franklin, *Reminiscences of an Active Life*, pp. 369, 502.

52. One must assume that Lynch conducted his business from his residence, since he is not listed at any other address in *Sullivan's Chicago Law Directory* (Chicago: Robert B. & Frank H. Sullivan, 1934–35).

53. William L. Dawson to author, Tuskegee Institute, Ala., Feb. 19, 1968. Dawson was a member of the Lynch household for several years.

54. Chicago *Defender*, May 12, 1928.

55. *Proceedings of the National Conference of Colored Men of the United States, held in the State Capitol at Nasvhille, Tenn. May 6–9, 1879,* quoted in Herbert Aptheker, ed., *A Documentary History of the Negro People in the United States* (New York: Citadel Press, 1951), pp. 723–24.

56. John R. Lynch, "Should Colored Men Join Labor Organizations?" *A.M.E. Church Review* 3–4 (Oct. 1886):165–67. For his role in promoting

business cooperation in the effort to solve the problems of unemployment, see August Meier, *Negro Thought in America, 1880–1915* (Ann Arbor: University of Michigan Press, 1963), p. 138.

57. John R. Lynch, *The Facts of Reconstruction* (New York: Neale Publishing Co., 1913), p. 11.

58. Lynch said he had received hundreds of letters complimenting him on his work. He does not indicate that any of them came from historians. John R. Lynch, *Some Historical Errors of James Ford Rhodes* (Boston: Cornhill Publishing Co., 1922), p. xiii.

59. Chicago *Defender*, Nov. 11, 1939.

60. New York *Times*, Nov. 3, 1939.

61. Chicago *Tribune*, Nov. 3, 1939.

Race and Faction in the Public Career of Florida's Josiah T. Walls

Hᴀᴅ Josiah Walls been a fictional character in a Reconstruction novel rather than a historical personality, he might have been a traditional carpetbagger. He was a Civil War veteran who remained in the South to seek his fortune, scaled to great political and economic height in a relatively short space of time, and plunged to poverty and obscurity with equal speed. Josiah Walls, however, was a black politician of considerable skill who fully recognized his limits as Florida's major Negro politician in the postwar era. Only by establishing the firm power base in Alachua County, Florida, that he never relinquished during his career, did Walls manage not only to survive but also to succeed in an age when neither survival nor success was guaranteed.

Between 1868 and 1884, Walls ran for Congress four times (twice elected and twice unseated), served in both houses of the state legislature, commanded white and black troops as a brigadier-general in the Florida militia, published two newspapers, owned and operated a sawmill that employed forty hands, practiced law with two black partners in his law firm, and lived with his wife and child on five-thousand acres of prime cotton and truck farmland in Alachua County. In this same period, he served also on the county commission, on the county school board, as mayor of Gainesville, as chairman of the county Republican executive committee, and on the Florida Republican state central committee. He was an active participant in the National Negro Convention movement in the 1870s, an ally of Frederick Douglass, and an acquaintance of President Ulysses S. Grant.[1]

The specifics of his birth and early years are unclear. Despite the claims of several biographical sketches, including the *Biographical Directory of the American Congress*, that he was freeborn, Josiah Walls was in fact born a slave on the plantation of Dr. John Walls (likely his father), a physician at the Winchester College of Medicine, Winchester, Virginia, on December 30, 1842. Most of the evidence supports this. A contemporary who lived in Alachua County wrote that the congressman often stopped in Virginia on his travels to Washington to "see his former master and mistress," whom he "always spoke of

. . . in the kindest of terms.'' While Walls himself once stated that his parents were free in 1842, he commented on a separate occasion that he never felt "the daylight of freedom" until his enlistment in the Union army in 1863. His military records note "free after 1863," a common heading in the files of black soldiers who had escaped slavery to enter the service.[2]

There is no hard evidence to suggest how Walls may have spent his youth. The Winchester region, which includes Darkesville, a small rural community to the north in present-day West Virginia where Walls grew up, posted the northern entrance to the fertile fields of the Shenandoah Valley. It was mostly a farm area that attracted slaveholders and nonslaveholders alike. Winchester developed into an entrepôt for the transfer of foodstuff to the eastern seaboard. Growing up in this community, Walls's formal education must have been limited, although his later speeches clearly indicate some degree of schooling. His only documented education was for a short time in Harrisburg, Pennsylvania, paid for by a "private source" and achieved "by his own application and industry." The mulatto son of the Winchester doctor gained more than simple rudiments, as his strong legible handwriting and mature vocabulary suggest.[3]

Although one biographical sketch claimed Walls had been impressed into Confederate service before being captured by Union troops in Virginia, concrete details of his life begin with his enlistment in the Third Infantry Regiment, United States Colored Troops, in July 1863 at Philadelphia. His regiment was the first of eleven black units raised in Pennsylvania, and his duty time from infantry private to artillery first sergeant spanned nearly the entire history of the regiment from inception to disbandment in Florida in 1865. Following its organization, Walls's regiment underwent a brief and inadequate training period at Camp William Penn before being dispatched to Morris Island, South Carolina. There it was stationed throughout most of 1863, employed primarily in seige work and fatigue detail; however, the regiment saw active combat in the assaults of Forts Wagner and Gregg that August and September.[4]

The Third Infantry Regiment, in which Josiah Walls served, suffered the problems and hardships endured by all black Civil War troops—improper training, ill-health, and discrimination in pay and promotion. Colonel Benjamin Tilghman, regimental commander, complained to his superiors that his men "begin to believe that they are not intended for soldiers, but merely drudges to do the hard and dirty work; whereas to make them reliable troops, their self-respect and

JOSIAH T. WALLS
P. K. Yonge Library of Florida History, University of Florida

pride in their profession should be cultivated in every reasonable way." Walls suffered from recurring, severely painful hemorrhoids and diarrhea, and an undiagnosed eye disease. He also never received the pay increase due with his promotion to sergeant.[5]

His regiment joined the Florida campaign of General Truman Seymour in February 1864 as part of the Union effort to deny the Confederacy the foodstuffs of middle Florida, salt from its coasts, and European goods that were siphoned through the northern naval blockade. Stationed first at Baldwin near the battle site of Olustee and then in Jacksonville, Walls's unit spent much of its time garrisoning the city and conducting slave raids up and down the St. Johns River.

After a relatively undistinguished record with no citations for merit or discipline, Walls mustered out of service on October 31, 1865, collecting $18.66 in back pay plus a service bounty of $100. He married Ella Ferguson soon afterward in Newnansville, Florida, and was employed briefly as a lumberjack on the Suwannee River and as a teacher in the Freedmen's Bureau School in Archer, Florida. His political career began with the passage of the Military Reconstruction Acts in March 1867.[6]

It is not at all difficult to account for Walls's entry into Florida politics. He was one of few reasonably qualified blacks available for political leadership. With emancipation, Elsie Lewis wrote, there arose a small cadre of blacks, mostly northern, sufficiently educated, and experienced in dealing with whites, who were able and willing to articulate the political, social, and economic demands of the new class; but in Florida, only Jonathan C. Gibbs, who did not live to see the end of Reconstruction, was recognized by both races as a competent spokesman. Josiah Walls was but one of a handful that included Charles Pearce, bishop of the African Methodist Episcopal Church, and John Wallace, author of *Carpetbag Rule in Florida*, who could provide adequate leadership.[7]

Walls's military experience and associations in the Civil War enhanced his political career from the outset. Two whites close to Walls during the war remained close politically in Reconstruction. Sherman Conant, who had been a company commander in Walls's regiment, later became a United States marshal in Florida and a prominent member of the Republican faction that Walls eventually joined. William K. Cessna, his Civil War platoon leader, gave Josiah Walls his initial postwar job as a lumberjack before each settled permanently in Alachua County. Moreover, Walls hired his former commanding general, William G. Birney, to edit one of his newspapers.[8]

A rough-and-tumble frontier style marked Florida politics during Reconstruction, contributing to the burdens facing Walls and the state Republican party. Florida, which one observer had called "the smallest tadpole in the dirty pool of secession," emerged from the Civil War still underpopulated and isolated. Fewer than 150,000 persons lived in the state, according to the 1860 census, and that figure included the slaves.[9] In 1865 Floridians still were living much as they had since 1565, scattered in pockets along the rivers and coasts. Communications and transportation were poor. Political issues tended to be narrow and somewhat parochial, and the statewide development of the Republican party tended to be hampered and factionalized, conditions similar in kind and degree to those found in Reconstruction politics elsewhere in the South. Republicans often fought more bitterly among themselves than with Conservatives and Democrats.

As military Reconstruction in 1867 approached, there was an awakening black interest in politics. Three principal Republican factions developed before the 1868 Florida constitutional convention, two of which survived in an altered state throughout Reconstruction. The first two of these were the freedmen factions: (1) the radicals—the "muleteam" faction led by two white treasury agents, Daniel Richards and Liberty Billings, and a black carpetbagger from Maryland, William Saunders; and (2) the Lincoln Brotherhood—the organization of freedmen under the leadership of Colonel Thomas Osborn, white head of the Freedmen's Bureau in Florida. The third original Republican faction consisted of moderate whites, mostly southern unionists centered in Jacksonville and led by Ossian B. Hart and the Union-Republican Club. After passage of the new state constitution in 1868, these three factions melted into two: (1) the "ring" faction of state officeholders who owed their political allegiances to the Reconstruction governors who appointed them; (2) and the "anti-ring" faction of federal officeholders who owed their political allegiance to the president of the United States and the congressional delegation of Florida.

Ring and *anti-ring* are difficult political concepts. Although the terms were used commonly enough by political participants and observers alike during Reconstruction to identify factional differences, and were popularized by the early histories of Florida's Reconstruction as a way to convey an image of self-serving politicians inured to the needs of people, they never were consistently applied. Two facts are clear: there were very loose ties among factions, even to the point of disintegration during election periods, and there were continual changes in alignment of key personalities. Walls was somewhat more

63

consistent: he began as a mule-team radical, joined the ranks of the moderate coalition that won control of the constitutional convention, and remained an anti-ring politician throughout Reconstruction.[10]

His initial presence in the radical faction is neither surprising nor mysterious. Richards, Saunders, and Billings had begun organizing the Florida freedmen, especially in the Tallahassee area, well before the constitutional convention was called. Their primary intent had been to capture Florida's electoral votes for Salmon P. Chase, secretary of the treasury, campaigning for president again in 1868. When the announcement for the state constitutional convention was published, the mule teamers were ready and first on the scene. Even before Republican moderates and a few Conservative whites who had been elected were able to gather in Tallahassee, Daniel Richards had nearly completed a draft of a new constitution. The Republican moderates, joined by the white Conservatives, eventually left the Tallahassee meeting, regrouped in nearby Monticello, wrote their own proposed constitution, and reclaimed the Tallahassee convention hall, touching off a dispute that was settled by the commanding general of the military district, George Gordon Meade.

Meade arrived in Tallahassee and accepted the resignation of the chairmen of the two factions, Richards and Horatio Jenkins, a moderate white Republican from Alachua County. Then he ordered all the delegates back to the convention hall and caused a roll to be taken of all "eligible" delegates. At this juncture the moderates gained control. Jenkins was reappointed chairman; Richards and the radicals were ousted, and the moderate draft became the guidepost for the state constitution.

There were two significant differences between the radical and moderate draft constitutions. First was the issue whether most state and county offices should be elective or appointive. The radicals wanted to make them elective because Negro voters were in the majority in Florida. The moderate plan sought to make these offices appointive by the governor, insuring that Negroes could not control the state government. Second was the issue of apportionment of representatives to the state legislature. Because the radicals demanded black control as much as possible, their draft constitution provided for representation on the basis of population, meaning expanded representation from the black belt counties. The moderate constitution, on the other hand, favored the smaller and less populated white counties by providing for restrictive representation. Each county was apportioned one representative, and no county could have more than four. The net effect was to insure that Reconstruction Florida under Republican administration continued fixed in white hands. Meade recommended to Congress that the moderate plan be adopted as the legitimate draft. Shortly thereafter, the radicals disappeared as a discrete faction, with each of its members lining up in either the ring or anti-ring group.[11]

Walls played only a minor role in the convention. He did not serve on any committees when the convention opened, although later he was appointed by the moderates to the finance and militia committees. His voting clearly shows the point at which he gave up the radicals and joined the more powerful moderate group. Walls voted with the radicals on all key roll-call votes save one—the final adoption of the moderate constitution. That decision not only preserved his political future, but it also marked the definable limits to his role as a black politician.[12]

There are two standard historiographic interpretations of the 1868 state constitutional convention and its aftermath in Reconstruction Florida. The traditional Dunningite view stresses that the convention fight, which resulted in separate meetings and two proposed documents, centered on race—the radicals wishing to impose "Negro rule" and the whites determined to resist. The modern revisionist view, on the other hand, emphasizes the political factionalism extant in the Republican party. Jerrell Shofner has argued that moderate Republicans and white Conservatives merged at Monticello because the radicals were "unbending" in their demands. "The radical leaders lost because they asked too much and could not accept less since their entire support came from Negroes."[13]

Neither interpretation is fully satisfactory. Of the twenty-one radicals at the convention, six were white: four were Union sympathizers during the Civil War and had suffered materially for their beliefs; three were deserters from the Confederate forces; and none were in sound financial condition. These white radicals may have been unyielding as a result of their previous treatment. The other radicals were black (five blacks were also listed in the original moderate-Conservative coalition), and the fact that they lost out in the convention does reinforce the Dunningite interpretation that it had been a struggle between races. Clearly, the state constitution was produced by a coalition of whites that guaranteed Florida's Reconstruction government would remain in white control. But the primary motivation for this coalition was not because the radicals were unwilling to modify their demands. Rather the coalition came about because of a previous political meeting of the Republican party held in July 1867.[14]

At the July platform meeting of the Republican party, the first state-wide political convention of the Reconstruction GOP, there had been a spirited debate over the issue of who should chair the convention. There had been three candidates, Ossian Hart of the Union-Republican Club of Jacksonville, Thomas Osborn of the Freedmen's Bureau, and Harrison Reed of the Direct Tax Commission and eventually the first governor under the new constitution. The radical mule-team faction chose not to nominate their own candidate, but to swing their votes behind Osborn, who won the chairmanship. It was to prevent the black radicals from continuing to exercise such a powerful position between moderate whites that the 1868 convention coalition of white moderates and conservatives came into existence. Thus, from the outset of Reconstruction, no black politician had an option other than to join with the moderate faction. Even after Republicans had split into ring and anti-ring groups, whites continued to maintain political control of each. This was the political reality limiting Josiah Walls's power and position. [15]

Because Republican factionalism produced a continuing instability in the constitutional convention's aftermath, moderate whites attempted a fence-mending campaign with Negro former radicals, including Josiah Walls. In Alachua County, which contained 12,000 whites and 5,000 blacks but had cast 979 black votes to only 8 white votes in the election for convention delegates, the local Republican executive committee was organized into a biracial structure that distributed power between whites and blacks. William K. Cessna, Leonard Dennis, and Horatio Jenkins represented the whites, while Walls and Henry S. Harmon—his friend, political confidante, and future law partner—led the blacks. Walls was nominated and then elected to the state legislature, as were Harmon, Cessna, and Jenkins, in an effort to promote party unity. [16]

At this juncture in his career, Walls began cementing his black power base in Alachua County. If his entry had been the result of being one of a handful of moderately educated and articulate Florida Negroes, his continued political success stemmed more from his accommodation with political reality. Unlike black former radicals who were unwilling to support the new state constitution or align with more powerful moderate whites, Walls returned to Alachua County after the convention and made strong speeches on behalf of its ratification. Three results then followed: (1) Alachua County blacks shared political power; (2) Walls won an overwhelming victory in his first state assembly race against a white opponent; and (3) he was afforded the opportunity to work for black advancement within the state legislature.[17]

Josiah Walls held to a sincere belief in the need to improve the political, economic, and civil status of blacks. As a member of the Florida legislature for two sessions in 1868–69, he supported a variety of measures that would guarantee rights for former slaves, including the Fourteenth Amendment. The major bill illustrating his efforts was one that, had it passed, would have allowed the people of Florida, "without distinction," to enjoy the use of all public facilities. House Bill 28 successfully worked its way through the house in 1869, but failed in the senate despite Walls's active support. A bill he also sponsored to enable black county clerks to practice law in Florida eventually passed; another bill to commit state funds to fight Ku Klux Klan terrorism did not pass. Walls's failure to achieve much for Florida freedmen did not detract from his commitment to try.[18]

His political success, although not his legislative success, can be compared with black ex-radicals who were unwilling to join moderate whites. A good illustration of the political conundrum for radical blacks in 1868 was the fall congressional campaign. Moderate Republicans nominated Charles Hamilton, a white agent in the Freedmen's Bureau, to Florida's single seat in Congress. William Saunders, one of the mule-team organizers, ran against him on an independent radical ticket. The overwhelming bulk of Florida freedmen refused to bolt the regular Republican slate, and Saunders was beaten decisively.

The next major step in the furtherance of his political career came when Walls was nominated to replace Hamilton in Congress in 1870, the result of changing political conditions. The expected Republican hegemony in Florida had failed to materialize. Instead, the party faced a struggle for survival, brought about because of the effectiveness of the KKK terrorist campaign in reducing black votes and the rising tide of white Democrats. To hold blacks in the Republican party, Florida moderate leaders agreed that a black should go to the House of Representatives.[19]

Joe M. Richardson has written of Josiah Walls that in 1870, when he won the nomination to Congress, he was "the natural choice" of his race. An examination of the 1870 nominating convention reveals, however, that he was far from that. He was not nominated until the eleventh ballot and then only after a riotous debate, at least one attempt to cheat on the count, and a near stampede caused by a convention hall fire.[20]

U.S. Senator Thomas Osborn's faction wanted another Negro, Robert Meacham, a former slave from Tallahassee, to succeed Hamilton. Hamilton himself had a bloc of support, as did three other blacks who were also candidates—Jonathan Gibbs, Charles Pearce, and Henry Harmon. Once it was clear to Negro delegates that Osborn's faction could be defeated only by black unity, Gibbs, Pearce, and Harmon withdrew in favor of Josiah Walls. Only then, a newspaper reporter wrote, did Walls become "the ascending luminary and his fortune was made." Jonathan Gibbs pointed out the significance of Walls's nomination, declaring it "not only a vindication of the honor and faith of the Republican Party in Florida," but also a marked triumph for blacks. "This was the great point sought after and gained." If it had been true that white moderate Republicans had decreed that a black should go to Congress, blacks alone determined that the man going would be Josiah Walls.[21]

Beyond the political circumstances that forced whites to choose a Negro congressional candidate, there were other reasons why the black delegates coalesced behind Walls. First, Walls had begun acquiring a degree of personal wealth, purchasing parcels of land in Alachua County in 1868–69. Second, he had clearly marked himself as a black who could not be controlled by white politicians. At the close of the second session of the state legislature in August 1868, Walls had made a public speech in which he had vehemently denied that William Cessna had exercised control over his legislative activity. He refuted the notion that he had been influenced and manipulated, and he defended his or any black man's right to a bold and independent stand. His role in the attempted passage of House Bill 28 bore witness to his belief. Third, Walls had taken a prominent position in the legislative impeachment efforts aimed at Governor Harrison Reed by moderate whites and their Democratic allies. The governor, a Wisconsin carpetbagger and sometimes cantankerous figure in Florida politics, had never maintained a strong alliance with any of the Republican factions. Walls and other Negro legislators voted to sustain Reed in office. Finally, Walls had given evidence of his intention to respond to white constituents as well as blacks. During his state legislative career, he had sponsored several individual white relief bills and the bill establishing the county seat for Levy County at Williston. Moreover, as a member of the education committee he had voted to establish a uniform system of common schools and the state's university.[22]

As his party's nominee for Florida's lone congressional seat in 1870, Walls faced opposition from political opponents within his own party, from his own race, and from Democrats. His first congressional race, successfully contested by Silas Niblack, his Democratic opponent, illustrates the pattern of Reconstruction politics in Florida.

The year 1870 marked the zenith of KKK terrorism in Florida. Klan violence was intended to eliminate Republican officeholders and supporters; in Alachua County alone nineteen murders and numerous less violent frays were credited to the Klan. By this time Walls shared county political power with Leonard G. Dennis, a white carpetbagger from Massachusetts, who had settled in Florida after the Civil War. Dennis rose to prominence nearly as rapidly as Walls and replaced him in the state legislature. The protracted internecine struggle between Walls and Dennis lasted until 1884 as both men maneuvered for control over the county GOP organization, Dennis leading the ring faction and Walls heading the anti-ring faction locally. Their political feud was temporarily overshadowed in 1870 by the fact that both were targets of the Klan. Dennis received several death threats, while Walls narrowly escaped being killed at a political rally when a bullet missed him by inches. As was the Republicans' pattern, both ring and anti-ring factions joined in time for general elections; and in 1870 Walls carried Florida against Niblack in a close election, winning by 627 votes out of 24,000 cast.[23]

Niblack appealed to the House of Representatives' Committee on Contested Elections. He specified a series of electoral fraud charges against Walls. Most significant was his claim that the Florida board of canvassers, composed of a Republican majority, had thrown out a sufficient number of Democratic votes from Duval, Manatee, Brevard, Calhoun, Monroe, Sumter, Suwannee, and Taylor counties to give Walls the election. Had they been counted, Niblack claimed, he would have won by 435 votes.[24]

Walls counterclaimed that he had lost some two thousand votes through Klan violence and intimidation. Blacks either had been turned away from the polls or feared to go there in large numbers in Columbia, Duval, Jackson, and Gadsden counties. U.S. Marshal Sherman Conant testified that "in some of the largest colored counties in the State hundreds of voters had been kept away from the polls by intimidation and violence—by hell raised in general." On January 29, 1873, unable to assess accurately how many potential votes Walls had lost and possessing evidence of fraudulent returns that discriminated against Niblack, the election was overturned by the House. Niblack was officially declared the winner by 137 votes.[25]

Even before this election was decided, the two men squared off again in the 1872 congressional election. By this time the Republican political arena had become much more complex. The national party organization had splintered with the creation of the Liberal Republican movement. Dissidents in the party attacked the excesses of the Grant administration and opposed the president's renomination for a second term. In Florida there were now two congressional seats available as a result of the 1870 census, and Walls and William Purman, the nominee from the First Congressional District (western Florida), were chosen by acclamation on the second day of the state Republican convention in Tallahassee in August 1872.[26]

Walls's 1872 congressional race was marred by party factionalism. Outgoing Governor Harrison Reed, who had faced four impeachment attempts by his own legislature since 1868, tried to wrest the Senate nomination from incumbent Thomas Osborn. At the convention Walls, "in a very excited and determined manner," threatened to withdraw his own candidacy if Reed was chosen over Osborn. Osborn was renominated, however, and Walls publicly apologized for his outburst. A second factional issue surfaced when Reed wanted to remove two white federal appointees—Marshal Sherman Conant and U.S. District Attorney Horatio Bisbee—from their posts in East Florida (the First Congressional District). Through Walls's efforts, they were reinstated by President Grant a month before the election.[27]

A third and in some measure more crucial split in 1872 appeared in the primary center of Congressman Walls's power base. The regular versus liberal Republican schism was manifested in Alachua County by the independent candidacy of Henry Harmon for the state senate. At a local meeting of the county GOP, Leonard Dennis removed another of Walls's supporters, Theodore Gass, from the regular ticket for a seat in the state assembly because Gass had endorsed Harmon. In the meantime, Walls, who had been busy traveling East Florida on his own behalf, returned to Alachua County to battle Dennis. Walls promised that if the move to dump Gass stood, he would stump the county for the entire week prior to the election for Harmon, causing "Rome to howl and the mountains to quake." Gass stayed on the ticket. Both he and Harmon won their seats in the state legislature; and Walls won another term in Congress from Niblack by more than 1,600 votes. He was at the pinnacle of his career.[28]

To appreciate fully Walls's racial concerns in Congress, one must first apprehend the prevailing black ideology of human rights. At the initial gathering of the National Negro Convention post–Civil War movement, held in October 1864 in Syracuse, a National Equal Rights

League was created to help establish an effective racial program. The commonly held view among those delegates was that black rights and equality rested upon the traditional notion of human rights and equality. Black rights, according to black leaders, were *restored* to Negroes, not *granted*, as a result of emancipation. Protection of their rights mandated black political participation, and the logical corollary following that was the need for the power of the franchise. Closely related was the black belief in the primary importance of education. Education not only meant responsible voting but also advancement economically. Furthermore, it should be pointed out that no black leader during Reconstruction advocated social equality; indeed, most, including Walls, separated social equality in the hope of allaying white fear about black equality in other spheres.[29]

Walls's congressional actions on civil rights were firm and uniform with the other black congressmen of Reconstruction. Walls participated in debate and voted for two potentially significant measures for black advancement—the establishment of the national education fund and Charles Sumner's 1871 supplementary civil rights bill. During the course of his remarks prepared in rebuttal to the view that an educational fund was an invasion of states rights by federal power, Walls argued eloquently for a national system of education: "I am in favor, Mr. Speaker, of not only this bill, but of a national system of education, because I believe that the National Government is the guardian of the liberties of all its subjects. And having within a few years ago incorporated into the body-politic a class of uneducated people, the majority of whom I am sorry to say are colored, the question for solution and the problems to be solved, then are: can these people protect their liberties without education; can they be educated under the present condition of society in the states where they were when freed? . . . Imagine, I say, your race today in this deplorable situation. Would you be considered as comprehending their desires and situation, were you to admit that their former enslavers would take an impartial interest in their educational affairs? I think not." Although Walls defended the measure as it was, only a last-minute provision (opposed by Walls) that permitted segregated school districts in the South enabled it to pass, 117 to 98, with 24 abstentions.[30]

Walls's action concerning Sumner's civil rights bill deserves attention, for it demonstrated a sophisticated but unsuccessful strategy. In December 1871 Walls asked that House Bill 374, which specified the removal of all penalties for Florida ex-Confederates affected by the Fourteenth Amendment, be attached as a rider to Sumner's bill. Joe

M. Richardson emphasized that Walls was attempting to cement relations with whites; and while this may be an entirely satisfactory answer for the many individual relief bills Walls and other black congressmen submitted, it is an unlikely primary motive for general amnesty. Walls meant to interface amnesty and civil rights. The Washington *New National Era*, edited by Frederick Douglass, recognized Walls's strategy by calling attention to his "coupling therein amnesty . . . with provisions securing to the outraged colored man the advantages and securities contained in Senator Sumner's bill supplementary to the Civil Rights Bill. We thank Mr. Walls for this happy suggestion."[31]

Walls did concern himself with nonracial issues, especially internal improvements for Florida. While in Congress, Walls introduced bills to establish post offices, customhouses, and courthouses in Jacksonville, Cedar Key, and Key West. He added legislation for improving harbors at Key West and Pensacola and the river systems along the Appalachicola and the St. Johns. Furthermore, he was instrumental in gaining for Florida seven new mail routes during Reconstruction as well as permission to sell public lands for a proposed state canal to be built from Fernandina on the Atlantic Ocean to the Gulf of Mexico. Even the normally partisan Democratic newspaper, Jacksonville *Florida Union*, said of Walls: "Mr. Walls adds his mite to what has gone before and does it well."[32]

In the very loose political milieu that was Reconstruction, it is not surprising to discover that Congressman Walls found specific occasions on which to advance his own financial interests as well as the material interests of his state. One such occasion involved a federal grant for a cross-state canal to be built by a corporation chartered by the state legislature in 1873. This corporation was composed of many prominent Florida Republicans, including Josiah T. Walls. The canal was never built, however. A second instance occurred in 1871 when the freshman congressman sponsored his first piece of legislation in the House of Representatives—a bill for public lands to be granted to the Great Southern Railway Company. It was designed to finance a railroad to run the entire length of the state, from the St. Marys River on the north to Key West and then to connect with other transportation to Cuba and nearby West Indian islands. The Great Southern Railway was a fraud, and it would strain credulity to suggest that Walls could have been an innocent party to the scheme. He was a member of the board of incorporators and received $150,000 of its stock. The Florida legislature approved the act of incorporation on November 24, 1870, upon approval of the trustees of Florida's Internal Improvement Fund. According to the charter's provisions, the Great Southern Railway Company received alternate ten-mile sections of land on either side of the proposed route and an additional five-mile swath if the land was improved. The company was capitalized at $10 million, divided among nineteen men, Walls among them, along with four members of the board of trustees of the state improvement fund.[33]

Walls's decline began with his third congressional campaign in 1874. His opponent, Jesse J. Finley, was a popular ex-Confederate and pre–Civil War Whig who had gained the respect of many East Florida whites and blacks. His campaign was low-key, lacking the typical displays of strident emotionalism that Reconstruction politics often produced. Walls, on the other hand, continued to face a number of intra-party problems. Both Dennis and Walls's former white ally William Cessna opposed his renomination, as also did a number of blacks in his district. The split was not clearly racial; ring and anti-ring groups included blacks and whites on each side. In Alachua County, for example, the postmaster was a white Walls supporter, while the county treasurer was a black Dennis supporter. There were physical encounters among Republicans; Walls and Robert Mayo, the treasurer, came to blows in a local blacksmith's shop. Their "scrimmage" was with sledges and pieces of scrap iron. Mayo was reported to have come out second-best.[34]

There were several points of contention about Walls during the campaign, including those who simply opposed his running for a third term. The Republican *Tallahassee Sentinel* editorialized its opposition on this basis. The paper noted that since 1870 Walls had received $24,000 in congressional salary. "There is not one of the number [of Walls's supporters] . . . who would object to a hack at the same butter." The Republican Jacksonville *Florida Union* indicted him for incompetence, saying that he had neither "the training nor the education, nor the application for mental work" required of a congressman.[35]

His critics leveled three specific charges against him. First was his nomination of William Saunders as a customs official at Cedar Key after initially trying to get Henry Harmon appointed. The second was that he had appointed the son of former Conservative governor David Walker to West Point, and the third was that he was culpable in the Archer post-office corruption scandal enveloping Edward Young. Young, the Archer postmaster, had been accused of misappropriating public funds. The first charge was of little or no consequence; it was common for political appointees to have ties to politicians in an era

73

prior to civil service. Walls in fact never appointed Acton Walker to West Point; he was Walls's second appointee to the Naval Academy after a Gainesville youth failed to appear for his entrance examination. Walker was also the nominee of Senator Simon Conover; thus Walls was not acting alone in this instance. Finally, the Archer post-office issue had been raised by Edward Cheney, editor of the *Florida Union*, who at one time had been removed by the Florida congressional delegation, including Walls, for embezzlement of funds while serving as postmaster at Jacksonville. There was no proof of Walls's connection to Young in any way.[36]

Walls also met opposition from two prominent East Florida blacks. John R. Scott and J. Willis Menard, both of Jacksonville, briefly conspired to oppose his third-term nomination in favor of Horatio Bisbee, a white Jacksonville lawyer. Bisbee eventually followed Walls to Congress. Despite these complications and Finley's own quietude, the 1874 campaign did indeed become a classic black-white encounter. Walls was accused of having penned "The Alachua Circular," an anonymous piece that was supposedly designed to inflame black solidarity and to create a black wing of the Florida Republican party. William Saunders and Henry Harmon were accused of managing Walls's campaign as though it were "a reign of terror." And there was some violence, especially in Lake City, where groups of black and white voters battled each other at the polls. The election was close; the results showed Walls the winner by only 371 votes out of more than 18,000 cast in East Florida. Finley successfully contested the outcome and was seated by the House of Representatives in March 1876.[37]

Although Walls was successful in winning an election to the state senate in 1876, would run again for Congress in 1884, and would serve as chairman of the Alachua County Republican organization until 1890, for all intents and purposes, his career declined rapidly after 1874. His brief stay in the state senate was of no consequence in terms of legislation, as the Republicans were in the minority; and following Florida's adoption of a new state constitution in 1885, which effectively disfranchised blacks, his role as Republican chairman was of even less significance. He carried only two precincts in 1890 when he ran the last time for the state legislature from Alachua County. By then most blacks were excluded from voting, and those few who still were able to cast ballots sold their votes to white candidates.

It would be too simplistic to explain Walls's eclipse only in terms of the historical forces that brought an end to Reconstruction and Negro participation in the governmental process. In Florida at least, blacks had been severely limited from Reconstruction's outset by white control of the Republican party's two factions as well as by white control of the state constitution.

Two things besides inevitable Negro failure in an era of white supremacy brought Walls down. First, the Republican party's stormy factional battles eventually ran too deep to be overcome by an anti-Democratic feeling in general elections. It was not uncommon for Republican opponents not to support each other in November. Second was the nature of Walls himself. While the man understood the limits of his power and prestige early in his career, he moved beyond them once too often. He nominated John Mercer Langston, a black man, to be President Grant's running mate in 1872 at a conference of black leaders in Columbia, South Carolina. He threatened an independent race in 1874 if he was denied the third-term nomination, and he even permitted a "New Departure" faction to be organized on his behalf. He ran in 1884 as an independent against the regular nominee of the GOP, Horatio Bisbee, and the Democratic nominee and eventual winner, Charles Dougherty. He lost sight, apparently, of the lesson he had learned at the 1868 state constitutional convention, when he had left the radicals for the moderate coalition and political survival; no black politician could successfully chart an independent course.[38]

Walls's last years were personally tragic. His first wife died after a long illness, and the 1895 freeze wiped him out financially. Walls and his second wife, who was fourteen-years old when he married her in 1885, moved at the turn of the century from Gainesville to Tallahassee, where he became director of the college farm at present-day Florida A&M University. His daughter broke off an affair with a married man only to kill him after a quarrel. She was sentenced to the state mental institution at Chattahoochee and passed away a short time later. Even his own death and burial on May 15, 1905, went unnoticed. Walls was buried in a small private Negro cemetery in Tallahassee. That same week the obituary columns in Florida's newspapers were filled with notices of the death of General Fitzhugh Lee, but no published record of Walls's end appeared. No will was ever probated and no death certificate was ever filed. Thus Josiah Walls died as he was born—in obscurity.

Notes

1. There are few biographical sketches of Josiah Walls. Two of the more detailed are found in Samuel D. Smith, *The Negro in Congress, 1870–1901*

(Chapel Hill: University of North Carolina Press, 1940), pp. 74–78; and Joe M. Richardson, *The Negro in the Reconstruction of Florida, 1865–1877* (Tallahassee: Florida State University Press, 1965), pp. 177–83. The only available full study is Peter D. Klingman, *Josiah Walls: Florida's Black Congressman of Reconstruction* (Gainesville: University Presses of Florida, 1976). The major sources of biographical material are the Josiah T. Walls service file, *General Index to United States Colored Troops*, microfilm copy 589, roll 90, and pension file, *General Index to Pension Files, 1861–1934*, microfilm copy T288, roll 495, both in the National Archives (NA), Washington, D.C.

2. *Biographical Directory of the American Congress, 1774–1961* (Washington; D.C.: Government Printing Office, 1961), p. 1769; James H. Roper to E. C. F. Sanchez, n.d., E. C. F. Sanchez Papers, misc. mss. box 12, P. K. Yonge Library of Florida History, Gainesville, Florida; *Tallahassee Sentinel*, Aug. 27, 1870; Josiah T. Walls service file.

3. Frederick Morton, *The Story of Winchester in Virginia: The Oldest Town in the Shenandoah Valley* (Strasburg: Shenandoah Publishing House, 1925), p. 147; Roper to Sanchez, n.d., Sanchez Papers.

4. William H. Barnes, *Our American Government: History of the Forty-third Congress*, 3 vols. (Washington, D.C.: W. H. Barnes Co., 1875), 3:216–17; Frederick M. Binder, "Pennsylvania Negro Regiments in the Civil War," *Journal of Negro History* 37 (Oct. 1952):383–417; "Orders, Letters, and Roster of Commissioned Officers, Endorsements, and Memoranda, Third Infantry Regiment, U.S.C.T.," NA.

5. Col. Benjamin Tilghman to Adj. Gen., Morris Island, S.C., Dec. 1863, "Orders and Letters"; "Company F Descriptive Book, Third Infantry Regiment, U.S.C.T."; Walls pension file.

6. *Fernandina Observer*, n.d., quoted in the Jacksonville *New South*, Aug. 26, 1874.

7. Elsie M. Lewis, "The Political Mind of the Negro, 1865–1900," *Journal of Southern History* 21 (May 1955):189–202. There are biographical sketches of Gibbs, Pearce, and Wallace in Richardson, *Negro in the Reconstruction of Florida*, pp. 179–98.

8. Klingman, *Josiah Walls*, pp. 6–11.

9. U.S., Bureau of the Census, *The Statistics of the Population of the United States* (Washington, D.C.: Government Printing Office, 1872), 1:19, listed for the 1860 census approximately 78,000 whites, 1,000 free colored, and 62,000 slaves.

10. The following works contain accounts of the political divisions in Reconstruction Florida: William Watson Davis, *The Civil War and Reconstruction in Florida* (Gainesville: University of Florida Press, 1913); Richardson, *Negro in the Reconstruction of Florida*; Philip Ackerman, "Florida Reconstruction from Walker to Reed, 1865–1873" (M.A. thesis, University of Florida, 1948); John Meador, "Florida Political Parties, 1865–1877" (Ph.D. diss., University of Florida, 1964).

11. Jerrell H. Shofner, "The Constitution of 1868," *Florida Historical Quarterly* 40 (Apr. 1963):356–74; id., *Nor Is It over Yet: Florida in the Era of Reconstruction* (Gainesville: University Presses of Florida, 1974), pp. 165–70.

12. Richard L. Hume, "Membership of the Florida Constitutional Con-

vention of 1868: A Case Study of Republican Factionalism in the Reconstruction South," *Florida Historical Quarterly* 51 (July 1972): 1–21.

13. Davis, *Civil War and Reconstruction in Florida*, pp. 491–513; Shofner, "The Constitution of 1868," pp. 372–73.

14. Hume, "Membership of the Florida Constitutional Convention," pp. 1–21.

15. *Tallahassee Sentinel*, July 15, 1867.

16. The small white-voter turnout resulted from a boycott of the general election by Conservatives, not from the political disfranchisement of former Confederates. Florida election law required that the 1868 constitution be ratified by a majority of registered voters. Conservatives believed that, by registering in larger numbers and then not voting, the constitution could be defeated. *Tallahassee Sentinel*, Mar. 19, 1868; Jacksonville *Florida Union*, Mar. 14, 1868.

17. Jacksonville *Florida Union*, Nov. 9, 1868.

18. *A Journal of the Proceedings of the Assembly of the State of Florida, at Its First Session . . . 1868* (Tallahassee: *Tallahassee Sentinel*, 1868), pp. 129–30, 132–35, 139; *Journal of the Senate, for the First Session, Fifteenth Legislature, of the State of Florida . . . 1868* (Tallahassee: *Tallahassee Sentinel*, 1868), pp. 129, 139, 169, 186.

19. Ralph Peek, "Election of 1870 and the End of Reconstruction in Florida," *Florida Historical Quarterly* 45 (Apr. 1967):352–68; id., "Aftermath of Military Reconstruction, 1868–1869," ibid., 43 (Oct. 1964):123–41.

20. Richardson, *Negro in the Reconstruction of Florida*, p. 178; *Tallahassee Sentinel*, Aug. 20, 1870, carried the complete account of the Gainesville nominating convention.

21. *Tallahassee Sentinel*, Aug. 20, 1870.

22. Klingman, *Josiah Walls*, pp. 21–29; Tallahassee *Weekly Floridian*, Aug. 11, 1868.

23. *Tallahassee Sentinel*, Nov. 5, Dec. 31, 1870. In 1870 there were approximately 96,000 whites and 91,000 blacks in Florida. See *Statistics of the Population of the United States*, 1:19.

24. George W. Paschall, *Contested Election: Silas Niblack v. Josiah T. Walls from Florida. Argument for Contestant* (Washington, D.C.: Government Printing Office, 1872), House Archives, NA, U.S., Congress, House, "Papers in the Case: Silas Niblack," 42d Cong., 2d sess., 1872, H. Misc. Doc. 34.

25. U.S., Congress, House, "Papers in the Case: Josiah Walls," 42d Cong., 2d sess., 1872; *Congressional Globe*, 42d Cong., 3d sess., 1873, pp. 949–52. A minority report was also filed by Congressman Arthur of Kentucky, who, while finding for Niblack, totalled a different vote margin. See *Congressional Globe*, ibid., app.

26. *Tallahassee Sentinel*, Aug. 10, 1872.

27. Horatio Bisbee to Henry S. Sanford, Oct. 9, 1872, Henry S. Sanford Papers, Box 136, P.K. Yonge Library of Florida History. Bisbee reported that Walls had seen President Grant. Sanford was Lincoln's first diplomatic appointment and a close acquaintance of Grant.

28. Tallahassee *Weekly Floridian*, Nov. 5, 1872.

29. *Proceedings of the National Convention of Colored Men Held in Syracuse, New York, October 4–7, 1864, with the Bill of Wrongs and Rights and Addressed to the American People* (Boston: G. C. Rand & Avery, 1864), passim.

30. *Congressional Globe*, 42d Cong., 2d. sess., 1872, pp. 808–10, 902–3.

31. Ibid., p. 168; Richardson, *Negro in the Reconstruction of Florida*, p. 188; Washington, D.C., *New National Era*, Dec. 23, 1871.

32. *Congressional Globe*, 42d Cong., 3d sess., 1873, index; ibid., 43d Cong., 1st sess. 1873, index; ibid., 42d Cong., 2d sess., 1872, p. 3939; Jacksonville *Florida Union*, Feb. 5, 1874.

33. *Minutes of the Board of Trustees, Internal Improvement Fund of the State of Florida*, n.p., n.d., pp. 443–47.

34. Gainesville *New Era*, Oct. 28, 1873.

35. Jacksonville *Florida Union*, June 30, Oct. 8, Nov. 21, 1874.

36. Klingman, *Josiah Walls*, pp. 58–61.

37. *Contested Election: Jesse J. Finly [sic] v. Josiah T. Walls. Second Congressional District—Florida. Brief for the Contestee*, House Archives, NA.

38. Klingman, *Josiah Walls*, pp. 122–40.

Loren Schweninger   4

James T. Rapier of Alabama and the Noble Cause of Reconstruction

Sᴵᴛᴛɪɴɢ at his office desk in Montgomery, Alabama, on July 7, 1872, black politician James T. Rapier, then thirty-five years old, recalled an earlier time when he had been a student in Canada. In a letter to his friend and former mentor William King, a white Presbyterian minister who had founded the Negro community of Buxton, Ontario, Rapier reminisced about studying Latin and Greek in the log schoolhouse, attending services at the Buxton Methodist church, enrolling in a Toronto normal school, and entering the teaching profession. In some ways it seemed as if a millennium had passed since then—the coming of the Civil War, the emancipation of 3½ million slaves, the defeat of the South, and the extension of citizenship rights to blacks—but in other ways it seemed like only yesterday, as he remembered so clearly how much he had matured under King's influence, and how, while in Canada, he had decided to devote his future to the cause of racial justice.[1]

To underscore this point, he traced his rise in Reconstruction politics. Only four months after Appomattox, in a keynote address to the Tennessee Negro Suffrage Convention, he had demanded that southern whites extend to Negroes the vote. Serving as chairman of the Platform Committee at the first Alabama Republican State Convention (1867), he helped draft a document, which, among other proposals, called for free speech, free press, free schools, and equal rights for all—white and black. As a delegate to the state's constitutional convention in 1867, he proposed an article promising Negroes equal access to public places, offered a resolution seeking debtor relief for black sharecroppers and tenant farmers, and sought to remove political disabilities (when Congress deemed it appropriate) from former Confederates who accepted the principle of racial equality as set forth in the Fourteenth Amendment. At the first National Negro Labor Union Convention held in 1869, he urged the president of the United States to create a federal land management bureau to assist former slaves in acquiring homestead land. In 1870 he received his party's nomination for secretary of state—the first black so honored—and though defeated, he later (1871) accepted a position as assessor of internal revenue for the Second District of Alabama, an important patronage office. "[Now]," he declared, "no man in the state wields more influence than I."[2]

Although several white Alabamians wielded at least as much influence as did Rapier, few observers would deny that by 1872 he had fashioned a powerful political organization and emerged as the state's most prominent black leader.[3] His primary responsibility as assessor of revenue was to determine the amount of tax money due the federal government from retail tobacco and liquor merchants, but his activities went beyond the levying of revenue.[4] During his travels through the Black Belt (his district included twenty-three counties), he met with Negro leaders, attended political meetings, and (along with his five assistants) conducted political canvasses.[5] During his stays at his office in Montgomery, he also discussed political matters with local black leaders. "Mr. Rapier is the best intellect under a colored skin in Alabama. His acquaintance among his race is more extensive than that of any man," proclaimed a reporter for the *New National Era* who was touring the South. Furthermore, he was the most articulate, best educated, and most well-known black in the state; he was "the head and front of the Negro Republican party."[6]

Actually there was no "Negro Republican party" in Alabama. Rapier depended on a number of white allies, including Senator George Spencer, congressmen Charles Buckley and Charles Hays, who (along with black Congressman Benjamin Turner) had been responsible for his appointment as assessor.[7] But he also struggled against a number of whites, including former senator Willard Warner, former governors Lewis Parsons and William Smith, and politicians John Keffer, Samuel Rice, and Alexander White, whom he described as "self-seeking office holders" and "quasi-Republicans."[8] They opposed President Grant, refused to accept freedmen as political equals, and, even worse, Rapier contended that they rejected the validity of the Reconstruction amendments. These were strong words. He was accusing members of his own party—the great party of Lincoln—of depravity. Yet, he clearly understood the anti-Negro sentiments of this group.[9] "I shall ever be at my 'Post'," he vowed, "battling for our cause."[10]

Aware of his position as a defender of Negro rights and confident of his standing among freedmen, Rapier launched a campaign in 1872 for a seat in the Forty-third Congress. Several months before the nominating convention, he established the Montgomery *Republican Sentinel*, a newspaper dedicated to the principle of black equality. "I issue 1000 copies weekly and flatter myself that much good has been accomplished," he confided to Republican National Committee Chairman William E. Chandler, "as we reach a class of reader who get no other paper [the *Sentinel* was free] and knowing mine to be edited by one of their own race have confidence in it."[11] The paper cost fifty dollars a week to produce, with twenty dollars coming from Chandler's committee and the remainder from his own pocket.[12] It was well worth the cost. Read and reread, the *Sentinel* became the anti-Conservative voice of many thousands. By the time the Republican nominating convention for the second district met in Eufaula, on August 16, 1872, it was a foregone conclusion that Rapier would be the nominee of the party.[13]

During the late summer and early fall, he carried his campaign to every corner of the district, to Fitzpatrick's Station, Chunnenugga Ridge, and Union Springs; to Farmersville, Hayneville, and Midway; to twenty-six towns and stations in a span of thirty-six days. In localities never before visited by a political leader, he discussed the issues with humor and irony as well as gravity.[14] Tall and handsome, with a dark frock coat and dark skin (despite being a mulatto), Rapier was described, even by his opponents, as an impressive, effective, and forceful speaker. One Conservative newspaper was almost effusive in its praise: "a fine looking man," knowledgeable and quick-witted, he made tremendously effective thrusts at the opposition.[15] Before hundreds, then thousands, of freedmen, he attacked the patronizing attitude of his Democratic opponent—the one-armed Confederate hero of Gettysburg, William C. Oates; he criticized the anti-Negro activities of fellow Republicans; and he "buried Horace Greeley," the Liberal Republican nominee for president opposing Grant.[16] In addition, he expressed his support for federal legislation to provide homesteads for Negro tenant farmers.

Toward the end of the campaign, as both sides pushed the canvass with unprecedented vigor, he reviewed his chances for success. The Republican party had a strong ticket in the field. It was more unified than at any previous time during Reconstruction. The Ku Klux Klan had been driven to cover by the federal district judge Richard Busteed acting under the Force Acts. And he had received the support of local blacks.[17] On election day (November 5, 1872), which was peaceful and calm everywhere in the district, Rapier won by 3,175 votes—19,397 to 16,222. He swept the Black Belt counties (Lowndes, Montgomery, Bullock, Barbour) two to one and polled 2,513 votes in the predominately white counties (Butler, Coffee, Crenshaw, Dale, Geneva, Henry, Pike). In a district where the black and white voters were about

81

evenly divided, he received the support of nearly 18,000 Negroes and 1,500 whites.[18] By achieving the organization of blacks within the Republican party, by campaigning vigorously and concentrating solely on the issues, by seeking to harmonize race relations without sacrificing principle, a Negro had won election to Congress from the capital of the old Confederacy.

Although elected in November 1872, Rapier would not take his seat until the Forty-third Congress convened in December 1873. He would thus have a full year to prepare himself and put his affairs in order. He was by no means idle during the interim. Early in 1873 he was appointed Alabama commissioner to the Fifth International Exposition in Vienna, Austria. In May he boarded a British liner for the Continent. "The moment I put my foot upon the deck of a ship that unfurled a foreign flag," he recalled in a House speech some months later, "distinctions on account of my color ceased."[19] After a two-month stay in Vienna and another two months touring Germany, France, and England, with a special view, he said, toward understanding the plight of working men in those countries, he returned to begin his duties as a congressman.[20]

Rapier took his seat in the United States House of Representatives on December 1, 1873. Joined by six other black congressmen (Joseph Rainey, Robert Elliott, Richard Cain, Alonzo Ransier of South Carolina, Josiah Walls of Florida, and John Roy Lynch of Mississippi), 183 other House Republicans, 88 Democrats, and 4 Liberals, he became part of the largest single party majority in fifty years.[21] With a coterie of able black colleagues, and with such a large Republican majority, he began his duties with great optimism. Only a few days after the opening session, he, along with several other members of the Committee on Education and Labor, submitted a proposal (H.R. 477) to improve the common school systems of the South. It would provide several millions of dollars to be distributed among the states with the highest illiteracy rates.[22] Later he offered legislation to aid businessmen in his section, requesting $50,000 to dredge the Pea and Chochawatche rivers, and additional funds to establish Montgomery, Alabama, as a federal port of delivery.[23]

His most important activities during the first session concerned his defense of Negro rights. He attended the National Negro Civil Rights Convention in Washington, D.C., on December 9, 1873.[24] He met privately with black leaders to discuss the pending equal rights bill (S. 1); and on June 9, in his first address to Congress, he spoke eloquently in favor of Negro equality.[25] Other nations, he said, had caste systems

JAMES T. RAPIER
Historical Pictures Service, Chicago

based on wealth, religious beliefs, or heredity, but distinctions in the United States were based entirely on skin color. The lowest, most ignorant, most dishonorable white man stood above the highest, most intelligent, noblest Negro. "I cannot willingly accept anything less than my full measure of rights as a man, because I am unwilling to present myself as a candidate for any brand of inferiority."[26] He urged his colleagues to support the efforts of blacks to gain equal access to restaurants, railway cars, theaters, schools, and places of public amusement.

Although there was little immediate response to his speech, nine days after he had given it the *New National Era* paid him a high compliment. It reported that he had delivered an address on civil rights second to none, and said it would be read by Negroes everywhere with a deep sense of pride.[27] Yet, as the first session drew to a close, neither his educational proposal, nor his river improvement bill, nor any civil rights legislation, had been brought before the House for a vote. Only his port bill (after a desperate struggle in the waning hours before adjournment) had been signed into law.

Encouraged by the inaction of Congress, Alabama Conservatives became more determined than ever to wrest control of the state from so-called Negro rule. Expressing the attitude of the overwhelming majority of Democrats, the *Montgomery Daily Advertiser* asserted that neither specious pleas nor vague sophistry could avert the inevitable confrontation between whites and blacks for political supremacy in the South.[28] The Mobile *Daily Register* put it simply when it said that the only issue in the coming campaign was whether the elevated white man or the debased Negro would govern the state.[29] In more frightening terms, the Conservative Montgomery *Daily Ledger* said that in the upcoming election, the physical, intellectual, and political supremacy of the white race would be decided forever. "We will ACCEPT NO RESULT BUT THAT OF BLOOD."[30]

Upon his return to Montgomery in July 1874, Rapier found that these frightening editorials were only part of the Democratic campaign to end Reconstruction. Whites were discharging Negro employees, disrupting Republican conventions, socially ostracizing white members of the party, and in some cases resorting to violence. "There was a Killing 7 miles from here last Saturday," Rapier's friend Elias M. Keils, a Barbour County judge, wrote. "The man killed was a colored man, rather earnest in politics."[31] Other racially and politically motivated murders occurred at various locations in the district; and as he began a round of speaking engagements, threats were made against

Rapier's life. "The Democracy told us that Rapier should not speak," former Republican Superintendent of Education N. B. Cloud testified before a congressional committee. "If he did they would kill him."[32]

Despite threats, Rapier launched a vigorous campaign for renomination. In an effort to calm racial tensions, he explained in several speeches that the pending Sumner civil rights bill did not require mixed schools, nor social equality, nor miscegenation, as the Democrats charged, but merely promised blacks an equal opportunity for education. In many states where there was a mixed school law, there was not a single mixed school, he pointed out, but state and federal funds in those states (the latter in the form of assistance to land-grant schools) were distributed to benefit Negroes as well as whites.[33] In other speeches, he urged his listeners to do nothing that might incite racial unrest.

Ironically, when the Republicans of the second district gathered in Union Springs on August 22, 1874, to nominate a candidate for Congress, the threat of disturbance came not from Democrats but from a group of Republicans. During the summer, bitter antagonisms had developed between two factions of Republicans in Montgomery County, one headed by the erratic young lawyer Robert Knox, who had earlier (1871) been convicted of jury tampering; the other led by Vienna-educated party stalwart Paul Strobach, who had served as state commissioner of immigration, a member of the general assembly, and sheriff. Both groups included Negroes, but the first found its major strength among a coterie of party members who opposed Rapier—Arthur Bingham, William Buckley, and Samuel Rice—while the second found its most ardent supporters among Negroes—Charles Steele, James Foster, and Peyton Finley. Besides the desire for local office, the main issue at stake between the two groups concerned the pending impeachment of Judge Richard Busteed, who had earlier been so effective in prosecuting Klan members. Though there were differences within each organization, Knox, who sought to placate his black followers, opposed impeachment, while Strobach, despite his admiration for the judge, reluctantly admitted that Busteed was probably guilty of several impeachable offenses.[34]

Determined not to be drawn into a local fight, Rapier had refused to support either group, maintaining that the decision concerning which faction should be recognized at the nominating convention should be left up to the state executive committee. But at Union Springs, Knox and his followers brandished guns, shouted "Traitor!" and "Scoundrel!" at the opposition and threatened to completely disrupt the proceedings. Rapier later recalled, "I had stood all day between angry disputants, sometimes even forcing them to put up their deadly weapons, and now the danger seemed more imminent than ever, if peace was not at once restored."[35] To avoid a bloody confrontation, he signed a pledge saying that he would do nothing detrimental to the Knox faction in the upcoming election.[36] Within a few days after receiving the nomination, however, he recanted this pledge, explaining that it had been made under duress. But by retracting his promise, no matter what the circumstances, he had committed a political blunder.

Still, the atmosphere of violence was the real issue. In the midst of the campaign, Rapier journeyed to Washington, reported the threats and violent acts to Attorney General George H. Williams, and pleaded for federal intervention—for detachments of U.S. soldiers to be sent immediately to the polling places to insure a fair election.[37] But on election day hundreds of frightened Negroes stayed away from the polls. When a group of freedmen attempted to vote in Eufaula, a race riot erupted; an estimated ten to fourteen blacks were killed and perhaps a hundred blacks and whites were wounded.[38] In the three counties where racial violence was most prevalent, the Republican vote fell off sharply compared to previous elections. As a result, Rapier lost to former Confederate Jeremiah N. Williams by 1,056 votes.[39] The Conservatives also took two of every three seats in the state legislature, all the state offices, and a majority of the other congressional seats. Rapier began proceedings to contest the election, but he eventually withdrew the contest when it became clear that the new Democratic House would reject his claim.[40]

The election of 1874 ended the four-year experiment with Reconstruction and so-called Negro rule in Alabama. The Democrats moved swiftly to consolidate their power. They gerrymandered nine Black Belt counties into six different congressional districts, and they grouped five others—Dallas, Hale, Lowndes, Perry, Wilcox—into a single, overwhelming, Negro district.[41] Since Rapier rented a plantation in Lowndes County in the new district, he decided to make another bid for Congress in 1876. Though nominated by the party, endorsed by the National Executive Committee, and supported by local blacks, he was opposed by another Negro, Jeremiah Haralson, a former slave who was a member of the Forty-fourth Congress. Many white Republicans, including former governor William Smith, Judge Samuel Rice, and editor John Saffold, and even a few white Democrats, campaigned for Rapier's black opponent.[42] Unlike "that darkie Rapier, who believes a negro is as good as a white man," one Conserv-

TABLE 1: *Comparison Showing Decline of Republican Votes in Areas of Racial Violence*

COUNTY	1872		1874		INCREASE/DECREASE	
	OATES	RAPIER	WILLIAMS	RAPIER	DEMOCRATIC	REPUBLICAN
Barbour	2349	2742	2791	2683	+442	-59
Bullock	1263	3100	1588	2497	+325	-603
Butler	1518	1097	2189	1470	+671	+373
Coffee	949	7	1382	72	+433	+65
Conecuh [Crenshaw]	1025	309	1615	382	+590	+73
Dale*	1194	266	1734	260	+540	-6
Henry	2022	281	2020	736	-2	+455
Lowndes	929	3726	1189	4158	+260	+432
Montgomery	3051	7047	3295	6184	+244	-863
Pike	1900	552	2377	727	+477	+175

*Geneva was included in the Dale County returns.
Source: Official Returns of Elections of State Officers and Congressional Election Returns, 1872, 1874, State Department of Archives and History, Montgomery, Alabama.

ative said, Haralson could at least be controlled by the superior intelligence of whites.[43] But in the end, in a district two-thirds black, despite receiving 60 percent of the vote between them, both black aspirants lost to Charles Shelley, a former Confederate general.[44] This was Rapier's last campaign for public office.

TABLE 2: *Congressional Election Returns, Fourth District, Alabama, 1876*

	SHELLEY	HARALSON	RAPIER
Dallas	2490	2979	67
Hale	2170	48	2340
Lowndes	1312	163	3904
Perry	2168	2563	261
Wilcox	1484	2922	664
TOTAL	9624	8675	7236

Source: Official Returns of Elections of State Officers and Congressional Election Returns, 1876, State Department of Archives and History, Montgomery, Alabama.

Turning away from politics, he devoted himself to managing his various business interests. Rapier could draw on a long family tradition of business enterprise. His slave grandmother Sally had operated a clothes-cleaning establishment in Nashville, and had saved enough money to purchase the freedom of her youngest child. His father, John H. Rapier, Sr., who was emancipated in 1829 by a barge master, had conducted a successful barbershop in Florence, Alabama, and accumulated $7,500 worth of property. Rapier's two brothers, Richard and John, Jr., who like himself were born free, both amassed substantial estates. One of his uncles, Henry K. Thomas, managed a thriving barbershop in Buffalo, New York, and wheat farm in Buxton, Canada. His other uncle, James P. Thomas, after gaining his freedom in 1851, married a wealthy St. Louis woman. He began speculating in city real estate; and by 1875, with assets totalling $250,000, had become one of the richest blacks in the United States.[45]

Having lived for several years with his slave grandmother, having always maintained a close relationship with his father, and having stayed with his Uncle Henry during his years in Canada, Rapier had observed firsthand these remarkable economic achievements.[46] Even as a student in Buxton, he had established a small potash (used in making glass) factory.[47] Upon his return to the South, Rapier rented cotton acreage in Maury County, Tennessee, and, later, on Seven Mile Island, near his hometown of Florence, where he also established a steamboat woodyard. In 1867 one newspaper ranked him among the most prosperous cotton planters in the Tennessee Valley.[48] But his entry into politics infuriated many whites. During the 1868 presidential campaign, he was forced to flee for his life from the Ku Klux Klan, losing his woodyard as well as a sixty-bale cotton crop. He recalled some time later: "One night four of us had been selected for hanging. By merest chance, I escaped."[49]

It took several years for Rapier to recover financially; but in the 1870s he secured loans from Lehman, Durr & Company, one of the largest cotton merchants in the region, and rented cotton acreage in Lowndes County.[50] Hiring black tenant farmers, whom he provided with mules, horses, and wagons, he personally supervised the planting and harvesting. Within a few years he was renting seven plantations, employing thirty-one tenant families, and harvesting five hundred bales of cotton each season.[51] His annual income rose to over seven thousand dollars.[52] Such profits elevated him to a position of wealth and economic standing even in the white-dominated society of post-Reconstruction Alabama.

Yet economic success and building a personal fortune meant little to him while the condition of blacks remained substantially unimproved. Throughout his career he had used personal funds to assist his brethren. He served on the advisory board of the Montgomery Freedmen's Savings Bank. After its failure he hired a lawyer and instigated several suits against loan-delinquent companies to compensate depositors.[53] With his own funds he established two newspapers—the Montgomery *Republican Sentinel* (1872) and the *Republican Sentinel and Hayneville Times* (1878). He edited the first himself and hired black Montgomery businessman Nathan Alexander to edit the second.[54] He assisted Negro tenants on his plantations by renting them land at well below the market rate and extending to them low-interest loans on amounts ranging up to a thousand dollars. He told a Senate committee in 1880, "I rent every man twenty-five acres of ground for one bale of cotton, exactly half of what my neighbors charge. I loan money at 22½ cents . . . , about one-quarter what my neighbors are charging."[55] In addition, he gave generously to Negro churches and schools. No person in the state, declared Montgomery Negro John Fitzpatrick, had more cheerfully aided blacks in constructing places of worship or erecting places of learning.[56]

These efforts in behalf of southern blacks and his long-time loyalty to the Republican party prompted several influential party members to urge his appointment as collector of internal revenue, a prestigious patronage position. Charles Pelham, a former congressman who had served with Rapier extolled him as the most competent, most highly esteemed, and most prominent black leader in Alabama, as also did George Spencer, a former senator; while Treasury Secretary John Sherman told President Hayes: "From my Knowledge of Mr. Rapier, formerly a colored member of Congress, he would make a most efficient officer."[57] Thanks to such support, Rapier received the appointment and was quickly confirmed by the Senate. Those who had recommended him so highly must have been pleased when Rapier received the highest praise from Revenue Commissioner Green B. Raum in 1882: "The excellent condition of your office, maintained under the pressure of extra work, indicate[s] a gratifying degree of energy and zeal on the part of yourself and four assistants. Your grade is first class."[58]

Yet, as in the past, Rapier used his office to further the cause of Reconstruction. During his travels throughout his district which included two-thirds of the state, he criticized white Democrats for drawing the color line in politics, attacked local laws designed to keep blacks in a subordinate position, and campaigned for the removal of incompetent and unfair public officials.[59] Especially repugnant to him was Lowndes County's Judge John McDuffie, a Republican who meted out long jail sentences to freedmen convicted of such petty offenses as selling produce after sunset. In a round of speeches in 1880, he urged blacks to reject the judge in the upcoming election.[60] At the same time he campaigned for presidential hopeful John Sherman, one of the authors of the original Reconstruction acts, casting his ballot in Sherman's behalf at the state and national Republican nominating conventions.[61] As collector of internal revenue (1878–83), Rapier was able to maintain his position as Alabama's leading black, even though the Republican party had long since ceased to be a viable force in the political life of the state.

About the time when Rapier began work for the Treasury Department, southern Negroes again became the focus of national attention. Protesting conditions in the post-Reconstruction South, blacks in Louisiana, Mississisippi, Alabama, Tennessee, and North Carolina left their home states, and in a great migration, moved to the North and West.[62] The exodus posed a dilemma for Rapier. He had always considered himself a southerner—"I was born in Alabama,"he said once, "I expect to stay here"[63]—and he had always viewed extreme proposals, such as the complete disfranchisement of former Confederates and the confiscation and redistribution of their property as unachievable, at least by the time he and the other black Reconstructionists had come to power. Now he was faced with perhaps the most extreme idea of the postwar era: the mass migration of blacks out of the South. But he quickly announced that he would do everything in his power to promote and keep in motion what became known as the Great Exodus.

In a grueling two-day examination before the Senate committee investigating the emigration, he explained why southern blacks were emigrating: they were faced with discriminatory laws, inadequate educational opportunities, and intolerable economic conditions. One Alabama statute, he said, stipulated that in certain predominately Negro counties a governor's commission would choose grand and petit jurors. "The proper heading of the law might have been 'An act to Keep Negroes off Juries'," he remarked sarcastically, adding: "It is the application of these laws and the opportunity they afford for oppression that we complain of, and from which the colored people are trying to get away."[64] He cited examples of the failure of state and local governments to provide adequate allocations for Negro education. He offered a list of figures to show how black tenant farmers, after paying for supplies, rent, and interest on borrowed money, were left with profits of $17.50 per year. "The colored people are leaving to better their condition, and I think they can do it anywhere except in the southern States."[65]

During the last few years of his life, despite failing health, Rapier became an active emigrationist.[66] Besides testifying on Capitol Hill, he attended the Southern States Negro Emigration Convention in Nashville, conferred privately with Negro leaders concerning the migration movement, and met with Minnesota Senator William Windom, chairman of the committee charged with investigating the exodus.[67] He journeyed to Kansas at least a dozen times, visiting Shawnee, Saline, and Wabaunsee counties; and on at least three of these sojourns he invited prominent blacks—Arkansas judge Mifflin Gibbs, Kansas editor John Henderson, and Alabama businessman William Ash—to help him evaluate the situation.[68] In 1880 he purchased eighty acres of land along the Kansas and Pacific Railroad for a possible Negro colony.[69] Returning to Alabama, he made a round of speeches urging blacks to leave their home state. "He might induce a few to go," a Democratic newspaper noted, "but those who have tasted the bitter disappointments realized in Liberia and Mississippi will never again leave the sunny plain of Alabama."[70] It seems ironic that Rapier, who had struggled so long to bring the two races together in the South, now became determined to settle blacks "anywhere except in the southern States."[71]

Even before this involvement, however, a campaign had been initiated to remove him from office as collector of internal revenue. A number of influential white Republicans led by Willard Warner charged Rapier with perfidy. "I can fight Enemies, but I am afraid of treachery," the former Senator wrote. "Rapier's [sic] stood where he could largely correct . . . the ignorant direction of negroes . . . but he has not done it."[72] In 1882 President Arthur suspended Rapier pending an investigation.[73] But when hundreds of Alabamians, white and black, came to his defense, extolling him as a man of superior ability, upright character, and administrative efficiency, he was reinstated. Typical among the letters written in his behalf was one by Jack Daw, a black tenant farmer, who asked poignantly: "Why is this ungrateful and unkind blow [struck] at him? What has he done? Is his office not clear? Has he not made a faithful and efficient officer? Is his Republican record not good? . . . . Is it not patent to every thinking mind that it is only for his color?"[74]

Indeed the stigma of color had confronted Rapier in all his efforts to better the condition of his race. With few exceptions, whites believed that even the most educated and talented blacks belonged to an unalterable lower caste in the social, political, and economic scale. Throughout his career whites had attacked him on racial grounds. Democrats accused him of trying to "Africanize Alabama," expressed great humiliation that a Negro might achieve a high state office, and promised in 1874 to redeem the state or "exterminate the niggers."[75] Always they claimed he stood for social equality and miscegenation.

Moreover, despite professions to the contrary, many white Republicans opposed him because of his color and his defense of Negro rights. Chester Arthur Bingham, Samuel Rice, Milton Saffold, William Smith, and Warner, among others, refused to campaign in his behalf, ignored his speeches in their newspapers, tried to block his confirmation as a revenue officer, and on occasion denounced him as "nothing but a nigger." In 1870, for instance, Smith told a gathering in Florence that unfortunately his only chance of becoming governor was "to run on the same ticket with a nigger."[76]

Many forces disrupted the Alabama Republican party during Reconstruction—the desire for office, squabbles over patronage, personality differences, inept and corrupt officials, the demand for lucrative railroad contracts—but perhaps the most significant was the intraparty dispute over the nature of black citizenship. Many white Republicans entertained grave doubts about the capacity of freedmen to exercise the rights of free men. Warner frankly admitted, "If we can

92

attain and shall represent all the political elements, except the Douglas Democrats and colored men, . . . Republicanism will prosper in the South."[77]

Rapier had always demanded full and complete recognition of the principles contained in the Reconstruction amendments. He had struggled tirelessly against Warner and other "quasi-Republicans." "After the enfranchisement of [blacks], white Republicans used every means to get up race prejudice," one perceptive party member noted, looking back over more than a decade of party discord. "They refused to support or affiliate with Colored Republicans. The demoralization of the party can be traced to this reason."[78] Indeed, the conflicts that plagued the party throughout its brief existence not only reflected the deep racial prejudices of many whites, but doomed Alabama Reconstruction to failure from the outset.

In the end Rapier became disillusioned and embittered. Like most black Reconstruction leaders, he suffered the emotional and mental anguish of being ejected from Pullman cars, of being refused admission to hotels, and of being ostracized by the white community.[79] Like other leaders, he, too, endured the pain of a tragic personal life. He never married: "the days of poetry are over with me and I must settle down to the stiff prose"; he made few, if any, intimate friends: "I have been surrounded by no one who cared for me or for whom I cared"; and he worked incessantly:"I am at my office nearly all the Time. Sleep there."[80] At the height of his political power and prestige he admitted that he occupied "a most responsible position under the Government and look forward for a summons from the people to come up higher."[81] He did not know what else to do. He would have to reap whatever pleasure there was in a political life. "My breast appears to be innocent of all those social feelings necessary to make our life happy."[82]

But his loss of hope went deeper than any personal sadness. Somehow he could not rid himself of the feeling that he had let down his race. As a young man in Canada, he had vowed that if ever given the opportunity, he would devote his life to assisting his brethren.[83] Having returned to the South with such buoyant spirits, having thrown himself so completely into the crusade for racial uplift, and having struggled so desperately to bring about racial equality, he had witnessed the Republican party's abandonment of the Negro, the violent overthrow of the Reconstruction governments, and the increase of poverty and misery among the black masses. As early as 1869, he had urged the creation of a new federal agency for the distribution of public land (fifty million acres) to propertyless blacks.[84] In 1871 he had pressed for massive federal assistance to Negro education, announcing to a convention of Negro labor leaders that he would not be adverse to having *UNITED STATES* printed above every schoolhouse door in the land to insure a proper education for black children.[85]

Yet these and other proposals—offered at conventions, in campaign speeches, at labor union meetings, and in Congress—went unnoticed. How deeply he felt the pain and suffering of his brethren is suggested by his bitter denunciation of the South as a land of inhumanity and economic oppression, his frantic efforts to resettle five million black people on the plains of Kansas, and his dispersing a personal fortune of probably $25,000 to various Negro schools, churches, newspapers, and emigration projects. Despite his success as a planter, at the time of his death on May 31, 1883, he lived in a small shack, on rented property, virtually penniless.[86]

His growing despair and alienation perhaps reflected the attitudes of most blacks, who joyously proclaimed a new and better life in the wake of freedom, generally accepted the values of hard work and individual initiative, and sought a harmonious relationship with whites. But they became disheartened as the years passed and it became clear that their most diligent effort could produce only a mere subsistence, that their families would live in physical danger, and that their condition would remain almost the same as it was in slavery.

Although his sacrifices and genuine sympathy for the downtrodden were accepted by blacks in his native land as they gathered by the thousands, even when their lives were in jeopardy, to hear him articulate their views and capture in words their aspirations, others have ignored Rapier's contribution. Contemporary whites castigated him as "a base radical" intent on inciting racial friction, while a few recent historians have rebuked him as a "class-conscious conservative" seeking to further his own interests.[87]

But such simplistic portrayals have done more to obscure than illuminate his role in Reconstruction. In the rapid pace of events following the Civil War, attitudes that could be termed *radical*, a few months later could be called *moderate*, and a year later *conservative*. By the time Rapier and other blacks came to power during the late 1860s and early 1870s, such extreme ideas as the complete disfranchisement of ex-Confederates and the redistribution of ex-Confederate property among freedmen had long since been rejected by Congress, the president, and the American people. The issues, then, as Rapier saw them, were how to harmonize the various elements within the Republican party (without sacrificing the integrity of the Reconstruction amendments) and how to make a majority of former slaves landowners. Anyone who supported full citizenship rights for blacks should be allowed to participate in the political process, he said, and the federal government should allow freedmen easy access to homestead land. These views made him neither a base radical nor a bourgeois conservative.

To his constituents Rapier was a hero, not because of his personal warmth and friendliness, nor even because of his individual sacrifices against tremendous odds, but rather because he stood with them in their struggle for political rights, economic opportunity, and social dignity. And it was to them—raggedly clad freedmen and women—that he spoke the words that have echoed down through the generations to our own day:

> Fight on in the noble cause, and we will anchor by and by. It is the old war over again, of right against the lie, but on our side is right and truth. Who can doubt the result? If all classes of us will only drop our political animosities, stop our bickerings, and work with a will for the good of the common country, ever holding fast to the great truths of liberty, a wide, deep sea of prosperity awaits our beloved State and nation.[88]

It was his "beloved State and nation" that failed to fight on, not James Rapier. Perhaps his greatest legacy was that he understood better than his contemporaries that the final reconstruction of the South would depend on racial equality—the noble cause of Reconstruction.

Notes

1. James Rapier to William King, July 7, 187[2], in "The Autobiography of William King," pp. 436–38, King Papers, National Archives of Canada, Ottawa, Ontario. This transcription was incorrectly dated 1870.
2. Ibid.
3. Some of the most influential white Republicans in the state during Reconstruction were state treasurer Chester Arthur Bingham, congressmen Charles Buckley, Charles Hays, Alexander White, governors William Smith and David Lewis, and U.S. senators George Spencer and Willard Warner. See Sarah Woolfolk Wiggins, *The Scalawag in Alabama Politics, 1865–1881* (University: University of Alabama Press, 1977); William M. Cash, "Alabama Republicans during Reconstruction" (Ph.D. diss., University of Alabama, 1973).
4. Montgomery *Alabama State Journal*, June 1, 1871.
5. Among the most politically active of his assistants was Montgomery black Henry Hunter Craig, doorkeeper at the 1867 Constitutional Convention, who spent most of his time before elections on street corners, at political

gatherings, or in drinking saloons, "talking politics with colored men." "Testimony of [R. D. Stanwood] at the Inquiry into the Affairs of the Office of Assessor of Internal Revenue for the Second District of Alabama, Montgomery, Alabama, November 2–4, 1871," pp. 2–10, Records of the Department of the Treasury (RDT), Assessor of Internal Revenue (AIR), Record Group (RG) 56, National Archives (NA), Washington, D.C.

6. Washington *New National Era*, June 20, 1872.

7. Charles Hays to George Boutwell, Mar. 14, 1871; George Spencer, Charles Buckley, Benjamin Turner to Ulysses Grant, Mar. 7, 1871, RDT-AIR.

8. James Rapier to George Spencer, Dec. 9, 1871, RDT, Applications for Collectors of Customs (ACC), RG 56, NA.

9. Shortly after the 1868 presidential election, secessionist Samuel Rice, long-time Democrat Lewis E. Parsons, and postwar Conservative Alexander White declared their loyalty to the Republican party. Rice believed Negro suffrage "would condemn itself"; Parsons told his followers "not to be suspicious of my intentions in regard to the negro"; and White contended that blacks would follow their former masters. Keffer, Smith, and Warner held similar views. *Elmore Republican*, Jan. 12, 1872; Sarah Woolfolk Wiggins, "Five Men Called Scalawags," *Alabama Review* 17 (Jan. 1964):45–55.

10. Rapier to Spencer, Dec. 9, 1871, RDT-ACC.

11. James Rapier to William Chandler, Aug. 30, 1872, Chandler Papers, Manuscript Division, Library of Congress (LC), Washington, D.C.

12. Ibid.

13. Two-term incumbent Charles Buckley received only nine delegate votes compared to Rapier's twenty-five. Montgomery *Alabama State Journal*, Aug. 23, 1872; Eufaula *Daily Times*, Aug. 17, 1872; Greensboro *Alabama Beacon*, Aug. 24, 1872.

14. Montgomery *Alabama State Journal*, Aug. 21, 30, 1872; Sept. 1, 18, 1872; Montgomery *Republican Sentinel*, Oct. 31, 1872; *Elmore Republican*, Sept. 27, 1872.

15. Union Springs *Herald and Times*, July 24, 1872. Both of Rapier's parents (John and Susan Rapier) were of mixed blood. He was born in Florence, Ala., on Nov. 13, 1837. See Loren Schweninger, "John H. Rapier, Sr.: A Slave and Freedman in the Ante-Bellum South," *Civil War History* 20 (Mar. 1974):23–34.

16. Montgomery *Alabama State Journal*, Sept. 1, 5, 11, 18, 21, 27, 1872; *Elmore Republican*, Sept. 27, 1872; Montgomery *Republican Sentinel*, Oct. 31, 1872.

17. Rapier to Chandler, Sept. 19, 1872, Chandler Papers. Among the local blacks who supported Rapier was Holland Thompson, who had congressional aspirations of his own but subdued them in the interest of party unity. Montgomery *Alabama State Journal*, Aug. 29, 1872.

18. Union Springs *Herald and Times*, Nov. 6, 1872; Official Returns of Elections of State Officers and Congressional Election Returns (Official Returns), Nov. 5, 1872; Alabama Department of Archives and History (ADAH), Montgomery, Ala.

19. U.S., Congress, House, *Congressional Record*, 43d Cong., 1st sess., 1874, p. 4784.

20. Washington *New National Era*, Oct. 9, 1873.

21. Washington *National Republican*, Apr. 26, 1874.

22. *Congressional Record*, 43d Cong., 1st sess, 1874, p. 104.

23. U.S., Congress, House, *Journal*, 43d Cong., 1st sess., 1874, 2:177, 1345.

24. Washington *Daily Critic*, Dec. 11, 1873.

25. *Congressional Record*, 43d Cong., 1st sess., 1874, p. 4785.

26. Ibid.

27. Washington *New National Era*, June 18, 1874.

28. *Montgomery Daily Advertiser*, quoted in Montgomery *Alabama State Journal*, Feb. 26, 1874.

29. Mobile *Daily Register*, Mar. 14, 1874.

30. Montgomery *Daily Ledger*, quoted in Montgomery *Alabama State Journal*, July 1, 1874.

31. Elias Keils to David Lewis, Aug. 25, 1874, Lewis Papers, ADAH.

32. U.S., Congress, House, *Reports*, 43d Cong., 2d sess., 1875, H. Rept. 262, 6:293.

33. Montgomery *Alabama State Journal*, July 23, 1874.

34. Ibid., July 29, 1874; *Montgomery Daily Advertiser*, June 18, 25, July 16, 17, 1874.

35. Selma *Southern Argus*, Sept. 4, 1874.

36. Union Springs *Herald and Times*, Aug. 25, 1874.

37. *Montgomery Daily Advertiser*, Sept. 1, 1874.

38. Ibid., Nov. 7, 1874; Montgomery *Alabama State Journal*, Nov. 4, 1874; Union Springs *Herald and Times*, Nov. 4, 1874; Mobile *Daily Register*, Nov. 7, 1874.

39. Official Returns, Nov. 3, 1874, ADAH; Mobile *Daily Register*, Nov. 4, 1874; Montgomery *Alabama State Journal*, Nov. 5, 6, 1874.

40. U.S., Congress, House, Committee on Elections, James T. Rapier v. Jeremiah Williams, Second District, Alabama, December 31, 1874, 44th Cong., 1st sess., 1874, H. Rept. 44A–F8.13, NA.

41. *Montgomery Daily Advertiser*, Aug. 20, 1876; Mobile *Daily Register*, Aug. 31, 1876.

42. *Marion Commonwealth*, Sept. 21, 22, 1876.

43. *Wilcox Vindicator*, Nov. 1, 1876.

44. U.S., Congress, Senate, *Reports*, 44th Cong., 2d sess., 1877, S. Rept. 704, 1:iii, 179–88.

45. See Loren Schweninger, "A Slave Family in the Ante-Bellum South," *Journal of Negro History* 60 (Jan. 1975):29–44.

46. John H. Rapier, Sr., to Henry K. Thomas, Feb. 28, 1843; James Rapier to John H. Rapier, Jr., Mar. 6, 9, June 26, 1857, Rapier Papers, Moorland-Spingarn Research Center, Howard University, Washington, D.C.

47. James Rapier to John H. Rapier, Jr., Mar. 3, 1857, ibid.

48. Montgomery *Daily State Sentinel*, Nov. 25, 1867.

49. *Senate Reports*, 46th Cong., 1st and 2d sess., 1880, S. Rept. 693, 8:470–71. The other three—freedmen Jack Bell, Porter Simpson, and Benjamin Cooper, who were also active in politics—were hanged from a bridge, their corpses left to dangle for a week with cards pinned to them warning blacks to behave themselves or suffer a similar fate. Huntsville *Advocate*,

Dec. 22, 1868; *Moulton Advertiser*, Oct. 2, 1868; Greensboro *Alabama Beacon*, Oct. 3, 1868.

50. Records of Lowndes County Court, Hayneville, Ala., Mortgages, 1877, 5:124–27.

51. Ibid., 1877, 10:103–6; 1878, CC:32.

52. Ibid., 1879, DD:203–5; 1880, LL:248; 1881, OO:488; 1882, 61:5.

53. Agency Committee Minutes, June 13, 1872, p. 10; R. H. T. Leipold to James Rapier, May 4, 1876, Commissioner's Correspondence, vol. 7, Records of the Office of the Comptroller of the Currency, Freedmen's Savings and Trust Bank, RG 101, NA.

54. Montgomery *Republican Sentinel and Hayneville Times*, Oct. 31, 1878. See Paul Strobach to William Chandler, Oct. 15, 1878, Chandler Papers.

55. Records of Lowndes County Court, Mortgages, 1881, YY:83; 1882, XX:501, VV:411; *Senate Reports*, 46th Cong., 1st and 2d sess., 1880, S. Rept. 693, 8:478.

56. John Fitzpatrick to Secretary of the Treasury, May 3, 1882, RDT–Collectors of Internal Revenue (CIR), RG 56, NA.

57. Charles Pelham to John Sherman, May 15, 1878, ibid.; John Sherman to Rutherford B. Hayes, May 15, 1878, ibid.

58. Huntsville *Gazette*, May 20, 1882.

59. James Rapier to Chester Arthur, May 31, 1882, RDT-CIR.

60. John McDuffie to Willard Warner, May 5, 1880, Sherman Papers, LC; James Rapier to John Sherman, May 4, 1880, ibid.

61. *Montgomery Daily Advertiser*, May 22, 1880; Huntsville *Gazette*, May 22, 1880; *Proceedings of the Republican National Convention, Held in Chicago, Illinois, June 3–8, 1880* (Chicago: John B. Jeffery, 1881), p. 46.

62. Robert Athearn, *In Search of Canaan: Black Migration to Kansas, 1879–80* (Lawrence: University of Kansas Press, 1978).

63. Demopolis *Southern Republican*, May 11, 1870.

64. *Senate Reports*, 46th Cong., 1st and 2d sess., 1880, S. Rept. 693, 8:468–69.

65. Ibid., 470–71.

66. Though a man of unusual energy and vitality, he seems to have been peculiarly susceptible to various illnesses. On at least three occasions (1870, 1873, 1883), he remained bedridden for a month or more with what were probably viral infections.

67. *Proceedings of the National Conference of Colored Men of the United States, Held in Nashville, Tennessee, May 6–9, 1879* (Washington, D.C.: Rufus H. Darby, 1879), pp. 21, 100, 101.

68. Montgomery *Alabama Republican*, Sept. 18, 1880; Topeka *Tribune*, Aug. 19, 1880; Topeka *Colored Citizen*, Aug. 16, 1879; Mifflin W. Gibbs, *Shadow and Light: An Autobiography* (1902; reprint ed., New York: Arno Press, 1968), pp. 181–82.

69. Records of the Wabaunsee County Court, Deeds, (Oct. 16, 1880), n.v.: n.p., Alma, Kan.; Montgomery *Advance*, Sept. 11, 1880; *Montgomery Daily Advertiser*, Aug. 19, 1880; Montgomery *Alabama Republican*, Sept. 18, 1880; Topeka *Tribune*, Aug. 19, 1880.

70. *Montgomery Daily Advertiser*, Aug. 28, 1879, Sept. 26, 1880; Huntsville *Gazette*, Apr. 15, 1882.

71. *Senate Reports*, 46th Cong., 1st and 2d sess., 1880, S. Rept. 693, 8:470–71.

72. Willard Warner to John Sherman, May 4, 1880, written at bottom of Robert Barber to Sherman, May 4, 1880, Sherman Papers.

73. Chester Arthur to James Rapier, Sept. 20, 1882, RTD–CIR; *Marion Standard*, Sept. 27, 1882.

74. Printed in Huntsville *Gazette*, Apr. 28, 1883.

75. Montgomery *Daily Mail*, Sept. 7, 1870; Mobile *Daily Register*, Oct. 27, 1874; Union Springs *Herald and Times*, Aug. 26, 1874; *House Reports*, 43d Cong., 2d sess., 1875, H. Rept. 262, 6:702.

76. Montgomery *Alabama State Journal*, Oct. 21, 1870.

77. Willard Warner to Carl Schurz, May 1, 1876, Schurz Papers, LC.

78. B. M. Long to Chester Arthur [1882], RDT-CIR.

79. *Congressional Record*, 43d Cong., 1st sess., 1874, pp. 4784–87.

80. James Rapier to Sarah Thomas, Jan. 10, 1872, Rapier Papers.

81. Ibid.

82. Ibid.

83. James Rapier to John H. Rapier, Jr., Feb. 28, 1858, ibid.

84. *Proceedings of the Colored National Labor Convention Held in Washington, D.C., December 6–10, 1869* (Washington, D.C.: New Era, 1870), p. 23.

85. *Senate Reports*, 46th Cong., 1st and 2d sess., 1880, S. Rept. 693, 8:146–47.

86. At the time of his death he owned no real estate, his total cash assets amounted to $235, and his other property holdings—cattle, horses, mules, and wagons used by his tenants as well as such personal items as furniture, clothes, and a gold watch—were valued at only $2,185. Records of the Montgomery County Court, Estates, 1883, 5:536–45, Montgomery, Ala.

87. See Thomas Holt, review of Loren Schweninger, *James T. Rapier and Reconstruction*, in *American Historical Review* 84 (June 1979):856; see also id., *Black over White: Negro Political Leadership in South Carolina during Reconstruction* (Urbana: University of Illinois Press, 1977).

88. Demopolis *Southern Republican*, May 11, 1870.

James O'Hara of North Carolina:
Black Leadership and Local Government

In the spring of 1900, Congressman William W. Kitchin felt a need to defend the good name of North Carolina, and in her defense inserted into the *Congressional Record* a speech justifying the state's efforts at suffrage restriction. In explaining "the problem confronting her good people," he cited the state's Reconstruction history. "Mr. Chairman," he said, "I remember when four out of the five commissioners of Halifax County were negroes, and one of them the chairman of the board." He added, "It was an era of extravagance and corruption."[1] The chairman of the Halifax Board of Commissioners was James Edward O'Hara, who served in that capacity from 1874 to 1878 and later also served in the Congress from 1883 to 1887. At the time of Kitchin's remarks, O'Hara was quietly practicing law in New Bern, North Carolina, and had not been an aspirant to public office for a decade.

On this occasion O'Hara was not called upon to defend his own good name. It is even possible that Kitchin's remarks may have escaped his attention. But it is easy to imagine an indignant O'Hara rising "to a point of personal privilege," as offended congressmen were wont to do, to inform the House that young Mr. Kitchin, when beginning that careful analysis of his performance as county commissioner, was all of eight years old! Yes, indeed, he might have retorted, there had been corruption, for he himself had been defeated in the 1878 race for Congress by Mr. Kitchin's father by means of dishonest ballot counting. But whatever O'Hara's reaction was to Kitchin's charges, the historical record is silent. In retirement O'Hara remained, as he had been throughout his career, a useful symbol to both friends and enemies, but a man whose personal voice was often ignored or misunderstood.

O'Hara's elusiveness, like that of most nineteenth-century black politicians, is largely a matter of missing or one-sided sources. In the seventy-five years since his death, most of his personal papers have disappeared. A few photographs survive—showing a confident, fair-skinned, bearded mulatto—and several scrapbooks and a family memoir have been preserved; but there is no O'Hara diary or significant collection of letters to illuminate his motives and ideals.[2] Halifax

County newspapers for the 1870s, which could provide valuable information to supplement such official sources as the minutes of the board of commissioners, are nearly all missing. Aside from several brief speeches in the House of Representatives in the 1880s, there is no complete O'Hara speech recorded, though he must have delivered hundreds in the course of his political career.

In his time O'Hara was far from an obscure man. He was, in fact, one of North Carolina's best known black leaders between 1875 and 1887. He was born in New York City, on February 26, 1844, the illegitimate son of an Irish merchant and a West Indian woman. Little is known of his youth, much of which he spent in the West Indies. (As late as 1871 O'Hara was giving his birthplace as St. Croix; but in the 1880 census he reported that he was born in New York. At some point between those two dates, he "found out that he was born in New York and his parents emigrated to the West Indies when he was an infant.") It is not clear when he returned to the United States, but in 1862 he visited Union-occupied eastern North Carolina in the company of New York missionaries and decided to stay permanently.

He taught school for several years, first in New Bern then in Goldsboro. His political experience began with work as engrossing clerk to the state Constitutional Convention of 1868 and the legislature of 1868–69. After about two years in Washington, D.C., working as a clerk in the Treasury Department and studying at Howard University, O'Hara returned to North Carolina and received his license to practice law in 1873. Peter M. Wilson, who later became a well-known journalist and was licensed at the same time, remembered O'Hara as a "colored man . . . who knew more law than I did."[3] The next year O'Hara won election to the Halifax County Board of Commissioners on an unopposed Republican slate of four Negroes and a white carpetbagger. This group chose O'Hara as its chairman. He also served as a delegate to the 1875 state constitutional convention. In 1876, as North Carolina was redeemed for Zebulon Vance and "the white man's party," Halifax County continued under black rule, with O'Hara gaining reelection both as commissioner and as chairman.

Halifax County was the most populous county in the Second Congressional District, a gerrymandered creation in eastern North Carolina that included several of the state's largest Negro counties. Formed in 1872, the district became one of the most remarkable centers of black political activity in late nineteenth-century America. Between 1872 and disfranchisement in 1900, the district elected four Negro representatives, including George H. White, the last Negro to represent

102

Second Congressional District Population, 1880

COUNTY	POPULATION	% NEGRO
Craven	19,729	66.2
Edgecombe	26,181	69.6
Greene	10,039	53.7
Halifax	30,300	69.8
Jones	7,491	57.1
Lenoir	15,344	52.6
Northampton	20,032	60.1
Warren	22,619	71.8
Wayne	24,951	48.6
Wilson	16,064	46.1
TOTAL	192,750	61.2

Source: Bureau of the Census, *Negro Population, 1790–1915* (Washington, D.C.: Government Printing Office, 1918), pp. 784–85.

the South in Congress until the 1970s. During the same period, numerous black Republicans served in county government or held federal patronage positions, and more than fifty Negroes represented the counties of the second district in the General Assembly. As O'Hara's tenure as a commissioner came to an end in 1878, he began the first five consecutive campaigns for the Republican congressional nomination in this often turbulent, "safe" Republican seat, ultimately succeeding in winning a place in the House from 1883 to 1887. After 1887 he held no other public office, but instead returned to the private practice of law. One black journalist commented that O'Hara refused to lie around Washington, like many other defeated politicians, begging for office. For a year or two O'Hara published a newspaper in Enfield, only one issue of which survives. He moved out of Halifax County in 1890 to New Bern, where he spent the last fifteen years of his life.[4]

The basic outline of O'Hara's career is clear enough; what is elusive is O'Hara the man—his character, his hopes, his ideals. One Democratic editor described him as a "living, foul-mouthed libel on honor, decency and truth" who was intent on "inflaming the worst passions" of ignorant Negroes; while another editor in the opposition observed: "He is a polite, intelligent colored man, conservative above his color." O'Hara was said to be "a shrewd darky, probably the most intelligent in the State if not in the South," a "mulatto with cheek a plenty." He was accused of making "highly incendiary and filthy" speeches, of using language "calculated to promote such feelings in the minds of his hearers as tend to trouble," of defying Democrats "in the most reck-less, bitter and venomous terms," though specific irresponsible expres-sions were never cited by a partisan press. On some occasions, newspa-per reports pictured him as assertive, as when he personally desegregated the main saloon on the Tar River steamer *Cotton Plant*, acting immediately after the 1875 Civil Rights Act went into effect. At one session of the Halifax Superior Court, he precipitated a fight by calling a certain white lawyer a liar. Yet Enfield tradition reports that O'Hara and his mulatto wife "always sat at the back" of the local Epis-copal Church (though he was a Catholic) "and took communion after the white people." A prominent white Republican stated that O'Hara "knows just how far to go without trespassing on the uncertain ground of race prejudice." "Everybody who knows him," the same observer said a few years earlier, "is aware of his ability and training, and apt-ness in affairs."[5]

The wide differences in these descriptions illustrate the difficulty of judging a man on incomplete evidence. It is certainly a challenging mental exercise, to say the least, to imagine a politely foul-mouthed incendiary conservative who is both reckless and accommodating. But then James O'Hara was a thing beyond the ordinary ken of most nineteenth-century Tarheels: a half-Irish, red-headed, Roman Catho-lic, freeborn, black carpetbagger!

However shadowy O'Hara *the man* is, his career provides an essen-tial perspective on black leadership during Reconstruction. The way in which he was continuously forced to be a symbol—for Democrats as well as for black and white Republicans—is in itself significant. At times his holding an office (or possibly dreaming about it) was a sign of the threat of Negro domination. In 1875 the Warrenton *Gazette* warned that if the Republicans controlled the state constitutional con-vention, O'Hara "will be our next judge as sure as the sun will rise to-morrow morning."[6] A year later second district Republicans honored O'Hara with an office that entailed no money and no power, but Dem-ocrats were still aghast at the thought of a Negro presidential elector.

When Democratic propaganda and Republican fears combined to cause O'Hara to resign from the electoral ticket, he became a new sort of symbol, this time representing, as the Democrats claimed, the hy-pocrisy of white Republicans. An editorial in the Democratic *Newber-nian* called upon colored fellow citizens to resent the insult of O'Hara's removal from the ticket; though a report on the next page referred to the mistreated O'Hara as an "imported montebank," an "ape," and an "Imp." The object of all this comment refused to blame his fellow

JAMES O'HARA
Regenstein Library, University of Chicago

Republicans for his resignation. Instead he commented: "I may have to a certain extent yielded to case prejudice, but by whom is this prejudice fostered, kept alive and used?"[7]

Two years later, in 1878, O'Hara's winning of the Republican congressional nomination was treated as evidence that Negroes were "drawing the color line."[8] Even after O'Hara was out of office, a Kinston newspaper used his name in an effort to frighten its readers out of voting for a popular Republican legislative candidate: "Our next legislature will elect a United States Senator. Suppose the majority is close and the Republicans tried to run in a Republican—suppose they tried to send the negro O'Hara to the Senate—who do you suppose, if Benj. Sutton was our representative, he would vote for? He would vote to send the negro to the United States Senate to represent North Carolina. Can any truly WHITE man vote for Benj. Sutton?"[9]

Not all of James O'Hara's battles were with Democrats. Within the Republican party, O'Hara's success or failure also took on symbolic significance, as white and black Republicans evaluated the racial tensions in the party and assessed the party's future development. O'Hara complained on one occasion, "There is always a combination between the white Republicans against any intelligent colored Republican who seeks to aspire to office." He told the 1874 congressional nominating convention that black candidates should not be set aside on account of their color; since voters were of both races, officeholders should also be so.[10] The convention went ahead and chose a Negro nominee, John A. Hyman, who, though elected, was not renominated in 1876; and no Negro was elected again until O'Hara's victory in 1882. If O'Hara had failed in 1882, in a confusing intraparty strife, the Second Congressional District might have become like other southern, black, Republican districts that almost never nominated Negroes. As it was, black congressmen served six terms after 1882 and only one before that year.

O'Hara's career as a county commissioner might be dismissed as a mere prelude to his more important service in the national legislature. But to do so would be to miss the vital significance of local government to all participants in the Reconstruction process. For a North Carolinian in 1875, the hub of political life was neither Raleigh nor Washington but the county seat. It was no accident that Congressman Kitchin turned to local government for his indictment of Reconstruction, that his remembrance mentioned the dreadful time when four Negroes sat on the board of county commissioners. For him and for most white southerners, Republican local government was the worst feature of

Reconstruction; because the Negro, as Kitchin said, had "filled offices which the best men in the State had filled. He was sheriff, deputy sheriff, justice of the peace, legislator, constable, county commissioner."

Although Kitchin admitted that during the two decades after Reconstruction certain black counties had elected "an occasional negro register of deeds or member of the legislature, and even district solicitor and member of Congress," he placed his main emphasis on local government. "The counties, towns, and cities were under absolute white control," he said, "and almost without exception under excellent government." But when he turned to the Negro domination that allegedly ruled in North Carolina in 1897 and 1898 under the aegis of Republican-Populist fusion, he spoke again primarily of local government. "Negro domination," he said, "does not mean that the government in every part of the entire State is under the control of negro influences. . . . When the great controlling element is the negro vote, and when that vote and its influences name the officials and dictate the policy of a town, city, or county, then it is dominant. When it elects negro officials of a town or county, there is negro domination."[11]

As North Carolina Democrats sought to undo Reconstruction, one of their most important goals was guaranteeing white control of local government. "It is absolutely necessary to the salvation of Warren, Halifax, Edgecombe, Craven and other counties similarly situated," a Black-Belt attorney wrote to a Democratic delegate in the 1875 state constitutional convention, "that the county funds be placed beyond the reach of the large negro majorities in those counties." He added that, if this were not done, extravagance, abuse, and corruption would be certain to result.[12] Sharing such sentiments, the Democratic majority succeeded in pushing through a constitutional amendment that centralized local government. Under the new arrangement, which was authorized by the voters in 1876, detailed in the next session of the legislature, and implemented in 1878, the General Assembly elected the local magistrates, who in turn elected the county commissioners. The other county officers—sheriff, clerk of the superior court, treasurer, and register of deeds—remained elective, but the body that controlled the taxes and financial policy was chosen indirectly.

Local self-rule subsequently became a major issue for Republicans in every election from 1878 to 1890. When a large group of dissident Democrats collaborated with Republicans in the Liberal movement of 1882 and 1884, the coalition made abolition of the Democratic system of centralized local government its main goal. The unpopularity of the county-government system contributed to the regular Democrats' loss of the state House in 1886 and nearly defeated the Democratic candidate for congressman-at-large in 1882.[13]

In short, O'Hara was more galling to Halifax County Democrats as chairman of the county commissioners than as a member of the United States Congress. Republicans agreed with Democrats in seeing county government as extraordinarily important; they, too, invested an ambitious politician in a local post with more than routine significance.

The importance of local government lay not only in its proximity and ubiquity but also in its broad and very real power. This power can be illustrated by the simple fact that county governments took more in taxation from the individual citizen than either the state or federal government. In Halifax County the state taxation was little more than $11,000 in 1879, while county taxes were nearly $15,000 and the only common federal taxes were internal revenue levies on liquor and tobacco.[14]

If the board of county commissioners did no more than set tax assessments, oversee the sheriff's collection of taxes, and provide certain exemptions from poll taxes, it would have been a very important body. But the commissioners' duties went far beyond taxes. They provided for maintenance of the poor, managed the prison, kept bridges and highways in repair, selected jurors, regulated retail liquor sales, evaluated officials' bonds, arranged payment of the county debt, served as board of education—the list goes on and on.

In this context Kitchin's charge of extravagance and corruption cannot be ignored as simple racist stereotyping. The question of how well O'Hara and his colleagues performed is a real one, one of several that demands an answer: Did a black-dominated board give Halifax County effective government? How did O'Hara gain and hold power? What was the relationship between O'Hara's service in county politics and his later success as a congressional aspirant? What was the basis for factional divisions among Republicans? Despite the limitations of the sources, they do provide adequate evidence to answer these questions.

There is a clear, prima facie case for the Democratic picture of a corrupt and extravagant O'Hara-led county government. Each year of O'Hara's tenure, for example, the commissioners levied taxes that were unconstitutionally high. Ignoring the requirement of the state's 1868 constitution that state and county taxes combined must never exceed $2.00 for the capitation (poll) tax or 66⅔¢ per $100 valuation for the property tax, O'Hara and his colleagues raised the poll tax to as high as $2.50 one year and charged as much as 90¢ in property tax.

Gross county taxes went up from $16,879 in 1874 to $20,446 in 1877. When a state supreme court decision reaffirmed the constitutional limit on taxation in 1876, the commissioners immediately cut county taxes by nearly half, only to return to excessive taxation within a few months. The Democratic board that succeeded O'Hara's group ordered the tax collector to collect no more than the legal amount and returned overpaid taxes from the previous year.[15]

Along with high tax levies went inefficient tax collection. Sheriff Lawrence F. Larkin, a northern-born white man, did so poorly at his duty of collecting taxes that his failures plagued county officials for several years after he was forced from office in 1878 for an insufficient bond. The state legislature passed "an act to collect arrears of taxes in the county of Halifax" in 1879, authorizing a special tax collector to handle the problem of unpaid taxes for the years 1875, 1876, and 1877, and rescinding Larkin's authority to collect these taxes. Another law was required the following year to cover tax arrears for 1878.[16]

One of the things that angered Democrats most about their black-majority board was its habit of voting money to county officers for "extra services." "Every device has been resorted to to swell the compensation of the county officials," declared an editorial that pointed to "Radical Government in Halifax County" as a reason for ratifying the Democratic changes in local government.[17] The first day on the job, O'Hara's board voted a $600 "ex officio allowance" to the Republican sheriff. When the sheriff died, the commissioners elected Larkin, the only white member of the board, to fill the vacancy; and after he had been in the post three months, they awarded him $800 for "ex officio services." The register of deeds, ex-officio clerk of the board, received $200 for extra official services one year and $250 another year. O'Hara himself collected $100 in extra services two months after taking office and again in January 1876, as well as receiving $800 in two years for serving as county attorney. He even managed to have himself voted $60 back pay for his work as clerk of the school committee for the years 1872 to 1874.[18]

The best example of extravagance and mismanagement, as far as many Democrats were concerned, was the board's handling of the salt bonds case. During the Civil War the Halifax commissioners had borrowed money upon the county's credit to purchase desperately needed salt for the people of the county. The county never paid this debt. Finally, in 1878, two of the county's creditors went to court with a demand for principal and interest amounting to about $12,000. The board responded by securing, in addition to the services of their own chairman, the services of two law firms, Day & Hall and Mullen & Moore. O'Hara was paid $400 and each of the firms $500 at the outset, with an additional payment of $100 made to O'Hara and $500 to each of the firms at the conclusion of the cases. One critic added up the figures and remarked, "In all a counsel fee of *$2500* when a $200 fee would be *ample*."

According to the same observer, inferior court prosecutor Spier Whitaker, when the public learned of this transaction, "there was deep and universal indignation against all concerned in this matter—in fact there was *no* one who even thought of defending them." William H. Day, one of the attorneys retained by the board, had been slated as the Democratic candidate for solicitor of the Second Judicial District; but in the brouhaha that followed, his name was dropped from the ticket. Day and his associates defended themselves by clever reinterpretation of the agreement with the county. Although the original statement had merely noted that "the decision in said suits will apply to a large number of similar claims against the County," Day, Hall, Mullen, and Moore claimed in an August statement that the true intent and meaning of the agreement was that the lawyers were to defend the county, not only in the pending cases, but also in all suits of a similar nature brought, presumably, by other bearers of salt bonds. The four attorneys also interpreted the earlier statement to promise $500 *in total* on the conclusion of the case—not $500 per firm as most readers took the document to mean.[19]

Not surprisingly, the men who served as Halifax's county commissioners in the years from 1874 to 1878 were ensnarled in numerous legal problems. "James O'Hara et al" were indicted at least fifteen times for malfeasance in office. The most serious difficulties came in September 1879, when the grand jury for the superior court found a true bill against the previous year's commissioners on three counts. About six months later charges were dropped against three of the former commissioners, leaving only O'Hara and his black colleague John H. Howard to face prosecution. The first of the three cases ended in a hung jury, with four of the twelve jurors voting not guilty, despite Spier Whitaker's "capital effort" for the prosecution. At the next term of the superior court, the state prosecutor dropped the cases against O'Hara and Howard after they pleaded nolo contendere and paid costs.

The available sources give few details of the charges against O'Hara, save that he was tried for fraudulent appropriation of county funds. Information is particularly sketchy for the twelve inferior court indictments, since minutes of the Halifax Inferior Court have not been pre-served. By all indications, however, he was not convicted in any of these cases, a fact that lends credence to O'Hara's 1878 explanation that the indictments then standing against him "were all alike, and were obtained for merely political purposes, that he had been acquit-ted in one case, and would be in all others when they dared to come to trial."[20] If Halifax County actually had as wretched a government as critics claimed, one would not expect O'Hara to evade conviction so consistently.

The fact is that O'Hara's board looks better upon closer examina-tion. Like the malfeasance indictments, the sweeping general charges of corruption and extravagance become more complicated and ambig-uous the more closely they are studied. Although the county com-missioners under O'Hara were in many respects ineffective, it is not always easy to find a sharp difference between the radical, Negro-dominated board of 1874–78 and its immediate successors. For example, the new Democratic board that took office in December 1878 failed to lower the high tax levy of the O'Hara board until angry tax-payers secured a restraining order. Spier Whitaker was not referring to Negro Republicans when he observed that the commissioners needed to learn "that they are not a law unto themselves." He added, "The people of our county have been sadly disappointed in the present board of Commissioners and there is running all over the County a loud and indignant cry of complaint."[21]

The tax rates charged by O'Hara and his associates seem less irre-sponsible when compared with rates in other counties. In 1879, when all county governments in North Carolina had been under Democratic control for a year, total county taxes amounted to just under one per-cent of the state's assessed valuation of real estate, the most important form of property for tax collectors. The O'Hara board's highest gross taxes came in 1877 when county taxes amounted to 1.02 percent of real estate valuation.[22]

County debt, however unwisely it may have been incurred, was 26¢ per capita in 1880 at the end of the O'Hara years, far below the state-wide mean of $1.09 or the $10.07 owed by every man, woman, and child in white-majority, Democratic Carteret County. Halifax, as one of the state's most important cotton-producing counties, was not a poor county, and by 1890 was able to erase its small debt entirely. A cooperative legislature aided this process in 1883 and 1885 by passing bills allowing the county to issue bonds and levy special taxes for retiring the debt. Needless to say, no such legislative remedy was available for James O'Hara from a Democratic General Assembly in the years 1874 to 1878.[23]

The Democratic wrath about pay for extra service also must be placed in perspective. Even after the county had been saved from black, Republican "misrule," some additional fees continued to be paid. Tax collector L. M. Long, for example, received $200 beyond his normal pay in 1879 for extra trouble in computing taxes." The legislature passed a bill in 1881 that allowed the board of magistrates in Halifax and two other counties to pay the chairman of the commissioners "such compensation as they deem proper and necessary," indicating perhaps that O'Hara's board was not entirely wrong in believing that its chairman deserved more than merely $2 a day and mileage. Furthermore, North Carolina law allowed significant flexibility in the matter of paying officers. As a supreme court decision of 1881 noted, a sheriff was expected to do many duties for which there was no provision for compensation, such as open and adjourn court, maintain order in the courtroom, accompany prisoners to court appearances, call witnesses into court and jurors to the box, and numerous other such services. Although a sheriff had no legal right to demand extra pay, the court noted: "In many of the counties it has been the practice of county authorities to make extra allowances to their Sheriffs for the performance of such services."[24]

The simple polemical categories *Republican waste* and *Democratic economy* conceal the fact that there were two philosophies of government in conflict, and the two did not precisely coincide with party lines. While the Democratic board that replaced James O'Hara et al endorsed retrenchment, it also continued in office many of the men who had been involved in the finances of the O'Hara years. The same board that ended relief payments for paupers outside the poorhouse, cut food expenditures for prisoners to 25¢ a day, and slashed the salary of the superintendent of the poorhouse from $400 per year to $150, also used William H. Day as county attorney and, as Whitaker noted, "appointed a man tax collector [L. M. Long] who had been Treasurer of the county (appointed by O'Hara & Co.) and as such had for *a whole year* failed to sue the Sheriff and his bondsman when he *knew* that the Sheriff was a defaulter for at least thirty thousand dollars."[25] This Democratic board came under heavy fire from men like Whitaker who advocated a consistent policy of minimal services and taxes. General David Clark, one of the county's major landowners and a leading non-Republican (who preferred to be called an Old Whig rather than a

Democrat), publicly criticized Halifax County government in 1880 for high taxes, wasteful expenditure—such as $200 extra for the tax collector and $600 for the sheriff—secretive procedure, and unresponsiveness to the public.[26] Board member Aaron Prescott entered his dissent on the minutes of the board, objecting to his colleagues' plans for bridge building, courthouse repairs, and poorhouse construction: "I think it the duty of public officers as well as individuals to be just before they are generous, and I feel that the first claim on this board to be considered is that of its creditors." He thought $500 would be enough to make the poorhouse comfortable for its inmates and urged that other repairs be deferred. Shortly thereafter Prescott resigned from the board.[27] When he returned to the board in 1882, serving for several years as chairman, it was a sign that Halifax County's "redemption" had entered a second stage.

The difference between Prescott and O'Hara was not that one was an honest man and the other a thief. At issue were two distinct notions of what government should do. O'Hara and his Negro associates were young men who had been children when the Civil War began. They were outsiders in one sense or another—mulattoes instead of blacks, artisans or professionals instead of farmers, ambitious but not wealthy men—tentatively defined in a society uncomfortable with ambiguity. They took for granted the expanded role of postwar government, looking to government at all levels for protection of their political and legal rights, and in particular their right to participate.[28]

Men like Whitaker, Prescott, and Clark, on the other hand, were secure men of property, whose participation in politics was not a way of raising their social status. They saw government as a technical problem, an exercise in efficiency, rather than an enterprise. They insisted on effective government but never asked the question Effective *for whom?* In some cases their demand for scrupulous accounting of county funds was matched by a curious tolerance for flagrant miscounting of Negro votes. Spier Whitaker, for example, was remembered by one associate as a "cynical and sarcastic" man who "thought it not wrong but smart to suppress the Negro vote," an art he "mastered in the Black District." In an election marked by very suspicious election returns, Whitaker was elected to the state senate in 1880, and W. H. Day and an associate were elected to the lower house. A federal grand jury later indicted seven Halifax election officials, with two of them ultimately paying fines.[29]

After 1878 James O'Hara and men like him had no further chance to control local government until the fusion upheavals of the 1890s.

Thanks to the constitutional and statutory changes that ended popular election of commissioners, taxes and expenditures were securely in Democratic hands for the next eighteen years. The most important executive positions, sheriff and clerk of the court, remained open to Republican politicians, but few blacks had the wealth or business connections necessary to secure the large bonds required for those offices. Several Eastern Carolina Negroes won places as registers of deeds, a lucrative office; but their victories did little to change the overall complexion of county government.

The centralization of local government did not, however, end the political ambition or influence of James O'Hara.[30] An aspirant for Congress as early as 1874, he finally won his party's nomination in 1878, only to lose the general election to Democratic fraud and Republican disunity. A host of enemies within the Republican party accused him of corruption and asserted that O'Hara, who had divorced his first wife, was actually guilty of bigamy. Late in the campaign some critics also claimed that he was not an American citizen. Included among O'Hara's Republican opponents were the incumbent congressman Curtis H. Brogden, formerly governor of the state, and John Hyman, the black former congressman. But his most damaging opposition may well have been that of the sheriff of Halifax County. Local elections took place three months before the congressional voting in 1878. In the August voting, Sheriff Larkin, an ally of O'Hara, was opposed by James T. Dawson, each man claiming to be the Republican nominee. Dawson, who was the victor in this bitter fight, worked to weaken O'Hara in Halifax County. The Democratic nominee for Congress was another Halifax man, William H. Kitchin, a lawyer-planter who was a close friend of Spier Whitaker. Kitchin had backed Dawson in local politics and had even stood surety on his official bond—an unusual action for such an intensely partisan Democrat—and Dawson reciprocated by supporting Kitchin for Congress.

The Republican executive committee made matters easier for the Democrats by calling a new nominating convention only three weeks before election day, after O'Hara's explanation of his divorce did not satisfy them. This new convention proceeded to nominate James H. Harris, a well-known black orator and veteran politician, as O'Hara's replacement. But despite rumors and accusations, and in the face of opposition from leaders in his own party, O'Hara stayed in the race and did remarkably well on election day. He won the election, in fact, until canvassing boards in the black majority counties of Edgecome, Halifax, and Craven drastically pruned his majorities in those counties, by rejecting hundreds of votes on flimsy technicalities.[31] These actions, combined with the Harris challenge, allowed Kitchin to win with only 43 percent of the vote. O'Hara considered local politics to have been the key to his loss. Dawson's friends, he said, "made a combination and counted me out. That was the reason Mr. Kitchen [sic] went on his bond."

O'Hara's attempts to undo this electoral larceny were all unsuccessful. After a mandamus suit pursued all the way to the state supreme court failed to bring redress, O'Hara contested Kitchin's seat in the House of Representatives. The Democratic majority on the Committee on Election did not report for more than two years after the election; then they voted against O'Hara with the observation that, although there were "very grave and important questions in dispute in the election," the available evidence was inadequate and ineligible.

O'Hara held no elective office from 1878 until he began his first term in Congress in 1883. An unsuccessful candidate for the congressional nomination in 1880, he bitterly opposed the man who defeated him, Craven Sheriff Orlando Hubbs, a northern-born white Republican, who won, in O'Hara's view, by an unfair parliamentary trick. O'Hara participated actively in state politics, when not distracted by his contested election case or malfeasance indictments. He took a central role in the antiprohibition campaign of 1881, in the Liberal coalition between Republicans and dissident Democrats that followed in 1882, and in black protests on Republican patronage policy. He finally won a second congressional nomination in 1882 after a furious battle with Representative Hubbs that featured a disorderly convention and several months of political civil war.

The conflict of 1882 was not atypical for either party in the North Carolina of the Gilded Age, as the prevailing political system seemed designed to produce chaos. Although there were minor differences in the organizational structure of the two parties, most political activity for either Republicans or Democrats was built around the convention—township, county, district, or state. These conventions, particularly at the lower levels, were open to the most flagrant abuses, including bribery of delegates, manipulation of credentials, and audience packing. An ambitious politician always had to be alert to potential tricks by his opponents, ranging from creative chairmanship to intervening crowds.

A Wilson lawyer complained in 1886, "We had a disgraceful squabble in the Township meeting." The friends of one aspirant had "opened all the Bar Rooms on the day of the meeting and filled the

Court House with a drunken rabble," making it impossible to transact business. Another politician commented on the nominating convention in the First Congressional District in 1878: "The Convention was extremely disorderly. It was sure from the beginning that I would be nominated, and some . . . [were] anxious to break up the Convention without a nomination." Such tactics could carry over to election day itself. "Money can be more effectively used in buying votes in this District than I ever knew," one Tarheel observed privately in 1880. "We don't propose to throw away money in barbeques and drinking, but to purchase directly the votes at the polls." Although these three comments fit the stereotype of black politicians, each was in fact made by a white, Democratic gentleman who at some time in his career served in Congress.[32]

O'Hara's fight with Hubbs illustrates not only the vagaries of the convention system, but also the complex factionalism that fissured the Republican party in the second district. The three major candidates for the 1882 congressional nomination represented three major groups within the Republican party. As a Negro, O'Hara could claim to be a racial spokesman for the vast majority of Republican voters, at least four-fifths of whom were black. Hubbs was one of a small number of influential northern immigrants. A third candidate, Lotte W. Humphrey, was a wealthy white southerner who had joined the party in 1876, at the close of Reconstruction. In 1878 and 1880 he had come within one vote of winning the congressional nomination.

Scalawag, carpetbagger, and black—these familiar categories of Reconstruction historiography were only the beginning of Republican factionalism. One of the basic facts of political life in the gerrymandered black second district was localism, and there was no neat, predictable racial pattern to political allegiances. A white northern politician living in Halifax, in fact, was more likely to support O'Hara than Hubbs, while an ambitious Craven County Negro would, for a variety of reasons, probably prefer Hubbs to the black candidate from the upper part of the district.[33] Democrats frequently asserted that blacks were a unified, monolithic mass in politics; but the charge obviously did not hold for internal Republican politics.

Hubbs, O'Hara, and Humphrey arrived at the district convention with no candidate controlling enough votes for a first-ballot victory, and the most ruthless jockeying for advantage resulted. The chairman of the district executive committee (elected by the district convention of 1880) called the session to order and appointed a pro-Hubbs credentials committee, which proceeded to decide a crucial dispute in the incumbent's favor. The Hubbs forces were then able to elect their candidate for permanent chairman over a man supported by the combined O'Hara and Humphrey forces. Three black delegates from Northampton, a county that had endorsed O'Hara, worked with the Hubbs forces, apparently induced by bribes or the promise of patronage. Humphrey, who had built up bitter resentment against Hubbs over the last two campaigns, counterattacked by withdrawing his name from the race and throwing his support to O'Hara. An alternate delegate, who was a Humphrey supporter and O'Hara's brother-in-law, used the sympathies of the pro-O'Hara, mostly black audience, to check the Hubbs supporters' moves. Climbing up on a table he announced, Humphrey's withdrawal. He pointed out that total number votes' from the five counties supporting the two men equalled an absolute majority by one vote and then moved the nomination of O'Hara by acclamation. Without the chairman's recognition, this motion was put to the delegates and audience, who roared their approval. The chairman boldly declared Hubbs the nominee and ordered the convention adjourned, as O'Hara pushed to the front to make an acceptance speech. Each side later issued victory manifestoes—signed by a majority of the delegates! The three Northampton men signed both statements.

In the bitter feuding that followed the convention, as each of the two men claimed to be the true nominee, O'Hara was able to prevail by taking hostage as many Republican candidates as possible. North Carolina Republicans were attempting an ambitious coalition with dissident Democrats in 1882—the Liberal movement O'Hara had done so much to promote—but now he and his supporters made it clear that they would not compromise. The Weldon *News* reported, "we have heard the negroes in this part of the district have openly declared that unless they are permitted to have their choice and elect O'Hara, they will not support the State ticket, but will, so far as they are concerned, allow it to be defeated." O'Hara supporters threatened to field schismatic candidates against any second-district Republican officeholder who refused to back O'Hara.[34] By the final days of the campaign it was clear that many Democrats were anxious to trade votes with the congressional rivals in order to help Democrats on the state and local levels. O'Hara's message was unmistakable—recognition of his claims would be good for the health of the party at several levels. O'Hara also had the support of Humphrey and other white Republicans who opposed Hubbs or the coalition movement or both. Former governor Brogden reportedly spent $1,800 in the effort to defeat Hubbs. Shortly before the election of 1882 Hubbs withdrew from the race; and, in the

117

absence of a Democratic candidate, O'Hara won the election virtually unopposed. "We are of the opinion that O'Hara is a man not easily subdued," a Democratic newspaper commented. "He has talent and irrepressible energy. . . . It is apparent that with the colored people he intends to rule or ruin." O'Hara was easily reelected in 1884, bringing to the faction-ridden second district four years of comparative calm.

In 1886, however, O'Hara faced renewed opposition, as a divided convention produced two Negro nominees and Democrats did their best to promote the split, apparently with secret financial help to one or both of the feuding Republicans. O'Hara's opponents complained that in Washington he had grown distant from the people. They asserted that he had failed to secure adequate patronage for the district's deserving politicos. In some cases they even made negative comparisons between his fair complexion and that of his darker rival, who they touted as being pure-blood Negro. More likely, his chief "failures" involved his distribution of the limited patronage available to him in a Democratic House and North Carolina's "unwritten law" (or prejudice) in favor of only two terms for a representative. Election day in 1886 was remarkably similar to that in 1878. Although O'Hara had three-quarters of the Republican votes, a Democrat—Furnifold Simmons—slipped into the House of Representatives with a mere plurality.[35] O'Hara remained involved in Republican party politics into the twentieth century, but he never regained the position of leadership he held in 1886.

During his dozen years or so in elective politics, O'Hara achieved little in the way of legislative initiatives or governmental innovation. In fact, he showed remarkably little interest in what are usually described as the great issues of the age: the tariff, the "money question," civil-service reform, railroad development, even the renewal of federal intervention in the South. He might momentarily seize upon one of these issues as an instrument for achieving some other goal, but his basic concerns lay elsewhere. For example, he denounced Orlando Hubbs as a high-tariff promoter in the campaign of 1882; but once he had captured a seat in Congress, he voted with the Republican majority against tariff reduction.[36]

O'Hara's only significant national attention came in December 1884, when, in another demonstration of ulterior motives, he offered a controversial amendment to the Reagan Interstate Commerce Bill providing that any railway passenger should "receive the same treatment and be afforded equal facilities . . . as are furnished all other persons holding tickets of the same class without discrimination." Helped by the votes of many northern Democrats, the amendment passed, although, after considerable debate, white southerners succeeded in tacking on another amendment making the point that equal could be separate. In this case O'Hara, whose concern was more with civil rights than railroad regulation, voted against the final bill.[37]

The most important issues for O'Hara, throughout his political career, were related to race relations, particularly on the local level. Influenced no doubt by his experience as a teacher and county education examiner, he urged Congress to vote federal aid for education. He advocated a constitutional amendment to undo the Supreme Court action in the Civil Rights Cases of 1883.[38] He fervently opposed the Democratic county government system, first in the convention of 1875, in almost every subsequent election, and especially in the Liberal movement of 1882 and 1884.

More than anything else, O'Hara was preoccupied with the process of gaining and holding political office. This preoccupation might have been mere opportunism or ordinary ambition if the Negro's right to participate were clearly, definitively settled. But little was ordinary for a black politician in the Bourbon era. Every nomination, election, or appointment was part of an evolving definition of the black man's place in the post-Reconstruction order. The question of black participation did remain open after Reconstruction; in fact, in some areas—the second district was one of them—the zenith of black political participation did not come until after Reconstruction.

James O'Hara was, perhaps, a rather parochial politician, with his interest in the near-at-hand and his own group. A nicer way to put that would be to say that O'Hara was an instinctive Burkean who held that "to be attached to the subdivision, to love the little platoon we belong to in society, is the first principle (the germ as it were) of public affections."[39] He had little other choice as long as black counties were ruled by white minorities, white Republicans monopolized patronage, or some Democrats saw the dangers of Negro domination in black judges, congressmen, and even presidential electors. In simplest terms, the question of how North Carolina could be both a white man's country and a free country was most often tested in relation to local self-rule.

In 1880 O'Hara had an unusual opportunity to express his own evaluation of the era in which he sought office. When a group of North Carolina blacks migrated to Indiana, a Senate committee investigated this exodus along with a larger movement to Kansas, and O'Hara was

119

one of the Negroes asked to appear before the committee. O'Hara's testimony showed mild optimism about the ability of blacks to prosper under the terms of the post-Reconstruction adjustment. Yes, prejudice against Negroes existed in North Carolina, he told the senators, but less so than in the North, and blacks voted freely and were quietly acquiring land. Negroes did not always receive justice from the courts, but then "a poor man, or an ignorant man, in any community, is at a disadvantage." Opposing black migration from the state as ill-conceived, he seemed to take for granted that the rights won by Negroes in Reconstruction would be permanent. It did not occur to him, apparently, that slow progress might be replaced by swift deterioration, that blacks and their leaders might ever again be excluded from the political game. His confidence in the enduring legacy of Reconstruction led him to declare, "I am one of those who think the American negro ought to be left to work out his own destiny, and that he had been a foundling and a ward too long already."[40]

The most important achievement of O'Hara's political struggles was his success at making the "black second" a stronghold of Negro officeholding. A man who refused to be subdued, he pushed his way, despite rebuffs, into offices few blacks held—presidential elector, county board chairman, congressman. In the process he helped change the political climate within the Republican party, shifting the expectations of both blacks and whites, so that after 1882 it was almost taken for granted that a Negro would be the nominee for Congress in the black second and blacks would take an ever-increasing role in party machinery and patronage. The question "What did O'Hara really *do* to change the lot of landless black laborers?" betrays a twentieth-century political mentality. What O'Hara *did* was give them rhetoric, a symbol of black progress, and cues about the future. In many ways he had little in common with his black constituents, but he was a convenient abstraction, a man defined as Negro in the right place, with the right skills—there was after all, only one other black lawyer in the whole county—who almost inevitably emerged as a black leader.[41]

Although O'Hara represented the increasing influence of black voters, he could never have gained power as a Negro candidate alone. His success came as a party candidate. Was he dependent upon white support? Yes. But, at the same time, white Republicans could not have prevailed in Halifax without the support of black spokesmen like O'Hara. It was not mere sentiment that kept O'Hara working within the confines of the Republican party even after he had been gravely disappointed by party leadership and practices. Political victory—at least victory with any substance—depended upon an organization that could confederate local interests and leaders, raise campaign funds, distribute rewards, and ordain nominees for lower offices (with their natural interest in fair elections and getting out the vote). Although the Republican organization was loose and at times chaotic, it was able to perform these functions. If O'Hara had won election to Congress as the leader of an independent Negro party, as in theory he might have done, he would have had no patronage at his disposal, few ties to networks of power outside his district, and uncertain access to political money. Furthermore, the absence of whites in O'Hara's hypothetical party would tend to exaggerate the element of racial conflict in every political dispute.

In the end O'Hara's experience in local government turned out to be a false start. His position as chairman of the board of county commissioners, rather than being a stepping-stone to his long-term goal of a seat in Congress, entangled him in local squabbles that gave an opening to election fraud. His alliance with Larkin, and the malfeasance indictments, also interfered with his plans. He might, perhaps, have found consolation in the fact that in one election after another Halifax delegates went to the congressional election committed to him, and might also have attributed some of this backing to relationships built up during his years as a commissioner.

A reporter from the Republican Raleigh *Signal* interviewed O'Hara just after he retired from Congress. O'Hara told the journalist that "local quarrels have done more to keep the Republican party out of power than anything else." The rich variety of Republican factionalism in the second district and in Halifax County certainly bore out the point. White Republicans were in frequent tension with black Republicans— that was obvious. But other fault lines in the party separated native white Republicans and immigrants, county from county, and even one ambitious Negro from another. Perhaps O'Hara remembered the previous year's sundered convention in Northampton, where one faction favored Robert E. Young, a wealthy white man from Vance County, and another demanded "a colored man or a choice from the county."[42]

O'Hara left office persuaded that success or failure for black politics hinged on county and local politics and the Republican party. When, thirteen years later, William W. Kitchin declared, "Mr. Chairman, I remember when four out of five commissioners of Halifax were negroes," he showed that he, too, shared that persuasion.

121

Notes

1. U.S., Congress, *Congressional Record*, 56th Cong., 1st sess., 1899–1900 (Washington, D.C.: Government Printing Office, 1900), app., p. 297.

2. James Edward O'Hara Papers, Regenstein Library, University of Chicago, Chicago.

3. Vera Jean O'Hara Rivers, " 'A Thespian Must Play His Role': A Biographical Sketch of Hon. James E. O'Hara; His Life, Work, and Family," pp. 2–9, O'Hara Papers; Joseph Eliot Elmore, "North Carolina Negro Congressmen, 1875–1901" (M.A. thesis, University of North Carolina, 1964), p. 42; U.S., Congress, Senate, *Report and Testimony of the Select Committee of the United States Senate to Investigate the Causes of the Removal of the Negroes from the Southern States to the Northern States*, 46th Cong., 2d sess., 1880, S. Rept. 693, pt. 1:56 (hereafter cited as Exodus Report); U.S., Congress, *Congressional Directory*, 49th Cong., 2d sess., 1886–87 (Washington, D.C.: Government Printing Office, 1886), p. 65; U.S., Department of Interior, *Official Register of the United States, 1869* (Washington, D.C.: Government Printing Office, 1869), p. 40; *1871* (1871), p. 39; Peter Mitchel Wilson, *Southern Exposure* (Chapel Hill: University of North Carolina Press, 1927), p. 89; Halifax County, Board of County Commissioners (HCC), Minutes, 1873–83 (microfilm), North Carolina, Division of Archives and History (NCDAH), Raleigh. On O'Hara's place of birth, see U.S., Dept. of Interior, *Official Register, 1871*; U.S., Bureau of Census, Manuscript Census Schedules, Tenth Census of the United States, 1880, Population, North Carolina, Halifax County, Enfield Township (west of railroad), p. 7; Goldsboro *Messenger*, Nov. 27, 1882; New Bern *Journal*, Sept. 17, 1905, clipping in scrapbook, O'Hara Papers. For information on O'Hara's teaching experience in New Bern, see Roberta Sue Alexander, "North Carolina Faces the Freedmen: Race Relations during Presidential Reconstruction, 1865–1867" (Ph.D. diss., University of Chicago, 1974), 2:636.

4. Eric Anderson, *Race and Politics in North Carolina, 1872–1901: The Black Second* (Baton Rouge: Louisiana State University Press, 1981); Salisbury *Star of Zion*, June 19, 1890.

5. Goldsboro *Carolina Messenger*, July 31, 1876; Tarboro *Southerner*, July 25, 1878; Goldsboro *Messenger*, Nov. 18, 1878; Goldsboro *Carolina Messenger*, Nov. 2, 1874, Nov. 2, 1876; Warrenton *Centennial*, Aug. 11, 1876; Goldsboro *Messenger*, Oct. 18, 1880; Tarboro *Southerner*, Mar. 12, 1875; Raleigh *Sentinel*, May 16, 1876; Ralph Hardee Rives to Peggy Lamson, Nov. 13, 1969, Halifax County Historical Association Papers, East Carolina University, Greenville, N.C.; telephone interview with John W. McGwigan, Enfield, Apr. 30, 1975; Washington, D.C., *National Republican* Sept. 27, 1886; Wilmington *Post*, Dec. 29, 1878.

6. Warrenton *Gazette*, July 30, 1875.

7. Raleigh *Sentinel*, Sept. 26, 1876; *Newbernian*, Oct. 25, 1876; Wilmington *Post*, Nov. 1, 1876.

8. New York *Times,* July 23, 1878.

9. Kinston *Free Press*, Sept. 27, 1888.

10. Exodus Report, p. 53; Goldsboro *Carolina Messenger*, May 18, 1874.

11. *Congressional Record*, 56th Cong., 1st sess., 1899–1900, app., pp. 297–98.

12. William Eaton to David Settle Reid, Sept. 20, 1875, David Settle Reid Papers, NCDAH.

13. For the Liberal platforms, see Wilmington *Post*, June 18, 1882; Raleigh *Register*, May 7, 1884.

14. U.S., Bureau of the Census, *Compendium of the Tenth Census* (1880), p. 1521.

15. HCC, Minutes, Apr. 7, 1875, Feb. 8, 1876, May 8, 1877, May 7, 1878; North Carolina, *Annual Report of the Auditor, 1875* (Raleigh: State Printer, 1876), p. 232; *1876* (1876), p. 179; *1878* (1879), p. 218; *1879* (1879), p. 133; French v. Commissioners, 74 N.C. 692 (1876); HCC, Minutes, Aug. 8, 1876, Jan. 6, 1879, Jan. 6, 1880.

16. As early as 1876 a group of taxpayers, charging that Larkin's bonds were insufficient, asked superior court judge S.W. Watts to review them. Watts ordered minor changes in the bonds but ruled in Larkin's favor. HCC, Mintues, Dec. 5, 1876. In September 1878, after three Republican commissioners resigned, a Democratic majority board demanded stronger surety from Larkin and, not receiving it, turned over tax-collection duties to a special tax collector. Ibid., Sept. 2, 3, 14, 1878. For the county's efforts to recover losses from Larkin, see ibid., June 9, 1879; Nov. 15, 1880; Mar. 21, 1881; Feb. 6, Apr. 4, 1882. North Carolina, *Public Laws, 1879*, ch. 304; *1880*, ch. 29.

17. Raleigh *Sentinel*, Oct. 3, 1876.

18. HCC, Minutes, Sept. 8, Dec. 7, 1874; Mar. 3, 1875; Nov. 3, 1874; Apr. 3, Jan. 4, 1876; Feb. (?), Jan. 4, 1875.

19. Brickell v. Commissioners, 81 N.C. 241 (1879). HCC, Minutes, June 3, 1878; Spier Whitaker to Walter Clark, July 25, 1878, Walter Clark Papers, NCDAH; HCC, Minutes, Aug. 6, 1878.

20. Halifax County Superior Court, Minutes, 1878–81, NCDAH; Goldsboro *Messenger*, Mar. 25, 1880; Tarboro *Southerner*, Apr. 1, 1880; Wilmington *Post*, Dec. 29, 1878. The inferior court indictments are mentioned in judicial fee lists in HCC, Minutes, Sept. 16, 1878, July (?), 1879.

21. Spier Whitaker to Walter Clark, Dec. 14, 1878, Clark Papers.

22. Computed from *Compendium of the Tenth Census*, p. 1521; N.C., *Annual Report of the Auditor, 1878*, pp. 218, 276.

23. U.S., Bureau of the Census, *Eleventh Census* (1890): *Wealth, Debt, and Taxation*, vol. 15, pt. 1, pp. 311–12; N.C., *Public Laws, 1883*, ch. 347; *1885*, ch. 13.

24. HCC, Minutes, Dec. 2, 1879; N.C., *Public Laws, 1881*, ch. 318.

25. Bryan v. Commissioners, 84 N.C. 106-7 (1881).

26. HCC, Minutes, Jan. 7, Feb. 3, Mar. 3, 1879; Whitaker to Clark, Dec. 14, 1878, Clark Papers; Raleigh *Signal*, Sept. 16, 30, 1880.

27. HCC, Minutes, July 5, Oct. 4, 1880.

28. Excluding George A. Brown, who resigned in 1875, and L. F. Larkin, who served only three months, seven men sat with O'Hara as members of the board of commissioners from 1874 to 1878; only one of them, John H. Howard, served the full four years. Of these eight commissioners, six were Negroes. I was unable to learn anything about John (Jack) Harvill aside from his

name and race. Four of the five remaining Negroes fit the generalizations in the above paragraph. Winfield F. Young (postmaster/farmer), Henry Clay (shoemaker), O'Hara (lawyer), and Howard (merchant) were all mulattoes 30 years of age or under in 1874. Stewart Hardy, a 44-year-old black farmer, is the only exception to the pattern. The white members of the board were much older, one being 54 the other 47, when they took office. Manuscript Census Schedules, 1880, Halifax County.

29. See Anderson, *Race and Politics in North Carolina*, pp. 91, 112.

30. Ibid. Except where otherwise noted, the following material on O'Hara's congressional campaigns is based on chs. 3–7 of that study.

31. The county canvassing board was selected in the following manner. The justices of the peace, meeting as a board, chose four election judges for each precinct, where possible selecting two Republicans and two Democrats. In turn the judges at each precinct chose one of their number to be a member of the county board of canvassers. The 1878 Halifax board of canvassers had a Republican majority, according to William H. Kitchin; but with a factional fight in the Republican party, this majority was useless for O'Hara. Sheriff Dawson was intimately connected with the mechanics of the election, his duties ranging from notifying election judges and registrars of their appointment to attending the canvassers' session. N.C., *Public Laws 1876–77*, ch. 275; *Congressional Record*, 46th Cong., 1st sess., 1879, p. 1297.

32. Frederick A. Woodard to Henry G. Connor, Aug. 26, 1886, Henry G. Connor Papers, Southern Historical Collection, University of North Carolina, Chapel Hill; Jesse J. Yeates to M. W. Ransom, Aug. 14, 1878, Matthew W. Ransom Papers, ibid.; Harry Skinner to Ransom, Aug. 27, 1880, ibid. Skinner was a Populist representative in the 1890s.

33. The Halifax County convention, chaired by a distinguished native white (John T. Gregory), gave O'Hara its undivided support. Wilmington *Post*, June 11, 1882. In contrast, Hubbs had the support of Craven and Jones counties, both with black majorities. E. R. Dudley, a black former legislator from Craven, supported Hubbs so strongly that O'Hara had him fired from his patronage post after the election. Anderson, *Race and Politics in North Carolina*, pp. 107, 115.

34. Weldon *News*, quoted in Raleigh *News and Observer*, Aug. 13, 1882; New Bern *Weekly Journal*, Aug. 3, 1882. Hubbs was willing to let the dispute be decided by a new nominating convention, but O'Hara refused to go along. *News and Observer*, Aug. 9, 1882.

35. The matter of skin color was not the primary issue in this campaign, as Furnifold Simmons later claimed. John C. Dancy has noted that O'Hara received "far more of the unadulterated black votes than did his opponent who was of unmixed Negro blood." J. Fred Rippy, ed., *Furnifold Simmons, Statesman of the New South: Memoirs and Addresses* (Durham: Duke University Press, 1936), p. 16; Salisbury *Star of Zion*, Mar. 24, 1887.

36. New Bern *Weekly Journal*, Aug. 3, 1882; *Congressional Record*, 48th Cong., 1st sess., 1883–84, p. 3908.

37. *Congressional Record*, 48th Cong., 2d sess., 1884–85, pp. 296-97, 316–23, 332–33, 339–43, 554. Ben H. Procter, biographer of the bill's sponsor, saw O'Hara's amendment as a "devious attempt to defeat" the bill. *Not without Honor: The Life of John H. Reagan* (Austin: University of Texas Press,

1962), p. 255. For an analysis of the votes on O'Hara's amendment, see Lawrence Grossman, *The Democratic Party and the Negro: Northern and National Politics, 1868–92* (Urbana: University of Illinois Press, 1976), pp. 110–12.

38. *Congressional Record*, 48th Cong., 1st sess., 1883–84, p. 282; ibid., 49th Cong., 1st sess., 1885–86, pp. 385, 3073.

39. Edmund Burke, *Reflections on the Revolution in France* (Harmondsworth, England: Penguin Books, 1968), p. 135.

40. Exodus Report, pp. 49–71.

41. The other black lawyer in Halifax was John H. Collins, who was elected district solicitor in 1878.

42. Raleigh *Signal*, July 21, 1887; *Blade*, July 23, 1886; and unidentified clipping in scrapbook, O'Hara Papers.

II

Collective Biography of
State and Local Leaders

Richard L. Hume   **6**

Negro Delegates to the State Constitutional Conventions of 1867–69

During a fifteen-month period, the vast changes unleased in the South by civil war, emancipation, Confederate defeat, and Congressional Reconstruction became apparent to all Americans. Beginning at the state capitol in Montgomery, Alabama (the very birthplace of the Confederacy) on November 5, 1867, and concluding in Austin, Texas, on February 8, 1869, conventions met to frame new constitutions for ten of the former Confederate states.[1] Authorized by Congress in the Reconstruction acts of March 1867, these bodies were to frame the new constitutions required to restore the southern states to the Union. The documents they were to draft were to guarantee what had been unthinkable at the beginning of the decade—the rights of southern Negroes to vote and to hold public office. The freedmen were to use their franchise for the first time to elect members of these conventions, and the first Afro-Americans ever elected to public office were among the delegates charged with drafting the new constitutions.

Many Americans perceived the great significance of the events begun by the calling of these bodies, which were often disdainfully labeled black-and-tan conventions by southern whites, who mocked their mixed racial composition.[2] From the assembling of the first of them in Montgomery to the adjournment of the last of them in Austin, reports of their proceedings—and of the activities of their Negro delegates—appeared frequently in the press. North Carolina's Republican papers noted with approval the election of delegate James H. Harris, a black from Wake County; Virginia Conservatives read apprehensively of the seating of delegate Lewis Lindsay, a Richmond Negro who had allegedly urged the freedmen to arm themselves. John A. Chesnut came to the convention in Charleston from Kershaw County, the home of the aristocratic Chesnut family whose name he bore. Various newspapers also noted that several Negroes were sent to the Mississippi convention from Warren County, the home of Jefferson Davis. The New York *Tribune* reported that about one-third of the Florida convention's delegates were Negroes, and numerous reports indicated that many Afro-Americans were elected to the Louisiana convention, which was to meet in New Orleans, the site of the 1866 race riot that helped doom Presidential Reconstruction. William H. Grey, a former slave of Governor Henry A. Wise of Virginia, appeared in the Arkansas convention; and Henry M. Turner, an articulate former Union-army chaplain, went to the one in Georgia. These reports and countless others informed Americans of the magnitude of the change underway in the former Confederacy. Such stories played a primary role in shaping the public image of the conventions and of the reconstruction process in general throughout the country.[3]

Indeed, the stunning significance of such news—of freedmen active in the formation of the South's new Republican party and of the presence of large numbers of Negroes in these important constitutional conventions—was discussed widely. To most northerners, to Afro-Americans themselves, and to a minority of southern whites, black enfranchisement was required to restore the South securely to the Union and to preserve the fruits of victory almost lost during Presidential Reconstruction. To a large majority of southern whites as well as to significant numbers of northern whites, these new Negro politicians and their constituencies of newly enfranchised freedmen represented, instead, a threat to a conservative restoration policy and to the continuation of white dominance. Whatever their perspective, though, all Americans—white, black, northern, and southern—were extremely interested in the role that Negroes, who constituted a quarter of the total membership of these ten reconstruction conventions, were to play in shaping a new South. Contrasting views of these new politicians, in fact, shaped the views (both the idealistic hopes and pessimistic fears) most Americans held about the future course of reconstruction.[4]

Racial attitudes have likewise shaped how historians have treated both these conventions and the events of Reconstruction in general. During the early 1900s Dunningites, who were quite critical of the entire program, viewed the Negro delegates sent to the conventions as ignorant, vindictive field hands and as the tools of dishonest carpetbaggers and scalawags. Revisionist scholars have recently pictured Reconstruction more positively. They have credited the members of these conventions with framing—with the aid of Afro-American delegates—progressive constitutions that instituted long overdue reforms throughout the former Confederacy.[5]

Despite their importance, however, historians have still generally given only limited attention to the black-and-tan conventions and the black and mulatto delegates who served in them. This essay therefore

130

ALABAMA CONSTITUTIONAL CONVENTION, 1867
Alabama Department of Archives and History, Montgomery

presents an overview of these delegates in all of the ten constitutional conventions of 1867–69. Both the delegates and the bodies in which they served deserve study. The conventions merit examination because they contained the first large biracial group of officials—Negroes and southern and outside whites—elected in the United States, and because their delegates confronted the basic issues of racial adjustment in the postwar South. Their Negro delegates deserve attention because they offer a sample of black and mulatto politicians throughout the South (one larger and more diverse geographically than any to date) on which to test current assumptions about Negro Reconstructionists. This sample can be used to compare Negro delegates as a group with other delegate factions and to determine more precisely the aspirations of the Afro-American political leaders—those of both greater and lesser prominence—who helped institute Congressional Reconstruction in the former Confederacy.

To begin this study, the manuscript census returns of 1870 were used[6]—along with selected manuscript collections, contemporary newspapers, secondary accounts, and federal and state documents—to classify all members of the conventions biographically. These sources indicated that the 1,011 delegates who participated in the ten conventions should be classified as follows: 552 southern whites (whites who had resided prior to 1860 in the states that formed the Confederacy), 258 Negroes (blacks and mulattoes),[7] 161 outside whites (whites who arrived in the region after 1860 from outside the former Confederate states), 34 unclassified whites (whites of unknown origin), and 6 unclassified delegates (of undetermined race). This delegate breakdown for each of the ten black-and-tan conventions is depicted in the following table.[8]

The voting patterns of individual delegates were then determined. This was done by examining convention journals, reports in contemporary newspapers, and monographs on reconstruction in particular states. Delegates classified politically as radicals were those who most frequently endorsed selected measures that guaranteed the political rights of freedmen, imposed restrictions on former Confederates, altered antebellum economic patterns, or strengthened the Republican party in the South. Conservatives were identified as those who most often opposed these programs; delegates who showed mixed voting patterns were classified politically as nonaligned.[9]

The process of biographical classification quickly revealed that the factional distribution of delegates differed considerably among various conventions (see table below). These differences reflected the particu-

Delegates to Southern Constitutional Conventions, 1867–69

STATE	TOTAL DELEGATES ELECTED	SOUTHERN WHITES	OUTSIDE WHITES	NEGROES	UNCLASSIFIED WHITES	UNCLASSIFIED DELEGATES	TOTAL DELEGATES PARTICIPATING
Alabama	100	52	24	17	6	–	99
Arkansas	75	45	17	8	–	–	70
Florida	46	15	13	19	3	–	50
Georgia	169	114	12	33	2	–	161
Louisiana	98	23	13	47	8	6	97
Mississippi	100	52	21	16	7	–	96
North Carolina	120	88	18	13	3	–	122
South Carolina	124	35	15	71	–	–	121
Texas	90	70	8	10	4	–	92
Virginia	105	58	20	24	1	–	103
TOTALS	1,027	552	161	258	34	6	1,011

lar postwar realities of each state in which a convention was held. In contrast to recent years, in which no state has had an Afro-American majority in its population, during the late 1860s three deep-South states—South Carolina, Mississippi, and Louisiana—did have such majorities. As a result of postwar white disfranchisement, five deep-South states—the three just listed and Alabama and Florida—actually had Negro majorities among electorates that selected convention delegates.[10] Since the composition of each black-and-tan convention was shaped largely by the nature of the constituencies that selected its members, the delegate factions of the bodies in the five states with Negro electoral majorities generally varied considerably from those that met where whites continued to represent a majority of registered voters.

Even so, in examining the delegate composition of the conventions as a whole, it is still important to note that, except in the South Carolina, Louisiana, and Florida conventions, southern whites made up the majority of delegates. They were especially numerous and influential in Georgia, in the upper-South states of North Carolina and Virginia, and in the trans–Mississippi River region of Arkansas and Texas.[11] Outside whites—the carpetbaggers—were much less numerous than native whites. Still, they appeared in significant numbers in Alabama, Florida, Mississippi, and Arkansas, the four scattered states in which they supplied at least 20 percent of delegate totals.[12] In general, Negro delegates represented constituencies in which the freedmen were most concentrated. They were particularly evident in the South Carolina convention, the only one in which they comprised an absolute majority (71 of 121) of participating delegates, and in Louisiana and Florida, where they accounted for almost half (47 of 97) and over a third (19 of 50) of the delegates respectively. In fact, over half of the entire Afro-American delegate strength was concentrated in these three deep-South states. Negro representation and influence tended to lessen correspondingly in other areas. There were, nonetheless, sizable blocs of black and mulatto delegates scattered among various conventions, most notably those in Alabama, Mississippi, Virginia, and Georgia (see table above).

In examining these delegates closely, it is first useful to note several significant characteristics of their constituencies. As noted, they generally came from districts where freedmen substantially outnumbered white voters. As a whole, their constituencies contained a two-thirds majority (a median of 64.3 percent) of freedmen among their electorates. Their Negro majorities were thus slightly greater than those of districts represented by carpetbaggers (as a median their electorates were 63.5 percent Afro-American), and they were markedly greater than those of districts represented by southern whites (which had a median figure of only 44.4 percent for Afro-Americans registered among their electorates).[13] Second, the counties where Negro delegates actually resided were generally notable for the high per-acre value of their croplands. The median 1860 per-acre value of such land in these counties was an impressive $22.[14] This was several times the $7 and $11 per-acre value of farmlands in the home counties of southern-white and outside-white delegates respectively. Finally, a number of Afro-American delegates came from urban districts, even though a large majority of the freedmen were actually employed as agricultural laborers in rural areas.

It is not surprising that these new politicians tended to come from districts with large Negro majorities among their electorates. It is, nonetheless, important to note this for two reasons. First, it shows that black political awareness had developed to a significant degree by 1867. The war had not only emancipated the freedmen, it had shown them—as two twentieth-century world wars would later demonstrate to colonial peoples—that whites were far from omnipotent. Conflict had not ended white dominance, but violence—the reality of whites killing whites—had certainly challenged elements of the creed of white supremacy. Although Negro delegates could be influenced by more experienced white politicians, the climate of opinion of the late 1860s guaranteed that, despite the traditional story to the contrary, they would not function simply as pawns of opportunistic white radicals. The psychological changes that accompanied emancipation and enfranchisement of the freedmen thwarted the development of any such tidy Republican coalition in which subservient former slaves meekly followed white leaders. Changed political realities, in fact, required that these new politicians strive to gain active and independent roles in framing these new constitutions.[15]

In addition to suggesting a rapid development of political awareness among the freedmen, the fact that these delegates often came from Negro-majority districts shows the importance of continued study of southern Reconstruction at the grassroots level. Even though relatively few Afro-Americans gained major elective positions throughout the region as a whole, the impact of these politicians was considerable at the local level, especially in districts where the freedmen comprised large majorities of voters. In such districts they were determined, to a degree only now being recognized, to hold local offices and to control

135

their own destiny. This determination influenced the entire course of Reconstruction. It impelled the freedmen to develop cadres of their own local leaders. It also intensified power struggles between Negroes and whites within the Republican coalition, and it strengthened Democratic efforts to overthrow "black rule" and restore white control throughout the South.[16]

The high value of agricultural lands in the districts of Negro delegates is also worthy of note, particularly when it is related to the large numbers of freedmen living in those constituencies. These areas were often the locations of the larger antebellum plantations. As claimed in several recent studies of slavery, it was here, among the slaveholdings of the larger planters, that Afro-Americans were perhaps best able to develop a sense of community and to maintain their cultural identity. It would appear that this identity was carried into the postwar years and given a political dimension during Reconstruction. Throughout such regions—districts of large plantations and many freedmen[17]—Negroes selected as delegates men from their own communities. In areas where smaller plantations and farms were more numerous, in contrast, the former slaves evidently found it more difficult to advance political leaders from within their own ranks. They apparently more often turned instead for leadership to white Republicans, especially the carpetbaggers.

Finally, Afro-American delegate constituencies were often in larger cities—New Orleans, Charleston, Richmond, and Savannah; they were also often in smaller hinterland centers—Pine Bluff, Macon, and Beaufort. A number of urban delegates, especially those from cities such as New Orleans and Charleston, had never been enslaved. Some, although formerly in bondage, had experienced a form of slavery which was probably less oppressive than that encountered by rural field hands. Others were rural Negroes—often former slaves—who had migrated to cities, attracted by economic opportunities, by hopes of aid from government agencies such as the Freedmen's Bureau, or by the desire to escape hardships of sharecropping and racial violence in rural areas. In addition, a small but important group of these urban delegates was comprised of nonsoutherners—Negro carpetbaggers who had arrived in southern cities with the Union army, with the Freedmen's Bureau, or with the various missionary societies. Whatever their individual backgrounds, though, these urban delegates soon found that cities offered unique opportunities to aspiring politicians. During the antebellum years, urban centers had often provided freedom (or at least a less harsh form of servitude). In the postwar years,

136

these centers offered economic advancement, often in state capitals or in larger cities that were also at the center of the political stage. It was no accident that a significant number of these new politicians, including some of those who were most articulate, entered political office from urban constituencies.[18]

An examination of the Negro delegates themselves would perhaps best begin with an overview of their racial backgrounds. The most striking fact here is that a large number of these delegates were mulattoes. Although only about 13 percent of the Negro population was so classified in the 1860 census, a slight majority of those delegates with identified racial backgrounds (100 of 192) were mulattoes.[19] The composition of Negro factions, nonetheless, varied from convention to convention. Those in Texas, Mississippi, and Georgia were apparently largely black; those in Virginia, Florida, North Carolina, and Alabama were divided about evenly. Still, the two conventions in which Negroes were most numerous contained mulatto majorities. Louisiana's mulatto contingent was strikingly large; and the South Carolina convention's Negro majority, as was the case with the much smaller minority contingent in Arkansas, contained a slight mulatto majority.[20] These racial divisions were important for at least two reasons. First, mulatto delegates—men such as John A. Hyman (N.C.), Francis L. Cardozo (S.C.), William H. Grey (Ark.), Pinckney B. S. Pinchback (La.), Charles Caldwell (Miss.), James T. Rapier (Ala.), Henry M. Turner (Ga.), and George T. Ruby (Tx.)—were frequently among the most articulate Negro spokesmen. Second, a number of mulattoes had experienced antebellum conditions different from those faced by most Negroes, and these differences could contribute to divisions over postwar priorities within Negro delegations. This problem was not particularly great in the conventions; these bodies finished their work as Reconstruction commenced. Still, it had the potential to weaken considerably the South's Republican state governments in the future.[21]

A second notable characteristic of Negro delegates was their antebellum status—whether they were slave or free. Evidence here is frequently difficult to locate and more readily available in some states than others. That located on slightly under two-thirds (158 of 258 or 61 percent) of these delegates, nonetheless points to two conclusions. First, a significant number—indeed a slight majority (79 of 158)—had not been enslaved; and at least an additional fourteen, although once in bondage, had obtained their freedom prior to the war. A second significant point becomes apparent when race and antebellum status are combined (for the purpose of comparison) on the 132 delegates on whom such information is available. A majority of blacks with known antebellum backgrounds (33 of 53) were formerly slaves; most mulattoes with ascertained backgrounds (48 of 79) had not experienced bondage.[22] Although a number of these delegates were former slaves, it is again clear that these men as a whole were not representative of the entire South's Afro-American population. Rather, in selecting their first political leaders, the freedmen tended to turn (as whites had also done traditionally) to individuals from the upper strata of their society. Their delegations often contained large numbers of antebellum free Negroes, of mulattoes, and of delegates who had connections with free Negro families in cities such as Charleston and New Orleans.[23]

The high literacy rate among Negro delegates again suggests that they were hardly typical of the southern freedmen. W. E. B. Du Bois estimated that only about five percent of the slave population was literate by 1860, but manuscript returns from the 1870 census, supplemented by other sources when available, indicate that about 85 percent of these delegates could read and write. It is probable, as Ralph A. Wooster has suggested, that census enumerators inflated the numbers of those new politicians who were actually literate. Still, the fact that at least 179 of them were apparently literate (while only some 34 are known to have been illiterate) reveals again that they often came from the upper levels of the Afro-American community.[24] Even so, it is important to note that the literacy rate varied, for obvious reasons, among different Negro delegate groups. All of the 46 antebellum free mulattoes whose literacy could be established were literate. In contrast, according to census returns, over a quarter (9 of 32) black delegates known to have been slaves could not read or write. Overall, though, a systematic accumulation of data on the literacy of these delegates challenges the traditional contention that they were simply throngs of ignorant field hands.

It is not surprising that the long-standing focus on the illiteracy of these new politicians is inaccurate and misleading. It is important, nonetheless, to deal with this aspect of the stereotype of postwar Negro leaders; it remains one of the most persistent elements of what has been called the tragic legend of Reconstruction. In fact, many of these delegates were literate, and it is clear that their ability to read and write was a tremendous asset. It allowed them to keep up with political developments; it allowed them in inform the masses of freedmen about these matters (while also promoting their own candidacies); and it enhanced their image within the party as potential Republican candidates. Literacy was thus a key factor in advancing the delegate careers of prominent Negro Republicans such as George Teamoh (Va.), Robert Smalls (S.C.), Josiah T. Walls (Fla.), and James T. Rapier (Ala.).[25] It was also important in securing the political advancement of less well-known politicians. As a group, these delegates would therefore be better viewed as ambitious men eager to take advantage of a once-in-a-lifetime possibility. Their general literacy contributed greatly to their awareness of this opportunity, and it often aided in their selection as candidates and in their campaigns to secure their convention seats.

The misleading nature of the traditional portrayal of these politicians—in which they are viewed as a monolithic group of ignorant and propertyless farm laborers—is again evident when their occupations are examined closely. Essentially, the 226 Negro delegates with ascertained occupations can be broken down into four groups of about equal size. The first of these, numbering some 50 delegates, was comprised of farmers. At least 12 of these men had no property and perhaps fit the traditional picture of the impoverished postwar Negro politician. As a group, though, their median property holdings in 1870 amounted to some $575 (ranging among those listing property from $150 to $8,000). This suggests that they were actually sometimes independent farmers; Thomas Holt has, in fact, shown that a number—such as Frederick A. Clinton, William H. Gray, William Nelson, and Augustus R. Thompson in South Carolina—did own small farms. According to various sources, others—Leopold Guichard and Theophile Mahier (La.), Benjamin A. Thompson (S.C.), and Benjamin F. Royal (Ala.)—were rather prosperous planters. Thus, there was actually considerable diversity within this group. It undoubtedly contained some impoverished sharecroppers, but its members would be most accurately categorized overall as a somewhat heterogeneous bloc that also contained farm owners and a few rather prosperous planters.[26]

Some 47 ministers made up a second major Negro delegate group. A small but interesting faction among them—men such as Francis L. Cardozo, Benjamin F. Randolph, and Richard H. Cain (S.C.), James W. Hood (N.C.), Thomas W. Stringer (Miss.), William Murrell (La.), James T. White and William H. Grey (Ark.), Tunis G. Campbell (Ga.), and Charles H. Pearce (Fla.)—were natives (or long-time residents) of the North who had generally entered (or returned to) the South with missionary societies or the Freedmen's Bureau. A second element—delegates such as William E. Johnston and Abram Middleton (S.C.)—was comprised of southern antebellum free Negroes. A third group was made up of former slaves—Robert Meacham (Fla.), James D. Barrett (Va.), Henry Eppes (N.C.), and Sancho Saunders and Isaac P. Brockington (S.C). Overall, these ministers were not especially prosperous; their median 1870 property holdings amounted to only $400 (ranging from $100 to $9,500 among the 37 listing assets). Despite their rather modest holdings, though, they were extremely important. Several, such as Francis L. Cardozo, had developed useful associations with influential white northerners.[27] Others—including both antebellum free mulattoes such as Cardozo and former slaves such as Robert Meacham—were highly respected leaders within their communities. As a whole, these men were also literate, and a number of them were among the most articulate Negro delegates.

A group of 54 skilled laborers formed the third and largest body of Negro delegates. Carpenters Charles M. Wilder (S.C.) and Joseph E. Oates (Fla.) had learned their trades while slaves. Others—barbers Robert C. De Large and Joseph H. Rainey (both S.C.), David Wilson (La.), and Ovid Gregory (Ala.)—had never been in bondage. Whatever their individual backgrounds, however, this faction contained significant numbers of carpenters, blacksmiths, barbers, shoemakers, and tailors—occupations open to antebellum free Negroes, to valued slaves, or to migrants into urban areas. As a whole these delegates were rather prosperous (with median 1870 holdings of $1,100 and a range of $100 to $20,000 among those actually listing property).[28] They were a diverse group, but their general prosperity suggests that they had been relatively successful, despite unsettled postwar conditions, in marketing their skills.

The final occupational group among Negroes—which included some 41 delegates—was made up of men employed in business and the professions. Sixteen teachers—including George T. Ruby (Tx.), W. Nelson Joiner (S.C.), and P. Francis Valfroit (La.)—comprised the largest single faction within this bloc. They were often aided in their quest for political office by their connections with the Freedmen's Bureau or other educational agencies. In addition, this group included a mix of businessmen and men with some professional training. Overall, these delegates were the most prosperous Negroes; their median 1870 holdings amounted to $2,180 (with a range of $200 to $14,388 among those listing assets). Several of them—New Orleans wine merchant E. Arnold Bertonneau, for example—were antebellum free Negroes. Others, such as George T. Ruby, were recent arrivals from the North. A few—such as brickyard owner William B. Nash (S.C.)—were former slaves. Whatever their origins, they represented an upper class, a tiny but obviously significant element that had already emerged within the postwar Negro community.[29]

In turning now to examine the role of Afro-American delegates within the conventions, it must be emphasized that their greatest assets were their relatively large numbers in several conventions and their overall political unity, which often allowed them to vote in bloc units. In the South Carolina convention, of course, they were in an absolute majority, and they formed the largest single delegate groups in Louisiana and Florida. Even in conventions in states such as Virginia where they were less numerous, Negroes sometimes comprised the largest single Republican faction (see table above). In various states their bloc votes on certain issues were therefore sometimes the key to Republican successes in incorporating reform articles into the new constitutions, often over the vocal opposition of well-organized Conservatives.

An analysis of voting patterns indicates that there was a median total of approximately 126 roll-call divisions in each convention, ranging from a low of about 21 in South Carolina to a high of approximately 775 in Texas.[30] A number of these concerned issues unique to a particular body. Virginia delegates, for instance, discussed at length whether Benjamin Butler, the controversial commander who had directed the recent wartime occupation of New Orleans, should be allowed to address them, and delegates in Austin debated for days the wisdom of dividing Texas into a number of smaller states.[31] In general, though, certain key issues were brought up in some form and voted on in each of the ten assemblies. From the perspective of Afro-American delegates, the three most important of these widely discussed issues were debtor relief and/or land reform, racial segregation, and the franchise.

The question of just which groups would be allowed to vote and which would not was debated in detail in almost every body. Although Congress had specified its requirements in regard to the franchise in March 1867, the issue of precisely which classes of whites should actually be disfranchised was discussed heatedly throughout the South. In conventions such as those in Alabama and Arkansas and, most generally, in those that contained sizable numbers of whites and relatively few Negroes, scalawags often attempted to restrict the political rights of additional former Confederates, whom they regarded bitterly as wartime oppressors.[32] With few exceptions, Negro delegates showed limited interest in restricting ex-Confederates and were reluctant to enter into these bitter debates among southern whites. This reluctance disappeared quickly, however, when Conservatives attempted to use racial fears to split scalawags away from other Republicans. When antireconstructionist delegates did this—with calls for Caucasian unity and Negro disfranchisement in the North Carolina, Alabama, Arkansas, and Virginia conventions, for example—articulate Negro leaders almost always entered quickly into the fray. They were aware that Congress was determined to protect their newly secured political rights, but they were also resolved to go on record themselves as representatives of a loyal segment of the southern population that was clearly entitled to its voting rights.[33]

Debtor relief, the economic question discussed most widely in the various conventions, sometimes resulted in long constitutional debates among whites. In Raleigh, for instance, this issue led carpetbagger Albion Tourgée to conclude that North Carolina was a territory and that its entire antebellum debt should be repudiated.[34] Afro-American delegates tended to be little interested in such abstract discussions; instead they showed more interest in pragmatic concerns, especially in the two conventions in which they were most numerous. In Louisiana they supported a proposal (which was eventually weakened) to force land lost for taxes to be sold in plots small enough to be purchased easily by yeomen.[35] Francis L. Cardozo and Richard H. Cain showed similar concerns when they spoke against one of several proposals for debtor relief in the South Carolina convention, arguing that large planters should be forced to sell land to small farmers. Cain also petitioned Congress to obtain land for the state's freedmen, and the convention eventually incorporated into the constitution a measure which authorized creation of a state land commission for that purpose.[36] Despite this interesting development, no similar agency was established in any other southern state. Although individual Negroes sometimes showed interest in land reform, most Republicans—including a number of middle-class Afro-American delegates themselves—held surprisingly orthodox nineteenth-century economic views. Despite the land hunger demonstrated by the general Negro population, members of the radical coalitions in the various conventions were generally unwilling to entertain seriously any such radical redistribution proposals.[37]

The rather modest economic programs advanced by convention delegates reveal several significant points that relate to the South's postwar Republican coalition and, in general, to the progress of southern reconstruction. Despite the relative affluence of some Negro delegates, for instance, it appears that the region's new Republican party was a mix of diverse economic interests.[38] Even with the wartime idealism of the carpetbaggers—and the wartime unionism of the scalawags—helping to hold it together, it would be difficult to build party consensus on economic policy. Prosperous outside whites frequently hoped to reshape Dixie's economy into something more closely resembling that of the North. Scalawags, who were generally yeomen whites from the hill-country regions of the Carolinas, Georgia, Alabama, and Arkansas, were also interested in economic change; but they were sometimes suspicious of the grandiose programs of carpetbaggers.[39] Meanwhile, economic distinctions among Negro delegates themselves could likewise work to frustrate development of agreement on economic policy. Hardly the vassals of white radicals, they sometimes evolved economic proposals of their own, especially in the conventions in which they were most numerous. In instances such as the debates involving the amount of property to be protected from attachment for debts, their leaders presented their programs with skill. Still, the resulting discussions showed divisions among radicals—between Negroes and whites and/or among Negroes themselves—on some economic matters.

Even more provocatively, the diversity of background and economic interest within the Afro-American delegate blocs themselves suggests a reason—one that needs further examination—why Republicans did not push more vigorously for racial equality. It has been argued correctly that the racial prejudices of scalawags and carpetbaggers often weakened their potential support for measures to attain that goal. While this is certainly true, it is also important to note that a number of Negro delegates themselves, such as those employed in businesses and professions, had an economic stake in the southern social system as it evolved by the late 1860s. In the abstract, racial equality was certainly an appealing ideal, especially in a decade during which so much had already been gained. Still, the livelihood of some of these delegates, such as those employed as teachers in schools established for the freedmen, actually depended on the continuation of segregation. These men were probably aware of the possibility that separation from the larger society allowed for more rapid development of a professional class, a business community, and a public-school system within the black community, just as similar divisions would later allow immigrants from southern and eastern Europe to develop these segments of their own communities in northern cities. They were also probably aware that without segregation it might have been more difficult for them to compete with white businessmen, educators, and professionals, who had much greater financial and political resources to bring to bear on any such rivalry.[40]

Thus Negro delegates offered a mix of responses when the issue of racial segregation was discussed in various forms in many of the conventions. In Arkansas and Alabama they were generally willing to support action against miscegenation, although they made clear at the same time their feelings that this problem associated with racial mixing was caused mainly by the sexual conduct of whites. In Louisiana they argued for a registration oath that required affirmation of a belief in racial equality, and in the Mississippi convention they were active supporters of a resolution designed to integrate places of public entertainment. Most frequently, however, the issue of racial separation surfaced in debates over the proposed public-school systems. In general, Afro-Americans were willing to accept racially segregated schools. Their leaders would allow racial separation—on the basis of a pragmatic mutual agreement with whites—to promote the continued development of black institutions (schools, churches, businesses) and to reduce the racial fears of whites, who threatened violence to prevent racial mixing. Although supportive of a segregated educational system in which they were included (which, after all, represented a considerable step forward from the antebellum system from which they were barred completely), Negro leaders spoke out in the various conventions against constitutional provisions that actually mandated racial segregation.[41] Despite the appeal of separation by mutual agreement as a means of reducing racial tension, they were much impressed by wartime gains and wished to keep open options for a future of greater racial understanding in which integration might become a realistic possibility. As Arkansas delegate William H. Grey noted, he hoped for an era of racial cooperation in which the freedmen would not be restricted legally by their color or by their previous condition.[42]

The ability Negro delegates demonstrated in formulating their political objectives was impressive, especially since they had very limited prior political experience. Even so, several political liabilities sometimes limited their effectiveness, despite their overall bloc voting patterns and their delegate numbers. Even with their general unity, political differences (such as those over the proper means of protecting property from attachment for debt) sometimes developed among them, between mulattoes and blacks or between former slaves and antebellum free Negroes. These differences revealed a serious problem that postwar Negro politicians never overcame, that of the gulf between poor freedmen who hoped for land confiscation and their middle-class leaders who would not support that policy.

Of more immediate importance, the radical leadership in the conventions as a whole was overwhelmingly white. Carpetbaggers, who believed they had done the most to secure victory in the recent war, and scalawags, who were certain they had suffered greatly under disloyal Confederates, assumed they should lead the new order and were not eager to give Negroes great power in the Republican hierarchy, even though the freedmen supplied the bulk of the party's rank-and-file voters. Consequently, Afro-Americans chaired a very small number of committees that drafted key articles for the new constitutions.[43] This lack of high-level influence, of course, compounded problems the generally inexperienced Negro delegates already faced. Thus, George Teamoh, an articulate former slave in the Virginia convention, noted that his fellow delegates, who were often isolated from the white party leadership, frequently became frustrated when trying to define constituent interests while following lengthy constitutional debates.[44]

It is difficult, of course, to determine the precise antebellum or wartime experiences of many Negro delegates. Their relative youth (their median 1870 age was 38)[45] and the fact that few of them—slave or free—were mentioned in antebellum sources often makes it impossible to establish precisely what paths led them to politics and resulted in their election to the conventions. It is clear, nonetheless, that their elevation to these bodies carried them into continued political careers. At least 179 of them later held other positions. A number—including eight congressmen, seven officers in the executive branches of state governments, and a state supreme-court justice—held high offices; the vast majority, some 93 state representatives and 37 state senators, took part politically in the reconstruction process at the state legislative level.[46] In contrast to carpetbaggers and scalawags, the Negro delegates—in spite of their numbers among Republican voters—were not able to secure a large share of political power, especially in high and important offices. Instead, they most often developed political careers in lesser local positions. The failure of Republicans to work out a true biracial coalition (a real sharing of offices at all levels) was a serious shortcoming. When federal support for Reconstruction waned during the 1870s, Negroes increasingly held power only in isolated legislative districts. This base could easily be eroded once white Conservatives replaced white radicals in high state offices.

The Conservative campaign to overthrow the South's radical governments depended in large part, as Allen Trelease has shown, on force and violence. Even though relatively few Afro-American politicians achieved positions of great political prominence in the postwar South, a systematic examination of the later careers of these delegates reveals that they, like other Negro leaders, were frequently victims of attacks by terrorist groups, such as the Ku Klux Klan. The systematic nature of this political violence is evident in the fact that at least 26 (over 10 percent) of the delegates here examined were actually victims of Klan-type attacks.[47] Most of these involved threats and loss of property, but at least six attacks—those aimed at Lee A. Nance and Benjamin F. Randolph (S.C.), John Gair and William R. Meadows (La.), and Charles Caldwell and William T.Combash (Miss.)—ended with the murder of Negro delegates (later in their political careers). Obviously, it took considerable commitment, dedication, and bravery to become identified as a black Republican leader, even at the local level, in the postwar South.

Despite such qualities, Afro-Americans were unable to maintain the political power they had gained initially in the conventions. Faced with fierce Conservative determination to restore native white supremacy, with the growing factionalism among scalawags, carpetbaggers, and Negroes within Republican organizations in the South, and with the waning of idealism among northern Republicans, the radical governments were routed by the mid-1870s. Most Negro politicians then returned to relative political obscurity. This story of Reconstruction as an opportunity missed is a sad story that is all too familiar. By the 1890s the postwar gains made by the freedmen appeared to be lost almost completely. An era of red-neck rule had commenced in the South, most southern Negroes remained impoverished sharecroppers, and most northerners had accepted the South's solution to the "race problem."

There is yet another side to the story, a side that offers a better perspective. Despite the Republican defeats in the South during the 1870s, these years were a beginning—a successful beginning in which Negro politicians shared. When the Civil War commenced, the vast majority of Afro-Americans were considered to be property, as the slave schedules of 1860 manuscript census returns reveal so strikingly. By 1870 they were, in contrast, legally recognized human beings— men, women, husbands, wives, children—and a number of them, including those examined here, had become active in politics. As members of the South's new Republican party, the first truly biracial political coalition in our history (whatever its defects in this respect), they had helped to frame, in an impressive flurry of activity equaled in the states only during the era of the American Revolution, a series of remarkably progressive new constitutions.[48] These documents and the later reforms that Negroes helped to secure while serving as legislators in the Reconstruction governments began to move the South from behind the barrier it had recently erected in its tragic defense of slavery. These beginnings, however illusory they appeared by the 1890s, were clearly of tremendous importance. They offered a vision of what might have been, and this vision was to be fulfilled, at least to some degree, during the twentieth century.

Notes

The author wishes to acknowledge assistance from the National Endowment for the Humanities, the American Council of Learned Societies, and the Graduate School of Washington State University for aid on a broader project of which this essay is a part.

1. Tennessee, the eleventh former Confederate state, had returned to the Union in 1866.

2. For an overview of the members of all these conventions, see Richard L. Hume, "The 'Black and Tan' Constitutional Conventions of 1867–1869 in Ten Former Confederate States: A Study of Their Membership" (Ph.D. diss., University of Washington, 1969).

3. These early reports on Negro delegates came from many sources. Most of them are noted in Hume, " 'Black and Tan' Constitutional Conventions."

4. For one of many examples of Conservative fears, see Raleigh *Daily Sentinel*, Jan. 15, 1868. For a more hopeful view of a convention and its Negro delegates (the Florida convention in this case), see New York *Tribune*, Feb. 5, 1868.

5. For a discussion of racial attitudes in Reconstruction historiography, see Thomas J. Pressly, "Racial Attitudes, Scholarship, and Reconstruction: A Review Essay," *Journal of Southern History* 32 (Feb. 1966):88–93.

6. Microfilm copies of the 1870 manuscript census returns for Alabama, Arkansas, Florida, Georgia, Louisiana, Mississippi, North Carolina, South Carolina, Texas, and Virginia are deposited in the library at Washington State University, Pullman, Wash.

7. The term *black* is used to denote full-blooded Afro-Americans, the terms *Negro* and *Afro-American* are used to denote all members of the race, and the term *mulatto* is used to denote Afro-American delegates of mixed ancestry.

8. These delegate totals differ slightly from those in my dissertation and in several articles. This is due to continued classification (or in a few cases reclassification) of delegates. In Florida, North Carolina, and Texas additional delegates were later appointed to the conventions. They replaced delegates who had died or been unseated.

9. For specific roll-call votes used in this classification process, see appropriate charts in Hume, " 'Black and Tan' Constitutional Conventions."

10. Data on overall population are taken from *Historical Statistics of the United States Colonial Times to 1970*, 2 vols. (Washington, D.C.: Government Printing Office, 1975), 1:24–36. Most data on voter registration are from U.S. Congress, Senate, *Executive Documents*, 40th Cong., 2d sess., 1868, no. 53. In-

complete figures in this report were supplemented with additional sources (see note 13).

11. See the chart in table on p. 133. Southern-white delegates—both scalawags (southern whites who supported Congressional Reconstruction) and Conservatives (southern whites who opposed Congressional Reconstruction)—are analyzed in Richard L. Hume, "Scalawags and the Beginnings of Congressional Reconstruction in the South," paper read at the annual meeting of the American Historical Association, San Francisco, Calif., Dec. 29, 1978.

12. For detail on carpetbagger delegates, see Richard L. Hume, "Carpetbaggers in the Reconstruction South: A Group Portrait of Outside Whites in the 'Black and Tan' Constitutional Conventions," *Journal of American History* 64 (Sept. 1977):313–30. Carpetbaggers were whites from northern and border states who settled in the former Confederate states and became Republican politicians.

13. Percentages of Afro-Americans registered to vote for convention delegates were obtained from several sources. Percentages on Arkansas, Florida, Mississippi, and the Carolinas were compiled from charts in *The American Annual Cyclopaedia and Register of Important Events of the Year 1867* (New York: D. Appleton & Co., 1868), pp. 54, 314, 517, 549, 699. Percentages by county on the Negro electorate in four other states were located in "Records of the United States Army Continental Commands, 1821–1920" Record Group 393, Old Military Records Division, National Archives; Washington, D.C. These four states were: Alabama ("Election Returns from the District of Alabama": figures on Alabama in the above cited encyclopedia are sometimes inaccurate because of later district changes); Georgia ("Miscellaneous Lists Relating to Registration in 1867"); Louisiana ("Tabular Statement of Registration in the State of Louisiana"); and Texas ("List of State and County Officers in Texas"). Virginia registration figures were located in *Documents of the Constitutional Convention of the State of Virginia* (Richmond: *New Nation*, 1867 [sic]), pp. 51–52. The figures on Mississippi in the *American Annual Cyclopaedia* omit three counties on which no returns could be found. Percentages on these three counties were compiled from population figures from U.S., Bureau of the Census, *A Compendium of the Ninth Census* (June 1, 1870) (Washington, D.C.: Government Printing Office, 1872), pp. 63–65. The totals on whites in these three counties were reduced by 20 percent (from the totals reported in the 1870 census) to compensate for white disfranchisement before arriving at percentages on Negro voters.

14. This information was not available on all delegates. In some cases a delegate's home county could not be determined (especially if he represented a multicounty district); in other cases land values for a known home county were not reported. These data were nonetheless available on 239 Negro delegates, 528 southern-white delegates, and 146 outside-white delegates. For per-acre county farmland values in 1860, see Thomas J. Pressly and William H. Scofield, *Farm Real Estate Values in the United States by Counties, 1850–1959* (Seattle: University of Washington Press, 1965).

15. For a study of the psychological changes that accompanied emancipation and their political ramifications, see Leon F. Litwack, *Been in the Storm So Long: The Aftermath of Slavery* (New York: Alfred A. Knopf, 1979).

148

16. For fresh insights into the importance of the Afro-American "control" of local offices in Mississippi, see, for example, William C. Harris, *The Day of the Carpetbagger: Republican Reconstruction in Mississippi* (Baton Rouge: Louisiana State University Press, 1979), 427–28.

17. Eugene Genovese, *Roll, Jordan, Roll: The World the Slaves Made* (New York: Pantheon Books, 1974), for instance, stresses constantly the family and cultural (especially religious) cohesion of the slaves on larger plantations. For a summary of literature relating the holdings of large planters to the higher per-acre values of farmland, see Randolph B. Campbell, "Planters and Plain Folk: Harrison County, Texas, as a Test Case," *Journal of Southern History* 40 (Aug. 1974): 369–98.

18. For comments on the appeal southern cities held for Negroes, see Howard N. Rabinowitz, *Race Relations in the Urban South, 1865–1890* (New York: Oxford University Press, 1978), pp. 18–30; Litwack, *Been in the Storm So Long*, pp. 311, 342.

19. Genovese, *Roll, Jordan, Roll*, p. 414. Data on the racial background of Afro-American delegates were most often obtained from manuscript census returns.

20. The numbers of mulattoes among Negro delegates (in relation to the numbers on which information on racial background was available were: Texas, 1 of 4; Mississippi, 3 of 10; Georgia, 6 of 15; Virginia, 8 of 17; Florida, 7 of 16; North Carolina, 5 of 11; Alabama, 5 of 12; Louisiana, 27 of 36; South Carolina, 33 of 64; and Arkansas, 5 of 7.

21. Thomas Holt, *Black over White: Negro Political Leadership in South Carolina during Reconstruction* (Urbana: University of Illinois Press, 1977), p. 17, noted such differences in the South Carolina convention but concluded that they became more important in later legislative sessions.

22. Census returns, unfortunately, do not indicate whether Negro delegates had been enslaved. Most of the information on this aspect of their lives was gathered from government documents, newspapers, convention speeches, and secondary accounts. Especially useful here were: Holt, *Black over White*, pp. 229–41; David C. Rankin, "The Origins of Black Leadership in New Orleans during Reconstruction," *Journal of Southern History* 40 (Aug. 1974):417–40; Richard G. Lowe, "Virginia's Reconstruction Convention: General Schofield Rates the Delegates," *Virginia Magazine of History and Biography* 80 (July 1972):341–60; Joseph M. St. Hilaire, "The Negro Delegates in the Arkansas Constitutional Convention of 1868: A Group Profile," *Arkansas Historical Quarterly* 33 (Spr. 1974):38–69; Elizabeth Balanoff, "Negro Legislators in the North Carolina General Assembly, July, 1868–February, 1872," *North Carolina Historical Review* 49 (Win. 1972):22–55; Howard James Jones, "The Membership of the Louisiana Legislature of 1868: Images of 'Radical Reconstruction' Leadership in the Deep South" (Ph.D. diss., Washington State University, 1975); Charles Vincent, *Black Legislators in Louisiana during Reconstruction* (Baton Rouge: Louisiana State University Press, 1976); U.S., Congress, Senate, "Affairs in the Late Insurrectionary States," *Senate Reports*, 42d Congress, 2d sess., 1872 (cited hereafter as Ku Klux Klan Report). The numbers of these delegates (black and mulatto) known to have never experienced bondage were (by convention): Virginia, 8; North Carolina, 2; South Carolina, 32; Arkansas, 2; Louisiana, 21; Missis-

sippi, 2; Alabama, 3; Georgia, 3; Florida, 4; and Texas, 2. The numbers of known former slaves (black and mulatto, including 14 individuals who gained their freedom before the war), were (by convention): Virginia, 13; North Carolina, 5; South Carolina, 37; Arkansas, 6; Louisiana, 2; Mississippi, 3; Alabama, 7; Georgia, 2; Florida, 3; and Texas, 0.

23. For example, delegates William McKinlay (father) and William J. McKinlay (son) were antebellum free mulattoes and Charleston natives. Delegates Robert and Thomas Isabelle, who represented New Orleans in the Louisiana convention, were brothers and antebellum free mulattoes.

24. Genovese, *Roll, Jordan, Roll,* p. 563. Most data on the literacy of these delegates came from the 1870 manuscript census, but some information was from secondary sources, such as Thomas Holt's *Black over White.* In comments on my paper on delegates in the Arkansas convention (presented on November 13, 1970, at the annual meeting of the Southern Historical Association at Louisville, Ky.), Wooster warned that census returns might exaggerate the literacy of the postwar southern population, both black and white. This may well be the case, but these returns remain the best source available on the literacy of large numbers of southerners. A number of Negro delegates who were Union-army veterans may have learned to read during the war. See John W. Blassingame, "The Union Army as an Educational Institution for Negroes, 1862–1865," *Journal of Negro Education* 34 (Spr. 1965):152–59.

25. Loren Schweninger, *James T. Rapier and Reconstruction* (Chicago: University of Chicago Press, 1978), for example, refers to numerous letters from Rapier to prominent Alabama Republicans.

26. Information on the occupations of Negro delegates was gathered from manuscript census returns and other sources. The group of farmers contained 46 delegates listed as farmers and 4 delegates listed as planters. The property holdings of 46 of these delegates were located in census returns and other sources, such as Holt, *Black over White,* pp. 229–41. In 1870 Guichard was worth $5,500, Mahier $8,000, Thompson, $6,376, and Royal $6,600.

27. Cardozo's school for Charleston's Negro children became a regular stop for visiting dignitaries. See Litwack, *Been in the Storm So Long,* pp. 495–96.

28. The property holdings of 39 skilled laborers have been located. The group of 54 delegates included 19 carpenters, 2 masons, 7 blacksmiths, a musician, an upholsterer, 8 shoemakers, 7 barbers, a tanner, 3 tailors, 3 coachmakers, a dyer, and a riverboat pilot.

29. The property holdings of 30 of these 41 delegates have been located. This group included 16 teachers, a dentist, 2 physicians, 4 merchants, a printer, 5 lawyers, a merchant-planter, a brick manufacturer, a wine merchant, 3 grocers, a newspaper owner, a cigar-store owner, an assistant newspaper editor, a ferryboat owner, a cotton broker, and a "businessman." In addition to farmers, ministers, skilled laborers, and delegates employed in business and the professions, there were 32 delegates with undetermined professions, 27 politicians (with undetermined nonpolitical professions), a porter, 3 laborers, a huckster, a domestic, and a shipping clerk.

30. An average of about eleven key roll-call votes was examined closely in each convention. They covered matters such as the franchise and racial issues (e.g., school segregation), economic questions, and votes relating directly to

implementation of federal reconstruction policy in the South. For detail on votes selected for analysis, see appropriate chapters in Hume, " 'Black and Tan' Constitutional Conventions." As a rule, Negroes voted as blocs (with somewhat greater frequency than did outside whites) on key roll-call divisions. Southern whites, of course, were badly divided between scalawags and Conservatives on many votes.

31. Ibid., pp. 137–38, 603–7.

32. For example, see *Official Journal of the Constitutional Convention of the State of Alabama Held in the City of Montgomery, Commencing on Tuesday, November 5th, A.D. 1867* (Montgomery: Barret & Brown, 1868), pp. 35–37.

33. For example, see Richard L. Hume, "The Membership of the Virginia Constitutional Convention of 1867–1868: A Study of the Beginnings of Congressional Reconstruction in the Upper South," *Virginia Magazine of History and Biography* 86 (Oct. 1978):465; id., "The Arkansas Constitutional Convention of 1868: A Case Study in the Politics of Reconstruction," *Journal of Southern History* 39 (May 1973):187.

34. Otto H. Olsen, *Carpetbagger's Crusade: The Life of Albion Winegar Tourgée* (Baltimore: Johns Hopkins University Press, 1965), p. 105; Jack B. Scroggs, "Carpetbagger Constitutional Reform in the South Atlantic States, 1867–1868," *Journal of Southern History* 27 (Nov. 1961):479.

35. Hume, " 'Black and Tan' Constitutional Conventions," pp. 100–101.

36. For detail on the land issue in South Carolina, see Carol K. Rothrock Bleser, *The Promised Land: The History of the South Carolina Land Commission, 1869–1890* (Columbia: University of South Carolina Press, 1969), pp. 1–20.

37. In early 1865 General William T. Sherman's famous "Special Field Order No. 15" set aside abandoned coastal land between Charleston, S.C., and Jacksonville, Fla., for the freedmen. This was supported enthusiastically by the freedmen in that region, who were generally impoverished field hands. More affluent Negro delegates were rather unenthusiastic about such confiscatory proposals. Imbued with the middle-class Victorian ideal of self-help, they preferred instead proposals designed to help hard-working, thrifty freedmen purchase small farms. For comments on the consequences of this division between the masses and middle-class leaders of the Negro community, see Litwack, *Been in the Storm So Long*, pp. 339–408; William Toll, "Free Men, Freedmen, and Race: Black Social Theory in the Gilded Age," *Journal of Southern History* 44 (Nov. 1978):571–96.

38. The median 1870 wealth of the 174 Negroes whose property was located in census returns or other sources was $650. For comparative purposes, the median holding for southern whites (radicals and conservatives combined) was $3,200, and the median 1870 holding for outside whites totaled $3,500. The property holdings of 413 southern-white delegates and 105 outside-white delegates were located in census returns and other sources. These figures vary slightly from those on page 323 of the article cited in note 12. This is due to the inclusion of new information on some delegates. Thomas Holt, *Black over White*, pp. 229–41, was especially important in supplying much of this new information.

39. As a group, scalawags (southern-white Republican delegates) were

markedly less prosperous than southern-white Conservative delegates, who opposed the implementation of Congressional Reconstruction in the South.

40. For detail on this point, see Rabinowitz, *Race Relations in the Urban South*, pp. 102–3, 181; id., "Half a Loaf: The Shift from White to Black Teachers in the Negro Schools of the Urban South, 1865–1890," *Journal of Southern History* 40 (Nov. 1974):565–94.

41. Hume, " 'Black and Tan' Constitutional Conventions," pp. 96–97, 339–40. For example, see p. 491 for the comments of delegate James W. Hood, a North Carolina black. For further detail on the integration/segregation issue, see William Prescott Vaughn, *Schools for All: The Blacks and Public Education in the South, 1865–1877* (Lexington: University of Kentucky Press, 1974), pp. 50–77; Howard N. Rabinowitz, "From Exclusion to Segregation: Southern Race Relations, 1865–1890," *Journal of American History* 63 (Sept. 1976):325–50.

42. Hume, "Arkansas Constitutional Convention of 1868," pp. 201-2.

43. Take three key commmittees, for example—those on education, the bill of rights, and the franchise. There was a total of 11 of each of these committees (one of each in nine conventions and two of each in the Florida convention, where Republicans divided into two separate conventions). Only four of these committees (totaling 33 in all) had black chairmen: education (Fla.), Charles H. Pearce; bill of rights (La.), James H. Ingraham; education (S.C.), Francis L. Cardozo; and franchise (S.C.), Robert C. De Large.

44. "George Teamoh Diary," Carter G. Woodson Papers, Manuscript Division, Library of Congress, pp. 254–71.

45. The ages of 200 Negro delegates were located in manuscript census returns and other sources. The median age for southern-white and outside-white delegates was 47.5 years and 36 years respectively. This information was located for 413 southern-white delegates and 105 outside-white delegates.

46. A number of Negroes, of course, held several different offices during this period. Their highest known offices have been selected for use in this summary. The eight congressmen were: Robert C. De Large (S.C.), Robert B. Elliott (S.C.), John A. Hyman (N.C.), Joseph H. Rainey (S.C.), Alonzo Ransier (S.C.), James T. Rapier (Ala.), Robert Smalls (S.C.), and Josiah T. Walls (Fla.). The state executive officers included: Caesar C. Antoine (lt. gov., La.), Francis L. Cardozo (sec. of state, S.C.), Pierre G. Deslonde (sec. of state, La.), Jonathan G. Gibbs (sec. of ed., Fla), Henry E. Hayne (sec. of state, S.C.), Landon S. Langley (st. school commissioner, S.C.), and Pinckney B. S. Pinchback (lt. gov., La.). Jonathan Wright (S.C.) was a state supreme court justice.

Data on offices held by blacks are scattered in various sources. Several of the most useful are: *Biographical Directory of the American Congress, 1774–1971* (Washington, D.C.: Government Printing Office, 1971); Lowe, "Virginia's Reconstruction Convention"; R. D. W. Connor, ed., *A Manual of North Carolina Issued by the North Carolina Historical Commission for Use of Members of the General Assembly Session 1913* (Raleigh: E. M. Uzzell & Co., 1913); Emily B. Reynolds and Joan R. Faunt, comps., *Biographical Directory of the Senate of the State of South Carolina, 1776–1964* (Columbia: South Carolina Archives Department, 1964); Holt, *Black over White;* Michael E. Thompson, "Blacks, Carpetbaggers, and Scalawags: A Study of the Membership of the South Carolina Legislature, 1868–1870" (Ph.D. diss., Washington State University, 1975); Carroll Hart, ed., *Georgia's Official Register, 1967–1968* (Atlanta: Georgia Department of Archives and History, n.d.); Thomas M. Owen, *History of Alabama and Directory of Alabama Biography,* 4 vols. (Chicago: S. J. Clarke Publishing Co., 1921); Sarah Woolfolk Wiggins, *The Scalawag in Alabama Politics, 1865–1881* (University: University of Alabama Press, 1977); David G. Sansing, "The Role of the Scalawag in Mississippi Reconstruction" (Ph.D. diss., University of Southern Mississippi, 1969); Vincent, *Black Legislators in Louisiana;* Jones, "The Louisiana Legislature of 1868"; C. Armitage Harper and Elizabeth Valachovic, eds., *Historical Register of the Secretary of State (Arkansas)* (Little Rock: Pioneer Printers, 1968); *Members of the Texas Legislature, 1846–1962* (Austin: Texas State Legislature, 1962).

In addition to the 146 Negro delegates noted as state officials, congressmen, or state legislators, 33 Negro delegates held other offices. They were county officials, local officials, or officials in the Republican party organization.

47. The most useful sources on this violence are Allen W. Trelease, *White Terror: The Ku Klux Klan Conspiracy and Southern Reconstruction* (New York: Harper & Row, 1971), and the Ku Klux Klan Report.

48. The black-and-tan conventions were comparable in several respects to the state conventions that instituted constitutional changes during the era of the American Revolution. Approximately thirteen of these assemblies met in eleven states between 1776 and 1784. See Francis Newton Thorpe, comp., *The Federal and State Constitutions, Colonial Charters, and Other Organic Laws of the . . . United States of America,* 7 vols. (Washington, D.C.: Government Printing Office, 1909), passim.

David C. Rankin 7

The Origins of Negro Leadership in New Orleans during Reconstruction

N EW ORLEANS, LOUISIANA, the greatest port and largest city of the South in 1860, is a natural choice for a detailed study of grass-roots Negro leadership during Reconstruction.[1] Captured by federal forces in late April 1862, scarcely a year after the fall of Fort Sumter, New Orleans was the first Confederate city to experience the humiliation of invasion and the ordeal of Reconstruction. With military occupation came the opportunity for the roughly 24,000 Negroes living in New Orleans to begin the earliest equal-rights campaign of the Reconstruction era; and unlike the Negroes residing on the abandoned Sea Islands off South Carolina, where another rehearsal for Reconstruction occurred prior to the close of civil war, they waged their struggle for equality in a community where Union officers found "all the elements of . . . society still in existence, but in a state of revolution and transformation." New Orleans in the summer of 1862, according to Commanding General Benjamin F. Butler, was a city "of a hundred and fifty thousand inhabitants, all hostile, bitter, defiant, [and] explosive."[2]

Focusing on the origins of the men who first accepted the challenge of Reconstruction, this study seeks to determine what it was in the antebellum lives of some Afro-Americans and not of others that prepared them to lead rather than follow. Merely discovering the names of these politicians proved a formidable task, but a close examination of contemporary newspapers yielded a list of 240 names.[3] The men included on the list were the ward officers and leading spokesmen of the major political organizations of the city: the *Club Unioniste Républicain*, the Union Radical Association, the National Equal Rights League, the Friends of Universal Suffrage, and the Republican party. Every effort was made to test the authenticity of claims to leadership and to avoid including on the list men, such as J. L. Davis, who claimed to be the popularly elected representative of the Eleventh Ward to the 1866 Radical Republican state nominating convention but had actually "nominated himself in a Grocery, where there were no persons present but himself and two others."[4]

The list was then checked against every available source that possibly contained information about the antebellum lives of these men: presidential papers, congressional reports, manuscript census returns, army muster rolls and pension files, municipal tax ledgers and conveyance records, city directories, church archives, private manuscript collections, birth certificates, marriage licenses, and obituary notices. Through this research, biographical data were collected on 201 of the men, the nucleus of Negro leadership in New Orleans during the 1860s.[5]

Virtually all these leaders were free before the war (see Table 1).[6] The antebellum slave who became a prominent politician in many southern states during Reconstruction was conspicuous in his absence from New Orleans, in spite of his disproportionately large representation in the Negro population.[7] In 1860, for example, over half of the Negroes living in New Orleans were slaves, and the proportion of ex-slaves to free men increased markedly during the war as countless former slaves migrated to the city from rural Louisiana. Five months after the Union invasion, Butler complained that runaway slaves were pouring into the city "by hundreds, nay thousands almost daily"; and in 1866 Dr. C. H. Tebault, health officer of the second district of New Orleans, remembered that during the war "tens of thousands of negroes forsaking their old homes in the country . . . flocked here." By 1870 the city's Negro population stood at over 50,000, double what it had been a decade earlier. Given this figure, the overwhelming preponderance of free men among these leaders is somewhat surprising. Yet it is worth remembering that free men of color had benefited from unusual advantages in antebellum New Orleans, which eased their path to political predominance during Reconstruction.[8]

TABLE 1: *Antebellum Legal Status of Negro Politicians in New Orleans during Reconstruction*

STATUS	TOTAL NUMBER	NUMBER OF KNOWN	PERCENTAGE OF TOTAL	PERCENTAGE OF KNOWN
Known	174		86.6	
Free		169		97.1
Slave		5		2.9
Unknown	27		13.4	
TOTALS	201	174		

Before the war, free men of color were set apart from slaves by what the New Orleans *Picayune* called "the mystic letters—f.m.c."—and by a number of special privileges which Louisiana legal codes had always recognized. Excluding minor restrictions, both the French code of 1724 and the Spanish digest of 1795 granted free coloreds "the same rights, privileges, and immunities" enjoyed by whites. As late as 1856, when the rights of free Negroes throughout the South were being abused, the Louisiana State Supreme Court ruled that "in the eye of the Louisiana law, there is (with the exception of political rights, of certain social privileges, and of the obligation of jury and militia service), all the difference between a free man of color and a slave, that there is between a white man and a slave." Thus, on the eve of the Civil War, free coloreds could make contracts, buy and sell property, acquire by inheritance and transmit by will, sue and be sued in civil courts, testify against whites in criminal cases; and like whites, they were exempt from testimony given by slaves.[9]

At least two of the politicians who were free before the war were born in bondage. Stephen Walter Rogers, a preacher, was a slave until May 18, 1852, when he was emancipated by his master's last will and testament; and James H. Ingraham, representative of Orleans Parish in the state Senate from 1868 to 1874, received his freedom in 1839 when only six years old. Ingraham, the son of a white slaveholder and his slave mistress, enjoyed a rather privileged existence even while enslaved. In 1872 Ingraham, after admitting "that it is true 'I was born a slave,' " declared that he had "never felt the 'whip' " or known the "inhumanities" of slavery.[10]

But, judging from their birth certificates and personal recollection, most of these men were born free. Blanc F. Joubert came from a long line of freemen. When asked if he had ever been a slave, Joubert, the son of a free colored slaveholder, retorted, "Never, and none of my family ever were." Another politician, when asked about his origins, responded, "I am a free man. I always was a free man, and my ancestors for generations were free." Similarly, Joseph A. Raynal boasted: "I am descended from more than five or six generations of freemen. . . . My ancestors came here with the first settlement." Such responses doubtless caused white citizens of Reconstruction New Orleans to wish they had listened to the *Picayune* in 1856 when it advocated removing all free Negroes from Louisiana because they were "a plague and a pest in our community, besides containing the elements of mischief to the slave population."[11]

The free colored population was not exiled, however; and at the outbreak of the Civil War, nearly all of these leaders lived in Louisiana, most of them in New Orleans (see Table 2).[12] Of those living in New

Orleans, over two-thirds lived in the Creole section of the city, on the downtown side of Canal Street (see Table 3). Moreover, many of the leaders who resided in the Crescent City in 1861 lived near one another, in and around the Vieux Carré.[13]

TABLE 2: *1860–61 Residence of Negro Politicians in New Orleans during Reconstruction*

RESIDENCE	TOTAL NUMBER	NUMBER OF KNOWN	PERCENTAGE OF TOTAL	PERCENTAGE OF KNOWN
Known	161		80.1	
Louisiana		156		96.9
(New Orleans*)		(155)		(96.3)
Northern state		3		1.9
Foreign country		2		1.2
Unknown	40		19.9	
TOTALS	201	161		

*See Table 3.

TABLE 3: *1860–61 New Orleans Residence of Negro Politicians in New Orleans during Reconstruction*

RESIDENCE	TOTAL NUMBER	NUMBER OF KNOWN	PERCENTAGE OF TOTAL	PERCENTAGE OF KNOWN
Known	119		76.8	
Downtown from Canal Street		84		70.6
Uptown from Canal Street		35		29.4
Unknown	36		23.2	
TOTALS	155	119		

Most of the city's Negro leaders were natives of Louisiana; nearly two-thirds were born and reared in New Orleans (see Table 4).[14] When asked how long he had lived in New Orleans, Jules Desalles, the grandson of a Frenchman, replied, "All my life; I was born here." Some claimed, as did Joseph Montieu and Edgar Davis, to have known each other since boyhood and to have "always been intimate friends." Others belonged to the oldest and most respected free colored families of Louisiana, "aristocratic families, whose condition," one New Or-

LOUISIANA OFFICEHOLDERS, 1868
New-York Historical Society

leanian observed in 1862, "cannot be improved (in this country at least)." Francis Ernest Dumas, who reportedly raised a regiment for the Union army during the war from among his own slaves, came from such a family. "Mr. Dumas," the Negro press reported in 1871, "is one of Louisiana's most esteemed citizens, and belongs to one of the best families in the State."[15]

TABLE 4: *Birthplace of Negro Politicians in New Orleans during Reconstruction*

BIRTHPLACE	TOTAL NUMBER	NUMBER OF KNOWN	PERCENTAGE OF TOTAL	PERCENTAGE OF KNOWN
Known	121		60.2	
Louisiana		95		78.5
(New Orleans)		(74*)		(61.2)
Southern state, excluding Louisiana		20		16.5
Foreign country		5		4.1
Northern state		1		0.8
Unknown	80		39.8	
TOTALS	201	121		

*The number born in New Orleans could be even greater, as fourteen of those born in Louisiana gave only the state and not a specific city or parish for their birthplace.

Many leaders came from colored families of French extraction, and a number of these families, such as the Bonseigneurs and the Glaudins, the Roudanezes and the Saulays, the Boisdores and the Estèves, the Canelles and the Adolphes, and the Raynals and the Belots, were intermarried long before the Civil War.[16] Singled out by observers as French-speaking, colored Catholics, these men were keenly aware of their uniqueness. The mulatto shoemaker Lazard Rodriguez, who knew of "no slave ancestors at all" in his family, informed a congressional investigating committee that he was "only a fourth African and three-fourth French." Before the same committee J. B. Esnard testified, "I was born in New Orleans, but am of French descent." In 1864 the Negro press described François Boisdore, whose father had paid taxes on property valued at $23,200 in 1836, as "a French gentleman, who was free born and raised in this city." The free colored historian Rodolphe Desdunes made much the same point about Armand Lanusse, editor of *Les Cenelles*, the first anthology of Afro-French poetry published in America. Though Lanusse had "visited France only through the prism of his imagination," according to Desdunes, "His pride in being Creole was more dear to him than his being Louisianian, or than anything else pertaining to his origin." Proud of their ancestors and their Creole heritage, these men represented what the Negro press called "an old population, with a history and mementos of their own, warmed by patriotism, partaking of the feelings and education of the white."[17]

Some leaders who were not natives of New Orleans had, nevertheless, lived most of their lives in the city. Lewis Banks, Jordan Noble, John Pullum, Sr., and Emperor Williams, for example, had all lived in the city for over twenty-five years when Louisiana seceded from the Union. Those born elsewhere were extremely anxious to identify themselves with the city. Pinckney Benton Stewart Pinchback, for instance, referred to New Orleans as "my old home" and claimed he had lived there since 1837. Actually, Pinchback was born in Georgia in 1837 and was less than a year old when he passed through the city with his family as they headed for Mississippi. Pinchback moved to New Orleans about 1850, and lived there for a while with his brother-in-law John Keppard, another Negro politician of the Reconstruction era.[18]

The few real outsiders to become political leaders in New Orleans during Reconstruction were exceptionally capable men. According to the Negro press George W. Levère, a New Yorker who came to New Orleans as chaplain of the Twentieth Regiment, United States Colored Troops, was a "true Christian, patriotic and learned gentleman." Robert I. Cromwell, who came in 1863, was an active abolitionist and a successful physician in Wisconsin before the war. John Willis Ménard, who arrived in 1865, was "a scholar and a good writer" as well as the Creole grandson of the first lieutenant governor of Illinois. Anatole Borée, who lived in New Orleans before the war but whose family was not old New Orleans, was the able grandson of Jean-Jacques Dessalines, the first emperor of Haiti. Other talented Negro leaders, such as J. Sella Martin, who before the war was pastor of the Joy Street Baptist Church in Boston, and T. Morris Chester, who was born in Pennsylvania and studied law in England, did not appear in New Orleans until the 1870s, long after the struggle for equality had begun.[19]

These newcomers did not pose a serious threat to local leadership; in general, they eagerly sought the favor of homegrown politicians. The response of old free colored leaders to an outsider who challenged their authority was, as the case of Dr. P. B. Randolph of New York illustrates, immediate and unequivocal. Recognized by the Negro press upon his arrival in New Orleans as "a man of education, an author, an able writer, and . . . an example to our young men anxious for intellectual acquirements and literary distinctions," Randolph made the mistake of publicly criticizing the free colored Creole leaders. Within the week they denounced Randolph, declaring him "unworthy [of] a place in *our* community."[20]

The free coloreds were more cautious in their dealings with Pinchback, Louisiana's most famous Negro carpetbagger, probably because of his immense popularity with the freedmen. But in 1892 Louis Martinet, a prominent free colored leader, singled out "Pinchback & the like" for special condemnation. "What," he asked, "have they ever done that has not been of more profit to them than to their race? *They have grown rich in fighting the race's battles*; that's the kind of patriots they are." The New Orleans *Times* thought it natural that the old free colored leaders despised Pinchback. "It was . . . simply idiotic," the paper observed in 1874, "to have supposed that men of culture, who long before the war had enjoyed the society on equal terms of cultivated white people in Europe, would ever forgive the attempt made by a colored man, not a native of Louisiana, not of French ancestry, and lacking education, to assume the right to speak for them."[21]

The majority of these politicians, newcomers as well as natives, were light-colored mulattoes (see Table 5).[22] This high percentage of mulattoes stands in sharp contrast to the color composition of the entire Negro population of New Orleans, which in 1860 was more than half black. But over three-fourths of the privileged free colored caste from which so many of these leaders sprang were mulatto in 1860. That so many mulattoes became leaders during Reconstruction would have come as no surprise to a number of perceptive foreigners who visited the city before the war. In 1832, for example, François Guillemin, the French consul at New Orleans, warned that "by repelling the mulattoes . . . the white aristocracy gives the slaves . . . the only weapon they need to become free: intelligence and leadership." In the same year Alexis de Tocqueville asked a group of New Orleans whites, "But do you not count upon making these *noirs blancs* someday your equals?" When they answered, "Never," he replied, "Then I much fear that they will one day make themselves your ministers."[23]

Many leaders roughly classified by census takers and others as mulattoes were actually quadroons or octoroons, some of whom could have passed for whites. Octave Belot, who another Negro politician said could "very easily pass for a white man," admitted, "I cannot trace my origin to any colored family." Jean B. Jourdain, who showed "little or no exhibition of African lineage" according to the colored press, told a congressional committee, "I am a colored man; . . . but

TABLE 5: *Phenotype of Negro Politicians in New Orleans during Reconstruction*

PHENOTYPE	TOTAL NUMBER	NUMBER OF KNOWN	PERCENTAGE OF TOTAL	PERCENTAGE OF KNOWN
Known	102		50.7	
Mulatto		93		91.2
Black		9		8.8
Unknown	99		49.3	
TOTALS	201	102		

my father is a white man and a gentleman." Another politician, when asked if he could not usually pass for a white man responded that "Strangers would very seldom take me to be a man of color." Still another, who was "whiter than nine-tenths of the native population" according to a northern visitor, said of his color, "I am what they call here a 'white nigger.' " Pinchback, who was a delicately featured quadroon, remembered that a befuddled policeman once stopped him and asked, "[A]re you a white man, or what are you." [24]

Some politicians and members of their families suffered uncertainty, if not anxiety, about their race. When asked if he was a colored man, light yellow J. B. Esnard replied, "I cannot answer that; I do not know exactly whether I am or not." Pinchback, according to his grandson Jean Toomer, the gifted Harlem Renaissance poet, "came of stock predominately Scotch, Welsh, and German," had no other member in his immediate family who "was, or was regarded, as a negro," and "by looks, color, and features, was evidently white." Still, Toomer declared his inability "to state as a fact that there was, or that there was not, some Negro or Indian blood in the family. I really do not know." [25]

Others were equally confused. Mrs. Edgar Davis said of her deceased husband when applying for his military pension: "On the question of his race, I am unable to testify positively. He had blond hair when young; when I met him first he was gray, his eyes were blue, complexion fair, height five feet eight inches and to all appearances was white. . . . In Louisiana, where there are so many variations of race, I will have to abide by whatever the records show concerning him, made long before my time." Surviving sketches and contemporary accounts suggest that Josephine Davis's uncertainty about her husband's race was warranted. In 1867 the *Republican* described Davis as "colored, but so near white that a stranger would not be able to perceive the color," and in 1901 a special examiner of the United States commissioner of pensions in Washington, D.C., said of Davis and his friends, "These are all white men & are of good reputations." But neither Davis nor his family challenged official records which held him to be legally colored. In contrast, Blanc F. Joubert's family went to court to prove that he was white. Joubert himself claimed that he was of "both races, although they called me in Louisiana a colored man"; but then he beclouded his issue by adding, "I cannot tell you whether I am a white man or a colored man."[26]

Fortunately, considering the demands which Reconstruction made upon Negro politicians, most of these men were in the prime of their lives when the Civil War began (see Table 6).[27] In 1861 their median age was thirty-five, and over three-fourths of them were in their twenties, thirties, and forties. Like the young men of the American Revolution, they were vigorous, impatient, and self-assured. Youthful Norbert Villère, for example, spoke at political meetings all over the city in the 1860s and was called an "indefatigable sentinel of freedom" by the colored press. In 1867 the *Republican* referred to 34-year-old Robert Cromwell as "one of the energetic colored champions of the party of progress." James Ingraham, only twenty-eight when the war began and labelled "*le Mirabeau des hommes de couleur de la Louisiana*" by a Belgian journalist, spoke for many of these young men when he said, "A man contending for his rights is never too energetic."[28]

TABLE 6: *Date of Birth of Negro Politicians in New Orleans during Reconstruction*

DATE OF BIRTH	TOTAL NUMBER	NUMBER OF KNOWN	PERCENTAGE OF TOTAL	PERCENTAGE OF KNOWN
Known	114		56.7	
1783–92		1		0.9
1793–1802		6		5.3
1803–12		17		14.9
1813–22		23		20.2
1823–32		33		28.9
1833–42		33		28.9
1843–52		1		0.9
Unknown	87		43.3	
TOTALS	201	114		

Even the older politicians were remarkably active. In 1871 one was still known, at the age of seventy, as "that rather young old man,

Jordan B. Noble." Another, Joseph Curiel, received the following tribute from the Negro press at the time of his death in 1867: "The cause of freedom has lost in Mr. Curiel a champion whose place will not easily be filled. Though the deceased was 74 years old, whenever there was a patriotic act to perform, he was always one of the first to come forward. Mr. Curiel was an ardent lover of all that was noble and great, and often showed the enthusiasm and vigor of a young man." [29]

Prior to the war these men apparently channeled their energy into learning trades and making money. Almost all of them held jobs that demanded skill or schooling (see Table 7).[30] The Negro press explained Émile Detiège's success as a mason by pointing out that "the old free colored population, of whom Mr. Detiège is a type, have been rather unique in the matter of occupation; following each in the trade of his predecessors, and progressing with a commendable spirit of emulation in the various branches of industry."[31]

TABLE 7: *1860–61 Occupation of Negro Politicians in New Orleans during Reconstruction*

OCCUPATION	TOTAL NUMBER	NUMBER OF KNOWN	PERCENTAGE OF TOTAL	PERCENTAGE OF KNOWN
Known	161		80.1	
Skilled labor		85		52.8
Business		38		23.6
Professional		35		21.7
Unskilled labor		3		1.9
Unknown	40		19.9	
TOTALS	201	161		

Although most of these leaders seem to have followed this pattern and relied upon a single occupation for their livelihood, a few mastered more than one trade. Emperor Williams, for example, was a bricklayer and a preacher; Louis Fouché and Joseph Abélard designed as well as built houses; and Pinchback, according to an interview of 1872, "followed various private avocations until the era of colored men in politics dawned." Incidentally, many of these men first encountered one another not at political rallies during Reconstruction, but at work before the war. Thus, Pinchback, William Barrett, and James Lewis became fast friends while working Mississippi riverboats; Eugène Rapp and Alphonse Fleury, Jr., ran a tailor shop together; Bernard Soulié and Édmond Rillieux were longtime business acquaintances; and others joined president Paul Trévigne at the meetings of the *Société des Secours Mutuels des Artisans.*[32]

Evidence from tax lists and census returns indicates that these politicians were financially more secure than the majority of Negroes in antebellum New Orleans (see Table 8).[33] They were, of course, vastly richer than the slaves. They were also better off than most of the city's free Negroes. Indeed, on the eve of the war these couple hundred men reported holdings valued at $883,790, nearly 40 percent of the wealth reported by the entire free colored population in1860.[34]

TABLE 8: *1860–61 Wealth of Negro Politicians in New Orleans during Reconstruction*

WEALTH	TOTAL NUMBER	NUMBER OF KNOWN	PERCENTAGE OF TOTAL	PERCENTAGE OF KNOWN
Known	75		37.3	
$ 1–500		17		22.7
501–1,000		11		14.7
1,001–2,500		19		25.3
2,501–5,000		6		8.0
5,001–10,000		7		9.3
10,001–25,000		9		12.0
25,001–50,000		2		2.7
50,001–100,000		1		1.3
over 100,000		3		4.0
Unknown	126		62.7	
TOTALS	201	75		

A few of these men were among the wealthiest people in New Orleans. Édmond Dupuy, for instance, paid taxes on personal and real estate valued at $171,000 in 1861. Bernard Soulié in that same year not only paid taxes on property assessed at over $100,000, but also loaned the Confederate government $10,000 to be repaid "on the convenience of the state." François Lacroix, another wealthy free Negro, reportedly owned "as much real estate as any man of any color in New Orleans." Lacroix, an octoroon who feigned poverty but traveled regularly to France, in 1861 held properties valued at $242,570. Thomy Lafon was extraordinarily generous as well as rich. Although he was born in poverty and wrote in 1835 that his "sole ambition" was "to leave this country," Lafon stayed in New Orleans, the city of his birth, established a dry-goods store, and left most of his $413,000 estate to charity. He contributed $500 to aid the Confederate army during the

Civil War. Not surprisingly, men of such economic standing were frequently unable to devote their full attention to politics. Bernard Soulié, Édmond Rillieux, and John Racquet Clay, for example, declined numerous political offices during Reconstruction because of pressing business commitments.[35]

Prior to the war at least twenty-three of these men had invested some of their wealth in slaves. In 1861, for instance, Drauzin Macarty owned five slaves, and Bernard Soulié, François Lacroix, and Édmond Dupuy each owned three. In that same year, John Racquet Clay, who was connected to the Negro race by a "somewhat remote link" according to the Negro press, sold a slave who had "the vice of running away"; and L. D. Larrieu bought a slave for his son. Another politician, who had himself never been a slaveholder, recalled that prior to abolition "Many friends of mine owned slaves."[36]

Most of these leaders could also read and write before the war (see Table 9).[37] Even the ex-slaves in this group were literate. Alexander Barber, for example, taught himself to read and write "from torn leaves out of a spelling book"; and while still a slave, Stephen Rogers compiled a fifty-page book of hymns and prayers entitled *Rogers's Compositions*. According to Rogers the book was "a daring piece of my own; . . . quite a curiosity, and a secret to the friends of freedom." Joseph Craig, also literate before the war, was educated by his master. A skilled printer, Craig was recognized even by the Negro-baiting *Times* as "a man of considerable intelligence."[38]

TABLE 9: *Antebellum Literacy of Negro Politicians in New Orleans during Reconstruction*

LITERACY	TOTAL NUMBER	NUMBER OF KNOWN	PERCENTAGE OF TOTAL	PERCENTAGE OF KNOWN
Known	106		52.7	
Literate		104		98.1
Illiterate		2		1.9
Unknown	95		47.3	
TOTALS	201	106		

Many leaders belonged to what the white press called "a sober, industrious and moral class, far advanced in education and civilization." Some had attended the private, free colored academies of New Orleans, where François Escoffié, Ludger Boguille, and others destined to become politicians taught before the war. A few studied in the

North and abroad. J. Willis Ménard attended Iberia College in Ohio, P. M. Williams went to Dartmouth, Francis Dumas studied in Paris, and Louis Charles Roudanez took medical degrees from both Dartmouth and the University of Paris. After completing their education, Armand Lanusse, Lucien Mansion, Adolphe Duhart, and Joanni Questy went on to become distinguished poets. V. E. Macarty was a musician as well as a poet. "Mr. M.," the Negro press wrote in 1865, "is one of the talented men who are an honor for our population, and of whom we are proud." Many New Orleanians agreed with Mortimer A. Warren, superintendent of public schools in 1866, when he boasted, "We have in our city the colored intelligence of the whole South."[39]

But these men did not need Warren or other whites to convince them of their ability. They firmly believed in themselves and during the formative years of Reconstruction sought to establish their political independence. "It is not," the Negro press warned in 1865, "the time to follow in the path of white leaders; it is the time to be leaders ourselves." J. Willis Ménard advised them to shape their own destiny and "to look at a white man as a mere common human being, and not as a ruler or superior." In the final analysis, Ménard argued, "most of the [white] Republicans, Radicals or Abolitionists, who are the well-wishers of the black man, only sympathize with him in his servile condition." The supreme self-confidence of these men was perhaps best expressed by Pinchback in 1873, when he reminded a convention of colored leaders: "We owe our successes, gentlemen, under God, first to ourselves. Without abatement to the meed [sic] or dues of the true [white] men that helped us in our distress, I affirm we possessed the elements in ourselves that needed the occasion only of a great revolution to develop them."[40]

The great revolution began, of course, with the Civil War, and fifty-nine of these leaders participated in that sanguine affair. They all eventually fought on the side of the Union, though a number of them, including E. Arnold Bertonneau, Noël Bacchus, and H. Louis Rey, initially served in the Confederate army. Jean Jourdain saw action at Vicksburg; Louis Snaer fought "like a lion" at Mobile; and Théodule Martin won the praise of his commanding officer for unusual bravery at Ship Island. Jordan Noble served in the Mexican War and the Battle of New Orleans as well as the Civil War. Six others had also fought with Andrew Jackson in 1815, and several were proud sons of men who had participated in that celebrated battle. During Reconstruction Lucien Jean Pierre Capla identified himself: "I was born and raised here; my father was one of the fighters of 1815." All of them appear to have taken soldiering seriously; a few were thoroughly imbued with the martial spirit. One of them, while a lieutenant in the Union army, shot and killed a young private for disobeying a minor order.[41]

Military service, in addition to offering the Negro positions of leadership and authority, also exposed him to the very real threat of disability or death. Even this, perhaps, helped prepare him for a career in politics, for he was about to enter a political arena where the bloodiest riot of the entire Reconstruction era occurred in 1866 and where, according to George E. Bovee, Louisiana secretary of state in 1868, a prominent Republican, if white, had "not much security," but "If he was colored, there was no security for him."[42]

The Negro politician of Reconstruction New Orleans thus differed markedly from most of those he sought to lead. At the beginning of the Civil War he was a freeman, not a slave; he was of light, not dark complexion. He was the son of an old New Orleans family, not an uprooted immigrant from rural Louisiana. He probably spoke beautiful French rather than a slave dialect. He possibly attended mass at St. Louis Cathedral, the oldest Catholic church in Louisiana, instead of Sunday night prayer meetings at St. James Chapel, the first African Methodist Episcopal church in New Orleans. He was literate, perhaps even well educated, not illiterate and previously denied the most rudimentary education. He was a successful artisan, professional person, or businessman, not an impoverished, unskilled laborer. Finally, he had possibly been a soldier during the Civil War, serving ultimately in the Union army, not a runaway slave, struggling to stay alive and searching for family, friends, and food.[43]

The politician of this study was, then, at the outbreak of the Civil War a young man of unusual ancestry, uncommon wealth, and exceptional ability. Through birth, marriage, friendship, and business acquaintances he was closely associated with the most sophisticated and exclusive free colored community in antebellum America. With the challenge of Reconstruction, he naturally looked inward, to himself, to his relatives, and to his friends, for leadership.

A full discussion of the relationship between antebellum origins and postwar behavior is beyond the scope of this essay, but it is clear that these leaders experienced great difficulty transcending their peculiar past.[44] Their struggle for political equality is a case in point: it was, until the inclusion of ex-slaves became imperative, for free coloreds only. To be sure, these leaders had from an early date championed the cause of the slaves by calling for emancipation; but from the beginning, they had also viewed slavery and suffrage as distinct issues. Indeed, they seem to have feared that the crusade against slavery would totally eclipse their own battle for political equality. Thus, on April 11, 1863, Paul Trévigne and his colleagues at the free colored newspaper *L'Union* praised Louisiana Unionists for demanding the abolition of slavery at numerous rallies, but they simultaneously expressed their dismay "that not one voice from the midst of these assemblies has been lifted to plead in favor of our rights."

Specifically, free colored leaders called upon white Unionists to support the immediate enfranchisement of "our population." When counseled to be patient, François Boisdore, the son of a free colored slaveholder, retorted on November 5, 1863, "We have already postponed long enough. . . . We have never been slaves." When advised to consider incorporating the freedmen in their cause and to "get rid of their own prejudices against those of their race who had been slaves," the men of *L'Union* responded by expressing their hope that someday there would be no invidious distinctions among different groups of people. "But in the meantime," they asked, "must a class which by its industry and education possesses all the qualifications necessary to exercise the right of suffrage in an intelligent manner be responsible for the ignorance that the laws of the Black Code have inflicted on the unhappy slaves? All those who . . . have lived in New Orleans long enough to be familiar with the [free] colored population of this city and appreciate its worth are in favor of endowing this population with the elective franchise."[45]

The first indication that any of these leaders had reconsidered their caste position on the question of suffrage did not come until March 1864 when Jean Baptiste Roudanez and E. Arnold Bertonneau petitioned Congress to enfranchise all Louisiana Negroes irrespective of their previous condition. Moreover, this new liberal ideology surfaced only after free colored leaders had exhausted every available option that might have led to free colored suffrage. By the spring of 1864 they had unsuccessfully taken their case not only to local Unionists who were reorganizing the civil government of Louisiana under Lincoln's plan of Reconstruction, but also to George F. Shepley, military governor of Louisiana, and Nathaniel P. Banks, commanding general of the Department of the Gulf. In fact, when Roudanez and Bertonneau presented their pathbreaking petition to Congress, they were themselves in Washington to deliver a memorial signed by over a thousand free coloreds asking for the enfranchisement of "all the citizens of Louisiana of African descent, born free before the rebellion." Only after meeting with Charles Sumner and other powerful Republican advocates of universal Negro suffrage did the two men call for the enfranchisement of freed as well as free Negroes, and they candidly explained in their petition that inclusion of ex-slaves in the electorate was "required not only by justice, but also by expediency, which demands that full effect should be given to all the Union feeling in the Rebel States, in order to secure the permanence of the free institutions and loyal governments now organized therein."[46]

Few free coloreds immediately embraced the new ideology put forth by Roudanez and Bertonneau. The history of the New Orleans *Tribune*—which succeeded *L'Union*, was owned by Roudanez's brother, and eventually led the campaign to unite the free and the freed—suggests how difficult it would be for free colored leaders to overcome their caste consciousness. In August 1864 the editors of the paper complained that "while we are of the same race as the unfortunate sons of Africa who have until now trembled under the bondage of a cruel and brutalizing slavery, one cannot, without being unfair, confuse the newly freed people with our intelligent population"; and as late as August 11, 1865, they were still singling out "the negro not 'emancipated,' and who was always free," as worthy of the right to vote. But gradually, through a series of articles that often mixed pragmatism with paternalism, the editors of the *Tribune* moved to a position advocating universal Negro suffrage. Recognizing that the freedmen, "our *dormant partners*," were destined to "hold the controlling political influence in Louisiana," they wrote in an extraordinarily revealing editorial that the free and the freed

> cannot be well estranged from one another. The emancipated will find, in the old freemen, friends ready to guide them, to spread upon them the light of knowledge, and teach them their duties as well as their rights. But, at the same time, the freeman will find in the recently liberated slaves a mass to uphold them; and with this mass behind them they will command the respect always bestowed to number and strength.

In another editorial the *Tribune* advised its free colored readers that "Binding the interests and the future of the freedmen to the prosperity and moral as well as social attainments of the old free colored people, is one of those ideas that it is the proper time for us to consider." The date was November 24, 1864, two and a half years after the Union invasion.[47]

At the very moment the men of the *Tribune* were calling for intraracial unity, other free colored leaders were advocating the enfranchisement of select groups within the Negro population. Some supported a movement to extend the vote to "all persons having not more than one-fourth negro blood." Appalled by this "spirit of aristocracy," the *Tribune* denounced those seeking "to enfranchise but themselves, and leave the masses outside." Others sought the suffrage for colored persons who qualified on the basis of military service, property qualification, and intellectual fitness; indeed, five thousand of them signed a petition requesting the enfranchisement of Negro soldiers who had served in the Civil War. And despite the *Tribune*'s declaration on the eve of the Convention of Colored Men of Louisiana that "the necessity of being united, and acting as one body, is now generally understood," the assemblage debated no less than three motions in behalf of selective suffrage, with the last one failing by the narrow margin of 38 to 27. After the convention another group of free coloreds petitioned the state legislature "claiming for certain classes of colored citizens the right of suffrage." When the petition failed in February 1865, the *Tribune* guardedly wrote, "The split in our population seems to be at an end." Four months later New York journalist Whitelaw Reid, after meeting with a group of leading free coloreds, observed, "Hitherto they have held themselves aloof from the slaves, and particularly from the plantation negroes. . . . 'But now,' as one of them very frankly said during the evening, 'we see that our future is indissolubly bound up with that of the negro race in this country; and we have resolved to make common cause, and rise or fall with them.'"[48]

Jean-Charles Houzeau, political editor at the *Tribune*, agreed that most free coloreds finally realized "the necessity of this alliance." But soon after Congress granted both free and freed Negroes the right to vote, the alliance collapsed. According to Houzeau, the freedmen had always "remained distrustful," and in 1868 even the *Tribune* encouraged their suspicion by supporting a white ex-slaveholder from Catahoula parish for governor and a free colored ex-slaveholder from France for lieutenant governor. Distressed by the paper's "illiberalism," Houzeau predicted that "Among the blacks the influence of the *Tribune* is naturally lost forever." On election day freedmen throughout Louisiana confirmed Houzeau's prediction by repudiating the paper's candidates. A disheartened Houzeau, who for three and a half years had worked at eradicating "this division between mulattoes and blacks," confided in his parents on April 2, 1868, that "the old aristocratic spirit of the mulatto has reappeared." An analysis of the free colored suffrage movement in New Orleans during Reconstruction suggests, on the other hand, that the old aristocratic spirit had never really disappeared at all.[49]

Notes

The author wishes to thank Professor David Herbert Donald for his comments on an earlier version of this essay.

Unless specified otherwise, all newspapers cited in these notes are New Orleans papers.

Throughout this essay the word *free*, when used to describe Negroes, refers exclusively to Afro-Americans who were free prior to 1861; the word *freed* refers to those Negroes who were freed as a result of the Civil War. The terms *Negro, Afro-American*, and *colored* describe all persons of African descent irrespective of phenotype or legal status. The word *mulatto* refers solely to persons of mixed ancestry, and the word *black* describes only Negroes of unmixed origins.

1. For years many studies of Reconstruction in Louisiana either dismissed Negro leaders as ignorant Africans recently removed from the civilizing influence of slavery or omitted them entirely. See, for example, John R. Ficklen, *History of Reconstruction in Louisiana (through 1868)* (Baltimore: Johns Hopkins University Press, 1910), pp. 175, 179; Ella Lonn, *Reconstruction in Louisiana after 1868* (New York: G. P. Putnam's Sons, 1918), pp. 21–26; Willie M. Caskey, *Secession and Restoration of Louisiana* (University, La.: Louisiana State University Press, 1938); Roger W. Shugg, *Origins of Class Struggle in Louisiana: A Social History of White Farmers and Laborers during Slavery and after, 1840–1875* (University: Louisiana State University Press, 1939). More favorable assessments include Rodolphe L. Desdunes, *Our People and Our History* (1911), trans. and ed. Sister Dorothea Olga McCants (Baton Rouge: Louisiana State University, 1973), pp. 124–39; A. E. Perkins, "Some Negro Officers and Legislators in Louisiana," *Journal of Negro History* 14 (Apr. 1929):523–28; Charles B. Rousseve, *The Negro in Louisiana: Aspects of His History and His Literature* (New Orleans: Xavier University Press, 1937), pp. 103–10, 113; Agnes S.Grosz, "The Political Career of Pinckney Benton Stewart Pinchback," *Louisiana Historical Quarterly* 27 (Apr. 1944):527–612; Clara L. Campbell, "The Political Life of Louisiana Negroes, 1865–1890" (Ph.D. diss., Tulane University, 1971); Joe Gray Taylor, *Louisiana Reconstructed, 1863–1877* (Baton Rouge: Louisiana State University Press, 1974), pp. 74, 135–38, 201, 219–22; Roger A. Fischer, *The Segregation Struggle in Louisiana, 1862–77* (Urbana: University of Illinois Press, 1974), pp. x–xi, 29; C. Peter Ripley, *Slaves and Freedmen in Civil War Louisiana* (Baton Rouge: Louisiana State University Press, 1976), pp. 160–80; Charles Vincent, *Black Legislators in Louisiana during Reconstruction* (Baton Rouge: Louisiana State University Press, 1976), pp. 29–38; Peyton McCrary, *Abraham Lincoln*

and Reconstruction: The Louisiana Experiment (Princeton: Princeton University Press, 1978), pp. 181–85, 229, 255, 296, 331. With the exception of Vincent, *Black Legislators,* all the studies cited above discuss only the state's most famous politicians; none explores in systematic fashion either the origins or the behavior of Negro leaders in New Orleans during Reconstruction. John W. Blassingname, *Black New Orleans, 1860–1880* (Chicago: University of Chicago Press, 1973), p. xv, largely ignores what the author inexplicably calls "the old and often-studied debate over politics."

2. U.S., Bureau of the Census, *Population of the United States in 1860* (Washington, D.C.: Government Printing Office, 1864), p. 195; James McKaye, *The Mastership and Its Fruits: The Emancipated Slave Face to Face with His Old Master* (New York: Loyal Publication Soc., 1864), p. 3; Benjamin F. Butler to J. G. Carney, July 2, 1862, quoted in *Private and Official Correspondence of Gen. Benjamin F. Butler during the Period of the Civil War,* 5 vols, comp. Jessie Ames Marshall (n.p., 1917), 2:35. For a sensitive discussion of Negro responses to emancipation on the Sea Islands, which whites fled after the Yankee invasion, see Willie Lee Rose, *Rehearsal for Reconstruction: The Port Royal Experiment* (Indianapolis: Bobbs-Merrill Co., 1964).

3. I began my list with names mentioned in existing studies of Reconstruction. Some of these studies contain errors, however. A. E. Perkins, "Oscar James Dunn," *Phylon* 4 (Sum. 1943):105; W. E. Burghardt Du Bois, *Black Reconstruction in America . . . 1860–1880* (New York: Harcourt, Brace & Co., 1935), pp. 469–70; John H. Franklin, *Reconstruction after the Civil War* (Chicago: University of Chicago Press, 1961), pp. 134–35; Roussève, *Negro in Louisiana,* p. 108; Campbell, "Political Life of Louisiana Negroes," p. 14; Fischer, *Segregation Struggle,* p. 57; and Taylor, *Louisiana Reconstructed,* p. 219, for example, all erroneously call Oscar J. Dunn an ex-slave. See U.S., Congress, House, *Testimony Taken by the Subcommittee of Elections in Louisiana,* 41st Cong., 2d sess., 1870, House Misc. Doc. 154, 2 pts., pt. 1:178 (hereafter cited as *Elections in Louisiana*); *Republican,* Jan. 17, 1869; and Marcus B. Christian, "The Theory of the Poisoning of Oscar J. Dunn," *Phylon* 6 (Fall 1945):255. Du Bois, *Black Reconstruction,* p. 462, also errs in calling William R. Crane a Negro. See *Tribune,* Dec. 13, 1865; *Republican,* May 29, Nov. 29, 1867. In addition to providing wrong initials for Louis Charles Roudanez, Du Bois (*Black Reconstruction,* p. 456), Shugg (*Origins of Class Struggle,* p. 215), and others have erroneously argued that Roudanez and his brother Jean Baptiste were Santo Domingan refugees. See Finnian P. Leavens, "*L'Union* and the *New Orleans Tribune* and Louisiana Reconstruction" (M.A. thesis, Louisiana State University, 1966), pp. 12–13. Vincent, *Black Legislators,* p. 25, misspells Charles Dalloz's name and incorrectly describes him as a black Texan. Dalloz was actually a pseudonym for a white Belgian named Jean-Charles Houzeau. See David C. Rankin, "Introduction," in Jean-Charles Houzeau, *The Black Journal in the United States from 1863 to 1870,* trans. Gerald F. Denault, ed. David C. Rankin (Baton Rouge: Louisiana State University Press, forthcoming). I drew the remainder (the bulk) of my list from newspapers, especially *L'Union,* Sept. 1862–July 1864; *Tribune,* July 1864–Feb. 1869; *Black Republican,* Apr.–Aug. 1865; and *Republican,* Apr. 1867–Dec. 1869. Also helpful were the petitions in Wm. H. Hire to John Covode, July 12, 1865, Andrew Johnson Papers, Manuscript Division, Library of

Congress, Washington, D.C.; and in C. Camp to O. O. Howard, Aug. 20, 1865, Papers of the Assistant Commissioner, Letters Received, Record Group (RG) 105, Records of the Bureau of Refugees, Freedmen and Abandoned Lands (BRFAL), National Archives (NA), Washington, D.C. (I am indebted to the late Marcus B. Christian for looking over one of my early lists of leaders.) For the names on which I eventually found data, see the biographical list following this essay.

    4. *Tribune*, Dec. 31, 1867.

    5. It should be noted that data were not available for all items on all individuals; hence, there is some disparity in the "known" totals in the tables that follow. The absence of complete biographical information on a number of leaders may have skewed the data so as to exaggerate somewhat the privileged background of this group.

    6. City directories, manuscript census returns, and registers of free colored persons were important but by no means the only sources used in determining prewar legal status. *New Orleans Directory*, 1855–62; see, for example, C. C. Antoine, Charles E. Logan, and George B. Taylor, ibid., 1861, pp. 36, 282, 424. U.S., Bureau of the Census, Manuscript Census Returns, Eighth Census of the United States, 1860, Louisiana, vols. 5–8, RG 29, NA (cited hereafter as Manuscript Census of 1860); see, for example, Pierre Canelle, François Escoffié, François Lacroix, J. B. D. Bonseigneur, and Robert Steptoe, ibid., 8:320, 464; ibid., 6:257, 276, 452; New Orleans, Mayor's Office, Register of Free Colored Persons Entitled to Remain in the State, vols. 1–3, 1856–64, City Hall Archives, New Orleans Public Library, New Orleans; see, for example, Oscar James Dunn, James Lewis, and Lewis Banks, ibid., vol. 1, entries of Jan. 22, Dec. 20, 1856; Jan. 18, 1858.

    7. For studies which argue that ex-slaves dominated the ranks of black Reconstruction politicians, see Alrutheus A. Taylor, *The Negro in the Reconstruction of Virginia* (Washington, D.C.: Association for the Study of Negro Life and History, 1926), pp. 5–7; Vernon L. Wharton, *The Negro in Mississippi, 1865–1890* (Chapel Hill: University of North Carolina Press, 1947), p. 164; August Meier and Elliott M. Rudwick, *From Plantation to Ghetto: An Interpretive History of American Negroes* (New York: Hill & Wang, 1966), pp. 152–53.

    8. *Population of the United States in 1860*, p. 195; U.S., Bureau of the Census, *A Compendium of the Ninth Census (June 1, 1870)* (Washington, D.C.: Government Printing Office, 1872), p. 53; Benjamin F. Butler to Henry W. Halleck, Sept. 1, 1862, quoted in *Correspondence of Gen. Benjamin F. Butler*, 2:243; *New Orleans Medical and Surgical Journal* 19 (1866):422.

    9. *Picayune*, Jan. 7, 1860, quoted in Lawrence D. Reddick, "The Negro in the New Orleans Press, 1850–1860: A Study in Attitudes and Propaganda" (Ph.D. diss., University of Chicago, 1939), p. 142; Charles Gayarré, *History of Louisiana*, 4 vols. (1866; reprint ed., New Orleans: Armand Hawkins, 1885), 1:540; Donald E. Everett, "Free Persons of Color in Colonial Louisiana," *Louisiana History* 7 (Win. 1966):49; *State v. Harrison* (Dec. 1856), quoted in Helen T. Catterall, ed., *Judicial Cases Concerning American Slavery and the Negro*, 5 vols. (Washington, D.C.: Carnegie Institution, 1926–37), 3:649–50; Donald E. Everett, "Free Persons of Color in New Orleans, 1803–1865" (Ph.D. diss., Tulane University, 1952), pp. 171, 175; John C.

Hurd, *The Law of Freedom and Bondage in the United States*, 2 vols. (Boston: Little, Brown, 1858), 2:159. For more on the slave system that granted free coloreds such wide-ranging freedom, see David C. Rankin, "The Tannenbaum Thesis Reconsidered: Slavery and Race Relations in Antebellum Louisiana," *Southern Studies* 18 (Spr. 1979): 5–31.

10. Freedom papers of Stephen W. Rogers, Louisiana Division, New Orleans Public Library; *National Republican*, Jan. 2, 1872.

11. U.S., Congress, House, *Testimony Taken by the Select Committee to Investigate the Condition of Affairs in the State of Louisiana*, 42d Cong., 2d sess., 1872, House Misc. Doc. 211 (cited hereafter as *Condition of Affairs in Louisiana*), p. 458; *Elections in Louisiana*, pt. 2:501, pt. 1:62; *Picayune*, Mar. 8, 1856.

12. The most valuable sources in determining residence were the Manuscript Census of 1860, city directories, and the press.

13. Whether a leader lived in the Creole or the American (uptown side of Canal Street) section of the city was based upon the ward in which he lived. As Table 3 illustrates, I was able to determine the home ward of 119 leaders. I was further able to plot the exact location of the homes of 106 politicians on an 1861 map. The map and most of the addresses came from *New Orleans Directory*, 1861. Indispensable in locating residences were *Insurance Map of New Orleans, Louisiana*, 2 vols. (New York: Sanborn Map & Publishing Co., 1876), and *Atlas of the City of New Orleans, Louisiana* (New York: E. Robinson, 1883). I am indebted to Samuel Wilson, Jr., of the School of Architecture, Tulane University, for introducing me to these maps.

14. Newspapers, the Manuscript Census of 1860, and birth records were of great assistance in determining place of birth. See esp. the newspapers cited in note 3 above and *Louisianian*, Dec. 1870–June 1882; see, for example, William Troy, C. C. Antoine, and Émile Detiège, *Tribune*, Feb. 5, 1865; *Republican*, July 23, 1876; and *Louisianian*, Feb. 20, 1875. See St. Louis Cathedral, Baptismal Register of Negroes and Mulattoes, vols. 23–28, 1831–40, Archives, St. Louis Cathedral, New Orleans; see, for example, Louis Doquéminy Larrieu and Antoine St. Léger, ibid., 24: 89, 79. See New Orleans, Office of Vital Records (OVR), Record of Birth (RB), vols. 2, 4, 6, 10, 1819–57, City Hall, New Orleans; see, for example, Noël J. Bacchus and Jean Pierre Cazelar, ibid., 2:35, 10:424.

15. U.S., Congress, House, *Report of the Select Committee on the New Orleans Riots*, 39th Cong., 2d sess., 1867, H. Rept. 16 (cited hereafter as *New Orleans Riots*), p. 332; deposition of Joseph L. Montieu, in Edgar Davis Pension, Records of the Veterans Administration, RG 15, NA; "A Lady of New Orleans" to editor, *Delta*, Sept. 7, 1862; Joseph T. Wilson, *The Black Phalanx: A History of the Negro Soldiers of the United States* (Hartford, Conn.: American Publishing Co., 1890), p. 169; *Tribune*, July 2, 1867; *Louisianian*, Sept. 10, 1871.

16. See New Orleans, OVR, RB, 6:444; 30:551; 44:367, 580. See also *Republican*, Nov. 17, 1869.

17. *Elections in Louisiana*, pt. 2:493, pt. 1:698; Erastus P. Puckett, "The Free Negro in New Orleans to 1860" (M.A. thesis, Tulane University, 1907), p. 58; *Tribune*, Sept. 1, 1864; Desdunes, *Our People and Our History*, pp. 13, 21; Edward M. Coleman, *Creole Voices: Poems in French by Free Men of*

Color, First Published in 1845 (Washington, D.C.: Associated Publishers, 1945); *Tribune*, Dec. 29, 1864.

18. New Orleans, Mayor's Office, Register of Free Colored Persons, vol. 2, entry of July 3, 1861; *Republican*, Mar. 12, 1872; Jan. 16, 1873.

19. *Tribune*, Mar. 21, Oct. 15, 1865, Apr. 14, 1867; *Republican*, Jan. 9, 1869; *Louisianian*, May 11, 1872; James M. McPherson, *The Negro's Civil War: How American Negroes Felt and Acted during the War for the Union* (New York: Random House, 1965), p. 23; *Republican*, May 27, 28, June 1, 1873.

20. *Tribune*, Mar. 10, 11, 1865 (the emphasis is mine).

21. Louis A. Martinet to Albion W. Tourgée, July 4, 1892, quoted in Otto H. Olsen, ed., *The Thin Disguise: Plessy v. Ferguson* (New York: Humanities Press, 1967), pp. 64–65; *Times*, Oct. 11, 1874. For a fuller discussion of dissension within the New Orleans Negro population, see David C. Rankin, "The Impact of the Civil War on the Free Colored Community of New Orleans," *Perspectives in American History* 11 (1977–78):377–416.

22. The Manuscript Census of 1860, newspapers, baptismal registers, birth records, and congressional investigations provided most of the information on phenotype.

23. In contrast, less than a quarter of the slaves living in New Orleans in 1860 were mulattoes, and less than 10 percent of the slaves living throughout Louisiana in 1860 were mulattoes. *Population of the United States in 1860*, p. 194; *Negro Population, 1790–1915* (Washington, D.C.: Government Printing Office, 1918), p. 209; George W. Pierson, *Tocqueville and Beaumont in America* (New York: Harper & Row, 1938), p. 631; Alexis de Tocqueville, *Journey to America*, trans. George Lawrence, ed. J. P. Mayer (New Haven: Yale University Press, 1960), p. 380.

24. *Elections in Louisiana*, pt. 1:178, 254; *Louisianian*, Feb. 13, 1875; *New Orleans Riots*, pp. 204, 209; *Elections in Louisiana*, pt. 1:62, pt. 2:501, 503; *Daily Delta*, Sept. 5, 1862; *Times*, Mar. 11, 1872.

25. *Elections in Louisiana*, pt. 1:689; Jean Toomer, "A Fiction and Some Facts" (1930), Jean Toomer Collection, Fisk University Library, Nashville, Tenn. (I am indebted to Steven W. Mintz of Oberlin College for the Toomer citation.)

26. Deposition of Josephine Davis, Edgar Davis Pension, RG 15; *Republican*, May 11, 1867; W. A. Pless to Commissioner of Pensions, Aug. 17, 1901, Francis E. Dumas Pension, RG 15; copy of judgment in *Marie F. H. Joubert v. Board of Health*, St. Louis Cathedral, Baptismal Register, 27:267; *Condition of Affairs in Louisiana*, pp. 456, 458. On Joubert, see also *Republican*, May 13, 1871; *Times*, Oct. 11, 1874. Excellent pictures of Davis, Montieu, Larrieu, Pinchback, Ménard, Lewis, Isabelle, Dunn, and other leaders may be found in *Frank Leslie's Illustrated Weekly* 15 (Mar. 1863):369; Langston Hughes, Milton Meltzer, and C. Eric Lincoln, *A Pictorial History of the Negro in America* (New York: Crown Publishers, 1968), pp. 176, 205, 209, 210; Edith Ménard, "John Willis Ménard: First Negro Elected to the U.S. Congress, First Negro to Speak in the U.S. Congress," *Negro History Bulletin* 28 (Dec. 1964):53; Ray Stannard Baker, *Following the Color Line: American Negro Citizenship in the Progressive Era* (1908; reprint ed., New York: Harper & Row, 1964), plate between pages 250 and 251.

SOUTHERN BLACK LEADERS OF THE RECONSTRUCTION ERA

27. Major sources on age were baptismal register, birth records, death records (also in OVR, City Hall, New Orleans), and obituary notices in the press.

28. Stanley M. Elkins and Eric L. McKitrick, "The Founding Fathers: Young Men of the Revolution," *Political Science Quarterly* 76 (June 1961):181–216; *Tribune*, May 12, 1867; *Republican*, Apr. 26, 1867; J.-C. Houzeau, "Le journal noir, aux Etats-Unis, de 1863 à 1870," *Revue de Belgique* 11 (May 1872):21; *Tribune*, Dec. 27, 1864.

29. *Republican*, Jan. 10, 1871; *Picayune*, June 21, 1890; *Tribune*, May 7, 1867.

30. Major sources on occupation were the Manuscript Census of 1860, city directories, and the birth records of the children of these men. The high number of ministers is misleading, for a number of them, such as Lewis Banks, Stephen Rogers, and Emperor Williams, had multiple occupations. Moreover, the preacher-politician never attained the preeminence in New Orleans during Reconstruction that he apparently attained elsewhere.

31. *Louisianian*, Feb. 20, 1875.

32. *Picayune*, July 16, 1859; *Republican*, Mar. 12, 1872; depositions of Josephine B. Lewis, P. B. S. Pinchback, and Thomas W. Wickham in William B. Barrett Pension, RG 15; *New Orleans Directory*, 1861, p. 367; New Orleans, Mortgage Office, Record Mortgage Office, 72:365, Civil Courts Building, New Orleans.

33. Data on wealth came from the Manuscript Census of 1860 and the New Orleans tax ledgers of 1860 and 1861. I relied upon tax-ledger data when available; see New Orleans, Treasurer's Office, Tax Ledger (TOTL), 1860–61, City Hall Archives, New Orleans Public Library.

34. For a fuller discussion of free colored wealth in 1860, see David C. Rankin, "The Forgotten People: Free People of Color in New Orleans, 1850–1870" (Ph.D. diss., Johns Hopkins University, 1976), pp. 110–20.

35. New Orleans, TOTL, 1861, A-E, p. 171; ibid., Q–Z, p. 220; *Daily True Delta*, Jan. 24, 1861; *Elections in Louisiana*, pt. 1:181; New Orleans, TOTL, 1861, L–P, 147–49; Thomy Lafon to P. Ovide Cherbonnier, May 11, 1835, quoted in Brief of Charles F. Hornberber in *Clarke C. Stayman v. Ceclia J. Parker Railey*, No. 561 (Probate Ct., Hamilton Cty., O., 1938), p. 34, copy, Special Collections Division, Tulane University Library, New Orleans; J. M. Murphy, "Thomy Lafon," *Negro History Bulletin* 7 (Oct. 1943):6, 20; *Daily Picayune*, Dec. 28, 1893; John D. Winters, *The Civil War in Louisiana* (Baton Rouge: Louisiana State University Press, 1963), p. 39; Bernard Soulié to H. C. Warmoth, Feb. 12, 1866, Henry Clay Warmoth Papers, Southern Historical Collection, University of North Carolina Library, Chapel Hill, N.C.; *Tribune*, Aug. 12, May 25, 1866.

36. New Orleans, TOTL, 1861, L–P, pp. 210, 147–49; ibid., Q–Z, p. 220; ibid., A–E, p. 172; *Louisianian*, Apr. 27, 1871; New Orleans, Conveyance Office, Record of Conveyance, 79:551, Civil Courts Building, New Orleans; ibid., 82:70; *Elections in Louisiana*, pt. 2:495. Both tax and conveyance records from 1859 to 1861 were helpful in determining slaveowners. See biographical list for the names of slaveowners.

37. Major sources in determining prewar literacy were the Manuscript

Census of 1860, birth records and baptismal registers of the children of these men, newspapers, and testimony before congressional committees.

38. *Republican*, Aug. 8, Sept. 25, 1873; Nathan Willey, "Education of the Colored Population of Louisiana," *Harper's New Monthly Magazine* 33 (July 1866):250; *Tribune*, Jan. 15, 1865; *Radical Standard*, Sept. 23, 1868; *Times*, July 8, Aug. 28, 1868.

39. *Picayune*, July 16, 1859; R. L. Desdunes, "Mme. Bernard Couvent," *Negro History Bulletin* 7 (Oct. 1943):7–9; Ménard, "John Willis Ménard," p. 53; Howard A. White, "The Freedmen's Bureau in New Orleans" (M.A. thesis, Tulane University, 1950), p. 87; Deposition of Adolph Victor, Francis E. Dumas Pension, RG 15; Leavens, "*L'Union* and the *New Orleans Tribune*," pp. 14–15, 55; Desdunes, *Our People and Our History*, pp. 13–29, 64–65, 68; *Tribune*, June 20, 1865; Mortimer A. Warren to Wm. De Loss Love, Jan. 12, 1866, Box 58, American Missionary Association (AMA) Archives, Amistad Research Center, Dillard University Library, New Orleans. Blassingame, *Black New Orleans*, p. 165, incorrectly states that Roudanez received a medical degree from Cornell University.

40. *Tribune*, Feb. 1, 1865, Oct. 31, 1866, Apr. 28, 1867; *Republican*, Nov. 18, 1873.

41. U.S., Office of the Adjutant General, *Official Army Register of the Volunteer Force of the United States Army for the Years 1861, '62, '63, '64, '65* (Washington, D.C.: Government Printing Office, 1865–67), pt. 8; Muster Rolls, Returns, and Regimental Papers, Volunteers, Civil War, U.S. Colored Troops, 73d, 74th, 75th, 76th, and 77th regiments, Boxes 5513–22, Records of the Adjutant General's Office, RG 94, NA; Pensions, RG 15; *Tribune*, May 14, 1865; Mary F. Berry, "Negro Troops in Blue and Gray: The Louisiana Native Guards, 1861–1863," *Louisiana History* 8 (Spr. 1967):165–90; *Louisianian*, Feb. 13, 1875; *Republican*, May 11, 1867; Everett, "Free Persons of Color in New Orleans," p. 309; *Daily Picayune*, June 21, 1890; *Tribune*, Jan. 10, 1865; *Picayune*, Apr. 24, 1853; *New Orleans Riots*, p. 119; New Orleans, Coroner's Office, Report Book, 1863, pp. 2, 6, City Hall Archives, New Orleans Public Library; *Daily True Delta*, Dec. 13, 1862. See biographical list for names of those who fought in the Battle of New Orleans and the Civil War.

42. *Elections in Louisiana*, pt. 1:22.

43. It is impossible to compare the origins of these men with those of Negro leaders from rural Louisiana with any degree of precision. Vincent's *Black Legislators* is helpful, but it deals almost exclusively with state legislators and does not purport to be a systematic investigation of Negro leadership at the grass-roots level. Some fragmentary evidence suggests that two important southern cities—Mobile, Ala., and Charleston, S.C.—produced Negro Reconstruction leaders whose origins closely resembled those of the men under consideration here. See Peter Kolchin, *First Freedom: The Responses of Alabama's Blacks to Emancipation and Reconstruction* (Westport, Conn.: Greenwood Press, 1972), pp. 163–67; E. Horace Fitchett, "The Traditions of the Free Negro in Charleston, South Carolina," *Journal of Negro History* 25 (Apr. 1940):150–52; Francis B. Simkins and Robert H. Woody, *South Carolina during Reconstruction* (Chapel Hill: University of North Carolina Press, 1932), p. 368; Joel Williamson, *After Slavery: The Negro in South Carolina*

during Reconstruction, 1861–1877 (Chapel Hill: University of North Carolina Press, 1965), pp. 316–17, 376–77; Thomas Holt, *Black over White: Negro Political Leadership in South Carolina during Reconstruction* (Urbana: University of Illinois Press, 1977), pp. 57–68.

44. For a full discussion of the themes briefly touched upon here, see David C. Rankin, "The Politics of Caste: Free Colored Leadership in New Orleans during the Civil War," in Robert R. Macdonald et al., eds., *Louisiana's Black Heritage* (New Orleans: Louisiana State Museum, 1979), pp. 125–38; and Rankin, "The Impact of the Civil War," pp. 377–416.

45. *L'Union,* Apr. 11, 1863; *Times,* Nov. 6, 1863, Jan. 6, 1864; *L'Union,* Feb. 11, 1864.

46. *L'Union,* Apr. 14, 1864; Boston *Liberator,* Apr. 1, 1864; U.S., *Congressional Globe,* 38th Cong., 1st sess., 34:1107; Donald E. Everett, "Demands of the New Orleans Free Colored Population for Political Equality, 1862–1865," *Louisiana Historical Quarterly* 38 (Apr. 1955):46–50; McPherson, *The Negro's Civil War,* pp. 278–79. Compare Blassingame, *Black New Orleans,* pp. 211–12, who calls the suffrage movement "a brilliant campaign to obtain the franchise" and writes enthusiastically of the petition carried to Congress by Roudanez and Bertonneau "calling for the right to vote which contained 5,000 [*sic*] signatures." Whereas Blassingame never mentions that the petition asked for the enfranchisement of only those Negroes who were born free, Vincent, in *Black Legislators,* p. 22, declares that the petition "urged suffrage for all black men, both the free and the former slaves." The fact is, of course, that only the "supplementary memorial" drawn up in Washington by Roudanez and Bertonneau advocated universal Negro suffrage.

47. *Tribune,* Aug. 4 (French ed.), 11, Dec. 29, Nov. 24, 1864.

48. Ibid., Nov. 12, 15, 16, 19, 1864, July 20, 1867, Jan. 8, 13, 15, 24, Feb. 5, 21, 1865; Reid, *After the War: A Tour of the Southern States, 1865–1866* (New York: Harper & Row, 1965), p. 244; Everett, "Demands of the New Orleans Free Colored Population," pp. 56–64.

49. Houzeau, "Le journal noir," p. 12; Houzeau to his parents, Apr. 2, 1868, Jean Charles Houzeau Papers, Centre National d'Histoire des Sciences, Bibliothèque Royale Albert 1er, Brussels, Belgium. (I am deeply indebted to Joseph Logsdon of the University of New Orleans for first showing me a copy of this letter.) See also Houzeau to Victor Bouvy, Mar. 2, 1868, in the J. B. Liagre Papers, Archives, Académie Royale des Sciences, des Lettres et des Beaux-Arts de Belgique, Brussels, Belgium, and Houzeau to N. C. Schmit, May 9, 1868, Correspondence J.C. Houzeau–N. C. Schmit, Service des Archives, Université Libre de Bruxelles, Belgium.

Biographical Information on Negro Leaders in New Orleans during Reconstruction

In the listings below the asterisk (*) means that the exact place of residence in New Orleans in 1860–61 is known for the person concerned; the dagger (†) means that the person was a slaveowner at some time before the Civil War. The abbreviations have the following meanings: F, free; S, slave; M, mulatto; B, black; N.O., New Orleans; L, literate; I, illiterate; C.W., Civil War; B.N.O., Battle of New Orleans.

NAME	ANTE-BELLUM LEGAL STATUS	PHENO-TYPE	DATE OF BIRTH	PLACE OF BIRTH	1860–61 PLACE OF RESIDENCE	1860–61 OCCUPATION	1860–61 WEALTH IN $	ANTE-BELLUM LITERACY	MILITARY SERVICE
Joseph Abélard*	F			N.O.	N.O.	Carpenter		L	
C. J. Adolphe				N.O.					
Joseph B. Alexis*	F	M	1825	N.O.	N.O.	Cooper		L	
James W. Allen						Minister			
Madison Allen*	F				N.O.	Painter			
Caesar Carpentier Antoine*	F	B	1836	N.O.	N.O.	Barber	700	L	C.W.
Félix C. Antoine	F	M	1839	N.O.	N.O.	Mechanic	1,900	L	C.W.
Charles Aubert	F		1822		N.O.	Carpenter	2,300		
Laurent Auguste*	F	M			N.O.	Cigar store	600		
Adolphe Augustin	F	M	1828	N.O.	N.O.	Cigar maker		L	
Moses B. Avery	F							L	C.W.
Noël Jacques Bacchus	F	M	1819	N.O.	N.O.	Carpenter	1,600	L	C.W.
Lewis Banks†	F	M	1808	Va.	N.O.	Minister			
Alexander Eusibius Barber	S	B				Steward		L	
William B. Barrett	F	M			N.O.	Barber		L	C.W.
Richard C. Baylor	S			N.O.	N.O.	Laborer		L	
Armand Belot*	F	M		N.O.	N.O.	Cigar factory		L	
Octave Belot*	F	M	1836	N.O.	N.O.	Cigar factory		L	C.W.

NAME	ANTE-BELLUM LEGAL STATUS	PHENO-TYPE	DATE OF BIRTH	PLACE OF BIRTH	1860–61 PLACE OF RESIDENCE	1860–61 OCCUPATION	1860–61 WEALTH IN $	ANTE-BELLUM LITERACY	MILITARY SERVICE
E. Arnold Bertonneau*	F	M	1834	N.O.	N.O.	Wine merchant			C.W.
Imanuel B. Bijou	F	B	1807		N.O.	Carpenter			
Thomas Bland*	F		1838	N.O.	N.O.	Drayman	550		
Ovide C. Blandin	F		1822	N.O.	N.O.				
Ludger B. Boguille*	F	M	1824	N.O.	N.O.	Teacher	600	L	C.W.
François Boisdore*	F	M			N.O.	Accountant	1,200	L	
Henry Bonseigneur*	F				N.O.	Cigar store	2,900		
J. B. D. Bonseigneur*†	F								
Paulin C. Bonseigneur*	F	M	1798	Haiti	N.O.	Grocer	19,400	L	B.N.O.
Anatole Louis Borée*	F	M	1805	La.	N.O.	Shoe store	3,800	L	B.N.O.
Pierre Boyer*	F	B		N.O.	N.O.	Tailor			
Numa Brihou	F		1832	N.O.	N.O.				C.W.
Bazile Brion*	F				N.O.	Shoemaker	1,000		
Clement Isaac Camp*	F				N.O.				B.N.O.
Edmund Campenel	F		1819	N.O.	N.O.	Mason	800	L	
J. Manuel Camps*†	F	M	1816		N.O.	Turner		L	
Pierre Canelle*	F	M	1810	N.O.	N.O.	Grocer	8,600	L	
Placide Z. Canonge*†	F				N.O.	Cotton weigher	1,500	L	
Lucien Jean Pierre Capla*	F	M	1821	N.O.	N.O.	Shoe store	1,300	L	
Edward Carter	F				N.O.	Shoe store	300	L	
Jefferson B. Carter	F			Ga.	N.O.	Minister		I	
St. Félix Casanave*	F	M	1835	N.O.	N.O.	Used furniture		L	C.W.

Jean Pierre Cazelar, Jr.	F	M	1824	La.	N.O.	Planter	41,000	L	
Eugène Chesse*	F				N.O.				B.N.O.
Charles B. Chevalier*	F	M	1831		N.O.	Carpenter		L	
Henry Chevarre*	F				N.O.		3,500		
Firmin C. Christophe	F				N.O.				
John Racquet Clay*†	F	M	1829	N.O.	N.O.	Broker	10,100	L	
David Copeland*	F				N.O.	Baker	1,800	L	
Myrtile Courcelle*†	F	M	1800	N.O.	N.O.	Broker	5,650	L	
Joseph A. Craig	S					Printer		L	
Robert I. Cromwell	F	B	1830	Va.	Wisc.	Physician			
Joseph Curiel*	F	M	1793	La.	N.O.	Grocer		L	
Victor Darinsbourg	F	M	1820	La.	N.O.	Carpenter	1,520	I	
Edgar Charles Davis	F	M	1830	N.O.	N.O.	Cooper		L	C.W.
L. Théodule Delassize†	F			N.O.	N.O.	Bldg. materials	1,300		
Jules Desalles*	F	M		N.O.	N.O.	Cigar maker	500	L	C.W.
Émile Detiège	F	M	1840	St. Martinville	N.O.	Mason		L	
W. A. Dove	F	M				Minister		L	
Adolphe Duhart	F					Teacher	150		
Francis Ernest Dumas*†	F	M	1837	France	N.O.	Clothing store		L	
Oscar James Dunn	F	M	1826	N.O.	N.O.	Plasterer		L	C.W.
Pierre G. Dupin*	F	M			N.O.	House furnishing	2,000	L	
Édmond Dupuy†	F	M	1819	Md.	N.O.	Warehouseman	171,000		
Joseph Ebb*	F	M			N.O.	Drayman			
James Edwards*	F				N.O.	Teacher			
François Escoffié*	F		1785	Opelousas	N.O.		4,900	L	B.N.O.
J. B. Esnard	F	M	1846	N.O.	N.O.	Tailor		L	
François Estève	F				N.O.			L	

NAME	ANTE-BELLUM LEGAL STATUS	PHENO-TYPE	DATE OF BIRTH	PLACE OF BIRTH	1860–61 PLACE OF RESIDENCE	1860–61 OCCUPATION	1860–61 WEALTH IN $	ANTE-BELLUM LITERACY	MILITARY SERVICE
Louis Ferry*	F				N.O.	Clerk			
Alphonse Fleury, Jr.*	F	M	1831	N.O.	N.O.	Tailor		L	C.W.
Florian Fleury	F	M	1842	La.	N.O.	Shoemaker		L	C.W.
Joseph Follin*	F		1809		N.O.	Carpenter			C.W.
William P. Forrest						Minister			
Louis Nelson Fouché*	F	M		Jamaica	N.O.	Mason	2,100	L	C.W.
Henry Francis			1812	N.O.	N.O.	Minister			
August Gaspard*	F	M		N.O.	N.O.	Mason			
Charles W. Gibbons*	F	M	1838	N.O.	N.O.	Painter		L	C.W.
Achille Glaudin	F				N.O.	Cigar store	4,500		
Clément Glaudin	F				N.O.				
Jean Baptiste Glaudin*†	F	M	1819	La.	N.O.	Cigar store	16,900	L	
Maurice Glaudin	F	M	1839	La.	N.O.	Cigar store	600	L	
Placide Glaudin	F		1840		N.O.	Cigar store			
Joseph C. Graves*	F				N.O.	Carpenter			
J. B. Grounx*	F				N.O.	Carpenter			
James H. Henry									C.W.
Joseph W. Howard									C.W.
Charles H. Hughes	F		1826	Washington City	N.O.	Baker			C.W.
James H. Ingraham	F		1833						
Robert Hamlin								L	C.W.
Isabelle	F	M	1837	Opelousas Attakapas					
Thomas H. Isabelle	F			S.C.		Merchant	200		C.W.
William C. Johnson	F	M	1820		N.O.	Mason			C.W.

Blanc F. Joubert†	F	M	1816	N.O.	France	Grocer		L	
Jean B. Jourdain*	F	M	1832	N.O.	N.O.	Cigar maker		L	C.W.
Victor Jourdain*	F	M	1827	N.O.	N.O.			L	C.W.
John F. Keating	F	M	1835	N.O.	N.O.	Mason	6,000	L	
John Keppard					N.O.	Cafe owner			C.W.
François Lacroix*†	F	M	1806	N.O.	N.O.	Tailor	242,570	L	
Thomy Lafon*	F	M	1810	N.O.	N.O.	Merchant	12,500	L	
J. Othello Lainez*	F			N.O.	N.O.	Shoemaker	50	L	C.W.
Louis Lainez	F								C.W.
Joseph Jean Pierre Lanna*	F	M	1807	N.O.	N.O.	Dry goods	5,500	L	C.W.
Armand Lanusse*	F	M	1812	N.O.	N.O.	Teacher		L	
Louis Duquéminy Larrieu*†	F	M	1831	N.O.	N.O.			L	C.W.
George W. Levère		B	1822	Va.		Minister		L	
A. W. Lewis	S		1832	Miss.		Physician			
James Lewis*	F	M		La.	N.O.	Steward		L	C.W.
Charles E. Logan*	F	M	1830	N.O.	N.O.	Plasterer	500	L	C.W.
Ernest Longpré, Jr.									
Drauzin B. Macarty*†	F	M	1811	N.O.	N.O.	Broker	60,900	L	
Victor Eugène Macarty*†								L	
Robert McCary, Jr.	F			N.O.	N.O.	Musician	1,300		
Joseph Francis Mansion						Minister			
Lucien Mansion*	F		1839	N.O.	N.O.	Cigar factory	5,300	L	
Théodule A. Martin*	F	M	1811	N.O.	N.O.	Barber		L	C.W.
Charles Martinez*	F		1836	N.O.	N.O.	Merchant		L	
Alexander Aristide Mary	F	M	1802	N.O.	N.O.	Real Estate	30,000	L	
J. A. Massicot	F		1823	N.O.	N.O.			L	C.W.
Eugène G. Meilleur*	F	M		N.O.	N.O.	Carpenter		L	C.W.

NAME	ANTE-BELLUM LEGAL STATUS	PHENO-TYPE	DATE OF BIRTH	PLACE OF BIRTH	1860–61 PLACE OF RESIDENCE	1860–61 OCCUPATION	1860–61 WEALTH IN $	ANTE-BELLUM LITERACY	MILITARY SERVICE
John Willis Ménard	F	M	1838	Ill.	Ohio	Minister		L	
Thomas A. Miles						Mason			
Louis Monde*	F				N.O.				
Julien J. Monette	F	M	1836	N.O.	N.O.	Tailor		L	C.W.
Félix Montégut*	F	M	1825	N.O.	N.O.	Mason			
Joseph Léonie Montieu*	F	M	1828	N.O.	N.O.	Clerk	5,300	L	C.W.
Manuel Moreau*†	F	M	1795	N.O.	N.O.			L	B.N.O.
Eugène Moret	F	M	1835	N.O.	N.O.			L	
C. Clay Morgan	F				N.O.	Lawyer		L	C.W.
Ernest C. Morphy*	F				N.O.				
George P. Nelson*	F	B	1810	Va.	N.O.	Soda shop	200		
Jordan B. Noble*	F	M	1800	Ga.	N.O.		1,500	L	B.N.O. & C.W.
Jacob A. Norager	F	M		La.	N.O.	Cabinetmaker			
John Parsons*	F				N.O.	Barber		L	
W. H. Pearne						Minister		L	
P. B. S. Pinchback	F	M	1837	Ga.	N.O.	Steward		L	C.W.
Armand Populus*	F		1839		N.O.	Mason		L	
Ulysse Populus*	F	M	1836	N.O.	N.O.	Barber	250	L	
François Porée*	F	M	1826	N.O.	N.O.	Clerk		L	
Paul Porée*	F	M	1827	N.O.	N.O.	Carpenter	1,000	L	C.W.
Thomas Médard Porée*	F	M	1815	La.	N.O.	Carpenter	800		
John Pullum, Jr.*	F			N.O.	N.O.	Barber			
John Pullum, Sr.*	F	M	1805	Va.	N.O.	Drayman			
Joanni Questy*	F		1818	N.O.	N.O.	Teacher		L	
James W. Quinn			1835	La.	La.				C.W.

P. B. Randolph	F				N.Y.	Reporter		L	C.W.
Eugène Rapp*	F	M	1836		N.O.	Tailor		L	C.W.
Robert Ray				N.O.	N.O.	Mason			
Joseph Auguste Raynal*	F	M	1836	N.O.	N.O.	Drygoods	3,350	L	C.W.
Eusèbe Reggio*†	F	B	1821	N.O.	N.O.	Mason	100	L	C.W.
Anthony Remoir	F	M	1830	La.	N.O.	Cigar maker	200		C.W.
Joseph Renaud	F	M	1831	N.O.	N.O.	Clerk		L	
Henry Louis Rey*	F				N.O.				
Octave Rey*	F	M	1837	N.O.	N.O.	Cooper	1,050	L	C.W.
Édmond Rillieux*†	F	M	1810	N.O.	N.O.	Drygoods		L	
Charles W. Ringgold*	F		1840		N.O.	Cigar maker	200		C.W.
Thomas P. Robinson*	F				N.O.				
Lazard A. Rodriguez*	F	M	1827	N.O.	N.O.	Shoemaker		L	C.W.
Stephen Walter Rogers*	F	M	1821	N.C.	N.O.	Minister	300	L	
Anthony Ross	F				N.O.	Minister			
Jean Baptiste Roudanez*	F	M	1815	N.O.	N.O.	Builder	2,500	L	
Louis Charles Roudanez*	F	M	1823	St. James	N.O.	Physician	14,000	L	
Antoine St. Léger	F	M	1835	N.O.	N.O.	Jeweler	800	L	C.W.
Henry Sanders	F					Minister			
Charles Satchell				Va.	N.O.	Minister			
Bernard Saulay*	F				N.O.	House furnishing	10,300		C.W.
Charles S. Sauvinet				N.O.	N.O.				C.W.
A. Lucien Scott									C.W.
John Scott*	F			Tenn.	N.O.	Carpenter			
John Sidney					N.O.				C.W.

NAME	ANTE-BELLUM LEGAL STATUS	PHENO-TYPE	DATE OF BIRTH	PLACE OF BIRTH	1860–61 PLACE OF RESIDENCE	1860–61 OCCUPATION	1860–61 WEALTH IN $	ANTE-BELLUM LITERACY	MILITARY SERVICE
William G. Smoot*†	F		1841		N.O.	Drayman	1,800		
Louis A. Snaer	F		1840	N.O.	N.O.				C.W.
Philomène S. Snaer	F	B			N.O.	Cigar maker			
Joseph Simon Soudé	F		1821	Ga.	N.O.	Carpenter		L	
Bernard A. Soulié*†	F	M	1803	N.O.	N.O.	Comm. merch.	100,150	L	
Victor Souterre*	F				N.O.	Clerk		L	
John F. Spearing†	F				N.O.	Sailmaker	22,150		
Eugène Staès*	F		1826	N.O.	N.O.	Clerk	200	L	C.W.
George W. Steptoe	F	M	1820	Va.	N.O.	Minister		L	
Robert H. Steptoe†	F	M	1810	Va.	N.O.	Minister	150	L	
Mitchell M. Sturgess	F				N.O.	Minister			
George B. Taylor*	F		1832	Alexandria	N.O.	Carpenter	800		C.W.
William W. Taylor	F				N.O.	Steward	500		C.W.
Sidney Thézan*	F		1821	N.O.	N.O.	Tailor		L	
Camille Thierry	F	M	1814	N.O.		Shoemaker	12,000	L	
Jacob L. Tosspot	F								
Pascal M. Tourné*†	F			France	N.O.	Railroad worker	6,400	L	
Moses Townsend	S				N.O.				
Paul Trévigne*	F	M	1825	N.O.	N.O.	Teacher	500	L	
Raymond Trévigne*	F	M	1830	N.O.	N.O.	Cigar maker			C.W.
William Troy	F			Canada	Canada	Minister			
Maure Parquitto Valentin*	F	M	1840	La.	N.O.	Shoemaker		L	
James Madison Vance	F		1818	Tenn.	N.O.	Minister	1,500	L	
Eugène Vessier*	F			N.O.	N.O.		1,050	L	
Charles Joseph Vèque*	F		1825	N.O.	N.O.	Painter		L	

William F. Vigers	F			N.O.	N.O.	Merchant	11,000	L
Norbert Villère*	F	M	1831	La.	N.O.	Lawyer	2,250	L
Henry White*	F	M	1815	Md.	N.O.	Drayman		L
Emperor Williams	F	M	1827	Tenn.	N.O.	Minister		
P. M. Williams	F					Teacher		L
David Wilson*	F				N.O.	Barber		
John F. Winston	F							L
Francis Xavier*	F	M			N.O.	Carpenter		
Adolphe Zémar	F	M	1835	La.	N.O.		100	L

Sources: Manuscript Census Returns, Eighth Census of the United States, 1860, Louisiana, Records of the U.S. Bureau of the Census, Record Group 29; Muster Rolls, Returns, and Regimental Papers, Volunteers, Civil War, U.S. Colored Troops, 73d, 74th, 75th, 76th, and 77th Regiments, Records of the Adjutant General's Office, Record Group 94; Pensions, Records of the Veterans Administration, Record Group 15; New Orleans, Mayor's Office, Register of Free Colored Persons Entitled to Remain in the State, 1856–64; New Orleans, Conveyance Office, Record of Conveyance, 1855–62; New Orleans, Treasurer's Office, Tax Ledger, 1859–61; New Orleans, Office of Vital Records, Record of Birth, 1819–57; New Orleans, Office of Vital Records, Record of Death, 1865–1900; St. Louis Cathedral, Baptismal Register of Negroes and Mulattoes, 1831–40; *New Orleans Directory*, 1855–62; New Orleans press, especially *L'Union*, 1862–64; *Tribune*, 1864–69; *Black Republican*, 1865; *Republican*, 1867–76; *Louisianian*, 1870–80; *Times*, 1873–80; and various other primary and secondary sources, published and unpublished.

Michael B. Chesson   8

Richmond's Black Councilmen, 1871–96

T HE RISE AND DECLINE of black officeholding in Richmond, Virginia, does not conform to generally held views concerning the nature of Reconstruction and Redemption. Reconstruction in a technical sense ended for Richmond in 1870, when Virginia was readmitted to the Union and white Conservatives regained full control of the city government. Yet no Negroes had won an elective municipal office from 1865 through 1870. The highest ranking black appointee was John Oliver, who became the messenger of the city council in May 1868. Two other blacks, Joseph Cox and Lewis Lindsay, were among the delegates elected from the city to the Virginia Constitutional Convention of 1867–68. Negroes held minor positions in the post office and as janitors and laborers in various city departments; but, unlike other parts of the state, Richmond sent no blacks to the General Assembly. Indeed, it was not until 1871, after the Redeemers had triumphed, that blacks first won positions of real power and influence. Most significantly, between July 1871 and June 1898, thirty-three blacks served on the city council.

The fact that black officeholding in the city's government did not begin until after the end of Reconstruction underlines the mildness of military and congressional policies in Richmond and further discredits the old but surprisingly resilient portrait of the tragic era. Furthermore, the legacy of Reconstruction was greater than has generally been recognized by scholars or admitted by local whites. Activities that historians have usually associated with Reconstruction continued well into the 1890s: black officeholding, widespread voting by Negroes, alliances with white Republicans of various factions, intense competition for office, increasing fraud and violence on the part of Democrats to reduce the black vote, and variously successful Republican appeals to Congress and the federal courts for relief from Bourbon oppression. Only the bluecoats and the gold spittoons were missing.

Though Republicans failed to win a presidential election after carrying the city and state for Grant in 1872, vigorous two-party warfare continued until 1896. Following the Panic of 1873, black political activity declined, at least in part because of worsening economic conditions.

The Republican vote dropped off in 1876, and no blacks were elected to the council in 1878. But in the 1880s, after the splintering of the Conservative-Democratic party into Funder and Readjuster wings, blacks became more active. Black leaders were more influential in Richmond in the 1880s and early nineties than they have been at any time before or since, until the present day. The extent and significance of their activities during this little-studied period of shadow Reconstruction will be the subject of this essay.

All thirty-three black councilmen were elected from Jackson Ward, which had been created in April 1871. Following Virginia's return to the Union in January 1870, the Redeemers had used fraud and violence to install their mayoral candidates in a series of elections. To eliminate the possibility of a Republican victory in a citywide contest, Richmond Conservatives agreed on a plan to create a new ward in addition to the five already in existence: Jefferson, Madison, Monroe, Clay, and Marshall. Over the opposition of three of the Republicans on the common council, the majority enacted this scheme, which owed something to a similar Republican move in 1867 when the legislature allowed the city to annex land and create the new wards of Marshall and Clay.[1]

The name Jackson had long been connected with an area that was annexed by the city in 1793. Joseph Jackson, a white contractor, built a house in the vicinity in the late 1790s. His son Joseph Jackson, Jr., was the proprietor of an entertainment resort called Jackson's Garden that was popular after the War of 1812. When builders developed the five-block-long area between Leigh and Jackson streets in the 1840s, it became known as Jackson's Addition, and was still so designated on city maps published in the 1870s. The name Jackson was subsequently applied to a much larger area.[2]

Until 1871 ward boundaries in Richmond ran on roughly parallel lines from the James River in a northerly direction to a creek and a series of hills. Jackson Ward was laid out at the northern edge of the city by slicing off the top of four of the old wards. The new ward boundaries were skillfully gerrymandered to include much of the black population and very few whites. By 1890 79 percent of the Jackson Ward inhabitants were black; whereas the five white wards had a median black population of only 30 percent. Jackson came to be known as the "black belt," the "shoestring ward," or simply "the ward." The line between it and the other wards has been compared to a rail fence struck by lightning.[3]

The gerrymandering of Jackson Ward insured white control of the five other wards and of the city government. It also meant that ward elections would be noncompetitive, since the Democratic nominees were chosen in a white primary. A safe Democratic majority was always a certainty, except in Jackson. In close citywide state and national contests, whites of the Conservative, Funder Democrat, and Democratic parties could concentrate their efforts on reducing the black vote in one ward.[4]

Unlike their counterparts in other Virginia cities, Richmond black councilmen were never part of a ruling Republican majority. Unionists and Republicans enjoyed a brief and tenuous hold on the council only in parts of 1868 and 1869. In Petersburg, however, white and black Republicans controlled the city council between 1870 and 1874, and Republicans carried the city in presidential elections in all but one contest until 1892. They were victorious in Norfolk in 1884 and 1888. The counties of the lower Peninsula, with the towns of Hampton and Newport News, were Republican strongholds into the 1890s, as was Henrico County itself, which surrounded Richmond. On the other hand, among large southern cities, Richmond was unusual in the degree to which blacks shared power and the length of time they held office.[5]

As in other southern cities, the 1870s and 1880s saw the use of the Democratic primary and, in consequence, lower turnouts in the regular elections. "Independents" who bolted the Democratic party to run for the council against the official nominees were objects of scorn, and there were few of them until 1879 when the Democrats split into Funder and Readjuster factions over the question of paying the state's antebellum debt. In 1886 the city's Democrats again split over temperance and the Knights of Labor. The Republicans offered regular opposition, but they ran complete tickets only in Jackson Ward, which they (or Readjusters) carried in all but one election from 1871 until 1896.[6]

Because of its largely black population and strong Republican organization, Jackson Ward was the scene of the most vigorous political contests in Richmond after the war. Independents of both parties were most likely to come from Jackson. After 1879 some Readjusters were nominated. But the Democrats were reluctant to concede control of the district despite, or perhaps because of, its black inhabitants. Registrars, election judges, and other Democratic officials challenged each black voter at length, to delay the segregated lines of Negro Republicans as long as possible. In each election hundreds would still be waiting to vote when the polls closed, even after standing in line the previous night. Bullies provoked black voters, as did the police, and the violence that often resulted was an excuse to arrest Negroes, who were released after the contest when charges had been dropped.[7]

Despite such Democratic efforts, the Republicans won in Jackson Ward, if nowhere else in Richmond, and usually a majority of the ward's council delegation was black. After 1874 the city council became an awkward bicameral body, with a common council as before, but with a board of aldermen, who had formerly sat only as members of the Richmond Hustings Court, serving as the upper chamber and passing on the items approved by the common council. Each ward elected five members for two-year terms on the common council, and two men for four-year and one for two-year terms on the aldermanic board.[8]

When most of the Richmond blacks were put into one ward, they lost their potential to recapture the city they and their white Republican allies had briefly controlled during Reconstruction. On the other hand, they were virtually guaranteed up to a maximum of eight seats on the council, seats that white Republicans might have continued to win had the majority of the black electorate not been united within one ward. Nor was it likely that whites of the Conservative party would have tolerated the continued challenge to their power that the Republicans presented in the turbulent year of 1870. Thus the creation of Jackson Ward was both an advance and a setback for black Richmonders. The gerrymandering of Jackson is probably about the best solution blacks could have hoped for, given the withdrawl of federal troops from Virginia and the attitudes of the national government on Reconstruction and the plight of the freedmen. There were other benefits for Afro-Americans in this concentration within one ward, such as the potential for increased development of racial pride and community spirit. After 1871 the growth in the number of organizations that were free of white control and led by blacks was one indication of the greater assertiveness of Richmond's Negro community, as was the rise of black entrepreneurs who served their own race rather than catering exclusively to white trade. The thirty-three men who were to represent Jackson on the city council for a generation were the political manifestation of this self-confidence and racial awareness.[9]

With the exception of John Oliver and a few others among the first blacks on the council, Richmond's Negro officeholders were not among the most notable leaders in the early years of Reconstruction. They were not inclined to play a prominent role or were simply too young. Exceptional orators like Richard Carter, Joseph Cox, Landon Johnson, and Lewis Lindsay and able organizers of street protests like

JOHN P. MITCHELL, JR.
Virginia State Library, Richmond

Henry Page and Ben Scott were not elected to the council. Some took jobs in the U.S. customhouse, while others dropped out of politics entirely. A few left the city. Neither were the Negro councilmen among the wealthy elite of the black business community. Entrepreneurs like liveryman Albert P. Brooks and the younger Giles B. Jackson became aware of the financial risks from open involvement in politics, even when working within the system as officeholders. Neither did conservative black ministers like J. W. Dungee and John Jasper nor the prosperous and more politically active Fields Cook hold office.[10]

The black councilmen occupied the middle ground politically and economically, although socially they ranked higher in the black community than did many postwar white councilmen in white society. Most were not militant, because as successful politicians they understood the limits of their power and knew that they must work not only with their few white Republican allies but also with their Democratic opponents and colleagues on the council. They carried little political baggage with them into the 1870s. Black voters generally chose to elect older, more established men of long residence in the city, after the turbulent experience of early Reconstruction. The Negro councilmen, with some notable exceptions, seemed to enjoy polite and even cordial relations with their white counterparts; but they were clearly representatives of the black community and visible symbols of Afro-American freedom. As such, they were occasional targets for ridicule of the white press, but the larger community seems to have ignored them as an affront to Caucasian dignity.[11]

Three-quarters of the councilmen came from the generation born between 1833 and 1863. Only two are known to have been born outside Virginia. Of the twenty-five whose racial background is known, sixteen were mulattoes and nine were blacks. These figures hardly indicate a strong trend toward leadership by either group, as in other cities, since the blacks and mulattoes served in more or less even proportions from 1871 to 1898. Still, there was a disproportionate mulatto representation on the council in terms of their percentage of the city's Negro population.[12] (See Table 1 for a profile.)

The thirty-three Negroes built up less seniority than did their white colleagues, serving an average of only 3.7 years, less than two terms on the common council or one long term on the board of aldermen. Alderman Josiah Crump and Richard G. Forrester of both bodies served ten (nonconsecutive) and eleven years respectively in the 1870s and 1880s. Sandy W. Robinson and John Mitchell each spent a total of eight years in both chambers. The remaining councilmen had six years or less in office, four with only one year.

The white councilmen elected with the blacks were of a different class than those who had served before the war. After the redemption of the city in 1870, politics was a less genteel calling. With blacks voting and holding office and Democrats using questionable tactics, members of the oldest and wealthiest families no longer felt obliged to sit on the council, as long as the city was under Conservative white rule. That disagreeable task was left to others. For example, about one-quarter of the white membership of the common council from 1871 through 1882 was merchants (grocers, coal and wood dealers, commission merchants) and one-quarter was manufacturers (tobacco, metals, food). Unskilled workers of either race were still rare on the council, but white-collar and skilled workers were now more numerous than professional men. The councils were increasingly of a middle- to lower-middle-class composition, reflecting that group's new importance in the postwar South, as C. Vann Woodward has noted. Such men were, perhaps, less paternalistic toward blacks than their aristocratic antebellum predecessors, but they might also have been less tolerant of them. Yet these clerks, carpenters, and machinists mixed with the black councilmen in the rough and tumble of city politics, sought black votes (with slight success) in the 1870s and 1880s, and may have come to a grudging respect for their Negro colleagues.[13]

The white members did serve longer than the blacks. In the five elections to the common council 1872 through 1880, for example, one-half of all incumbents were returned; yet only five blacks held office for two or more successive terms. Postwar white incumbents did not remain in office as long as did those who served in the antebellum era; but there were still men with lengthy service, like John M. Higgins, who represented Jefferson Ward for eighteen years. While Higgins's tenure was unusual, many of the same names appear on council minutes for six or eight consecutive years, or reappear after a short absence. Also, if an old member is missing from a usual spot in the ward delegation, he has often been replaced by a brother, son, or other close relative.[14]

The reasons for the correspondingly high turnover among the black councilmen include chronic factionalism in Jackson Ward that was caused by personal rivalries, differing religious and fraternal affiliations, and the various white Republicans and even Democrats with whom different black leaders allied. Antebellum status and color may also have been important determinants of political success, but to

TABLE 1: *Personal Characteristics of Black Councilmen, 1871–98*

NAME	BLACK/ MULATTO	SERVED ON COUNCIL	OCCUPATION IN OFFICE	BIRTH DATE(S)	CENSUS YEAR(S)
John Adams	M	1882–88	plasterer	1847	1860, 1880
Joseph Allen	B	1882–84	grocer	1836	1860, 1880, 1900
Edinboro Archer	B	1882–88	wheelwright	1833	1880
Landrum Boyd	M	1872–73	brickmason	1839	1870
Andrew Brown	?	1888–90	postal clerk	1840	1900
Edward Carter	M	1888–90	postal clerk	1859/45	1870, 1900
Isaac Carter	?	1888–90	carpenter	1845	1900
Josiah Crump	M	1876–84 1888–90	postal clerk	1838	1860, 1880
Morton Deane	M	1894–96	ironworker	1853/59	1880, 1900
Joseph Farrar	M	1886–88	carpenter	1832	1860, 1870, 1880
Richard Forrester	M	1871–82	carpenter	1826	1860, 1870, 1880
Jackson Foster	B	1874–78 1880–82	grocer	1835	1880
Joshua Griffin	B	1886–88	shoemaker	1851/53	1870
James Hayes	?	1886–90	lawyer	1858	—
Benjamin Jackson	B	1890–96	grocer	1839/41	1870, 1900
Thomas Jeter	M	1890–92	plasterer	1852	1880
Robert Johnson	B	1874–78	shoemaker	1825	1880
Robert Jones	?	1886–88	doctor	1860	—
Henry Layne	?	1890–92	laborer	?	—

Name	Color	Occupation	Birth	Council	Census
James Lewis	M	barber	1852	1884–86	1880
John Mitchell	M	editor	1863	1888–96	—
Henry Moore	M	carpenter	1856/58	1892–98	1880, 1900
John Oliver	M	notary public	1834/15	1872–73	1870, 1880
Edwin Randolph	M	lawyer	1862/50	1882–86	1900
Jordan Robinson	?	barber	?	1884–86	—
Sandy Robinson	B	huckster	1845	1880–88	1880
Alpheus Roper	B	plasterer	1830	1871–72	1860
William Smith	?	barber	1848	1892–96	—
Andrew Thompson	B	saloonkeeper	1860	1890–92	—
Alfred Thornton	?	caterer	1802	1872	—
William Tinsley	M	barber	1853	1880–82	1880
Nelson Vandervall	M	grocer	1820	1873–78	1860, 1870, 1880
Royal White	M	carpenter	1835	1890–94	1870, 1900

Sources: U.S., Bureau of the Census, Manuscript Census Schedules, Population, 1860, 1870, 1880, 1900, Virginia, Henrico County, City of Richmond; Richmond *Dispatch*; Richmond *Planet*; annual city directories; Luther Porter Jackson, *Negro Officeholders in Virginia, 1865–1895*; Richmond Common Council, Minutes; Board of Aldermen, Journal.

The middle initials and variant spelling of names have been dropped. Color is as indicated in the 1860, 1870, and 1880 census. The years of council service have been compiled from the sources above; membership on the common council has not been distinguished from the board of aldermen. Some men served on both bodies. Occupation in most cases is that held while in office, or the nearest date possible, as compiled from sources. In a number of cases, members resigned to accept federal appointments as required by presidential directive or Virginia law; in other cases they do not seem to have resigned. If no other occupation could be found, the federal appointment is listed, particularly when held in the same period. Birth dates are given as in the 1860 census, if listed; otherwise in the order found in the census for 1870, 1880, and/or 1900. The first three give the age at the last birthday, so that ages may vary by a year either way depending upon when polled. The 1900 census gives a month and a year. Jackson often lists dates at variance with the census, and census dates also differ.

what extent is not clear. In some cases black voters were probably dissatisfied with the performance of their representatives, who were confronted with a nearly perpetual Democratic majority. Other incumbents failed to build the personal following required for a strong political base because they were overconfident, lazy, or lacked a job that afforded daily contact with large numbers of constituents. Some councilmen simply chose the wrong side in a given year. A few may have found service on the council personally unfulfilling.

Many blacks did want to serve. Competition in Jackson was probably more intense than in the white wards, where nominees were chosen in the primary if not by prearrangement among bosses. Of the black councilmen, John Oliver dropped out of politics, Landrum Boyd and Edward R. Carter resigned to accept federal appointments, and Joseph E. Farrar was chosen to replace Jordan A. Robinson because of the latter's chronic absenteeism. Alfred L. Thornton and Josiah Crump died in office. Most of the others simply failed to win renomination from one of the Republican factions. In most years a spot on the regular Republican ticket was tantamount to election.[15]

All but Tredegar ironworker Morton Deane and laborer Henry Layne, each of whom served only two years, were in occupations with high visibility. In the daily course of their jobs, each of the other thirty-one councilmen would meet many potential supporters. This was especially true for the nine men in the building trades, seven in service jobs, or seven others who supplied food and drink. Many of the officeholders worked at a number of different occupations while in Richmond, but like their white colleagues they were almost uniformly from the petty bourgeoisie of small businessmen and tradesmen.[16]

Only four black professionals, including two lawyers, a doctor, and a newspaper publisher held office. Yet, in addition to the physician and the lawyers who had received advanced training, plasterer John H. Adams was a graduate of Lincoln University, and most of the rest had probably attended Richmond's locally famous Colored Normal and High School. Only four councilmen were listed as illiterate in the census.[17]

At least one-quarter, including the seven listed in the 1860 census and shoemaker Robert W. Johnson, were free before the war. Almost one-third of the remainder were born in the last ten years of the slavery era, in some cases so late (Mitchell in 1863) as to have few if any memories of life under the peculiar institution, if indeed their parents were slaves.[18]

Most of the councilmen, if their occupations are any indication, enjoyed a comfortable or even wealthy status in the black community. The 1870 census shows, for example, that two of the oldest men to serve were fairly well off. Dairyman and carpenter Richard G. Forrester had $1,800 in real estate and $200 in personal property, while grocer Vandervall had $2,000 in real property and $300 in personal effects. Younger men had acquired less, like carpenter Joseph E. Farrar, who had only $300 in personal property, and Benjamin Jackson, a hotel waiter, who had only $100 in real estate before he became a caterer, grocer, and insurance collector. Some younger men had successful fathers. The tobacconist Valentine Griffin had $800 in real and $600 in personal property, while his son Joshua R. Griffin worked in a tobacco factory. Others were less fortunate. Edward R. Carter's father was a hotel waiter with only $100 in personal property.[19]

In 1900 at least six of the former councilmen, including Joseph Allen, Isaac W. Carter, Morton Deane, Benjamin Jackson, Henry J. Moore, and Edwin A. Randolph were listed as owning their own houses, and several had paid off their mortgages.[20] Many of the councilmen knew each other before serving as officeholders. They were born and grew up in the same neighborhood, were classmates in school, and had settled in the same precincts. Huckster Sandy W. Robinson and wheelwright Edinboro Archer lived next door to each other while serving on the common council and board of aldermen in the 1880s. While rising young black leaders may not have had an "old-boy network," some did have models from the previous generation. Richard Forrester, who had been a page in the state capitol in the 1860s, occupied a position of public prominence in the 1870s when he lived at 319 College Street. Edwin A. Randolph, who became the first editor of the Richmond *Planet* and who graduated from the Yale law school, lived at 311 College Street. Although a generation younger, Randolph doubtless knew who the distinguished gentleman with the white moustache and elegant mutton chops was, and he probably played with Forrester's sons.[21]

The relationship between Joseph E. Farrar and young Henry J. Moore is documented. Farrar, a carpenter and general contractor, lived at 810 Fourth Street. The 25-year-old Moore, a carpenter employed by Farrar, lived at 808 Fourth Street and boarded with Farrar's family. The younger man undoubtedly benefited not only from his apprenticeship in carpentry, but also from the political lore that Farrar had accumulated in a career stretching back to Monroe and Clay ward caucuses in 1867.[22]

With a sample of only thirty-three councilmen, it is difficult to detect economic trends in the type of blacks elected, but the development of Negro political leaders seems to have gone through at least four phases between 1865 and 1896. The years 1865 through 1870 were dominated by orators and firebrands, some of whom were relatively poor and uneducated, whereas wealthier or more moderate men increasingly shunned politics. The 1870s were characterized by men like Thornton, Forrester, and Vandervall, who had established themselves in business, were generally older, and, as in the case of the latter two, had sometimes played minor roles as moderates in the early years of Reconstruction. They worked under the direction of white Republican leaders who decided larger policies and distributed patronage.

In the years from 1882 to 1890 the "new-issue" Negroes, who were born in the closing days of slavery or after emancipation, came to prominence. Examples of such men on the council included attorneys James H. Hayes, Edwin A. Randolph, and physician Robert E. Jones. These men were often prominent members of the customhouse gang; but they had more influence and independence in their own right, as befitted their backgrounds, and in these cases, their professional status.[23]

The final type of black leader, who was not always a "new issue," overthrew the ruling clique in Jackson Ward, partly by using racial pride against white bosses outside the ward and partly by allying with independent local Republicans in Jackson. Men like John Mitchell worked with whites like James Bahen, a grocer and ward boss, against the city branch of William Mahone's state machine and increasingly against the policies of the national Republican party.[24]

John Mitchell, Jr., was among the most prominent Negroes and was perhaps, the most assertive black to sit on the council. He was more likely to ridicule white pretensions than to be the butt of Democratic jokes. His older colleagues had learned diplomacy; but in August 1888, only a month after taking his seat on the common council for the first time, young Mitchell cast the lone vote against an expansion of the all-white police force. He thought that some black patrolmen should be appointed, a proposal that had not been made since the days of the carpetbagger mayor George Chahoon. Because of his aggressive attitude, many of the proposals he made while on the council were either rejected or buried in committee. Mitchell was an example of an activist black councilman, yet the changing fortunes of his career illustrate the rampant factionalism among politicians of both races and the inevitable limits that the system placed on even a leader of his remarkable talent and energy.[25]

In many ways Mitchell was typical of the new-issue Negroes. Born in 1863 of slave parents, the young mulatto had few if any memories of slavery, though he grew up in the home of his wealthy former master. Like others of his generation who came of age in the 1880s, he was often more militant than his elders who had known slavery. The new generation was solidly middle class, like most of their parents, but they tended to be better educated. Because of his activities as a newspaper editor, and Ann Field Alexander's as yet unpublished biography of him, more is known about Mitchell than any of the other black political leaders.[26]

After a slow start, Mitchell excelled at the city's Colored Normal and High School, from which he graduated in 1881. Founded by northern whites and supported by the Peabody Fund, Colored Normal had been taken over by the city; but before its decline in the mid-1880s (caused by a cut in municipal funding), it continued to provide black students with a superior education. It was still run by its first principal, Ralza M. Manly, a Vermonter who had been chaplain of a black regiment in the Union army and a superintendent of Freedmen's Bureau schools in Virginia. Manly was also an early member of the council from Jackson Ward and served on the city school board. As a student under Manly, Mitchell exhibited many talents, including a gift for public speaking, as shown by the debating medals that he won.[27]

During the brief reign of the Readjusters, Mitchell got a teaching job in one of the city's black schools, but he was dismissed after a year, in 1884, by the new all-white school board following the victory of Funder Democrats in the state elections the previous fall.

At the end of 1884 Mitchell took over the debts and editorship of the struggling Richmond *Planet*, the newest of three black newspapers in the city. He was to remain its editor and publisher until his death in 1929. The black community in Richmond soon came to know Mitchell better through his militant editorials against lynching and his sarcastic references to the double standard in race relations. For Mitchell the newspaper editor, publicity proved to be less of a problem than it was for most Negro politicians. His control of the paper, as well as his urbanity, intelligence, and polished oratory made him attractive to white Republican leaders.[28]

In 1888, before he was twenty-five, Mitchell gave a rousing speech to the Republican state convention in Petersburg. He was also placed on the Republican ticket from Jackson Ward for a seat on the common council. Mitchell won his first election in May and in July traveled as a delegate to the Republican National Convention.[29]

It is doubtful that Mitchell could have achieved such prominence so quickly without the backing of William Mahone, Republican party chairman for Virginia. Despite his promising start and the debt he probably owed Mahone, Mitchell joined other Virginia blacks who broke with the diminutive boss in the fall of 1888. Mahone had not only refused to endorse, but actively tried to prevent a black, John Mercer Langston, who was president of Virginia Normal and Collegiate Institute in Petersburg, from being elected to the congressional seat from Virginia's Fourth District. When Mahone ran for governor in 1889, Mitchell's support was weak. The hostility of Mahone and his Richmond allies would eventually contribute to Mitchell's loss of power.[30]

In 1890 Mitchell ran for alderman and won at the head of the regular Republican ticket. His ticket was opposed by an all-black Independent Republican slate that included James H. Hayes (who had tried to gain control of the *Planet*), Joshua R. Griffin, and Joseph E. Farrar. The black bolters claimed they were opposed to the rule of white ward boss James Bahen, a Mitchell ally; but they were also friendly with Mahone; and some of them were encouraged to run by Democrats. Spotting this split in Republican ranks, the Democrats ran a full ticket in the ward on short notice, hoping that enough blacks would vote for the Independents, so that Bahen, Mitchell, and a few other leaders would be defeated. To avoid such splits in the future (and to protect himself), Mitchell urged the Republicans to hold regular primaries like the Democrats. His suggestion was adopted to the extent that precinct caucuses were held, where delegates to the city's Republican conventions were instructed which nominees they should support. But bolting from the regular Republican ticket continued, especially by members of the customhouse gang, despite their obvious lack of support in the ward. The competition for elective and appointive office among Richmond's black leaders was still spirited in the 1890s and resembled the contests in the early years of Reconstruction. Negroes sought the relatively high salaries of federal jobs as well, along with the prestige and status that went with such positions.[31]

In 1889 Mahone secured the appointment of Otis H. Russell, son-in-law of R. M. Manly, as postmaster of Richmond. Mitchell was angry when Russell initially failed to appoint blacks to postal positions, but he was later placated when some jobs were given to Negroes. The editor soon found that the postmaster was building a local political machine as an adjunct to Mahone's state organization. Fewer and fewer Republicans were being elected to office, so patronage became an increasingly important factor in holding together what remained of the party in Virginia.

Richmond, the state capital, was particularly vital as a patronage center. The post office, with its dozens of positions for letter carriers and clerks, had the most jobs to offer, but the U.S. customhouse was in the same building, and a federal circuit court and an internal revenue office were also in the city.

The carpetbaggers with Washington connections and their black colleagues in the 1860s and 1870s were said to be members of the "customhouse gang." With the decline of Richmond's port in the 1880s, the customhouse became less important and required fewer personnel, but the needs of the post office continued to grow with the city's population. Thus Mahone's black and white supporters of the 1890s were often said to belong to the "post office gang." The term was also used to describe any federal employee, such as U.S. Marshal Edgar ("Yankee") Allan, who became Republican city chairman in 1890. His friend and fellow attorney, Judge Edmund Waddill, was a former congressman and city chairman. Although attorney James Hayes himself did not work in the post office, his wife worked there; and he was perhaps the most important black member of the gang. Robert A. Paul, whom Mitchell defeated in the 1892 council race, was a former aide to Readjuster Governor William E. Cameron, whom he helped to elect, and another member of the gang.[32]

In the 1890s Mitchell was regularly opposed by tickets of the postal group. The white bosses downtown may have thought they represented the Republican party in Richmond, but it was Mitchell and his cohorts who carried the ward with the most party members year after year. In 1892 his slate beat that of Hayes, and his 1894 ticket won by an even larger margin. Even in 1896, when the Democrats finally succeeded in redeeming Jackson Ward, the post-office's candidates finished third, behind Mitchell's.

Although John Mitchell was undeniably idealistic and committed to the cause of his race, he was also an ambitious and realistic politician. Though a representative of the reform element in Virginia's Republican party, Mitchell held political power for eight years in Richmond because of his well-oiled machine, known locally as "the whiskey ring." His closest ally by 1890, perhaps as early as his break with Mahone, was, ironically, a white man, James Bahen.[33]

Bahen was the most powerful of the Irish, German, and Italian grocers and liquor dealers who lived in Jackson Ward among the blacks and played leading roles in politics, as did grocers of both races else-where in the city. Bahen was born in Ireland in 1848, served as a team-ster in the Union army, and settled in Virginia by 1871. His store, known as Bahen's Hall, became a popular gathering place for black voters. Elected to the common council in 1882, along with four new black members who defeated longtime Negro incumbents, Bahen moved up to the board of aldermen in 1886. He was a member of Rich-mond's Irish National Republic Club. Investing in real estate in Rich-mond and other Virginia cities had made Bahen a wealthy man at his death in 1907.[34]

Traditionally Democrats in the North, many of the city's Irish, and other ethnic groups gravitated toward the Republican party. In 1896, out of eighteen white delegates to the state Republican convention from Richmond, eight were Irish. Many native whites resented their influence, as did some blacks. John Mitchell, as well, recognized Ba-hen's power, admitting in the *Planet* that the Independent Republican campaign of 1890 began with attacks on "James Bahen . . . who has virtually controlled politics in the Ward." The two men lived in differ-ent precincts and were thus not direct competitors, but in 1890 they joined forces against the candidates of the post-office gang and Demo-cratic interlopers. In 1892 Bahen and Mitchell campaigned with arms linked in marches through the ward and rode in the same carriage in a victory parade after the triumph of their ticket in the May city elec-tions. In the 1896 contest Bahen declared his black ally to be "the greatest man now living." Mitchell supplied the militant editorials, speeches, and appeals to racial price, while Bahen fueled the Jackson Ward rallies with his liquor and food.[35]

The working-class whites of Jackson Ward often supported the Mitchell-Bahen machine. In return they demanded representation on the council. In addition to Alderman Bahen, they had Mordecai T. Page, a huckster and later a saloon keeper, who served on the common council. Before Bahen's time, the ward's whites had been represented by alderman-grocers John Rankin and Oswald Gasser.[36]

More socially prominent and prosperous white Republicans who lived outside the ward supported Hayes, Paul, and others of the post-office gang who tried to "purify" the liquor-tainted district in the 1890s. These whites were allies of Mahone and enemies of Mitchell, but they cared little about the council elections in Jackson. They were willing to accept an all-black post-office ticket against the mixed slates of their party rivals, Bahen and Mitchell.

The post-office gang could also depend on the moral support of many black religious leaders and the help of William W. Browne in their attempts to beat "the rum dealers." Browne began his career as a temperance advocate in Alabama and became head of the United Order of True Reformers, the largest black fraternal and charitable organization in Richmond. Yet the gang failed in its campaigns, losing to Mitchell by margins of about seven to one. By the 1890s most ministers were unwilling to do the street-level political work and perform the arduous duties at the polls that political success required. In an 1886 vote on local option, most blacks apparently followed Mahone's orders and supported the wets, though which side ministers like John Jasper took is in some doubt, as is their ability to deliver their congregations to a particular political faction.[37]

Despite his short-lived candidacy for Congress in 1890 against Mahone's wishes, in 1892 John Mitchell still expected to be chosen as usual as a delegate to the Republican National Convention. Normally one man of each race was elected to represent the Third District. The white usually lived outside Richmond, while the black resided in Jackson Ward. Mitchell began his campaign for a convention seat in April 1892 with a white ally and running mate, James D. Brady. Brady was a collector of internal revenue for the eastern district of Virginia and a recognized anti-Mahone leader. When the district convention met in Richmond in May 1892, Judge Waddill and city chairman Edgar Allan were elected. Mitchell was selected as a nonvoting alternate, along with C. W. Harris of Manchester, who was a loyal black supporter of Mahone.[38]

The year proved to be a bad one for Republicans, as Grover Cleveland carried Richmond at the head of a Democratic landslide, and Republicans temporarily lost their patronage in the city. Mitchell, now cynical and bitter, was not overly concerned. He supported Edmund C. Cocke, the Populist candidate, for governor in 1893, probably because there was no Republican nominee. In 1894 Mitchell again dared to question Mahone's policy of not nominating congressional candidates, a ploy designed to bring federal intervention. As a result he lost his usual seat on the district's Republican committee and was formally expelled from the party.[39]

The angry editor had now been personally defeated on two issues crucial to Virginia blacks: their right to run for elective office, and their right to hold positions in the Republican party. Mitchell also failed in his attempt to protect a share of the patronage for Negroes. Federal appointments were controlled by the post-office gang, but Mitchell and other Jackson Ward leaders had long been able to get some city jobs for their own candidates. By the mid-1890s, however, whites held virtually all municipal jobs, including the cleaning of spittoons. Black laborers were even excluded from city construction projects, such as the new city hall, which was completed in 1894 with nonunion, white day laborers only.[40]

Such favoritism had always characterized committee appointments on the city council. The duties of black councilmen were theoretically the same as those of their white counterparts. John Mitchell and other members from Jackson Ward appeared to receive routine appointments to the joint standing committees of the common council and board of aldermen. Those serving for the first time were usually given only one or two committees, while council veterans received as many as three assignments. Table 2 shows the number of blacks appointed to committees upon the seating and organization in July of fourteen new councils from 1871 (every two years after 1872) until 1898. The Negro members were most often appointed to the market committees, because so many of their constituents were hucksters, and thus they knew conditions in the city's First and Second Markets better than most whites. But these were also committees low in prestige. (The Third Market, located in Clay Ward in the expanding West End, was not completed until 1891.) Blacks were almost as numerous on the Committee on Elections, perhaps for purposes of token representation, in hopes of stilling black protests over election fraud. The only other committee in which blacks always had representation was Claims and Salaries, another body that was low in prestige.

Blacks were usually appointed to the Committee on Streets Generally, which oversaw the maintenance, improvement, and extension of city streets, as requested by subsidiary ward committees. More often than not, they served on the Police Committee, where they were potential guards against the regular abuse of Negroes by law officers, as were those on the Health and Fire committees, which periodically tried to tighten controls over black sanitary facilities and housing. A less prestigious committee dealt with Shockoe Creek, but this tributary of the James devastated black housing in the creek bottom during periodic floods and Negro members on this committee proved useful. The Fire Alarm and Police Telegraph, and Accounts and Printing committees were neither prestigious nor of direct benefit to blacks.

More important committees on which blacks served less than half of the years they were on the council included the School Committee, which gradually cut funding for black students; the Public Grounds and Buildings Committee; the Committee on Lunatics, which ran the

TABLE 1: *Number of Blacks Appointed to Twenty-Five Standing Committees (Joint after 1874) of the Richmond City Council, 1871–98 (Fourteen New Councils)*

COMMITTEE	FROM COMMON COUNCIL	FROM BOARD OF ALDERMEN	TOTAL	BLACK % OF COMMITTEE MEMBERSHIP*
First Market	11	9	20	30
Second Market	10	10	20	30
Elections	12	6	18	26
Claims and Salaries	5	9	14	21
Streets Generally[1]	7	3	10	6
Police	5	5	10	15
Health	5	5	10	14
Fire	6	3	9	10
Shockoe Creek (established 1887)	5	3	8	19
Fire Alarm and Police Telegraph	5	3	8	12
Accounts and Printing	3	4	7	11
Schools (established 1872)	6	0	6	7
Public Grounds and Buildings	1	5	6	7
Lunatics (established 1878)	5	0	5	10
Retrenchment and Reform	5	0	5	7
Ordinances	2	3	5	8
Cemeteries	3	0	3	4
Relief of the Poor	1	2	3	3
Third Market (established 1891)	1	1	2	17
Finance	0	0	0	0
Light (abolished 1892)	0	0	0	0
Water	0	0	0	0
Board of Public Interests[2]	0	0	0	0
Improvement of James River[3]	0	0	0	0
St. John's Cemetery (white, inactive)	0	0	0	0

Sources: Richmond Common Council, Minutes; Board of Aldermen, Journal; *Rules of the Board of Aldermen and Common Council of the City of Richmond* (1887); Richmond *Planet*; Richmond *Dispatch*.

Committee members were chosen by the president of each chamber, a majority from the larger common council, and thus aldermen appear on fewer committees. The finance chairman was a nonvoting ex officio member of all other committees.

*Of the 564 seats on the city council for both chambers that were filled by regular election from 1871 through 1896, 56 (or 10 percent) were won by blacks.

[1]One member from each ward in each chamber.

[2]Presidents appoint 2 aldermen, 3 councilmen; board elects 2 nonmembers and council 3; common council president is ex officio chairman.

[3]Presidents appoint 3 aldermen, 4 councilmen; chamber of commerce elects 7 nonmembers.

white and black asylums; and the important Committee on Retrenchment and Reform, which decided where the city budget could be cut. Blacks rarely served on the Committee on Ordinances, which drew up new laws and amended old ones. Only three blacks ever sat on the Cemetery Committee, so Negroes seldom had a spokesman to ask for the expansion or preservation of a black burying ground, or a site for a new one. Because so many blacks were among the needy, it was important to have a Negro on the Poor Committee; yet blacks rarely served on this body, as was noted by the Richmond *Planet* in 1890 when no Negro was appointed.[41]

Blacks never served on what were arguably the most powerful committees, including the all important Finance Committee, the influential Board of Public Interests, the Light and Water committees, and the James River Committee, whose members spent tens of thousands of city dollars on a hopeless cause.

The minutes of the Richmond Common Council do not reveal that black members were treated in any special way or singled out in any manner other than for committee assignments. Without knowing their identities, there are few cases in a twenty-year period where a reader would know that one member was white and another black. The exceptions were the tributes paid by the council to deceased black members. The death of Alfred L. Thornton in December 1872 was the occasion for a special meeting of the common council called by president Thomas Hicks Wynne. Three colleagues from Jackson Ward were appointed to draw up appropriate resolutions. The council voted to attend Thornton's funeral in a body and to send a copy of the adopted resolutions to his family. Alderman Josiah Crump, who was born a slave and died in February 1890, a time of hardening racial attitudes, also received a tribute from the mayor and resolutions of mourning from his fellow aldermen, who attended the funeral. In each of these instances the procedure recorded in the minutes is the same as that which followed the death of a white member or other Richmond notable.[42]

The powers that Thornton, Crump, and other blacks shared on the bicameral city council were extensive, as set forth in the city charter and ordinances. In practice they were somewhat weakened by bickering between the two chambers and by disputes between either or both of those bodies and the mayor, who ordinarily had relatively little power. The council, through its committees, chiefs, and superintendents, passed city ordinances, provided for municipal services, and supervised the employees in each office and department. There is no evidence to suggest that the black men elected to exercise these powers outwardly perceived their roles as being any different from those of whites. They each took an oath to perform the duties of their office honestly and to the best of their ability. Yet the black councilmen tried to further the interests of their constituents and the welfare of Jackson Ward, while white members tried to maintain Conservative-Democratic control of the city. Some black council members were naturally less conscientious than others, but the minutes and the white press do not reveal their involvement in any scandals, as was the case with a number of white councilmen and city officials.

The blacks on the council encountered seemingly insurmountable odds in accomplishing their goals. As both Negroes and Republicans, they were twice damned in the eyes of their colleagues; but since whites had created Jackson Ward and had thereby ensured their presence, the white majority went along with some of their requests. The blacks were tolerated into the 1890s because they had relatively little power as long as the Democrats were united, and whites outside the council simply ignored them, as have most historians of Richmond. Yet black councilmen and aldermen were crucial in achieving some aims of Afro-Americans, even though they never numbered more than seven on a forty-eight member council. The representatives of Jackson Ward were able to get the city to build a new school for blacks in the Navy Hill area, as well as a night school for children who worked during the day. They saw to it that poor blacks received fuel during the winter along with indigent whites. The streets in Jackson Ward were improved and better lighted because of their presence. Still, as a tiny minority of the council, they had little impact on white racial policies and attitudes.[43]

The black councilmen, unlike white Republican members during Reconstruction, were not inclined to be obstructionists; neither could they be, given their small number. They often split their votes; and when they did vote as a bloc, it was almost always on an issue directly affecting their constituents. In 1872, for instance, a resolution calling for a fifty-cent poll tax was passed unanimously. Forrester and Roper might well have objected, but they did not. Under this proposal, no child was to be enrolled in a city school whose father had not paid the tax for that year. The payments were to be kept in a separate account, which was to be used to defray school expenses. In the same year, however, Forrester and John Oliver voted with two whites against a measure stopping city medical payments for the poor. The motion passed twenty to four. In 1873 Forrester and Vandervall voted with their white colleagues from the ward to repeal extra tax assessments for the extension of gas and water pipes, because they thought ward residents were being unfairly charged for utilities to which they had a right of access.[44]

Black members helped to defeat a proposal to locate a new smallpox hospital in Jackson Ward in 1873, although they probably owed their success as much to white memories of the city's battle to keep the Confederacy from putting a similar facility within city limits as to their own objections about a nuisance in their ward. A later group of Negro members objected when a plan to build a city incinerator for garbage and dead animals was presented in 1890. None of the white wards wanted the smelly crematory, so the white majority placed it in Jackson, despite John Mitchell's attempts to delay action in 1891. By 1892 he was protesting the effects of the new structure on his neighborhood.[45]

Legislation that had the effect of discriminating against blacks became more common in the late 1880s. In 1886, acting on the complaint of a white grocer in the ward, the council passed an ordinance forbidding homeowners to connect their flush toilets to the city sewer system unless they had specific kinds of fixtures. Those with privies were also more closely regulated; but, as the minutes state, most white residents already had properly installed equipment, whereas most blacks did not. In 1890, over the objection of some Jackson men, including Mitchell, a law was passed requiring building permits for frame structures to be approved by the Fire Committee, unless at least two of the aldermen and three members of the common council from the ward in question approved the structure in writing. The council's action seemed to be aimed at having such structures concentrated in Jackson Ward. Mitchell apparently feared that the committee would discriminate against black contractors and prospective homeowners. Two months later he and two other ward representatives were appointed to the Fire Committee, perhaps in answer to his objection that blacks did not often sit on the body.[46]

On the other hand, black councilmen were instrumental in stopping the illegal practice of grave robbing, which was limited almost entirely to black cemeteries. Negro councilmen publicized the issue, along with editorials in the *Virginia Star*, a black Richmond newspaper. Black members also supported resolutions for special cemetery guards. In 1882 the matter came to a head when a Negro janitor at the Medical College of Virginia in Richmond and several white medical students were arrested with cadavers. The Conservative white press joked about the matter or pontificated on the necessities of medical research and training, while ignoring the fact that none of the students were black and that virtually all of the corpses they dissected were. Eventually the state worked out an agreement to furnish the chief culprits, the Medical College and the University of Virginia medical school, which had been supplied by regular nocturnal rail shipments, with unclaimed bodies from the poorhouse and city hospital. Even this plan resulted in abuses for the black inmates. In 1886 Negroes on the council also secured the end of the chain gang in Richmond; they objected to the spectacle of convicts, all black, cleaning the city's streets. Readjuster legislation had abolished the whipping post and poll tax four years earlier.[47]

In important matters affecting the good of the city as a whole, the Negro councilmen could generally be counted upon to support the views of the white majority. The deepening of the James River channel to Richmond was an important, though unsuccessful, project in the postwar city, and black members regularly voted funds for the work. They also supported appropriations for the Yorktown centennial and the visit of the president, his cabinet, and distinguished French visitors to the city.[48]

Black councilmen could even be generous toward the Confederacy. In 1889 Royal White and other blacks voted for resolutions honoring Jefferson Davis after his death and appointing Mayor James T. Ellyson to attend his funeral in New Orleans as the city's representative. In 1893 Alderman Mitchell, who repeatedly criticized devotees of the Lost Cause in his *Planet*, voted for a $4,000 appropriation to bring the Confederate president's body to Richmond for final interment. But blacks could also draw the line on support for Confederate creditors and former rebels. In 1872 John Oliver argued against paying a company that had supplied the city with salt during the war. When the council was asked to vote $10,000 to defray the expenses of a Confederate veterans organization in celebrating the cornerstone ceremony for their new building, the Jackson men refused. Five blacks on the common council joined with ten whites to defeat the motion.[49]

They might have been more agreeable if whites had not so consistently obstructed some of their most important requests. The issue of an armory for black military clubs illustrates how difficult it could be for Jackson Ward representatives to achieve their goals, even in the late eighties, at the height of their influence on the council. Numerous attempts were made to have a building erected for the First Colored Battalion of the Virginia State Militia or to have an existing building modified for them. These proposals were either summarily rejected by the white majority or, as was more often the case, pigeonholed in the Finance or Grounds and Buildings committees, only to be presented again in the next council.[50]

An armory for the First Battalion was finally erected in 1895, but it was a pitifully small structure compared with the enormous buildings paid for by the city and used by such elite white units as the Richmond Grays, Howitzers, and Light Infantry Blues. Ironically, this victory came only a year before blacks were eliminated from the common council.[51]

Jackson Ward's representatives failed in their persistent attempts to obtain a city park for their district. By the mid-1880s, as black leaders pointed out, every ward except Jackson had a tastefully decorated and landscaped park where children played and weary adults went on hot summer nights to hear band concerts. Jackson never shared in this municipal largess. The matter was discussed three times in 1884, four times in 1887 and 1888, and once in 1890. There was still no city park in a black neighborhood of 15,000 people in 1910. Jackson Ward ceased to exist as a political entity in 1903. It was gerrymandered out of existence, just as it had been created; but its spirit lives on in the newly designated National Historic District, which includes part of the old ward.[52]

Events in Virginia began to undermine black influence in the city even before it reached its peak. After the collapse of the Readjusters in 1883, the number of black voters in the state declined steadily. Only one Negro, an incumbent who had been elected in 1887, remained in the Senate after the state elections in 1889. There were only four Negroes in the House of Delegates and twenty-four Republicans in all. By 1891 no blacks and only three Republicans were in the General Assembly.[53]

Though scholars differ over the actual motivations of Conservatives and Funder Democrats, various measures enacted by them did have the effect of reducing the number of black voters in Richmond. In 1876 petty larceny was added to the list of felonies that were grounds for disfranchisement. In Richmond about one thousand blacks were disfranchised between 1870 and 1892 by conviction of petty larceny or felony, while another thousand lost the vote after being convicted of petty larceny alone in the Richmond police court. Failure to pay the poll tax, until it was repealed, or to be assessed for tax purposes was also used to deny the ballot, despite the warnings of the *Virginia Star*.[54]

The Anderson-McCormick law, passed in 1884 over the veto of

Governor Cameron and rewritten to meet a court challenge, ensured that Democrats would appoint local election officials. The stuffing of ballot boxes and other frauds became more common in the late 1880s, to the extent that "counting out" Republicans developed into a fine art.[55]

Black strength in Richmond also weakened because Negroes continued to leave the city for better opportunities elsewhere. Richmond was thus an exception to the trend in the postwar urban South. Except for the boomtown of Atlanta, it may have been the only large southern city where the percentage of the total population that was black declined before 1900. With cheap transportation by rail and water readily available, the city's blacks left for nearby northern cities. In 1870 Richmond's population was 45 percent black and in 1880 44 percent, an insignificant drop. By 1890 only 40 percent of the residents were Afro-Americans and in 1900 only 38 percent, the same proportion as in 1860. The black community also grew more slowly. Its rate of growth was 20 percent in the 1870s and 16 percent in the 1880s. In the 1890s there was an absolute decline in the number of blacks.[56]

Yet, despite restrictive legislation and a gradual decline in the size of the black population, Republican strength in Richmond persisted, and even increased, as shown by the 1888 presidential election, when Benjamin Harrison polled 6,273 votes in losing the city, more than any Republican candidate up to that time. The Democrats had to use increasingly blatant tactics to limit black voting, and the defeat of the Force Bill in 1890–91 indicated that the federal government would not interfere in southern elections. In 1891 Henrico County was finally redeemed, and a federal judge dismissed the Jackson Ward cases—a series of indictments against local Democratic officials who had been charged with conspiring to defraud voters in the contested 1888 congressional election between incumbent Democrat George D. Wise and Republican Edmund Waddill. Judge Robert M. Hughes, an editor of a Radical Republican newspaper during Reconstruction, ruled that attempts to inhibit voting, even in national elections, were not federal crimes but matters for regulation by state and local courts. The effect of the events of 1891 can be seen in the city's Republican vote for president the next year, which declined by 48 percent to 3,289.[57]

The Republicans tried to fight back with a variety of weapons, including forms filled out by blacks upon leaving the polls, certifying that they had voted the Republican ticket. Collections of such documents proved useful, as when city Republicans successfully contested the 1888 congressional election and got Waddill seated in place of Wise.[58]

215

The Walton Act of 1894, however, was designed by the Democrats to end the need for open fraud and the potential for embarrassing reversals. It called for a modified Australian ballot that served as a literacy test. The Democrats also used a new and confusing tactic, printing false names similar to those of Republican candidates on the ballots that were now supplied to all voters regardless of party. Even the best informed Republicans found it difficult to properly mark their ballots in the short time that each man was allowed in the voting booth.[59] John Mitchell thought all blacks should have the right to vote, and he approved of any method that would enable them to find the Republican candidates on a deliberately confusing ballot. But Mitchell, like John Mercer Langston, eventually sanctioned the idea of having party workers screen out uneducated and poorly dressed blacks. Illiterate voters slowed the long lines of Negroes at the polls because they were more likely to be successfully challenged by Democratic election judges. Such voters often could not mark their complicated ballots in the prescribed manner and allotted time or without the assistance of Democratic poll workers. The long lines of black voters could have been somewhat shortened if Jackson had been given an additional precinct, as was done for some white wards. But in 1890 when Clay Ward was given a fifth precinct in a surprise move by the council, Bahen and Mitchell were unable to win a fifth precinct for Jackson.[60]

As early as 1894 there were signs that Negroes would not be allowed to remain on the council much longer. After their ranks had split in 1886 over support for local option and organized labor, the Democrats began to use the caucus to avoid such damaging interparty warfare. In 1895 Democratic councilmen angered the Jackson Ward delegation by electing a new gas-works superintendent in a party caucus. Offended by such discourtesy, the Republicans boycotted council meetings in the future when they discovered the Democrats in closed session; but the whites found that they could govern without them.[61]

Republican state boss William Mahone died in October 1895, but John Mitchell and the other black councilmen did not profit from his death. In the city election of May 1896, they were at last counted out by their Democratic foes in an unusually well-organized campaign of police intimidation, delays and persistent challenges of Negro voters, and other harrassment. A lone black, incumbent Alderman Henry J. Moore, served out his four-year term and then lost his seat in 1898. For the first time in twenty-seven years, since the creation of Jackson Ward in 1871, there would be no Afro-American on the Richmond city council. The increasing militancy of leaders like Mitchell, the alliances they all had with various white Republican factions, and their demands for a proportional share of the city budget for their ward made it necessary for whites to remove them from office. Mitchell and a few others would run for council again, but campaigns and editorial protests were ineffectual. After the turn of the century Mitchell became more conservative and held an awkward position midway between that of Giles B. Jackson, a follower of Booker T. Washington, and the more strident James H. Hayes. Virginia Negroes were not finally disfranchised until the Constitutional Convention of 1901–2; but for whites and blacks in the former Confederate capital, the last vestiges of Reconstruction had been swept away in 1896.[62]

The difference between black political activity in the early years of Reconstruction and after 1870 is that rhetoric and protest characterized the earlier period, whereas political maneuver, compromise, and some substantive accomplishment in municipal government marked the later era. Blacks did not even begin to vote in Richmond until the fall of 1867 and then only on a limited basis. Carpetbaggers and scalawags often dropped black nominees from tickets and replaced them with white Republicans. By 1870 Negroes were voting regularly and in large numbers and with the creation of Jackson Ward, they successfully demanded more offices and a larger share of the patronage. They elected not only councilmen and justices of the peace, but also United States senators and representatives and at least one Virginia governor. Before July 1871 they had held no elective office in city government. After that date dozens of blacks helped to run the city, and yet the world did not end. Reconstruction in Richmond was not as "black" and the following two and a half decades as lily white as was once thought; neither did the two-party system collapse without a fight.

The black councilmen's accomplishments were relatively modest, but their limited success is a tribute to their ability as well as to the willingness of a generation of local white politicians to work with them. Few white Republicans who could serve as allies were elected from wards other than Jackson; and the Democrats rarely split, so the Jackson men had little active white support. Yet they persevered. Their activities over a 35-year period are less well known and certainly less dramatic than events of the first postwar years in which Negroes played a part; but with Afro-Americans once again on the Richmond City Council, the legacy of the first black councilmen may well prove more significant and lasting.

Notes

All newspaper citations herein are from Richmond newspapers unless specifically noted otherwise.

1. Richmond Common Council (RCC), Minutes, Apr. 17, June 19, July 13, 1871, City Clerk's Office, City Hall, Richmond. On the "Municipal War" in the spring of 1870, see the *Daily Dispatch*, especially Mar. 17 to May 31, 1870. The best account by a contemporary is John S. Wise, *The Lion's Skin* (New York: Doubleday, Page & Co., 1905), pp. 271–83; see also Jack P. Maddex, Jr., *The Virginia Conservatives, 1867–1879* (Chapel Hill: University of North Carolina Press, 1970), pp. 89–90; Howard N. Rabinowitz, *Race Relations in the Urban South, 1865–1890* (New York: Oxford University Press, 1978), pp. 267, 275–77. Most of the black councilmen are listed in Luther P. Jackson, *Negro Officeholders in Virginia, 1865–1895* (Norfolk: Guide Quality Press, 1945), p. 57–58.

2. Samuel Mordecai, *Virginia, Especially Richmond, in By-Gone Days* (2d ed.,1860; reprint ed., Richmond: Dietz Press, 1946), pp. 121, 222; Mary Wingfield Scott, *Houses of Old Richmond* (Richmond: Valentine Museum, 1941), pp. 28–29, 43; id., *Old Richmond Neighborhoods* (Richmond: Valentine Museum, 1950), pp. 223, 255–57, 267; *Office Map of the City of Richmond* (Richmond: J. F. Z. Caracristi, 1873); *Map of Richmond, Manchester, and Suburbs* (Richmond: F. W. Beers, 1877). Following the long established precedent of naming wards after national figures, the new ward's name was probably intended to honor Andrew Jackson, who would have been acceptable to both southerners and Unionists. Confederate Richmonders may have thought otherwise, and an argument could be made for Stonewall Jackson. Neither man is mentioned in the minutes, perhaps in a deliberate bit of ambiguity. Nor is there contemporary evidence that the ward was named for Giles B. Jackson, a young black supposedly befriended by Ulysses S. Grant during the Civil War. Giles Jackson was prominent by the 1890s as a businessman and attorney. He testified before Congress in 1923, as a very old man, that Grant had indeed named the ward for him, though not while he was president. The story has been repeated in various secondary sources; but the ward was created during Grant's first term. Jackson is listed as twenty-seven in June 1880. See U.S., Bureau of the Census, Manuscript Census Schedules, Population, 1880, Virginia, Henrico County, City of Richmond, Jackson Ward, 1st Precinct, p. 29; U.S., Congress, House, "Statement of Mr. Giles B. Jackson," in *To Create a Negro Industrial Commission*, 67th Cong., 4th sess., 1923, H. Rept. 2895, ser. 46, Jan. 25, 1923 (Washington, D.C.: Government Printing Office, 1923), pp. 3, 7; William P. Burrell, *Twenty-Five Years History of the Grand Fountain of the United Order of True Reformers, 1881–1905* (Richmond: Grand Fountain, 1909), p. 47; New York *Times*, Jan. 27, 1980, "Virginia Capital's Jackson Ward: Change in a Historic Black Area."

3. *Daily Dispatch*, June 19, 1867, Nov. 1, 1884; RCC, Minutes, Dec. 30, 1867, May 9, 1870, Apr. 21, 1871; U.S., Bureau of Census, *Compendium of the Eleventh Census, 1890* (Washington, D.C.: Government Printing Office, 1896), pt. 1:742–43; Ann Field Alexander, "Black Protest in the New South:

John Mitchell, Jr., (1863–1929) and the Richmond *Planet"* (Ph.D. diss., Duke University, 1973), pp. 193–94.

4. Alexander, "Black Protest," pp. 194–96.

5. William D. Henderson, *The Unredeemed City: Reconstruction in Petersburg, Virginia, 1865–1874* (Washington, D.C.: University Press of America, 1977), pp. 205–6, 225–31, 233–40, 270–71; Robert F. Engs, *Freedom's First Generation: Black Hampton, Virginia, 1861–1895* (Philadelphia: University of Pennsylvania Press, 1979), pp. 192–98; Alexander, "Black Protest," p. 245; *Planet*, June 13, 1891; Clarence A. Bacote, "William Finch, Negro Councilman," *Journal of Negro History* 40 (Oct. 1955):352, 364; Eugene J. Watts, "Black Political Progress in Atlanta: 1868–1895," *Journal of Negro History* 59 (July 1974):268–86; Rabinowitz, *Race Relations*, pp. 265–66, 329–30; W. Dean Burnham, ed., *Presidential Ballots, 1836–1892* (Baltimore: Johns Hopkins Press, 1955), pp. 822–23, 826–27, 838–43.

6. "Independents" (editorial), *Daily Dispatch*, Nov. 5, 1874; Leon Fink, " 'Irrespective of Party, Color or Social Standing': The Knights of Labor and Opposition Politics in Richmond, Virginia," *Labor History* 19 (Sum. 1978):325–49. The years 1878–79 were exceptions to Republican hegemony in Jackson Ward; see *Daily Dispatch*, May 23–24, 1878; Rabinowitz, *Race Relations*, pp. 324–25.

7. Dr. C. A. Bryce, "Good Old Days When Jackson Ward Was a Political Battleground," *Times-Dispatch*, May 8, 1921.

8. RCC, Minutes, July 1, 6, 1874.

9. Thomas Eugene Walton, "The Negro in Richmond, 1880–1890" (M.A. thesis, Howard University, 1950), pp. 47–59; Peter Rachleff, "Black, White, and Gray: The Rise and Decline of Working Class Activity in Richmond, Va., 1865–1890" (M.A. thesis, University of Pittsburgh, 1976), pp. 152–53.

10. On Oliver, see Manuscript Census Schedules, 1870, Madison Ward, p. 297; ibid., 1880, Jackson Ward, p. 48; Engs, *Freedom's First Generation,* pp. 33, 48–49, 63–64, 91. On the orators, see Jackson, *Negro Officeholders,* pp. 9, 25; *Daily Dispatch*, Apr. 18, July 27, Oct. 15, 1867; May 7, June 7, 25, Nov. 22, 1869; and Leslie Winston Smith, "Richmond during Presidential Reconstruction, 1865–1867" (Ph.D. diss., University of Virginia, 1974), pp. 141–44. On Scott, see Manuscript Census Schedules, 1880, Jackson Ward, p. 15; *Daily Dispatch*, Dec. 13, 1866; May 8, July 24, 1867; Apr. 7, 1868. On Brooks, see *Daily Dispatch*, Oct. 1, 1867; Luther Porter Jackson, *Free Negro Labor and Property Holding in Virginia, 1830–1860* (New York: D. Appleton-Century Co., 1942), p. 77n; Smith, "Presidential Reconstruction," pp. 144–45. When Giles B. Jackson tried to speak at a celebration of the Fifteenth Amendment on April 20, 1877, he was hooted down and chased away by a black crowd; see Rachleff, "Black, White, and Gray," p. 153. On Dungee, see Richmond *State*, Nov. 10, 1876; a former Republican, he and his family were chased out of town after he supported the Democrats in the presidential election. On Jasper, see Edwin Archer Randolph, *The Life of Rev. John Jasper* (Richmond: R. T. Hill, 1884); or Richard Ellsworth Day, *Rhapsody in Black* (Valley Forge: Judson Press, 1953). On Cook, see Smith, "Presidential Reconstruction," pp. 139–40; *Daily Dispatch*, Mar. 14, 1866; Jackson, *Free Negro Labor*, p. 151n; and John Thomas O'Brien, Jr., "From Bondage to Citizenship: The Rich-

mond Black Community, 1865–1867" (Ph.D. diss., University of Rochester, 1975), pp. 164, 426, passim.

11. Herbert Tobias Ezekiel, *Recollections of a Virginia Newspaperman* (Richmond: H. T. Ezekiel, 1920), pp. 86–89.

12. In addition to Thornton, who was born in 1802, and Forrester, Johnson, and Vandervall, all of whom were born in the 1820s, John Oliver is listed as thirty-seven years old, Manuscript Census Schedules, 1870, p. 297, and as sixty-five years old, ibid., 1880, Jackson Ward, p. 48. Since Oliver was still active as a teacher and trustee at the Moore Street Industrial School in the 1890s, the age given in 1870 is probably more accurate.

13. RCC, Minutes; *Daily Dispatch; Gillis's Directory, 1871–72; Chataigne's Directory, 1881;* C. Vann Woodward, *Origins of the New South, 1877–1913* (Baton Rouge: Louisiana State University Press, 1951), p. 151.

14. On Higgins, see Manuscript Census Schedules, 1870, Jefferson Ward, p. 205; *News Leader*, July 21, 1906.

15. RCC, Minutes, Feb. 24, May 27, 1873; Mar. 25, 1890; Feb. 1, Mar. 22, 1886; Dec. 19, 1872; Alexander, "Black Protest," pp. 206–7; *Planet*, May 24, 31, 1890; May 7, 28, 1892; May 19, 26, 1894.

16. Manuscript Census Schedules, 1880, Jackson Ward, p. 37; ibid., 1900, Jackson Ward, p. 4909B, 3–105–3; *Chataigne's Directory, 1891.*

17. Those listed as illiterate were Brown, Jeter, Moore, and White. Manuscript Census Schedules, 1870, Jefferson Ward, p. 331, for Jeter; Clay Ward, p. 14, for White; 1900, p. 3180, 3–101–A, for Brown; p. 3959, 136A, 3–102–17, for Moore.

18. Jackson, *Negro Officeholders*, p. 57; O'Brien, "Black Community," p. 324.

19. Manuscript Census Schedules, 1870, Jefferson Ward, pp. 84, 119, 151; Monroe Ward, pp. 66, 88; Clay Ward, p. 24.

20. Ibid., 1900, Jackson Ward, pp. 238A, 267B, 4909B, 6156BH, 3959, 3189.

21. Ibid., 1880, Jackson Ward, pp. 62, 76; *Chataigne's Directory, 1881.*

22. Manuscript Census Schedules, 1880, Jackson Ward, p. 47; RCC, Minutes, May 28, 1892; *Planet*, May 28, 1892, May 19, 1894; Alexander, "Black Protest," p. 264; *Daily Dispatch*, Oct. 1, 9, 1867; June 5, 9, 25, 1869.

23. Charles E. Wynes, *Race Relations in Virginia, 1870–1902* (Charlottesville: University of Virginia Press, 1961), p. 9; *Daily Dispatch*, May 4, 1867; Alexander, "Black Protest," pp. 77, 122–25, 203–4, 218, 369.

24. Alexander, "Black Protest," passim.

25. RCC, Minutes, Aug. 6, Dec. 3, 1888.

26. Alexander, "Black Protest," esp. chs. 5–6, pp. 185–266; see also August Meier, "Negro Class Structure and Ideology in the Age of Booker T. Washington," *Phylon* 23 (Fall 1962):258–66.

27. Alexander, "Black Protest," pp. 24–37.

28. Ibid., pp. 67, 84–97.

29. Ibid., pp. 185–87.

30. Ibid., pp. 190–91, 196–97, 232–33, 239–44.

31. *Planet*, May 24, 31, June 7, 1890.

32. Alexander, "Black Protest," pp. 217–19, 253–58; on Allan, see *Daily Dispatch*, Aug. 14, 1869; and William T. Alderson, Jr., "The Influence of Mil-

itary Rule and the Freedmen's Bureau on Reconstruction in Virginia, 1865–1870" (Ph.D. diss., Vanderbilt University, 1952), pp. 111–12, 198–99. For figures reflecting Richmond's decline as a port, see the reports of the harbormaster; *Daily Dispatch,* Jan. 1, 1871–1901; *Statistical Abstract of the United States, 1892* (Washington, D.C.: Government Printing Office, 1893); ibid., *1900* (1901).

33. Alexander, "Black Protest," pp. 258–59.

34. Manuscript Census Schedules, 1880, Jackson Ward, p. 35; Bryce, "Good Old Days"; Lyon G. Tyler, ed., *Encyclopedia of Virginia Biography,* 5 vols. (New York: Lewis Historical Publishing Co., 1915), 5:683–85.

35. Alexander, "Black Protest," pp. 201, 225–26, 259–60.

36. Ibid., p. 261; *Chataigne's Directory, 1881* and *1891,* on Gasser, Rankin, and Page. In 1875 Gasser was among the wealthiest persons in Jackson Ward; his house, store, and lots were assessed at $5,105; only fourteen residents in the ward were above the $5,000 level. See Richmond City Land Book, 1875, Jackson Ward, Virginia State Library, Richmond.

37. Alexander, "Black Protest," pp. 261–63; Fink, "Party, Color or Social Standing," pp. 334–35; cf. Rabinowitz, *Race Relations,* p. 318; and W. Asbury Christian, *Richmond: Her Past and Present* (Richmond: L. H. Jenkins, 1912), p. 398, on the position of the Rev. John Jasper on local option. On blacks and prohibition elsewhere in the South, see Hanes Walton, Jr., and James E. Taylor, "Blacks and the Southern Prohibition Movement," *Phylon* 22 (Fall 1971): 247–59.

38. Alexander, "Black Protest," pp. 246–51.

39. Ibid., pp. 252–53.

40. Ibid., pp. 212, 253–54; *Daily Dispatch,* Jan. 1, 1890; RCC, Minutes, Jan. 3, Mar. 7, 1887.

41. *Planet,* July 12, 1890.

42. RCC, Minutes, Dec. 19, 1872; *Planet,* Feb. 22, 1890; Alexander, "Black Protest," pp. 206–7

43. Jackson, *Negro Officeholders,* pp. 83–84; RCC, Minutes, Apr. 1, 1889.

44. RCC, Minutes, Apr. 8, Aug. 15, Nov. 25, Dec. 9, 1872.

45. Ibid., June 9, 23, 1873; Feb. 3, Sept. 1, 1890; Alexander, "Black Protest," pp. 212–13.

46. RCC, Minutes, Sept. 6, 1886; May 5, 1890.

47. *Daily Dispatch,* Dec. 1, 1886, Jan. 21, 1888; *Weekly Dispatch,* Jan. 9, 1880; *Virginia Star,* Dec. 16, 1882; RCC, Minutes, Feb. 1, 1886; Wynes, *Race Relations in Virginia,* pp. 22–25.

48. RCC, Minutes, Apr. 4, July 21, 1881.

49. Ibid., Sept. 5, 1887, Dec. 9, 1889.

50. Ibid., May 26, 1882; Feb. 5, 1883; Sept. 7, 1885; Feb. 2, Sept. 6, 1886; Dec. 5, 1887; Jan. 3, Feb. 6, May 7, Sept. 3, 1888; Dec. 2, 1889; Mar. 3, 1890.

51. See Paul S. Dulaney, *The Architecture of Historic Richmond* (Charlottesville: University Press of Virginia, 1968), pp. 104, 111, for pictures of two white armories and the First Battalion armory. See also Christian, *Richmond,* pp. 371, 442; and John A. Cutchins, *A Famous Command: The Richmond Light Infantry Blues* (Richmond: Garrett & Massie, 1934), pp. 209–10, 214.

52. RCC, Minutes, Apr. 7, May 5, Aug. 4, 1884; June 6, July 5, Sept. 5, Oct. 3, 1887; Jan. 3, June 7, Aug. 6, Sept. 3, 1888; Apr. 1, 1889; Apr. 7, 1890;

Andrew Buni, *The Negro in Virginia Politics, 1902–1965* (Charlottesville: University Press of Virginia, 1967), pp. 24–25.

53. Wynes, *Race Relations in Virginia*, pp. 42, 49.

54. Many whites in Richmond were also disfranchised by such legislation. For the argument that these measures were not aimed specifically at blacks, see Robert R. Jones, "James L. Kemper and the Virginia Redeemers Face the Race Question," *Journal of Southern History* 38 (Aug. 1972):393–414; and Ralph Clipman McDanel, *The Virginia Constitutional Convention of 1901–02* (1912; reprint ed., New York: Da Capo Press, 1972), p. 28. But see also Wynes, *Race Relations in Virginia*, pp. 24–25, 45–46, 136; Rachleff, "Black, White, and Gray," p. 158; and James Hugo Johnston, "The Participation of Negroes in the Government of Virginia from 1877 to 1888," *Journal of Negro History* 14 (July 1929):264–66. An undated and unidentified newspaper clipping, with the report of the auditor for public accounts for 1873, listing capitation tax delinquents, states that of 6,186 registered black voters in the city, 5,483 had not paid the tax. See George W. Bagby Scrapbooks, sec. 36, Virginia Historical Society, Richmond. The editor of the *Virginia Star*, May 11, 1878, appealed to his readers to pay the tax and described the complicated procedure.

55. McDanel, *Constitutional Convention*, p. 28; Wynes, *Race Relations in Virginia*, pp. 39–42.

56. *Compendium of Eleventh Census, 1890*, 1:742–43; Reynolds Farley, "The Urbanization of Negroes in the United States," *Journal of Social History* 1 (Spr. 1968):241–58.

57. Alexander, "Black Protest," pp. 237–38, 244–46; Burnham, *Presidential Ballots*, p. 843.

58. Alexander, "Black Protest," pp. 202, 221.

59. Ibid., pp. 197–99.

60. Ibid., pp. 199–203; *Planet*, Jan. 14, 1890.

61. Fink, "Party, Color or Social Standing"; see also Melton Alonza McLaurin, *The Knights of Labor in the South* (Westport, Conn.: Greenwood Press, 1978), pp. 41–42, 48–50, 86–91, 135, 143–47; Kenneth Kann, "The Knights of Labor and the Southern Black Worker," *Labor History* 18 (Win. 1977): 49–70; and Sidney H. Kessler, "The Organization of Negroes in the Knights of Labor," *Journal of Negro History* 37 (July 1952):248–76; Alexander, "Black Protest," pp. 213–15.

62. Alexander, "Black Protest," pp. 263–66, 300–317.

Thomas C. Holt 9

Negro State Legislators in South Carolina during Reconstruction

Rᴇᴄᴏɴsᴛʀᴜᴄᴛɪᴏɴ ᴡᴀs "a frightful experiment which never could have given a real statesman who learned or knew the facts the smallest hope of success."[1] Daniel H. Chamberlain, the last Republican governor of South Carolina, wrote this post-mortem a quarter of a century after he had been driven from office by a violent and fraudulent campaign to restore native whites to power in the fall and winter of 1876–77. Undoubtedly his view was colored by the social milieu of America at the turn of the century, when racism of the most virulent type had become the intellectual orthodoxy. On the other hand, these later reflections do not differ much from his assessment just two months after he had been forced to relinquish his office. In June 1877 he explained to William Lloyd Garrison that "defeat was inevitable under the circumstances of time and place which surrounded me. I mean here exactly that the uneducated negro was too weak, no matter what his numbers, to cope with the whites." In later years he described that weakness more explicitly: blacks were "an aggregation of ignorance and inexperience and incapacity."[2]

The story of Reconstruction in South Carolina and elsewhere has been considerably revised since Chamberlain presented his analysis of its failure; yet, his basic premise is still shared by many revisionists. "The failure of the Radical government . . . was due not so much to its organization as to its personnel," Francis B. Simkins and Robert H. Woody wrote in 1932.[3] Given the armed support of the federal establishment and the overwhelming black majority in South Carolina, the failure of the Republican regime could only have been caused by the venality, ignorance, and corruption of the leadership. Northern adventurers, mediocre scalawags, and uneducated, "excitable" freedmen constituted a legislature so guilty of mismanagement and fraud that the white minority rose up in justifiable wrath to put it down. Simkins and Woody were more charitable to the achievements of the Reconstruction regime than Chamberlain, but they leave little doubt that the inexperienced, undisciplined ex-slaves were the weak link in the Republican coalition.

While Simkins and Woody read the supposed incapacities of the slave into the failures of Reconstruction, a recent revisionist history of slavery reverses the process: the failures of the postemancipation political order help confirm a controversial description of the slave regime. Eugene Genovese, in *Roll, Jordan, Roll*, evokes a seminal, sometimes brilliant picture of the slave's worldview; but the essence of his argument is that that worldview was conditioned by a basically paternalistic master-slave relationship. Furthermore, the long-term consequence of that paternalism on blacks was to transform "elements of personal dependency into a sense of collective weakness." Although the slaves were able to manipulate the masters' paternalism in ways that reaffirmed their individual manhood, "they could not grasp their collective strength as a people and act like political men." This "political paralysis," this absence of "a stern collective discipline," not only accounts for their failure to mount significant slave revolts or to take advantage of their masters' strategic weakness to strike for freedom during the Civil War, but also explains their failure to "organize themselves more effectively in politics" after the war.[4] In short, the behavior of the freedman confirms the conditioning of the slave.

But it is difficult to reconcile any of these views with events in South Carolina during Reconstruction. Certainly the cause of its failure cannot be laid to the political incapacity and inexperience of the black masses. They were uneducated. They were inexperienced. But they overcame these obstacles to forge a formidable political majority in the state that had led the South into secession. During the Reconstruction era 60 percent of South Carolina's population was black. This popular majority was turned into a functioning political majority as soon as Reconstruction legislation was put into effect with the registration for the constitutional convention in 1867. Despite violence and economic intimidation, the black electorate grew rather than declined between 1868 and 1876. The only effective political opposition before the election of 1876 came from so-called reform tickets, especially in 1870 and 1874. On these occasions, black and white Republican dissidents fused with Democrats to challenge the regular Republican party. But the strength of these challenges was generally confined to the predominantly white up-country counties and Charleston with its large white plurality and freeborn Negro bourgeoisie. Indeed, many observers condemned the unflinching, "blind" allegiance of black Republicans as evidence of their lack of political sophistication. But given the political alternatives and the records of so-called reform and fusion candidates, the black electorate could just as easily be credited with a high degree of political savvy. For South Carolina certainly, Frederick Douglass was right: the Republican party—despite its weaknesses and inadequacies—was the deck, all else the sea.

In an era when primaries were almost unknown and the nomination of party candidates was subject to manipulation by various intraparty factions, the voters had little leverage on the selection of their political leadership beyond the general election. It is difficult, therefore, to discern the political thinking and preferences of the masses of voters in any systematic fashion. However, one revealing report from an army chaplain just after the first election of Reconstruction offers some clues to the newly formed political mind of the ex-slaves. Chaplain F. K. Noble's literacy class for enlisted men of the 128th United States Colored Troop in Beaufort was polled on the advisability of immediate suffrage for illiterates. While "the more intelligent" favored a literacy qualification for voters, he observed, "those who learned less easily were in favor of immediate suffrage."

> One of the speakers—a black thick-lipped orator—commenced his speech as follows: "De chaplain say we can learn to read in short time. Now dat may be so with dem who are mo'heady. God hasn't made all of us alike. P'raps some *will* get an eddication in a little while. *I knows de next generation will.* But we'se a downtrodden people. We hasn't had no chance at all. De most uf us are slow and dull. We has bin kept down a *hundred years* and I tink it will take a *hundred years to get us back agin.* Dere fo' Mr. Chaplain, I tink we better not wait for eddication."[5]

Despite efforts by some of their elected leaders to include literacy and poll-tax qualifications for suffrage in the new constitution, the 1868 Constitutional Convention vindicated the views of Chaplain Noble's class by bestowing the right to vote on all male citizens of the state.

Activities other than partisan politics also demonstrate the freedmen's capacity for collective political action. For example, in the lowland rice-growing areas, cash-poor planters instituted a system wherein their workers were paid in scrip rather than currency. The scrip or "checks" could be redeemed only at designated stores in exchange for goods priced significantly above normal retail items. Although the legislature made some attempts in 1872 and again in 1875 to reform and control the system, its essential features remained unchanged: the workers exchanged low-paid labor for high-priced goods. Since their political representatives appeared to be unable to correct this problem, in July 1876 the workers took matters into their own hands. They struck. The strike was widespread and involved considerable violence against nonstrikers. Governor Chamberlain sent in the militia and had the strike leaders jailed. He also sent Negro Congressman Robert Smalls to convince the strikers to renounce violence and concede scabs their right to work. Smalls reported to the governor that he had succeeded in his mission, but subsequent reports of continued violence suggest that the right-to-work principle was attended more in the breach than in the observance. Eventually the planters capitulated and abolished the scrips system.[6]

There had been earlier efforts to organize black laborers. In 1869 South Carolina workers organized to send delegates to the National Colored Labor Convention in Washington, D.C., and to pressure the state's General Assembly for changes favorable to workers' rights in agriculture and the trades. However, in this instance, it is less clear to what extent the freeborn bourgeoisie, rather than ex-slaves, and politicians, rather than workers, initiated and controlled the agitation.[7]

Thus it is difficult to see how freeborn whites could have utilized the political system to fulfill their aspirations and to satisfy their needs—given its inherent limitations—any more more effectively than did the black ex-slaves. They identified and articulated their needs quite clearly and forcefully: they wanted land, economic justice, and education. They shrewdly discerned the organized political force most favorable to their objectives, the regular Republican party. They supported that party faithfully, despite the constant threat and reality of violence and economic reprisals. Whatever lessons their paternalistic masters had tried to instill did not paralyze them politically nor rob them of collective will. The black ex-slaves of South Carolina were, and acted as, political men.

Ultimately the failures of South Carolina Republicans must be laid not to their black ex-slave constituents but to the party leadership. Thus Simkins and Woody are partly right when they blame the personnel of the South Carolina government, but they are wrong to the extent that they find venality, corruption, ignorance, and inexperience as the primary causal factors. Surely there were venal men. Clearly corruption was rife. But there were corrupt Democrats before, during, and after Reconstruction, including the architects of the Democratic campaign of 1876, Martin W. Gary and M. C. Butler.[8] Republican corruption merely offered a propagandistic advantage in the Democratic efforts to discredit the Radical regime. With the possible exception of the land-commission frauds, corruption was secondary to the major failures of that regime while in office and to its ability to sustain office.[9]

SOUTH CAROLINA REPUBLICAN LEGISLATORS, 1868
Library of Congress

TABLE 1: *Membership of House of Representatives and Senate, 1868–76*

SESSION	68 SPEC.	68–69	69–70	70–71	71–72	72–73	73 SPEC.	73–74	74–75	75–76
HOUSE										
Democrats	15	14	15	14	10	21	20	21	34	34
White Republicans	34	33	32	35	35	23	25	25	20	18
Negro Republicans TOTAL	$\frac{75}{124}$	$\frac{74}{121}$	$\frac{76}{123}$	$\frac{77}{126}$	$\frac{75}{120}$	$\frac{81}{125}$	$\frac{80}{125}$	$\frac{80}{126}$	$\frac{70}{124}$	$\frac{71}{123}$
SENATE										
Democrats	6	6	6	5	5	8	8	8	8	8
White Republicans	15	15	14	15	15	9	9	10	8	8
Negro Republicans TOTAL	$\frac{10}{31}$	$\frac{10}{31}$	$\frac{11}{31}$	$\frac{12}{32}$	$\frac{12}{32}$	$\frac{16}{33}$	$\frac{16}{33}$	$\frac{15}{33}$	$\frac{17}{33}$	$\frac{17}{33}$

Source: Reprinted from Thomas Holt, *Black over White: Negro Political Leadership in South Carolina during Reconstruction* (Urbana: University of Illinois Press, 1977), p. 97.

These figures represent persons who actually served; consequently, vacancies and contested elections caused variations in the total membership from session to session. There were 124 seats in the House throughout the period; the increases in Senate membership reflect the admission of new counties in 1870 and 1872.

Very likely native whites viewed the fact that blacks wielded political power as itself a form of corruption of governmental process.

South Carolina was unique among American state governments in that blacks enjoyed control over the legislature and many other political entities. Of the 487 men elected to various state and federal offices between 1867 and 1876, 255 were black. While it is true that they never succeeded in elevating any of their number to the U.S. Senate, they did fill nine of the state's fifteen congressional terms between 1870 and 1876, including four of the five seats available from 1870 to 1874. J. J. Wright was elected to one of the three positions on the state supreme court in 1870, which he held until 1877. However, no black was ever even nominated for the governorship, and all of the circuit judges, comptrollers general, attorneys general, and superintendents of education during this period were white. Only a handful of blacks served in the important county offices of sheriff, auditor, treasurer, probate judge, and clerk of court. More commonly blacks were elected to such local offices as school commissioner and trial justice; but even among these they were not a majority.[10]

Clearly blacks enjoyed their greatest power in the General Assembly. Their membership averaged from just over one-third during the first five sessions of the Senate to about one-half during the last five; but in the House of Representatives they were never less than 56 percent of the membership. (See Table 1.) More important than their membership was their growing control of key committees and leadership posts in both branches of the General Assembly. Samuel J. Lee became the first black Speaker of the House in 1872; he was succeeded by Robert B. Elliott from 1874 to 1876. The president pro tem of the Senate was a black after 1872, as was the lieutenant governor, who presided over that body. Better than two-thirds of the respective committee chairmanships were held by blacks in the House after 1870 and in the Senate after 1872. Furthermore, in both houses the key committees—those controlling money bills or the flow of major legislation—generally had black chairmen.

Little wonder then that former slaveholders viewed the new order with alarm. Indeed, the displaced local whites often became hysterical in their denunciations of the new order. For example, when William J. Whipper was elected to a judgeship in the important Charleston circuit, the *News and Courier* ran a banner headline declaring its "Civilization In Peril." As a deliberate Republican policy, the judicial system had been kept inviolately white and conservative. The election of a black radical to fill one of the most important of these posts was the first step toward the creation of "an African dominion," indeed "a new Liberia." Here, as elsewhere in the South, to involve blacks in the political process was "to Africanize" the social system.[11]

The biographical profile of the Negro leadership justifies neither the fears of white contemporaries nor the charges of many historians of that era. While the overwhelming majority of their constituents were black, illiterate, and propertyless ex-slave farmworkers, most of the political leadership was literate, a significant number had been free before the Civil War, many were owners of property, and most were employed in skilled or professional occupations after the war. At least one in four of the 255 Negroes elected to state and federal offices between 1868 and 1876 were of free origins. Indeed, counting only those for whom information is available, one finds that almost 40 percent had been free before the Civil War. Of those whose educational attainments are known, 87 percent were literate, and the 25 identifiable illiterates approximately matched the number who had college or professional training. Information on property ownership is available for little more than half the legislators.[12] Seventy-six percent of these men possessed either real or taxable personal property, and 27 percent of them were worth $1,000 or more. Indeed, one in four held over $1,000 in real property alone. (See Table 2.)

Among both ex-slaves and legislators of free origin whose prewar occupations can be identified, artisans were the most numerous group. The numbers of common laborers, fieldhands, and domestics were far fewer than among the Negro population as a whole. After the war the largest proportion took up professional occupations, mostly teaching and preaching. Farmworkers composed the second largest group, but 60 percent of these owned their farms. Better than 1 in 5 remained in skilled trades, especially carpentry and tailoring. However, there were significant occupational discontinuities between legislators of free origin and those who were formerly slaves. About 70 percent of the former were employed in professions, most of them as teachers, as compared with only 24 percent of the ex-slaves, who were mostly preachers. Only 9 of the 64 leaders of free origin whose occupations are known were farmers, and just 2 were tenants. Thirty-eight percent of the 90 ex-slaves worked on farms, 12 of them as tenants. About equal proportions of both groups (21 and 24 percent) were skilled tradesmen. (See Table 3.)

These occupational differences reflect other variations in the antebellum backgrounds of ex-slaves and those who had been free before the war. Despite various legal regulations and economic harassment

230

TABLE 2: Biographical Summary of Negro Legislators, 1868–76

		COLOR			EDUCATION			
---	BLACK	MULATTO	UNKNOWN	ILLITERATE	LITERATE	COMMON	PROFESSIONAL	UNKNOWN
Free	65	23	37	5	2	22	20	18	3
Slave	105	63	33	9	14	69	8	4	10
Unknown	85	17	8	60	9	22	7	2	45
Totals	255	103	78	74	25	113	35	24	58

		REAL PROPERTY			PERSONAL PROPERTY			
---	NONE	UNDER $1,000	$1,000 AND OVER	UNKNOWN	NONE	UNDER $1,000	$1,000 AND OVER	UNKNOWN
Free	65	11	17	17	20	12	20	9	24
Slave	105	35	23	17	30	25	46	7	27
Unknown	85	12	10	2	61	6	16	0	63
Totals	255	58	50	36	111	43	82	16	114

Source: This summary is drawn from Holt, *Black over White*, appendix A.

TABLE 3: *Primary Postwar Occupations of Negro Legislators, 1868-76*

OCCUPATION	SLAVE	FREE	MISSING DATA	TOTALS
Professional				
Lawyers	1	8	1	10
Doctors	0	1	0	1
Teachers	4	17	3	24
Ministers	17	9	6	32
Others	1	3	3	7
TOTALS	23	38	13	74
Agricultural				
Farm Owners	18	6	11	35
Tenants	12	2	1	15
Others	5	1	1	7
TOTALS	35	9	13	57
Artisan				
Blacksmiths	3	0	1	4
Carpenters	8	2	2	12
Tailors	0	7	1	8
Masons	2	1	1	4
Others	9	4	1	14
TOTALS	22	14	6	42
Other				
Merchants	4	2	2	8
Laborers	6	1	2	9
TOTALS	10	3	4	17

Source: Reprinted from Holt, *Black over White*; p. 39.

during the antebellum period, many free Negroes had been able to acquire impressive educations and property. Only 3 percent of the free-born legislators were illiterate and 29 percent had acquired education or training beyond the common-school level; at least 14 percent of the ex-slaves were illiterate and only 4 percent had gotten better than a grade-school education. Legislators of free origin were more likely to own property (76 percent versus 53 percent) or to come from propertied families. William McKinlay, who represented Charleston in the 1868 Constitutional Convention and in the House of Representatives from 1868 to 1870, was probably the wealthiest of the Negro politicians with $15,320 in taxable real estate in 1860. The McKinlay family—which included McKinlay's son and fellow representative William J.—paid taxes on real property worth $40,000 during the 1870s. Other free-born legislators had more modest holdings. Henry Jacobs of Fairfield owned $1,200 in real property and personal items worth $2,500 in 1860. Although Thaddeus K. Sasportas and Florian Henry Frost, who were still in their twenties when elected to the House, owned little property, they were both scions of property-holding families. Joseph Sasportas owned $6,700 in real property in 1860, and Henry Maine and Lydia Frost left their son an estate worth $2,000 in the mid-1870s. While these sums were not particularly impressive to South Carolina's white ruling class, they mark a considerable gap between the ex-slaves and their freeborn colleagues. The median financial worth was $1,100 for the 45 legislators of free origins, but only $300 for the 75 ex-slaves.

Nevertheless, the freedmen moved very aggressively to close the gap between themselves and their freeborn colleagues. Several of them took advantage of schools established by missionary societies, the Freedmen's Bureau, and the army after the war. Others may have emulated Robert Smalls, who hired a tutor. They also seized various opportunities for enterprise in the postwar period. Hastings Gantt, a plantation slave in Beaufort before the war and its state representative after the war, had acquired an 84-acre farm worth $900 by 1870. He was elected president of the St. Helena Planters Society in 1871. William R. Jervay owned only the shirt on his back when he fled his owner to join the Union army; by the mid 1870s he owned a 275-acre plantation and a lucrative construction business. William Beverly Nash, a hotel porter during slavery, acquired a brick manufacturing plant after the war. It should be noted, however, that those legislators who had been employed as artisans or house servants during slavery appear to have been most successful in acquiring property after the war. In some way, then, though slaves, their occupational profiles are similar to the successful freeborn legislators.

Thus, while there were differences in their respective social and economic backgrounds, neither the freeborn nor ex-slave legislators conform to the traditional stereotype of ignorant, pennyless sharecroppers rising from cotton fields to despoil the legislature and plunder the state. In truth, most of the freeborn and many of the slaveborn were a "middle" class of artisans, small farmers, and shopkeepers located on the social spectrum somewhere between the vast majority of Negro sharecroppers and the white middle and upper classes. Indeed, because of their education, class position, and general aspirations, they were more likely to embrace than reject the petty bourgeois values of their society.

But while their political opponents have distorted the social and economic backgrounds of the Negro leadership, charges that they were politically inexperienced can scarcely be denied. Northern as well as southern blacks had few if any opportunities to gain experience in partisan politics during the antebellum period. Most could not vote in the state in which they resided, and they were unlikely to hold office in any state. In various ways, employees of the missionary societies and churches, the army, and the Freedmen's Bureau gained experience in public life and in serving and mobilizing constituents. Between 1865 and 1868 about one-fourth of the black elected officials had been affiliated with one or more of these institutions, as also had more than 37 percent of those who served in the first Republican government in 1868. But, of course, while these affiliations could help prepare men for public service, they were no substitute for direct legislative and partisan political experience.

The black legislator's lack of prior political experience was further exacerbated by the likelihood of an abbreviated service for most of their number. The high turnover in the House of Representatives suggests the volatility of that body. Only two black members, William M. Thomas of Colleton and Joseph D. Boston of Newberry, served the entire four terms of the Reconstruction period. Eight other men served three terms; but 61 percent of the 212 blacks elected to the House between 1868 and 1876 were one-term members. Only 15 of these advanced to higher elective offices in the state senate or executive branch or at the federal level. Clearly, for most of its sessions, the House of Representatives was composed of a disproportionate number of freshmen legislators.

It is difficult to evaluate the political impact of this rather high turnover in membership. Generally, a low turnover rate is evidence of significant institutionalization in a legislature that is reflected in strong party leadership and discipline.[13] Conversely the relatively weak party discipline of the South Carolina Republican party would appear to be congruent with the high turnover of its members. Certainly the evidence of intraparty dissension and weak leadership among Republican legislators is formidable by almost any standard. The index of relative cohesion developed by sociologist Stuart Rice in the 1920s provides one way of measuring unity or conflict within a party or subgroup. On the Rice scale a score of 100 indicates unanimity of the group, while a score of 0 indicates a perfect split, half of the members voting for a measure and half against it. Throughout the Reconstruction era, Democrats voted together more consistently than did Republicans. While the Democrats' average score was never less than 68, the Republicans never exceeded 50.[14]

Although the Rice index is a useful indicator of the overall performance of a political party or subgroup, it does not identify the sources of that disunity or unity. An alternative way to examine legislative voting behavior is to count how often specific pairs of legislators agreed with each other on roll-call votes. These agreement scores are superior to Rice cohesion indices to the extent that individual performances can be highlighted as well as the aggregate performances of the party or various subgroups. It is conceivable, for instance, that a small group of maverick party members would vote consistently against their party and thereby lower the aggregate cohesion score of the whole group. Thus there might be solidarity in the party as a whole which a small bloc of dissident members might obscure. Was the Republican weakness relative to the Democrats caused by a weak link within its ranks? Were the politically inexperienced freedmen that link?

Apparently they were not. A comparison of the agreement scores of the two parties in the 1876 session of the House of Representatives not only confirms the same overall pattern of Republican disunity and Democratic solidarity shown by the Rice index, but shows that pattern to be pervasive and continuous among all Republican members. The 1876 legislative session was particularly significant because it occurred in a period of clear and present danger for Republicans when the necessity for unity was self-evident. When the legislature convened in December 1875, South Carolina was one of only three southern states still under Republican control. There was every reason to expect that the violent crusade Mississippi Democrats had launched to "redeem" their state would be extended to South Carolina during the fall. If Republicans were ever to be united, the time was at hand.

Despite the obvious incentives for party unity, on "critical" roll calls the 89 Republican legislators voted with each other an average of 43.2 percent of the time as compared with 56.8 percent for the Democrats.[15] Furthermore, the party's relative weakness does not appear to have been caused by any consistent bloc of dissidents. An examination of individual pairings of legislators reveals a lack of cohesion throughout the membership; there were hardly any strong pairs among Republicans comparable to pairings among Democrats. Twenty-eight percent of all possible Democratic pairs voted together on more than 80 percent of the roll calls, while only 3.9 percent of the Republican pairs scored as high. Furthermore, only 2 pairs of Republican members (0.06 percent) agreed on 90 percent or more of the roll calls, while there were 33 such pairs (6.6 percent) among Democrats.[16] It is unlikely that the high turnover among the Republican membership is responsible for the difference between their political performance and that of the Democratic membership. The proportion of Democratic freshmen in the 1876 legislature was even greater than that of inexperienced Republicans, and veteran Republicans appear to have broken party ranks as frequently as did freshmen. The question remains then: Why were Republicans so fractious, especially when faced with the challenge of a reviving Democratic party?

Although no single bloc or segment of the Republican party was solely responsible for its weakness, there were political differences within the party that diminished its strength. Evidence suggests that the lack of party solidarity revealed on legislative roll calls reflected differences in aspirations and ideological orientations of various subgroups within the party. From the beginning of Reconstruction there had been conflict between white and Negro Republicans and between Negroes with roots in the freeborn mulatto bourgeoisie and the black ex-slaves.[17] During the early meetings between 1865 and 1868, Negro aspirations for greater representation and power clashed with white efforts to maintain political control, and the demands for universal manhood suffrage and land reform articulated by black ex-slaves did not always resonate with the policy objectives and ideological orientation of their freeborn colleagues. At the end of the Reconstruction era, such differences in interests, perceptions, and orientation still undermined party unity. The cohesion indices for all ten legislative sessions and the agreement scores for the 1876 session generally reflect these conflicts. For instance, by calculating the average number of times a given subgroup voted with other Republicans, one can uncover the breaks in the party's ranks. In 1876 the average agreement score for white Republicans was 37.3 as compared with 44.6 for Negroes. Similarly, black former slaves scored 46.9 as compared with 38.7 for mulattoes of free origin.[18] Clearly, what little political stability Republicans could lay claim to was provided not by the better educated and more experienced whites or by the brown bourgeoisie, but by the blacks of slave origin.

Internal conflict plagued Republicans outside the legislature as well. John Morris, an agent of the Republican National Committee visiting South Carolina on the eve of its first Reconstruction election, was dismayed by its vehemence. Any other state party would be doomed by the internecine warfare, he observed; only South Carolina's overwhelming black electoral majority insured a Republican victory.[19] Even at the party's founding convention in 1867, Francis Cardozo found it necessary to warn his colleagues:

236

From the unhappy state of things which has existed here in the enjoyment of this new privilege the colored find themselves divided and disunited by a variety of sentiments and feelings. Whatever may be a man's social status, whatever may be his religious views, whatever may be the state of his knowledge, if he will come with you and vote for this platform, unite with him, if it be Satan himself. (Cheers.) Let no cause of dissension, no feeling of animosity, no objection to social condition, prevent you from securing to yourselves and your children the liberty that has been committed to you.[20]

Much of the intraparty conflict to which Morris and Cardozo referred was idiosyncratic, caused by personal competition of politically ambitious men. But some of the more important disagreements reflected overtones of racial and class antagonism. This was true certainly of the rather consistent deviation in the voting behavior of white and Negro Republicans. On critical roll calls a majority of the white Republicans opposed a majority of Negroes on at least one of every three votes. From 1872 to 1874 they opposed each other on an astounding 60 percent of the critical votes. Since white legislators constituted about a fifth to a third of the Republican legislative majority, such general and continuous defections could prove devastating to the party's fortunes.

It is not surprising that white Republican legislators did not see eye to eye with their black colleagues; there was ample evidence of distrust and animosity between these segments of the party. During the early years of Reconstruction, whites actively discouraged blacks from seeking their appropriate share of offices and power. On several occasions during the first two years of Republican rule, whites tried to exclude blacks from major state executive offices, congressional seats, judgeships, and even key party leadership posts.[21] During the 1870 campaign Negroes rebelled against this policy and demanded their fair share of state and party offices. Nevertheless, during the final year of Republican rule, the party again would be split badly by the governor's effort to deny an important judicial post to William J. Whipper, a northern black lawyer.[22]

Such conflicts cannot be traced solely to racial animosities, but there is evidence that racism was a contributing factor. For example, in 1868 Franklin J. Moses, Jr., Speaker of the House and governor of the state from 1872 to 1874, advised Governor Robert K. Scott to appoint only native whites to state judicial posts.[23] In 1871 State Representative T. N. Talbert was even more explicit. "My policy," he wrote the governor, "is to get as many of the native whites of the state to unite with us as we can and try and induce Northern men to come and settle among us. There is not enough virtue and intelligence among the Blacks to conduct the government in such a way as will promote peace and prosperity."[24]

Given the nation's racial climate it is not surprising, perhaps, that tensions would develop between Negro and white Republicans or that they would often perceive policy issues differently; but there was no reason to expect that Negro legislators would be so much less cohesive among themselves than their Democratic rivals. For much of the Reconstruction period a unified Negro leadership could have dominated the legislature. Their overwhelming majority in the House together with a consistently large plurality in the Senate should have enabled Negroes, given inevitable absenteeism and defections among white Republicans and Democrats, to attain most of their major legislative objectives. But in fact Negro leaders were often at odds on legislative objectives, political policies, and ideology. Furthermore, the nature of their disunity followed a consistent pattern from the earliest political meetings and is best explained by reference to differences in their socioeconomic status and antebellum experience.

The most visible, though not necessarily most significant, divisions were between the black ex-slaves and those mulattoes who had been free before the war. The number of freeborn brown officeholders was far out of proportion to their share of the state's population, especially in the early conventions and legislative sessions, and their control of leadership positions was even more striking. In the 1868–70 House of Representatives, for example, half the committee chairmanships held by Negroes were filled by freeborn mulattoes. Between 1868 and 1876, over half the Negro state senators were drawn from this class and their average term of service was longer than that of black freedmen. Five of the seven Negroes elected to the state executive branch were freeborn brown men as well as four of the state's seven Negro congressmen.

Obviously, free brown men successfully offered themselves as prominent leaders of a predominantly black ex-slave electorate, but their very success aroused jealousy and political divisiveness within the party. In 1871 black leader Martin R. Delany complained to Frederick Douglass about mulatto dominance of patronage positions. In 1870 William H. Jones, Jr., black representative from Georgetown, publicly ridiculed Joseph H. Rainey, his mulatto rival for the state Senate, because of his extremely light complexion. State Senator William B.

Nash, a black ex-slave, once referred to his mulatto colleagues as "simply mongrels."[25]

It is misleading, however, to consider these intraracial tensions as merely a consequence of differences in skin color and antebellum origins. The fact is that among South Carolina Negroes a light complexion and free origins correlated very strongly with other indicators of bourgeois class status; mulattoes and those who had been free before the war were more likely to own property and thus to enjoy higher status than black ex-slaves, who were more likely to be propertyless. These general patterns were reflected in the General Assembly, where legislators of free origins were generally better educated than the freedmen, more likely to own property, and more likely to be employed as artisans or in a profession rather than as farmworkers. These objective differences, as minor as they might have appeared to whites, generated not only consciousness of class differences but social institutions that confirmed and reinforced those differences. The Brown Fellowship Society was one such institution. Founded in 1790, the society limited its membership to free brown men, providing them with a variety of financial services as well as social connections. At least three legislators belonged to the Brown Fellowship Society, and several others were members of social clubs with a similar orientation though less prestige.[26] Church affiliation was another indicator of status aspirations if not class position. Thomas W. Cardozo, brother of Francis L. Cardozo and a representative of the American Missionary Association in 1865, complained to his superiors that he could not "worship intelligently with the colored people [meaning black freedmen]" and urged the formation of a separate missionary church for himself and his teachers.[27] The pattern of religious affiliation among Negro legislators suggests that Cardozo's prejudices were not uncommon. Of the legislators whose religious affiliations can be identified, all but one of the freeborn were Catholic, Presbyterian, or Episcopalian, while 70 percent of the former slaves were either Methodist or Baptist.[28]

It appears that these differences in social background and status produced differing perspectives on public policy. During the 1868 Constitutional Convention, for example, black ex-slave delegates voted with other Negro delegates an average of 72 percent of the time, while freeborn mulatto delegates averaged 67.9 percent. The differences in voting behavior were more dramatic when sensitive issues of land reform and confiscation were debated. Robert C. De Large's resolution to halt the disfranchisement of ex-Confederates and the confiscation of their property was one early test of radical and conservative tendencies in the convention. Although De Large's motion was opposed by a majority of the Negro delegates, it drew its heaviest support from mulatto delegates who had been free before the war, about 40 percent of whom supported the resolution, and its heaviest opposition from those blacks who had been slaves, about 75 percent of whom opposed it.[29] Debates on whether to impose literacy and poll-tax requirements for voting reveal similar divisions. Delegates from the antebellum free class argued strenuously, though unsuccessfully, that illiterates and persons failing to pay a poll tax should not be allowed to vote.

The biographical profile of Negro delegates is far too incomplete to construct a composite index of class status for all ten legislative sessions; nevertheless, a variety of indicators reveal a consistent tendency over several sessions: the higher a member's social status the more likely was he to support conservative positions. In 1876, for example, Governor Chamberlain sponsored a series of conservative measures designed to placate and attract the support of Democrats for his gubernatorial bid. He wanted to cut funds for education, place the local school commissions in the hands of planters, eliminate the scholarship program at the state university, and reinstitute convict lease. When Chamberlain's measures came to a vote in the House, his main supporters were white Democrats and Negro legislators of high social status. Negro planters of moderate means like John Westberry, Jacob C. Allman, and Thomas Hamilton and merchants like William J. Andrews supported the governor and the Democrats on most of these measures.[30]

Undoubtedly, for many of these men their political positions reflected specific class interest. Thomas Hamilton, for example, was a rice planter in Beaufort; his view of labor issues was, as one would expect, quite different from that of most of his constituents. During the violent strike in the summer of 1876, Hamilton lectured his workers and constituents about the common interests of employers and laborers. "You complain now that you don't get enough for your labor, but would you not have greater cause of complaint if you destroy entirely their [the planters'] ability to pay you at all? I am a rice planter, and employ a certain number of hands. Now, if my work is not permitted to go on, how can I gather my crops and pay my laborers, and how can my laborers support their families: They are dependent upon their labor for support; they are not calculated for anything else; they can't get situations in stores as clerks; they can't all write, nor are they fitted for anything else. There is but one course for you to pursue, and that is

240

to labor industriously and live honestly."[31] Evidently Hamilton later recognized some affinity between his interests and those of white planters; he joined the Democratic party after the election of 1876.

For most Negro leaders, however, the differences probably resulted less from specific class interests than general differences in consciousness and modes of perception. Negro and white Republicans shared generalized, though not clearly articulated, "progressive" values and orientations. Negroes were unanimous in their support for civil rights and free public education, for example. There was also general support for expanded social services, such as mental asylums and almshouses, and for state-sponsored economic developments, such as railroad construction and phosphate mining. But as we have seen, measures to regulate the new farm-labor system and to reform land ownership, both of which were critical issues for the majority of their constituents, produced no unified positions and no effective programs from the legislators.

A closer examination of two issues, education and labor legislation, suggests the political difference that social class differences made in South Carolina. The establishment of an educational system was one of the most striking successes of the Republican regime. The system did not function as well as its founders had hoped, but its creation firmly established the principle of free public education in a state that had not had such a system before the war. It also provided the infrastructure on which later systems could be based. The freedmen enthusiastically took advantage of the new opportunity, and their leaders endorsed public schooling as a major goal of the postwar period. A resolution passed at one of the early conventions declared, "Knowledge is power."[32] Curiously, in the view of some leaders, the endorsement of education as a major objective for the new black citizens served also to set off the uneducated as degraded and unfit to participate in public life. Thus convention delegates who advocated literacy and poll-tax qualifications for suffrage, all of whom were freeborn brown men of well-to-do backgrounds, were motivated by a desire to encourage education among the masses. According to this view, uneducated adults would be encouraged to go to school to avoid disfranchisement and the poll taxes levied on registered voters would pay the costs of maintaining the school system.[33] As we have seen, the black freedmen in the convention as well as those in Chaplain Noble's class perceived the issue differently. A literacy requirement would be political suicide for a largely illiterate black electorate, so they decided they "had better not wait for eddication."

241

Despite their differences, legislators were successful in passing laws establishing schools for all. But their efforts to regulate the evolving free-labor market were much less productive. Two of the scores of bills introduced on labor subjects serve to illustrate the differing perceptions among Republicans. One, introduced by James Henderson, a Negro farmer from Newberry County, on January 8, 1870, would have established labor-contract agents to directly supervise and monitor relations between planters and workers. Several days later a substitute bill was introduced by George Lee, a Negro lawyer from Charleston. Lee's bill relied on the regular court system to settle contract disputes and gave the laborer a ninety-day lien on the crop at harvest. Thus, rather than direct state intervention to resolve labor disputes, the disputants had to assume the initiative and expense of litigation themselves. Normally the planter was better situated to undertake such risks than was the worker.[34]

Clearly, many of the legislators preferred a laissez-faire approach to regulating the labor market. John Feriter, a white native Republican, declared that the "law of supply and demand must regulate the matter"; and Reuben Tomlinson, a white northern Republican and former abolitionist, insisted, "I don't believe it is in the power of the General Assembly to do anything except to give them [farmworkers] equal rights before the law." Apparently a majority of both white and black legislators agreed with Feriter and Tomlinson; they voted for Lee's bill, which approached this laissez-faire ideal, and against Henderson's bill, which advocated state regulation. However, the minority voting for Henderson's bill included 48 percent of the ex-slaves as compared with only 11 percent of the freeborn, and 35 percent of the blacks in contrast with only 18 percent of the mulattoes. It would appear then that those whose origins were closer to the masses of the electorate saw labor problems differently than their colleagues from more privileged backgrounds.[35]

The 1876 legislative session was the last opportunity Republicans had to ensure economic justice for their constituents. Elected by a very close margin in 1874, Governor Daniel Chamberlain moved openly to build a political coalition of conservative Republicans and Democrats. His "reform" policies won general approval among Democrats. Chamberlain sought to cut government spending by reducing social services and education programs. He removed Republicans from important local offices and replaced them with Democrats. These policies won Democratic support but alienated and demoralized Republicans. J. W. Rice's despondent letter to Chamberlain protesting the appointment of several Democrats to Laurens County offices formerly held by Republicans was typical of the governor's correspondence during this period: "I am at last discouraged and thinking about resigning."[36] Generally, the party morale declined and dissension increased. During the spring of 1876, Democrats watched gleefully as Republican conventions often tottered on the brink of physical violence. As A. P. Aldrich told a cheering audience, the Democrats planned "to keep Chamberlain and some of the carpetbaggers fighting, till they eat each other up all but the tails, and that he would keep the tails jumping at each other, until Southern raised gentlemen slide into office and take the reins of government."[37]

Aldrich proved a true prophet. Both Wade Hampton, the Democratic gubernatorial candidate, and Daniel Chamberlain, the Republican, claimed victory after the November election that year, but only the Democrats possessed the unity and strength to enforce their claim. For five months there were two governments in South Carolina competing for control of the state and recognition by federal authorities. Although Republicans controlled the state house and the machinery of government, years of intraparty strife and rivalry had finally taken their toll. Unfavorable decisions by Republican-elected judges and defections and resignations of Republican officeholders weakened Chamberlain's authority, while Hampton grew more formidable as the crisis stretched from weeks into months. Hampton's unofficial militia of red-shirted gunmen imposed bloody curfews on blacks in much of the countryside, while Chamberlain's militia was disarmed and ineffective. Hampton collected $100,000 in state taxes, while Chamberlain was unable to command the allegiance of taxpayers or tax collectors.[38] By March newly elected Republican President Rutherford B. Hayes had decided already to concede the disputed elections in the South in exchange for the presidency, but it is doubtful that he could have decided otherwise in South Carolina even had he wanted to. By that time only a massive show of federal force could have saved the Republican regime; probably, such action was not politically feasible in 1877, nor is it clear that it could have been more than a temporary expedient.

The failure of South Carolina's Reconstruction then was not caused by a weak and ignorant electorate. Despite the economic threats and physical terrors of the 1876 campaign, black freedmen turned out in force and delivered a record vote to Republican candidates. True, there was "political paralysis," an absence of "stern collective discipline," and a failure of will; but these were shortcomings of the Republican leadership, not of the masses of black voters. Divisions among the leaders—between white and black and among Negroes themselves—diminished the power these voters had entrusted to them and betrayed the aspirations they had clearly articulated. The freedmen made an amazing transformation after the Civil War; slaves became political men acting forcefully to crush the most cherished illusions of their former masters. The tragedy of Reconstruction is that they received so much less than they gave.

Notes

This paper was prepared while the author was a Fellow at the Center for Advanced Study in the Behavioral Sciences at Stanford, California. I am grateful to the Center, to the National Endowment for the Humanities, and to the Andrew W. Mellon Foundation for their support.

1. Daniel H. Chamberlain, "Reconstruction in South Carolina," *Atlantic Monthly* 87 (Apr. 1901): 476.

2. Id. to William Lloyd Garrison, June 11, 1877, quoted in Walter Allen, *Governor Chamberlain's Administration in South Carolina: A Chapter of Reconstruction in the Southern States* (New York: G. P. Putnam, 1888), p. 504; id., "Reconstruction in South Carolina," p. 477.

3. Francis Butler Simkins and Robert Hilliard Woody, *South Carolina during Reconstruction* (Chapel Hill: University of North Carolina Press, 1932), pp. 112–13.

4. Eugene Genovese, *Roll, Jordan, Roll: The World the Slaves Made* (New York: Random House, 1974), pp. 149, 154.

5. F. K. Noble to George Whipple, Sept. 29, 1868, American Missionary Association (AMA) Papers, Amistad Research Center, Dillard University, New Orleans, La. (Italics in original.)

6. Thomas Holt, *Black over White: Negro Political Leadership in South Carolina during Reconstruction* (Urbana: University of Illinois Press, 1977), pp. 168–69.

7. Ibid., pp. 158–59.

8. Ibid., pp. 147–48, 195–96.

9. The major incidents of corruption involved bribes to gain favorable action on railroad legislation or election to the U.S. Senate. However, the Land Commission case involved the theft of funds appropriated to assist farm tenants acquire land. Even after the frauds were uncovered and stopped, the fund had been so depleted as to render the program ineffective. See Carol K. Bleser, *The Promised Land: The History of the South Carolina Land Commission, 1869–90* (Columbia: University of South Carolina Press, 1969), pp. 47–58.

10. For more detailed information on officeholding, see Holt, *Black over White*, ch. 5.

11. Charleston *News and Courier*, Dec. 24, 1875.

12. These percentages are based on those legislators for whom information

is available. If all 255 legislators are taken as the base, then 46 percent owned real or personal property and 33 percent owned real estate. One-fifth had taxable property valued in excess of $1,000, and 11 percent had $1,000 or more in real property alone.

13. Cf. Nelson W. Polsby, "The Institutionalization of the U.S. House of Representatives," *American Political Science Review* 62 (Mar. 1968):144–68; Morris P. Fiorina, David W. Rohde, and Peter Wissel, "Historical Change in House Turnover," in *Congress in Change: Evolution & Reform*, ed. Norman J. Ornstein (New York: Praeger, 1975).

14. The index of relative cohesion is calculated by taking the absolute difference between the percentage of a group or party present and voting who voted yea on a roll call and the percentage who voted nay. See Lee F. Anderson, Meredith W. Watts, and Allen Wilcox, *Legislative Roll-Call Analysis* (Evanston: Northwestern University Press, 1966), pp. 32–39.

15. The critical roll calls are those that were most sharply contested. William Riker's coefficient of significance was used to separate these from more routine or procedural votes. The degree of participation and closeness of outcome determine the value of the coefficient. Here all roll calls with a value above 0.39 were selected as critical; this corresponds to a situation where absenteeism was less than 25 percent among Republicans and the split was less than 2 to 1. Ibid., pp. 81–86. The average agreement score for a party or subgroup is calculated by adding the average score of each legislator and dividing by the total number of persons scored. An individual legislator's average score is determined by adding all the scores for that member with all other members (excluding scores not based on at least half the roll calls) and dividing by the total number of pairs. When two members did not vote on half the roll calls, their score is treated as zero; that is, it is not counted in the totals. Thus absenteeism poses a problem, since a common denominator (the total number of possible pairs) is used to make the averages comparable. Therefore, a member with an excessively large number of absences will have a low score. In extreme cases, such members have been excluded from the calculation. There is still an appreciable difference for individual members in the values when averages are based on differing denominators; that is, absentee effects are excluded. However, the relative performance of subgroups is the same; for instance, Democrats still score higher than Republicans, although the specific values change. For this reason I will give both sets of scores. When the absentee effect is controlled, the Republican score is 60.1 and the Democrat score is 80.2.

16. The denominators for these ratios are the total possible pairs within a given group or party. The general formula for total pairs is $N(N–1)/2$. Thus the total possible pairings among the 32 Democrats scored was 496, and among the 82 Republicans scored, 3,321.

17. See Holt, *Black over White*, pp. 16–22.

18. When absenteeism is controlled, these gaps narrow appreciably, but the relative positions remain the same. White Republicans score 58 and Negroes 61, ex-slaves score 62 and mulattoes of free origin 58.

19. John Morris to William Claflin, Sept. 14, 1868, William E. Chandler Papers, Library of Congress, Washington, D.C.

20. Charleston *Daily Courier*, Mar. 22, 1867.

21. See Holt, *Black over White*, pp. 103–8.

22. Ibid., pp. 185–89.
23. Franklin J. Moses to Robert K. Scott, Aug. 17, 1868, Governor Robert K. Scott Papers, South Carolina Archives, Columbia.
24. T. N. Talbert to Robert K. Scott, Jan. 12, 1871, ibid.
25. "Letter to Major Delany," *The Life and Writings of Frederick Douglass: Reconstruction and After*, 4 vols., ed. Philip S. Foner (New York: International Publishers, 1955), 4:279; Charleston *Daily Courier*, Apr. 4, 1870; *Beaufort Republican*, Jan. 30, 1873.
26. State representatives Robert C. De Large, William McKinlay, and Dr. Benjamin A. Boseman were members of the Brown Fellowship Society. State Senator Henry Cardozo was a member of the Bonneau Society, and Representative Charles Wilder was president of the Friendly Union Society. See Holt, *Black over White*, pp. 65–66.
27. Thomas W. Cardozo to S. Hunt, June 23, 1865, AMA Archives.
28. Information on religious affiliation was uncovered for 18 percent of the 255 legislators; 38 were former slaves and 34 were freemen.
29. Holt, *Black over White*, pp. 125–31.
30. Incomplete data makes the calculation of a precise quantitative index of social status excessively difficult if not impossible. *High status* here means that a given member can be identified as either mulatto or of free origins *and* the owner of real property or a person employed in a skilled trade or profession. *Low status* means the members are black or of slave origin and have no property or trade. Thirty members were classified as of high status and twelve as of low status.
31. *Beaufort Tribune*, Oct. 4, 1876.
32. *Proceedings of the Colored People's Convention of the State of South Carolina Held in Zion Church, Charleston, November, 1865* (Charleston: South Carolina Leader Office, 1865), p. 9.
33. *Proceedings of the Constitutional Convention of South Carolina* (Charleston: Denny & Perry, 1868), pp. 735–38, 825–35.
34. Holt, *Black over White*, pp. 162–63.
35. Ibid.
36. J. W. Rice to Daniel H. Chamberlain, Jan. 3, 1876, Governor Daniel H. Chamberlain Papers, South Carolina Archives, Columbia.
37. Samuel Jones to Chamberlain, Aug. 13, 1876, ibid.
38. Holt, *Black over White*, pp. 202–5.

III

Individual State and Local Leaders

Howard N. Rabinowitz   **10**

Holland Thompson and Black Political Participation in Montgomery, Alabama

F EW SOUTHERN CITIES during Reconstruction could match the extent and longevity of Republican rule found in Montgomery, Alabama. Between 1868 and 1875 its mayor was a Republican, and for all but two years its city council was Republican controlled. Montgomery County, likewise, was under Republican rule until 1877, and no Democrats were sent to the state legislature until the following year. Because blacks were an integral part of the Republican coalition, an examination of the role of Montgomery's black councilman and state legislator Holland Thompson reveals much about the basic issue in Reconstruction politics of the relationship between black leadership and white sponsorship. The backgrounds of Thompson and his black contemporaries in Montgomery also provide documentation of the recruitment patterns among black leaders. Finally, Thompson can be viewed as a certain type of political leader found in local government throughout the South during Reconstruction. Exploring the reasons for his success as well as the forces that restricted his further advancement can deepen our understanding of the period's social and political life.

Holland Thompson was born a slave in Alabama around 1840.[1] His parents were evidently brought from South Carolina during the 1830s by William H. Taylor, a former South Carolinian who became a wealthy planter in Montgomery County. At the end of the Civil War, Thompson still belonged to Taylor and was working as a waiter at the Madison House hotel. This must have seemed a natural position for him given his handsome appearance. No photographs of him have been located, but he was later described as a "pure African, nearly as black as they are ever made, six feet high, and with a rather good-natured expression."[2] Enjoying more freedom than most slaves, Thompson learned to read and write and was able to forge strong family ties. Although he was not legally married until August 1865 to Binah Yancey, a literate mulatto former slave of the secessionist leader William Lowndes Yancey, the couple already had a son, Holland Jr., in 1862.[3]

Thus Thompson was well prepared for a political career when emancipation came. He was physically imposing, literate, and had made a socially advantageous marriage. He also had greater financial security than did most former slaves. Whether he drew on savings he had accumulated while a slave or whether he perhaps benefited from the help of his former master is not known, but by 1866 he had opened a small grocery that soon became one of the most prosperous Negro firms in the city. As of 1870 he owned city and rural real estate worth at least $500 and personal property worth $200.[4] Slavery had prepared Thompson for postwar politics in one final important way. As a slave he had been prominent in the Negro branch of the First Baptist Church, a congregation whose more than four hundred black members far outnumbered the whites.[5] After emancipation his fellow congregants would form the core of his political base.

Once free, Thompson quickly emerged as a major political leader who urged blacks to assert their rights and claim what was rightfully theirs even if that meant acting independently of white allies. In November 1865 he was a delegate to a Negro convention in Mobile and on January 1, 1866, told an Emancipation Day rally in Montgomery that "The colored race . . . must not stand waiting for others to push them along."[6] In August 1866 he called for the summoning of a national Negro convention so that blacks could "consult upon their condition, prospects, interests and course of action." He saw the need for blacks to combat the policies of the Johnson Administration and, unlike many black leaders, placed the highest priority on making the new southern homestead law a more effective means of providing land for the freedmen.[7] Thompson's early emphasis on economic mobility and self-help continued to be a persistent theme in his speeches and letters to newspapers. Blacks, he argued in 1867, had to work industriously, educate their children, avoid whiskey, and cease "bickering among yourselves."[8] By then, however, if not earlier, Thompson realized that blacks needed the right to vote, for "In no other way can they find protection for life and property." Furthermore, there "must . . . [be] a thorough organization of all colored voters or many will not be able to cast their votes understandingly."[9]

Yet Thompson never neglected to allay white fears in order to reduce white opposition to black progress. While urging blacks to vote for the new state constitution drafted by white and black Republicans and opposed by most whites, he also spoke out against confiscation of white-owned property, asked blacks to end hard feelings toward "our conservative friends," and called only for civil and political rights, since social rights "will work [themselves] out in good time." Despite

250

FIRST COLORED BAPTIST CHURCH
Alabama Department of Archives and History, Montgomery

the fact that his recently deceased older brother Frederick had been captain of a Negro militia company, Thompson criticized such companies because they worried whites. Blacks, he said, should get a piece of land instead of a gun.[10]

Thompson's speeches and letters quickly attracted the attention of both white and black Republicans; even white Democrats were impressed. This helps account for Thompson's selection in October 1867 as one of the first two blacks to serve on the Montgomery City Court grand jury.[11] Thompson must have welcomed such recognition of his growing stature within the community, but he probably appreciated even more his increasing political influence. As leader of the Union League's Lincoln Council, an all-black political club that struggled for parity with the city's two all-white Republican clubs, he could not be ignored. In May 1867 he was chosen as a delegate to the first Union Republican State Convention. In September, at the Montgomery County convention, he won approval for his plan to nominate two northerners, two southern whites, and one Negro to serve as delegates to the state constitutional convention. Earlier he had capped his rise to political prominence by being chosen as one of the handful of blacks on the first state Republican Executive Committee.[12]

Although Thompson's public stands had gained the respect of his fellow blacks and had given him a reputation among whites as a moderate spokesman for his race, the key to his continued success in politics was the base he developed within the world of Baptist church politics. As a member of the Negro branch of the First Baptist Church, Thompson helped organize and became the first president of the First Colored Baptist Sabbath School in May 1865.[13] The following year he was one of four Negro trustees for the Negro branch who purchased two lots from the parent church for $600.[14] The break between the two congregations was completed in 1867 when Thompson joined seven hundred of his fellow congregants in founding the entirely separate First Colored Baptist Church, the cornerstone of which was laid in May 1867.[15] Thompson was chosen church clerk and continued as superintendent of the rapidly expanding sabbath school. Two years later he became president of the 180-member missionary society attached to the school. He also was instrumental in founding and organizing the Second Colored Baptist Church, which became known later as the Dexter Avenue Baptist Church and was made famous by the Reverend Martin Luther King, Jr.[16]

Thompson's involvement in church affairs transcended local boundaries. He was a member of a fifteen-man committee which summoned the first Convention of Baptist Colored Churches that met at the First Colored Baptist in December 1868. Out of that meeting came the Colored Baptist Missionary Convention of the State of Alabama. Thompson served as its corresponding secretary between 1868 and 1872, and subsequently as clerk of the executive board and treasurer. Even more significantly, for several years he was superintendent of state Negro Baptist Sunday schools, an office that is indicative of his interest in education and further expanded his network of statewide contacts. He used his position within the convention to advocate the importance not only of education but also of temperance and a Bible-based fundamentalist religion.[17] Thompson's central role in the Alabama convention was all the more remarkable because he was the only nonminister in the inner circle of leaders.[18]

Thompson's religious and educational activities brought him into contact with northern missionaries who came south after the war. At the 1869 meeting of the State Colored Baptist Convention, Thompson made a motion in support of the American Baptist Home Missionary Society of New York, of which he claimed to be an agent. The following year he called for greater dedication to educational efforts and urged closer ties with northern Baptists.[19] In these early years his interest in education and missionary work led him to cross sectarian bounds and resulted in close contact with Congregationalist missionaries of the American Missionary Association who arrived in Montgomery in 1866. In 1868 Thompson received Sunday school papers and religious tracts from the AMA and sought the help of local missionaries to get a new organ for his church. Thompson was not above mixing religion and politics as he reported in 1871 to AMA field secretary E. M. Cravath, in a letter primarily concerning the organ, that "we expect to carry the City by a long-magority [*sic*]. I am glad that New York have [*sic*] gone Republican."[20] The close ties between Thompson and the AMA were further evident in his selection as president of the Swayne School Association in 1869, a group that oversaw operations at the school founded and staffed by AMA representatives.[21]

When the Republican state legislature declared all municipal offices vacant in August 1868, Thompson's influence with white and black Republicans combined with his relatively good standing among white Democrats to make him a likely choice for one of the seats on the new city council. Over the opposition of many whites who refused to serve with a Negro, Mayor Thomas Glasscock chose Thompson, who was already a state legislator, to become one of the two black councilmen from the Fifth Ward, a heavily black ward that contained the First Colored Baptist Church.[22] This council, composed of two blacks and ten whites, served until the first municipal election open to black voters was held in December 1869. Thompson's power was evident as he became one of only three councilmen to join Mayor Glasscock in making the transition from appointed to elected officeholder. Thompson and his new black running mate from the Fifth Ward, fellow First Baptist member and state legislator Latty Williams, were elected handily, despite claims that "The white rads . . .[were] awful mad because the black rads nominated . . . [them]." Drawing on a favorable ward population base that in 1870 contained 1,429 blacks and only 1,168 whites in a city 49 percent black, Thompson and Williams gained reelection as the council's only blacks in 1871 and 1873. Republicans controlled the council for all but two years during the four terms that Thompson served and elected their mayoralty candidate every time.[23]

Thompson was never appointed to a prestigious committee and usually had to settle for the Hospital and Cemetery committees. Nevertheless he played a central role in council affairs. He was, for example, one of three members appointed to fix rates of assessment on personal property and one of two who prepared a new city code. Following the death of Mayor Glasscock, he joined the new mayor and a white councilman in drafting suitable resolutions and making arrangements for the funeral that included selection of an all-white group of pallbearers.[24]

Thompson often demonstrated his concern for blacks. He took special interest in the condition of streets in Negro areas of the city. An advocate of relief for the poor, he favored city soup kitchens and visited homes to determine eligibility for aid, a role that undoubtedly had a positive political impact. He succeeded in increasing the wages of street workers, most of whom were black, from $1 per day to $1.25 and sought to fund new tasks that would increase the numbers of workers. His dismay at the poor condition of the Negro section of the city cemetery led him to call for the creation of a new cemetery entirely for blacks, thus demonstrating a belief held by many black leaders that separate treatment should at least be equal treatment. Similarly, rather than seek desegregation of the city hospital, he sought to improve facilities for black patients there.[25]

Thompson's years on the council were most noteworthy for his interest in the composition of the police force and his concern for the development of public education. Prior to appointment of the Republican controlled council in 1868, only whites had served on Montgomery's police force. At the new council's first meeting, Thompson moved that blacks should comprise half the members of the force. He essentially got his way, as his colleagues agreed to hire five white and four black day-policemen and eight night-policemen of each race. Seeking to soften the impact of having black policemen, one of the city's most prominent native white Republicans offered a resolution that required the mayor to instruct black policemen to arrest only blacks unless called upon by other law enforcement officials to arrest whites. Thompson then moved to amend the resolution by adding that "the white policemen arrest only white parties except when called upon by the Marshal or colored policemen." Though adopted in amended form, the entire resolution restricting the powers of the police was rescinded on a motion by Thompson at the next meeting. As a result, Democratic leader James H. Clanton was soon complaining that "negro police—great black fellows—[are] leading white girls around the streets of Montgomery and locking them in jail."[26]

In subsequent years Thompson persisted in his attempt to equalize the number of blacks and whites on the police force. Often he succeeded, and even when he failed he was able to secure a relatively even division, including a ten-to-six split in December 1871, when the Democrats controlled the council. He was also instrumental in returning the force to full strength following cuts necessitated by the depression of 1873.[27] He was unable, however, to end the policy of forcing policemen to pay for their own uniforms, a burden that was unduly hard on blacks.[28] More importantly, Thompson could not prevent the eventual removal of black policemen and reversion to the whites-only policy. In 1875 the lame-duck Republican administration dropped the black policemen as part of a temporary economy move, only to have the new Redeemer council restore the positions and fill them with whites.[29]

Thompson's contributions in the field of education were more long lasting, for he helped initiate and supervise the city's system of public education. Prior to the creation of the public system, Thompson was closely identified with the private education of local Negroes. In addition to his service as superintendent of his church's Sunday school and as president of the Swayne School Association noted earlier, he was chairman of the second anniversary celebration of the founding of Negro schools in Montgomery in 1868.[30] This interest in education moved him to action in 1870 after the state board of education made the City of Montgomery a separate district, distinct from the county, and authorized the city council to appoint a school board for the racially segregated system. The council adopted Thompson's proposal that $4,000 be given to the new board of school commissioners, along with his proviso that the money be divided between the black and white schools in proportion to the number of children of each race attending.[31] Thompson's leadership role prompted his fellow councilmen to choose him as the only black member of the city's first five-man school board. When the board was increased to six members in 1871, Thompson was again chosen as the only black, as was the case the following year even though the Democrats controlled the council.[32] His presence undoubtedly helped account for the fact that throughout Reconstruction the per-pupil expenditure and conditions in the schools remained relatively equal for blacks and whites.[33]

Nevertheless Thompson's tenure was marked by controversy due to his bitter quarrel with local AMA missionaries and teachers, who had initially welcomed his prominence in educational affairs. Swayne School had become part of the new system, with the AMA providing the building free of charge and furnishing the teachers who were paid by the city; and it was expected that Thompson's close ties with the school would prove an asset. At first Thompson did not disappoint. It was he who notified the AMA workers of the council's decision to appropriate the $4,000, and he requested that the AMA send two more teachers to the city. He also sought to get Peabody Fund money to help the Negro public schools.[34] But friends and representatives of the AMA soon came to fear and resent Thompson.

The reasons for Thompson's break with the AMA are not altogether clear. Judging from reports of AMA supporters and from what is known of Thompson, religious differences were the cause. According to School Commissioner Henry M. Bush, when the school board met in September 1872 to organize schools for the year, Thompson charged that teachers were encouraging students to join the Congregational Church and to attend their sabbath school rather than his. No action was taken except to pass a resolution opposing sectarian religious influence by teachers during school hours. Bush felt that "Thompson and his church" would continue to oppose Swayne until "the church matters are settled or this sectarian influence broken down." Yet Thompson could not be ignored and Bush asked the AMA, "Can you humor his whims by sending a Baptist teacher among the ones sent?"[35] Although there is no indication that such a step was ever taken, there soon was ample evidence to suggest that such action was unnecessary.

In November 1872, the Reverend G. W. Andrews of the AMA's Congregational Church reported that opposition to his church among blacks was lessening, since "Holland Thompson is rapidly losing his influence and a more generous and liberal spirit is coming in its stead."

With evident glee, though with some trepidation, the Reverend Andrews reported a year later that "Holland Thompson has been expelled from the Baptist church cause [?] the personal use of church funds and personal obstinancy in relation to the whole matter. The Baptist Church seem [*sic*] now much happier and more united [?] and I am heartily glad of it but I fear he may get back into the church again."[36] Andrews's fears were warranted. The resilient Thompson, who had been barred from the 1872 Baptist State Convention, was back as a delegate from the First Baptist Church the following year. As if to absolve him of any guilt in financial matters, his fellow delegates, in addition to selecting him for other important offices, elected him for the first and only time to the post of treasurer.[37] But by then Thompson was no longer a member of the city school board, and while he probably played a key role in encouraging opposition to the AMA in subsequent years,[38] the loss of his position undermined his effort to challenge the organization he had evidently come to view as a rival for the religious, educational, and, perhaps, political affections of the black masses.[39]

Thompson's temporary expulsion from the First Colored Baptist Church and the evident internal dissension that preceded it no doubt were major reasons, along with unreported but probably active opposition of the AMA and its supporters, for his failure to win reelection to the school board in January 1873.[40] His weakened position within his church also must have influenced the decision of Republican slate makers not to nominate him for state legislator in November 1872 after he already had served two terms as a state representative.[41] A look at Thompson's legislative career and a discussion of Republican factionalism in Montgomery County will provide additional reasons for his surprising absence from the 1872 ticket.

Thompson was elected to the state house of representatives in February 1868 and reelected in November 1870. During both terms he was one of three blacks in the five-man Montgomery delegation.[42] Like most freshmen legislators, he moved cautiously through the first year in office, offering no bills of consequence and only one resolution and serving inauspiciously on the Military Affairs Committee. In the 1869–70 session, however, Thompson emerged as a prominent member, setting the pattern for his second term. He was active in debate, demonstrated a shrewd understanding of parliamentary maneuvers, introduced several controversial pieces of legislation, and was appointed to the prestigious Finance Committee, in addition to the Capitol and Corporations committees.[43]

Much of Thompson's activity in the legislature was typical of the behavior of all legislators, regardless of race. He introduced bills for the relief of white and black residents of Montgomery County, for the issuance of county bonds, for expediting construction of railroads in the state, and for payment of deficiencies in the Montgomery city school fund.[44] As a partisan politician, he skillfully blocked consideration of a resolution of censure against the Republican *Alabama State Journal*; and as a typically patriotic Republican, he sponsored a successful resolution to have the American flag flown daily over the capitol while the legislature was in session. Then, combining partisanship and patriotism, he led a losing effort to prevent the seating of Mobile's Alexander McKinstry, a former Confederate colonel, who only five months earlier had left the Democratic party.[45] And like many other legislators, Thompson saw no conflict of interest in challenging legislation that negatively affected his business. A grocer himself, he sought unsuccessfully to defeat a bill regulating the hours of groceries.[46]

Nevertheless, as he did in the city council, Thompson took special interest in matters directly or indirectly affecting blacks. In December 1869, he sponsored a bill establishing a savings association in Montgomery. When the bank opened as a branch of the National Freedmen's Savings and Trust Company Bank in June 1870, Thompson was one of the two blacks on its executive committee.[47] Other proposed legislation indicated Thompson's appreciation of the special problems confronting blacks as poor people. He unsuccessfully sought to establish the office of county advocate for Montgomery County to defend persons unable to hire counsel. After failing to postpone consideration of a bill to increase revenue rates in the state, Thompson offered an amendment to exclude from taxation dogs, so ubiquitous among poor blacks, and substitute diamond rings.[48] He was equally unsuccessful in trying to defeat legislation aimed at impeding the growth of black political power. He opposed an effort to require voters to vote in the precinct in which they resided and, concurrently, in the Montgomery City Council sought to water down a 1872 bill that tightened other voting requirements and procedures in Montgomery County.[49]

Like most black legislators, Thompson was especially concerned about overt racial discrimination. In 1871, for example, he requested that the Judiciary Committee be instructed to report "if it is not a violation of the Constitution . . . to arrest persons of different color for intermarrying, and if the different sections of the Code of Alabama relating to the punishment of marriages between white persons and negroes . . . are still in force in this state." With the chamber now solidly in Democratic hands, the motion was tabled by a vote of 69 to 17.[50] Thompson was no more successful in his persistent efforts to ban unequal treatment of blacks on the state's railroads. In one of his first votes in the legislature in 1868, he voted for Representative Stewart's bill to punish common carriers that discriminated among passengers. The bill carried despite opposition from many Republicans, but was blocked in the Senate. Therefore, in February 1870, Thompson shrewdly offered an amendment barring racial discrimination on railroads to a popular bill authorizing state aid for the construction of railroads. Though adopted in the House, the amendment failed to win Senate approval.[51]

In March 1871, Thompson introduced what was essentially the Stewart bill, providing penalties for "making unjust and illegal distinction, based on color, race and previous condition." The heavily Democratic chamber killed the bill, but Thompson reintroduced it in December 1871. This time he won Judiciary Committee approval for an amended version and was able to secure special consideration for the bill shortly before the session was scheduled to end. Moves to table or recommit failed, but the bill was further amended to require separate compartments for the races on all public conveyances. After additional debate and maneuvering, the words *railroad companies* replaced *common carriers*, the substitute bill as amended was adopted, and the bill was ordered to a third reading. But the delaying tactics had succeeded; the House adjourned before a vote could be taken.[52]

The *House Journal* does not indicate whether or not Thompson approved of the amendments providing for separate but equal accommodations. Given his attitude toward segregated cemeteries, hospitals, and public schools expressed as a councilman, it is likely that he did. It is not known whether Thompson believed there were potentially positive aspects to segregation or simply thought it fruitless to challenge its existence, but in the past he had sought to end the exclusion of blacks from public facilities and/or force equal treatment without demanding integration. It is therefore reasonable to conclude that he would have been satisfied with equal access rather than integration on railroad cars. Another piece of Thompson legislation considered on the same days as the common carriers bill provides further support for this assumption.

Thompson's interest in Negro education and his opposition to unequal treatment of blacks, particularly exclusion, led him in December 1871, to offer an amendment to a bill to establish a state agricultural and mechanical college at Florence, a facility meant for whites only.

259

Rather than explicitly calling for integration, Thompson's amendment required that "the same *or* equal facilities and advantages of instruction be given to all students making application at such college, whether white or colored." The amendment was tabled and the bill was subsequently passed without any mention of race. Not one to give up easily, in February 1872, Thompson sought to add a proviso to the bill requiring that "no applicant for admission . . . shall be excluded on account of race, color, or previous condition." The House adjourned before a vote could be taken. When it reconvened Thompson substituted for his original amendment one requiring the appropriations for the college "to be divided between the white and colored race in the State equally." Even this seemingly clear-cut expression of a separate but equal philosophy was handily rejected by the Democratic majority, as was Thompson's final proposal to have a board of Negro trustees administer a pro-rata share of funds for agricultural and mechanical education.[53]

Thompson had performed ably as a state legislator. He handled the mundane housekeeping chores common to all legislators, looked after the interest of his district, defended his party, and accurately reflected the desires of his primary supporters. Even such staunch Democrats as P. T. Sayre thought of Thompson as "a very respectable negro."[54] But Thompson had, no doubt, made most Democrats and many white Republicans uncomfortable with his stands in the House. He had raised the specter of miscegenation, had reminded whites of their responsibility to provide equal education for blacks, and had sought to ban racial discrimination on the state's railroads. Above all, unlike most of the black legislators, he was constantly in the forefront of the proceedings. Perhaps white Republican leaders found him a bit too pushy, and perhaps he aroused the envy of some of his fellow blacks. If so, this would have been a factor in his failure to gain renomination in 1872.

Thompson was also a victim of the persistent factionalism that dominated Montgomery and, indeed, all of Alabama Republican party affairs. This is not the place for an in-depth analysis of the Byzantine world of Montgomery Republican politics. It needs to be emphasized, however, that alliances within the local party were constantly shifting and there were few long-term associations. Carpetbaggers and scalawags were prominent in both major factions, though the latter were more conspicuous in the faction led by carpetbag U.S. Senator Willard Warner and scalawag Governor William H. Smith. Sometimes the factions were separated by issues; more often they were separated by a scramble over offices with the ins versus the outs. Whatever the causes, these factions, though led by white officeholders, had black lieutenants and depended on the masses of black voters. For the period under discussion, Thompson was associated with the more militant and pro-Negro wing led on the state level by U.S. Senator George E. Spencer, a carpetbagger from New York and Iowa, and on the local level by Paul Strobach, an Austrian immigrant who served in numerous county, state, and federal offices.[55]

Although the Montgomery Republicans had been relatively united in 1868, the obvious opportunities for political office in a city, county, and congressional district distinguished by a great excess of black over white voters soon encouraged vicious nomination fights and, eventually, competing Republican slates in the general elections. In 1870 Thompson, Latty Williams, and a third black—former city councilman Henry H. Craig—had gained the three positions on the legislative ticket assigned to blacks only after defeating a number of black challengers, including incumbent George W. Cox and the popular Hales Ellsworth. Indicative of the serious split between city and county blacks, most of the challengers were from outside the city, with Ellsworth the evident rural counterpart of the urban Thompson. The previous year, for example, Thompson and Williams, along with Peyton Finley, another important black leader, had called for a new meeting to select a delegate to a national Negro convention after Ellsworth had been chosen at the original meeting, which Thompson had not attended.[56]

In 1871 Thompson, at the height of his power, became more deeply enmeshed in factional strife as he sought to increase his political influence. In January he was a member of the Committee on Permanent Organization of the Colored Labor Convention, which recommended him for convention president. However, he encountered for the first time the formidable figure of James T. Rapier, fresh from his recent statewide campaign for secretary of state. Rapier, who was soon to be appointed assessor of internal revenue, was already on his way to becoming one of the most influential black politicians in the nation. A compromise offered by Latty Williams would have made Rapier president and Thompson vice-president, but it was tabled and a slate headed by Rapier, without Thompson, was chosen. Thompson, who could not be totally ignored, was chosen treasurer of the Alabama Negro Labor Union, which was founded at the convention. In that capacity he served under president Jere Haralson of Selma, who like Rapier later became a congressman. Nevertheless, Thompson was left off the new organization's executive committee, which included Rapier, Williams, and Henry H. Craig.[57]

Later in the year Thompson was elected chairman of one of the Republican precinct conventions that served as the first stage in the process of nominating candidates for the fall 1871 county campaign. Chosen because he was "thought to be neutral" in the fight between the Strobach faction and the one headed by sheriff Charles H. Scott and former state commissioner of industrial resources John C. Keffer, a Pennsylvania carpetbagger, Thompson proceeded to pick a committee heavily weighted with Strobach people to select delegates to the county nominating convention. The opposition forces left the convention, taking with them a new enmity toward Thompson. Three days later Thompson challenged the white Republican candidate of the Scott-Keffer wing for chairmanship of the county convention. The convention dissolved with each faction nominating its own county ticket. In November the Strobach nominees won handily.[58]

Thompson believed he had earned the right to seek his party's nomination for congressman, an office then held by white Republican Charles W. Buckley. Although Buckley, a Montgomery carpetbagger and former Freedmen's Bureau chaplain, had steered a careful course between the district's rival factions, his patronage policies and position on issues had endeared him to the Scott-Keffer wing, making him vulnerable to attack by the stronger Strobach element. This was not the first time Thompson had thought about Congress or challenging Buckley. As early as 1869 the Democratic *Montgomery Daily Advertiser* had used the presence of Congressman Buckley to taunt local Republicans. How could the party ignore the claims of "Holland Thompson . . . or any colored man of intelligence whose name is suggested as a congressional Representative from this district?" Thompson must have been making at least token moves toward a campaign, for he waited three weeks before announcing in the Republican *Alabama State Journal* that he was "*not* a candidate for Congress." Rather he urged "all good Republicans" to stand beside the regular nominees of the party "and lay aside all family quarrels," as he reminded the party of the Breckinridge-Douglas split in 1860. The following year he again wrote to the *Journal* taking himself out of consideration for that year's regular congressional election and declaring support for Buckley, thus earning a salute for his unselfish behavior from the editor, who urged other Republicans to follow Thompson's example of "selfless sacrifice."[59]

Now, in 1872, at the age of 32, with four years of experience in the state legislature and city council, a strong base among urban blacks, and factional strife irreparable, Thompson had decided the time had come to challenge for Congress. Unfortunately he faced two major obstacles—one, of course, was the incumbent Buckley; the other, a more formidable and popular member of his own Spencer-Strobach wing, James T. Rapier. Urged on by his growing self-confidence, Thompson launched unproductive attacks against both men. In the spring of 1872 he fought Rapier's selection as president of the congressional district convention called to select delegates to the Republican National Convention on the ground that Rapier could use the office to press his candidacy for Congress. The *Daily Advertiser* pointedly noted that Thompson forgot to say that he himself also had congressional aspirations, as it reported the designation of Rapier with only four dissenting votes.[60] Undeterred, Thompson set about to defeat prospective Buckley delegates to the district nominating convention. But after a Buckley slate defeated Thompson supporters in Thompson's home precinct, the *Daily Advertiser* concluded that the "carpet-bag crew . . . [was] out to destroy Thompson's influence among his people because of his independent ideas."[61] The feebleness of Thompson's effort against both men was evident at the district nominating convention where, though placed in nomination, he received no votes, as the convention became a battleground between Buckley and Rapier supporters. In the end Thompson further angered the Buckleyites by supporting his victorious fellow black faction member without regaining much of the ground he had lost with Rapier.[62]

In retrospect it is easy to see why Thompson had little chance against Rapier. As a successful planter from Lauderdale County, Rapier enjoyed far more support in the rural districts outside of Montgomery. He could also probably count on the backing of certain important Montgomery blacks, including the city's wealthiest Negro, James H. Hale.[63] And while Thompson held two important elective offices, Rapier's position as assessor of internal revenue had much greater political impact in terms of favors and patronage he could dispense. Finally, Rapier was less threatening to the white leaders of the Spencer-Strobach faction and to whites in general. In vivid contrast to the slightly younger Thompson, Rapier was a former free Negro, a mulatto, and well-educated. The fact that his stands on racial issues were more moderate than Thompson's buttressed the view that if there had to be a Negro congressman the "refined" Rapier was the man.[64]

Thompson had lost more than a congressional nomination. He had alienated key members of the two major factions of the party. At the same time, he had been taking increasingly militant stands in the state legislature. Worse still, it was already evident that he was encountering dissension within his church and opposition from northern missionaries. On the eve of the convention to nominate state legislative candidates, he was thus extremely vulnerable. It must have come as no surprise to him when he was omitted from the ticket that included his close associate Latty Williams and his old rival from within the Spencer-Strobach wing, Hales Ellsworth.[65] Thompson was nevertheless extremely bitter; and because he evidently let his feelings be known, he had to write to the *Journal* on the eve of the election in response to charges that he had called leading Republicans—including Strobach and Rapier—thieves and fools. He naturally denied the charge and advised all his friends to support the nominees of the Republican party.[66] But the fact that he spoke at none of the rallies during the campaign suggests that either he had few friends left or else he had decided to vent his displeasure through inaction.

Still a member of the city council, however, Thompson continued to use that forum effectively. Even at the lowest ebb of his fortunes in early 1873, he was popular enough to be chosen orator of the day at the annual parade and banquet of Grey Eagle No. 3, the city's only black fire company. In a flowery speech he revealed once again the power he shared with other successful black politicians to move an audience.[67] By the summer he was confident enough to announce as candidate for the vacant seat of state senator from Montgomery, while joining Latty Williams in a controversial attack on the Warner-Smith faction.[68] Nothing came of his senate bid, but that fall Thompson was reelected to his fourth term on the city council.[69]

Thompson continued to mend his fences at the church during the following year, and his political fortunes again began to rise. By the summer of 1874 he was once more at the center of Montgomery politics. In June he served on the credentials committee of the State Equal Rights Association, though it was Ellsworth and not Thompson who addressed the convention. The next month, prior to the legislative nominating conventions, Thompson edited a Republican newspaper, the *Republican Banner*, aligned with the Strobach wing and supposedly owned by blacks. As an indication of Thompson's return to the fold, he was one of three blacks nominated for the legislature on the Strobach ticket.[70] More important, in July, following the designation of Montgomery as a port of delivery in the Mobile District, Thompson was appointed deputy collector at a salary of $350 a year, the only patronage plum he ever received from the party he so ardently served. The *Daily Advertiser* correctly saw this appointment as a victory for the Strobach forces, as it noted that Thompson, in his newspaper, had thanked Senator Spencer for his efforts on his behalf.[71] Unfortunately for Thompson, the Warner-Smith faction evidently regained the ear of President Grant in December 1874, for he was replaced by a white Republican.[72]

All Thompson now had left was his council seat, and that too was soon lost. Thompson and his allies on the council had been unable to prevent a steady tightening of the voting requirements aimed at undercutting Republican strength. Even more damaging was the escalating intraparty strife that sapped the party's strength. Thus, in the May 1875 municipal election, the Democrats swept the Republicans out of every office and redeemed the city for the forces of white supremacy. The key element in the Republican defeat was the defection of an estimated 450 blacks and a number of prominent white Republican county and federal officeholders.[73]

For the first time since August 1868, Holland Thompson's Fifth Ward council seat was to be occupied by a Democrat when power officially changed hands in December 1875. What is most striking, however, is that Thompson had not even been a candidate in that memorable 1875 contest, a fact unfortunately left unexplained by the press of both parties.[74] On the face of it, such a campaign could have been expected. Thompson was still popular in his ward and, despite the stiffer voting requirements, registered black voters for the election outnumbered whites by 288 to 267. Nevertheless a citizens' meeting chose two white council candidates to join the rest of the all-white Republican council slate. Where in 1873 Thompson and Williams had received 326 and 325 votes respectively versus 221 and 214 for their Democratic opponents, their white Republican successors drew 218 each as compared to the victorious Democratic totals of 251 and 234.[75] Obviously a number of Thompson's supporters either had crossed over or simply sat out the election. Thompson did serve as one of the six ward vice-presidents of the central council of the party for the election, but there is no evidence that he actively campaigned for the ticket.[76]

Thompson was not to have any glorious last hurrah. For the years following the disastrous 1875 municipal canvass there are only two extant indications of any political activity on his part. In what evidently signaled a shift to the anti-Spencer wing, Thompson was among the signers of an August 1875 circular sent to "reliable Republicans" that blamed the party's troubles on divisions and poor leadership. And in

1876 Thompson was forced to write to the *Alabama State Journal* to deny rumors that he had sent a petition to Washington to prevent troops from coming to Montgomery.[77] Given what was happening in the city and in his ward, it is understandable why Thompson chose not to return to the political wars. Despite successes in presidential elections until 1888, local Republicans failed to capture a single municipal office after 1875. Although white Republicans ran respectable races in the Fifth Ward and occasionally in other wards as late as 1879, the percentage of black voters in the Fifth and in the city-at-large continued to decline, thanks to new legal and illegal techniques employed by the Democrats.[78]

But there was perhaps more to Thompson's political inaction than mere demographics or increased white hostility. Many of his black contemporaries remained politically active, and as late as 1876 three of them were elected to the state legislature from Montgomery County.[79] It would seem, therefore, that changes in Thompson's personal life might have played the determining role in limiting his post-1875 political participation and might even hold the key to understanding his "abdication" in 1875. First, death claimed several members of his family. In March 1873 his wife Binah died, evidently as a result of childbirth complications.[80] In 1875 his oldest son, Holland, Jr., perhaps already quite ill before the municipal election, died shortly before the fall county elections.[81] In the interim between the deaths of his wife and son, Thompson, then the father of five young children including an infant, remarried. Yet remarriage brought new personal tragedy. In 1876 an eight-month-old daughter died followed the next year by a five-month-old son. Thereafter Thompson and his new wife, Charlotte, who was only 37 in 1880, had no more children.[82] Whether this was a conscious decision brought on by the series of losses he suffered is unknown, but given the circumstances it is not unlikely. There is also the possibility that Thompson's own physical, if not mental health, had begun to fail. Perhaps the cancer that was to take his life in 1887 had already begun to affect him in the late 1870s.

Thompson's declining economic fortunes and his abandonment of statewide religious activity provide indirect support for the theory that personal factors rather than the changed political climate caused his withdrawal from politics and replacement by a new group of black leaders. As late as 1873, Thompson's house and shop on Jefferson Street were assessed at $800 and his merchandise valued at $400. By 1876 and 1877 there was only $100 worth of goods; and each year thereafter, with the exception of 1881, the value continued to fall, until in

266

the half decade before his death it was always under \$40.[83] It is unlikely that a healthy, highly motivated Thompson would have let his business suffer such a disastrous decline. Nor would he have forsaken religious politics as happened soon after the death of his infant son. Thompson was still quite active at the 1875 meeting of the State Baptist Convention, but at the 1876 meeting he made few motions; and although chairman of the Committee on Temperance, he did not address the body, held no convention office, and was no longer listed as a trustee of the Alabama Baptist Normal and Theological School (Selma University). He seemed to regain some of his old drive at the 1877 meeting, where he served on a number of committees, addressed a local sabbath school, and was again appointed general superintendent of Sunday schools for the following year. Nevertheless this proved to be only a parting flurry. Thompson was not even present at the 1878 meeting; there is no mention of him in the minutes or in the lists of executive board members, trustees of Alabama Baptist Normal and Theological School, or even of Sunday school board members. He never again attended a meeting of the convention he had helped to create and build.[84]

The 1877 Baptist meeting virtually ended Thompson's public career. In 1881 he served as vice-president of the Industrial State Fair Association (Colored) that was organizing a Negro fair. The other officers included such major leaders of the black community as Democratic editor James A. Scott and the rising star in Republican politics Charles O. Harris. In his final public appearance, Thompson gave one of the eulogies at an 1885 service held at the AMEZ Church honoring the memory of U. S. Grant.[85]

Two years later Thompson died at the age of 48. A short and partially inaccurate obituary in the Democratic *Daily Dispatch* revealed that he had spent the previous five years preaching and teaching young blacks to read and write. The only other acknowledgment of the death of the city's most important black leader of Reconstruction was a brief announcement in the *Montgomery Daily Advertiser* under the small heading "Funeral Notice": "The friends and acquaintances of Rev. Holland Thompson are requested to attend his funeral this Sunday afternoon at 3 o'clock from the First Colored Baptist Church."[86]

One might have expected at least a perfunctory obituary for a former city councilman and state legislator, but none was carried by either the paper or the *Huntsville Gazette*, the state's major black newspaper, which had a Montgomery correspondent and regularly reprinted material from no longer extant issues of Montgomery's black

267

paper *The Herald*. The State Baptist Convention, which commonly passed resolutions in memory of less prominent departed members, evidently did not even mention Thompson's passing in its minutes; and subsequent histories of the organization and of the state's Baptists merely list him as a former convention officer.[87]

No will or inventory of Thompson's estate was filed with local authorities. Although his burial location in the Negro section of the city graveyard is mentioned in the records, it is no longer possible to identify his final resting place. And where the house and grocery once stood on Jefferson Street, there is now a vacant lot, the only one on a block of late nineteenth-century houses.[88] It is as if he had never existed.

But Holland Thompson did exist, and he and other forgotten black leaders of Reconstruction deserve to be remembered both for their own personal identity and for what they tell us about a critical period in our history. Thompson was at the center of Reconstruction in Alabama and this meant being at the center of black life. In a brief period that lasted no more than ten years, he emerged from slavery to forge an impressive public career built on a close association with the basic institutions of black life—church, Freedmen's Bank, secular and religious schools, and volunteer organizations such as fire companies. He gained additional access to black voters through relief activities and the operation of his successful neighborhood grocery, traditionally a launching pad for ethnic politicians in nineteenth-century America. He reached still other blacks as a newspaper editor, powerful orator, and inveterate writer of letters to the editor. And he was constantly visible to blacks as a city councilman and state legislator.

There is, of course, no question that Thompson benefited from the sponsorship of white men like Mayor Glasscock, Paul Strobach, and Senator Spencer. One could argue, however, that he attracted attention because of his own personal qualities and, even more important, because of the bloc of black voters he commanded. Throughout the South there were black leaders who were mere puppets manipulated by white masters, but this was not the case with Thompson or numerous men like him. Neither was he, as some Democrats claimed, the force behind the throne, controlling white colleagues in a city that had been "Africanized."[89] Rather, like Atlanta's William Finch and Raleigh's James H. Harris, he was a skillful politician who, despite the desires of white Republicans and Democrats alike, insisted on putting his own advancement and the advancement of his people ahead of injunctions to keep a low profile and stay in his place.[90]

In the end, however, both the black masses and the white leaders

268

kept Thompson from rising to greater political heights. His momentary loss of power within the church that was never fully regained combined with the attractiveness of James T. Rapier to rural blacks and white Republicans and denied him any real chance to gain the congressional nomination he sought. Then the abuses of Redemption and the misfortunes of his personal life left him a political has-been at the remarkably young age of thirty-six. Here again Thompson was not unique, for a surprising number of black Reconstruction leaders throughout the South, whether because of death, disillusionment, poor health, emigration, or other interests, ended their political careers prematurely, depriving other blacks of much needed leadership.[91]

But Thompson's legacy remains today in the form of the First Colored Baptist and Dexter Avenue Baptist churches, the Alabama State Baptist Convention (black), and the Montgomery public school system. They are reminders that long before the arrival of Martin Luther King, Jr., Montgomery had strong black leadership.

Notes

The author wishes to thank the National Endowment for the Humanities and the University of New Mexico Research Allocations Committee for financial assistance during the preparation of this essay.

All newspapers cited herein are Montgomery newspapers unless specifically noted otherwise.

1. Sources differ as to the exact year of Thompson's birth. The 1870 census listed Thompson's age as 30, the 1880 census as 39, and his 1887 death certificate as 48. U.S., Bureau of the Census, Manuscript Census Schedules, Ninth Census of the United States, 1870, Population, Alabama, Montgomery County, City of Montgomery, Ward 5, p. 61; ibid., 1880, Fifth Ward, p. 59; Oakwood Cemetery, Montgomery, Ala., Record of Interments, 1876–92, pp. 427–28, Alabama Department of Archives and History (ADAH), Montgomery.

2. *Daily Advertiser*, Dec. 3, 1873, identifies Thompson's owner and wartime occupation and provides the quoted physical description. For Thompson's parents' birthplaces, see Manuscript Census Schedules, 1880, Montgomery, Fifth Ward, p. 59; for information about Taylor, see Thomas McAdory Owen, *History of Alabama and Dictionary of Alabama Biography*, 4 vols. (Chicago: S. J. Clark Publishing Co., 1921), 4:1653–54; Manuscript Census Schedules, 1860, Free Inhabitants, Alabama, Montgomery County, City of Montgomery, First Division, p. 175; ibid., Slave Inhabitants, First Division, p. 181; ibid., Productions of Agriculture, First Division, p. 17.

3. Montgomery County, Colored Marriage Licenses, bk. 1 (1865–67), p. 7,

Records Management Division, ADAH; Manuscript Census Schedules, 1870, Montgomery, Ward 5, p. 61. Identification of Binah Thompson's former owner is based on her last name and the fact that one of William Lowndes Yancey's thirty slaves in 1860 was an 18-year-old mulatto female, while ten years later Binah is identified in the 1870 census as a 28-year-old mulatto. Manuscript Census Schedules, 1860, Montgomery, Slave Inhabitants, First District, p. 126.

4. Montgomery County Tax Book 1866, supp. sec., beat 4, n.p., ADAH; 1867, p. 73; 1868, p. 41; ibid., 1869, Assessment of Taxes on Real Estate and Personal Property, 1:161; *Alabama State Journal*, July 22, 1869; Manuscript Census Schedules, 1870, Montgomery, Ward 5, p. 61. Although the 1870 tax book and Thompson's own estimate of his wealth in the 1870 census agree on the $500 and $200 figures for Thompson's urban property, the tax records also list Thompson as co-owner of 150 improved and 150 unimproved acres of rural land valued at $2,000. Although Thompson still owned the rural property as late as 1872, it had been sold by 1873. Montgomery County Tax Book, 1872, 1:53; 1873, 1:165, 266. Thompson probably did get some financial help from his master, a not uncommon occurrence in the immediate postwar years, for Thompson seems to have thought highly of Taylor. Although he took neither his former master's name, politics (Democrat), nor religion (Methodism), Thompson named his second son William H. Ironically his third son was named after prominent abolitionist Wendell Phillips. Manuscript Census Schedules, 1870, Montgomery, Ward 5, p. 61. For a discussion of surnames and naming practices among blacks, see Herbert G. Gutman, *The Black Family in Slavery and Freedom, 1750–1925* (New York: Pantheon Books, 1976), esp. pp. 185–201, 230–56. Efforts to link Thompson with the family of the famous white southern historian of the same name proved unsuccessful, and the genesis of his name remains a mystery.

5. Alabama Baptist Association, *Minutes of the Forty-First Annual Session . . . 1860 . . . and of the Bible Society . . . Held at the Same Time and Place* (Montgomery: Montgomery Mail Steam Press, 1860), n.p., microfilm, Samford University Library, Birmingham, Ala.; id., *Minutes of the Forty-Sixth Session . . . 1865* (Montgomery: Barrett's Book & Job Office, 1865), p. 19.

6. Mobile *Nationalist*, Jan. 25, 1866.

7. Holland Thompson to editor, ibid., Aug. 30, 1866. This letter, like Thompson's other early published letters, was either written by someone else or severely edited prior to publication. These letters are characterized by perfect spelling, correct sentence structure, and an elegant style; the few extant handwritten letters Thompson sent to other people during these early years, including some quoted in this essay, are characterized by poor spelling, weak sentence structure, and improper grammar. Nevertheless, the ideas expressed in the letters to editors are consistent with those found in his reported speeches and accurately reflect his thinking. Scholars of black political life during Reconstruction need to be more aware of the problems involved in the use of published letters allegedly written by blacks.

8. *Daily State Sentinel*, July 23, 1867. See also Thompson to editor, Mobile *Nationalist*, Mar. 28, 1867, and the report of one of Thompson's speeches in the *Daily State Sentinel*, July 23, 1867.

9. Thompson to editor, Mobile *Nationalist*, Mar. 7, 28, 1867. According to August Meier the black masses initially were mainly concerned about land and education, whereas their leaders gave a higher priority to enfranchisement. If this was so, Thompson was an exception, and his views reflected his close ties with the masses, perhaps as a result of his being both black and a former slave. August Meier, *Negro Thought in America 1880–1915* (Ann Arbor: University of Michigan Press, 1966), pp. 3–16, esp. pp. 5–6, 11–12.

10. *Daily State Sentinel,* July 23, 1867. For Frederick Thompson's death and brief obituary, see ibid., July 2, 1867.

11. Ibid., Oct. 7, 1867.

12. *Weekly Advertiser,* May 21, 1867; *Daily State Sentinel,* Sept. 17, June 19, 1867. For Thompson's role as leader of the Lincoln Council, see *Daily State Sentinel,* Sept. 7, 1867.

13. Alabama Baptist Association, *Minutes of the Forty-Seventh Annual Session . . . 1866* (Montgomery: Barrett & Brown, 1866), p. 20; *Alabama State Journal,* May 7, 1869.

14. Alfred Lewis Bratcher, *Eighty-Three Years: The Moving Story of Church Growth* (Montgomery: Paragon Press, 1950), p. 8.

15. Ibid., p. 7; *Daily State Sentinel,* May 31, 1867.

16. *Daily State Sentinel,* Aug. 20, 1867; *Alabama State Journal,* May 7, 1869. Thelma Austin Rice, ed., *Dexter Echo: Centennial Souvenir Program* (Montgomery: Dexter Avenue Baptist Church, 1977), pp. 3–4, 19. The First Colored Baptist Church also drew a major twentieth-century black civil-rights leader to its pulpit—Ralph David Abernathy.

17. *Alabama State Journal,* Sept. 29, 1868; Colored Baptist Missionary Convention of Alabama, *Report of the First . . . Convention . . . 1868* (Montgomery: Barrett & Brown, 1869), p. 2, microfilm, Samford University Library; id., *Report of the Second . . . Convention . . . 1869* (1869), p. 2; id., *Report of the Third . . . Convention . . . 1870* (1870), n.p., p. 6; *Report of the Fourth . . . Convention . . . 1871* (1872), p. 2; id., *Report of the Fifth . . . Convention . . . 1872* (1872), p. 2; Colored Missionary Baptist Convention of Alabama, *Minutes of the Seventh Session . . . 1874* (Mobile: Shields Co., 1875), p. 10, app.; id., *Minutes of the Tenth Session . . . 1877* (Montgomery: Smith, Allred & Beers, 1877), p. 24; Charles Octavius Boothe, *The Cyclopedia of the Colored Baptists of Alabama* (Birmingham: Alabama Publishing Co., 1895), pp. 37–40 and passim; Nathaniel Reid Stevenson, *History of Colored Baptists in Alabama: Including Facts about Many Men, Women and Events of the Denomination Based upon the Careful Study of the Highest Recognized Authority within Reach* (Gladsen, Ala., 1949), p. 37. Thompson's temperance and educational stands are found scattered throughout the Baptist Convention's published reports (called *minutes* beginning in 1873) between 1868 and 1877; but for the clearest statement of his religious philosophy, see his circular letter in defense of the statement "We believe that the Scriptures, comprising both the Old and the New Testament are the word of God; the only Rule of Faith and Practice," Colored Baptist Missionary Convention of Alabama, *Report,* 1871, pp. 17–22.

18. Although the *Daily Dispatch,* Mar. 14, 1887, claimed that Thompson spent part of his final five years preaching, there is no firm evidence that he served as a minister in the antebellum or immediate postbellum years. Thomp-

son's funeral notice referred to him as *Rev.*, as does a recent authority on Alabama Black Baptists. *Daily Advertiser*, Mar. 13, 1887; Reid, *History of Colored Baptists*, p. 37. Nevertheless, Thompson was always called *Brother* or *Bro.* rather than *Rev.* or *Dr.*; and he was never listed among the "Ordained or Licentiated Ministers" in Alabama Colored Baptist Missionary Convention (ACBMC) Reports, 1868–72; Alabama Colored Missionary Baptist Convention (ACMBC), *Minutes*, 1873–77. An earlier expert on Alabama Black Baptists and a contemporary of Thompson's always listed him as *Bro.* and failed to include him among Montgomery's former slave preachers. Boothe, *Cyclopedia of Colored Baptists*, pp. 27–28, 37–40, 57–58. See also Peter Kolchin, *First Freedom: The Responses of Alabama Blacks to Emancipation and Reconstruction* (Westport, Conn.: Greenwood Press, 1972), p. 153; Bratcher, *Eighty-Three Years*, pp. 7–9; *Daily State Sentinel*, Aug. 24, 1867; *Daily Advertiser*, May 28, 1871.

19. ACBMC, *Report . . . 1869*, p. 11; *1870*, pp. 11–12. Despite Thompson's claim to represent the American Baptist Home Missionary Society (ABHMS), the society's records do not list him as an agent. James D. Leachman, director of ABHMS, to author, Apr. 26, May 10, 1977.

20. Holland Thompson to Edward P. Smith, Sept. 30, Oct. 8, 1868; id. to E. M. Cravath, Nov. 27, 1871, microfilm, American Missionary Association (AMA) Archives, Amistad Research Center, Dillard University, New Orleans, La. See also A. B. Ackley to Edward P. Smith, June 4, 1868; T. C. Stewart to Smith, Sept. 4, 1868; Mary L. Santley to Smith, Aug. 27, 1869, ibid.

21. *Alabama State Journal*, Feb. 5, 1869.

22. *Daily Advertiser*, Aug. 8, 11–14, 1868; Montgomery City Council (MCC), Minutes, Aug. 15, 1868, ADAH. Glasscock (in some records Glascock) had previously served with Thompson on the first state Republican Executive Committee and had nominated him for secretary of the city convention that began the process of selecting delegates for the state constitutional convention. *Daily State Sentinel*, June 19, Sept. 7, 1867. The other black councilman was Henry Hunter Craig; see n. 56.

23. *Daily Advertiser*, Dec. 7, 1869; quotation, Oct. 29, 1869; Dec. 5, 1871; Dec. 2, 1873. In 1870 the city contained 5,183 blacks and 5,405 whites; the only one of the other five wards with more blacks than whites was the First Ward, where the margin was much narrower than that in the Fifth. U.S., Bureau of the Census, *Ninth Census: Population* (Washington, D.C.: Government Printing Office, 1872), 1:81. Latty (whose name appears in some records as Lattie or Laddie) Williams, was a Georgia-born mulatto and a literate former slave. Twenty-five years old in 1869, he listed no occupation in the 1870 census, but he was a prolific officeholder. Active in politics as early as May 1867, he was already a state legislator when elected to the council. He served in the legislature and council until his death from hepatitis in 1874 and was appointed to several patronage positions. *Daily State Sentinel*, May 21, July 5, Nov. 14, 1867; *Daily Advertiser*, May 9, 1869, Dec. 3, 1873; *Alabama State Journal*, June 16–17, 1874; Manuscript Census Schedules, 1870, Ward 5, p. 4; Oakwood Cemetery, Interment Record 1874–81, p. 152. By a straight party vote of 9–3, Williams was succeeded by another Georgia-born Negro, a 44-year-old mulatto barber, Alfred Billingslea. *Alabama State Journal*, June 23–24, 1874; Manuscript Census Schedules, 1870, Ward 5, p. 17. Billingslea's

selection may well have been a personal victory for Thompson, for a meeting of twenty-six ward residents had previously recommended another black, grocer Randall Chilton, for the position. During the regular 1873 election campaign, Chilton had challenged Thompson and Williams for one of the ward's council seats. *Alabama State Journal,* June 21, 1874; Sept. 19, 23, 25, Oct. 2, 14, 1873.

24. MCC, Minutes, Aug. 1, 1870, Feb. 6, 1871; *Daily Advertiser,* Sept. 24, 1870. For committee assignments, see, for example, MCC, Minutes, Dec. 21, 1869, Dec. 19, 1871; *Alabama State Journal,* Jan. 6, 1874.

25. See, for example, MCC, Minutes, Oct. 19, Nov. 2, 1868; Mar. 1, May 3, June 7, Aug. 16, 1869; Apr. 13, 1870; Feb. 12, 1872; *Daily Advertiser,* May 6, 1870, Mar. 20, 1874. For the support other black leaders gave to separate but equal facilities for blacks, see Howard N. Rabinowitz, *Race Relations in the Urban South, 1865–1890* (New York: Oxford University Press, 1978), pt. 2 and passim.

26. MCC, Minutes, Aug. 15, 24, 1868; *Daily Advertiser,* Aug. 16, 25, 26, 1868; testimony of James H. Clanton, in U.S., Congress, *Testimony Taken by the Joint Select Committee to Inquire into the Condition of Affairs in the Late Insurrectionary States,* 42d Cong., 2d sess., 1872, vol. 8, hereafter cited as KKK Hearings. Thompson, however, failed to achieve support for an effort to assign one Negro and one white policeman to each beat. *Daily Advertiser,* Aug. 25–26, 1868.

27. See, for example, MCC, Minutes, Dec. 21, 1869; May 1, 20, Dec. 19, 1871; *Alabama State Journal,* Dec. 16, 1873; *Daily Advertiser,* Dec. 16, 1873. Near the end of Democratic control of the council, however, only six of the twenty policemen were black. *Alabama State Journal,* July 31, 1873.

28. MCC, Minutes, Jan. 16, 1872.

29. *Daily Advertiser,* June 9, 15, Sept. 7, 1875; Jan. 11, 1876; Montgomery, "Report of the Committee on Police," *Annual Message of the Mayor of Montgomery and Reports for the Various City Officers and Standing Committees of the City Council for the Fiscal Year Ending April 30, 1877* (Montgomery: Barrett & Brown, 1877), p. 26.

30. ACMBC, *Report . . . 1869,* p. 26.

31. MCC, Minutes, Sept. 5, 19, 1870.

32. Ibid., Sept. 19, 1870, Jan. 2, 1871, Jan. 3, 1872.

33. *Daily Advertiser,* Sept. 8, 1871, Apr. 10, 1873; MCC, Minutes, Apr. 7, 1873.

34. Clarinda Wilkins to E. M. Cravath, Sept. 22, 1870, AMA Archives; Henry M. Bush to Cravath, Aug. 27, 1870, ibid.; Montgomery, Board of City School Commissioners, Minutes, Nov. 3, 1870, County Board of Education Building, Montgomery.

35. Bush to Cravath, Sept. 2, 1872, AMA Archives. See also J. M. McPherron, a Swayne teacher, to Cravath, Oct. 8, 1872, ibid. In 1874 Rev. G. W. Andrews, pastor of the Congregational Church associated with Swayne and the AMA, wrote Cravath that his church was thriving and that the recent addition to his congregation of three prominent former members of First Colored Baptist *"is the turning point in the history of our church."* Andrews to Cravath, May 11, 1874, ibid. (italics in original). As early as October 1870, Thompson had warned the Colored Baptist Missionary Convention of the need to have

black Baptists "take over control of our own education" rather than leaving it to others. He was probably referring to the AMA, since in the same speech he urged closer ties with northern Baptists. ACBMC, *Report . . . 1870*, pp. 11–12.

36. Andrews to Cravath, Nov. 18, 1872, Nov. 10, 1873, AMA Archives.

37. ACMBC, *Minutes . . . 1873* (Mobile: Thompson & Powers, 1874), passim; *1874*, pp. 10–11, 16–17, 19, app., and passim.

38. For black opposition to the AMA's religious and educational efforts, see, for example, Mrs. G. W. Andrews to Cravath, June 17, 1875; G. W. Andrews to M. E. Streiby, July 11, 1875; J. D. Smith to Streiby, Sept. 20, 1876, AMA Archives. For Thompson's earlier involvement in the conflict between local blacks and northern teachers in the Congregational Church, see Alice Abercrombie to Cravath, June 10, 1872, ibid.

39. Thompson's religious and educational rivalry with the AMA is quite clear. Conjecture about a political rivalry is based on the close relations between the AMA and school-board member H. M. Bush, a *"National Republican . . . [who] has never mixed in Montgomery Radicalism."* "Citizen Patrons" to editor, *Daily Advertiser,* Jan. 9, 1876 (italics in original). See also n. 56 for the tie between one of Thompson's chief black rivals and the AMA. There is, however, no evidence of direct AMA involvement in local politics.

40. MCC, Minutes, Jan. 10, 1873.

41. *Alabama State Journal,* Aug. 4, 1872.

42. *Daily Advertiser,* July 14, 1868 (although the election was held in February, the defeat of the radial constitution delayed the swearing in of victorious candidates until July), Nov. 13, 1870. Thompson is incorrectly identified as a three-term state legislator in Kolchin, *First Freedom,* p. 153. Approximately 26 other blacks served with Thompson in the first Reconstruction House and 18 in the second. There was also one Negro in the state senate. Sarah Woolfolk Wiggins, *The Scalawag in Alabama Politics, 1865–1881* (University: University of Alabama Press, 1977), pp. 147–50.

43. *Journal of the House of Representatives . . . 1868* (Montgomery: John G. Stokes, 1869), p. 24 and passim; *House Journal,* 1869–70, (1870), pp. 114–15 and passim.

44. *House Journal,* 1868, pp. 202, 278, 404, 199; 1869–70, pp. 395, 436, 465; 1870–71 (Montgomery: W. W. Screws, 1871), p. 216; 1871–72 (1872), pp. 65, 250.

45. Ibid., 1870–71, pp. 300, 262; 1869–70, pp. 165–66.

46. Ibid., 1870–71, pp. 281–82; 1871–72, p. 124.

47. Ibid., 1869–70, p. 116; *Daily Advertiser,* June 18, 19, 1870. The other black member was Henry Duncan, about whom little is known. More noteworthy because it is indicative of the interlocking nature of Reconstruction leadership in the city was the fact that the two whites on the committee were Mayor Glasscock and school-board member Henry M. Bush.

48. *House Journal,* 1871–72, p. 337; 1869–70, p. 161.

49. Ibid., 1870–71, pp. 138–39; 1871–72, pp. 47, 451–52. Cf. MCC, Minutes, Jan. 22, 1872.

50. *House Journal,* 1870-71, pp. 269–70.

51. Ibid., 1868, pp. 102–3; 1869–70, pp. 433–34.

52. Ibid., 1870–71, p. 451; 1871–72, pp. 202, 547, 549–51, 555–57.

53. Ibid., 1871–72, pp. 497–98, 551–52, 554. As of 1872 blacks were barred from the state-supported Alabama Baptist Orphans Home and the Institution for the Deaf and Dumb and Blind and lived in unequal segregated quarters at the Insane Hospital. When blacks were finally admitted on a segregated basis to the Institution for the Deaf and Dumb and Blind in 1892, a six-man Negro Advisory Board was established, a pale version of what Thompson had in mind for the agricultural college. Rabinowitz, *Race Relations in the Urban South,* pp. 135, 137, 145, 148.

54. Testimony of P. T. Sayre, in U.S., Congress, KKK Hearings, 8:357.

55. No separate study of the Montgomery Republican Party exists; however, rabid factionalism among local party members is treated as part of the larger problem of Alabama Republican intraparty conflict in Loren Schweninger, *James T. Rapier and Reconstruction* (Chicago: University of Chicago Press, 1978); Wiggins, *Scalawag in Alabama Politics*; William M. Cash, "Alabama Republicans during Reconstruction: Personal Characteristics, Motivations, and Political Activity of Party Activists, 1867–1880" (Ph.D. diss., University of Alabama, 1973). Both Republican and Democratic newspapers in Montgomery emphasized the importance of factional divisions. See esp. *Daily Advertiser,* Nov. 28, 1871; *Alabama State Journal,* Nov. 5, 1871.

56. *Weekly State Journal,* Aug. 19, 1870; *Alabama State Journal,* Dec. 5, 1868, Jan. 2, 4, 1869. Craig, like most of Montgomery's important black politicians, was a former slave. A South Carolina–born mulatto, he was the leading barber in Montgomery before the Civil War. He served an abbreviated term as city councilman, a full term as state legislator, and enjoyed a variety of patronage appointments that included doorkeeper at the 1868 Constitutional Convention, county registrar, railroad mail agent, and city tax assessor. He died in 1876 at the age of sixty. Oakwood Cemetery, Record of Interments, 1876–92, pp. 63–64; *Daily Advertiser,* May 9, 1869, Aug. 11, 1876; *Alabama State Journal,* Aug. 10, 1876; *Daily State Sentinel,* Nov. 6, 1867, Jan. 21, 1868; MCC, Minutes, June 5, 1871.

Finley, a black farmer, was born in Georgia in 1824. Elected as Montgomery's sole Negro delegate to the 1868 Constitutional Convention, he later served as the only black member of the state board of education and held a variety of local elective and patronage offices. See, for example, Manuscript Census Schedules, 1870, Montgomery County, Township 16, p. 13; *Daily State Sentinel,* Sept. 14, 1867; *Daily Advertiser,* Dec. 4, 1870; *Alabama State Journal,* June 21, 1872; Mar. 13, June 6, 1873. See also Finley's first letter to the editor, *Alabama State Journal,* Mar. 12, 1874, in which he complains about the efforts of some white men to undermine the independence of black politicians.

Hales (in some records Hale or Hailes) Ellsworth was a black farmer born in Alabama in 1820. Like Thompson he had a mulatto wife and was comparatively well off financially in 1870, with $500 in real estate and $300 in personal property. He served as chairman of the county Republican Executive Committee in 1869, was one of two directors of the county board of education in 1871, and was elected to the state legislature in 1872 and the county commission in 1874. Unlike Thompson he retained close ties with the AMA until at least as late as 1873. Manuscript Census Schedules, 1870, Montgomery

County, Township 16, p. 110; *Daily Advertiser*, Aug. 2, 1869, Mar. 7, 1871; *Alabama State Journal*, Nov. 9, 1872, Nov. 12, 1874; Hales Ellsworth to E. M. Cravath, Jan. 8, Sept. 5, 1873, AMA Archives. For evidence of the split between rural and urban Republican blacks, see *Daily Advertiser*, Jan. 15, Feb. 24, 1874; *Alabama State Journal*, Dec. 19, 30, 1873. Somewhat later the correspondent of the Watertown (N.Y.) *Times* visited the city and wrote, "The city darkey and the country darkey are frequently on bad terms." Reprinted in *Daily Advertiser*, Mar. 24, 1880.

57. *Weekly State Journal*, Jan. 6, 1871.

58. *Daily Advertiser*, Aug. 6, 9, Nov. 8, 1871; quotation, Aug. 6, 1871.

59. Thompson to *Alabama State Journal*, May 25, 1869; id. to *Weekly State Journal*, Aug. 26, 1870 (italics in original); *Daily Advertiser*, May 8, 1869. See also *Daily Advertiser*, Aug. 21, 1870.

60. *Daily Advertiser*, May 16, 1872.

61. Ibid., July 28, 1872; quotation, July 29, 1872.

62. *Alabama State Journal*, Aug. 20, 1872; Thompson to editor, ibid., Aug 28, 1872.

63. Evidently a former slave, James Hale was born in South Carolina in 1830. By 1870 he was a prosperous carpenter with $2,500 in real estate and $400 in personal property. Along with Rapier, he was one of a few mulattoes among the predominantly black Negro leadership of Montgomery. There is no direct evidence of Hale's support for Rapier; but in 1870 Rapier lived with the Hale family and subsequently was active in emigration efforts with William H. Ash, who was identified as Hale's son-in-law in the 1880 census. Manuscript Census Schedules, 1870, Montgomery, Ward 4, p. 41; 1880, p. 23; *Weekly Advance*, Sept. 11, 1880; Rabinowitz, *Race Relations in the Urban South*, pp. 87, 94, 143, 249.

64. Schweninger, *James T. Rapier*, passim, esp. pp. 37–150.

65. *Alabama State Journal*, Aug. 4, 1872.

66. Thompson to editor, ibid., Oct. 29, 1872.

67. Ibid., May 24, 1873.

68. Ibid., Aug. 26, 1873. In a letter to the Mobile *Watchman*, Williams attacked Republican treatment of black politicians. The Democratic *Daily Advertiser* publicized the letter and used it to needle Republicans, especially the *Alabama State Journal*, about their neglect of black rights. The *Journal* editor and the black opponents of Williams used the *Journal* pages to condemn Williams for character assassination and for helping the Democrats. See, for example, *Daily Advertiser*, Sept. 5, 7, 20, 1873; *Alabama State Journal*, Sept. 6–10, 12–14, 23, 25, 1873. Although this was primarily Williams's fight, the *Journal*, Sept. 7, 1873, alluded to Thompson's support for Williams's views without actually naming him.

69. *Alabama State Journal*, Dec. 6, 1873. Williams was reelected along with Thompson despite efforts of their opponents to deny at least one of them renomination. "Voter" to editor, ibid., Sept. 25, 1873; "Peeping from the Watchtower" to editor, ibid., Oct. 2, 1873; ibid., Sept. 19, Oct. 5, 1873. Earlier the *Journal* editor and his supporters had been unable to prevent the unanimous election of Williams as chairman of the city's central council of the Republican party.

70. *Alabama State Journal*, June 26, 1874; *Daily Advertiser*, July 14, 16, 23,

28, 1874. Thompson resigned from the ticket after receiving a federal appointment. By this time the Strobach forces had become the minority wing of the local party, thanks to the defection of several white county officials led by Patrick Robinson, Strobach's old ally. The alliance of Robinson and longtime Strobach opponents gave them an overwhelming majority in nominating meetings and enabled their choices to be designated the regular Republican candidates. Prominent among the "regular" Republicans was Hales Ellsworth, who was elected treasurer of the new county Republican Executive Committee. The regulars received more votes in the November elections than the Democrats and the Strobach Republicans combined. *Alabama State Journal,* June 3, July 26, 29, Sept. 3, 11, Nov. 12, 1874. Both a cause and result of the rift between Strobach and Robinson was the indictment of county officials by a Strobach-controlled grand jury, which included Holland Thompson. *Alabama State Journal,* May 12, 1874. For fights between blacks belonging to the Strobach and Robinson factions, see *Daily Advertiser,* Sept. 29, 1874.

71. *Daily Advertiser,* Aug. 6, 1874, reported Thompson's appointment as deputy collector but incorrectly stated that Montgomery had been made a port of entry and gave Thompson's salary as $1,500, the figure Congress had set as the maximum for the position. (I want to thank William F. Sherman of the National Archives for providing me with the correct information.) Thompson was given the added responsibility of distributing relief supplies to victims of flooding in his district. Ordinarily this could be viewed as another patronage position, but he was given the job because "He is a gov[ernment] officer and would do it without pay." C. C. Sheets, Deputy Collectors Office, 2d Dist., U.S. Internal Revenue Service, to Gov. David Lewis, July 13, 1874, Alabama Governor's Correspondence, David Peter Lewis, Gen. Corres., July-Sept. 1874, ADAH; see also *Daily Advertiser,* Jan. 30, 1875, for a largely favorable assessment of the way in which Thompson performed his duties. The only other patronage matter I have found involving Thompson is an 1882 petition from sixty-five blacks asking for Thompson's appointment as collector of internal revenue for the Second Collection District of Alabama. Collector of Internal Revenue Applications, Holland Thompson, Alabama, Second District, 1882, Record Group 56, National Archives. (I want to thank Michael Les Benedict for bringing this petition to my attention.) This effort on Thompson's behalf was probably part of a broader effort to remove James T. Rapier from the position. Schweninger, *James T. Rapier,* pp. 173–75. Considering the abundance of federal, state, and local patronage given to other local black politicians, it is especially surprising that the party so inadequately rewarded Thompson. The neglect was perhaps due to his independent ideas, but it also may have been in response to Thompson's own desires. His thriving grocery business and family responsibilities, for example, precluded acceptance of such typical jobs as railroad mail agent. Financially, he didn't need jobs as much as others did, especially when most positions were minor ones that would have nevertheless left him beholden to party leaders. This is, of course, speculation; but it is a reminder that we need to know much more about the handling of grass-roots patronage during Reconstruction, especially as it affected the relationship between whites and competing groups of blacks.

72. *Daily Advertiser,* Jan. 5, 1875; William F. Sherman to author, Aug. 8, 1979. The Warner-Smith faction was most likely responsible for Thompson's

replacement, but two letters by Paul Strobach contain tantalizing suggestions (without mentioning him) that Thompson may have been a victim of Senator Spencer's efforts to attract white support from the opposite wing of the party; his hypothesis is given further support by Thompson's later break with Spencer. Strobach to William E. Chandler, May 7, 14, 1875, William E. Chandler Papers, Library of Congress. (I am grateful to Michael Les Benedict for mentioning these letters to me.)

73. *Daily Advertiser*, Feb. 20, 28, Apr. 26, May 5–6, 1875; *Alabama State Journal*, May 5, 1875. Although the election was held in May, victorious candidates did not take office until the usual time in December. This unprecedented move was evidently aimed at taking advantage of the momentum established by the November 1874 redemption of the state government and at preventing potential black voters from meeting the stiffer residency requirements. For charges of Democrats buying Negro registration slips and using economic intimidation, see *Alabama State Journal*, Apr. 7–8, 14, 1875; *Daily Advertiser*, Apr. 28, 1875.

74. *Alabama State Journal*, Apr. 30, 1875, claimed that no Negro was seeking office; and the only one who had even announced for an office had allegedly been promised an appointive position by the Democrats.

75. *Daily Advertiser*, Apr. 26, May 5, 1875; *Alabama State Journal*, Apr. 13, 1875.

76. *Alabama State Journal*, Apr. 3, 7, 1875.

77. *Daily Advertiser*, Aug. 22, 1875; Thompson to editor, *Alabama State Journal*, Sept. 15, 1876. Joining Thompson as signers of the circular were Patrick Robinson and Hales Ellsworth.

78. *Daily Advertiser*, Nov. 8, 12, 1876; Apr. 8, 29, May 2, 3, 1877; Aug. 6, 11, 1878; May 7, 1879; Aug. 8, Nov. 3, 10, 1880; Apr. 8, 1883; Nov. 5, 11, 1884; Nov. 7, 1888.

79. Ibid., Aug. 8, 1876. The three blacks were H. V. Cashin, C. O. Harris, and Captain Gilmer. Further evidence of continued Radical strength was the vote on holding what would be a Redeemer-controlled constitutional convention; Montgomery County returned a 3,380 vote majority against the convention, the second largest margin among the fourteen counties that opposed it. Ibid., Aug. 20, 1875.

80. Oakwood Cemetery, Record of Interments, Card 854, Mar. 6, 1873, Sexton's Office, Montgomery City Cemetery. No cause of death was mentioned, but the 1880 census lists Thompson as having a daughter named Binah, age seven. Manuscript Census Schedules, 1880, Montgomery, Fifth Ward, p. 59. A Montgomery AMA worker reported to her superior that "Mrs. H. Thompson has died quite suddenly since you were here." E. C. Ayer to E. M. Cravath, Mar. 18, 1873, AMA Archives.

81. Oakwood Cemetery, Interment Register, 1874–81, p. 136, ADAH.

82. Ibid., 1876–92, pp. 413–14; Manuscript Census Schedules, 1880, Montgomery, Fifth Ward, p. 59. Thompson probably remarried around 1875, but a search of Montgomery County marriage licenses between 1872 and 1880 revealed no certificate. It is likely that the new Mrs. Thompson was from another county, where the marriage took place. It is also possible that participation in the Alabama Colored Missionary Baptist Convention brought the couple to-

gether. See ACMBC, *Minutes . . . 1874*, p. 9; Boothe, *Cyclopedia of Colored Baptists*, p. 48.

83. See, for example, Montgomery County, Tax Books: 1871, 1:48; 1872, 1:53; 1873, 1:165; 1875, 1:78; 1876, 1:90; 1877, 1:103; 1878, 1:108; 1881, 1:174; 1882, 1:163; 1885, 1:153; 1887, 1:228.

84. Colored Missionary Baptist Convention of Alabama, *Minutes of the Eighth Annual Session . . . 1875* (Mobile: Henry Farrow & Co., n.d.), pp. 6, 8–9, 11–12; id., *Minutes of the Ninth Annual Session . . . 1876* (Montgomery: Advertiser Book & Job Office, 1877), pp. 14–15, 17, 19; id., *Minutes of the Tenth Annual Session . . . 1877* (1878), pp. 7, 11, 15, 18, 24, 33. One of the three delegates from the First Colored Baptist Church at the 1878 session was William Thompson, who was probably Holland's son. If he was, his presence rather than his father's provides further evidence that illness and/or personal problems cut short Thompson's public carrer. Id., *Minutes of the Eleventh Annual Session . . . 1878* (Selma: Jas. S. Jacob, 1879), p. 5.

85. *Advance*, Sept. 3, 1881; *Huntsville [Ala.] Gazette*, Aug. 15, 1885. Charles O. Harris also gave one of the Grant eulogies. Harris was a Georgia-born mulatto who was listed in the 1880 census as a school teacher. Though only twenty-seven years old in that year, he had already established himself as Montgomery's most important Negro politician along with his close friend Hershel V. Cashin. Harris was educated at Oberlin and Howard University, served as assistant enrolling clerk in the General Assembly between 1870 and 1874, was secretary of the city Republican central council for the 1875 election, and was elected to the state legislature in 1876. In 1885 he served as superintendent of mail carriers under Postmaster Charles W. Buckley and in 1890 as chairman of the county Republican Executive Committee. Manuscript Census Schedules, 1880, Montgomery County, Elan Beat, p. 22; *Weekly State Journal*, July 8, 1870; John W. Beverly, *History of Alabama* (Montgomery, 1901), pp. 204–5; *Alabama State Journal*, Apr. 7, 1875; *Daily Advertiser*, Aug. 8, 1876; June 13, 1880; Sept. 1, 2, 1885; Aug. 3, 1890. Like his friend Harris, H. V. Cashin was a Georgia-born mulatto. He was the same age as Harris but was a lawyer rather than a teacher. Because he came from the city and Harris lived in the country, their alliance eliminated much of the political competition between urban and rural blacks. Elected to the legislature in 1874 and 1876, Cashin was president of the Republican party's central council for the 1875 election and enjoyed several postoffice patronage jobs. As early as April 1875, he and Harris were identified by the Democratic *Advertiser* as Montgomery's two most important black politicans. Manuscript Census Schedules, 1880, Montgomery, Fourth Ward, p. 70; *Alabama State Journal*, Nov. 12, 1874, Apr. 7, 1875; *Daily Advertiser*, Apr. 29, 1875, Aug. 8, 1876; *Huntsville Gazette*, Jan. 12, July 12, 1884, Apr. 9, 1887. For Scott, see Rabinowitz, *Race Relations in the Urban South*, pp. 232, 301–2, 307.

86. *Daily Dispatch*, Mar. 14, 1887; *Daily Advertiser*, Mar. 13, 1887.

87. See, for example, *Huntsville Gazette*, Mar. 12, 19, 26, Apr. 2, 9, 1887; Boothe, *Cyclopedia of Colored Baptists*, pp. 55–57 and passim; Reid, *History of Colored Baptists*, passim. Unfortunately the Baptist convention minutes are no longer available for 1887; however, no mention of Thompson's passing was made in the detailed extracts from the minutes in Boothe's compilation;

neither was there any reference in the 1888 minutes. It is possible that Boothe may have borne Thompson some personal animosity and therefore refused to immortalize his contribution. Thompson's political contribution has been equally unappreciated by succeeding generations of Montgomery blacks. The chapter on politics in a commemorative history of the city's black community fails to mention Thompson's service as councilman, gives incorrect dates for his terms in the legislature, and erroneously reports that he ran for alderman as a Democrat in 1882, a year in which there wasn't even a municipal election. J. M. Brittain, "The Negro in Politics," in *A Century of Negro Progress in Montgomery City and County: Centennial Edition 1863–1963,* ed. B. S. Thompson, Sr. (Montgomery: Centennial Celebration, 1963), p. 18.

88. Oakwood Cemetery, Record of Interments, 1876–92, pp. 427–28. The following records for the relevant years, all located in the Montgomery County Court House, contain no reference to Thompson's death: Montgomery County Will Books; Executor's Record; Administrator's Record; Probate Court Record; Estate Files.

89. For example, following the Republican victory in the 1873 municipal campaign, the *Daily Advertiser,* Dec. 2, 1873, announced: "For the next two years the city Administration will be completely in the hands of the African Party, with none to check their doings. . . . Beyond doubt, while Messrs. Faber and Hughes [mayor and city clerk], and certain white men are given position, Holland Thompson and Laddie Williams are the overseers of the white gang!"

90. Clarence A. Bacote, "William Finch, Negro Councilman, and Political Activities in Atlanta during Early Reconstruction," *Journal of Negro History* 40 (Jan. 1955):341–64; ch. 12 of this study; Rabinowitz, *Race Relations in the Urban South,* pp. 145, 166, 174, 221, 264, 265, 277, 286, 313, 316, 403.

91. See, for example, Thomas Holt, *Black over White: Negro Political Leadership in South Carolina during Reconstruction* (Urbana: University of Illinois Press, 1977), pp. 38, 218–19; William C. Harris, "James Lynch: Black Leader in Southern Reconstruction," *Historian* 34 (Nov. 1971):40–61; Schweninger, *James T. Rapier;* Peggy Lamson, *The Glorious Failure: Black Congressman Robert Brown Elliott and the Reconstruction in South Carolina* (New York: W. W. Norton & Co., 1973); Joe M. Richardson, "Jonathan C. Gibbs: Florida's Only Negro Cabinet Member," *Florida Historical Quarterly* 42 (Apr. 1964):363–68.

Joseph P. Reidy   **11**

Aaron A. Bradley: Voice of Black Labor in the Georgia Lowcountry

A VAST LITERATURE describes the antebellum adventures of runaway slaves; but for a variety of reasons, little information survives on the later lives of most. Least, comparatively, is known about fugitives who returned south after the war. Such repatriates brought with them wide varieties of experience, borne of their bids for freedom, their travels, and their achievements and failures in the North, Canada, and Europe. They conveyed to former slaves a determination to enjoy freedom to its fullest. They helped organize churches, schools, and—after Radical Reconstruction commenced—Republican party clubs. Moreover, they instilled in freed people knowledge of their rights, privileges, and responsibilities under a republican form of government and a determination to settle for nothing less than full enjoyment of those rights. In important ways the relatively anonymous fugitives fermented the emancipation process, linking the southern struggle with the national black campaign for equal citizenship and with the worldwide republican movement.

Several fugitives returned to the Georgia lowcountry. Georgia- and South Carolina–born members of the Fifty-fourth and Fifty-fifth Massachusetts Volunteers, the most celebrated northern black regiments, settled in the Savannah-Charleston area, where they had served. Richard W. White, for example, a South Carolina native, resided in Savannah after the war and became an important figure in the black effort to hold elective office during Reconstruction.[1] Similarly, William and Ellen Craft, antebellum Georgia's most celebrated fugitives, established a school along the coast in the early 1870s that survived into the twentieth century.[2] Of all Georgia's returned runaways, none played a more instrumental role in the adjustment to freedom than Aaron Alpeora Bradley.

Details of Bradley's antebellum life remain obscure. He was apparently born around 1815 in Edgefield District, South Carolina, a mulatto slave of Francis Pickens, the state's Civil War governor. Bradley also worked for a time as a shoemaker in Augusta, Georgia. Sometime in the mid 1830s he escaped slavery and found his way to Boston, where he eventually studied law and made the acquaintance of prominent New England abolitionists. He was determined both to advance his legal career and overturn barricades of discrimination; but as he became increasingly abrasive in those pursuits, he had several brushes with the law that jeopardized his status as an attorney.[3]

At the end of the Civil War, Bradley decided to settle in Savannah, the place through which he probably made his northward escape. An opponent of planter domination from his youth, he returned with a knowledge of law that he intended to wield against their power. He seized the opportunity offered by the revolutionary context of the times, creatively drawing upon his legal training to reshape plantation society. He made his living serving the legal needs of lowcountry blacks. Building a constituency among them and establishing himself as a political agitator in their behalf, he led a checkered career as delegate to the Reconstruction constitutional convention, state senator, and candidate for Congress.

Georgia blacks, unlike their neighbors in South Carolina, did not constitute a majority of their state's population. While blacks formed an aggregate majority in Georgia's lowcountry no less than in South Carolina's, the black and white populations in Chatham County, where Savannah was located, were almost equal in 1860. In the city itself, whites outnumbered blacks by nearly 50 percent in 1860 and as late as 1870 still held a slight lead. Only in 1880 did black Savannah residents numerically nudge ahead of their white neighbors.[4] Hence, Reconstruction's promise differed markedly in the two states. During Presidential Reconstruction, white Georgian natives and recent northern immigrants pieced together a Republican party based upon unchallenged black allegiance and the support of former governor Joseph E. Brown and, it was hoped, his upper piedmont constituents. With their political base thus established, Republicans stood ready to make a bid for state power.[5]

In the meantime blacks had perfected their own political organization. With the support of Freedmen's Bureau officers, Georgia blacks formed the Georgia Equal Rights and Education Association, pledged, as its title indicated, to securing for southern blacks full enjoyment of citizenship rights. From January 1866 to May 1867 the organization held three statewide conventions. Intense white opposition forced the organization to alter its name in the fall of 1866 and drop the emphasis on equal rights; nonetheless, its continued educational work kept freedmen aware of the course of struggle.[6] In March 1867 Geor-

Electioneering at the South
Harper's Weekly, July 25, 1868

gia blacks stood prepared to join white Republicans in reconstructing the state.

White Republican chicanery coupled with outright Democratic opposition largely curtailed the promise of black political participation during Reconstruction. In September 1868 the state legislature voted to expel its black members, thereby provoking Georgia's third reconstruction. The move threw black politics into confusion as political leaders scrambled to regain lost ground. No sooner had blacks regained office than Radical rule in Georgia ended. In 1872, when Democrats regained full control of the state government, blacks lost all illusions of using politics to reconstruct their lives and their society. Instead they turned to other avenues open to change by building kinship and community institutions and by concentrating on economic rather than political power. The economic struggle primarily involved shaping the evolving tenancy system to maximize black autonomy from planter control. In the rice lowcountry, specifically, it took the form of the struggle for land and the preservation of the antebellum task system.

Bradley moved to Savannah in December 1865, at the most critical stage of the land-settlement issue. Reconstruction in the lowcountry followed contours determined by antebellum plantation development. Slaves and masters along the coast, unlike those in upland cotton areas, developed a unique labor system, fashioned out of geographical isolation and the labor requirements of the rice crop. Predicated on a longstanding black majority and the absence of whites during the lengthy malarial season, the system rested on a compromise in which slaves exchanged fidelity for a large degree of autonomy, which gave black drivers plantation supervision and allowed field hands control over their own time after completing daily tasks fixed by custom. The task system provided the social basis upon which slaves grew vegetables and raised animals for market, accumulated a modicum of property, and established terrain essentially free from white control. Throughout the antebellum period, geographical isolation fostered a tightly knit, interrelated, highly aristocratic and self-conscious planter elite and a closed, stable, homogeneous slave population with strong cultural and family ties of its own. Whites held title to the land and reaped its richest rewards, but blacks occupied and effectively controlled it for most of the growing season.[7]

The Civil War shattered this world and inaugurated the great transformation in which sea-island blacks and Bradley would play so crucial a part.[8] In December 1864 General William T. Sherman of the Union army captured Savannah. After an interview with Savannah black leaders, Sherman issued his celebrated Special Field Order No. 15, which allocated coastal land for black settlement. By summer 1865 General Rufus Saxton, administrator of the order, had settled an estimated 40,000 freedmen on forty-acre family plots. In the fall, however, fugitive planters began returning, demanding that President Andrew Johnson restore their property. Both Saxton and Freedmen's Bureau Commissioner General O. O. Howard insisted upon the government's obligation to honor Sherman's order. Nonetheless, Johnson determined to return the land to its original owners, and he directed Howard to devise a restoration policy. After visiting the islands in October, trying unsuccessfully to persuade freedmen to relinquish their land claims voluntarily, Howard reluctantly resorted to force. His plan involved dispossessing blacks claiming land under Sherman's order, permitting planters to repossess all land except that sold under the direct tax laws, issuing warrants for twenty acres of land in South Carolina to holders of valid Sherman grants, and enforcing compliance through threats of military action.[9]

Bradley arrived on the scene at the peak of black resistance to restoration. Seeing himself as a champion of all blacks' causes, he cast his interests broadly, establishing loose contacts with black churches and soon opening a school. He began agitating for black suffrage, joining forces with the vote campaign begun in the wake of the Sherman interview. He proposed impeaching President Johnson, whom he saw as obstructing Reconstruction by virtue of his partiality toward former Confederates at the expense of loyal southerners, black and white.[10]

Bradley held the city authorities of Savannah in no higher esteem than he did President Johnson and recommended their removal as well. He accused the city police and the mayor's court of discrimination toward blacks, mentioning especially the mayor's habit of sentencing blacks to work city streets in ball and chain for the slightest offense. Bradley charged the Savannah Freedmen's Bureau court with similar irregularities and requested inauguration of appeal procedures, offering his services as judge. He held little hope of success, nonetheless, inasmuch as the court had decided that no black should argue cases before it. As Bradley commented, "Thus they Rob us with impunity in our own Court."[11]

At the same time that he took such broad interest in the problems of Savannah blacks, he encountered rice-plantation freed people, from whom he gained new insight into the Sherman land issue. As important as he considered the entire range of black grievances, his contact with plantation folk convinced him of the importance of land to any meaningful enjoyment of freedom. Hence, while he actively sought just treatment for all Savannah blacks at the hands of both civil and Freedmen's Bureau authorities, he began concentrating his efforts against President Andrew Johnson's land restoration plan. Viewing the seceded states as territories and considering Sherman's order a military action, he insisted that only Congress or military authorities and not the president had jurisdiction over the land question. At a mass meeting of blacks early in December, which he had called to discuss blacks' rights to vote, to have jury trials, to testify in state courts, and to keep their Sherman land, he advised freedmen to remain on the land rather than make unfavorable contracts with planters. Witnesses accused him of counseling resistance to removal, even at the points of federal bayonets; and military authorities promptly charged him with using seditious and insurrectionary language, tried and convicted him before a military commission, and sentenced him to one year's confinement in Fort Pulaski. He protested his conviction to Secretary of War Edwin M. Stanton, to Attorney General James Speed, and to President Johnson; and on December 29, 1865, he was paroled on the condition that he remain in Savannah and report daily to the city's provost marshal. General Davis Tillson, recently appointed head of the Freedmen's Bureau in Georgia, tried unsuccessfully to alter the parole's terms, arguing that only removal from the state would neutralize Bradley's troublesome presence.[12]

Bradley chafed under the restrictions, which, he insisted, disrupted his educational work. It appears, in fact, that the restrictions effectively destroyed his school. Nonetheless, he obtained permission to attend the state's first freed people's convention in Augusta on January 10, 1866. Convention delegates discussed the land question, but chose not to speak forcefully on the issue. They ultimately resolved in favor of making federal lands available to freedmen, "at such rates, and upon such terms, as will enable them to pay for them without embarrassment; and thus to secure to themselves and their children permanent homes." At some point in the proceedings Bradley made disparaging remarks about the late President Abraham Lincoln and Secretary of War Stanton. Tillson, a guest at the convention, reported to Stanton, who ordered Bradley to serve the remainder of his sentence at Fort Pulaski or leave the state. Bradley chose the latter alternative. He returned to Boston and did not again set foot in Georgia until late December 1866, when the Supreme Court's *Ex parte Milligan* decision invalidated military trials of civilians.[13]

In Bradley's absence Georgia Assistant Commissioner Tillson adopted a policy of returning land to original owners, consolidating Sherman land grantees on certain sections of plantations in anticipation of removal to South Carolina warrant lands after harvest, allowing owners to cultivate unoccupied areas of their plantations unobstructed, and forcing freed people without Sherman grants to make contracts with planters.[14] Both planters and Freedmen's Bureau and federal military authorities insisted that blacks remain producers of market staples. Planters believed that abandonment of staple production would create social chaos by removing blacks from the beneficial influence of whites and would thus cause former slaves to retrogress to lower levels of civilization. Conversely, while northern Bureau and military officers entertained less sanguine estimates of white tutelage, they saw market participation as essential to economic progress and political democracy in a society that adhered to laissez-faire economics and republican institutions. Out of their joint desire to keep blacks growing cotton and rice, both planters and federal officials struck common ground in recognizing as legitimate the land claims of fugitive white owners rather than those of loyal black possessors.[15]

While absent in the North, Bradley continued agitating the cause of the Sherman land grantees. Appealing to Bureau Commissioner Howard for favorable consideration of black land claims in light of passage of the Homestead Act, Bradley exhorted: "My great object is, to give you Back-bone, and as the Chief Justice of 4 millions of Colored people, and Refugees; You can not, and must not, be a Military Tool, in the hands of Andrew Johnson."[16] By the same token, when Bradley learned of continuing deterioration of the situation in the lowcountry, he appealed to the commander of the Military District of South Carolina to permit blacks to bear arms and form military companies.[17]

When Bradley returned to Savannah at the end of the year, he gave new life to the lowcountry freedmen's struggle for land. Over the course of 1866, bureau officials had permitted blacks to occupy scattered plantations that still had not been repossessed, but the end of the harvest season smoothed the way for the removal of black intransigents to South Carolina warrant lands. Blacks felt the rumble of federal force on the horizon and braced for battle, and Bradley's reappearance offered hope. In his inimitable way, he would draw public attention to the Sherman grantees' plight and force federal policymakers at the highest levels to take a stand.

The conflicting parties joined battle on Charlotte and Isabella Cheves's Savannah River Delta Plantation. The Cheveses decided to circumvent earlier difficulties over crop settlements by leasing Delta to white agents for 1867. The lessees attempted to entice the freed people into making contracts by offering to hire them for either a share of the crop or monthly wages. According to local bureau agent Captain Henry C. Brandt, the blacks "positively refused" the offer, pledged to "hold the land for 1867 as before in 1866," and insisted that "no Officers of the Freedman Bureau or Military forces could drive them off." The freedmen employed Bradley to write a petition for them to bureau headquarters. Within days of his return, Bradley, the "notorious character" and "troublemaker" (as Brandt styled him), was back in the fray.[18]

In addition to his appeals for Savannah River blacks, Bradley petitioned in behalf of freedmen on Wilmington, Argyle, and Sapelo islands, complaining about injustice in the warrant-transfer system and the settlement of accounts for improvements and crops. Addressing pleas to President Johnson, Senator Benjamin Wade, Bureau Commissioner Howard, and assistant commissioners Tillson in Georgia and R. K. Scott in South Carolina, Bradley and the petitioners sought redress, quoting at length from the Freedmen's Bureau Bill, the U.S. Constitution, and the recently passed Civil Rights Bill. In a typical passage, Bradley argued: "We your humble Petitioners come and pray that you will be pleased to '*Extend military protection*,' under the 14th section Bureau bill of June 11th 1866, that we may have 'full and equal benefit, of all laws and proceedings for the security of *Persons* and property': (Civil Rights bill sec 1)." Similarly, he insisted that the bureau had a legal obligation to "*Extend Military* Protection over all cases, *questions* (and stay outrages as now practiced) concerning free enjoyment of Equal Rights and Immunities." He requested the formation of courts with partial black membership to adjudicate land claims and to fix compensation for improvements.[19]

He appealed to Wade: "We are the producers of all that is exported of any value. We are the loyal men who can save Georgia, if you will let us do it." He complained that Tillson forced Savannah blacks to work plantations against their will and without due process of law, and he asked permission for blacks to form a militia for self-protection. Tillson denied the charges and accused Bradley of fomenting discontent by threatening bloodshed unless injustice against blacks ceased. Tillson's successor, Assistant Commissioner Caleb C. Sibley, defended his predecessor's record but characterized the blacks' mood as one of "more or less dissatisfaction . . . mainly due to their extreme reluctance to leave the plantations and give up to original owners." He reported that some blacks who had originally vacated their Sherman holdings along the South Carolina side of the river had since returned and insisted on remaining. Bureau agent Brandt concluded that only two of the twenty petition signers on Delta Plantation had valid possessory titles; the rest not only had no valid claims to land but also had entered contracts with a planter on another plantation. Endorsing Brandt's demand that the petitioners leave, South Carolina Assistant Commissioner Scott accused Bradley of exploiting them for his own gain by charging them a dollar each to affix their names. Regardless of the countercharges, Bradley's attack on Tillson helped sustain his leadership of the land struggle.[20]

Bradley's petitions for the rice freedmen illuminate the nature of his relationship with them. By inclination drawn toward confrontation, he gave special attention to the land claims of the Sherman grantees. Versed in the law, he realized how vulnerable the recently emancipated slaves were before it. He saw his role as one of legal counselor and petitioner in their behalf. He argued the validity of their claim on the basis of recent congressional legislation and Sherman's order. Thus he clothed their claim in its strongest legal garb, at the same time acquainting the petitioners with their newly acquired rights as citizens under a republican form of government.

Not inclined to shy away from public conflict, Bradley moved along paths more timid leaders feared to travel. Moreover, he lacked institutional ties that confined other leaders, pressuring them to capitulate on the land issue. For instance, the Freedmen's Bureau often used its few black officers to quell plantation discontent in the wake of restoration. In South Carolina, Major Martin R. Delany, who in July 1865 reportedly urged black landholders to resist white removal efforts, by the end of the year found himself traversing the islands persuading recalcitrant blacks to forsake land claims and make contracts. Former army lieutenant Stephen A. Swails performed similar service on the islands, as did Lieutenant James M. Trotter working for the army's Orangeburg District Labor Commission. Tunis G. Campbell, civilian agent on St. Catharine's Island, Georgia, managed to escape that role largely because of the success of his self-governing black colony, first established on the island but later forced to move to mainland McIntosh County. In the effort Campbell managed a unique demonstration of land ownership—which, however, degenerated into a leasing rather than owning operation before foundering in the 1870s—while at the same time circumventing the contract business. Nonetheless, despite the important legacy of Campbell's experiment to McIntosh County blacks, it was so small in scale, and so far down the coast, that it had little effect on land developments in the more strategic Savannah area.[21]

Northern black leaders in the South provided the same link with national republican traditions that Bradley did, but none matched his grass-roots involvement in the land struggle. African Methodist Episcopal missionary Richard H. Cain in Charleston, for example, remained a consistent champion of land for blacks, yet his style of leadership denied him the place in the fight that Bradley occupied. Closely linked with his congregation, Cain preferred using his pulpit and his newspaper, the *Missionary Record*, to agitate the land issue. Moreover, he opposed confiscation, favoring instead a federal loan to sponsor black land purchases. He carried his interest in the land into the 1868 South Carolina Constitutional Convention, later tried unsuccessfully to make land available to freedmen by speculating in a 2,000-acre tract, and eventually built upon Charleston District's black voter majority to serve two congressional terms. Yet in 1865 and 1866, when the prospect of holding office stood shrouded in an uncertain future, Cain's intellectual support carried little practical weight in the rice districts. On the other hand, Bradley's presence in the field provided the strongest impetus to the rice laborers' claim for land. No other state-level black leader in either South Carolina or Georgia cultivated the relationship with rice freedmen that Bradley did; neither did any espouse their cause with his passion and militancy.[22]

In the thick of Bradley's land offensive of early 1867, Congress passed the Reconstruction acts thereby opening a new line of attack to black land strategists. On the surface the Reconstruction acts took the unprecedented step of remanding the seceded states to military rule and enfranchising southern black men. But, lurking barely beneath the surface, the acts held potential for even more change in the South. While making no mention of land, the acts did offer to southern blacks hope of using their votes to legislate land reform. In Savannah, for example, even though whites outnumbered blacks in the total population, black registrants outnumbered whites 3,091 to 2,240 in 1867.[23] In the black-majority lowcountry, land aspirants anticipated using their new political weapon to counterbalance planter economic superiority. At the time, few freedmen appreciated how the acts would channel black land agitation within the confining legislative process, where redistribution stood little chance of success.

Bradley did nothing to dissuade freed people's faith in their ability to vote fundamental change; and casting aside any such misgivings of his own, he laid plans to capture elective office. To lay a firm foundation

290

for black political power, he broadened the basis of his agitation. First, in the name of the "right of self-government" granted by Congress, he reopened his case for judicial reform in Savannah, requesting the removal of rebel judges and their replacement by "loyal civil Tribunals."[24] Harking back to his earliest interests among Savannah blacks, he announced a program calling for federal protection of black civil and political rights designed to appeal to all blacks regardless of class position. Second, he formed an alliance with the black urban working class by forging links with Savannah longshoremen, who in late 1865 had struck for higher wages and now (with Bradley's assistance) protested their victimization by a recently passed, oppressive city tax.[25] In his new appeal Bradley apparently hoped to build a power base that in time might both assure him office and prove strong enough for him to take radical steps regarding land distribution, education, civil and political rights, and other issues of vital importance to blacks.

Taking his cue from the unilateral nature of the Reconstruction acts, Bradley tested black political strength by requesting military authorities to remove Savannah's mayor, Edward C. Anderson, a former Confederate colonel, who had arrested Bradley on several occasions and whose mayor's court had proved a scourge to black Savannah. Arguing that Anderson showed favoritism toward fellow rebels to the detriment of loyal blacks and whites, Bradley insisted that the mayor's "oppressive acts have reached a point at which our indurence fails to be a verture in free men"; he asked, "Are we yet Slaves or are we free American citizens?" After repeated petitions in that vein, in January 1868 the War Department ruled that the Reconstruction acts did not require removal of disloyal officeholders, even though newly elected officials were required to swear loyalty to the Union. Therefore military authorities would take no action to remove Anderson.[26] Thereafter Bradley and his supporters would have to resort to electoral politics to change the city's officers, in the same way they would have to struggle for land reform.

Throughout his 1867 campaign against Anderson, as well as during his land activities, Bradley agitated his cause in the streets. He repeatedly risked arrest but insisted on sustaining black political power through massive, potentially explosive, public meetings. His political style included flashy clothing (beaver hat and kid gloves, for example) and a retinue of lackeys and bodyguards.[27] His critics considered him excessively vain and flamboyant, but his supporters both condoned and encouraged his eccentricities. His physical appearance and ceremonial bearing displayed a sense of decorum befitting a person with his political influence. Thus Bradley fits easily into the tradition of urban politicians of a later time who made such overt public demonstrations of the trappings of power. What critics perceived as idosyncratic antics in fact constituted the essence of his leadership style, one to which his constituents from both urban and rural backgrounds responded enthusiastically.

Bradley's campaign against city authorities attracted a wide spectrum of support among Savannah blacks.[28] But by late 1867, his activities contributed to growing political factionalism that reflected the process of class stratification among blacks and the success of relentless white opposition to black political unity. Bradley did not share the traditional bases of support enjoyed by other Savannah leaders—for example, the ministers. Under the restrictive provisions of his release from Fort Pulaski, his school apparently failed. Moreover, no surviving evidence suggests his membership in any one of Savannah's black churches.[29] Finally, in all his surviving petitions and reports of his speeches, he does not once invoke the name of God; and his only biblical references—several allusions to himself as the widow's son during 1867 shortly after his father died—may have referred to Lincoln's Second Inaugural Address as much as to the Book of Exodus.[30] Clearly Bradley was one of the most secular black leaders of the nineteenth century. Yet, despite his aloofness toward regular leadership channels and his light color, his active involvement in land and labor struggles promised him a large working-class constituency. Moreover, his willingness to engage in mass political organizing, replete with tactics of street theater and public confrontation, struck a responsive chord among rice-plantation workers and urban laborers. Such an organizing style gave physical coherence to black political unity and physical evidence of black-voter power at the same time that it mocked old slave-code restrictions on black assemblies. Hence his constituency grew.

At the same time, however, numbers of blacks began to repudiate Bradley's variety of mass politics, the volatile and unpredictable nature of which produced increasingly fewer tangible results, threatened public peace, and most of all tended to lessen whites' opinions of blacks in general. The disenchanted did not favor abandoning struggle, but they did wish to cloak black political activity with respectability. They increasingly eschewed Bradley's tactical antics and his larger protest strategy.

Anderson took advantage of these incipient divisions to isolate Bradley from more "respectable" black elements. With white support, the mayor met Bradley's tactics head on, publicly confronting him on occasion and obstructing his efforts to hold mass political meetings at every turn. For example, in September 1867 the mayor asked military authorities to interdict a planned meeting of freedmen under Bradley's sponsorship. Anderson warned of its "revolutionary and agrarian . . . character" and estimated that it would draw some three thousand laborers from the fields during the crucial harvest season. Finally, he cited the inevitable disruption of the city's commerce that would result from the presence of such a multitude on the public streets. Military authorities decided to take no prohibitive action, but the tense atmosphere guaranteed trouble. The meeting ended in disorder, apparently as a result of an outbreak of violent black factionalism. Even without military intervention, the rally's outcome played into Anderson's hands.[31]

The specific causes of the disorder remain unknown, but witnesses accused Bradley of making disparaging remarks about the Union League in Savannah, which in turn prompted some of its members to violence. Bradley maintained a curious but not entirely clear relationship with the Savannah black league, the earliest club of which dates from the summer of 1865, months before Bradley entered the city.[32] At times he argued against incorporating the league's activities into larger efforts on the part of Georgia blacks, for example, into the Georgia Equal Rights and Educational Association, which grew out of the January 1866 freedmen's convention. At other times, especially during and after 1867, he had a close relationship with the longshoremen's league and even on occasion affixed league symbols after his signature. According to the records of the Savannah branch of the Freedmen's Savings and Trust Company, Bradley served as secretary of one of the league clubs from August to September 1867. Significantly, the trouble at the public meeting occurred less than one month after he left that office.[33] In the end his relationship with the various factions apparently depended upon his changing estimation of their threat to his political organization and ambition.

Bradley's factional infighting diluted the power of the black voting majority as well as his own impact on city hall. In turn Mayor Anderson, backed by white property, wielded his administrative and judicial power to force an increasingly higher price upon black practitioners of confrontation politics, especially Bradley. In October 1867, for example, the city passed an ordinance prohibiting assemblies between sunset and sunrise without prior written permission of the mayor and enforced the ordinance against black political meetings. Six months later Anderson threatened to arrest Bradley's landlady on a charge of operating a disorderly house unless she removed Bradley from her premises. The mayor claimed that she agreed to do so on the grounds that she herself found his presence objectionable. Bradley argued that Anderson had forced her hand; but, reluctantly, the agitator had to accept defeat.[34] For a time Bradley's approach enhanced his image among his lower-class constituents and magnified his political threat. In the long run, though, the frequent gatherings of armed rural laborers that threatened recurrent violence as well as increased black political factionalism promised only to estrange the "respectable" black element, an increasingly important social byproduct of emancipation's structural effect on Savannah's black community.[35]

Yet changes in black political life resulting from secular trends in the developing black social structure did not diminish Bradley's threat to translate black votes into political power. The congressional Reconstruction acts mandated elections for delegates to constitutional conventions; and throughout summer and fall 1867 battles with Savannah authorities, Bradley had his eye on a convention seat. The specter of having Bradley serve in the convention sent shivers down the spines of white Georgians. Bradley's election confirmed white fears, inasmuch as agent Brandt reported that the balloting had produced "the greatest excitement" among Savannah River freedmen "because their Apostle Bradley is elected and now all land and property will be restored to these freedpeople, at least 100 acre land & one mule." Brandt reported hundreds from his South Carolina district as having registered in Savannah so they could vote for Bradley, as well as having formed armed militia companies to foster their political interests and land ambitions.[36]

The reaction to Bradley's election illustrates how he linked the quest for land with the exercise of political rights in the eyes of lowcountry blacks. Through his political success they hoped to realize their land aspirations. Despite the symbolic importance of voting, casting ballots carried much graver weight. When necessary, voters would use political power to protect newly acquired citizenship rights; but to the children of Sherman's legacy, securing homesteads far outweighed any other possible reward for voting.

Despite his mandate, Bradley apparently realized that state conventions could take no effective action, so at the convention he did not agitate the land issue. Instead he focused on safeguarding blacks from the more obvious manifestations of oppression, for example, discrimination in state courts and on public carriers and unjust and cruel confinement of black prisoners. Land would have to await either congressional action or formation of a radical legislative coalition in Georgia. From the start of the convention, Bradley practiced politics as the art of compromise, in deference to impositions of the republican legislative process. He did not shy away from sharp, heated exchanges with his political enemies; his abrasive debating tactics in reality aimed at establishing a fundamental level of civil and political rights for all citizens, black as well as white, both in the convention and in society at large. He refused to permit whites to treat him or other blacks as slaves.

Yet, while he insisted on equal treatment for blacks, he forsook all other issues, however dear to his constituents, that stood little chance of obtaining convention endorsement. Moreover, he prepared to trade votes and bargain with white delegates to secure approval of his measures. Basically, Bradley intended to support white Radicals' debt-freeze and homestead measures in exchange for endorsement of safeguards for civil and political rights. By adopting the Radicals' strategy of appealing to upcountry yeomen, Bradley attempted to strike an alliance fraught with political, economic, and social implications for southern whites as well as blacks. He admitted that black voters had nothing to gain personally from either stay or homestead laws, inasmuch as such legislation applied only to property owners. Moreover, he conceded that the blacks' perceived worst enemies, the planters, could turn such legislation to their own advantage at the freedmen's expense. Nonetheless, he realized that only such a politically based coalition of poor whites and blacks could muster enough strength permanently to subdue the planter class. Only with the former slave owners neutralized could freedom become a reality and could poor farmers and laborers hope seriously to legislate land reform. Short of congressional action, politicians on the state level had few other options for securing radical change.

Bradley's frank willingness to compromise in such a way shocked most of his black colleagues, who insisted upon voting according to principle rather than expediency. Bradley did not convince them of the need to bargain—in the long run to the blacks' disadvantage. Nearly all black delegates eventually endorsed the yeoman strategy, but failing to follow Bradley's lead left them with virtually nothing in return. Most significantly, they failed to get a constitutional guarantee of blacks' right to hold elective offices, a failure that cost them dearly throughout the remainder of Radical Reconstruction.[37]

In the midst of the debate over compromising votes, white convention delegates taught Bradley and his constituents another crude lesson in the realities of American politics. Dredging criminal charges from his past, they strove to expel him from the convention. In defending himself, Bradley indiscreetly insulted various delegates who then managed to have him ejected. The move effectively closed all doors to Bradley's working within the confines of the newly opened legislative process. His expulsion made him a martyr among Savannah blacks; and in the elections for state offices that accompanied passage of the constitution in April 1868, his constituents promptly elected him to a seat in the state Senate. Later, the Senate, following the convention's lead, also expelled him, several weeks before both houses joined hands in ejecting all black senators and representatives. The collective expulsion drove home to Georgia blacks the duplicity of their nominal friends. Moreover, Bradley's experience indicated how precariously a radical black teetered on the pinnacle of political office. Neither enjoying strong constituent support nor tailoring his program to withstand the rigors of legislative compromise could permanently shield Bradley. With little provocation and relative ease, white opponents could manipulate the legislative process and silence him or any other black official.[38]

The November 1868 national elections only served to heighten black frustration. Shut away from polling places throughout the state and subject to fraudulent counts even where they could cast ballots, blacks grew increasingly restive. Beginning to see the futility of expecting change through the political process, rice laborers in southern Chatham County's Ogeechee River district revolted. Claiming inspiration from Bradley, they assumed that by taking armed control of the countryside, Congress would sustain their possession of it. They operated virtually unchecked for over a month before federal authorities captured the leaders and thereby checked the rebellion. In all, civil authorities reportedly issued some 1,300 arrest warrants and lodged nearly 100 prisoners in jail. The action permanently ended hopes of taking land by force. Moreover, it forced Bradley again to flee north for his life. He found it safe to return to Georgia only in January 1870 to retake his Senate seat as Georgia entered its third reconstruction.[39]

For the remainder of Radical Reconstruction, particularly during the reconvened legislative session, Bradley challenged civil authorities' injustice toward blacks and continued his campaign to remove Mayor Anderson. He sponsored measures to relieve laborers from excessive taxation, to reduce the length of the work day to eight hours, and to protect blacks' civil and political rights, none of which passed; but, apparently viewing land redistribution as an increasingly futile

296

cause, he did not so much as enter a measure in its behalf. Over the course of the legislative session, he began to find greater fault with Governor Rufus Bullock's Republican regime. At the beginning of the term, he had joined Tunis G. Campbell, George Wallace, William H. Harrison, and James M. Simms in addressing a memorial in behalf of Georgia's black legislators in Bullock's favor, defending him from detractors' charges of corruption. Nonetheless, by the end of the year, Bradley opposed Bullock's efforts to prolong his administration by postponing scheduled elections. Moreover, he condemned the governor for inaugurating "A New System of Chain Gang Slavery"—the convict lease system.[40]

Viewing the Chatham County Republican organization as a reflection of Bullock's corrupt Atlanta operation, in the fall of 1870 Bradley severed his ties with Savannah party regulars, led by Congressman Joseph W. Clift and Collector of Customs T. P. Robb. Bradley set up a rival independent Republican organization with support from some disenchanted white Republicans as well as most black party members. The independents held a nominating convention that put forth a mixed black-white ticket for all county offices, including black candidates King Solomon Thomas for sheriff, James Porter for assistant clerk of superior court, and John H. Deveaux for county ordinary. The convention also advanced an all-black slate for Congress and the state legislature, including Bradley as candidate for the 42d Congress, Ulysses L. Houston for the 41st Congress, James M. Simms for state senator, and Charles L. DeLamotta for state representative. Alone among important black politicians, Richard W. White, prominent in the earlier struggle to establish blacks' office-holding rights, remained loyal to the regulars and ran as one of their congressional candidates. Bradley's move threw the Savannah party into disarray, with blacks dividing allegiances between Clift's regulars and Bradley's independents, and Democrats stepping in to endorse Bradley, thereby further contributing to Republican confusion. With Republicans thus divided, the Democrats won handily; only Simms and Thomas defeated their Democratic rivals.[41]

The election took its toll. Growing numbers of blacks became entirely disenchanted with Republican politics, and in the face of increasing Democratic intimidation and chicanery, many let their party memberships and voter registrations lapse.[42] Moreover, defeat convinced many black politicians of the dangerous consequences of division within party ranks, and many rebels returned to the regular fold. DeLamotta, Thomas, Porter, and Deveaux joined White among the regulars and increasingly came to represent a new breed of professional politician, light-skinned and tied more closely to white Republican patronage than to the party's black rank and file. The *Savannah Tribune*, edited by Deveaux, L. B. Toomer, and L. M. Pleasant, became the major voice of the new breed, as well as a significant force in Georgia and southern black life into the twentieth century.[43] Moreover, Baptist minister-politicians like James M. Simms and U. L. Houston faced mounting pressure from their congregations to forsake politics in favor of church work.[44] Consequently Bradley's independents increasingly came to represent only his most loyal constituents, the rice-plantation workers and urban laborers.

If the 1870 election gave crude shape to new black political alignments, Bradley's 1871 campaign to remove Robb from the customs collectorship solidified them.[45] Beginning in the summer of 1871, both white and black Republicans began taking sides in the impending battle over Robb's continuation in office. Among white Republicans, both John E. Bryant, longtime friend of Georgia blacks, and M. H. Hale, one of Robb's subordinates, wanted his ouster. Late in September Bradley, signing himself "the Peoples Deligate," petitioned President Grant for Robb's removal, reminding the president of black Republican voter strength in Georgia and suggesting himself and two white Republicans as possible replacements.[46] During the first week in October, Bradley organized a petition campaign calling for Robb's removal, accusing him of using his office "to divide the Republican party in the first Congressional District of Georgia," and recommending six possible replacements, again including Bradley. Rice-plantation workers on Skidaway Island drew up a supplementary petition also denouncing Robb, characterizing his five black customhouse employees as persons "who *demoralized, corrupted,* divided and destroyed the Union League in Savannah" and bought black votes for the Democracy at one dollar apiece during the October 1871 mayor's election.[47] Later several blacks accused Bradley of enticing them to sign the petition under false representations, then refusing to permit them to retract their signatures after discovering his true intentions.[48]

Under Richard W. White's inspiration, petitions began circulating in Robb's behalf. Delegates to the Southern States Convention of Colored Men in Columbia, South Carolina, in October 1871 signed one. Meanwhile, White and his cohorts circulated several pro-Robb petitions in Savannah that collectively amassed approximately 3,000 signatures of black Republicans.[49] Robb was acquitted of any wrongdoing in connection with the Bradley petition campaign, but Bradley maintained relentless pressure for his removal. At the end of the year Bradley submitted another deposition to the president accusing Robb's black henchmen of disrupting political meetings and trying to kill him, arguing that they "defy all civil law and keep the colored people of the city of Savannah and country of Chatham in great Terror!" Again Bradley called for Robb's removal. Finally, after months of defending his record as customs collector, Robb resigned in February 1872.[50]

Robb's successor, James Atkins, represented Georgia's insurgent Republicans; nonetheless, he maintained Robb's alliance with the regular black customhouse faction, reappointing most of them to the positions they had held under Robb. For a time under Atkins, Bradley served as a special customs inspector, but personal disagreements between Bradley, Atkins, and the other insurgents (including Bryant and Hale) led to Bradley's dismissal and his efforts to remove Atkins from office.[51] Bradley applied constant pressure on customhouse officials to favor his independent faction of Chatham County Republicans. At the same time, however, most black politicians had deserted him, making peace with white Republicans in power at any given time and denying Bradley and his followers even the crumbs of federal patronage. Bradley's antics reflected a growing sense of bitterness on his part that did not aid his case, either among the blacks whom he had apparently tricked into signing petitions or among the Savannah black population at large.

At bottom these changes reflected class forces at work in the black community and its Republican party organization. The growing and disproportionately light-skinned professional group (which the White-Deveaux faction represented) led the more respectable black Republican elements back into the regular camp, at the same time awaiting results of John E. Bryant's bid for greater power in the party's executive committee. Dark-skinned rice workers, on the other hand, unmoved by the significance of patronage to plantation hands and either unaware or uninterested in Bryant's moves, stayed loyal to Bradley. Two black Republican parties took shape: one representing elite urban blacks and tied to patronage politics, the other representing the lowest orders of urban and rural laborers and loyal to Bradley.

Viewing the disastrous demise of Radical power in Georgia, Bradley hoped that President Ulysses S. Grant's administration would come to the assistance of southern blacks. Its failure to do so only sharpened black disenchantment and dulled Bradley's prestige. At each election during the early 1870s, whites raised the specter of Bradley leading armed blacks in full-scale revolt. Their fears proved groundless, for the end of Radical rule in Georgia in 1872 proved a turning point both in Bradley's career and in the larger adjustment to freedom. It drove home the painful lesson that the realities of southern politics made radical change through the legislative process all but impossible. It also indicated how little Washington intended to do in behalf of southern blacks, in terms of both political rights and land claims.[52]

In September 1874 Bradley penned a lament to the deteriorating condition of affairs: "There was a time, when I could and did lead the Republican party to Victory in this first District, but I have resigned my leadership to others whoes political *wisdom* time will revele."[53] For Bradley the old party was dead, a victim of its own opportunism and corruption. Fleeing the new generation of professional black politicians in Savannah, Bradley stumped his old South Carolina constituents seeking a seat in the 44th Congress, running on a platform of reducing the cotton tax that weighed so heavily on southern blacks, ending fraudulent Indian land appropriations as well as bank and railroad swindles, and letting "All persons be free and equal before the laws of the State and Nation." His attempt to capture congressional office again failed.[54]

Rice-country blacks saw their collective political ambitions, which they had pinned to Bradley's early political success, plummet with their "Apostle's" career. By 1872 they realized that politics—even when mediated through Bradley—could offer no hope of obtaining the land Sherman had promised. South Carolinians could turn to the state land commission to fulfill their dream, but they would have to leave their cherished lowcountry homes for that land. As Radical Reconstruction in South Carolina failed, blacks there began to search for a promised land across the ocean in Liberia. By 1875 Bradley, too, had become interested enough in migration to sponsor an unsuccessful colonization movement to Florida. At the end of the decade he attempted to muster support for the Kansas Exodus movement that gripped southern blacks from 1879 to 1881. Failing to gain followers, he decided to migrate himself, making it as far as St. Louis, where he died in 1881.[55]

The story of Bradley's last years provides a fitting epitaph for the course of blacks' desire for land in the postbellum South. Despite involvement in Republican politics and his aggressive attempt to obtain civil rights and civil justice for the freedmen, Bradley viewed those struggles as secondary actions to protect blacks against white depredations. For him, as well as the Delta Plantation workers, the Ogeechee district insurrectionists, and all lowcounty freedmen, possession of

300

land served as a much surer guarantee of freedom than civil or political rights. Without land, freedom stood compromised and blacks had to resort to cosmetic guarantees of just treatment. Ultimately Bradley refused to abandon his vision of the importance of land and committed himself to a thousand-mile journey in its pursuit.

Barred from direct land ownership at first, the rice-plantation freedmen that he left behind strove instead to maximize their independence as free workers. In the long run, planters and laborers again made their peace under the task system. Yet larger economic forces spelled the doom of the compromise, as competition from upland rice in Louisiana and Arkansas, coupled with a series of disastrous hurricanes beginning in the early 1880s, undermined lowland rice. As the rice empire crumbled, blacks finally came to possess their cherished land, but economic changes consigned them to bare subsistence and dire poverty. Peasant proprietorship provided a social basis for continued cultural isolation, and Bradley's secular message of changing society through conscious human effort retreated in the face of a renewed upsurge of supernatural explanations of personal relations and social causation.[56]

Bradley's urban constituents, on the other hand, fashioned their own means to contend with their particular problems. For dock workers, the longshoremen's union provided both a labor and social organization, serving the dockside black community and providing the framework for militant strike action like that of 1891, for example.[57] For the rest of the community, development of family, church, fraternal, and social institutions and preservation of the skeletal black Republican party offered solace in the face of Jim Crow and provided bases from which to attack segregation as, for example, during the 1906–7 streetcar boycott.[58] In some ways these developments differed markedly from Reconstruction-era protest; but that notwithstanding, they took their inspiration from that peculiar and promising time when southern blacks carved out the terrain of freedom. No single lowcountry black played a more instrumental role in that process than did Aaron A. Bradley.

Notes

The author wishes to thank J. Scott Strickland for material on Bradley's activities in South Carolina, Sara Dunlap Jackson and Mary Giunta for help with National Archives sources, and participants in the February 1980 Georgia Studies Symposium for comments on an earlier draft. He also thanks his colleagues on the Freedmen and Southern Society Project, Ira Berlin and Leslie Rowland, for their collaboration, criticism, and encouragement.

1. Richard W. White to Chas. J. Folger, Mar. 13, 1882, enclosed in T. F. Johnson to Chas. J. Folger, Mar. 13, 1882, Custom House Nominations, Savannah, Ga., General Records of the Department of the Treasury, Record Group (RG) 56, National Archives (NA), Washington, D.C.; Elizabeth Studley Nathans, *Losing the Peace: Georgia Republicans and Reconstruction, 1865–1871* (Baton Rouge: Louisiana State University Press, 1968), p. 153.

2. R. J. M. Blackett, "Fugitive Slaves in Britain: The Odyssey of William and Ellen Craft," *Journal of American Studies* 12 (Apr. 1978):41–62.

3. In 1867 Bradley reported his age as fifty-one. Registers of Signatures of Depositors in Branches of the Freedmen's Savings and Trust Company, Savannah, Georgia Branch, Records of Insolvent National Banks, Records of the Office of the Comptroller of the Currency, RG 101, NA. See also E. Merton Coulter, *Negro Legislators in Georgia during the Reconstruction Period* (Athens: Georgia Historical Quarterly, 1968), pp. 37–38.

4. U.S., Bureau of the Census: *Population of the United States in 1860* (Washington, D.C.: Government Printing Office. 1864), 1:72, 74; *Ninth Census, Statistics of the Population of the United States* (1872), 1:20–21, 100; *Statistics of the Population at the Tenth Census* (1883), 1:385, 417. Between 1860 and 1880, the Savannah white population hovered around 15,000. The 1860 black population of over 8,000 increased to 13,000 in 1870 and to more than 15,000 in 1880. By 1870, however, there were almost 50 percent more blacks than whites in the county as a whole.

5. This and the following summary of Georgia Reconstruction come primarily from Nathans, *Losing the Peace*.

6. *Proceedings of the Freedmen's Convention of Georgia, Assembled at Augusta, January 10th, 1866* (Augusta: Loyal Georgian, 1866); *Proceedings of the Convention of the Equal Rights and Educational Association of Georgia, Assembled at Macon, October 29th, 1866* (Augusta: Loyal Georgian, 1866); Macon *Georgia Weekly Telegraph*, May 10, 1867.

7. Ira Berlin, "Time, Space, and the Evolution of Afro-American Society on British Mainland North America," *American Historical Review* 85 (Feb. 1980):58–66.

8. See Clarence L. Mohr, "Georgia Blacks during Secession and Civil War, 1859–1865" (Ph.D. diss., University of Georgia, 1975), esp. chs. 2 and 3, portions of which appear in Clarence L. Mohr, "Before Sherman: Georgia Blacks and the Union War Effort, 1861–1864," *Journal of Southern History* 45 (Aug. 1979):331–52. See also George Alexander Heard, "St. Simons Island during the War between the States," *Georgia Historical Quarterly* 22 (Sept. 1938):249–72.

9. For an account of the Sherman meeting with the black ministers, see New York *Tribune*, Feb. 13, 1865; *Christian Recorder*, Feb. 18, 1865; or "Colloquy with Colored Ministers," *Journal of Negro History* 16 (Jan. 1931):88–94. Fuller accounts of the Sherman order and its consequences appear in Claude F. Oubre, *Forty Acres and a Mule: The Freedmen's Bureau and Black Land Ownership* (Baton Rouge: Louisiana State University Press, 1978), pp. 46–71; William McFeely, *Yankee Stepfather: General O. O. How-*

ard and the Freedmen (New Haven: Yale University Press, 1968), chs. 4–8; Joel Williamson, *After Slavery: The Negro in South Carolina during Reconstruction* (Chapel Hill: University of North Carolina Press, 1965), pp. 54–63, 142–59. See also Manuel Gottlieb, "The Land Question in Georgia during Reconstruction," *Science and Society* 3 (Sum. 1939):356–88; James S. Allen, *Reconstruction: The Battle for Democracy* (New York: International Publishers, 1937), ch. 2; W. E. B. Du Bois, *Black Reconstruction in America: An Essay toward a History of the Part Which Black Folk Played in the Attempt to Reconstruct Democracy in America, 1860–1880* (New York: Harcourt, Brace & Co., 1935), passim.

10. Asa L. Cotton to House of Representatives, [Dec. 1865?], Andrew Johnson Papers, Duke University, Durham, N.C. Bradley returned to the impeachment theme soon afterward. In a petition he originated in the District of Columbia early in 1866, he called for Johnson's resignation, encouraging Congress to pay him the rest of his salary for his unexpired term of office. Bradley to ?, [early 1866], 39A-H10.2, Petitions and Memorials, 39th Congress, Records of the U.S. Senate, RG 46, NA.

11. Abraham Winfield to Maj. Gen. Howard, Jan. 27, 1866, W-46 1866, Letters Received, Commissioner, Records of the Bureau of Refugees, Freedmen, and Abandoned Lands, RG 105, NA. In this and future quotations, capitalization, punctuation, and spelling peculiarities of the original manuscripts will appear without the use of [*sic*].

12. Bradley to E. M. Stanton, [Dec. 1865], Bradley to Mr. Speed, Dec. 24, 1865, B-2 1866, Letters Received, Comr., RG 105, NA; id. to Andrew Johnson, Dec. 27, 1865, S-42 1866, Letters Received, Records of the Adjutant General's Office, RG 94, NA; Tillson endorsement, dated Jan. 4, 1866, on Col. H. F. Sickles to Capt. W. W. Deane, Jan. 2, 1866, W-91 1866, Letters Received, RG 94, NA. The territorial status for the conquered South theme appears clearly in the proceedings of Bradley's military commission in the Savannah *National Republican*, Dec. 14–17, 19, 1865, also in the Asa Cotton petition of [Dec. 1865] cited in note 10 above.

13. The published proceedings of the convention do not report debates in their entirety. Aside from indicating several of Bradley's barbs at his chief rival, the Rev. Henry McNeal Turner, the proceedings only mention his support for a defeated proposal calling for Congress to treat the seceded states as territories. *Proceedings of the Freedmen's Convention of Georgia,* Jan. 10, 1866., pp. 3, 28. Tillson explains Bradley's convention role and removal in his endorsement, dated Jan. 23, 1867, on Bradley to Sen. Benjamin Wade, Jan. 3, 1867, W-17 1867, Letters Received, Comr., RG 105, NA. After the court delivered its Milligan ruling, Bureau Commissioner Howard desired to test whether or not the decision would apply to seceded and loyal states alike. At the advice of Georgia Assistant Commissioner Caleb C. Sibley, they used Bradley as their test case, but federal district court judge John Erskine refused to authorize a military trial of the black civilian and the issue was dropped. See George R. Bentley, *A History of the Freedmen's Bureau* (Philadelphia: University of Pennsylvania Press, 1955), pp. 164–65.

14. See Tillson to O. O. Howard, Feb. 6, 1866, and id. to agent W. F. Eaton, Apr. 17, 1866, Reports, Ga. Asst. Comr., RG 105, NA. For accounts of rice planters adjusting to the new order, see Frances Butler Leigh, *Ten*

Years on a Georgia Plantation since the War (1883; reprint ed., New York: Negro Universities Press, 1969); James M. Clifton, ed., *Life and Labor on Argyle Island: Letters and Documents of a Savannah River Rice Plantation, 1833–1867* (Savannah: Beehive Press, 1978), pp. 351–65; Robert Manson Myers, ed., *The Children of Pride: A True Story of Georgia and the Civil War* (New Haven: Yale University Press, 1972), pp. 1273–423. For a general survey of the transformation of the rice industry in the postbellum era, see Clifton's introduction to *Life and Labor on Argyle Island.*

15. For the antebellum background of the northern view, see Eric Foner, *Free Soil, Free Labor, Free Men: The Ideology of the Republican Party before the Civil War* (New York: Oxford University Press, 1970); for its postbellum application, see id., "Reconstruction and the Crisis of Free Labor," in id., *Politics and Ideology in the Age of the Civil War* (New York: Oxford University Press, 1980), pp. 97–127.

16. Bradley to Chief Justice O. O. Howard, Sept. 9, 1866, B-210 (No. 2) 1866, Letters Received, Comr., RG 105, NA. Bradley addressed Howard figuratively as ex officio chief justice of Freedmen's Bureau courts; Howard himself did not claim the title.

17. Bradley to Gen. [R. K.] Scott, Oct. 22, 1866, Letters Received, Mil. Dist. of S.C., Records of U. S. Army Continental Commands, RG 393, pt. 2, no. 132, NA.

18. For 1865 difficulties, see Charlotte S. Cheves to Davis Tillson, Oct. 7, 1865, Unregistered Letters Received, Ga. Asst. Comr., RG 105, NA; Capt. A. P. Ketchum to Wm. H. Tiffany, Oct. 28, 1865, Records of Capt. A. P. Ketchum, A.A.G., re Restoration of Property, Savannah, Subasst. Comr., ibid. On general developments in the Savannah River rice area during 1866, see Brandt to Lt. Col. H. W. Smith, Aug. 31, Nov. 1, 1866, and id. to Bvt. Maj. E. L. Deane, Dec. 29, 1866, vol. 260, Letters Sent, Rice Hope Plantation, S.C., ibid. An account of the 1867 difficulties coincidental with Bradley's return appears in id. to Lt. Col. H. W. Smith, Jan. 10, 1867, ibid.

19. York Sherman to O. O. Howard and Davis Tillson, [Jan. 1867], Unregistered Letters Received (filed under agent Magill, Jan. 22, 1867), Ga. Asst. Comr., RG 105, NA; Captain Shige to O. O. Howard, Jan. 16, 1867, S-37 1867, Letters Received, Comr., ibid. For another petition in Bradley's hand, see Charles Frazer to Assistant Commissioner of South Carolina, [Jan. 1867], B-22 1867, Letters Received, S.C. Asst. Comr., ibid.

20. Bradley to Wade, Jan. 3, 1867, with Tillson endorsement of Jan. 23, 1867, W-17 1867, Letters Received, Comr., ibid. See also Edw. E. Howard to J. E. Bryant, Jan. 26, 1867, John Emory Bryant Papers, Duke University. Sibley's endorsement, dated Feb. 2, 1867, appears on Captain Shige to O. O. Howard, Jan. 16, 1867, S-37 1867, Letters Received, Comr., RG 105, NA. Bureau agent H. C. Brandt (Feb. 12, 1867) and Assistant Commissioner Scott (Feb. 16, 1867) endorsed Adams Humes to O. O. Howard and R. K. Scott, [Feb. 1867], B-16 1867, Letters Received, Comr., ibid. Savannah newspapers also covered the Savannah River area unrest. See, for example, the account of Oglethorpe Plantation difficulties in the *Savannah Republican,* Jan. 31, 1867.

21. On Delany, see Victor Ullman, *Martin R. Delany: The Beginnings of Black Nationalism* (Boston: Beacon Press, 1971), pp. 327–46, 365–66. On Swails, see G. R. Whitridge to Gen. Charles Devens, Jan. 6, 1866, S-165 1866,

Letters Received, Dept. of the South, RG 393, pt. 1, NA; Williamson, *After Slavery*, pp. 82–83. On Campbell, see Tunis G. Campbell, *Sufferings of the Rev. T. G. Campbell and His Family, in Georgia* (Washington, D.C.: Enterprise Publishing Co., 1877), as well as his numerous reports to bureau officers Rufus Saxton and A. P. Ketchum, in Records of Capt. A. P. Ketchum, re Restoration of Property, Savannah Subasst. Comr., RG 105, NA.

22. For Cain's position on land at the convention, see *Proceedings of the Constitutional Convention of South Carolina* (1868; reprint ed., New York: Arno Press, 1968), pp. 107–10, 136–38, 376–81, 417–24. On his other activities, see Williamson, *After Slavery*, pp. 206–7.

23. C. Mildred Thompson, *Reconstruction in Georgia: Economic, Social, Political 1865–1872* (1915; reprint ed., Savannah: Beehive Press, 1972), p. 171n.

24. The loyal tribunals quotation appears in Bradley to Maj. Gen. G. H. Thomas, Mar. 21, 1867, A-209, Letters Received, Bureau of Civil Affairs, 3d Military District, RG 393, pt. 1, NA; the right of self-government quotation appears in Bradley to Maj. Gen. John Pope, May 28, 1867, A-481, ibid. See also Bradley to Pope, May 21, 1867, and June 5, 1867, A-417 and A-562, respectively, ibid.

25. James Mackey to Col. C. C. Sibley, [early 1867], Affidavits and Petitions, Ga. Asst. Comr., RG 105, NA, published in Edward Magdol, *A Right to the Land: Essays on the Freedmen's Community* (Westport, Conn.: Greenwood Press, 1977), app. 6. The *Savannah Republican* reported both strikes: Sept. 5–6, 1865, and Jan. 28–30, 1867.

26. Bradley to Gen. John Pope: May 28, 1867, A-481, Letters Received, Bur. Civil Affairs, 3d Mil. Dist., RG 393, pt. 1, NA; May 21, 1867, A-417, ibid.; Oct. 17, 1867, A-1868, ibid.; Oct. 26, 1867, A-1936, ibid. Id. to Gen. George G. Meade, Jan. 25, 1868; id. to U. S. Grant, Jan. 20, 1868; and Asst. Judge Advocate Gen. W. M. Drum to Bvt. Brig. Gen. R. C. Drum, Jan. 28, 1868, B-29 1868, Letters Received, 3d Mil. Dist., RG 393, pt. 1, NA. For testimony and report in an investigation of charges against Anderson made in another Bradley petition (Jan.-Feb. 1868), see file E-13 1868, ibid.

27. The hat and gloves characteristic appears in Coulter, *Negro Legislators in Georgia*, p. 82; the lackey reference ibid., p. 119; the bodyguard references in the May 16, 1868, endorsement of Maj. Geo. A. Williams, provost marshal general of the 2d Mil. Dist., on Bradley to Gen. [E. R. S. Canby], May 7, 1868, B-6 1868, Letters Received, Dept. of the South, 2d Mil. Dist., RG 393, pt. 1, NA.

28. Many blacks retained an interest in the anti-Anderson campaign. See, for example, petitions and testimony contained in files E-13 1868 and E-18 1868, Letters Received, 3d Mil. Dist., RG 393, pt. 1, NA. Moreover white Republicans also petitioned for Anderson's removal for their own reasons. See F. S. Hesseltine to Maj. Gen. John Pope, Oct. 3, 1867, enclosed in J. W. Clift to Maj. Gen. John Pope, Oct. 4, 1867, Applications Received for Civil Positions in the Counties, Bur. of Civil Affairs, ibid.; and citizens of Savannah to Maj. Gen. Geo. G. Meade, May 29, 1868, S-275 1868, Letters Received, ibid.

29. Alone among Savannah black leaders, Bradley lacked ties to any black social, religious, or benevolent organization. See John W. Blassingame, "Be-

fore the Ghetto: The Making of the Black Community in Savannah, Georgia, 1865–1880," *Journal of Social History* 6 (Sum. 1973):476–77.

30. "Ye shall not afflict any widow, or fatherless child." Exodus 22:22. But cf. Lincoln, Mar. 4, 1865: "With malice toward none; with charity for all . . . let us strive on . . . to care for him who shall have borne the battle, and for his widow, and his orphan." Abraham Lincoln, *The Collected Works of Abraham Lincoln*, 8 vols., ed. Roy P. Basler (New Brunswick, N.J.: Rutgers University Press, 1953), 8:333.

31. E. C. Anderson to Gen. John Pope, Sept. 18, 1867, S-99 1867, Letters Received, 3d Mil. Dist., RG 393, NA. On the meeting, see *Savannah Republican*, Oct. 1, 1867.

32. See notice of an upcoming meeting in *Savannah Republican*, July 5, 1865; also report of various Union League clubs' participation in the annual Liberian Independence Day Celebration, ibid., July 27, 1865.

33. See n. 25 above and Bradley to Maj. Gen. John Pope, May 28, 1867, A-481, Letters Received, Bur. of Civil Affairs, 3d Mil. Dist., RG 393, pt. 1, NA; Registers of Signatures of Depositors in Branches of the Freedmen's Savings and Trust Company, Savannah, Georgia Branch, RG 101, NA.

34. On the ordinance, see Bradley and J. H. Grant to Gen. Pope, October 17, 1867, A-1868, Letters Received, Bur. of Civil Affairs, 3d Mil. Dist., RG 393, pt. 1, NA. For Anderson's enforcement of the ordinance against black assemblies, see statement of Moses Bentley, [Feb. 1868] in E-18 1868, ibid.; and statement of Bradley, Feb. 8, 1868, B-29 1868, ibid. For the matter with Bradley's landlady, see Bradley to Maj. Gen. Geo. G. Meade, Apr. 24, 1868, and Edw. C. Anderson statement, May 2, 1868, B-176 1868, ibid.

35. For statements suggesting black opposition to Bradley, see Capt. H. C. Cook to Lt. John E. Hosmer, Oct. 3, 1867, S-109 1867, ibid.; and *Savannah Republican*, Oct. 1, 1867. On stratification in the black community, see Blassingame, "Before the Ghetto," 466–68. On the role of whites in shaping the views of certain blacks in an antipolitical direction, see James M. Simms, *The First Colored Baptist Church in North America* (Philadelphia: J. P. Lippincott, 1888), p. 190.

36. Brandt to Bvt. Maj. E. L. Deane, Oct. 31, 1867, vol. 260, Letters Sent, Rice Hope Plantn., RG 105, NA; Z. Haynes to Gen. Canby, Nov. 30, 1867, H-69 1867, Letters Received, Dept. of the South, 2d Mil. Dist., RG 393, pt. 1, NA; Brandt to Deane, Dec. 26, 1867, vol. 260, Letters Sent, Rice Hope Plantn., RG 105, NA.

37. The journal of the Constitutional Convention of 1867 gives no indication of the political maneuvering involved in the proceedings. For such information it is necessary to consult the daily reports of convention business in the Atlanta newspapers, especially the Atlanta *Intelligencer*. Bradley's position on the issues discussed above appears in the proceedings for December 13 and 16, 1867, and January 8, 10, 15, 25, and 29, 1868. See Coulter, *Negro Legislators in Georgia*, pp. 43–61. See also Bradley's defense against the charges in his statement and supporting petition, Feb. 12, 1868, J-38 1868, Letters Received, Bur. Civil Affairs, 3d Mil. Dist., RG 393, NA. On the Republican relief strategy, see Nathans, *Losing the Peace*, pp. 40–44, 60–63; on black officeholding, see ibid., pp. 66–69, 152–53.

38. On blacks in Georgia politics, see John M. Matthews, "Negro Republi-

cans in the Reconstruction of Georgia," *Georgia Historical Quarterly* 60 (Sum. 1976):145–64; and, in many ways more valuable, his unpublished essay "The Negro in Georgia Politics, 1865–1880" (M.A. thesis, Duke University, 1967). See also Nathans, *Losing the Peace,* passim; Coulter, *Negro Legislators in Georgia,* pp. 55–80.

39. The Savannah *Morning News* gave almost daily accounts of the insurrection during December 1868 and January 1869.

40. Bradley statement of resolutions, Jan. 18, 1870, B-7 1870, Letters Received, Dept. of the South, RG 393, pt. 1, NA; Coulter, *Negro Legislators in Georgia,* pp. 81–99; broadside, "A New System of Chain Gang Slavery," Boston Public Library. Bradley's personal disenchantment with Atlanta politics increased with the unsuccessful effort of his fellow senators to expel him, again for alleged prior crimes. See his protests: Bradley to Gen. Alfred A. Terry, May 4, 1870, B-7 1870, Letters Received, Dept. of the South, RG 393, pt. 1, NA; and Bradley to Maj. Gen. Alfred A. Terry, July 25, 1870, filed with W-91 1866, Letters Received, Adjt. Gen. Office, RG 94, NA. Terry's name appears as Bradley wrote it; his middle initial was actually H.

41. Savannah *Morning News,* Oct.-Dec. 1870, esp. Oct. 6, 1870; Coulter, *Negro Legislators in Georgia,* pp. 91–99. Houston ran simultaneously as candidate for state representative from Bryan County and was elected. To some extent Bradley's independence paralleled that of white party stalwart John E. Bryant; but the latter, unlike Bradley, was a serious contender for the customhouse collectorship. See Ruth Currie McDaniel, "Georgia Carpetbagger: John Emory Bryant and the Ambiguity of Reform during Reconstruction" (Ph.D. diss., Duke University, 1974).

42. This trend continued, so that by mid-decade only 600 of the estimated 6,000 eligible black voters were registered. See Matthews, "Negro in Georgia Politics," p. 109–10.

43. Olive Shadgett draws a clear distinction between these new leaders and their Reconstruction forebears but stresses continuing factionalism among black Georgia Republicans. Olive Hall Shadgett, *The Republican Party in Georgia from Reconstruction to 1900* (Athens: University of Georgia Press, 1964), pp. 78, 79–97. See also Robert E. Perdue, *The Negro in Savannah 1865–1900* (New York: Exposition Press, 1973), pp. 90–93; Clarence A. Bacote, "The Negro in Georgia Politics, 1880–1908" (Ph.D. diss., University of Chicago, 1955).

44. Simms, *First Colored Baptist Church,* pp. 156–71.

45. The following discussion of the anti-Robb campaign comes from documents in his appointment file: Custom House Appointments, Savannah, General Records of the Department of the Treasury, RG 56, NA.

46. The Peoples Deligate to President U. S. Grant, [late Sept. 1871], ibid.

47. Bradley petition, [Oct. 11, 1871], with attached petition of Peter Parker, Oct. 11, 1871, ibid. Ninety names besides Bradley's appear on the former; eighty-one accompany Parker's on the latter.

48. Paul Gordon deposition, Oct. 16, 1871; Preamble and Resolutions of Chatham County Republican Executive Committee, Oct. 16, 1871; James Washington deposition [154 names in all], Oct. 21, 1871, ibid.

49. John H. Deveaux to the President of the United States, [Oct. 1871], Oct. 21, 1871; R. W. White petition, Oct. 18, 1871, ibid.

50. Bradley deposition addressed to President Grant and his cabinet, Dec. 29, 1871; T. P. Robb to the President, Feb. 18, 1872, ibid.

51. Coulter, *Negro Legislators in Georgia*, pp. 106–7. To illustrate further Bradley's continued popularity among rice workers, in January 1872 he spoke at a rally opposing congressional efforts to repeal the duty on foreign rice and proposed petitioning the House Ways and Means Committee. See Savannah *Morning News*, Jan. 23, 1872.

52. Bradley to President Grant, [Sept. 1869], Letters Received from the President, Atty. Gen.'s Papers, RG 60, NA; id. to Maj. Gen. Terry, Dec. 29, 1869, B-27 1869, Letters Received, Dept. of the South, RG 393, pt. 1, NA; id. to Gen. Alfred H. Terry, Feb. 12, 1870, B-7 1870, ibid. For fears of Bradley-led unrest, see Mayor John Swain to Gov. James J. Smith, Sept. 1872, Gov. Smith's Corres., Georgia Dept. of Archives and History.

53. Bradley to Charles F. Conant, Sept. 14, 1874, Custom House Nominations, Savannah, RG 56, NA.

54. Bradley election broadside in Bryant Scrapbooks, Bryant Papers, Duke University.

55. See Duncan Clinch Heyward, *Seed from Madagascar* (Chapel Hill: University of North Carolina Press, 1937), pp. 141–42, on the importance of the home place among lowcountry blacks. The best account of the South Carolina land commission is Carol K. R. Bleser, *The Promised Land: The History of the South Carolina Land Commission, 1869–1890* (Columbia, S.C.: University of South Carolina Press, 1969); of the Liberian Exodus movement, George B. Tindall, *South Carolina Negroes, 1877–1900* (Columbia: University of South Carolina Press, 1952), pp. 153–68, 169–85. For the Florida scheme, see Coulter, *Negro Legislators in Georgia*, p. 108.

56. A twentieth-century rice planter observed that her renters all owned small plots. Patience Pennington [Elizabeth W. Allston Pringle], *A Woman Rice Planter* (New York: Macmillan Co., 1913), p. 5. Clearly the plots did not provide sufficiently to free blacks from engaging in the dying rice economy. On manifestations of cultural isolation, see Lorenzo D. Turner, *Africanisms in the Gullah Dialect* (Chicago: University of Chicago Press, 1949); on the strong influence of the supernatural, see Georgia Writers Project, *Drums and Shadows: Survival Studies among the Georgia Coastal Negroes* (Athens: University of Georgia Press, 1940).

57. See Philip S. Foner and Ronald L. Lewis, eds., *The Black Worker: A Documentary History*, 4 vols. to date (Philadelphia: Temple University Press, 1978–), 3:366–405.

58. Clarence A. Bacote, "Negro Proscriptions, Protests and Proposed Solutions in Georgia, 1880–1908," *Journal of Southern History* 25 (Nov. 1959):471–98; August Meier and Elliott Rudwick, "The Boycott Movement against Jim Crow Streetcars in the South, 1900–1906," *Journal of American History* 55 (Mar. 1969):756–75; John Dittmer, *Black Georgia in the Progressive Era 1900–1920* (Urbana: University of Illinois Press, 1977), pp. 17–19.

William Finch of Atlanta:
The Black Politician as Civic Leader

ALTHOUGH the career of William Finch and the politics of nineteenth-century Atlanta have already been investigated by historians, Finch is an appropriate figure for a much needed examination of black urban politicians in the Reconstruction South. A prominent organizer of the local Republican party and councilman in 1871, Finch was representative of a pioneering group of black leaders in Reconstruction Atlanta who regarded political activity a civic duty rather than a means to promote Republican party interests or their own careers. Finch's leadership cannot be understood without paying close attention to the political environment in which he operated and the needs and nature of the black community he served. His political behavior and public career also were shaped by his personality and background.[1]

Like many of Altanta's black leaders of the immediate postbellum period, William Finch was a newcomer who migrated to the city in the late 1860s. He was a mulatto born October 1, 1832, in Washington, Georgia, a small town in Wilkes County, where he spent the first sixteen years of his life. His father was a white man named Finch; his mother, Frances, was a slave.[2] In 1844 he went to live with a local judge and a few years later he was apprenticed to a tailor. This apprenticeship prepared Finch for his lifetime vocation. In 1848 Joseph H. Lumpkin, the chief justice of the Georgia Supreme Court from its inception in 1845 until his death in 1867, purchased Finch and brought him to Athens.[3]

Finch's experience in Athens (1848–66) profoundly shaped his life. The Lumpkin family taught him to read and write. He became convinced that literacy was the key to Afro-American advancement and devoted much of his life to championing educational causes. He also became involved in church activities. He underwent a religious conversion in 1848 and embarked upon a life-long career as a church leader.[4]

Little is known about Finch's family life in Athens. He married Laura Wright in 1854. Three children were born to the couple before the Civil War, and two more were born during the war. Except for

Finch's service with Lumpkin's son in the Confederate army, the judge made little attempt to interfere with his slave's family.[5]

As a skilled slave, Finch avoided many of the hardships of the fieldhands, and it is quite possible that he hired his own time. The outbreak of the Civil War disrupted the southern economy, and Finch utilized his tailoring skill to take advantage of the demand for artisans. The war brought him and his family increased freedom and greater prosperity. By 1865 he had amassed over $135 in gold.[6]

Finch thought highly of his owner, accepted many of his values, and ascribed "much of his success in his business life to the conversations which used . . . to occur between himself and Chief Justice Lumpkin." Yet at the same time that Finch internalized white bourgeois values he also felt a keen sense of loyalty to his race. He might appreciate the opportunities Judge Lumpkin afforded him and loyally serve with the judge's son in the Confederate army, but when the army of liberation came through Athens, Finch welcomed it with enthusiasm, presenting a United States flag to the 144th New York Regiment.[7]

It did not take Finch long to break the ties of slavery. By the summer of 1865 he was on his own, purchasing a home in Athens for his family. He immediately immersed himself in community affairs; with Daniel Bridges he established a freedmen's school. By August he had persuaded Bernard Jacobs, a drum major in a New York regiment, to serve as the school's teacher. "I don't suppose that any colored school has been opened anywhere under more Difficult Circumstances than this, without any help and hardly any Books," Finch wrote the Georgia Freedmen's Bureau, "but with a firm Determination that we would open our School and do what we could toward Educating our Selves."[8] Finch worked hard to make the school a success; and when Jacobs returned north, he recruited two southern white ladies to replace the drummer. He actively solicited financial support from the Freedmen's Bureau and sought as much aid as possible from local blacks.[9]

In light of William Finch's educational endeavors, it is not surprising that he soon became politically involved. In late 1865 the freed people of Clarke County elected Finch chairman of a four-man delegation to a convention in Augusta. The convention had been called by John Emory Bryant, a white Union officer and bureau agent, to discuss the freedmen's political and social problems. Meeting in January 1866, black representatives from 18 of Georgia's 132 counties organized the Equal Rights Association, a forerunner of the Republican party in the state. The group issued a series of demands that included the enfranchisement of blacks and the establishment of "equal justice without

310

ADVERTISEMENT, *Atlanta City Directory*, 1892
Atlanta Historical Society

WILLIAM FINCH
Atlanta Historical Society

311

any equivocation or evasion of natural rights." Finch was chosen as one of the group's vice presidents and later served as authorized agent in Clarke County for the association's newspaper, *The Loyal Georgian*.[10]

Soon after becoming active in the Equal Rights Association, Finch moved to Augusta. It appears likely that his move was in part political. Because Finch had distinguished himself at the January convention, Bryant might have promised him a job. The position never materialized, however; and failing to prosper as a tailor, he moved again in 1868, to Atlanta, where he remained for the rest of his life.

Finch's motive in moving twice in the late 1860s probably related to his desire to advance himself. Athens, a small town, offered fewer opportunities to a tailor than did Augusta or booming Atlanta. Moreover, his children would soon outgrow the freedmen's school in Athens, and in Atlanta they could acquire more than just a rudimentary education. Arriving in Atlanta fifty dollars in debt, Finch formed a partnership with Danwell Byrdie and opened a tailor shop on Whitehall Street. He soon was so successful that he could branch out on his own. He opened his own business (perhaps buying out Byrdie), sent for his family in Athens, and settled permanently in Atlanta.[11]

The majority of Reconstruction Atlanta's black population did not escape poverty or illiteracy as did Finch. Less than 19 percent of the city's black male household heads in 1870 owned property, and the median property holding of those who did was only $400. Nearly 85 percent of the city's black household heads in the same year were illiterate. Clearly Finch, with property valued at $1,000, was part of the economic and educated elite of black Atlanta.[12]

One other characteristic of Atlanta's black community which influenced the evolution of its political leadership was that many of its members were newcomers. Only 1,914 slaves and 25 free Negroes lived in the city in 1860. The Afro-American population swelled during and after the Civil War; by 1870, the city's black population stood at 9,929.[13] This population influx had important consequences for black politics. Politically active newcomers such as Finch, James Tate, George Graham, and Jackson McHenry did not have to contend for leadership roles with an older and exclusive elite. Especially notable by its absence was any kind of black aristocracy made up of those who had lived in antebellum Atlanta as free Negroes. Initially, therefore, black Atlantans were more politically unified than were blacks in other southern cities.[14]

Concentrating on his business, Finch's involvement in politics was minimal for the first several years of his residency in Atlanta. Yet until 1870 there was little reason for him to become politically active. Black Atlantans acquired the right to vote in 1867 but exerted only a minimal influence on most elections. Unlike other cities in the state, Atlanta did not have a black electoral majority, a situation that encouraged the newly formed Republican party there to ignore the freedmen and concentrate on attracting white voters. In the fall of 1867 black Atlantans, irritated about being taken for granted, decided to nominate their own ticket for the state constitutional convention. Only after white Republicans made some concessions did blacks agree to support the party's choices for the convention. The seeds of distrust had been planted, and tension between white and black Republicans weakened party efforts in Atlanta.[15]

A change in Atlanta's municipal election law shortly after the freedmen's enfranchisement also dissipated black political strength. Before 1868 voters in each ward had elected their own representative to the city council. Fearing the election of Republican councilmen from the Third and Fourth wards where black voters were in the majority, local Democrats in 1868 persuaded the Georgia legislature to alter municipal election procedures in Atlanta. Under the revised procedure, councilmen ran in citywide elections; and since white voters outnumbered black voters in Atlanta, Afro-American political influence was effectively minimized.[16]

Few freedmen voted in the 1868 and 1869 city elections. Shortly before the 1868 election, the city attorney discovered that Atlanta's 1847 municipal charter did not recognize blacks as voters. Although the city council resolved to suspend the election until the state legislature corrected the charter, the Democratic party ignored this resolution and held the election. The following year whites erected a new obstacle to black voting in Atlanta in the form of a city ordinance requiring a poll tax. Blacks participated in both the Democratic primary and the general election anyway; and according to the *Constitution*, "the colored population was out in strong numbers" during the latter election. In fact, enough blacks turned out that the police became alarmed and arrested some in an effort to hold down the count.[17]

Despite this interest on the part of black voters, Republicans had little chance to capitalize on their political strength in the Third and Fourth wards as long as councilmen were elected in citywide contests. Changes in the Georgia legislature allowed the party to alter the city's election laws. These changes occurred after the legislature had expelled twenty-eight of its thirty-two black members in September

1868. Congress ordered a second Reconstruction of Georgia, enabling Governor Rufus Bullock to purge the Conservative element in the legislature and reseat the expelled black members. With Radicals in control, Henry C. Holcombe, a Republican representative from Fulton County, maneuvered through the legislature a bill that restored the old procedures in Atlanta's elections; and Governor Bullock signed the measure on October 25, 1870. Thus the upcoming election of councilmen in Atlanta would be by wards instead of by citywide contests.[18]

With his business flourishing and his family comfortably settled in Atlanta, Finch became politically active during the summer of 1870. In August he helped to organize the Mechanics' and Laborers' Union, a predominantly black Republican group, served as its assistant secretary, and was elected a delegate to the National Labor Convention in Cincinnati. Several months later, when Republican ward clubs met in Atlanta, Finch served as chairman of the Fourth Ward club. It was this organization that nominated him and D. D. Snyder, a white federal revenue officer, to run for the council.[19]

Finch's political rise only two years after he came to the city was not unusual in Atlanta. With rapid population growth, class lines within the black community were fluid, and leaders were often newcomers. Thus William Finch, with his experience in the Equal Rights Association and the Mechanics' and Laborers' Union, a growing tailor trade, membership in Bethel Church, the dominant black institution in the Fourth Ward, and residency in Shermantown, the black enclave of that ward, was a figure of some renown; and it is not surprising that he was nominated for the city council.

After the Republican nominations for city council, Finch and other black political leaders, such as James Tate, a Fourth Ward grocer, and Jackson McHenry, a drayman and candidate for city council from the Fifth Ward, spoke at several city rallies. At these rallies Finch praised the party and called for blacks to unite behind the Republican candidates for office. He also identified his candidacy with the proposed public school system, calling for "educational facilities for *all*," whether the students be "laborers' children" or "colored children."[20]

While the inclusion of Finch and two other black candidates—McHenry from the Fifth Ward and George Graham, an illiterate carpenter from the Third Ward—stimulated black enthusiasm for the Republican municipal ticket, it made it difficult to attract a candidate for mayor. Four Republicans refused to accept the nomination, and at least two of them probably did so because of the presence of blacks on the ticket. Unable to find a white Republican, party leaders eventually decided to endorse Dennis F. Hammond, who had entered the mayor's race as an independent. Hammond had been a Democrat for thirty years, but in 1869 he voted for the Republican candidate for mayor.[21]

With black majorities in both the Third and Fourth wards, Finch and the other three Republican candidates from those wards seemed assured of victory on election day. Nevertheless, both municipal officials and police worked to offset the black numerical advantage and prevent a number of Republicans from voting. Election officials checked the residence of each black Republican voter while they permitted any Democrat to vote unimpeded. When a prominent politician brought his house servant to the polls, the servant's ballot "was received without a word, as he voted the Democratic ticket, but when a colored man wanted to vote a Republican ticket he was compelled to prove where he lived." In addition, officials tried to collect poll taxes from Republicans in direct violation of instructions from the Georgia legislature.[22]

The police assisted election officials, intimidating black voters and keeping some from the polls. Their actions were especially effective in the Fifth Ward, where Jackson McHenry was running a strong race. After police arrested and assaulted one voter, blacks followed them to the city jail. The crowd refused to disperse, and when one of their leaders was arrested, they hurled bricks at the police. The lawmen opened fire, killing two bystanders and wounding five others. Only after the disturbance was over did United States troops appear, prompting the *Methodist Advocate* to comment sarcastically: "Probably their services were not needed until a few 'Niggers' had been killed."[23]

Such tactics undoubtedly enabled the Democrats to maintain control in the Fifth Ward. Had either Jackson McHenry or the white Republican candidate won, the council would have been evenly divided between Republicans and Democrats. By carrying the Fifth Ward, Democrats ensured that they would be in the majority, outnumbering the Republicans six to four on the city council. This situation obviously limited the Republicans' ability to carry out some of the planks in their platform, which, in addition to commitments to inaugurate a public school system, municipal water works, and city hospitals, also included promises of a uniformed police force and street improvements.[24]

Although outnumbered, the Republicans could hope to implement some of these planks if they consistently voted as a unit, persuaded a few Democrats to support them on key issues, and gained the support or at least the neutrality of Mayor Hammond, whose independent candidacy the party had championed. Finch manifested a shrewd awareness of these facts at the very outset of his term and was not intimidated by the prospect of serving on a political body dominated by white Democrats. During the campaign he had made a special point of appealing to white working-class voters on the school issue. In accepting his nomination he announced his intention to promote the concerns of all Atlanta's citizens regardless of race or party.[25]

Probably Finch was encouraged by Mayor Hammond's impartial assignments of councilmen to the standing committees, committees that administered most of the functions and services of Atlanta's government in 1871. Hammond made a genuine effort to divide equitably between Republicans and Democrats positions on these committees. While no Republican was assigned to the most powerful of these committees—Finance, which apportioned municipal revenues to the various departments—Finch was put on the important street committee, which throughout the nineteenth century spent the lion's share of the city's income. His other committee duties were less impressive. Graham, the other black councilman, was relegated to committees on Printing and Wells, Pumps, and Cisterns. Because of his illiteracy, Graham was unable to serve effectively on these committees or contribute significantly to the council's proceedings.[26]

Perhaps most pleasing to black Atlantans was Mayor Hammond's appointment of a Republican, D. D. Snyder, as chairman of the Police Committee. With Snyder at the head of that committee, blacks could hope to have a sympathetic ally in complaints brought against the police. Maintaining that the appointment of Snyder would lead to the hiring of black policemen, Democrats reacted quickly to overturn the mayor's decision. On January 20, 1871, they voted Snyder out and installed a fellow Democrat instead.[27]

Snyder's behavior in this dispute must have raised questions in the minds of Finch and other black leaders about the commitment of white Republicans to the party's platform and racial reform. When his appointment as chairman of the Police Committee was discussed at the very first meeting of the city council, Snyder remarked that he had "no interest in serving on the committee." At the next council meeting, when he was deposed, he was not even present to record his vote on the matter. Thereafter his attendance at council meetings was sporadic, as was that of S. W. Grubb, the other white Republican councilman. Unlike Finch and Graham who had perfect attendance records at council

316

meetings, both Snyder and Grubb were absent when key votes were taken on public schools, municipal water works, and other important issues. Both white Republicans seemed much more interested in state politics than in municipal affairs.[28]

The indifference of the two white Republicans to local concerns forced Finch to seek alliances with his Democratic colleagues on the council. The hostile reception those colleagues gave to each and every motion or resolution Finch proposed during the first few months of 1871 would have caused a less patient man to abandon all hope of compromise. The very first statement by Finch recorded in the official minutes of the council was an innocuous suggestion that the marshal be asked to restrain the "nocturnal wanderings" of Atlanta's numerous streetwalkers. Although similar complaints about *nymphs du pave* were routinely voiced in council minutes before and after Finch's term of office, on this occasion Finch was curtly informed that "everybody had a right to be on the streets at night!"[29] During another meeting of the council, Finch persuaded his colleagues to deny extension of the license of Joe Rutledge's "Educated Hog and Snake Show" on Humbug Square, an area near the city's center. At the next council meeting, however, an appearance by Rutledge, a white man, led to the reversal of Finch's motion. In yet another council meeting, Finch offered a resolution thanking the ladies of Atlanta for their efforts in relief of the poor. This resolution was rejected, too, by a strictly partisan vote of the councilmen.[30]

The most humiliating insult that Finch had to absorb from his Democratic associates occurred after a policemen, C. M. Barry, threatened to arrest him. Barry, who several years earlier had been briefly discharged from the force for beating a pregnant freedwoman, assaulted Finch at a session of the mayor's court. Finch had gone behind the bar of the court during the trial of several black prostitutes and was forcibly ejected by Barry—on the ground that no one but the accused, witnesses, and necessary legal officers had a right to be in that area of the courtroom.[31]

Despite his status, Finch had been treated as a common vagrant. But when he appealed to his colleagues to reprimand the policeman, urging the council to "look upon this case not in relation to color or Republicanism" but as an affront to one of its members, his appeal fell on deaf ears. With other Republicans strangely silent, the Democrats dismissed the case against Patrolman Barry for lack of jurisdiction. On other occasions the same councilmen tried and fired policemen charged with lesser offenses. Finch's political position, however, had

317

neither afforded him protection from police harassment nor allowed him to redress his grievances.[32]

Although he did launch a few stinging barbs of his own during one council meeting, Finch otherwise managed to keep his temper and brush aside ugly incidents such as the Barry affair. He frequently supported Democratic proposals to the council that he believed would benefit all of Atlanta's people. These proposals included booster-oriented projects such as a $7,000 municipal appropriation to encourage the state agricultural society to locate its fairs in Atlanta and a resolution in support of the Georgia Western Railroad, which received a $300,000 subscription from the city government. Finch and the three other Republicans joined the Democrats in unanimous approval of both of these projects.[33]

In a surprising number of instances Finch broke party ranks during council meetings and sided with the Democrats on votes pertaining to street improvements and routine municipal business. Finch was the only Republican to join the Democrats in voting for a resolution to secure a list of male Atlantans subject to the street tax and to force all defaulters to work the streets without pay. This resolution was aimed at Atlanta's impoverished black males. Finch was also the only Republican to vote in favor of a motion authorizing an appropriation of $17,150 for the widening of Broad Street in the central business district. Moreover, he vigorously defended the Democratic chairman of the Street Committee, Nicholas L. McLendon, against both Republican and Democratic criticism during two lively controversies. McLendon was charged on one occasion with ordering city-street cart hands to construct terraces on a lot belonging to his brother-in-law and in the other instance with illegally keeping a wooden shanty and a delivery stable within the fire limits.[34]

Finch's motive in defending McLendon and siding with the Democrats at times clearly involved building up political debts that would be paid to the account of his own constituents. Not long after Finch had voted for widening Broad Street, the Street Committee reported in favor of building a rock culvert on Jackson Street on the city's outskirts, near the property of William Jennings, a white Republican. One Democratic councilman spoke against this measure, complaining of the want of "a good sewerage in the business part of the city" and stating his opposition "to lobbying such things through." That statement touched Finch in a sensitive spot, with the result that he "got his blood up, pitched his voice to a high key, and indignantly insisted that he knew nothing at all about the lobbying."[35] Despite his denials, the

318

minutes of the city council in 1871 contain abundant evidence of Finch's skill at lobbying: a successful motion to remove obstructions from Stephens Street in a black neighborhood; approval of another motion to build a rock culvert on Markham Street near a black Baptist church; and acceptance of yet another resolution to lay a sidewalk in front of Bethel AME Church. Quite possibly none of these municipal improvements would have been delivered without Finch's lobbying.[36]

Even his stance on McLendon's wooden shanties had benefits for his constituents. Housing was expensive and transportation poor in Atlanta during the 1870s. Many blacks were forced to live in shanties near the city's center. Strict enforcement of fire-limit regulations would have eliminated housing and employment opportunities for many blacks. Finch, who was on the Fire Committee as well as the Street Committee, was thus understandably lenient about enforcement of the fire limits.[37]

Finch's constituent services also included the introduction or support of numerous petitions from black organizations for the use of City Hall to hold fairs and festivals. He frequently brought to the council's attention those who were in need of assistance from the Relief Committee. His last two motions to the city council (both adopted unanimously) requested the purchase of an ax and a saw for a blind sawyer and a pair of boots for a Fourth-Ward street hand.[38]

Perhaps the hardest battle in defense of black interests occurred during the spring and early summer of 1871. Finch and his Republican colleagues fought a rear-guard action to prevent Democrats from extending Mitchell Street through the campus of Atlanta University, a black school founded in 1867. Had Mitchell Street been extended, it not only would have divided the campus property, but it would have destroyed a valuable classroom and dormitory building. Several prominent whites attacked Finch for his efforts, but his delaying tactics gave the school administrators time to obtain a court injunction. The issue was resolved finally in the courts to the advantage of the school.[39]

In addition to his support for Atlanta University, Finch as councilman was a leading advocate for public education. Although the inauguration of public schools had been overwhelmingly approved by Atlanta voters in 1870, the Democratic councilmen at first failed to act on the approved referendum. At a March 1871 council meeting, Finch made clear his commitment to schools for all races and classes. Perhaps because of his efforts, the council several months later recommended that city officials incorporate two missionary schools for blacks into the Atlanta school system.[40]

ATLANTA UNIVERSITY WITH PATH THAT WOULD HAVE BECOME MITCHELL STREET EXTENSION
Atlanta Historical Society

By the time of its dissolution, the 1871 council had achieved a record of positive accomplishments: a plan for inaugurating public schools, a uniformed police force, and street and sanitation improvements in long neglected neighborhoods. Although a minority member of the minority party, Finch had succeeded in advancing the interests of his constituents. In short, given the limited power of his position, Finch did an excellent job of squeezing concessions from his Democratic associates on the council.

One reason Finch worked well with the Democrats was because he frequently sought the approval and support of southern whites. Believing that the activities of black political figures could help to elevate the race, Finch walked a thin line between political realism and accommodation. He realized that his presence on the city council would not immediately usher in a new millennium in race relations, but he hoped that as whites saw black councilmen act in a law-abiding, responsible manner, their respect for Afro-Americans would grow to the point where they might concede them more rights. When the interests of black Atlantans were threatened, such as in the attempt to divide the Atlanta University campus, Finch persistently defended black concerns. On other occasions, however, he urged conciliation and compromise with whites, and did his best to appease those on the council. Such an approach quite possibly had been perfected before the Civil War when Finch had been the slave of Judge Joseph H. Lumpkin. Thus it seems likely that Finch's paternal relationship with the chief justice shaped his political thinking while on the council.

Above all Finch feared group protests and demonstrations. Such confrontations only hardened white attitudes and proved to be counterproductive. Consequently, on several occasions he tried to disperse black mobs. During the city election of December 1870, for example, Finch worked arduously to avoid conflict. He noted: at a time "when disturbances were looked for, I advised and talked with those of my race. In fact, some prominent white persons sent for me to go to the calaboose. I went and spoke to the colored people, and used every exertion to try and disband them." The police shootings during that election no doubt further convinced Finch of the futility of street demonstrations.[41]

Eight months later, in August 1871, Finch again intervened to calm angry blacks and persuade them to disband. A crowd of persons who were upset about the senseless death of a fellow black Atlantan had formed outside the courthouse at the trial of James Alexander, a chain-gang guard who had beaten a prisoner to death and then at-

321

tempted to conceal the murder. Those who could not find seating inside the courthouse gathered outside, milling around, and shouting at Alexander when the police brought him from the courthouse to the jail.[42] Fearful that his motives might be misunderstood, Finch at first ignored white requests that he intervene; but as the tension increased Finch "advised and counseled the colored people to go to their homes and to let the law take its course."[43]

The councilman's efforts as conciliator earned him a blistering attack in the Atlanta *Sun*. Characterizing Finch as a villain, a cutthroat, and "a notorious leader of bad men," the paper found it evident that Finch and another black Republican "were leading spirits of the contemplated movement" of disorder. Several days later the paper thundered, "If a crowd of savage, worthless, irresponsible negroes are to intimidate the law-abiding citizens of this place, . . . [p]rompt and determined actions on the part of the officers will go far toward quieting the riotous proclivities of these negroes."[44] Police interference, of course, was precisely what Finch hoped to avoid and was why he urged the group to go home.

The *Sun*'s attack was particularly painful because Finch had intervened at the request of whites. During the Alexander trial "prominent men in Atlanta, and Democrats too, . . . asked me to counsel with the colored people and try and influence them to behave—and I have done so." Finch perceived this action as a way to promote harmonious race relations in Atlanta. "On each and every occasion," he declared, "I have exerted myself to preserve and keep up the kindest feeling between the white and colored people." Pointing to his effort eight months earlier, on election day, to avoid a racial confrontation, Finch concluded, "I have endeavored to do my duty on all occasions where law and order is concerned and shall so continue to do." Yet his efforts, as far as the *Sun* was concerned, were detrimental, leaving him to wonder why the *Sun* should "so persistently attack and misrepresent" him.[45]

In defending himself against the *Sun*'s attack, Finch also gave clues why he dropped out of Republican party politics a few years later. "I have my shop and am in it and at work every day," he wrote, "and am glad to say, that the greater part of my patronage is from white men, and the greater part of it from Democrats."[46] By associating with the Republican party and running for office he undoubtedly lost some customers. Such an economic price perhaps appeared worthwhile when Republicans had a chance of winning local elections; but as the party's chances for victory became more and more remote, Finch probably decided that party work was not worth the loss in customers at his tailor shop. In late 1871, Democrats, who had gained control of the state legislature, rewrote Atlanta's election law. Council members now were to run in citywide races; consequently, Republicans had little chance of winning seats on the city council. During crucial state and federal elections of 1872 and 1874, Democrats in Atlanta resorted to force and intimidation to ensure victory. Finch's identification with the Republican party had become an economic liability and his interest in party politics gradually waned.[47]

Finch's waning interest in the Republican party contrasted sharply with that of his close political associate, James Tate, a Fourth-Ward grocer. Tate, who had arrived in the city sometime in 1865, taught in a freedmen's school for a year and then embarked on a successful career as a grocer. After serving as Fulton County representative to the Equal Rights Association, he joined the Republican party. In 1870 he became a candidate for the state legislature. Although he had little chance of winning, he campaigned actively. Tate and Finch made an effective team, and the two men spoke at several mass meetings. Their efforts brought a large number of blacks to the polls, ensuring the election of Republican councilmen from the Third and Fourth wards.[48]

Unlike Finch, Tate maintained his affiliation with the Republican party for the rest of his life. He supported its efforts in local affairs long after the state legislature had changed Atlanta's election law that made council races at-large instead of ward elections. In 1875, in an attempt to revitalize the party, he advocated support of certain acceptable Democratic councilmen. Tate urged blacks "to vote for any democrats which the republican executive committee might place upon their ticket on the grounds that although they were democrats in name, still the party that elected them would have claims upon them which they would be bound to respect." Such a strategy proved a failure, however, and the Republicans ceased to be a threat in local elections. Despite these setbacks, Tate continued his party work well into the 1880s.[49]

With his grocery on Decatur Street conveniently adjacent to the growing black settlement of Shermantown, Tate could remain active in politics and suffer no loss in business. Finch, however, faced a different problem. In 1871 he asked, "Why should I quarrel with those, or be estranged from those from whom I earn my bread, or why try and bring about trouble among the races?"[50] It became obvious to him that his party work was becoming incompatible with his profession. Although Finch ran for the city council in 1871, 1872, and 1879, he dropped out of the party after attending the Republican National Convention as a Georgia delegate in 1872. Three years later, when James Tate was organizing Republican ward clubs and plotting a new strategy to enhance black political influence in the city, Finch was conspicuously absent. In 1884, after the Republicans mentioned him as a possible candidate for the state legislature, he told a reporter: "If they want to make a fool of anybody they must find someone else. They can't put me up by myself to be shot at."[51]

After his term on the city council, William Finch became a less visible figure in black leadership circles. He searched for other avenues in which he might achieve the prestige of councilman, but he never duplicated his earlier success. In the 1870s he worked to improve the Atlanta public schools. His efforts kept the school issue before city officials and made the white community conscious of black desires.

Education had always been a central concern to Finch. As councilman he had shrewdly tied the question of black education to that of public schools for both races and all classes. By 1872 Atlanta officials supported in principle the idea of black elementary education. The board of education paid the teachers' salaries in two northern missionary schools; however, they refused to add an extension to the missionary buildings or to open another school. Finch, with the support of other black leaders, worked to improve the schools and to staff them with black teachers.

In fall 1872 William Finch and other parents who had children of high school age approached the city council with a request to either establish a high school or to make arrangements with Atlanta University to educate qualified students. A week later the parents met at Bethel Church, elected Finch as their chairman, and decided to send formal petitions to both the council and the board of education. Although the group won the support of the Atlanta *Constitution* and several councilmen for their cause, the board of education, after some delay, rejected the petition. The following fall Finch led a drive to increase the number of grammar schools, but the board again rejected the petition.[52]

Some black Atlantans, faced with these unsuccessful attempts to obtain public secondary education and increase the number of grammar schools, decided to concentrate on improving pedagogy and, in the process, expand job opportunities for educated blacks. Beginning in 1874 they mounted a campaign to employ black teachers in black schools. Finch joined the effort, but his role gradually became less prominent. In 1875 he worked closely with Francis J. Peck, the minister of Bethel Church, to request "that colored teachers be employed in all the colored schools under the charge of the Board." Three years later, however, a group of black Baptists and Methodists failed to select Finch as one of their leaders to negotiate with the school board. Finch attended the meeting and signed the petition requesting black teachers for black schools but had no significant leadership role. Thus by the late 1870s his position within the black community had begun to decline.[53]

Finch also experienced a diminishing leadership role in his church activities. A member of Bethel AME Church, he worked harmoniously with Rev. Francis J. Peck, who served as pastor for two terms during the 1870s. Finch found it difficult to get along with other ministers, however, and sometimes ran afoul of the church leaders. In 1874, shortly after Peck left, the congregation brought charges against Finch for disorderly conduct and disturbing the worship service. Finch admitted his guilt and paid the court costs. Several months later the new minister unsuccessfully attempted to reprimand the tailor for crude language. Although ordained as a minister in 1868 and as a presiding elder in 1876, Finch apparently never served either as a trustee of the church or as a member of its board. Perhaps his confrontations with authority made the congregation leery of giving him much power.[54]

His unhappiness with church leadership came to a head in the early 1880s, when Wesley J. Gaines returned as pastor of Bethel Church. Gaines, who had done much in the late 1860s to build Bethel into one of the largest and most prestigious black churches in the city, quickly clashed with the former councilman. Allegedly concerned about Finch's character, Gaines suspended him from preaching and eventually expelled him from the church. It seems likely that the charge that Finch had led "a vicious life" was a smear, and that Gaines really discharged him because the hot-tempered tailor found it hard to exercise the proper deference around the autocratic and overbearing minister. "I am not the only minister of many years standing this Caesar has tried to kill," Finch wrote in an angry letter to the *Constitution.* "I no more recognize what Gaines and his intimidated underlings have done than if they had whistled a corn song. I will preach whenever I feel like it." He concluded that Gaines did "not give me a fair trial. I would be cleared by a committee of angels, much less men, for he has nothing to try me for."[55]

After his expulsion, Finch joined the Northern Methodist Loyd Street Church. In 1885, however, he joined a group of dissenters at Bethel Church to bring back Francis J. Peck. The dissidents,

dissatisfied with Gaines's hand-picked successor, hoped to either install Peck at Bethel or to establish a rival church with Peck as minister.
Gaines quickly quashed the move and drove Peck out of Atlanta. Such
methods antagonized many black Atlantans and gave credence to
Finch's earlier charge that Gaines acted as a Caesar. The *Defiance*, the
city's major black newspaper, editorialized, "Now the Reverend
[Gaines] should know that he only owns a spot of land in Atlanta, not
the entire city, nor Bethel church either." It added, "There are plenty
of good men belonging to Bethel who will not be governed by one
man."[56] Despite the support of the *Defiance*, Finch's attempt to rejoin
the African Methodist Episcopal denomination ended in failure. He
remained a Northern Methodist for the rest of his life but became less
involved in church matters.[57]

During the 1880s Finch withdrew from public life and concerned
himself with his business and his family. His first wife, Laura, died in
1876. Five years later he married Minnie Vason of Madison, Georgia.
It is difficult to determine what impact the death of his son William had
on him, but perhaps this personal tragedy made Finch more with-
drawn. After attending Atlanta University, William had left Georgia
and worked as a barber at Fort Sill, Arkansas. He was arrested as a
horsethief, escaped, but in the process killed several soldiers. Later the
army recaptured him. The fact that his father persuaded citizens in Atlanta, Augusta, and Savannah to sign a petition of pardon and obtained support from both of Georgia's U.S. senators suggests that the
charges against William were not clear-cut; nevertheless, he was exe-
cuted in the summer of 1883.[58]

Although generally inactive in Atlanta politics after 1879, Finch
made one last sortie in 1886. Prohibition was the sole issue in the city
election that year, and as a lifelong teetotaler, the former councilman
could not resist getting involved. Both wet and dry organizations
feared that continued agitation might disrupt the city's economy. They
agreed to select twenty-five delegates from each side to serve as a Committee of Fifty to nominate all candidates for municipal office. Finch
participated in the effort to get blacks on the nominating committee.[59]

At the October 27 meeting where details of the compromise were
worked out, Finch reminded the audience of the support black voters
had given the prohibition cause in the 1885 referendum. "The better
element of the colored people," he noted, "when they see anything
which promises well for the city, are ready to cooperate to push it.
They helped you win the prohibition battle and they are ready to help

326

you maintain it." In his effort to place blacks on the Committee of Fifty, Finch shrewdly disarmed whites with a reference to the Civil War. "I fought, bled, and died as a soldier in the confederate army," he exclaimed. "I want to stand by you in the fight for good government in the city. . . . Our colored friends mean to do that. I hope that there will be some representation accorded them on that committee, and I move that it be done."[60] Ironically, Finch's speech led to the appointment of his rival, Wesley J. Gaines (as well as a Baptist minister), but his efforts had indeed ensured black representation.

Finch appeared at the November 5 meeting to defend the fusion ticket from attack by the Knights of Labor. So raucous was the meeting that his speech could not be heard above the din, but he managed to move acceptance of the ticket, which went on to victory in the December election.[61]

William Finch's efforts in 1886 marked the passing of a man anachronistic to the times. He was a transitional figure in black-Atlanta affairs. The turmoil of the Civil War and the massive influx of newcomers disrupted the antebellum black leadership. With class lines in disarray, a man such as Finch, with political experience, skills, and education, could quickly move to the forefront. As the black community grew, however, he was replaced by other leaders whose economic and social ties were more directly related to the community. Finch resented this change and perhaps his campaign in 1879 for the city council was an attempt to regain the status he once had enjoyed. With his expulsion from Bethel Church in 1881, he no longer commanded much of a following, and his leadership role was taken over by others, including Wesley J. Gaines.

William Finch was representative of a group of political leaders in Atlanta during the late 1860s and early 1870s who became politically active out of a sense of civic duty and saw politics as one aspect of service to their community. Charles Morgan and Jacob Fuller, for example, were just as involved in the First Congregational Church as they were in the Republican party; in addition, both men served as trustees of Atlanta University. Hampton Hall, a Second-Ward carpenter active in the party, provided St. Paul's AME Church with a plot of land and became one of its trustees. When Dr. Henry E. Baulden was not caring for patients, he could be found at a meeting, speaking out forcibly on the issues. In addition to political work, Baulden took a strong interest in education. James Tate divided his time between his grocery store, the church where he served as a trustee, and the Republican party.

Mitchell Cargile, Sr., successful cabinetmaker and undertaker, ran twice for city council. Cargile, who was a powerful figure in Bethel Church, helped to expel Finch in 1881.[62]

Many of those who participated in politics occupied a high economic position within the black community. Of the thirty-one politically most active individuals between 1870 and 1877, twenty-two owned property in 1873. Three years later most continued to hold land despite the severe depression of the mid-1870s. Such men did not enter politics out of hope for personal gain; instead they saw politics as a means to advance their race. William Finch told an audience in 1870 that he failed to comprehend how an Afro-American could be anything but a Republican. Politics was a responsibility of citizenship and these men took their responsibility seriously. They organized and spoke at mass rallies, ran for local office, and participated in the internal affairs of the party.[63]

With the defeat of Republican candidates for the city council in 1875 and the division of the state Republican organization into two warring factions the next year, some blacks followed Finch's example and dropped out of party politics. Death claimed other important Republicans. Consequently black politics in Atlanta went through a change in leadership between 1876 and 1880.

A resurgence of black political activity occurred in Atlanta in 1880 when William A. Pledger, editor of the Athens *Blade* and a former Atlanta resident, became chairman of the Georgia Republican Central Committee. With an Afro-American in a powerful party position, the possibility for patronage increased, and blacks hoped the party would become more responsive to their needs. Ward clubs sprang up in the black settlements of the city, and Afro-Americans dominated Fulton County party functions.[64]

With Pledger's accession to power, a class of professional black politicians emerged in Atlanta. These men were attracted to politics out of more than just a sense of civic duty; over 25 percent of those active between 1878 and 1884 held federal jobs. Of these generally young men who had attended Atlanta University, few had exerted leadership in the earlier period. Despite their age, two-thirds of them owned property.[65]

Of those who had previously participated in Atlanta politics, most were followers rather than leaders or ran for local office and had little to do with Republican politics in general. Among the earlier civic leaders only Jackson McHenry and C. C. Wimbish became professional politicians. McHenry, who ran with Finch in 1870 for the city council, saw his work in politics as a means to advance both the race and himself. His efforts met with partial success; in 1891 he was awarded the post of head janitor at the customhouse.[66]

C. C. Wimbish had joined the Republican party during his student days at Atlanta University, and it was probably his political connections that aided him in securing a position in the post office. In 1880 the Atlanta *Constitution* identified him as one of the leaders who had helped Pledger gain control of the central committee. Perhaps because he owed his post-office appointment to white Republicans, Wimbish did not always support the Pledger faction in the early 1880s; but he nonetheless retained the respect of most black Atlantans. Like McHenry, with whom he sometimes battled, Wimbish remained an important figure in party circles for several decades.[67]

Unlike many of the earlier civic leaders, the professional politicians were more direct in articulating the concerns of their community. In dealing with black problems, William Finch frequently sought alliances with whites. While the professional politicians also saw a practical need in seeking such alliances, they were more likely to organize and discuss grievances in the open. In 1880, for example, after a band of white terrorists murdered two blacks outside Jonesboro, Georgia, some twenty miles from Atlanta, black Atlantans gathered to protest the outrage. Republican politicians dominated the evening meeting. James Treadwell served as chairman and C. C. Wimbish, Richard J. Henry, Henry A. Rucker, and others called on the governor to prosecute the terrorists. Jackson McHenry declared that blacks when attacked needed to stand up for their rights "by resorting to powder and ball arguments."[68] As the speakers feared, however, a Jonesboro jury refused to convict the murderers.[69]

A protest that black politicians organized several years later was more successful. In 1882, when a rumor spread through the city that whites might attempt to lynch a black prisoner, two Republicans, William D. Moore, a federal clerk, and Richard J. Henry, a porter, organized a meeting. From there the blacks went en masse to the mayor's home, where they demanded that he provide adequate protection for the prisoner, and then marched to the county jail to stand guard themselves. Later the police became upset over the number of blacks outside the jail and arrested those who refused to disperse; Moore and Henry posted bail for them and secured their release. The protest helped to ensure the prisoner's safety, and he eventually obtained his freedom.[70]

Overall, however, the young professional politicians proved to be no more successful than were their civic-minded predecessors of the 1870s in obtaining concessions for black Atlantans. In fact, after the prohibition controversy ended in the late 1880s, white politicians, fearful that blacks might become a balance of power in city elections, began to restrict Afro-Americans at the polls. By 1900 they had reduced black registration to about nine hundred voters, and those blacks were too few to influence Atlanta politics.[71]

While black political power in Atlanta steadily declined, Finch spent the last two decades of his life quietly tending to business and personal affairs. He continued to work as a tailor, attended Loyd Street (later Central Avenue) Methodist Church, and resided at the same Edgewood Avenue address. If the traumas of the 1906 Atlanta race riot affected his view of whites, Finch kept it hidden. When he died in 1911 several newspapers praised him for having "a host of white friends." The Atlanta *Journal* referred vaguely and without hostility to his service on the city council; the *Constitution* failed to note it.[72]

Finch was an important figure in Atlanta only for a decade. Because of his economic ties to the white community and his sometimes accommodating manner, he was unable to articulate forcefully the demands of the black community. Yet during his term on the council he served his constituents well and, given his limited base of power, succeeded in extracting all that could have been obtained from the Democrats.

The experience of William Finch indicates that in some southern cities an indigenous antebellum elite failed to dominate the postwar black social structure. In Atlanta, class lines in the black community remained open for a while, allowing newcomers to advance rapidly. Frequently these successful newcomers went into politics, not in pursuit of personal gain, but because they saw Republican party work as a means of benefiting their community. Concerns about patronage came later in Atlanta black politics and to a different group of individuals. What is striking about William Finch and his colleagues is the strong sense of idealism that motivated them during the Reconstruction politics of the early 1870s.

Notes

All newspapers cited herein are Atlanta papers unless specified otherwise.

1. Studies of black politics in nineteenth-century Atlanta include Clarence A. Bacote, "William Finch, Negro Councilman and Political Activities in Atlanta during Early Reconstruction," *Journal of Negro History* 40 (Oct. 1955):341–64; id., "The Negro in Atlanta Politics, 1869–1955," *Phylon* 16

(Dec. 1955):330–50; Eugene J. Watts, "Black Political Progress in Atlanta, 1868–1895," *Journal of Negro History* 59 (July 1974):268–86; and John Hammond Moore, "The Negro and Prohibition in Atlanta, 1885–1887," *South Atlantic Quarterly* 69 (Win. 1970):38–57. An early biographical sketch of William Finch appeared in E. R. Carter, *The Black Side: A Partial History of the Business, Religious and Educational Side of the Negro in Atlanta, Ga.* (1894; reprint ed., Freeport, N.Y.: Books of Library Press, 1971), pp. 74–77.

2. Account 1421, Atlanta, Ga., Signature Depositor Cards of Freedmen's Savings Bank, Records of Comptroller General, (microfilm) M816, roll 6, Record Group (RG) 101, National Archives (NA).

3. Carter, *The Black Side*, p. 75.

4. Ibid., p. 6. It is not clear which denomination he affiliated with in the 1840s; it was certainly not, as Carter asserts, the African Methodist Episcopal Church. Because Judge Lumpkin was a Presbyterian who actively proselytized among the slaves, Finch might have become a Presbyterian. Robert Manson Myers, ed., *The Children of Pride: A True Story of Georgia and the Civil War* (New Haven: Yale University Press, 1972), pp. 411–12, 1599.

5. Carter, *The Black Side*, p. 75; *Constitution*, Jan. 12, 1911; *Journal*, Jan. 11, 1911.

6. William Finch to Gen. Davis Tillson, Nov. 17, 1865, Letters Received, 1:143, Assistant Commissioner for Georgia, Records of the Bureau of Refugees, Freedmen, and Abandoned Lands, 1865–69, M798, roll 11, RG 105, NA.

7. Carter, *The Black Side*, pp. 77, 75.

8. William Finch, Report of the Colored Schools of Athens, Ga., Oct. 19, 1865, Letters Received, Superintendent of Education for Georgia, 1865–70, M799, roll 8, RG 105, NA.

9. Daniel Hough to Supt. G. L. Eberhart, Oct. 22, 1865, ibid.

10. Elizabeth Studley Nathans, *Losing the Peace: Georgia Republicans and Reconstruction, 1865–1871* (Baton Rouge: Louisiana State University Press, 1968), pp. 25–27; Augusta *Loyal Georgian*, Jan. 20, 27, 1866.

11. Carter, *The Black Side*, p. 76. Although Finch's deposit records in the Freedmen's Bank made mention of his stay in Augusta, records for two of his children did not. Probably his family remained in Athens while he was in Augusta and joined him only after he was settled in Atlanta. Accounts 1421, 2, 77, M816, roll 6, RG 101, NA.

12. By way of comparison, roughly 53 percent of white male household heads in Atlanta held some property in 1870, and their median holding was $2,000. Statistics on property holding, illiteracy, and mulattoes are based on sample data drawn from the 1870 manuscripts of the U.S. population census. These statistics are drawn from a 10 percent sample of all household heads (N = 532) in Atlanta in 1870.

13. U.S., Bureau of the Census, *The Statistics of the Population of the United States, Ninth Census* (Washington, D.C.: Government Printing Office, 1872), 1:102.

14. Neither did Reconstruction Atlanta have any kind of mulatto aristocracy. Only 6.2 percent of the city's Negro household heads in 1870 were mulattoes. There is no evidence that this mulatto population had any political advantage or disadvantage in Atlanta during the early 1870s. See also Howard N.

Rabinowitz, *Race Relations in the Urban South, 1865–1890* (New York: Oxford University Press, 1978), pp. 248–49.

15. *Daily Intelligencer*, Sept. 27, Oct. 1, 1867; Clara Mildred Thompson, *Reconstruction in Georgia: Economic, Social, Political, 1865–1872* (1915; reprint ed., Gloucester, Mass.: Peter Smith, 1964), p. 187; E. A. Ware Diary, Apr. 23, 1868, cited in E. T. Ware, "Sketch of the Life of Edmund Asa Ware," 26, Box 2, Edmund A. Ware Papers, Trevor Arnett Library, Atlanta University, Atlanta.

16. Watts, "Black Political Progress," pp. 272–73.

17. *Constitution*, Dec. 2, 1869; *Daily Intelligencer*, Nov. 24, 1869; *New Era*, Nov. 29, Dec. 2, 4, 1868.

18. Bacote, "William Finch," pp. 343–44; Howard N. Rabinowitz, "From Reconstruction to Redemption in the Urban South," *Journal of Urban History* 2 (Feb. 1976):177–78.

19. *New Era*, Aug. 10, Nov. 12, 1870.

20. Ibid., Nov. 16, Dec. 2 (quote), 6, 1870; *Constitution*, Dec. 6, 1870.

21. *Constitution*, Nov. 20, Dec. 2, 3, 4, 1870; *New Era*, Nov. 20, 1870; *True Georgian*, Nov. 23, 26, 1870.

22. *New Era*, Dec. 10, 1870; see also *Daily Sun*, Dec. 8, 1870; for the Democrat's response, see *New Era*, Dec. 11, 1870.

23. *Methodist Advocate*, Dec. 14, 1870; *Constitution*, Dec. 8, 1870; *Daily Intelligencer*, Dec. 8, 1870; *New Era*, Dec. 8, 1870.

24. *New Era*, Jan. 7, 1871.

25. Ibid., Nov. 15, 1870.

26. *Constitution*, Jan. 11, 1871. Finch was also on the committees for Lamps and Gas, Market, and Fire Department. For comments on Graham's illiteracy, see ibid., Jan. 8, 1871; *New Era*, Mar. 15, 1871; *Daily Sun*, Mar. 14, 1871.

27. *Constitution*, Jan. 21, 1871.

28. *New Era*, Dec. 24, 1871; *Constitution*, Jan. 14, 21, Nov. 18, 1871.

29. *Daily Sun*, Jan. 13, 1871; *Constitution*, Jan. 14, 1871.

30. *Constitution*, Feb. 18, Mar. 12, 19, 1871; *New Era*, Feb. 19, Mar. 12, 1871.

31. *Daily Sun*, Mar. 29, 31, 1871. Barry committed a number of assaults on the freed people of Atlanta, and the Freedmen's Bureau forced the city council to fire him in 1867. The following year the council quietly rehired him. Atlanta, City Council (ACC), Minutes, Sept. 6, 1867, July 31, 1868, Atlanta Historical Society, Atlanta.

32. *Constitution*, Apr. 1, 1871.

33. Ibid., May 3, 6, June 2, 1871; *New Era*, Oct. 10, 1871.

34. *Daily Sun*, Feb. 15, 18, June 3, 1871; *Constitution*, Apr. 15, 22, 29, 1871.

35. *New Era*, June 24, 1871.

36. Ibid., Jan. 14, 1871; *Constitution*, June 24, 1871; ACC, Minutes, Sept. 15, Nov. 10, 1871.

37. James M. Russell, "Politics, Municipal Services, and the Working Class in Atlanta, 1865 to 1890" (paper read at Organization of American Historians convention, Apr. 11, 1980).

38. *New Era*, Jan. 14, Feb. 25, 1871; ACC, Minutes, Oct. 27, Dec. 16,

1871; Jan. 5, 1872.

39. *Constitution*, May 27, 1871; *New Era*, June 17, 24, 1871; E. A. Ware to E. M. Cravath, May 13, 22, 29, June 9, c. Oct. 10, Nov. 4, 11, 1871, (microfilm) roll 7, Georgia, American Missionary Association (AMA) Archives, Armistad Research Center, Dillard University, New Orleans, La.

40. *New Era*, Mar. 25, 1871; *Constitution*, May 6, 1871, Jan. 6, 1872.

41. *New Era*, Aug. 22, 1871.

42. Ibid., Aug. 18, 24, 1871; *Constitution*, Aug. 12, 19, 22, 1871.

43. *New Era*, Aug. 22, 1871.

44. *Sun*, Aug. 24, 1871; *New Era*, Aug. 22, 1871.

45. *New Era*, Aug. 22, 1871.

46. Ibid.

47. Jerry Thornbery, "The End of Political Reconstruction in Georgia: The View from Atlanta" (paper read at Georgia Studies Symposium, Atlanta, Feb. 15, 1980).

48. Augusta *Loyal Georgian*, Jan. 20, 1866; *New Era*, Nov. 13, 18, 1870.

49. *Constitution*, Dec. 1, 1875.

50. *New Era*, Aug. 22, 1871.

51. *Constitution*, Sept. 30, 1884.

52. Ibid., Sept. 14, 20, Oct. 5, 12, 1872; Sept. 13, 1873; Atlanta, Board of Education, Minutes, Sept. 26, 1872, (microfilm) roll 1, Georgia Department of Archives and History (GDAH), Atlanta; E. A. Ware to Board of Education, Oct. 3, 1872; W. L. Scruggs to Ware, Oct. 4, 1872, Box 1, Atlanta University Papers, Trevor Arnett Library, Atlanta University, Atlanta.

53. Atlanta, Board of Education, Minutes, July 10, 1875; June 13, 1878, (microfilm) roll 1, GDAH.

54. *Constitution*, Mar. 3, 7, Aug. 9, 15, 1874; Carter, *The Black Side*, pp. 76–77.

55. *Constitution*, Jan. 1, 1882. The official board of Bethel Church accused Finch of "living a vicious life" in a letter to the *Constitution*, Dec. 27, 1881.

56. *Defiance*, quoted in Atlanta *Constitution*, Jan. 12, 1885; also see *Constitution*, July 8, 9, 1885; *Christian Recorder*, Feb. 11, 1886.

57. Bacote, "William Finch," pp. 363–64.

58. Carter, *The Black Side*, pp. 75–76; *Constitution*, June 6, 30, 1883. During the 1880s Finch apparently dropped out of the movement to place black teachers in all of Atlanta's black schools. No doubt the fact that his nemesis, Rev. Wesley J. Gaines, headed the movement, coupled with events in his family life, made him reluctant to get involved.

59. *Constitution*, Oct. 26, 28, 1886; see also Moore, "Negro and Prohibition in Atlanta," pp. 38–57; Watts, "Black Political Progress," pp. 276–79; Rabinowitz, *Race Relations in the Urban South*, pp. 314–18.

60. *Southern Recorder*, Oct. 29, 1886.

61. *Constitution*, Nov. 6, 1886.

62. Ibid., Dec. 1, 1874, Dec. 4, 1877, Dec. 27, 1881; Records of First Congregational Church, Atlanta; Deed Records and Mortgages, Superior Court of Fulton County, Ga., 10:10 (microfilm), GDAH; *Sun*, Mar. 14, 1872; Edward R. Carter, *Biographical Sketches of Our Pulpit* (1888; reprint ed., Chicago: Afro-Am Press, 1969), pp. 135–44.

63. *Constitution*, Dec. 6, 1870; Jerry Thornbery, "The Development of

Black Atlanta, 1865–1885" (Ph.D. diss., University of Maryland, 1977), pp. 253–54.

64. Ruth C. McDaniel, "Black Power in Georgia: William A. Pledger and the Takeover of the Republican Party," *Georgia Historical Quarterly* 62 (Fall 1978):225–39; Olive Hall Shadgett, *The Republican Party in Georgia: From Redemption through 1900* (Athens: University of Georgia Press, 1964), pp. 76–89.

65. Thornbery, "Development of Black Atlanta," pp. 259–60.

66. Ibid., p. 261; Carter, *The Black Side*, pp. 178–80.

67. *Constitution*, Apr. 23, 24, 1880; June 9, 28, 1882; Mar. 23, 1884; Shadgett, *Republican Party in Georgia*, pp. 58, 193n.

68. *Constitution*, Aug. 3, 1880. Wimbish, McHenry, and Rucker all at one time held federal jobs. Rucker, a barber and federal clerk in the 1880s, later served as collector of internal revenues in Atlanta between 1897 and 1910. Treadwell, a supporter of the Pledger faction, sought a federal job but apparently never obtained one. Henry, a wealthy porter, was active in numerous Republican functions in the 1880s.

69. Ibid., Sept. 12, 18, 1880.

70. Ibid., May 2, 1882, June 29, 1883.

71. Watts, "Black Political Progress," pp. 275–86.

72. *Journal*, Jan. 11, 1911; *Constitution*, Jan. 12, 1911.

Dr. Benjamin A. Boseman, Jr.:
Charleston's Black Physician-Politician

T HOUGH ECLIPSED in fame and prominence by at least a half dozen
other black South Carolina politicians, Dr. Benjamin A. Boseman,
Jr., was a critical figure in Reconstruction Charleston. Boseman was
the only politician—black or white—from Charleston to be elected to
three consecutive terms in the state House of Representatives during
Reconstruction. In 1873 he was appointed postmaster of Charleston
and served until his death in 1881. During a successful political career
he managed the difficult feat of treading the uneasy line between
whites who were apprehensive about any specific indications of black
advancement and blacks who were impatient to improve their status
after the war. Whites usually regarded him as properly conservative
and accommodating, perhaps because of his civil and dignified manner. But on more than one occasion he advocated measures that most
whites found utterly reprehensible. Boseman's political career suggests the kinds of opportunities that were available to black Reconstruction leaders as well as the sorts of limitations that were imposed
upon them in a decade of unprecedented political developments that
unfolded in postwar Carolina.

Boseman was born in New York City on July 30, 1840.[1] He spent his
formative years in Troy, N.Y., where his family moved in the early
1840s. Troy, located directly across the Hudson River from Albany,
was a bustling town in mid-nineteenth century with a population of
nearly 29,000, of whom only 509 were black.[2]

Benjamin grew up in a stable nuclear family, the oldest of five children. He was a light-skinned child, though there is no indication that
either of his parents was white. His father, Benjamin, Sr., had been
born in Florida in 1816 and his mother, Anneretta, was a native New
Yorker who was one year younger than her husband.[3] The elder Boseman served for a number of years as a waiter and steward on board the
Empire, a steamboat that plied the Hudson River.[4]

Young Boseman, with his two brothers and two sisters, probably attended a segregated public school in Troy in the 1840s and 1850s.[5] Jim
Crow educational facilities notwithstanding, Troy was a center of abo-

litionist activity in the antebellum era. Noted black nationalist and abolitionist Henry Highland Garnet settled in Troy in 1840 and became pastor of the Liberty Street Presbyterian Church. A National Negro Convention was organized by Garnet and held in the city in 1847. Though Garnet left Troy in 1848, abolitionists remained active in the community. Frederick Douglass spoke in the city before a Negro State Convention in 1855 and appealed to blacks to participate more actively in organized politics.[6] There is no evidence that any members of the Boseman family were associated with or took an interest in the abolitionist movement, but it is likely that the twin legacies of segregation and abolition left their mark on young Benjamin.

As an adolescent, Boseman embarked on a medical career. In 1857, at the age of sixteen, he was accepted as a medical apprentice by Troy's most prominent physician, Dr. Thomas C. Brimsmade.[7] Boseman's affiliation with Brimsmade was typical for a prospective medical doctor in the mid-nineteenth century, though his color surely added an unusual dimension to the relationship. Medical education of that era combined apprenticeship with attendance at medical college.[8] Boseman served for more than seven years under Brimsmade as a "doctor, student + companion." During that time he read extensively and attended one course of medical lectures at Dartmouth College.[9]

Boseman reached a decisive point in his life in early 1864 when he decided to continue his medical education. The decision would not only advance his professional career but it would also create the opportunity for him to make a personal contribution to a nation caught up in a prolonged and bitter Civil War. Combining professional growth and advancement with public service would mark much of Boseman's adult life. The 23-year-old Boseman informed Brimsmade that he wanted to complete his medical training at the Medical School of Maine and then serve as a physician with one of the Negro regiments in the war. Brimsmade promptly provided authorities at the Maine school with a glowing letter and indicated that "Boseman's preliminary education has been better than that recommended by the Amer. Med. Association." Brimsmade extolled his apprentice as "a young gentleman of unexceptionable habits + great moral worth."[10] Boseman was accepted by the school.

The Medical School of Maine, which operated under the auspices of Bowdoin College, was generally well regarded by medical practitioners of that day.[11] Though very few blacks attended medical school at that time, Boseman was not the first black student to enroll at the

DR. BENJAMIN A. BOSEMAN, JR.
Library of Congress

Medical School of Maine. More than a decade earlier, Charles Dunbar of New York City had attended the institution.[12]

Boseman spent a term attending medical lectures in Maine in 1864.[13] He probably took courses in chemistry, anatomy, and physiology.[14] The major shortcoming of nineteenth-century medical education was the lack of laboratory and clinical training; it is, therefore, unlikely that Boseman or any of his fellow students had an opportunity to conduct any serious laboratory work.[15] But like students at most reputable medical schools, Boseman was required to write a thesis.[16] His forty-page handwritten thesis, "The Importance of Medical Statistics," does not deal directly with statistics as the title implies. Instead it is an aggressive argument for the necessity of maintaining complete medical records.[17] Most nineteenth-century physicians were extraordinarily lax in keeping and consulting medical records in their diagnosis and treatment of disease.[18] Boseman's topic was consequently an issue of considerable medical concern.

Once he completed requirements for the medical degree, Boseman turned his attention to gaining an appointment as a physician to a Negro regiment in the Union army, although he was not altogether certain that a black man would be accepted for such a position. He wrote Acting Surgeon General Joseph K. Barnes, indicating that he had seen advertisements for surgeons and assistant surgeons for Negro troops and that he was unaware of any regulations prohibiting black men from serving in such a capacity. He recounted his medical training and asked to appear before the Army Medical Board in New York City.[19]

To bolster his chances with the army, Boseman enlisted the support of his local congressman and two physicians. John A. Griswold, a Democrat (who would soon turn Republican) and a member of the U.S. House from Troy, recommended Boseman as "a colored young man of this city" who "in all respects—education, respectability of character etc.—is entitled to consideration."Griswold indicated that he hoped Boseman could be accepted as a surgeon with a colored regiment.[20] The two physicians also enthusiastically endorsed Boseman. William F. Leyrumous, a professor of obstetrics at Berkshire Medical College, considered Boseman "unusually well informed for his years." Dr. Charles E. Simmons wrote, "I deem him fully qualified for the position."[21]

Boseman subsequently appeared before the Army Medical Board and was administered an essay examination that dealt with diphtheria, which he passed. He was approved and recommended by the board for appointment as a contract surgeon in August 1864.[22] Altogether more than 5,500 contract surgeons served in the Union army during the Civil War. They were not commissioned, though they sometimes wore officers' uniforms; but because they were not officers, there was no opportunity for promotion.[23]

Boseman spent most of the next thirteen months examining black recruits at Hilton Head Island, South Carolina. He quickly found the work tedious and not sufficiently challenging to his medical skills. Within seven months of his arrival, he wanted to leave South Carolina. He appealed to Congressman Griswold again and asked, in March 1865, for aid in gaining a transfer "to one of the colored hospitals at Washington, or Alexandria or even to Norfolk or Portsmouth." Boseman suggested that working in a hospital would contribute to the further development of his medical knowledge.[24]

Boseman was not transferred. Either the congressman did not intervene or, if he did, his efforts failed. In any event, Boseman remained at Hilton Head until mid-September 1865, when his thirteen-month contract expired and he left the army.[25] Boseman then moved to Charleston, where he apparently established a medical practice.[26] Soon thereafter he was invited to serve as an honorary delegate to a state Negro convention held in the city with several other black luminaries, including Francis L. Cardozo, Richard H. Cain, and Martin Delany.[27]

Then Boseman fades from the scene and does not reappear for nearly two years. He reemerges in October 1867 serving as chairman of a Republican ward meeting in Charleston.[28] But by that time he was somewhat of a latecomer to Reconstruction politics; Republican political activity was well underway. Most of the black and white leaders who would achieve prominence in Charleston and South Carolina politics already had been deeply immersed in Republican affairs for more than eight months. Black leaders such as Robert Brown Elliott, Robert De Large, Francis Cardozo, Richard Cain and others had been organizing and enlisting support for themselves and the Republican party since March and April, after the first Reconstruction Act was passed. Boseman's presence was not noted at any of the initial Republican gatherings, nor was he a member of the nearly all black Committee of Thirteen that served as a steering committee and drew up a party platform for the Republicans during their early weeks in South Carolina.[29] Furthermore, he was not one of the several black speakers and participants at a key mass meeting held in Charleston in late March to ratify the Republican platform.[30]

Boseman's belated entrance into politics was probably a factor that prevented his election to the Constitutional Convention of 1868. Competition among Republicans in Charleston for nomination as one of nine delegates to the convention was fierce. Nomination assured election, because the Democrats largely boycotted the election.[31]

Boseman's absence from the convention did not diminish his interest in politics. He joined with other Republicans from across the state in party caucuses held in Charleston during the concluding sessions of the convention in March 1868 at which candidates were nominated for state and local offices. There was intense competition among potential Republican candidates because the Democrats had decided against participation in the upcoming April elections in the desperate hope that a low voter turnout would make it impossible to ratify the new state constitution. Therefore, nomination as a Republican was again tantamount to election because a significant majority of the state's population was black.[32]

Thus with a Republican sweep in the elections all but inevitable, it is surprising that black leaders fell back and openly deferred to white Republicans in the quest for elective offices. Black leaders pursued what they perceived a wise and sound political strategy by refusing to accept nominations for major offices. Prominent blacks agreed that if any of their number were precipitously thrust into influential political positions, white sensibilities would be outraged and the long-term prospects for successfully establishing a biracial Republican party would be seriously damaged.

Francis Cardozo consequently refused to consider accepting the nomination for lieutenant governor. Benjamin Boseman and Robert De Large strongly condemned the nomination of Jonathan J. Wright, a black lawyer from Beaufort, for lieutenant governor. Their arguments were persuasive, and a native white Republican was nominated instead. Martin Delany confessed that though he was preeminently qualified to serve in the U.S. House of Representatives, he would refuse to accept the nomination out of consideration for whites who were not prepared to accept a black congressman.[33]

But self-imposed political restraint had its limits. Black leaders did decide to accept one significant state office, that of secretary of state.[34] Moreover, black politicians showed considerable interest in the 154 seats in the state legislature. Thirteen black men—including Benjamin Boseman—were among the eighteen Republicans nominated by the caucus for the state House of Representatives from Charleston County. All eighteen were easily elected.[35]

In the nearly five years Boseman spent in the state House, he established a mixed political record. He was a source of effective leadership

340

in efforts to enact productive legislation. But he also advocated blatantly partisan measures and attempted to use his position for personal though not illegal advantage. Shortly after the first Reconstruction legislature (the Forty-eighth General Assembly) convened in special session in July 1868, Boseman introduced a civil-rights bill. The proposal was intended "to prevent discrimination between persons by those carrying on business under license on account of race, color, or previous condition." With Boseman's concurrence, William Whipper, a black legislator from Beaufort, amended the bill to include common carriers in its provisions. The *Charleston Daily Courier* charged that the legislation would admit blacks to hotels, houses of entertainment and amusement, as well as to public conveyances.[36] But as it would turn out, Boseman and other black leaders were less concerned with racial integration than with eliminating discrimination, which they equated with exclusion.

The bill created a pronounced disagreement over the black man's role in postwar society. Many white Republicans indicated their opposition to equal rights by first refusing to debate the issue lest they offend their black colleagues and then by refusing to vote either for or against the bill. The *Daily Courier* reported that the black Republicans were disgruntled at the lack of white Republican support for the Boseman bill. William Whipper in a House speech accused white Republicans of purposely refusing to participate in the legislative proceedings, thereby making a quorum difficult to muster.[37]

Not all white Republicans tried to evade the issue. The Rev. B. F. Jackson, a white representative from rural Charleston County, was unequivocal in his support. "I deny the Bill contemplates social equality. Its object is simply to secure in every business transaction equal and exact justice without any invidious discrimination on account of race, color or previous condition." But in blunt opposition to the bill, John Feriter, a white Republican from Sumter County, let it be known that "If other white men dodge the question I will not." He claimed that the bill would disrupt trade and business and especially harm hotel keepers who, henceforth, would be compelled to admit black guests.[38] Despite much passive white opposition, the bill passed in the House, where there was a black majority, and was sent to the Senate.[39]

The bill faced very tough opposition in the Senate, where it was tabled, and a substitute passed. The initiator of this legislative maneuvering was D. T. Corbin, the white Republican senator from Charleston. Black senators, with the notable exception of Richard Cain, worked energetically for the passage of Boseman's original bill. Benjamin F. Randolph, a black senator from Orangeburg County, demanded legal equality with Caucasians and, furthermore, wanted no hotels closed to him.[40] Stephen Swails of Williamsburg County and Henry E. Hayne of Marion County recalled that they and their black colleagues had been discriminated against on trains, in hotels, and in billiard parlors. But Cain, Charleston's black senator, evoked bitter and lingering opposition from fellow black legislators when he vigorously opposed the Boseman bill as well as the Corbin substitute by arguing that prejudice could not be legislated out of existence.[41] However, Corbin did succeed in derailing Boseman's bill. Corbin's vague substitute, which guaranteed to protect "all persons in the State in their civil rights," weathered the hectic debate that followed and finally passed in the predominantly white Senate.[42]

Boseman's desperate efforts to revive his original legislation in the House failed. The black doctor, who had not actively participated in the previous debates, preferring to manage the bill from behind the scenes, rose in the House to speak for his bill after the Senate returned Corbin's bill. Grabbing for straws and resorting to uncharacteristic histrionics, he warned that he was not intimidated by the rumored threat of the resignation of forty white legislators should his bill pass.[43] As it turned out, neither bill could attract sufficient legislative support during the remaining days of that special legislative session to pass in both houses.

It was nearly a year and a half later and well into the third session of the Reconstruction legislature before a major civil-rights bill drew enough support to survive the legislative gauntlet, but it was not Benjamin Boseman who sponsored the new legislation. However, Robert Smalls, the black representative from Beaufort, introduced a bill that was very similar to the initial Boseman proposal.

Passage of civil-rights legislation in 1870 may have been prompted primarily by repeated instances of racial discrimination encountered by prosperous and prominent blacks in postwar Carolina. Two black aldermen in Charleston were given very slow service at a local barroom and then were charged double the regular price for their drinks. Black people who attended the Academy of Music, which was a concert hall and auditorium in Charleston, were seated separately, high up in the hall. They let it be known that they wanted seating comparable to that of whites down closer to the front of the room though not necessarily among the white patrons.[44] Several black legislators, including Jonathan Wright and Robert De Large, had also recently confronted discrimination on railroad trains in Virginia and South Carolina.[45]

Although the Smalls measure, like the Boseman legislation, was a comprehensive bill designed to end racial discrimination in public accommodations, neither bill was a legislative attempt to integrate those facilities. When the Smalls bill became law, it prohibited discrimination by common carriers, and it specified that no special quarters or accommodations could be set aside. Yet it did not rule out separate accommodations if they were equal. Accommodations "must be equal in every respect to that furnished by him [the carrier] to any other person, for like compensation or reward." Separate but equal facilities also would be acceptable in any theater, place of amusement or recreation. The proprietor of such an establishment could not "refuse or deny to any person lawfully applying therefor [*sic*], accommodation equal in every respect to that furnished at such place for a like reward to any other person, on account of race, color or previous condition."[46]

Though the bill faced stiff and acrimonious opposition, it did pass.[47] It is clear that what most black leaders favored was not racial integration but admission to and acceptance at facilities that previously refused them and attempted to continue to do so or provided them with facilities demonstrably inferior to those provided whites even though blacks paid the same price. It is apparent in the case of the Academy of Music, for example, that black leaders would accept segregated seating if their seats were equal to those of white customers. Black legislators like Boseman and Smalls, in resolutely advocating an end to racial discrimination, were not insisting on the kind of race mixing that so many whites—including white Republicans—found deplorable and usually labeled "social equality."[48]

Boseman's attempts in 1868, as chairman of the House Medical Committee, to secure legislation affecting medicine and health care in the state were more successful and less controversial than his efforts on behalf of civil rights. He sponsored the first measure to regulate the practice of medicine in the postwar era.[49] The act established minimum standards of medical education. A prospective physician was required to have completed two courses of medical instruction as well as either to have graduated from a U.S. or foreign school of medicine or to have a certificate of qualification from a state medical society.[50]

Boseman was active in other medical matters as well. He was appointed physician to the Charleston City Jail in 1869 by Governor Robert Scott, a patronage position he held until he was appointed postmaster four years later. As chairman of the House Medical Committee, he dealt with such varied problems as the establishment of a state pharmaceutical association, the practice of veterinary medicine, and state payments for post-mortem examinations.[51] He was not, however, a member of the relatively inactive, all white South Carolina Medical Association.[52]

Of much greater concern and importance was health care in South Carolina, particularly among the poor. A large though undetermined portion of the state's population remained destitute in the years after the war. The Freedmen's Bureau had ceased to provide substantial aid by 1868. The ill and infirm of the state who were without financial resources had nowhere to turn but to private charity. In 1870 Boseman and Reuben Tomlinson, a white Republican representing Charleston, introduced separate pieces of legislation to provide medical aid for the poor, and both measures passed.[53] The Boseman measure placed the main responsibility for medical care on the counties. County commissioners were required, "when in their judgement necessary," to appoint one or more physicians to furnish medical treatment to the poor of that county.[54]

There is no precise way of knowing how effective Boseman's measure was in providing health care. The legislation in effect gave county commissioners the option of whether or not to furnish medical service for the poor. Thus it is not unreasonable to assume that in many South Carolina counties, the legislation had no impact on the delivery of health care. And given the general state of medical knowledge and practice in the nineteenth century and the usual reluctance of people to seek medical attention except when gravely ill, the beneficial effect of the Boseman measure was probably limited even when and where care was provided.[55]

Boseman and a handful of other legislators also showed a deep interest in the care of the mentally incompetent and insane. But their efforts to improve conditions at the segregated state insane asylum, while earnest and sincere, were largely futile. In late 1869 Boseman was elected as one of the five blacks on the nine-member Board of Regents of the Lunatic Asylum.[56] In 1871–72 Boseman served on both a special committee assigned by the regents to examine conditions at the asylum and a legislative committee that investigated the institution. In each instance the committee's report described the conditions at the asylum as deplorable and inadequate while praising the performance of the asylum's superintendent, Dr. J. F. Ensor.[57]

The legislature responded to these investigations and appropriated additional funds for the institution for the next fiscal year, 1872–73. Yet that money, the Board of Regents' committee later reported, was diverted elsewhere by state officials. The report went on to castigate bitterly those authorities who had manifested "an indifference to the cruel consequences of their action utterly unbecoming the rulers of a civilized people."[58]

Boseman's service on a special committee investigating the all black State Orphan Asylum in Charleston was similar to his experience with the insane asylum. The committee found the kitchen, dining room, washroom, beds and bed clothing all unfit for use. No medicine was available. The buildings were in dilapidated condition. The five-man committee placed blame for the situation on the trustees of the asylum who "in whole or in part have been terribly derelict in their duty." The legislature subsequently passed a resolution recommending the appropriation of $20,000 to construct a new asylum in Charleston.[59]

Boseman did not demonstrate the same kind of interest in education—particularly higher education—that he did in care for the insane and orphans. He was elected by the legislature in March 1869 to the seven-member Board of Trustees of the University of South Carolina along with Francis Cardozo and five white Republicans.[60] Though he and Cardozo were among the two best educated Republicans in Reconstruction South Carolina, they took no special interest in the administration of the university. No fundamental changes were made in university policies during their four-year tenure as trustees. Remarkably, neither Boseman nor Cardozo demonstrated any concern about admitting black students to or hiring black faculty for the all white institution. Boseman was elected secretary to the board in 1872, but he missed four of five meetings held that year.[61] It was not until after Boseman and Cardozo failed to win reelection to the board in 1873 that the university was "radicalized" and began to admit black students and hire black faculty.[62]

The black doctor's interest in civil rights, in improving medical care, in providing better facilities for the mentally ill and orphans, and his less than overwhelming concern with education reflect only one side of his multifaceted political character. He was also a partisan, thoroughly committed to Republican politics. He advocated and initiated proposals that were created solely to benefit the Republican party. For example, Boseman was an earnest supporter of a legislative measure to lower the residency requirement for voting in Charleston elections from sixty to ten days.[63] It was obvious that this maneuver would make it possible to transport voters into Charleston temporarily from the predominantly black rural areas of the county to take part in municipal elections. When Governor Robert Scott vetoed the residency bill,

345

Boseman unsuccessfully appealed to fellow legislators to override the veto. Though the whole Charleston delegation—with the exception of Robert De Large—supported the effort to override, the veto was sustained.[64]

In 1871 Boseman introduced a bill that was as blatantly partisan as any measure proposed during Reconstruction in South Carolina. The bill passed despite angry opposition from local whites. It shifted the date of Charleston's municipal election from October to the first Wednesday in August.[65] Republicans and Democrats alike were well aware that the change would adversely affect Democrats, because affluent and influential white citizens fled Charleston during the summer months in the hope of avoiding the scourge of yellow fever. Since the white male population was only slightly larger than the black male population, the shift in election dates was considered essential in maintaining Republican control of the city.[66] Prominent white Democrats as well as the *Daily Republican* complained to no avail that the change was grossly unfair because the new date was in the middle of "the hottest and sickliest season of the year."[67]

But Boseman did not support every partisan measure that Republicans devised. When a bill was introduced in 1872 to create a metropolitan police force for the city of Charleston, Boseman was one of only three members of the Charleston delegation who voted against it. Twelve voted for it.[68] The bill failed, but had it passed it would have created an enormous reservoir of patronage for Republicans by establishing a separate police force composed of several dozen officers under the authority of the state legislature and not city officials at a time when Democrats controlled the city.[69]

For politicians like Boseman, support of the Republican party meant not only political survival; it also represented a legitimate means to take advantage of their official positions and influence to create financial opportunities for themselves. Reconstruction leaders were motivated not only by political ambition but by the desire to pursue entrepreneurial activities as well.

Boseman joined with twenty-eight other blacks and two prominent white Charleston Republicans in the formation and incorporation of the Enterprise Railroad Company in 1870.[70] Among the founders who were important black politicians were Robert De Large, Alonzo Ransier, William Whipper, Robert Brown Elliott, and Joseph Rainey. Boseman was one of the eleven blacks on the twelve-man board of directors. All the original officers were black, including the president,

Richard Cain, the AME minister.[71] The Enterprise was created to provide horsedrawn freight service in Charleston between the Cooper River wharves on the city's east side and the South Carolina Railroad terminal at the city's northern boundary.[72] Boseman purchased twenty-five shares of stock in the corporation at a cost of $625.[73]

The company encountered difficulties from its inception and never operated as a black venture. Evidently there were problems in raising sufficient capital to begin construction. A prominent white Republican, Timothy Hurley, replaced Cain as president in 1871.[74] Local black draymen organized to oppose the railroad, which they viewed as potentially ruinous competition. The draymen succeeded in enlisting the support of several Republican aldermen, which led to further delays in construction and operation.[75] Finally, for reasons that are not entirely clear, the railroad was taken over by a group of white businessmen led by S. S. Solomon, and it was operated as a passenger line.[76]

There were numerous accusations concerning the Enterprise's problems as a black corporation. Boseman pointed the finger at Hurley and charged him with fraudulently manipulating the company's stock in obtaining 6,000 shares for himself. But no official explanation was forthcoming, and Boseman remained a stockholder even after majority ownership passed from black hands.[77]

Before the fiasco with the Enterprise and heady with prospects for financial success in the early 1870s, black leaders took part in the rush to create phosphate mining companies in the Carolina lowcountry. Immense phosphate deposits, which were a valuable source of fertilizer in the nineteenth century, had been discovered in the river beds of the state in the late 1860s. Boseman himself introduced a bill in late 1869 "to incorporate the South Carolina Chemical and Mining Company." However, it died in committee.[78]

Undaunted, Boseman and several of the state's other prominent black politicians (many of whom were also involved with the Enterprise Railroad) formed the South Carolina Phosphate and Phosphatic River Mining Company in 1870. Robert Smalls, Robert Brown Elliott, William Whipper, Beverly Nash, Edward Mickey, and Boseman among others combined with at least five whites to incorporate the company. They agreed to pay the state a royalty of one dollar for every ton of phosphates mined in the state's navigable rivers. The corporation was authorized to issue $2 million of capital stock in shares of $100 and to begin functioning when $300,000 in stock had been subscribed.[79] Apparently raising funds was more difficult than anticipated. There is no evidence that the company commenced operations and no record that Boseman owned stock in it, though it is conceivable that money he may have invested was lost.

The Enterprise Railroad and the South Carolina Phosphate Company were conspicuous by their failures as black businesses. But if the companies did not succeed, individual black men like Benjamin Boseman did. According to tax records for 1874, Boseman had acquired $2,500 in real estate and $350 in personal property. He owned a house and an adjacent lot on Coming Street near Calhoun Street in central Charleston.[80]

Economic and political success was matched by social acceptance. By the mid-1870s Boseman was a family man. He and his mulatto wife Virginia had two children, a son Christopher and a daughter Ada.[81] Boseman joined and became a vestryman at St. Marks Episcopal Church. Founded by free blacks in 1849, it was the most fashionable church among Charleston Negroes.[82] As a mulatto and a man of some means, he was invited to join the exclusive Brown Fellowship Society. The society had been founded in 1790 by well-to-do brown men as a social, benevolent, and self-help organization. It provided education, insurance, and a burial ground for the families of its members. Boseman had the distinction of being the only non–South Carolina native initiated in the society during Reconstruction and perhaps during its history. However, other notable native mulatto politicians were among its members, including Robert De Large, William McKinlay, and Malcolm Brown.[83]

It is also worth pointing out that a lighter or darker skin complexion sometimes did serve as a divisive issue among Charleston's Negro leaders. Martin Delany placed blame for loss in the 1871 municipal election on brown men who, he charged, cooperated too eagerly with white Democrats. Thus it was the brown men who "have received all the places of honor, profit and trust, intended to represent the race." That brought an angry response and rebuttal from light-skinned leaders. But if skin color sometimes divided Negro leaders, prewar status seems to have been an even more critical factor in postwar politics in Charleston. Virtually no ex-slave rose to any position of power or prominence in the city after the war. Virtually all the significant Negro politicians—whether black or brown, whether natives of the city or not—had been freemen in the antebellum period.[84]

By the early 1870s, Boseman was apparently no longer practicing medicine on a full-time basis. He was wholly consumed by politics, and he managed to survive and even prosper in a turbulent and chaotic postwar political world where the attrition rate among politicians was high. Boseman's success in politics can be attributed at least in part to his ability to adjust to the shifting and often bitter factional struggles that marked Republican politics during Reconstruction in Charleston.

The single most striking feature of Republican politics was intra-party warfare and the constant struggle for patronage. As the Republican party organized in Charleston in 1867 and 1868, it split into two factions that, despite changes in composition and leadership, persisted for the next decade. One group was largely made up of northerners—both black and white—who had come to Charleston after the war. Because a sizable number of them had come from Massachusetts, that faction was dubbed for a time the Massachusetts party. Boseman consistently supported this group during Reconstruction. The competing faction, the Charleston Ring, was composed mostly of natives of the city—both black and white—and it constantly challenged the Massachusetts party for political dominance and for patronage in Reconstruction Charleston and South Carolina.

Republicans split for the first time during the U.S. Senate election in the special session of the legislature in the summer of 1868. The Massachusetts party, including Boseman, joined in support of Frederick Sawyer, who was a native of Massachusetts and a Harvard graduate. Sawyer had spent the 1850s in Charleston as superintendent of schools and had been appointed collector of internal revenue in Charleston by President Johnson in 1865. Opposing him was the leading native white Republican of Charleston, A. G. Mackey. Mackey had supported the Union during the secession crisis and had been appointed collector of the port in 1865 by President Johnson. After a lengthy contest involving eight ballots, Sawyer won the bitter, critical election.[85] More important, he and the Massachusetts party won control of federal patronage.

But if geographical differences that divided the Republicans were not enough, the party fabric was further torn by interracial discord prior to the 1870 elections. Black leaders who had acquiesced to white leadership before the 1868 elections and thereby permitted white Republicans to monopolize major offices now chafed in frustration and anger. Black politicians led by Robert De Large and Martin Delany insisted on a greater allotment of offices and greater political influence. De Large lashed out at white Republicans, "If the white men in the party think that the Republican party was made for them, for their special benefit, they are badly mistaken." Delany argued that black politicians from South Carolina deserved to hold one U.S. Senate seat, two seats in the U.S. House, the lieutenant governor's chair, and a reasonable quota of state and local offices.[86]

Boseman initially and eagerly supported the efforts of black leaders to secure a larger share of political power. He spoke out enthusiastically in the state House on behalf of Jonathan Wright's nomination to the state supreme court in 1870. Wright, a black lawyer from Beaufort, was subsequently elected by the legislature over another black candidate, William Whipper.[87]

But Boseman's willingness to support Negro candidates was tempered by his commitment to the Massachusetts faction of the party. By 1870 Christopher C. Bowen, a white congressman representing Charleston, had emerged as leader of the faction. However, Bowen's nomination for reelection was challenged by assertive black politicians led by Robert De Large. Several prominent blacks had gathered in an all black meeting in Charleston in June 1870 and agreed to support De Large as the party nominee for Congress against the incumbent Bowen. If Boseman attended the black gathering he remained decidedly silent, but chances are that he was not present.[88] Boseman declined to support De Large's candidacy, deciding in this instance that loyalty to faction was more important than loyalty to race.

Boseman supported Bowen in the divisive campaign that followed in 1870 and was a candidate for reelection to the state House on the Bowen ticket. Two separate Republican slates of candidates were put forward by the contending factions. The Charleston Ring, led by E. W. M. Mackey, the thirty-year-old son of the collector and senatorial candidate A. G. Mackey, backed De Large. Each slate was composed primarily of black nominees for state and local offices. Boseman ran on a ticket in which sixteen of the twenty-four nominees were black.[89]

Futile attempts were made prior to the election to resolve the intraparty dispute and to offer only one Republican ticket and one nominee for Congress.[90] However, there was no compromise, even though Democrats threatened the divided Republicans with a ticket of their own. In the election that followed, Bowen's ticket swept every race with one significant exception—his own. De Large won the seat in Congress in a controversial, disputed election; but Boseman and the other candidates on the Bowen ticket were elected. The fears that a revitalized Democratic party might defeat the fragmented Republicans did not materialize.[91]

The scenario in the 1872 elections was similar, and once again Boseman was aligned with the winning faction. Party divisions intensified and expanded to the statewide races that year, as two Republican tickets vied with each other for political supremacy. The so-called Regular Republicans, supported by the Mackey faction from Charleston, nominated Franklin J. Moses, Jr., for governor and Richard Gleaves, a black man from Beaufort, for lieutenant governor. Several prominent black leaders, including Richard Cain and Robert Brown Elliott, lined up in support of the Regulars' ticket.[92]

But Boseman and the black and white Republicans connected with the Bowen faction would have no truck with the Regulars. With the nominations of Moses and Gleaves, the Bowenites—designating themselves Reformers—bolted the state Republican convention and met in a rump convention. Ostensibly offended at the corruption that tainted the Regulars' nominees, but in reality eager to dominate the party machinery, the Reformers proceeded to nominate a separate ticket. Reuben Tomlinson, a white legislator originally from Philadelphia and a former superintendent of schools for the Freedmen's Bureau, was nominated for governor.[93]

Benjamin Boseman was the Reformers' first choice for lieutenant governor; but for reasons that were not explained, he refused to consider or accept the nomination. James N. Hayne, a black legislator from Barnwell, was selected instead.[94] Boseman satisfied himself with nomination and reelection to the House on a Bowen ticket composed of thirteen black and five white candidates. He was one of only three blacks on that ticket whom the *Charleston Daily News* was willing to support editorially.[95]

Boseman and the other Bowen candidates to the state legislature and county offices won their races, but in the statewide races Tomlinson and Hayne were defeated.[96] Nevertheless, even though the Reformers had bolted the Regular Republican convention, they were the recipients of federal largess in the form of patronage in the aftermath of the election. Four months later, in March 1873, President Grant appointed Benjamin Boseman postmaster of Charleston. Shortly before Boseman's appointment, Frederick Sawyer had been named assistant secretary of the Treasury, and James L. Orr, the former governor and Confederate senator who had supported the Reformers in 1872, was appointed minister to Russia.[97] In all likelihood Boseman was nominated postmaster on advice of Senator John J. Patterson, who was just beginning his term. Generally during the Grant administration, Republican members of the House were given the opportunity to select postmasters in their congressional districts.[98] But in March 1873 only the Senate was in session; and furthermore, Charleston and South Carolina's second district seat in Congress was vacant, making it all but certain that Patterson played a critical role in the appointment of Boseman, Sawyer, and Orr.[99]

Patterson's surprising influence as a new senator was probably due to his close relationship with Grant. He had won Senate election in December 1872 amid allegations that he had indulged in wholesale bribery of legislators. The Charleston delegation, with its thirteen blacks—including Boseman—and five whites, had voted unanimously for Patterson, although there was a black candidate in the field—Robert Brown Elliott.[100]

Black and white Republicans who supported the Bowen faction were naturally pleased with Boseman's appointment. However, the reaction of local whites was unexpected. They greeted the naming of a black postmaster with equanimity, even though Boseman replaced a popular white resident and longtime postmaster, Stanley G. Trott. If the *Daily News* is an accurate indicator, many whites were willing to accept Boseman's appointment and were convinced that he would perform his duties creditably. It reported: "He has commanded a good share of the respect of citizens of all shades of political complexion, and it is expected that in the important post to which he has now been appointed, he will prove a conscientious, trustworthy and competent officer."[101]

Boseman's eight years as Charleston's postmaster were both uneventful and remarkable. With one notable exception, no correspondence whatsoever concerning the conduct of the Charleston Post Office in the nineteenth century has survived. But apparently Boseman supervised its operations competently and satisfactorily. After his death the *News and Courier* commented, "In his position as postmaster he was civil and accommodating, and, as far as his capacity went, was an excellent public officer."[102]

Incredibly, however, Boseman's tenure as postmaster was not marked by any significant involvement in patronage or Republican politics. The close connection between patronage and politics in the Post Office Department is one of the most enduring and widely known features of U.S. political history. In a majority of late nineteenth-century American cities, the postmaster was the majority party's foremost political operative.[103] But that was most certainly not the case in Charleston from 1873 until 1881.

During Boseman's first six years as postmaster there was exactly one change in post office personnel. The only surviving piece of post office correspondence is a response to an inquiry concerning "Rules Governing Appointments and Promotions." In it Boseman, in 1879, informed

President Rutherford B. Hayes's personal secretary, W. K. Rogers, that one new clerk had been hired the previous year after the death of the former clerk. That was the only change among post office employees since Boseman had been appointed postmaster.[104]

Moreover, Boseman's name rarely surfaced in accounts of local and state politics in Charleston's major newspaper, *The News and Courier,* after he became postmaster. In one instance, in August 1875, he did serve as vice-president of the Ward 5 Cunningham Campaign Club.[105] George I. Cunningham was the Republican mayor and candidate for reelection. But Boseman's participation in the campaign was not particularly noteworthy or crucial.

What accounts for Boseman's decidedly inactive role in politics while serving in a post that was commonly regarded as awash with intense political activity? The chief explanation is that in Charleston and, in all probability, other coastal cities the main center of patronage and politics was not the post office but the customhouse. The bulk of federal patronage was dispensed through the collector of customs. Therefore, whichever Republican faction controlled the customhouse in Charleston had a distinct advantage in Republican politics. During most of the Reconstruction decade, the Bowen-Sawyer faction (the Massachusetts party) dominated the customhouse through Collector George W. Clark and challenged the Mackey wing or Charleston Ring for supremacy in the Republican party in Charleston and South Carolina.

Thus, while Bowen and Mackey—the leading white Republicans in Charleston—competed for control of the local party through their respective factions, one of the city's most prominent and effective black leaders was relegated to the post office—not an insignificant position but certainly not as influential as or exercising the authority of the collector of customs.

After Redemption in 1877 Boseman continued to maintain a low political profile. He attracted little publicity and avoided stirring up racial animosity that was sometimes directed against black postmasters in South Carolina during the post-Reconstruction years.[106] In 1878, however, he did offer effusive words of praise for Wade Hampton, who was running for reelection as governor and had made an open appeal to black voters. But Boseman did not make an outright commitment of political support for the Democrat. He said: "You may quote me as expressing absolute confidence in Gov. Hampton and entire satisfaction with his course. We have no complaint whatever to make. He has kept all his pledges."[107] In the meantime, Boseman had been reappointed postmaster by President Hayes in 1877. He served in that capacity until his death from Bright's disease at the age of forty on February 23, 1881.[108]

It would be easy to dismiss Benjamin Boseman as a conservative, middle-class black man who was essentially a sychophant of white interests and was, thus, hardly representative of the 255 black men who held state and federal office in South Carolina during Reconstruction.[109] Though not unfamiliar with segregation and discrimination in his hometown of Troy, N.Y., Boseman by education and financial standing appeared to have more in common with prosperous and articulate whites than poor and illiterate freedmen. He demonstrated no overwhelming interest in the two prime concerns of most freedman, land and education. Rather, he appeared more concerned with satisfying his own middle-class aspirations by involvement with the Enterprise Railroad and the South Carolina Phosphate Mining Company.

But, with the possible exception of Francis Cardozo, Boseman was the most successful black politician in Charleston in winning the respect of a suspicious white population while simultaneously earning the confidence and support of the black community, especially its middle-class elements. Boseman was a self-effacing, taciturn man. He lacked the flamboyance and personal magnetism possessed by some other black politicians, but he also was not perceived as the same sort of threat as such black leaders as Robert Brown Elliott, Robert De Large, and Richard Cain frequently were. There is little doubt that Boseman had a well developed facility for getting along with whites. He had grown up in the midst of an enormous white majority in Troy. He had evidently established a reasonably close personal relationship with Dr. Thomas C. Brimsmade as well as, perhaps, Congressman John A. Griswold; and he was able to take advantage of their patronage. Later as a legislator he performed his duties judiciously and competently. He engaged in no emotional and personal tirades against whites. He did not earn the enduring enmity of white leaders. After Reconstruction ended, no effort was made to replace him as postmaster.

Yet a one-dimensional perception of Boseman as a conservative who consistently accommodated to white interests is misleading. Though usually quiet and restrained, Benjamin Boseman was a solid and loyal supporter of the Republican party. He participated wholeheartedly in Republican activities and factional struggles up to the time when he was appointed postmaster in 1873. As a legislator he initiated and strongly defended an unprecedented civil-rights measure in 1868

354

to guarantee equal access to public accommodations. He led an effort to improve the quality of medical care in South Carolina and supported attempts to improve the treatment of the mentally impaired.

Moreover, he was the advocate of baldly partisan measures intended solely to place Democrats at a disadvantage. He succeeded in winning passage of legislation to shift the date of Charleston's municipal election to the summer months and give clear advantage to the Republicans. Yet he managed this feat without arousing strident criticism from whites, although they regarded such measures as abominable. Finally, as Charleston's postmaster for eight years, Boseman was largely removed from the turbulent world of partisan politics and did not play a crucial or influential role in Republican affairs.

Local political figures like Boseman have been virtually unrecognized among significant Reconstruction leaders. Even though he was never elected to a major state or federal office and never achieved the notoriety of a Robert Smalls, Robert Brown Elliott, or Francis L. Cardozo, Benjamin Boseman's erudition, legislative record, role in Republican politics, and appointment to an important federal position justify his inclusion in the pantheon of six or eight most important black politicos in Reconstruction South Carolina.

Notes

Unless otherwise specified, all newspaper citations in these notes refer to Charleston papers.

1. Medical School Roster, Medical School of Maine, Special Collections, Bowdoin College Library, Brunswick, Me.

2. The black population was 1.7 percent of the total population of Troy. U.S., Bureau of the Census, *The Seventh Census of the United States: 1850* (Washington, D.C.: Robert Armstrong, 1853), p. 105.

3. Mary Livingston, who had been born in the West Indies, also lived with the family. Perhaps she was the maternal grandmother of Benjamin, Jr. U.S., Bureau of the Census, Manuscript Census Schedules, 1850, Rensselaer County, Troy, Seventh Ward, pp. 258–59.

4. *Prescott and Wilson's City of Troy City Directory for the Year 1848–49* (Troy: Prescott & Wilson, 1848), vol. 20.

5. The Seventh Census indicates that Benjamin, Jr., and his oldest brother and two sisters were enrolled in school in 1850. The Fourteenth Amendment brought an end to segregated public education in Troy. Rutherford Hayner, *Troy and Rensselaer County, New York: A History,* 3 vols. (New York: Lewis Historical Publishing Co., 1925), 2:284.

6. For Garnet's activities in Troy, see Joel Schor, *Henry Highland Garnet: A Voice of Black Radicalism in the Nineteenth Century* (Westport, Conn.:

Greenwood Press, 1977), pp. 28–31, 89–92; Earl Ofari, *"Let Your Motto Be Resistance": The Life and Thought of Henry Highland Garnet* (Boston: Beacon Press, 1972), pp. 10–11, 45–49. Among the sixty-seven delegates to the convention were Frederick Douglass, Alexander Crummell, and William C. Nell. Floyd Miller, *The Search for a Black Nationality: Black Emigration and Colonization 1787–1863* (Urbana: University of Illinois Press, 1975), pp. 187–90; Howard Holman Bell, *A Survey of the Negro Convention Movement 1830–1861* (New York: Arno Press, 1969), pp. 85–91, 188–89; Benjamin Quarles, *The Black Abolitionists* (New York: Oxford University Press, 1968), pp. 40, 189, 225–26.

7. For more on Brimsmade's impressive medical career, see Samuel Rezneck, *Profiles out of the Past of Troy, New York, since 1789* (Troy: Chamber of Commerce, 1970), pp. 147–50.

8. William F. Norwood, *Medical Education in the United States before the Civil War* (1944; reprint ed., New York: Arno Press, 1971), pp. 10, 381, 404–6; John Duffy, *The Healers: A History of American Medicine* (New York: McGraw-Hill, 1976; paperback ed., Urbana: University of Illinois Press, 1979), pp. 166–67; William G. Rothstein, *American Physicians in the Nineteenth Century: From Sects to Science* (Baltimore: Johns Hopkins University Press, 1972), pp. 19, 85–86, 88–93.

9. Dr. T. C. Brimsmade to P. A. Chadbourne, M.D., Feb. 24, 1864, Medical School of Maine Records, Special Collections, Bowdoin College Library; Office of Alumni Records, Dartmouth College, to author, May 16, 1979.

10. Brimsmade to Chadbourne, Feb. 24, 1864.

11. For a brief history of the Medical School of Maine, see Norwood, *Medical Education*, pp. 201–4. See also "Program Commemorating the Medical School of Maine and Seth Adams Hall," Bowdoin College, June 11, 1965, Special Collections, Bowdoin College Library.

12. Martin Robison Delany, *The Condition, Elevation, Emigration and Destiny of the Colored People of the United States* (1852; reprint ed., New York: Arno Press, 1968), pp. 134–35.

13. *Catalogue of the Officers and Students of Bowdoin College and the Medical School of Maine,* Fall 1864 (Brunswick: J. Griffin, 1864), p. 25. Though listed for the fall term, Boseman undoubtedly had attended the previous spring term. In later correspondence (see note 19) he indicated that he had already graduated by the summer of 1864. Medical School of Maine records list him in the class of 1864. *General Catalogue*, Medical School of Maine, Brunswick, p. 480.

14. Courses in bacteriology, pathology, and pharmacology did not yet exist. Norwood, *Medical Education*, p. 396.

15. Rothstein, *American Physicians*, pp. 18, 125; Norwood, *Medical Education*, p. 398.

16. Norwood, *Medical Education*, p. 404.

17. Benjamin Antonio Boseman, Jr., "The Importance of Medical Statistics" (M.D. thesis, Medical School of Maine, 1864). The Bowdoin College Library has the original thesis.

18. For the typical methods of diagnosis and treatment of disease in the first half of the nineteenth century, see Rothstein, *American Physicians*, pp. 41–45; Duffy, *The Healers*, pp. 98–99.

356

19. Boseman to Joseph K. Barnes, M.D., July 1, 1864, Records of the Adjutant General's Office, Medical Officers' Files, Record Group (RG) 94, National Archives (NA), Washington, D.C.

20. John A. Griswold to Maj. Gen. B. F. Butler, July 19, 1864, ibid. James L. Harrison, comp., *Biographical Directory of Congress, 1774–1949* (Washington, D.C.: Government Printing Office, 1949), p. 1240. Griswold was reelected in 1864 and 1866 as a Republican.

21. Both letters are dated July 1, 1864, and are contained in Boseman's file, Adjutant General's Office, Medical Officers' Files, RG 94, NA.

22. The four-page exam is in Boseman's army file. Approval and Recommendation, August 8, 1864, ibid.

23. George Washington Adams, *Doctors in Blue: The Medical History of the Union Army in the Civil War* (New York: Henry Schuman, 1972), pp. 174–75.

24. Boseman to Griswold, Mar. 13, 1865. Adjutant General's Office, Medical Officers' Files, RG 94, NA.

25. Contract: Assistant Surgeon, Aug. 16, 1864, to Sept. 16, 1865, ibid.

26. Boseman was not listed in the first city directory published in postwar Charleston, but his absence is not surprising. Generally, no careful or conscientious effort was made to include blacks in Charleston directories. *Charleston City Directory for 1867–68* (Charleston: Jno. Orrin Lea & Co., 1868).

27. *South Carolina Leader,* Nov. 25, 1865. Two black conventions were held in Charleston in September and November 1865. Most of the delegates to the conventions had been free before the war and were skilled tradesmen and working people. They appealed unsuccessfully to the constitutional convention and subsequently to the state legislature for equal treatment and equal rights under the law. *Proceedings of the Colored People's Convention of the State of South Carolina* (Charleston: South Carolina Leader Office, 1865); Herbert Aptheker, "South Carolina Negro Conventions, 1865," *Journal of Negro History* 31 (Jan. 1946):93.

28. *Daily News,* Oct. 29, 1867.

29. Ibid., Mar. 22, 1867; *Daily Courier,* ibid.; *Advocate,* Mar. 23, 1867.

30. It is, of course, possible that Boseman was present in the nearly all black crowd that numbered approximately 2,000. *Daily Courier,* Mar. 27, 1867; *Advocate,* Apr. 6, 1867.

31. The five black nominees were Alonzo J. Ransier, Robert De Large, Richard Cain, Francis Cardozo and William McKinlay. All had been free before the war. Three—Ransier, Cardozo, and McKinlay—were natives of Charleston. The four whites nominated were Frederick A. Sawyer, A. G. Mackey, Gilbert Pillsbury, and C. C. Bowen. *Daily Courier,* Nov. 4, 1867; *Daily News,* ibid.

32. The Second Reconstruction Act of March 23, 1867, provided that at least one-half of all registered voters would have to vote on the question of ratification. Henry Steele Commager, ed., *Documents in American History* (New York: Appleton-Century-Crofts, 1963), 1:488–89.

33. *Daily News,* Mar. 9, 12, 21, 1868.

34. Two black Charlestonians, Francis Cardozo and William McKinlay, were nominated for secretary of state. Cardozo won the nomination. Ibid., Mar. 12, 1868.

35. *Daily Courier,* Mar. 28, 1868; *Daily News,* Apr. 15, 17, 1868. House members represented the county at large. However, the Charleston delegation was informally divided up among rural and urban representatives. Two state senators were also elected—Richard Cain was black and David T. Corbin was white.

36. *Journal of the House of Representatives of the State of South Carolina, Special Session of 1868* (Columbia: John W. Denny, 1868), pp. 112–13, 218–19. *Daily Courier,* Aug. 31, 1868.

37. The evidence only partially supports Whipper's assertion. In a roll call on his amendment to include common carriers in the bill, 29 legislators failed to vote, 16 of whom were white. Then, on the third reading of the bill, 35 legislators did not answer the call; of these only 18 were white, although 20 of 22 who voted against the bill were also white. *Daily Courier,* Aug. 17, 1868; *House Journal,* spec. sess., 1868, pp. 218–19. I used Thomas Holt's racial breakdown of black political leaders to determine the color of each lawmaker. Thomas Holt, *Black over White: Negro Political Leadership in South Carolina during Reconstruction* (Urbana: University of Illinois Press, 1977), pp. 229–41.

38. *Daily Courier,* Aug. 17, 1868.

39. *House Journal,* spec. sess., 1868, p. 243; *Daily Courier,* Aug. 18, 1868. There was no roll call on the House vote.

40. *Daily Courier,* Aug. 31, 1868.

41. *Journal of the Senate of the State of South Carolina, Being the Special Session of 1868* (Columbia: John W. Denny, 1868), pp. 272–76; *Daily Courier,* Sept. 5, 1868.

42. *Senate Journal,* spec. sess., 1868, pp. 254–56, 272–76, 314, 347.

43. *Daily Courier,* Sept. 16, 1868.

44. *Daily News,* Sept. 29, 1869; *Daily Republican,* Dec. 10, 17, 1869, Jan. 5, 1870.

45. *Daily Republican,* Dec. 13, 1869, Jan. 31, 1870; *Daily News,* Jan. 19, 1870.

46. *Acts and Joint Resolutions of the General Assembly of the State of South Carolina . . . 1869–70* (Columbia: John W. Denny, 1870), pt. 1, pp. 386–88.

47. *House Journal,* 1869–70 (Columbia: John W. Denny, 1870), pp. 284, 289, 298–99.

48. South Carolina's experience with civil rights and public accommodations supports the contentions of Howard Rabinowitz in his study based primarily on the urban communities of Atlanta, Montgomery, Raleigh, Richmond, and Nashville. Rabinowitz argues that Reconstruction policies which established separate but equal facilities drew the support of black political leaders because they represented a significant improvement over antebellum measures that usually prescribed exclusion of Negroes. Howard N. Rabinowitz, *Race Relations in the Urban South, 1865–1890* (New York: Oxford University Press, 1978), pp. xv–xvi, 171, 182–97.

49. Antebellum legislation had required medical doctors to be licensed by a state-authorized board of physicians. But that regulation had been unenforced since 1838, when a measure had been enacted repealing penalties imposed on physicians who practiced without a license. *Acts and Joint Resolutions of the General Assembly, 1817* (Columbia: Daniel & J. J. Faust, 1818), pp. 31–34;

Acts and Joint Resolutions, 1838 (Columbia: A. H. & W. F. Pemberton, 1839), pp. 39–40; Joseph I. Waring, *A History of Medicine in South Carolina, 1825–1900* (Columbia: South Carolina Medical Assn., 1967), pp. 95, 99–101; Richard H. Shryock, *Medical Licensing in America, 1650–1965* (Baltimore: Johns Hopkins University Press, 1967), pp. 33–34; Rothstein, *American Physicians*, pp. 107–8.

50. *House Journal,* 1868–69, pp. 51, 107, 128, 129, 399; *Acts and Joint Resolutions,* 1868–69, pp. 196–97.

51. *Daily Courier,* Mar. 29, 1869; *House Journal,* 1872–73 (Columbia: Republican Printing Co., 1873), pp. 264, 274, 292, 385, 404; ibid., 1870–71, pp. 372, 585, 599; *Reports and Resolutions of the General Assembly, 1869–70* (Columbia: John W. Denny, 1870), pp. 1483–86.

52. Waring, *History of Medicine in South Carolina,* pp. 144–45.

53. "A Bill to Provide for the Care of the Poor," *House Journal,* 1869–70, pp. 204, 229, 248, 251, 264, 289, 333, 554, 573. The Tomlinson bill, which carried over from the 1868–69 session, made it the responsibility of county commissioners to provide a poorhouse and appoint overseers of the poor. *Acts and Joint Resolutions,* 1869–70, pt. 1, pp. 369–72; "Joint Resolution to Provide Medical Aid for the Indigent Sick in the Respective Counties in the State," *House Journal,* 1869–70, pp. 259–60, 267, 271, 518.

54. *Acts and Joint Resolutions,* 1869–70, pt. 1, p. 421.

55. Duffy, *The Healers,* pp. 119, 123.

56. *House Journal,* 1869–70, pp. 168–70. Other blacks on the board were Robert Brown Elliott, S. B. Thompson, Robert De Large and the chairman, Beverly Nash.

57. "Report of the Committee of the Board of Regents of the Lunatic Asylum," *Reports and Resolutions . . . , 1871–72* (Columbia: Republican Printing Co., 1872), pp. 137–38; "Report of the Joint Committee on the Lunatic Asylum and Medical Affairs," ibid., pp. 889–90.

58. *Reports and Resolutions . . . , 1872–73* (Columbia: Republican Printing Co., 1873), p. 7.

59. Ibid., pp. 477, 803–5.

60. *House Journal,* 1868–69, p. 489; *Daily Courier,* Mar. 10, 1869.

61. Board of Trustees, Minutes, 1869–73, microfilm, South Caroliniana Library, University of South Carolina, Columbia, S.C.

62. *House Journal,* 1872–73, pp. 460–67, 475–79. Pamela Mercedes White, " 'Free and Open': The Radical University of South Carolina" (M.A. thesis, University of South Carolina, 1975). Daniel Hollis, *University of South Carolina,* 3 vols. (Columbia: University of South Carolina Press, 1956), 2:50–52.

63. *House Journal,* spec. sess., 1868, p. 123; *Daily Courier,* Aug. 18, 1868.

64. *Daily Courier,* Sept. 1–3, 1868; *House Journal,* spec. sess., 1868, pp. 332–34.

65. *House Journal,* 1870–71, pp. 326, 381, 559, 570, 629; *Acts and Joint Resolutions . . . , 1870–71* (Columbia: Republican Printing Co., 1871), p. 579.

66. In the 1870 census, there were 26,139 blacks and 22,749 whites in the city of Charleston. But the white male population was 10,967 and the black male population was 10,779. U.S., Bureau of the Census, *The Statistics of the Population of the United States* (Washington, D.C.: Government Printing Office, 1872), p. 258.

67. *Daily Republican*, Mar. 8, 1871. Blacks were not as susceptible to yellow fever as whites. See Peter Wood, *Black Majority: Negroes in South Carolina from 1670 to the Stono Rebellion* (New York: Alfred A. Knopf, 1974), p. 91.

68. *House Journal*, 1871–72, pp. 335, 369, 371, 376–77; *Daily News*, Feb. 8–9, 1872. When a roll call was taken on striking the enacting clause of the bill, Boseman was one of 69 (of the 90 who voted) who voted to strike the clause.

69. *House Journal*, 1871–72, p. 355; *Daily News*, Feb. 2–3, 1872.

70. *Senate Journal*, 1869–70, pp. 365, 397, 403, 410, 431–32, 435–36, 450, 507–9, 517; *House Journal*, 1869–70, pp. 445, 475, 479, 494.

71. *Acts and Joint Resolutions*, 1869–70, pt. 1, 391–92; *Daily Republican*, Mar. 24, 1870.

72. *Acts and Joint Resolutions*, 1869–70, pt. 1, pp. 391–92. Antebellum regulations prohibited the operation of steam engines in the city. Thus railroad trains did not enter Charleston.

73. The company was authorized to subscribe stock up to a total of $250,000. Boseman's will indicates that he still owned twenty-five shares when he died. But there is no way to determine the exact date when he purchased the stock; it seems likely that he bought it while the Enterprise was still a black business.

74. *Daily Republican*, Apr. 27, Aug. 3, 1871; Jacob Schirmer Diary, May 6, 25, 1871, South Carolina Historical Society, Charleston, S.C.

75. *Daily Republican*, June 14, 15, 21–24, 26, July 3, 18, Aug. 3, 15, 1871; *Daily News*, June 14, 1871.

76. *News and Courier*, Aug. 26, 1873, Jan. 2, 1874; Schirmer Diary, Sept. 20, 1873, Jan. 2, 1874.

77. *Daily News*, Feb. 7, 1873.

78. *House Journal*, 1869–70, p. 209.

79. *Acts and Joint Resolutions*, 1870–71, pp. 688–89.

80. County Auditor's Tax Duplicates, 1874, Charleston County Court House, Charleston, S.C.

81. Will of Benjamin Boseman, Feb. 10, 1877, Probate Records, ibid.

82. *News and Courier*, Feb. 24, 1881; Marina Wikramanayake, *A World in Shadow: The Free Negro in Antebellum South Carolina* (Columbia: University of South Carolina Press, 1973), p. 130.

83. Brown Fellowship Society, Minute Books, photocopy, Charleston County Public Library, Charleston. The original minute books are contained in the rare-book room of the Robert K. Smalls Library at the College of Charleston.

84. Thomas Holt emphasizes the differences between black and brown leaders, *Black over White*, pp. 43–71. For the angry exchanges in the Delany controversy, see *Daily Republican*, Aug. 15–18, 21, 1871; *Daily News*, Aug. 16, 1871.

85. *House Journal*, spec. sess., 1868, pp. 93–94; *Daily Courier*, July 16–18, 1868.

86. *Daily Republican*, June 24, 1870; *Daily News*, June 25, 1870.

87. *Senate Journal*, 1869–70, pp. 333–34; *Daily Republican*, Feb. 2, 1870. The legislature elected the justices to the three-man court in joint session.

88. Among those in attendance were Alonzo Ransier (chairman of the meeting), Martin Delany, and Richard Cain. *Daily Republican,* June 22, 1870.

89. Ibid., Sept. 13–14, 1870; *Daily News,* Sept. 13–16, 1870.

90. *Daily Republican,* Aug. 12, 15, 19–20, 24, 29, Sept. 12, Oct. 3, 13, 1870.

91. *Daily News,* Nov. 2, 8, 1870. Robert H. Woody, "The South Carolina Election of 1870," *North Carolina Historical Review* 8 (Apr. 1930):168–86. The Republicans were not split in the statewide races. Robert Scott was re-elected governor. Alonzo Ransier was elected the state's first black lieutenant governor.

92. *Daily News,* Aug. 16, 23, Sept. 5, 7, 1872.

93. Ibid., Aug. 24, 1872; Willie Lee Rose, *Rehearsal for Reconstruction: The Port Royal Experiment* (Indianapolis: Bobbs-Merrill Co., 1965), pp. 98, 390–92.

94. *Daily News,* Aug. 24, 1872.

95. Ibid., Sept. 27, Oct. 4, 7, 18, 1872. The Democrats did not participate in the 1872 state elections; neither did the party offer a slate of candidates in Charleston County. Thus the *Daily News* selected and supported a combination of what it regarded as the best candidates from the Bowen and Mackey tickets.

96. Ibid., Oct. 28, 1872.

97. Ibid., Mar. 19, 1873. The *Daily News* was puzzled by federal patronage policies and wondered editorially if Grant was openly encouraging insubordination within the party.

98. Dorothy Ganfield Fowler, *The Cabinet Politician: The Postmasters General 1829–1909* (New York: Columbia University Press, 1943), p. 145; Wayne E. Fuller, *The American Mail: Enlarger of American Life* (Chicago: University of Chicago Press, 1972), p. 293.

99. The 1870 U.S. House election between Bowen and De Large had been the subject of a lengthy congressional investigation after De Large had been sworn in. The investigation finally determined that numerous illegal activities had occurred in both camps. The seat was therefore declared vacant in January 1873. *Daily News,* Jan. 20, 1873; Samuel Denny Smith, *The Negro in Congress, 1870–1901* (Chapel Hill: University of North Carolina Press, 1940), pp. 50–51; *Biographical Directory of Congress,* p. 1073.

100. *House Journal,* 1872–73, p. 86; *Senate Journal,* 1872–73, p. 95. *Daily News,* Dec. 12, 1872, Jan. 28, 1873. See also *Report of the Joint Investigating Committee on Public Funds and Election of Hon. J. J. Patterson Made to the General Assembly of South Carolina at the Regular Session* (Columbia: Calvo & Patton, 1872), pp. 908–15.

101. *Daily News,* Mar. 19, 1873.

102. No correspondence concerning the Charleston Post Office is contained in the Post Office Department records in Record Group 28 in the National Archives. *News and Courier,* Feb. 24, 1881.

103. Fowler, *Cabinet Politician,* p. 146; Fuller, *American Mail,* pp. 293–94, 302, 314; Morton Keller, *Affairs of State: Public Life in Late Nineteenth-Century America* (Cambridge, Mass.: Harvard University Press, 1975), pp. 310-11; Clyde Kelly, *United States Postal Policy* (New York: D. Appleton & Co., 1932), p. 193.

104. Boseman to W. K. Rogers, Nov. 5, 1879, Rutherford B. Hayes Papers, Rutherford B. Hayes Library, Fremont, O.

105. *News and Courier,* Aug. 14, 1875.

106. George Brown Tindall, *South Carolina Negroes 1877–1900* (Columbia: University of South Carolina Press, 1952), p. 65.

107. *Columbia Daily Register,* Apr. 19, 1878, quoted in Tindall, *South Carolina Negroes,* p. 25. Boseman's obituary in the *News and Courier,* Feb. 24, 1881, indicates that Hampton had appointed him surgeon to the First Regiment of the State National Guard in 1876.

108. Thomas A Smith, manuscripts librarian, Rutherford B. Hayes Library, to author, Apr. 19, 1979. *News and Courier,* Feb. 24, 1881.

109. Holt, *Black over White,* p. 38.

14

George T. Ruby and the Politics of Expediency in Texas

IN THE POST–CIVIL WAR ERA no black man in Texas exercised more political power than did George Thompson Ruby. An astute politician, Ruby built a base of power in the black community of Galveston, then used that support to make himself a major force in the state at large. He was a forceful advocate of civil and political rights for his race, but he knew when to compromise to gain his larger goals, and he moved carefully among hostile white politicians in his efforts to expand opportunities for black people. In the context of his time and place, his goals were radical, but he was hardly a political fanatic. His entire career demonstrated responsibility and moderation. In the end his work failed and he left Texas for a more favorable environment, but rather than any personal character flaws or lack of depth in his vision, forces outside his control undercut his efforts. The refusal of whites to compromise on racial matters, the white majority of the state, and Ruby's steadfast willingness to adhere to democratic politics prevented his attaining the goals he sought. His career is instructive, not only in that it shows how at least one black politician gained power during Reconstruction, but also because it indicates the problems that beset both Ruby and the southern Republican movement in their efforts to establish a viable political alternative to the white-dominated Democratic party.[1]

Ruby was not a native Texan, but arrived in the state after the Civil War. He had been born in New York City in 1841, and he maintained that he was the son of a wealthy white father. More probably his parents were Ebenezer and Jemima Ruby, his father a clergyman and farmer with land on the outskirts of Portland, Maine. They had moved there in 1851 and Ruby grew up in this predominantly white community. He claimed that he received a sound and liberal education, and it may be assumed, given the small number of blacks in the area, that he spent his youth in an atmosphere of relatively little racial hostility. His later career, however, demonstrated that he early became aware of the problems that beset his race throughout the country.[2]

At the age of twenty, Ruby became involved for the first time in efforts to improve the condition of blacks in the United States. In 1860 he moved to Boston and obtained a job on the *Pine and Palm*, the official newspaper of James Redpath's Haitian migration project. Redpath wanted Haiti to provide the world with an example of the ability of blacks. Ruby went to the island to report on the experiment, which Redpath believed would provide a base from which blacks could move toward a "position of perfect Social, Political, and National Equality and Power with the Whites." Ruby's later career, pursuing economic opportunity and legal and political rights, showed views similar to those of the English reformer and suggests the importance of Redpath in the development of Ruby's analysis of social problems. Ruby always believed that until some sort of economic base was established, political and other rights could be undercut. He may also have learned something about the impediments to achieving equality when Redpath's experiment collapsed in 1862, lacking financial support, facing opposition from black leaders in the United States, and suffering from hostility between the immigrants and native Haitians.[3]

Ruby returned to the United States after the Haitian scheme failed, but he continued to work for black improvement by moving to Louisiana where an invading Union army had liberated large numbers of slaves. Along with other northerners, Ruby went south to educate the freedmen in the responsibilities of freedom. He first taught in a school for adults that met in a Baptist church in New Orleans. When General Nathaniel Banks took over the local black schools and attempted to expand operations into the interior of the state, Ruby went to St. Bernard's Parish. Following the war, when the army dropped its support of the educational effort, Ruby returned to New Orleans, where he taught at the Fort Douglas school for freedmen run by the American Missionary Association. After Thomas W. Conway organized the Freedmen's Bureau schools, Ruby joined the bureau and worked as a teacher and school agent. He found the life of a bureau member difficult and for the first time encountered overt hostility to his efforts. When he tried to start a school in East Feliciana Parish, a white mob carried him from his home to a nearby bayou and threw him in, proclaiming that they did not want "any damned nigger school in that town."[4]

In September 1866, after a financial crisis closed the Louisiana schools, Ruby joined the Freedmen's Bureau schools in Texas. Ruby chose Texas because so many of the people who had been a part of the military schools in Louisiana were working out of Galveston for Superintendent Edwin M. Wheelock, the former supervisor of General

GEORGE T. RUBY
Gonzales Historical Museum, Gonzales, Texas

Banks's system. Wheelock and other old associates from New Orleans provided Ruby with an already existing network of friends with whom he could work. He received an appointment as school organizer and operated in Galveston and the surrounding counties. This job placed him in the heart of the black belt of Texas and helped him establish contacts with the local black community. During this time he gained a reputation, even among whites, as a man of integrity. A Unionist newspaper cited him as "a colored man of education, character, and ability, and . . . an honest man." One local Democratic newspaper begrudgingly viewed him as a good fellow among a bad lot. General Charles Griffin, assistant commissioner of the Freedmen's Bureau in Texas, wrote of his agent, "He is an energetic man and has great influence among his people." At this time Ruby began to build the base for his later political activities.[5]

In spring 1867 Ruby turned from education to politics, apparently urged by white friends in the bureau and on the staff of General Griffin. Congress supplied the opportunity for this shift on March 2, when it passed its first reconstruction measure. In its call for new constitutional conventions in the South, Congress stipulated that delegates should be elected by all male citizens above the age of twenty-one, without regard to race, color, or previous condition.[6] The introduction of black people into the political process meant that successful politicians would have to attract their votes. Ruby, who had emerged as an individual with contacts throughout the black belt, proved an excellent intermediary between the freedmen and ambitious white politicians.

Ruby's first office was president of the Galveston chapter of the Union League, and the league would thereafter remain the center of his power. As the league's local president, Ruby served essentially as the spokesman to blacks for the state's Unionist politicans. James H. Bell, an associate of Andrew J. Hamilton, President Johnson's provisional governor, and Elisha M. Pease, a prewar governor, brought the organization to Texas to use to mobilize blacks, and Bell was the first state president. The league was a secret organization with elaborate rituals—mechanisms that allowed freedmen to be instructed in patriotism toward the Union and the Republican party, marched to the polls, and protected from outside white interference.[7]

At the beginning Ruby appears to have been little more than an instrument used by the Unionists and other white politicians. His relationship with political leaders in Galveston during the period affirms this. His closest associates were federal military personnel and civilians

366

connected with the bureau. Ruby joined them in May 1867 in forming the National Republican Association of Galveston to prepare for the election of delegates to the constitutional convention. These men, although they publicly supported the doctrine of political and civil equality of blacks, hardly carried out these ideas in practice. With few exceptions they did not approve of black officeholding and did not see blacks as filling leadership roles even within the party. Local Democratic newspapers charged them with demagoguery.

While Ruby probably realized the incongruity of his friends' public and practical positions, he defended them nonetheless, leading to accusations that he was nothing more than "a yellow negro, a tool." He may have been just that, but at that time his political power lay with the white Republicans, no matter how insincere they may have been, and he remained loyal. He faithfully turned out the league for party rallies and conventions.

Eventually he began to receive rewards, although modest. At the first state Republican convention, in July, he received an honorary vice-presidency. Later he solicited and obtained an appointment as a notary public for Galveston. His pursuit of the position of notary public indicated his ties to the white leaders. His application possessed the endorsement of General Griffin, Griffin's adjutant general, Oscar F. Hunsacker, and the president of the Galveston street railroad, B. Rush Plumly. Griffin's note praising Ruby's service in the political cause, written to E. M. Pease, whom the general had just placed in the governor's office after having removed James W. Throckmorton, was sufficient to gain the office. Although the beginnings were small, Ruby had shown that he could organize black voters, and he had been rewarded. The offices, as minor as they were, in turn showed blacks that he had access to white political leaders, and this bolstered his support among them.[8]

The composition of the electorate following the initiation of Congressional Reconstruction added to Ruby's importance to white politicians. The required registration of voters proceeded through the spring and summer of 1867 and certified over a thousand blacks in Galveston. Potential white registrants outnumbered blacks, but restrictions imposed by the Reconstruction Act passed March 23 and the refusal of many, who were otherwise qualified, to swear to the oath provided by that law, limited the number of those actually registered to about two-thirds of the blacks.[9] To be elected required the support of black voters; therefore, the man who could deliver that support possessed political power.

As Ruby used his bureau position to organize local Union leagues around the Galveston area in preparation for the convention election, he became less satisfied with his role as a spokesman for white interests. In autumn 1867 he finally announced that he intended to run for one of Galveston's seats in the convention. His associates argued against a black man representing such an important county, suggesting that if he ran, the men in business and industry whom they hoped to attract to their party would be dissuaded from joining. Ruby countered that he was the only true representative of the great majority of loyal men in Galveston, and it was his right to run and their right to have him run. He refused to back out of the race and, thus, precipitated a vitriolic fight between himself and his friends in the Galveston Republican Association.

To minimize Ruby's threat and undercut his power, association leaders immediately attempted to broaden white participation in the organization's activities by bringing in individuals not yet eligible to vote. When Colonel A. P. Wiley, a "father of secession," applied for membership, association president Oscar Hunsacker and George W. Honey, a school organizer for the American Missionary Association, heartily endorsed his admission and called for the acceptance of all converts to the Republican cause. If enough such men came in, black power would be severely reduced. Ruby, along with B. Rush Plumly, who had served as chairman of General Bank's board of education in the Department of the Gulf and considered himself a protector of blacks, fought the move. Plumly argued that Wiley's application was premature and would lead to the rapid return of old Confederates to power. When the association admitted Wiley anyway, Ruby resigned and charged that the association's leaders had sold out to the rebels.[10]

Cut out of the Republican association, Ruby determined to run for the convention without its backing. He believed that the Union League actually controlled black voters, and he knew that he controlled the league; therefore, he believed that he could win the election despite the opposition of white Republicans. He obtained some white support. Plumly continued to work with him, and a convert to his cause was Dr. Robert K. "Revenue" Smith of the customhouse. On December 21, 1867, the Galveston Union League met to decide whom it would support for the convention election. Ruby demanded that it endorse him, whereas association leaders desperately tried to prevent such a move. However, Ruby showed that he controlled this group when the members announced that their choices for the convention were he and Smith.

368

But the nominee was not satisfied simply with the league's endorsement; he quickly moved to take over the rest of the machinery of the local Republican party. He and Smith called a meeting of the Galveston Republican Association to ratify the league nominations. Honey and others condemned the call as being without authority and designed to force upon the party "conditions which are highly objectionable," but Ruby had found his strength and could not be thwarted. Over opposition of the white leadership, the association joined with the league and approved Ruby and Smith as the convention nominees.[11]

The campaign that followed was relatively quiet, with the election of Ruby a foregone conclusion. Many white Republicans, however, refused to support him and joined a coalition of conservative Unionists and Democrats that called itself the Conservative party. Given the electorate, they did not believe they could elect a majority of the delegates to the convention and instead urged whites to register to vote, to vote against a convention, but to vote for delegates who would oppose black suffrage in the event that the convention received enough support to be called. At Galveston this coalition put up James A. McKee and Colonel John T. Brady to oppose Ruby and Smith. Neither, however, actively canvassed and, despite the urging of Conservative leaders, few whites went to the polls. Voting probably took place largely along racial lines; the results indicated that less than one-third of the eligible white voters cast their ballots. Given the white boycott, Ruby won easily, defeating McKee 900 to 245.[12]

Ruby had run for the constitutional convention as a candidate of the black community. When he arrived at Austin, most people believed he was a radical politician who was primarily interested in securing equal rights and suffrage for blacks. His actions proved him a strong advocate of both of these goals, but he did not turn out to be the firebrand that whites had expected. He was an active participant in debate, a forceful behind-the-scenes manipulator, yet an acute observer of the political situation and a spokesman for moderation. His work in the convention made him an important figure in the state Republican political scene for the next five years and marked his transformation to the state level of leadership. A man of medium height, with a light olive complexion, his most noteworthy physical feature was his face, which was described as sharp and incisive, with a hawklike nose. By the end of the convention his face was known throughout the state.[13]

The Constitutional Convention of 1868 provides the first opportunity to examine Ruby's ideas concerning the problems of blacks and the ways to rectify them. He envisioned a comprehensive program of education, economic development, and legal protection. Perhaps because of his background in education, he placed the development of a system of public schools at the center of his program. In this he was typical of others, of both the North and the South, who believed that education was the panacea that would help blacks climb out of the darkness of slavery. After the convention's committees had already been named, he solicited an appointment as an additional member of the Committee on Education, and he helped draft the constitutional mandate for a public-school system for the children of all races.

Yet Ruby was not content to rely solely upon education. He supported provisions to make available public lands for homesteading, which would give blacks an opportunity to become landowners. Understanding from personal experience how artificial and legal barriers could be built to exclude blacks from full participation in the community, he also worked to prevent legal or other kinds of discrimination. Just prior to the convention he had been denied first-class passage on a steamship to New Orleans. Now he obtained a place on the Committee on General Provisions and helped draft a section that would have made the exclusion of blacks from public conveyances, places of public business, and businesses licensed by the state illegal. That committee also produced a section that called for equal rights for all free men, with no man or set of men entitled to exclusive separate offices or privileges.

On the convention floor, Ruby also repeatedly supported investigations of violence and favored all measures to suppress these less subtle actions against blacks. While he believed in democratic political processes, he thought the restoration of former Confederates to their civil rights would lead inevitably to the imposition of limits on his own race; consequently, he argued that their continued exclusion from the franchise and officeholding was necessary and proper as punishment for their treason. With some modification, Ruby worked for these goals in 1868 and continued to pursue them through the rest of his career.[14]

Given the fact that in the convention eighty of the ninety delegates were white, Ruby had little chance to secure the provisions he sought. Unable to carry out his plan in full, Ruby's major accomplishment in the convention was working for a coalition with whites that would aid him in carrying out as much of it as possible. He demonstrated in this effort mature political abilities, successfully exploiting for his own ends the factionalism among the white members of his own party.

The split of white Republicans into numerous interest groups provided the basis for Ruby's political operations in the constitutional convention. Regional jealousies, agrarian and urban interests, and personal ambitions made white Republicans members of a very unstable coalition held together most of the time only by the common need to protect themselves from Democratic attacks. Early in the convention it was evident that regionalism was the most important factor dividing the whites. Three major blocs emerged, centered around Edmund J. Davis, former governor Andrew J. Hamilton, and James W. Flanagan. Davis's supporters came, for the most part, from the western portion of the state, a region that felt it had been neglected by antebellum state government. Hamilton represented the central portion of the state, the region that had dominated Texas economically and politically since statehood. Central Texas was the home of most of the state's urban population, its richest farmlands, and the greatest plantations. Flanagan represented the east, a section with worn-out farms and suffering from the same resentment toward the central section that characterized the constituency of the west.[15]

One issue was a source of particular irritation among these groups—the legality of secession and the legislation of subsequent state governments, known locally as the *ab initio* question. Two positions developed. One group argued that secession and subsequent governmental actions were illegal from the beginning, or ab initio, and the other, that, except for secession, laws and other government acts since 1861 had to be considered legal for practical purposes to prevent disruption of economic life. Enormous economic stakes depended upon the particular interpretation. As an example, the legislature had passed laws during the war that allowed the seizure of lands from Unionists who refused to pay taxes, donated significant portions of the public lands to individuals and corporations, and granted corporate monopolies to railroad builders, bridge companies, and private schools. On the one hand, ab initio could break these interests; on the other, it would renew the prospects of those cut out during the war. After the war, the legislature had provided for the collection of wartime taxes at the specie value when levied, rather than at the value of the Confederate currency of the time. Again, the issue touched the pocketbooks of many Texans.

Of all the legislation and executive actions touched by ab initio, the one that most concerned political leaders in 1868 was an act passed in 1864 which allowed six railroads indebted to the state school-fund to pay the interest due on their loans in state and Confederate warrants, rather than in specie as required by the original legislation. The act required that the treasury accept this practically worthless paper at face rather than actual value, thus making it possible for the railroads to dump over $300,000 in Confederate and state paper on the school fund, relieving themselves of much of their indebtedness and bankrupting the fund dedicated to the education of the children of the state.

Republican delegates from the central part of the state, where most of the railroads were located, wanted the payments recognized as valid. Delegates from the east and west, lacking transportation and needing the school fund restored so that it could serve as a source of postwar construction loans, wanted the law declared invalid. In addition, various agrarian elements of the party and land speculators, who realized that the railroads would be built with tax money if the fund was not restored, envisioned a rapid increase in taxes and consequently entered the ab initio camp. In the convention, supporters of the ab initio position, who were in a minority, repeatedly failed to push their measures through committee; but the issue was too important to be dropped, and the proponents began to look to the electorate as a means of gaining their end when thwarted in the convention.[16]

The factionalism of the white Republicans and the split over ab initio provided an avenue along which Ruby could move to greater power. Two events aided him in this rise—his unexpected takeover of the state Union League on June 15, 1868, only two weeks after the beginning of the constitutional convention, and the formal split of the white Republicans into two parties in the state convention in August.

Under the leadership of white Unionist politicians, the state Union League had never been particularly responsive to the aspirations of its black members. Following the removal of Governor Throckmorton in 1867 and his replacement with E. M. Pease, these Unionists had been even less interested in the blacks and went about their business distributing offices among white loyalists. Pease's administration and, consequently, the state league under the direction of Pease's associate Bell lost popularity among blacks because of its reluctance to give public offices to blacks, its weak stand on civil rights, and its hesitation in prosecuting white terrorists. This discontent provided the background for the annual league convention at Austin in 1868, where Ruby became the spokesman for those wanting change.

When Ruby discovered the extent of the unrest, he announced his candidacy for Bell's office. The action caught administration supporters by surprise and, unaware of Ruby's potential challenge, they were unprepared to beat him back. White leaders tried to restrain the black delegates and managed to hold many in line; but by a vote of 91 to 90, Ruby took over the state league organization. The administration regrouped and elected Alfred Longley, editor of the *Austin Republican,* as vice-president; but that victory did not diminish the fact that Ruby now controlled the league. At this point the implications of his triumph were not clear, but most of Pease's supporters believed that it spelled potential disaster.[17]

Their fears were realized at the state Republican convention that August. Governor Pease's forces controlled the convention, holding the votes of most of the delegates and most of the proxies. Ab initio forces, however, decided to push their idea before the party, since it was stalemated in the constitutional convention. E. J. Davis proposed on behalf of the ab initio faction that the party platform include a resolution in favor of nullifying all legislation passed during the war and, specifically, the law that authorized the payment of debts to the school fund in state warrants. As expected, the administration-dominated convention refused to incorporate these resolutions into the platform, and Davis led those who supported him out of the meeting.

Ruby supported ab initio, in large part because he wanted schools established and believed that would be possible only when the school fund was restored; but he refrained from endorsing either side. Trying to secure concessions on issues closer to his interest, Ruby announced that he would not decide which group to support until each side had published its platform. The regulars either did not understand or did not feel they could make concessions, for they gave little, in fact producing a platform dangerous to blacks that included reenfranchisement of former Confederates, support for railroads, and only general statements concerning civil rights. The bolters, on the other hand, called for continued disfranchisement, support for a free public-school system, and rigid enforcement of the laws.

Democrats accused Davis of currying favor with Ruby and the league, and perhaps their assessment was correct. Given the choice, Ruby threw his and the league's support to the bolting camp, where he helped form the Radical Republican party to oppose the regulars. For the regulars the full meaning of this takeover of the state league organization was now apparent, for in only a day the ab initio supporters had gained access to the majority of Republican voters.[18]

The regular party leadership realized too late the extent of Ruby's power and the importance of his league presidency. In an effort to rectify the situation, they attempted, after the party convention adjourned, to undermine his base of power at Galveston. Smith, Ruby's running mate the previous spring, led the attack, returning to Galveston, where he accused his colleague of corruption and selling out his black constituents. Ruby denied the accusations and appealed to league members for support. Smith quickly found himself in the midst of outraged blacks who refused to believe the charges and, when called upon to affirm the course of their leader at Austin, overwhelmingly voted their approval. Following an evening league meeting, an altercation between Smith and Ruby led to a riot in which the police had to intervene to prevent outraged blacks from killing Smith. Unable to convince league members that Ruby had betrayed them, administration supporters abandoned their immediate campaign. Although Ruby would face administration efforts to regain control of the league, he felt strong enough that autumn to volunteer to the national Republican committee to go north as a speaker in the presidential election. He had easily survived the first attack upon his base of power.[19]

The constitutional convention continued despite the Republican party's collapse. On August 31, 1868, the delegates recessed until December 8, then reconvened on that date and continued to meet until the following February. The regulars controlled the convention; therefore, the document they produced reflected their interests. The proposed constitution did not incorporate ab initio. Rather than Ruby's proposals for a clear statement on the extent of an individual's civil rights, the draft incorporated a general resolution recognizing the equality of all persons before the law. A proposal by blacks to include a resolution that would not require mandatory segregation—not because they wanted mixed schools but because they realized in some counties economic and demographic conditions would make two separate school systems impossible—was not included. Most portentous for blacks, the proposed constitution included a provision allowing all adult males to vote, except those explicitly disqualified by the United States Constitution. Given the white majority in Texas, this section paved the way for the ultimate failure of Ruby and his program.[20]

Ruby, who considered the draft constitution a disaster for blacks, joined with twenty-two other convention delegates who opposed it on other grounds. Along with an official commission from the convention, he went to Washington to appeal to Congress to reject the proposed constitution and to delay any ratification election. The bolters or Radical Republicans met with President Grant and testified before the House Committee on Reconstruction. Ultimately, however, events in other southern states worked more effectively in favor of their efforts than any action of their own. Heated battles were also underway in Virginia and Mississippi between Republican factions. Grant, unclear on the best course to take in those states, decided to postpone elections in Texas until the results could be seen in the other two contests. Ruby and the Radicals thus obtained a delay; but the final defeat of the constitution was not assured.[21]

Once it became clear that Grant did not intend to rush a Texas election, Ruby returned to the state to put the league's organization together in order to defeat the constitution. He urged league leaders to instruct members to vote against the constitution but to select candidates in legislative races who favored the Radical cause in the event a majority of voters ratified the document. As president, Ruby issued new league charters and harangued members throughout the state to reorganize, meet regularly, and prepare for an active campaign.

A major task was to break away any residual black support from Pease and Hamilton. Hamilton became the focus of Ruby's attacks upon the administration's forces after he announced his intention of running for governor. Ruby characterized Jack Hamilton as the archetypal white man who could be anything he wanted to be, rebel or loyalist, a man without principles and totally untrustworthy. In a speech at Galveston, Ruby warned blacks that they could never vote for a politician who had tried to convince Congress that no Negroes were being killed in Texas. No black man, he reasoned, could afford to remain in the regular party organization. In his charge to local leaders, Ruby indicated that he believed the fight would be hard but that with organization and dedication blacks could defeat the constitution and its authors.[22]

By spring of 1869 the ground upon which Ruby was fighting was quicksand. Ruby discovered, as he warmed to the fight, that political conditions were rapidly changing. Through the Galveston Republican Association, Ruby had helped to plan a convention of bolting Republicans for May 11, 1869. He supported Morgan Hamilton, brother of Jack, who urged that the Radicals organize to oppose the constitution but make no nominations for public office until the president called for an election. Morgan Hamilton believed that delaying the whole process would delay the time when the constitution would be considered and that time was on the side of the Radicals. If the election were postponed, he thought Grant would become aware of the political results implied in the constitution's ratification—the return of the Confederates to power.

Within the Radical group, however, a strong movement had emerged, led by James G. Tracy of Houston and Edwin Wheelock, to accept the constitution and bring about a compromise between the two factions. The middle-road movement had strong support, including

375

General Joseph J. Reynolds, commander of the Fifth Military District, and, implicitly, Reynolds's close friend, President Grant. Grant appears to have tired of the internal squabbles within the southern-state party organizations and, unable to decide which group to back, began to pressure them to cooperate. Wheelock and Tracy called for a state nominating convention to meet at Houston on May 24, then delayed it until the first Monday in June.

Ruby realized that a shift was taking place. If General Reynolds and the president wanted compromise, to stick with Morgan Hamilton opened up the possibility of being left isolated. As a result, Ruby attended the middle-party convention and backed its nomination of E. J. Davis for governor, and its decision no longer to oppose the constitution. Ruby indicated that he believed united action was now necessary to settle the local political situation, and he was willing to compromise. "Whenever unnecessary," he wrote to Morgan Hamilton, "I do not believe in open force among those claiming to be with us, *at this time.*"[23]

Unfortunately for the Republicans, the middle-party movement did not accomplish the compromise it sought. Morgan Hamilton refused to join in the convention. Pease and A. J. Hamilton sent observers; but when they saw they would not emerge as leaders, they also opted to stay out. Still, while these leaders would not compromise, many of their supporters appear to have been drawn to the movement because of its logic. The full slate of delegates nominated indicated a willingness by these Republicans to let past political differences be forgotten and to move on against the Democrats. After placing Davis at the top of the ticket, the delegates carefully distributed the remaining offices among the various factions that joined in, trying to build as broad based a party as possible.[24]

Having joined the middle-party movement, Ruby was at the center of activity after President Grant, in midsummer, ordered the Texas election for the following November. Ruby quickly found that mobilizing the Union League was a task of considerable difficulty and encountered a problem that plagued the Republican organization throughout its early history. At the heart of the problem was inadequate financing. Organization required the printing of campaign materials, the circulating of them, and the placement of agents in the field to coordinate local activities. All of these required money, and the black constituents who furnished the majority of Republican support did not have resources to defray the costs. Ruby found that the subordinate league councils did not provide enough money even to keep traveling agents in the field, let alone to support printing. Ruby sought alternative funding in the North, but found Republicans there reluctant to help. He called upon the national council of the league, claiming that the perpetuation of freedom in Texas depended upon their willingness to give money; but the support did not come, indicating that while northern Republicans desired their party to prosper in the South, they would not furnish, or did not have, the resources to bail out the local organizations. Without financing, organization was practically impossible, and Ruby would discover that the league was always more efficient in its reputation among its antagonists than it was in actuality.[25]

In addition to handling league work, Ruby decided to run for a seat in the Senate from the Twelfth District. The Twelfth consisted of Galveston, Brazoria, and Matagorda counties; and while Galveston did not contain a large black population upon which to draw support, the other two were old black-belt counties with large black majorities. Ruby faced the same arguments he had encountered in his run for the convention, in particular that the time had not come for black men to put themselves forward for public office. Even friends who had urged him to take over the state league and to run for the constitutional convention now opposed him. Major Plumly denounced him at a Galveston Republican meeting on August 25, 1869, for leading blacks to political ruin, playing the demagogue, and creating a black man's party.

Although facing strong opposition, Ruby responded vigorously and refused to abandon the race. Accusing his opponents of being motivated by their own thwarted ambition, he effectively manipulated league chapters in his district to keep voters in line behind him. His candidacy created an excited response throughout the black community, one which frequently could not be controlled. When A. P. McCormick, a supporter of Jack Hamilton and a candidate for the House, tried to address blacks in favor of Hamilton's campaign, Ruby's supporters kept him from speaking. Hamilton had become a traitor in their eyes, and his appeal was not worth hearing. Ruby denied that he was trying to create a black man's party, but the backing he received among blacks convinced whites that he was doing just that. Ruby's campaign raised fears among whites, who complained that throughout the district blacks had become more defiant.[26]

The chances of success for Ruby appeared good, but the campaign of the middle-party languished through the summer of 1869. Ruby possessed good possibilities for election to the state Senate, but unless the Davis ticket did well throughout the state he would be in the minority. The middle-party movement received a major boost in September, when President Grant responded to election disasters in Mississippi and Virginia and finally gave his open support to it. While encouraging compromise, Grant had refrained from any action when Jack Hamilton had refused to withdraw from the race. The national Union League pressured the president to end his hands-off policy and received support from Cabinet officers. Still Grant delayed, until finally his man in the field, Reynolds, informed him that he had given up all hope of compromise and that he blamed Hamilton for the stalemate. The president then threw all his support and the offices in his control behind the Radicals.[27]

Grant's decision to back Davis worked immediately to Ruby's advantage. At Galveston the Treasury replaced the pro-Hamilton collector of customs with a Davis man, Nathan Patten, who had worked with Ruby in the constitutional convention; and Patten appointed the senatorial candidate a special deputy collector. For the next four years Ruby would be the chief arbiter of appointments to positions as clerks, inspectors, weighers, watchmen, and messengers in the customhouse. The president's recognition of the middle-party group placed in Ruby's hands the ability to provide tangible rewards to his supporters, and thus gave him another powerful tool to promote party loyalty. The appointment proved a mixed blessing, however, for it also served as a source of irritation among those who did not receive jobs they thought they deserved.[28]

Ruby still faced a difficult election campaign and the candidate had to adjust to changing political realities if he hoped to maintain power. Whites who had been reluctant to register and vote in 1867 were returning to the polls. While black voters still outnumbered white voters in adjacent counties, last minute registration in Galveston placed more whites than blacks on the lists. In addition, Ruby confronted both more vocal and racist opposition in the newspapers. The *Galveston News* reported that Ruby's opponent had to have every Conservative vote in order to keep the city from being represented by a "turbulent negro incendiary in the State Senate." When the returns came in, Ruby's opponent carried Galveston County, 1,597 to 1,554; but Ruby's majority in Brazoria and Matagorda insured him the seat he sought. Despite the victory, the election of 1869 indicated that politics based solely on black power was no longer possible in the Twelfth District and that Ruby would have to adjust his politics to meet the new situation.[29]

In March 1870, Congress accepted the proposed Texas constitution and noted the state's ratification of the Thirteenth and Fourteenth amendments. It also restored Texas to its regular place in the Union and recognized the government of Edmund J. Davis that had been elected the previous November. When the state Senate met at Austin in a special session, George Ruby faced a difficult problem. He had to work for measures that would insure his continued control over his black constituency but at the same time act to make inroads among white voters. As senator from the Twelfth District, Ruby would work to develop a new image, one of a conservative politician who looked after not only the interests of blacks, but also whites in his community. During his four-year term he worked to tie himself and his constituents closer to the white business interests of Galveston in párticular, seeking an alliance that would benefit all three.

Ruby tried several new approaches and techniques in rearranging his base of power. A major goal was to decrease his reliance upon the Union League. Whites did not like the organization because they saw it as a somewhat corrupt institution in which they could have little say. More important, the league's political power was based too exclusively on black voters. If it could bargain only with votes it could deliver, the possibility existed for whites to argue in favor of disfranchising blacks rather than making concessions to secure black support. The fact that whites would not join the league and that its power was based on an unstable commodity—the franchise—caused Ruby to move away from it. He began efforts to weld blacks in his district into an organization that whites could not ignore and would have to deal with politically and economically—a labor union. He believed that if he could create a situation of mutual economic interdependence between blacks and white businessmen blacks would have a greater chance to maintain political power. In his effort the urban nature of his district was important; black workers in an urban economy could make demands that unskilled and unorganized workers in rural areas could not. Dependence on organized black labor would, theoretically, force white businessmen and industrialists to help maintain black political rights.

Ruby turned to the docks in his efforts to organize blacks. Whites had dominated the work on the Galveston wharf prior to the war, but in the postwar period large numbers of blacks moved into these jobs. If he could control this labor force, he would obtain power that even the most grudging white politician would have to recognize. The idea behind the experiment with a labor union appears to have originated in efforts made at this time by national black leaders to encourage unionization throughout the South. In December 1868 Ruby had attended the Colored National Labor Convention at Washington, D.C., and had been a member of the executive committee. The group had emphasized the desirability of organizing labor and encouraging education as important means of improving the condition of blacks. The convention had asserted that improvement would be possible only when the labor of blacks was dear and whites had to bargain for it. "Labor must be made more scarce," the delegates had argued. Organization of the work force and the movement of contract workers in the countryside to their own farms were the only ways to improve the local situation. The following May, associates of Ruby, including John DeBruhl and Richard Nelson, organized the Labor Union of Colored Men at Galveston. The wharf was and remained the center of their activity, although they sought to expand the union, especially to nearby Houston.[30]

Ruby's organizational activities unified black workers on the docks, but the philosophy of the local union movement limited its effectiveness. Ruby did not see the union as a device for confrontation, but rather as an institution to make possible an alliance with Galveston's white businessmen. The Galveston union denied the need for strikes but argued, rather, that the union provided capital with an organized work force. Politically, the union suffered from many of the charges of corruption and political manipulation that plagued the league, charges that worked against the alliance Ruby envisioned. Information about black activities on the wharf during this period is practically nonexistent, but at least one former dock worker remembered how he was used politically. On election days, leaders appeared and took the workers to picnics, gave them whiskey, cigars, and marked ballots, then took them to cast their votes. William H. Thomas remembered: "Fix up de way us was, us would vote to put us back in slavery. And de nigger that didn't vote, after all dat, him am in for de fixin'. I means he gets fixed. Dey pounds he head till him won't forgit to do it right next time." Despite his hopes, Ruby never used the union effectively to support his own political power. The work he accomplished, however, would provide a base for his young protégé, N. Wright Cuney, who would dominate the wharf in the 1880s and 1890s.[31]

In addition to seeking economic interdependence that would link blacks and whites, Ruby tried to build his ties to whites by establishing himself as a power broker between them and the newly installed Davis administration. While Davis was in power, Ruby was the intermediary between the state government and the local community, providing direct access to Governor Davis when appealed to. Ruby also oversaw the appointment of local officials and worked tirelessly to insure that they acted in the party's interest. Unfortunately, rather than strengthening his position, this role worked against him, for it irritated many whites who complained of having to rely upon a black man. When he traveled north in the autumn of 1870, for example, the delay in the appointment of a local judge, whom Ruby reserved the right to approve, outraged white Galvestonians. Another weakness of this particular approach to the local businessmen was that it required continuation of the Davis administration to remain effective. Ruby therefore linked himself irrevocably with Davis, and the popularity of the Davis regime was a matter over which he had little control.[32]

Ruby also attempted to improve his connections with white business interests by working for them in the legislature. He held major assignments on committees concerned with the judiciary, militia, and public lands. He was assiduous in his efforts in behalf of railroads, banks, and insurance companies connected with Galveston. He introduced bills that incorporated the Galveston and El Paso; the Galveston, Houston, and Tyler; and the Galveston, Harrisburg, and San Antonio railroads. On the legislation that incorporated the International and Great Northern, the Southern Pacific, and gave concessions to the Texas Central, Ruby shifted from opposition to support in order to establish himself as an advocate of Galveston's interests. Despite his earlier association with the agrarianism of Morgan Hamilton within the Republican party, Ruby had become as strong a railroad man as anyone else in the party. Ruby acted with a combination of administration men and Democrats in behalf of these transportation interests and helped to obtain stronger ties between his city and the rest of the state.[33]

While trying to establish some sort of working relationship with the economic leaders of Galveston, Ruby had few illusions about the benevolence of these or any other white Texans. He made concessions on such issues as railroads, but he remained a strong advocate of measures designed to protect blacks in their civil rights and to provide equal opportunities. With Matthew Gaines, the other black member of the Senate, and backing from the Davis administration, Ruby helped pass bills that created a state militia, the state police, and a public-school system. He never believed these were enough to protect blacks, but he found whites unwilling to go further. When he attempted to pass a bill that would have enforced the compliance of public carriers with constitutional provisions that demanded equal access by all peoples, he found that his most ardent white supporters were not interested in helping. Ruby worked this bill through the Judiciary Committee and saw it reported to the floor, but the bill never even came up for a vote.

381

Thus, while he was willing to compromise with whites, he did not forget his black constituents and pushed as far as he could in trying to protect them.[34]

But in spite of his work for blacks, as Ruby tried to appease the white community his position among blacks became less secure. The interests of a landless agrarian, and urban work force, which comprised the bulk of Ruby's backing, were inimicable to the interests of the planter and merchant groups Ruby had to approach for support. The education and self-help programs Ruby sought for his black constituents were hardly in the interest of the whites, since they would serve to make the former slaves more independent. The state aid for railroads and public improvements demanded by white businessmen, on the other hand, took away money needed to support the programs intended to aid blacks. Funding to support the interests of both groups was not possible, since the tax base in the state was too narrow. Ruby was forced to make concessions; and as he provided support for white interests, he sacrificed some of the goals of his black constituents, who were denied educational opportunities, office, and greater economic freedom. As a result, his position drew fire from blacks. Compromise gained him little from whites also; for no matter what he did, businessmen continued to view him as an upstart and a threat.

In the congressional elections of 1871, a revolt among Ruby's supporters forced him to back away from his efforts in the white community. In 1869, in an effort to attract Galveston businessmen, Republicans had run for Congress William T. Clark, a Union general with business ties in the North. Clark had an interest in railroad construction and had worked for this and other business interests of the Third Congressional District. Ruby had supported Clark, but once the general got to Washington, he neglected Ruby and the people who had provided the votes that sent him there. Clark's insensitivity and Ruby's activities in the legislature caused many blacks to question their leadership and provided grounds for a movement against them under Louis W. Stevenson, a white former Freedmen's Bureau agent and organizer for the Union League. In a letter to Secretary of State James P. Newcomb, who had succeeded Ruby as the head of the state Union League in 1870, Stevenson charged that Ruby had sold out to railroad interests of the state and was enriching himself at the expense of the public. That Ruby had returned from the first session of the legislature and bought a house and two lots was all the proof Stevenson needed of the senator's corruption. He likewise condemned Clark. Newcomb did not encourage Stevenson's rebellion, but it continued and served as the basis for a major challenge to Ruby's power.[35]

Over objections of the Davis administration, Stevenson decided to run against Clark for Congress. While Davis was not particularly pleased with Clark, Stevenson was unattractive because he was too closely associated with the Union League and was consequently unattractive to many whites. When told that the administration would try to prevent his running, Stevenson informed Newcomb that he intended to try to cut black voters away from the administration, Clark, and Ruby. "If it becomes necessary to make war," he wrote, "so be it, but the field will not only be where you have been firing missiles, it will be transferred to Africa." With others who opposed the administration, Stevenson formed a new state Union League and claimed that it was the legitimate representative of loyal people in Texas. Morgan Hamilton was among the dissidents who joined Stevenson, and his conversion broadened the goals of the movement into one of "reform." Hamilton started a newspaper, *The Reformer*, in Austin. In it he attacked the railroad "monopolists" in the party, demanded that the leadership be purged, and supported Stevenson and any other politician who attacked the administration. Stevenson worked his contacts among black people, encouraging the formation of antiadministration Union leagues. Even the Labor Union of Colored Men became a battleground when Stevenson tried to wrest its control from Ruby.[36]

Ruby did not particularly care for Clark, since the congressman had largely ignored him, but Stevenson's activities were a threat to his own base of power. Ruby, in a vigorous response, campaigned in favor of Clark and insured his control over black voters in the Galveston region; but he frightened many whites as he wielded his club to insure party conformity. Clark quickly realized that he had to make peace with Ruby. He went to Galveston, where he talked with him, "frankly avowing his error and asking if [he] could give him [his] support." Content with Clark's amends, Ruby set about using every tool at his disposal to crush his opponent.[37]

On June 8 the senator mobilized black laborers behind Clark. He took advantage of the annual labor convention at Houston to patch up differences between Clark and black workers. When N. Wright Cuney took over the chairmanship of the convention, it was evident that Ruby had prevented any of his opponents from capturing the labor movement. While the convention considered the plight of laborers in Texas, Clark attended daily, working the floor in behalf of his candidacy. Accompanied by Ruby and party secretary James G. Tracy, the congress-man assured black leaders that he supported their aspirations. The convention did not make political endorsements, but the delegates ad-journed leaving the impression that they favored Clark. Clark had been given an opportunity to mend fences, while Ruby had stood in the background and overseen the operation.[38]

After retaining control over the labor movement, Ruby moved to reorganize the Union League and make sure that the local chapters supported Clark. State president Newcomb provided him with a free-hand, issuing and removing charters wherever the best good could be served. When Stevenson's backers took over the Galveston chapter, Ruby obtained a new charter and installed N. Wright Cuney as presi-dent of the pro-Clark league. Newcomb declared the Stevenson league to be irregular; and when the Stevenson group appealed to the national league officers to recognize their organization as the rightful represent-ative of loyal Texans, Newcomb dissuaded the leaders from interven-ing. Through effective propaganda and use of state officers against lo-cal dissidents, Ruby quickly routed the Stevenson forces who sought to undercut his control over the league.[39]

Ruby also appropriated a new mechanism for political purposes, the newly created public-school system. This activity greatly offended whites, who feared Ruby's increased power. The school system was a potentially important political tool because of the valuable patronage associated with it. The supervisor of schools in each district appointed local school boards that had tremendous power—they chose teachers, leased buildings, and made contracts for books and construction. At Ruby's request, Davis appointed Captain William H. Griffin supervi-sor of education at Galveston because he was a party loyalist, in addi-tion to being a good school officer. When Griffin arrived at Galveston, he joined Cuney's chapter of the Union League, legitimizing its official status, and appointed a proadministration school board: Ruby; George Lawrence, a Union League organizer; Nathan Patten of the customhouse; N. Wright Cuney; and F. C. Mosebach, a German Re-publican businessman. From this position Ruby used school patronage to party advantage. Already hostile to the costs of public education, white businessmen were further alienated by Ruby's blatant use of the schools for political ends. Ruby managed to hang onto power, but he also undid work that was aimed at pacifying local whites.[40]

The Labor Union of Colored Men, the Union League, and the pub-lic schools provided Ruby with the "grease" to ensure Clark's renomination, but Ruby acted in 1871 almost as though the challenge to his power was an outrage that he wanted to completely destroy. With the support of Davis, the senator had the state police brought into his district to make sure that Stevenson's faction could not disrupt the conventions or stage popular demonstrations that might sway a meeting in his opponent's favor. When Republicans met at Galveston to select delegates to the district convention, fifty policemen attended also. Although Stevenson supporters received seats in the convention, whenever the opposition tried to stir the delegates in favor of their candidate, the police, who were all Ruby men, quickly put them back in their seats. Even the Democratic *Galveston News* admired Ruby's skillful political maneuvering. When Stevenson's men realized that their candidate had no chance in the convention, they withdrew, and the remaining delegates named Ruby and Cuney to attend the Houston convention and declared their support for Clark. At Houston, Ruby ran an equally tight operation. The delegates, for the most part, were committed to Clark, and the galleries were filled only with Clark supporters; Ruby sat at the box office handing out tickets only to the congressman's friends. As expected, the convention renominated Clark and denounced those who would disrupt the Republican party, while Ruby presided as convention chairman.[41]

Despite his efforts in favor of Clark, the changing electorate that threatened Ruby also worked against his candidate. The growing white majority turned the election into a Republican debacle. Clark received more votes throughout the district than he had in 1869, but his Democratic opponent received twice the votes of his party's candidate in the previous election. When all the returns were in, the Democrat had won by a narrow margin. The state returning board disallowed votes in five counties because of various kinds of fraud, and Davis issued Clark a conditional certificate of election. But a congressional committee found in favor of the Democrat, and the Republicans lost control over the Third District. In Galveston County, intimidation and black distrust of Clark had cut into the number of Republican votes, decreasing the party poll from nearly one thousand in 1869 to only 304. Other counties made the election close, but the Galveston returns indicated approaching disaster for Ruby. Despite what he had done for Galveston's business leaders, they were not coming into the Republican party and he could not count on them for votes. It was also apparent that he could no longer muster black voters in full strength. While he would continue to be an important figure in state politics until 1874, the election of 1871 marked the collapse of his independent power. His political base had been eroded, both in real numbers and in the importance of the black vote relative to the total electorate.[42]

After 1871 Ruby's power depended increasingly upon his connections with the national Republican leadership and with the Davis administration. In his continued bid for power, he now turned to Washington and Austin rather than to activity in the local community. To assure national support, he campaigned in 1872 for President Grant's reelection and saw that his contributions were recognized. For the presidential election he inaugurated a short-lived newspaper, the *Galveston Standard*, the primary goal of which was the renomination and reelection of the president. He also attended the Colored Men's National Convention at New Orleans, where he served as secretary and helped bring the National Labor Union of the United States in line behind the Republican party for the election. Through contacts he had made in Washington he solicited aid from the national party to send speakers to Texas, holding out the hope that Texas might yet be kept in the Republican column, and he also volunteered to speak in the North in behalf of Grant. Even though Texas did not vote for Grant, Ruby had made a strong case for his party loyalty.[43]

Ruby also provided continued support for Governor Davis, managing his renomination for the general elections in 1873 despite strong opposition. Davis was in trouble within his own party, and his unpopularity among whites had grown as administration programs brought about increased taxation. Federal officeholders did not believe he could be reelected and sought to dump him from the ticket. Of all the white politicians, Davis had done more than any other to recognize Ruby as a political equal, and the senator threw his support behind him. Davis was largely responsible for a convention of blacks that met at Brenham on July 4, 1873, to consider the political role of blacks in Texas. The delegates named Cuney chairman, and Ruby received a place on the Credentials Committee and the Committee on Address, indicating who controlled the convention. Despite suggestions that blacks form a racial party, Ruby kept the delegates in line behind Republicanism and Davis. His address, endorsed by the convention, resounded with themes he had put forward throughout his career, the condemnation of violence against blacks and reassertion of the blacks' claim to basic civil rights. In addition, he encouraged blacks to acquire land and homesteads as a means of securing complete freedom. But at the heart of his address was loyalty to Republicanism. To Democrats who encouraged blacks to break with the Republican party, Ruby responded that the former should not be surprised to find blacks aligned against them, since they were men who had from the "day of the acquisition of our liberty set their faces in steadfast opposition to our political education and social progress, with a blind spirit of malignant opposition." Ruby united blacks behind the Republican party and Governor Davis, and he led them into the state convention at Dallas, where they overwhelmed the governor's opponents. Davis received the party's renomination, and Ruby had provided him with the votes.[44]

However, neither Grant nor Davis could protect Ruby's office in his predominantly white district. From members of his own party, pressure increased for the senator to step aside in 1873 for a white candidate in the general election. A group of German Republicans, who demanded that the party recognize their claims to office, advocated that Judge Chauncey B. Sabin be put up for the Senate instead of Ruby. Because Ruby himself realized the unlikelihood of his reelection and thought that Sabin might have a chance, he refused to stand for renomination. When the district convention met at Brazoria, blacks insisted that Ruby be renominated, but he refused to campaign against Sabin, and Sabin secured the nomination. Ruby strongly endorsed Sabin, the party's desire to send good legislators to Austin, and the aspirations of the local Germans for a place on the ticket. As a result, Ruby's fall from power came at the hands of his own party rather than the Democratic opposition.[45]

In the general election of 1873, Texans voted Davis out of office. Sabin lost despite Republican hopes that the judge was attractive enough to be elected. The Democratic administration of Richard Coke set about dismantling much of the Republican administration's programs, including the final dismemberment of the police force that had been introduced to protect black voters. Under Coke, Texas was not a promising place for a former black senator. Ruby remained in Galveston through the spring of 1874 and continued to participate in local politics, but he had begun to look for opportunities elsewhere. When a seat in the state House of Representatives opened in April, blacks hoped that Ruby would run. White Democrats feared the Republicans had developed a conspiracy in which Ruby would announce his candidacy the morning of the election and blacks would march on the polls led by the Union League. If whites did not show up, Ruby could overwhelm the Democratic candidate. White fears were groundless, however; and despite the pleas of his supporters, Ruby refused to run. Still he polled 69 votes among the 742 cast.[46]

Shortly after the special election, Ruby moved to New Orleans, where he found conditions more congenial to his efforts in behalf of blacks. He received an appointment in the customhouse, perhaps a reward from Grant for his prior services; but he spent most of his time working on newspapers in behalf of Republican and black causes. Until 1878 he edited P. B. S. Pinchback's *State Register*. He later edited his own paper, the *New Orleans Observer*, which he used to support Senator John Sherman's candidacy for the presidency in 1880. He cut most of his ties with Texas Republicans, except for an occasional letter soliciting subscriptions to his newspaper, although he did return to the state in 1880 to work for Sherman in the state party convention. His return in 1880 indicated, however, that he no longer had any authority in Texas, and the delegates stampeded in favor of former president Ulysses S. Grant. The *Observer* folded shortly after the 1880 election, but Ruby found another patron and in 1880 started the *Republic*, which supported local Republican congressional candidates.[47]

The Exoduster Movement of the late 1870s occupied much of Ruby's time. He became a prominent figure in the promotion of black migration from Louisiana to Kansas. In his newspaper, at public meetings, and before Congress he argued that the only way for blacks to obtain complete freedom was to leave the South. Kansas provided the economic opportunities and land ownership that were the ultimate base of freedom. For those who remained behind, the exodus promised benefits also, for Ruby believed the decrease in labor force would drive up the price of labor. Clearly, by 1880 Ruby had come to see improvement in the social relations of races in the South as hinging on increased respect of whites for black economic power. Before a congressional committee that investigated the black exodus to Kansas, Ruby stated that the migrations would end only when black people's civil rights were recognized. Without those rights blacks had no alternative but to pursue a course that would ultimately secure them.[48]

Ruby's work in New Orleans continued the fight that had occupied him from his youth—for economic opportunities and civil rights for black people. His politics were those of expediency; the men he supported and the course he pursued changed with shifting conditions. But his political opportunism always aimed at securing goals to which he remained dedicated. Alliances changed, but the ends changed very little. Unfortunately the people he had to work with were not as willing to compromise. In 1882, at forty-one years of age, Ruby promised to be a prominent leader among blacks for many years to come, a man who could lead, a model of educated and astute political ability. That promise would never be fulfilled, however, for on October 31, 1882, after a short attack of malaria, Ruby died in his home at 125 Euterpe Street.

The man who had left his family in Maine to work in behalf of blacks throughout the nation, who had helped to turn the South upside down, received only a short notice in the white newspapers of New Orleans when he died.[49] His life had reflected the dream of black people for a new place in American society. His death came at the time when that vision began to blur amid violence, increased segregation, and disfranchisement.

Notes

1. George T. Ruby was clearly the most important black politician in Texas during Reconstruction in terms of power and ability. He was one of only thirteen black legislators, serving with Matthew Gaines in the Senate and eleven others in the House. (While J. Mason Brewer, in *Negro Legislators of Texas* [Dallas: Mathis Publishing Co., 1935], pp. 31–49, notes only nine blacks in the House, my own examination of the postwar legislature shows eleven: Mitchel Kendall, Richard Allen, R. Goldsteen Dupree, Silas Cotton, Henry Moore, Shep. Mullins, Benjamin F. Williams, James McKee, Jeremiah J. Hamilton, Richard Williams, and John Mitchel—see Galveston *Flake's Bulletin*, Jan. 14, 1870.) Despite his importance, Ruby has attracted relatively little attention among historians. Charles W. Ramsdell, *Reconstruction in Texas* (New York: Columbia University Press, 1910), and William C. Nunn, *Texas under the Carpetbaggers* (Austin: University of Texas Press, 1962), deal with him peripherally and play down his role in Reconstruction. Barry A. Crouch, "Self-Determination and Local Black Leaders in Texas," *Phylon* 39 (Dec. 1978):344–55, and Randall B. Woods, "George T. Ruby: A Black Militant in the White Business Community," *Red River Valley Historical Review* 1 (Aut. 1974):269–80, focus on limited periods of Ruby's career—Crouch on early efforts at organizing the freedmen and Woods on his work in the legislature.

2. Walter P. Webb, ed., *The Handbook of Texas* (Austin: Texas State Historical Association, 1952), 2:513; U.S. Bureau of the Census, Manuscript Census Schedules, Eighth Census of the United States 1860, Population, Maine, Cumberland County, New Gloucester Township, p. 567; id., Tenth Census of the United States, 1880, Population, Louisiana, Orleans County, New Orleans, p. 45; *Flake's Bulletin*, Apr. 22, 1868; *Houston Union*, July 30, 1870. Ruby does not appear in the 1860 Maine census. Only two families by the name of Ruby lived in the area at that time—Isaiah B. Ruby, a black mariner, aged 64, who lived in the city of Portland, and Ebenezer Ruby, aged 44, a clergyman and farmer, who had $300 in real property and $350 in personal property. The Ebenezer Ruby household consisted of a wife, Jemima, aged 47, a son, Arthur T., 15, and Margaret Ruby, 63, who had $900 in real and $35 in personal property. Ruby supposedly had a brother named Arthur, thus making this family more likely to be his. With regard to the race of his parents,

both are listed as black in this census. The census of 1880, however, lists a George W. Ruby in New Orleans, who is probably George T., and he is classified as a mulatto. Except for the middle initial, every particular suggests that George W. and George T. Ruby are the same. At the time of the census he was 39, was married to a Virginia woman, Lucy V. Ruby, 29, and had three children, Mabel, 8, born in Texas, George, 5, born in the District of Columbia, and Victor T., a newborn. Every member of the family is listed as mulatto.

3. Boston *Pine and Palm*, June 22, 1861, quoted in Willis B. Boyd, "James Redpath and American Negro Colonization in Haiti, 1860–1862," *Americas* 12 (Dec. 1955):169–82; Rodney P. Carlisle, *The Roots of Black Nationalism* (Port Washington: Kennikat Press, 1975), p. 75; U.S. Congress, Senate, *Reports*, 46th Cong., 2d sess., 1880, S. Rept. 693, pt. 2, p. 37, cited hereafter as Exodus Hearing.

4. Exodus Hearing, p. 53; Howard Ashley White, *The Freedmen's Bureau in Louisiana* (Baton Rouge: Louisiana State University Press, 1970), p. 169.

5. Quote from *Flake's Bulletin*, May 14, 1867; see also ibid., May 15, 16, 17, 1867; *Galveston News*, May 16, 1867; Charles Griffin to O. O. Howard, May 24, 1867, quoted in Crouch, "Self-Determination and Local Black Leaders," p. 347.

6. U.S., *Statutes at Large* (Boston: Little, Brown & Co., 1868), 14:428.

7. [Illegible] to A. J. Hamilton, Nov. 29, 1867, Andrew J. Hamilton Papers, University of Texas Archives, Austin.

8. *Flake's Bulletin*, May 2, 14, 15, 16, 17, June 4, July 2, 4, 5, Sept. 5, Dec. 22, 1867; *Galveston News*, July 5, 6, 7, 1867; G. T. Ruby to Elisha M. Pease, Aug. 16, 1867, Governor's Papers, Texas State Archives, Austin; id. to Pease, Oct. 12, 1867, Pease-Graham-Niles Papers, Travis County Collection, Austin Public Library.

9. U.S. Army, Fifth Military District, *General Order No. 73: Tabular Statement of Voters Registered in 1867 and at the Revision of the Lists in 1867–'68–'69, Showing Also the Number Stricken Off the Lists; And, of Votes Cast at Elections Held in the State of Texas, under the Authority of the Reconstruction Acts of Congress* (Austin: Tracy, Siemering & Co., 1870).

10. *Flake's Bulletin*, Oct. 12, 15, 17, 1867.

11. Ibid., Dec. 19, 22, 25, 1867.

12. Ibid., Jan. 5, 1868; *Galveston News*, Jan. 5, Feb. 16, 1868; Ernest W. Winkler, ed., *Platforms of Political Parties in Texas* (Austin: University of Texas Press, 1916), pp. 102–3.

13. *Houston Union*, July 30, 1870; *Flake's Bulletin*, May 18, 1870.

14. *Journal of the Reconstruction Convention Which Met at Austin, Texas, June 1, A.D. 1868* (Austin: Tracy, Siemering & Co., 1870), 1:270, 279, 485, 496–98, 609; ibid., 2:483; *Flake's Bulletin*, Apr. 22, May 2, 1868.

15. Carl H. Moneyhon, *Republicanism in Reconstruction Texas* (Austin: University of Texas Press, 1980), chs. 1 and 5.

16. *Journal of the Reconstruction Convention*, 1:28, 49–59, 61–63, 126–28, 134, 138, 143, 150, 154, 157, 188, 241–42, 632; *Biennial Report of the Comptroller of Public Accounts, State of Texas, from September 1, 1867, to August 31, 1869* (Austin: Tracy, Siemering & Co., 1870), p. 5, tables 2, 18–23.

17. *Flake's Bulletin*, June 20, 28, 1868; *Galveston News*, June 23, 1868.

18. *Austin Republican*, Aug. 13, 15, 22, 1868; *Flake's Bulletin*, Aug. 15, 16, 19, 1868; *San Antonio Express*, Aug. 21, 1868; *Galveston News*, Aug. 22, 1868; *Proceedings of the Republican State Convention Assembled at Austin, August 12, 1868* (Austin: Daily Republican Book & Job Office, 1868), pp. 3–7.

19. *Flake's Bulletin*, Aug. 22, Sept. 9, 10, 1868; G. T. Ruby to Edward McPherson, Sept. 8, 1868, William E. Chandler Papers, Library of Congress, Washington, D.C.; id. to William E. Chandler, Sept. 23, 1868, ibid.

20. *Journal of the Reconstruction Convention*, 1:696–97, 902; 2:483.

21. *Galveston News*, Mar. 2, 3, 4, 18, 1869; *Flake's Bulletin*, Feb. 17, 1869; *Memorial to the Senators and Representatives of the Forty-first Congress from the Commissioners Elected by the Reconstruction Convention of the State of Texas to Represent the Condition of the State and the Wants of the Loyal People* (Washington, D.C.: J. L. Pearson, 1869).

22. G. T. Ruby to James P. Newcomb, May 6, 1869, James P. Newcomb Papers, University of Texas Archives; *Flake's Bulletin*, May 4, 1869.

23. Quote from Ruby to Newcomb, May 16, 1869, Newcomb Papers; see also M. C. Hamilton to Newcomb, May 14, June 19, 26, 1869, ibid.; George C. Rives to Newcomb, June 18, 1869, ibid.; *Flake's Bulletin*, May 9, 11, 12, June 12, 1869; *San Antonio Express*, May 16, 21, June 15, 16, 1869.

24. *Flake's Bulletin*, June 12, 1869; *San Antonio Express*, June 15, 16, 1869.

25. Ruby to Newcomb, July 1, Sept. 12, 1869, Newcomb Papers; id. to Subordinate Councils, Union League of America, Aug. 11, 1869, ibid.; id. to Thomas Baker, July 15, 1869, Chandler Papers.

26. Id. to Newcomb, Sept. 12, 1869, Newcomb Papers; *Galveston News*, Aug. 27, 28, Sept. 5, Oct. 8, 17, 1869.

27. Moneyhon, *Republicanism in Reconstruction Texas*, pp. 113–16.

28. *Galveston News*, Nov. 2, 5, 1869; Elias Blouver to E. J. Davis, Jan. 18, 1870, Governor's Papers.

29. *Galveston News*, Nov. 27, 30, Dec. 4, 7, 8, 1869.

30. Quote from W. E. B. Du Bois, *Black Reconstruction* (New York: Harcourt Brace & Co., 1935), p. 365; Austin *State Journal*, May 24, 1870, May 6, 1871; *Flake's Bulletin*, June 18, 1871; *New York Tribune*, Jan. 10, 1871.

31. George Rawick, *The American Slave: A Composite Autobiography* (Westport, Conn.: Greenwood Press, 1972), 5:98; *Flake's Bulletin*, June 18, 1871; Maude Cuney Hare, *Norris Wright Cuney: A Tribune of the Black People* (New York: Crisis Publishing Co., 1913).

32. Ruby to Newcomb, June 7, 13, 29, July 7, 13, Aug. 18, 1871, Mar. 12, 1872, Newcomb Papers; W. P. Ballinger Diary, Feb. 18, 1871, William P. Ballinger Papers, University of Texas Archives; *Flake's Bulletin*, Oct. 20, 1870.

33. *Senate Journal of the Twelfth Legislature, Called Session, 1870* (Austin: Tracy, Siemering & Co., 1870), p. 562; *Senate Journal . . . First Session, 1871* (Austin: Tracy, Siemering, 1871), pp. 319–21, 1148.

34. *Senate Journal*, 1871, pp. 353, 668.

35. *Galveston News*, Apr. 23, 25, 1871; Louis W. Stevenson to Newcomb, Aug. 28, 1870, Newcomb Papers.

36. Stevenson to Newcomb, May 26, Feb. 12, 13, 1871, Newcomb Papers; Joseph M. Gibbs to Newcomb, Apr. 30, 1871, ibid.; Austin *Reformer*, June 17, July 1, 15, 22, 1871; *Flake's Bulletin*, June 23, July 19, 1871.

37. Ruby to Newcomb, June 13, 29, 1871, Newcomb Papers.

38. *Galveston News*, June 9, 13, 18, 1871; Austin *State Journal*, Aug. 9, 1871.

39. Ruby to Newcomb, July 6, 27, 1871; George Lawrence to Newcomb, July 11, 1871, Newcomb Papers.

40. J. G. Tracy to Newcomb, June 1, 1871, ibid.; Ruby to Newcomb, July 6, 1871, ibid.; H. C. Hunt to Newcomb, July 15, 1871, ibid.; James Walker to Newcomb, Aug. 2, 1871, ibid.; *Flake's Bulletin*, June 29, 1871.

41. *Galveston News*, July 30, Aug. 3, 1871; *Flake's Bulletin*, Aug. 3, 1871; Ruby to Newcomb, Aug. 4, 1871, Newcomb Papers.

42. Ruby to Newcomb, Aug. 18, 1871, Newcomb Papers.

43. Nathan Patten to Newcomb, Mar. 2, 1871, ibid.; Ruby to Newcomb, Mar. 12, 1872, ibid.; A. W. Kempton to Newcomb, Mar. 26, 1872, ibid.; Ruby to William E. Chandler, June 6, 1872, Chandler Papers; *Galveston News*, Apr. 11, May 2, 1872; Austin *State Journal*, Apr. 15, 1872; Dallas *Norton's Union Intelligencer*, May 25, 1872; *San Antonio Express*, May 21, Nov. 14, 1872.

44. *Galveston News*, June 12, 20, July 4, 5, 6, Aug. 20, 21, 1873; Austin *Weekly State Journal*, July 10, 1873; Winkler, *Platforms of Political Parties in Texas*, pp. 148–51, 155–57.

45. *Galveston News*, Oct. 31, Nov. 5, 1873.

46. Ibid., Apr. 16, 17, 1874.

47. Ibid., Apr. 28, 1878; Exodus Hearing, pp. 37–38; Ruby to John Sherman, June 23, 1879, May 2, 1880, John Sherman Papers, Library of Congress; id. to D. B. Fearing, Mar. 24, 1880, ibid.; D. B. Fearing to E. M. Pease, May 17, 1880, Pease-Graham-Niles Papers; *New York Times*, Mar. 25, 26, 1880; Austin *Democratic Statesman*, Mar. 26, 1880.

48. Exodus Hearing, pp. 51–52.

49. Death certificate in Louisiana Division, New Orleans Public Library; New Orleans *Daily Picayune*, Nov. 1, 1882.

August Meier

Afterword: New Perspectives on the Nature of Black Political Leadership during Reconstruction

As Howard Rabinowitz observes in his introduction, for decades chroniclers of the black experience during Reconstruction had dedicated themselves to correcting W. A. Dunning's racist interpretation by rehabilitating the careers and contributions of the Negro politicians who were active in the South during the post–Civil War years. Nearly two decades ago, the need to go "beyond redemption" and to employ the kinds of questions raised by sociologists and political scientists in order to understand how black Reconstruction leaders actually functioned in the arena of party and state politics, was raised at the University of Illinois conference on new frontiers in Reconstruction history.[1] Now, finally, a new generation of political and social historians has begun addressing this fundamental question as this pioneering anthology reveals. As Rabinowitz has put it in his introduction, an examination of how black political leaders "functioned in Reconstruction politics and within the Republican Party . . . is the most crucial" aim of this volume.

It is true that a handful of older essays and monographs, though cast in the "rehabilitation" mode, do provide a good deal of the kind of data that are helpful in analyzing the way in which black leaders functioned in southern politics during and after Reconstruction.[2] It is also interesting to note that in at least a couple of cases—Klingman's biography of Walls and Schweninger's volume on Rapier[3]—the authors represented in this volume originally presented their work within the redemptionist framework. Now both of these historians have recast their findings into a more functional analysis. Similarly, even the other essays in this anthology that still reflect vestiges of the rehabilitationist school—most notably Reidy's highly illuminating study of the much maligned A. A. Bradley—address themselves to the larger questions. Consequently the findings of the contributors to this volume, supplemented with data gleaned from the older studies cited, help to chart some of the tentative conclusions that can now be drawn, and at the same time point the way for future avenues of research into the history of the black political experience and race relations in the post–Civil War South.

From a perusal of the contributions to this book, certain themes emerge as important for consideration in analyzing the role of black political leaders during and after Reconstruction. Most or all of the essays take up the social origins and subsequent social and occupational characteristics of these racial leaders; analyze the power base from which they operated; demonstrate the importance of both the alliances these men made, and also the cleavages within the Republican party and among the black politicians, as central to any understanding of how they functioned during the Reconstruction period; and how in the final analysis, no matter how influential blacks as individuals or a group might have been in a state or city's politics, Negroes failed to retain their political foothold.

· On the subject of origins and social characteristics, it is clear that as a group the political leaders were an elite far more fortunate than the overwhelming majority of freedmen. A highly disproportionate number of them were antebellum free persons of color, and most of the rest were ex-slaves who had occupied relatively advantaged positions. These findings emerge from the accounts of individual careers, but are especially well illuminated in the collective profiles developed in the essays by Holt on South Carolina, Rankin on New Orleans, and Hume on the delegates to the state constitutional conventions. Yet this volume also contains the results of pioneering work on the diversity within this leadership group. Holt stresses the cleavages among them arising from different origins to be found in analyzing the Negro leaders of the Palmetto State. And Hume not only carefully distinguishes several categories of leaders whose interests were far from identical, but also makes the important point that there were significant differences in the kinds of delegates elected from the various states, a phenomenon rooted in the striking contrasts in numbers of free Negroes to be found in the several southern states before the Civil War.[4]

It is also clear that the politicians as a group were unusually fortunate in terms of occupation and wealth, especially during the active period of their political careers. Some in fact demonstrated remarkable upward economic mobility. The entrepreneurial propensities of these men are evident both among the planters who went to Congress—like Rapier, Bruce, and Walls—and also among leading city politicians like Thompson of Montgomery, Finch of Atlanta, and Mitchell of Richmond. And while some—like Rapier, Walls, Thompson, South Carolina congressman Robert Brown Elliott, and the former congressman and lieutenant governor of the same state, Alonzo J. Ransier—displayed striking downward economic mobility

394

afterwards, many of them were in comfortable economic circumstances for the rest of their lives. Examples of the latter pattern range from U.S. Senator Bruce, who remained a wealthy plantation owner, to Richmond councilman Mitchell, who played a prominent role as a newspaper editor and banker well into the twentieth century.

In every case the black politicians had their essential base in the black community. Walls had his base in Alachua County of black-belt Florida; Rapier, among the masses of freedmen in the plantation counties of Alabama; Bruce and both James and John R. Lynch, in the heavily Negro Mississippi and Yazoo valley counties in western Mississippi; both Ruby of Texas and Bradley of Georgia, in the rural folk and urban black workers of their districts; Robert Smalls and other South Carolina leaders, in the majority-black population of that state, especially in the heavily Negro coastal areas; the city councilmen, in wards with Negro majorities. Several, as some of these essays explicitly indicate, were excellent speakers and must have been endowed with a kind of charismatic quality that gave them a solid base in their black constituency; even the conservative and rather accommodating James Lynch, as Harris points out in his article of a few years ago, had a charismatic appeal for the freedmen of Mississippi.

The routes by which these men achieved their political prominence were varied. In all categories—city councilmen, state legislators and cabinet officers, and congressmen—there were individuals who first established themselves and seemingly developed a constituency through their work in the black churches and in the schools (both in those established by the Freedmen's Bureau and later in the educational systems set up by the states). Yet it would seem difficult to ascertain whether the church and school were actually crucial to the political prominence these individuals achieved. As Holt perceptively observes elsewhere, "It was less a matter of the churches themselves being a base for organizing a constituency than simply the attractiveness of the church for black men of ambition and leadership potential."[5] The same would be equally valid of those who first established their prominence in educational activities; like the church, the schoolhouse was one of the few avenues of opportunity open for ambitious men interested in achieving leadership. Some, in fact, were clearly economically and politically ambitious persons who came from other states because they saw an opportunity for acquiring wealth and power, and then quickly established themselves in politics. This pattern was to be found both in a state like South Carolina, with its own substantial indigenous leadership elite, and also in Mississippi, where an individual like Bruce

395

moved into an area characterized by a vacuum of trained and sophisticated local blacks, quickly established himself in politics as sheriff and
tax collector, then became county superintendent of schools, and rapidly moved into state and national office, while along the way making
himself a wealthy man. Again, to cite the case of an individual who was
the very antithesis of Bruce, the militant champion of the black masses
A. A. Bradley singlehandedly developed his leadership without strong
connections to school or church.

Yet it is also evident from these essays and the handful of other
works that shed some light on how post–Civil War southern black politicians actually functioned, that a base in the black community, however it was achieved, was not sufficient for a black political leader to
exercise significant influence or achieve high political position. Everywhere a cooperative attitude toward whites in general or alliances with
particular white leaders or factions were essential. This was true even
in the three states with Negro majorities, most notably South Carolina,
where blacks not only formed a preponderance of the population, but
where their particularly talented and articulate representatives formed
a majority in the constitutional convention, controlled the state legislature and chaired most of the important committees in it for several
years during the early seventies, and where they sent more Negroes to
Congress than any other southern state.

The patterns of black/white alliances and cooperative relationships
were, of course, highly varied. At the city-council level, blacks were
consistently in a distinct minority; and, in order to secure legislation to
benefit their constituents, they proved quite adept at horse-trading,
lobbying, and voting with white Democrats. In Richmond's Jackson
Ward there developed the curious situation where black politicians actually shared political power within their own district with a white businessman whose store was situated in the black residential area. At
higher levels the patterns revealed in this volume were more varied.
There was a man like Bruce, who cultivated friendly relationships with
white planters and Democrats in the Delta, and stood above the factions led by highly placed whites in the state's Republican party. The
two Lynches also proved singularly cooperative with Mississippi
whites. Similarly Jonathan Gibbs of Florida won his state school super-
intendency and J. J. Wright of South Carolina secured his post on the
supreme court because of acceptability to whites; while Benjamin
Boseman and Francis Cardozo of the same state maintained a cooperative and friendly position toward whites, evidently viewing this as the

best way to both advance their own ambitions and accomplish things for the race.

Others played the factional game in the Republican party—siding with one white leader or another and often switching from one faction to the next in the process. Robert Brown Elliott, probably the most powerful black political leader in South Carolina in his day, formed alliances with three successive white governors who achieved the gubernatorial office amidst the Republican factional wars of the state, even though his relations with each were ambiguous, unstable, and tinged with personal opportunism and compromise. P. B. S. Pinchback had a similar role and experience in Louisiana.

The cases of Florida's Congressman Walls, Montgomery's councilman Thompson, and Texas's state legislator Ruby, are all particularly instructive in this regard. As Klingman observes, Walls switched from a radical to a moderate faction with marvelous timing and thus established himself as an important black leader (even though he subsequently made missteps and misjudgments in the factional conflicts that led to his downfall). Even more illuminating is Moneyhon's analysis of Ruby, who, building on his solid base among the rural freedmen, formed an alliance with the state's governor and, when the occasion warranted it, rearranged his strategy to include the urban black workers and white mercantile elements in his coalition. Ruby's failure to retain office stemmed not from lack of personal skill and judgment, but from the difficulty of simultaneously serving the interests of both his black and white constituencies with their diverse and contradictory needs and wants. In the end, the increasing size of the white electorate proved to be something he could not withstand, with his former white supporters deserting him partly because they disliked his stand on racial issues and partly because they could simply outvote his black supporters. Similarly on a local level, Thompson essayed to be cooperative toward whites and simultaneously represent the interests of his black constituents, though his espousal of the latter and his personally aggressive manner eventually undercut his acceptability to influential whites and he lost out to the more palatable Rapier in the struggle to serve in Congress. Rapier, for his part, obtained his seat in Congress from an electorate about equally divided between blacks and whites, succeeding in his campaign with the support of 1,500 white voters along with 18,000 blacks. Even a militant like Bradley in Georgia, who consistently espoused the cause of the black farmers and urban workers of Chatham County, at times felt he had to act in an opportunist fashion and make appropriate compromises with influential white politicians.

The dependence upon whites was, of course, even more extreme for most of those Negroes who remained in political office during the post-Reconstruction years, as in the "fusion" arrangements between white Democrats and black Republicans in both South Carolina and Mississippi, and the informal alliance that developed in late nineteenth-century Georgia between the Redeemers and the black Republican leader and newspaper editor William A. Pledger, despite the latter's reputation as a militant crusading journalist. In fact, in border-state Missouri, the former radical Republican and minister to Liberia, J. Milton Turner, in the 1880s actually joined the Democratic party. The Bruce-Hill-Lynch triumvirate in Mississippi was particularly famous; controlling patronage that they doled out principally to Mississippi whites, they maintained a significant role through the 1880s until constitutional disfranchisement in 1890 snuffed out all possibility of blacks exercising any political influence.

This dependence on alliances with white factions and leaders, even in states with black majorities, poses the interesting question of why Negroes were unable in any state to obtain the coveted office of governor and, except for a few instances, others of the very highest offices like a national senator or state supreme court justice. Yet it should be emphasized, as Anderson so perceptively points out in his essay on post-Reconstruction congressman O'Hara, that the relationship between whites and blacks was a two-way street—was one of mutual interdependence; that ambitious white politicians in the Republican party needed black support as much as blacks seemed to need theirs. The moderate white faction in Florida needed Walls and his black voting strength as much as he needed them; white Democrats in city councils needed black Republican support to obtain necessary majorities against white Republicans who opposed their proposals. Perhaps the most stark example of this phenomenon is the way in which the Mississippi legislature, though in a state with a black majority, was itself composed of a white majority. Yet it was the pressure stemming from the hopes of the mass of black voters that put Hiram Revels and then Bruce in the Senate, and John R. Lynch in the Speaker's chair of the Mississippi House. Not surprisingly, on the other hand, all three men were moderates—Republican stalwarts, as John Hope Franklin describes John R. Lynch—but individuals whom whites perceived as posing no threat to them. Franklin's description of the youthful, moderate Lynch rising quickly in the Mississippi House and playing a key role in its affairs before reaching the speakership suggests something of the tactful, politically astute, but not very militant character of this popular spokesman for the blacks from southeastern Mississippi. Finally, the mutually complementary nature of the support of both black and white elements as accounting for the success—and often ultimately the failure—of some of the most skillful and dedicated black Reconstruction leaders is perhaps most clearly seen in the cases of Ruby and Thompson. They were individuals who sincerely tried to benefit their black constituencies by cooperating with important white elements; but in the end, as Rabinowitz says of Thompson, the loss of support from both the black voters and the white leaders limited their accomplishments and achievements and cut short their careers.

One reason for the necessity of alliances with whites—particularly in states with black majorities—was the existence of cleavages and factionalism among the Negroes. This question comes up in nearly every essay in this volume, and few were the black politicians able to rise above the factional fights. The case of Rapier, who first defeated Thompson in the struggle for the congressional seat and then a few years later fought another rival black, the conservative Jeremiah Haralson, only to have both lose to a white candidate in a two-thirds black constituency, is, of course, simply one extreme example of this factionalism. The causes for it were many. Factionalism, in the first place, is common, if not inevitable, in a republican polity—though, as Holt points out, the Democrats showed far more unity, and the factionalism among Republicans and even between black Republicans was particularly severe during Reconstruction. As Holt says, much of this cleavage and conflict was idiosyncratic, due to personal rivalries and ambitions; yet it was also rooted in other causes. Part of it was based on rivalries among white Republican leaders, all of whom sought black support and whose own struggle for leadership often would have been hopeless without factionalism among the blacks themselves. At least some of this factionalism was, as Holt also indicates, rooted in class differences within the Negro community—though South Carolina and New Orleans may well represent extreme cases of this phenomenon. The essays here do not systematically examine these kinds of explanations, yet all of them may well have been generally operative: as Reidy concludes for Bradley in Georgia, the political leader's own "activities contributed to growing political factionalism that reflected the process of class stratification among blacks and the success of relentless white opposition to black political unity."

The whole question of class divisions is itself of considerable importance, as both Holt and Rankin make clear. Rankin vividly demonstrates not only the gulf in social origins between the black masses and their leaders, but the difficulty such leaders had in representing the interests of the masses. The same could be said of a man like Bruce, as well as less obviously of others. On the other hand, the findings of most of the authors suggest that, despite the gulf in social origins, many if not most of the leaders sought somehow to reconcile their personal ambitions with service to their constituency. Of course, some service to their black constituency was necessary if they were to remain in office, though one is impressed in reading these essays by the diversity of the degree to which black leaders did so. But there were enough differences in style among black politicians, enough differences in the kinds of alliances they made, and enough differences in their stand on issues, such as the land question, which were of fundamental interest to the masses they all had as their constituency so that at this stage of our knowledge it is difficult to make adequate generalizations. Moreover, the striking difference in the evaluation of Rapier's motivations by Schweninger and Rabinowitz suggests that differences in scholarly perspective will continue to cloud our vision on this as on so many other issues.

In addition, the very conditions, and contradictory constraints and motivations, under which the black politicians operated inherently served to limit both their effectiveness as leaders and what they could deliver to their black constituencies. Thus the right to vote, the franchise itself, was a militant demand for blacks and freedmen in the mid-nineteenth century; yet, paradoxically, American politics is a politics of compromise between competing and varied interest groups and, accordingly, the radical step of enfranchising the freedmen was likely at best to produce only limited advances for them. Secondly, the black political leaders were functioning in a white-dominated society. The national government was white dominated and not inclined to give full and unequivocal support to Radical Reconstruction. In only three states were blacks a majority of the electorate; and, even in those three states, influential whites, with their connections to higher federal authorities or for other reasons, retained much of the power. We do know that certain black politicians were influential—for example, Elliott, Pinchback, Ruby, Walls, Finch, and Thompson—in their own way; yet in every case this influence was limited by the white-dominated political milieu in which they worked. The operations of the Bruce-Hill-Lynch triumvirate were simply a particularly stark example of this phenomenon. Finally, there were the natural ambiguities arising from the fact that black politicians were normal human beings; even those most sincerely bent on serving the race were personally ambitious men who wanted to gain prestigeful posts and political power. Several had entrepreneurial interests of their own that could be helped by state and congressional legislation; and a few essays in this book point to specific cases where, like so many of their white counterparts, blacks did support legislation for their own direct economic interest. It would be naïve to think that these black leaders during Reconstruction lacked the normal impulses of even the most idealistic and socially responsible political leaders; and one of the virtues of this volume is that it illuminates so well the complex and ambiguous ways in which late nineteenth-century black political leaders in the South functioned.

On the basis of the information thus far accumulated we can attempt a tentative model of what the individuals who gained prominence in political life were like. They were men of relatively fortunate origins, compared to the mass of their Negro constituents. They were likely, but not necessarily, to have come to prominence through work in the Freedmen's Bureau, the Union leagues, the church, or the school. As a class they were relatively well-educated, ambitious men. They were likely to be successful artisans, farmers, and professionals, and in a few cases at least achieved considerable wealth. However they achieved power, they all operated from a black base. Yet all found it necessary for reasons suggested above to find allies among whites, even though white factions and leaders also needed them as long as Congressional Reconstruction lasted.

In their expressed interests in the legislative chambers there was some variation, depending on the kind of office held. Congressmen emphasized civil rights and protection of the ballot, and protested against white violence, while approving internal improvements that would benefit their white constituents. Those on the state level stressed civil rights and education; the land issue also loomed in importance at this level, but on this subject the leaders were highly divided. On the local level the city councilmen seemed to concern themselves not with civil rights but with welfare issues—access to education, positions on the police force, and adequate sanitation and street improvements. To what degree patronage interests governed the actions of these politicians is not clear—some of the contributors to this anthology note its importance, others ignore it, though common sense would suggest that it must have been of some interest to politicians at all levels.[6]

401

Overall, the typical late nineteenth-century black political leader in the South was a moderate. All were practical men who saw the necessity of compromise. They were also ambitious men who needed white support to advance themselves and the interests of their black constituents. Even the most militant spokesmen—like the two Georgians, Bradley during Reconstruction and Pledger afterwards—found astute compromise essential to obtain the benefits desired either personally or for the race. The intersection of personal rivalries among blacks, class cleavages, the activities of whites—both Democrats and Republicans—and the very nature of the American political system made inevitable the emergence of a typically moderate political type. Ultimately they all failed, partly because of the factionalism among them, although actually this only played into the hands of southern whites because the dominant forces in the national government were so moderate and northern public opinion was lukewarm at best.

This is, of course, a tentative model; further case studies of individual politicians and group profiles are essential to see if it will be sustained. For example, the black politicians as a group were likely darker and contained more ex-slaves than the sampling here reveals.[7] New Orleans and Charleston were atypical, in fact; and Hume's essay suggesting differences in the various states points future researchers in the right direction. In this connection we also need more study of the routes of upward political mobility and, in particular, of a group of prominent politicians not represented here except marginally in the case of Thompson—religious leaders like Henry Turner of Georgia and R. H. Cain of South Carolina.

We also need to do some really hard digging and thinking to ascertain how much political power these men actually had; it is often difficult to ascertain this from offices held. Rabinowitz makes a good case for the influence of Thompson, though he sat on no prestigious council committees. On the other hand, a man like South Carolina supreme court justice Wright, despite his exalted post, exercised little if any real power, for the most part going along with his two white colleagues on the court. In every case critical examination of this issue is necessary. Were the black lieutenant governors in Mississippi and South Carolina impotent, while those in Louisiana (Oscar Dunn and Pinchback) wielded considerable power? Was there any correlation between a militant style and political power or effectiveness, or might a more conservative spokesman, in some cases at least, have obtained more concrete benefits for the black masses? I would suspect that underneath the moderate style that seemed to characterize so many of

402

the men who achieved political eminence lay substantial differences in what they aimed—and were able—to deliver. In addition, as Anderson's essay on O'Hara so uniquely points out, we cannot understand how much power blacks wielded unless we study the structures in which they operated. In fact, it would appear that O'Hara was more powerful as a local county official than as a congressman. Such analysis only hints at the wealth of illuminating information in store if proper research is done along these lines for other states as well. Finally, Anderson's suggestion about black politicians functioning as symbols suggests fruitful lines for additional research. But I would go further than Anderson; for I think that by playing a symbolic role for blacks as well as whites, many of the Negro political leaders were able to give the impression of influence and power, when actually they may, in many cases, have had relatively little of it.

As the preceding paragraph suggests, we need many studies of how black political leaders functioned at the local—city and county—level. Moreover, explicit attention should be paid to the complex mix of motives and tactical considerations that characterized all of these men in the varying contexts in which they operated. Such information may be difficult to find, but at least we should start to address ourselves very systematically to this question, for this is the only way to understand a militant who could compromise or an accommodationist who used militant rhetoric, and to understand the interplay between the ways the political leaders functioned as political realists on the one hand and as symbols on the other.

In this connection I would like to suggest that a systematic examination of the positions various politicians took on the land question—including their response to the Kansas Exodus—might be quite productive. Clearly this topic reveals a cleavage among the elite who held political office. Yet one might speculate further that this cleavage reflected ideological and tactical differences within the black leadership elite, with those supporting land reform and migration being more attuned to the masses than those who, opposing land expropriation and the Kansas Exodus, tended more to go along with the southern white establishment. Examination of the reasons for this cleavage—and its possible relationship to other cleavages within the black political elite—might lead to some very illuminating conclusions on the nature of black leadership in the Reconstruction era.[8]

Broader questions also emerge. How did these political leaders function in comparison with other blacks who have historically, officially or unofficially, played political roles? Leslie H. Fishel's article on the Negro in northern politics in the late nineteenth century pictures them primarily as ambitious men seeking personal advancement. This was subsequently certainly true for most of the men Booker T. Washington had appointed to political office and for Booker T. Washington himself—though some of his appointees, most notably James Weldon Johnson, were strongly motivated in the direction of advancing the race.

The role of the southern nineteenth-century black politician should also be viewed in comparison with the kind of politician who emerged in the North in the twentieth century, as black migration made salient the demand for black representation in city halls, state legislatures, and Congress. The analyses thus far of politics based on a constituency of the northern black urban masses suggest the salience of opportunistic personal motivations.[9]

One might ask, too, how does the newest breed of black political leader, arising both from the migration to the North and the growth of the ghettoes on the one hand, and the fruits of enfranchisement in the South on the other—and operating in a far more permissive context than their nineteenth-century predecessors—actually function? Perhaps, as David Gerber has perceptively suggested in a recent article, underneath the variations in the behavior of black political figures in different areas and at different times, there has always been a basic underlying similarity bottomed on black powerlessness and the patterns of American race relations—what Gerber describes as "a politics of limited options."[10]

Finally, given the new interest in the history of ethnicity and ethnic leadership in this country, it will be instructive to compare how blacks, with their very different and unique history, functioned politically as compared with other ethnic groups. Studying changes over time, such investigations should stress both the similarities arising from the common features associated with being underprivileged minorities and the differences based upon variations in minority groups' cultural values and community cohesiveness, as well as the intersection of these with changing attitudes of the dominant native-white majority and that dominant majority's varying attitudes toward different minority groups.

In this connection I find John Higham's interest in the marginality of ethnic leadership suggestive.[11] Black Reconstruction politicians were a special group—clearly more prosperous, more educated, more assimilated on the whole to white American culture than the mass of freedmen. Their very attainments, as Higham suggests, separated

404

them from the masses and made it hard for them to properly or effectively represent the interests of the masses. Yet I think the matter is more complex than Higham describes it—for it was this marginality that made it possible for them to deal with the dominant white group, however varied their dealings (from accommodation to militancy, from representing the interests of the race to focusing on their own personal interests in practice if not in rhetoric) might be. Thus the very marginality of the black political leaders in the post–Civil War era might serve as an important key to understanding the complex nature of their patterns of behavior.

Notes

1. August Meier, "Comment on John Hope Franklin's Paper," in *New Frontiers of the American Reconstruction*, ed. Harold M. Hyman (Urbana: University of Illinois Press, 1966), pp. 77–86.

2. These include two "revisionist works" not truly rehabilitationist by later standards: R. H. Woody, "Jonathan Jasper Wright, Associate Justice of the Supreme Court of South Carolina, 1870–77," *Journal of Negro History* 18 (July 1933):114–31; and Agnes Smith Grosz, "The Political Career of Pinckney Benton Stewart Pinchback," *Louisiana Historical Quarterly* 27 (Apr. 1944):527–612. Useful items more clearly redemptionist in intent are Edward F. Sweat, "Francis L. Cardozo: Profile of Integrity in Reconstruction Politics," *Journal of Negro History* 41 (Oct. 1961):217–32; Joe M. Richardson, "Jonathan C. Gibbs: Florida's Only Negro Cabinet Member," *Florida Historical Quarterly* 43 (Apr. 1964):353-68; William C. Harris, "James Lynch: Black Leader in Reconstruction," *Historian* 34 (Nov. 1971):40–61; Peggy Lamson, *The Glorious Failure: Black Congressman Robert Brown Elliott and the Reconstruction in South Carolina* (New York: W. W. Norton, 1973). Clarence Bacote, "The Negro in Georgia Politics, 1880–1908" (Ph.D. diss., University of Chicago, 1955), in its realistic assessment of the activities of William Finch, W. A. Pledger, and others, prefigures the tone of the present anthology. Finally there is Gary Kremer's recent "A Biography of James Milton Turner" (Ph.D. diss., American University, 1978), which though in my judgment utilizing an unfortunate conceptualization, nevertheless offers an illuminating analysis of how a prominent black border-state political leader functioned in the post–Civil War years.

3. Peter D. Klingman, *Josiah Walls: Florida's Black Congressman of Reconstruction* (Gainesville: University Presses of Florida, 1976), and Loren Schweninger, *James T. Rapier and Reconstruction* (Chicago: University of Chicago Press, 1978).

4. Charles Vincent, *Black Legislators in Louisiana during Reconstruction* (Baton Rouge: Louisiana State University Press, 1976), in his epilogue points to differences between social origins of the black political leaders of Louisiana and Mississippi.

5. Thomas Holt, "Afro-Americans," in *Harvard Encyclopedia of Ameri-*

can Ethnic Groups, ed. Stephan Thernstrom (Cambridge, Mass.: Harvard University Press, 1980), p. 13.

6. William Hine, "Frustration, Factionalism and Failure: Black Political Leadership and the Republican Party in Reconstruction Charleston, 1865–1877" (Ph.D. diss., Kent State University, 1979), indicates that as far as the extant sources indicate, on the municipal level patronage interests were perhaps the leading interest of Charleston black politicians.

7. Orville Vernon Burton, "Ungrateful Servants? Edgefield's Black Reconstruction: Part I of the Total History of Edgefield County, South Carolina" (Ph.D. diss., Princeton University, 1976), for example, indicates that upcountry, local southern Negro politicians were black ex-slaves rather than light-skinned antebellum free persons of color.

8. In the formulation of this question I am greatly indebted to the analysis of Negro elite behavior by Joe William Trotter in "The Making of an Industrial Proletariat: Black Milwaukee, 1915–1945" (Ph.D. diss., University of Minnesota, 1980), to be published in revised form by University of Illinois Press.

9. Leslie H. Fishel, Jr., "The Negro in Northern Politics, 1870–1900," *Mississippi Valley Historical Review* 42 (Dec. 1955):466–89; August Meier, *Negro Thought in America, 1880–1915* (Ann Arbor: University of Michigan Press, 1963), chs. 7, 10, 13, passim; Ralph J. Bunche, "The Political Status of the Negro," memorandum for the Carnegie-Myrdal study of the Negro in America, 1940 (copy in Schomburg Collection of New York Public Library), published in abbreviated form as *The Politics of the Negro in the Age of FDR*, ed. Dewey W. Grantham (Chicago: University of Chicago Press, 1973); and the following specific studies that deal in some detail with black politics in the twentieth-century northern cities: Harold F. Gosnell, *Negro Politicians: The Rise of Negro Politics in Chicago* (Chicago: University of Chicago Press, 1935); Allan H. Spear, *Black Chicago: The Making of a Negro Ghetto* (Chicago: University of Chicago Press, 1967); Gilbert Osofsky, *Harlem: The Making of a Ghetto* (New York: Harper & Row, 1966); Kenneth Kusmer, *A Ghetto Takes Shape: Black Cleveland, 1870–1930* (Urbana: University of Illinois Press, 1976); James Q. Wilson, *Negro Politics* (Glencoe, Ill.: Free Press, 1960); and id., "Two Negro Politicians: An Interpretation," *Midwest Journal of Politics* 4 (Nov. 1960):346–69; Charles R. Branham, "The Transformation of Black Political Leadership in Chicago, 1864–1942" (Ph.D. diss., University of Chicago, 1981), to be published in revised form by University of Illinois Press. For an illuminating case study, see David M. Katzman, *Before the Ghetto: Black Detroit in the Nineteenth Century* (Urbana: University of Illinois Press, 1973), ch. 6; in this midwestern Republican city, a united black elite secured a relatively good share of political patronage and elective office until progressive political reforms undermined the power of the party's political machine at the turn of the century.

10. David A. Gerber, "A Politics of Limited Options: Northern Black Politics and the Problem of Change and Continuity in Race Relations Historiography," *Journal of Social History* 14 (Win. 1980):235–55.

11. John Higham, ed., *Ethnic Leadership in America* (Baltimore: Johns Hopkins University Press, 1978), p. 14.

The Contributors

ERIC ANDERSON (Ph.D., University of Chicago) is on the faculty of the history department at Pacific Union College, Angwin, California. He is the author of *Race and Politics in North Carolina, 1872–1901: The Black Second*, and is a contributor to the *Dictionary of North Carolina Biography*.

MICHAEL B. CHESSON (Ph.D., Harvard University) is on the faculty of the history department at the University of Massachusetts in Boston. He is the author of *Richmond after the War, 1865–1890*.

JOHN HOPE FRANKLIN (Ph.D., Harvard University) is John M. Manly distinguished service professor at the University of Chicago and senior Mellon fellow at the National Humanities Center. His numerous publications include *From Slavery to Freedom: A History of Negro Americans; Reconstruction after the Civil War; The Militant South;* and *A Southern Odyssey: Travelers in the Antebellum North*.

WILLIAM C. HARRIS (Ph.D., University of Alabama) is on the history faculty at North Carolina State University. His publications include *Leroy Pope Walker: Confederate Secretary of War; Presidential Reconstruction in Mississippi;* and *The Day of the Carpetbagger: Republican Reconstruction in Mississippi*.

WILLIAM C. HINE (Ph.D., Kent State University) is on the history faculty at South Carolina State College. His articles have been published in *South Carolina Historical Magazine, Phylon* and *Cleveland Magazine*.

THOMAS C. HOLT (Ph.D., Yale University) is on the faculty of the University of Michigan at Ann Arbor, where he teaches history and Afro-American studies. He is the author of *Black over White: Negro Political Leadership in South Carolina during Reconstruction* and is a contributor to the *Harvard Encyclopedia of American Ethnic Groups* and *Black Leaders of the 20th Century*.

RICHARD L. HUME (Ph.D., University of Washington) is on the history faculty at Washington State University. His articles have appeared in

Journal of American History, Journal of Southern History, and in state journals; he has also contributed to *The Encyclopedia of Southern History.*

PETER D. KLINGMAN (Ph.D., University of Florida) is on the social science faculty of Daytona Beach Community College, where he also serves as chairman of faculty affairs. He is the author of *Josiah Walls: Florida's Black Congressman in Reconstruction.*

AUGUST MEIER (Ph.D., Columbia University) is university professor of history at Kent State University. He is the author of *Negro Thought in America, 1880–1915* and co-author (with Elliott Rudwick) of *From Plantation to Ghetto; CORE: A Study in the Civil Rights Movement, 1942–1968;* and *Black Detroit and the Rise of the UAW.*

CARL H. MONEYHON (Ph.D., University of Chicago) is on the history faculty at the University of Arkansas in Little Rock. He is the author of *Republicanism in Reconstruction Texas.*

HOWARD N. RABINOWITZ (Ph.D., University of Chicago) is on the history faculty at the University of New Mexico. He is the author of *Race Relations in the Urban South, 1865–1890,* and a contributor to several other books, including *The City in Southern History,* and a forthcoming book on blacks in North Carolina.

DAVID C. RANKIN (Ph.D., Johns Hopkins University) is on the history faculty of the University of California at Riverside. His articles have appeared in *Journal of Southern History, Southern Studies,* and *Perspectives in American History.*

JOSEPH P. REIDY (Ph.D., Northern Illinois University) is on the history faculty of the University of Maryland at College Park, where he serves as associate editor for the Freedmen and Southern Society Project. He is the author of " 'Negro Election Day' and Black Community Life in New England, 1750–1860," in *Marxist Perspectives.*

JAMES MICHAEL RUSSELL (Ph.D., Princeton University) is on the history faculty of the University of Tennessee at Chattanooga. He is a contributor to *Towards a New South?: Studies in Post–Civil War Southern Communities; Dictionary of Georgia Biography;* and *Encyclopedia of Southern History.*

LOREN SCHWENINGER (Ph.D., University of Chicago) is on the history faculty of the University of North Carolina at Greensboro. He is the author of *James T. Rapier and Reconstruction.*

JERRY THORNBERY (Ph.D., University of Maryland) teaches American history and history of the South at Gilman School in Baltimore. He is the author of "Northerners and the Atlanta Freedmen, 1865–69," in *Prologue*.

Index

Abélard, Joseph, 165
Adams, John H., 200
Adolphe family, 160
Alabama: and Rapier, 79–99;
    Republicans in, 80, 85–86; racial
    tensions in, 84; violence in, 86;
    comparison showing decline of
    Republican votes in areas of racial
    violence, 87; congressional election
    returns, fourth district, 1876, 88;
    constitutional convention, 1867, 131
Alabama Negro Labor Union, 261
Alabama Republican State Convention,
    79
Alabama State Baptist Convention, 269
Alabama State Journal, 258, 262, 266
Alachua County, Florida: and Walls, 66
Alcorn, James Lusk, 4, 6, 9, 10, 12
Aldrich, A. P., 243
Alexander, Ann Field, 203
Alexander, James, 321–22
Alexander, Nathan, 89
Allan, Edgar, 205, 207
Allen, Joseph, 201
Allison, Senator William B., 32
Allman, Jacob C., 240
Ames, Governor Adelbert, 12, 13, 15;
    and Bruce, 6, 10–11; and Lynch, 42
Anderson, Mayor Edward C., 291, 292,
    296
Anderson-McCormick law, 214–15
Andrews, Rev. G. W., 256–57
Andrews, William J., 240
Antebellum literacy of Negro politicians
    in New Orleans during
    Reconstruction, 167
Archer, Edinboro, 201
Arthur, President Chester A., 49, 50, 92
Ash, William, 91
Association for the Study of Negro Life
    and History, xiv, xv
Athens, Georgia: and Finch, 310
Athens *Blade*, 328
Atkins, James: and Bradley, 299

Atlanta: Finch in, 312–30; politics in,
    313–24, 328–29
Atlanta *Constitution*, 313, 324, 325, 330
Atlanta *Journal*, 330
Atlanta *Sun*, 322
Atlanta University, 319, 320, 321
Austin Republican, 373

Bacchus, Noël, 168
Bahen, James, 202, 204, 205–6, 216
Banks, General Nathaniel P., 170, 364
Banks, Lewis, 161
Baptist church: and Thompson, 250,
    252–53, 257, 267
Barnes, Joseph K., 338
Barrett, James D., 140
Barrett, William, 165
Barry, C. M., 317–18
Baulden, Dr. Henry E., 327
Bell, Jack, 97
Bell, James H., 366, 372
Belot, Octave, 162
Belot family, 160
Bertonneau, E. Arnold, 140, 168, 170,
    171
Bethel AME Church, 325
Billings, Liberty, 63, 64
Bingham, Arthur, 85
Bingham, Chester A., 92
Biographical information on Negro
    leaders in New Orleans during
    Reconstruction, 181–89
Birney, William G., 62
Birth of a Nation, 55
Bisbee, Horatio, 70, 74, 75
Black councilmen in Richmond, 191–222;
    characteristics of, 196–202;
    achievements of 211–14
Black leaders: and Dunning studies, xii,
    xiv; and South Carolina, xv; in New
    Orleans, 155–89; in South Carolina,
    characteristics of, 230–34; origins and
    social characteristics of, 394;
    occupations and wealth of, 394–95;

411

and black community, 395; and churches and schools, 395; and whites, 396, 398; and Republican party, 397; and class differences, 399, 400; and their constituencies, 400; and civil rights and education, 401; as moderates, 402–3; and land issue, 403; and migration, 403

Black masses: and Bruce, 26–27; and New Orleans politicians, 169

Black police: and Thompson, 255

Black political power: and Bradley, 290–92

Black politicians in New Orleans: characteristics of, 156–69; age of, 164–65; literacy of, 167; as slaveowners, 167; education of, 167–68; military service of, 168–69; and black masses, 169; and suffrage, 170–73; biographical information on, 181–89

Black Reconstruction, xv–xvi

Blacks: and politics in South Carolina, 224–29; and other ethnic groups, 404

Black state legislators: in South Carolina, 223–46

Black teachers: and Finch, 324–25

Black workers: and Ruby, 379–80

Blaine, James, 30, 50

Blair bill, 28

Bland-Allison Silver Purchase, 21

Boguille, Ludger, 167

Boisdore, François, 160, 170

Boisdore family, 160

Bonseigneur family, 160

Borée, Anatole, 161

Boseman, Ada, 348

Boseman, Anneretta, 335

Boseman, Benjamin A., Sr., 335

Boseman, Christopher, 348

Boseman, Dr. Benjamin A., Jr., 335–62; early life of, 335–38; and politics, 339–55; in state legislature, 340–46; and civil rights, 341–43; and racial discrimination, 343; and health care, 344; and the insane and orphans, 344–45; and higher education, 345; business interests of, 346–48; wealth of, 348; and other black leaders, 349–50; as postmaster, 351–53; and whites, 354

Boseman, Virginia, 348

Boston, Joseph D., 234

Bovee, George E., 169

Bowdoin College, 336

Bowen, Christopher C., 350

Bowers, Claude G., xiii, 55

Boyd, Landrum, 200

Bradley, Aaron A., 281–308, 393; early life, 281–82; and land issue, 285–90, 300–301; educational work of, 286; and black political power, 290–92; and constitutional convention, 294–95; and Robb, 298–99; and Atkins, 299; and migration, 300

Brady, Colonel John T., 369

Brady, James D., 207

Brandt, Captain Henry C., 288, 294

Bridges, Daniel, 310

Brimsmade, Dr. Thomas C., 336, 354

Brockington, Isaac P., 140

Brodgen, Curtis, H., 114, 117

Brooks, Albert P., 196

Brown, George A., 123

Brown, Joseph E., 282

Brown, Malcolm, 348

Brown Fellowship Society, 239

Browne, William W., 207

Bruce, Blanche K., 3–38; Houston on, xix; early life, 3–4; appearance of, 6; wealth of, 7–8; and education, 8–9, 27–28; and U.S. Senate, 11–22; and 1876 Republican convention, 17; and Hayes, 17–18; and Lynch and Hill, 19; and racial progress, 22; and migration, 22–26; and black masses, 26–27; preference for white society, 27; and self-help, 27–28; and 1880 presidential election, 29–30; as register of the treasury, 30–31; and 1888 presidential campaign, 31; as recorder of deeds for District of Columbia, 31

Bruce, Josephine B. Willson, 27

Bryant, John E., 298, 299, 310

Buckley, Charles, 80, 262

Buckley, William, 85

Bullock, Governor Rufus, 297, 314

Burgess, John W., xiii

Bush, Henry M., 256

Busteed, Richard, 81, 85

Butler, Benjamin F., 14, 15, 141, 155, 156

Butler, M. C., 226

Byrdie, Danwell, 312

Cain, Richard H., 82, 139, 142, 290, 339, 341, 342, 347, 351, 354, 402

Caldwell, Charles, 137, 146

Calhoun, John, 43

Calkins, William H., 49
Cameron, Gov. William E., 205
Campbell, Tunis G., 139, 289, 297
Canelle family, 160
Capla, Lucien Jean Pierre, 168–69
Cardozo, Francis L., 137, 139, 140, 142,
    236–37, 239, 339, 340, 345, 354, 355
Cardozo, Thomas W., 239
Cargile, Mitchell, Sr., 328
Carpetbag Rule in Florida, 62
Carter, Edward R., 200, 201
Carter, Ham, 9, 11
Carter, Isaac W., 201
Carter, Richard, 194
Cassidy, Hiram, 44
Les Cenelles, 160
Cessna, William K., 62, 66, 68, 73
Chahoon, George, 202
Chalmers, General James R., 47, 48
Chamberlain, Governor Daniel H., 223,
    226, 240, 242, 243
Chandler, William E., 81
Charleston: and Boseman, 339–62
Charleston Daily Courier, 341
Charleston Daily News, 351
Chase, Salmon P., 64
Chase, W. Calvin, 32
Cheney, Edward, 74
Chesnut, John A., 129
Chester, T. Morris, 161
Cheves, Charlotte, 287–88
Cheves, Isabella, 287–88
Chinese exclusion bill: and Bruce, 21
Cincinnati *Commercial*, 26
Civil rights: and Walls, 71–72; and
    Rapier, 82–84, 85; and O'Hara, 119;
    and Thompson, 250–52; and
    Boseman, 341–43; and black leaders,
    401
Civil Rights Bill, 1874: and Lynch, 45–46
Civil War: and Walls, 60–62
Clanton, James H., 255
Clark, General David, 112
Clark, General William T., 382, 383,
    384–85
Clark, George W., 353
Clay, Henry, 124
Clay, John Racquet, 167
Clayton, Powell, 50
Cleveland, Grover, 31, 51, 207
Clift, Joseph W., 297
Clinton, Frederick A., 139
Club Unioniste Républicain, 155
Cocke, Edmund C., 207
Coke, Richard, 387

Colored Labor Convention: and
    Thompson, 261
Colored Men's National Convention,
    New Orleans, 386
Colored National Labor Convention,
    1868, 379–80
Combash, William T., 146
Compromise of 1877, 18
Conant, Sherman, 62, 69, 70
Congressional Record, 101
Conkling, Roscoe, 12–13, 14
Conover, Senator Simon, 74
Constitutional conventions. *See* State
    constitutional conventions
Convention of Colored Men of
    Louisiana, 172
Conway, Thomas W., 364
Cook, Fields, 196
Cooper, Benjamin, 97
Corbin, D. T., 341, 342
Cotton Plant (steamer), 104
Coulter, E. Merton, xxiii
Council, William H., 53
Cox, George W., 261
Cox, Joseph, 191, 194
Craft, Ellen, 281
Craft, William, 281
Craig, Henry H., 95, 261, 262, 275
Craig, Joseph, 167
Cravath, F. M., 253
Cromwell, John W., 53
Cromwell, Robert I., 161, 164
Crump, Josiah, 196, 200, 210
Cuney, Norris Wright, xiv, 53, 380, 383,
    384, 385, 386
Cunningham, George I., 353
Curiel, Joseph, 165

Daily Dispatch, 267
Daily Republican, 346
Davis, Alexander K., 11
Davis, Edgar, 158, 163–64
Davis, Governor E. J., 371, 373, 376,
    377, 378, 379, 380, 381, 386–87
Davis, Jefferson, 213
Davis, J. L., 155
Davis, Mrs. Edgar, 163–64
Daw, Jack, 92
Dawson, James T., 114, 115
Day, William H., 110, 112, 113
Deane, Morton, 200, 201
DeBruhl, John, 380
Debtor relief: and black delegates to
    constitutional conventions, 142
Defiance, 326

413

DeLamotta, Charles L., 297
Delany, Martin R., 238, 289, 339, 340, 348, 349
De Large, Robert C., 140, 239–40, 339, 340, 342, 346, 348, 349, 350, 354
Dennis, Leonard, 66, 69, 70, 73
DePriest, Oscar, 53
Desalles, Jules, 158
Desdunes, Rodolphe, 160–61
Dessalines, Jean Jacques, 161
Detiège, Èmile, 165
De Tocqueville, Alexis, 162
Deveaux, John H., 297, 298
Dexter Avenue Baptist Church, 252, 269
Dixon, Thomas, 55
Dougherty, Charles, 75
Douglass, Frederick, xviii, 22–23, 27, 32, 238; and Walls, 59, 72; and Republican party, 225; in Troy, 336
Du Bois, W. E. B., xv–xvi, 138
Duhart, Adolphe, 168
Dumas, Francis Ernest, 160, 168
Dunbar, Charles, 338
Dungee, J. W., 196
Dunning, William A., xi, 393
Dunningites, xii–xiv; and Du Bois, xx; and Florida, 65; and black delegates to constitutional conventions, 130
Dupuy, Édmond, 166, 167
Dutcher, Silas P., 50

Education: and Bruce, 8–9, 27–28; and Walls, 71; and Rapier, 82; and O'Hara, 119; of black politicians in New Orleans, 167–68; of black legislators in South Carolina, 233; and black legislators in South Carolina, 240–41; and Thompson, 255–56; and Bradley, 286; and Finch, 310, 319, 324–25; higher, and Boseman, 345; and Ruby, 364–66, 384; and black leaders, 401
Elliott, Robert Brown, xvii, 82, 229, 339, 346, 347, 351, 352, 354, 355, 397
Ellisville Eagle, 49
Ellsworth, Hales, 261, 264, 275
Ellyson, Mayor James T., 213
Enforcement Acts of 1870–71, 10
Ensor, Dr. J. F., 344
Enterprise Railroad Company, 346–47, 354
Eppes, Henry, 140
Escoffié, François, 167
Esnard, J. B., 160, 163

Estève family, 160
Ex parte Milligan decision, 286

Factionalism: and Republican party, 399
The Facts of Reconstruction, 54–55
Farrar, Joseph E., 200, 201, 204
Feriter, John, 242, 341
Fifth International Exposition, Vienna, 82
Finch, Laura Wright, 309, 326
Finch, Minnie Vason, 326
Finch, William, 268, 309–34; early life, 309–10; and education, 310, 319, 324–25; and politics, 310, 314–24; in Atlanta, 312–30; and Barry, 317–18; on city council, 317–22; and whites, 321, 329; and church activities, 325–26, 327; and prohibition, 326
Finch, William (son), 326
Finley, Jesse J., 73, 74
Finley, Peyton, 85, 261, 275
First Colored Baptist Church, Montgomery, 250, 251, 252, 269
Fishel, Leslie H., 403–4
Fitzhugh, Robert, 44
Fitzpatrick, John, 89
Flanagan, James W., 371
Fleming, Walter L., xiii, xiv
Fleury, Alphonse, Jr., 165
Florey, H. T., 7
Florida: and Walls, 59–78; politics in, 62-70
Forrester, Richard G., 196, 201, 202, 211
Foster, James, 85
Fouché, Louis, 165
Franklin, John Hope, xvii
Freedmen: in Mississippi, 40–42; and collective political action, 225–26
Freedmen's Bureau, 40
Freedmen's Saving and Trust Company, 258, 293
Freedmen's Savings Bank, 21–22
Friends of Universal Suffrage, 155
Frost, Florian Henry, 233
Frost, Lydia, 233
Fuller, Jacob, 327

Gaines, Matthew, 381
Gaines, Wesley J., 325, 327
Gair, John, 146
Galveston News, 378, 385
Galveston Standard, 386
Gantt, Hastings, 233
Garfield, James A., 29
Garner, James W., xiii, 54–55

Garner, Henry H., 336
Garrison, William Lloyd, 223
Gary, Martin W., 226
Gass, Theodore, 70
Gasser, Oswald, 206
Genovese, Eugene, 224
Georgia: and Bradley, 281–308; land issue in, 285–90
Georgia Equal Rights and Education Association, 282, 293
Gerber, David, 404
Gibbs, Jonathan, xvii, 62; on Walls, 68
Gibbs, Mifflin, 91
Glasscock, Mayor Thomas, 253, 254
Glaudin family, 160
Gleaves, Richard, 351
Gleed, Robert, 9
Gordon, John B., 22
Graham, George, 312, 314, 316
Grant, Ulysses, 29, 80, 81, 191, 265, 299; and Mississippi, 13–14; and Walls, 59; and Boseman, 351; and Texas politics, 374–75, 376, 378; and Ruby, 386, 387
Gray, William H., 139
Greeley, Horace, 81
Greenville *Weekly Times*, 12
Gregory, Ovid, 140
Grey, William H., 130, 137, 139
Griffin, Captain William H., 384
Griffin, General Charles, 366, 367
Griffin, Joshua R., 201, 204
Griffin, Valentine, 201
Griswold, John A., 338, 339, 354
Grossman, Lawrence, xviii
Grosz, Alice, xvi
Grubb, S. W., 316–17
Guichard, Leopold, 139
Guillemin, François, 162

Haitian migration project, 364
Hale, James, 263, 276
Hale, M. H., 298
Halifax County, N.C., 102; county commissioners, 123–24
Hall, Hampton, 327
Hamilton, Andrew J., 366, 371, 376
Hamilton, Charles, 67, 68
Hamilton, Jack, 375, 377, 378
Hamilton, J. G. De Roulhac, xii, xiv
Hamilton, Morgan, 375, 376, 381, 383
Hamilton, Thomas, 240
Hammond, Mayor Dennis F., 315, 316
Hampton, Wade, 243, 353

Haralson, Jere, 261
Haralson, Jeremiah, 86
Hardy, Stewart, 124
Hare, Maud Cuney, xiv
Harmon, Henry, 66, 68, 70, 73, 74
Harris, Charles O., 267, 279
Harris, C. W., 207
Harris, James H., 114, 129, 268
Harris, John R., 47
Harrison, Benjamin, 31, 51, 215
Harrison, William H., 297
Hart, Ossian B., 63, 66
Harvill, John, 123
Hayes, James H., 202, 204, 205, 217
Hayes, Rutherford B., 29, 243, 353; and Bruce, 17–18; and Rapier, 90
Hayne, Henry E., 342
Hayne, James N., 351
Hays, Charles, 80
Health care: and Boseman, 344
Henderson, James, 242
Henderson, John, 91
Henry, Richard J., 329, 334
Herbert, Hilary A., xii, xiii
Hewett, T., 47
Higgins, John M., 197
Higham, John, 404–5
Hill, James, 9; and Bruce, 19; and Lynch, 43
Holcombe, Henry C., 314
Holt, Thomas, 26, 139, 395
Homestead Act, 287
Honey, George W., 368
Hood, James W., 139
Houston, David G., xv
Houston, R. W., 45
Houston, Ulysses L., 297, 298
Houzeau, Jean-Charles, 172–73
Howard, General O. O., 285, 287, 288
Howard, John H., 110, 123, 124
Hubbs, Sheriff Orlando, 115, 116–17, 118
Hughes, Judge Robert M., 215
Human rights: and Walls, 70–71
Humphrey, Lotte W., 116–17
Hunsacker, Oscar F., 367, 368
Huntsville Gazette, 269
Hurley, Timothy, 347
Hyman, John A., 106, 114, 137

"The Importance of Medical Statistics," 338
Indians: and Bruce, 21
Industrial Cotton Centennial Exposition, 28

Ingraham, James H., 157, 164
Ireland, Samuel J., 4

Jackson, Andrew, 168
Jackson, Benjamin, 201
Jackson, Giles B., 196, 217
Jackson, Joseph, 192
Jackson, Joseph, Jr., 192
Jackson, Rev. B. F., 341
Jacksonville *Florida Union*, 72, 73, 74
Jackson Ward, Richmond, Va., 192–94
Jacobs, Bernard, 310
Jacobs, Henry, 232–33
Jasper, John, 196, 207
Jenkins, Horatio, 64, 66
Jennings, William, 318
Jervay, William R., 233
Johnson, Andrew, 285, 286, 287, 288, 349, 366
Johnson, James Weldon, 404
Johnson, Landon, 194
Johnston, William E., 139
Joiner, W. Nelson, 140
Jones, Robert E., 202
Jones, William J., Jr., 238
Joubert, Blanc F., 157, 164
Jourdain, Jean B., 162, 168
Journal of Negro History, xiv

Kansas Exodus, 388, 403; and Bruce, 23–24, 26; and Bradley, 300
Keffer, John, 80, 262
Keils, Elias M., 84
Kellogg, William Pitt, 16
Keppard, John, 161
King, Martin Luther, Jr., 252, 269
King, William, 79
Kitchin, William H., 114, 115
Kitchin, William W., 101, 106–7, 121
Klingman, Peter D., 393, 397
Knox, Robert, 85, 86
Ku Klux Klan: in Florida, 69; in Alabama, 81; and Rapier, 89; and delegates to constitutional conventions, 146

Labor legislation: in South Carolina, 242
Labor Union of Colored Men, Galveston, 380, 383
Lacroix, François, 166, 167
Lafon, Thomy, 166
Lamar, L. Q. C., 20–21, 30, 49
Land issue: and Thompson, 250; and Bradley, 285–90, 300–301; and Ruby, 370; and black leaders, 403

Langston, John Mercer, 18, 75, 204, 216
Lanusse, Armand, 160, 168
Larkin, Sheriff Lawrence F., 109, 114, 121, 123
Larrieu, L. D., 167
Lawrence, George, 384
Layne, Henry, 200
Lee, General Fitzhugh, 75
Lee, George, 242
Lee, Samuel J., 229
Levere, George W., 161
Lewis, Elsie, 62
Lewis, James, 165
Leyrumous, William F., 338
Liberia: and Bruce, 24–26; and Bradley, 300
Lincoln, Abraham, 286
Lindsay, Lewis, 129, 191, 194
Lodge, Henry Cabot, 50
Long, L. M., 112
Longley, Alfred, 373
Louisiana officeholders, 1868, 159
The Loyal Georgian, 312
Lumpkin, Chief Justice Joseph, 309, 310
Lynch, Cora Williamson, 53
Lynch, Ella Somerville, 52
Lynch, James, 3, 9
Lynch, John R., xiii, xiv, 15, 27, 39–58; 82; and Bruce, 9, 19, 32; and Hayes, 18; early life, 39–40; in Mississippi House, 42–43, 44–45; in U.S. House, 43–44, 45–47; and civil rights, 45–46; and 1875 election, 46–47; and 1876 election, and 1880 election, 47–48; and 1882 election, 49; wealth of, 51–52; later life, 51–58; in army, 52; on blacks in Congress, 53; in Chicago, 53–54; and labor organizations, 54; and Reconstruction history, 54–55

Macarty, Drauzin, 167
Macarty, V. E., 168
McCary, William, 44
McCormick, A. P., 377
McDuffie, Judge John, 90
McHenry, Jackson, 312, 314, 315, 328, 329
McKee, George C., 11
McKee, James A., 369
Mackey, A. G., 349, 350
Mackey, E. W. M., 350
McKinlay, William J., 232, 348
McKinley, President William, 31, 32, 52
McKinstry, Alexander, 258
McLendon, Nicholas L., 318, 319

Mahier, Theophile, 139
Mahone, William, 202, 204, 205, 207, 216
Maine, Henry, 233
Manley, Ralza M., 203, 204
Mansion, Lucien, 168
Martin, J. Sella, 161
Martin, Théodule, 168
Martinet, Louis,162
Mayo, Robert, 73
Meacham, Robert, 68, 140
Meade, George Gordon, 64, 65
Meadows, William R., 146
Mechanics' and Laborers' Union, 314
Medical School of Maine, 336
Ménard, J. Willis, 74, 161, 168
Methodist Advocate, 315
Mickey, Edward, 347
Middleton, Abram, 139
Migration: and Bruce, 22–26; and
    Rapier, 90–91; and O'Hara, 119–20;
    and Bradley, 300; and Ruby, 388; and
    black leaders, 403
Military service: of black politicians in
    New Orleans, 168–69
Missionary Record, 290
Mississippi: and Bruce, 3–38;
    Republicans in, 10; state politics,
    1873, 10; 1875 election, 13–14, 16–17;
    and Lynch, 39–58; freedmen in, 40–42
Mississippi River Improvement
    Association, 20–21
Mitchell, John P., Jr., 195, 196, 202–8,
    211, 213, 216, 217
Montgomery, Alabama, 249–80; Swayne
    School, 251
Montgomery Daily Advertiser, 84, 262,
    263, 265, 267
Montgomery *Daily Ledger*, 84
Montgomery *Daily Register*, 84
Montgomery *Republican Sentinel*, 80, 89
Montieu, Joseph, 158
Moore, Henry J., 201, 216
Moore, William D., 329
Morgan, Charles, 327
Morris, John, 236, 237
Morton, Oliver P., 14, 16–17
Mosebach, F. C., 384
Moses, Franklin, Jr., 237, 351
Mulattoes: as delegates to state
    constitutional conventions, 137; in
    New Orleans politics, 162–64; in
    South Carolina, 238
Murrell, William, 139

Nance, Lee A., 146

Nash, Beverly, 347
Nash, William B., 140, 233, 238–39
The Nation, 30
National Colored Labor Convention, 226
National Conference of Colored Men:
    and Lynch, 53
National Equal Rights League, 70–71,
    155
National Labor Convention, 314
National Negro Civil Rights Convention,
    1873; and Rapier, 82
National Negro Convention, 336; and
    Thompson, 250
National Negro Labor Union
    Convention: and Rapier, 79
National Republican Association,
    Galveston, 367
Negro. *See* Black
Negro History Bulletin, xvi
The Negro in Congress 1870–1901, xiii
Nelson, Richard, 380
Nelson, William, 139
Newbernian, 104
Newcomb, James P., 382, 383, 384
New National Era, 80, 84
New Orleans: origins of black leadership
    in, 155–89; antebellum legal status of
    Negro politicians in, during
    Reconstruction, 156; characteristics
    of Negro politicians in, 156–69; free
    colored population in, 157–58;
    1860–61 residence of Negro
    politicians in, during Reconstruction,
    158; birthplace of Negro politicians
    in, during Reconstruction, 160;
    mulattoes in, 162–64; phenotype of
    Negro politicians in, during
    Reconstruction, 163; date of birth of
    Negro politicians in, during
    Reconstruction, 164; 1860–61
    occupation of Negro politicians in,
    during Reconstruction, 165; 1860–61
    wealth of Negro politicians in, during
    Reconstruction, 166; black politicians
    as slaveowners, 167; Ruby in, 388
New Orleans Observer, 388
New Orleans *Picayune*, 156, 157
New Orleans *Times*, 162
New Orleans *Tribune*, 171–72
News and Courier, 229, 352, 353
New York *Times*, 15; on Bruce, 32; on
    Lynch, 55
New York *Tribune*, 22, 129
Niblack, Silas, 69, 70
Noble, Chaplain F. K., 225, 241

417

Noble, Jordan B., 161, 165, 168
North Carolina: and O'Hara, 101–25; second congressional district population, 1880, 103; politics in, 105–18; 1878 election, 114–15; 1882 election, 116–18; 1886 election, 118
Number of Blacks Appointed to Twenty-Five Standing Committees . . . of the Richmond City Council, 209

Oates, Joseph E., 140
Oates, William C., 81
Occupations: of black delegates to constitutional conventions, 139–40; of Negro politicians in New Orleans, 165; of black leaders in South Carolina, 230, 232
O'Hara, James Edward, 101–25; early life, 102; character, 103–4; political career, 104–18; as county commissioner, 106–14; and 1878 election, 114–15; and 1882 election, 116–18; and 1886 election, 118; and race relations, 118–19; and civil rights, 119; and education, 119; and migration, 119–20; achievements of, 120–21
Oliver, John, 191, 194, 200, 211, 213
Orr, James L., 351
Osborn, Thomas, 63, 66, 68, 70

Page, Henry, 196
Page, Mordecai T., 206
Parsons, Lewis, 80, 96
Paternalism, 224
Patten, Nathan, 378, 384
Patterson, Senator John J., 351, 352
Paul, Robert A., 205
Pearce, Charles, 62, 68, 139
Pease, Elisha M., 366, 367, 372, 373, 375, 376
Peck, Rev. Francis J., 324, 325
Pelham, Charles, 89–90
Perce, L. W., 43, 44
Phylon, xvi
Pickens, Francis, 281
Pike, James S., xii, xiii
Piles, J. W.: on Lynch, 44
Pinchback, Pickney B. S., 137, 161, 162, 163, 165, 168, 397; Grosz study of, xvi; seating of, and Bruce, 14–15, 16; and Ruby, 388
Pine and Palm, 364

Pleasant, L. M., 298
Pledger, William A., 328, 398, 402
Plumly, B. Rush, 367, 368, 377
Political: experience and black delegates to state constitutional conventions, 144–45; experience of black legislators in South Carolina, 234; power and black leaders, 402–3
Politics of limited options, 404
Porter, James, 297
Powers, Governor Ridgley C., 10
Prescott, Aaron, 113
Press: and constitutional conventions, 129–30
The Prostrate State . . ., xii
Pullum, John, Sr., 161
Purman, William, 70

Quantrill, William C., 4
Questy, Joanni, 168

"The Race Problem," 28
Race relations: and O'Hara, 118–19
Racial discrimination: and Rapier, 92–94; and Thompson, 258–60; and Boseman, 343
Racism: and Republican party in South Carolina, 237–38
Railroads: and Ruby, 381
Rainey, Joseph, 82, 140, 238; and Enterprise Railroad Company, 346
Raleigh Signal, 121
Ramsdell, Charles William, xii
Randolph, Benjamin F., 139, 146, 341–42
Randolph, Dr. P. B., 161–62
Randolph, Edwin A., 201, 202
Rankin, John, 206
Ransier, Alonzo J., 82, 346
Rapier, James T., xxi, 79–99, 137, 139, 393; and Hayes, 18; early life, 79; as assessor of internal revenue, 79–80; and politics, 79–88; 1872 campaign, 80–81; and homesteads for black farmers, 81; and education, 82; and civil rights, 82–84, 85; in U.S. House, 82–84; business interests of, 88–89; and KKK, 89; and aid to other blacks, 89–90; as collector of internal revenue, 89–90; and migration, 90–91; and racial discrimination, 92–94; despair and alienation of, 94–95; and Thompson, 261, 263, 269
Rapier, John H., Sr., 88
Rapier, John H., Jr., 88

Rapier, Richard, 88
Rapp, Eugéne, 165
Raum, Green B., 90
Raynal, Joseph A., 157
Raynal family, 160
Reconstruction: negative image of,
    xi–xvi; Dunningite view of, xii–xiv;
    Rehabilitation School, xiv–xvi, 393;
    and revisionism period, xv–xviii; in
    South Carolina, and Simkins and
    Woody, xvi; and biographies,
    xvii–xviii; history, and Lynch, 54–55;
    and Dunning, 393
Reconstruction in Mississippi, 55
"The Reconstructionists and Their
    Measures," xv
Redeemers, 14
Redpath, James, 364
Reed, Governor Harrison, 66, 68, 70
The Reformer, 383
Rehabilitation School, xiv–xvi, 393
Reid, Whitelaw, 172
Reminiscences of an Active Life (Lynch),
    47, 48, 55
Republic (New Orleans), 388
Republican, 164
Republican Banner, 264
Republican party: in Mississippi, 10,
    13–15; national convention, 1884, and
    Lynch, 50–51; in Florida, 63; in
    Alabama, 80, 85–86; and economic
    policy, 142–43; and racial equality,
    143; in New Orleans, 155; and
    Jackson Ward, Richmond, 194; and
    blacks in South Carolina, 224–29; in
    South Carolina, 234–38; in
    Montgomery, 249, 260–61; in
    Georgia, 283, 297; and Boseman, 346;
    in Charleston, 349, 352; in Texas,
    368–69, 376; and black leaders, 397;
    and factionalism, 399
*Republican Sentinel and Hayneville
    Times*, 89
Revels, Hiram Rhoades, 3, 9, 12, 20
Revisionist School, xv–xviii; and black
    delegates to constitutional
    conventions, 130
Rey, H. Louis, 168
Reynolds, John S., xiv
Reynolds, Joseph J., 376, 378
Rhodes, Jack Ford, xii, xiii
Rice, J. W. 242–43
Rice, Samuel, 80, 85, 86, 92, 96
Rice, Stuart, 234

Rice index, 234–35
Richards, Daniel, 63, 64
Richardson, Joe M., xvii; on Walls, 67,
    71–72
Richmond, Virginia: black councilmen,
    1871–96, 191–222; Jackson Ward,
    192–94; characteristics of black
    councilmen, 196–202; white
    councilmen, 197; personal
    characteristics of black councilmen,
    1871–98, 198–99; committee
    appointments of black city councilors,
    208–10; powers of city council,
    210–11; achievements of black city
    councilmen, 211–14; decline in
    number of blacks in, 214–17
Richmond *Planet*, 201, 203, 206, 210, 213
Rillieux, Édmond, 165, 167
Robb, T. P., 297; and Bradley, 298–99
Robinson, Jordan A., 200
Robinson, Sandy W., 196, 201
Rodriguez, Lazard, 160
Rogers, Stephen Walter, 157, 167
Rogers, W. K., 353
Roger's Compositions, 167
Roll, Jordan, Roll, 224
Roosevelt, Theodore, 50
Roudanez, Jean Baptiste, 170, 171
Roudanez, Louis Charles, 168
Roudanez family, 160
Royal, Benjamin F., 139
Ruby, Ebenezer, 363
Ruby, George Thompson, 137, 140,
    363–92; early life, 363–64; and
    education, 364–66; and politics,
    366–87; and land issue, 370; in state
    Senate, 379; and black workers,
    379–80; and whites, 380, 382; and
    railroads, 381; and public school
    system, 384; and migration, 388; in
    New Orleans, 388
Ruby, Jemima, 363
Rucker, Henry A., 329, 334
Russell, Otis H., 204
Rutledge, Joe, 317

Sabin, Judge Chauncey, B., 387
Saffold, John, 86
Saffold, Milton, 92
Sasportas, Joseph, 233
Sasportas, Thaddeus K, 233
Saulay family, 160
Saunders, Sancho, 140
Saunders, William, 63, 64, 67, 73, 74

Savannah Tribune, 298
Sawyer, Frederick, 349, 351
Saxton, General Rufus, 285
Sayre, P. T., 260
Schweninger, Loren, 393
Scott, Ben, 196
Scott, Charles H., 262
Scott, James A., 267
Scott, John R., 74
Scott, Robert K., 237, 288, 289, 343, 345
Seal, Colonel Roderick, 46
Segregation: and black delegates to
  constitutional conventions, 143–44
Senate Committee on River
  Improvements, 20–21
Seymour, General Truman, 62
Shelley, Charles, 88
Shepley, George F., 170
Sherman, General William T., 151,
  284–85; Special Field Order No. 15,
  285
Sherman, John, 29, 90, 388
Shofner, Jerrell, 65
"Should Colored Men Join Labor
  Organizations?" 54
Sibley, Caleb C., 288–89
Simkins, Francis Butler, xvi, 223–24, 226
Simmons, Dr. Charles E., 338
Simmons, Furnifold, 118
Simms, James M., 297, 298
Simpson, C. A., 50
Simpson, Peter, 97
Skin color: and division among blacks,
  348
Slaves, fugitive: return to South, 281
Smalls, Robert, xvii, 18, 139, 226, 233,
  347, 355; and Boseman, 342, 343
Smith, Dr. Robert K., 368, 373–74
Smith, Governor William H., 80, 86, 260
Smith, Samuel Denny, xiv
Snaer, Louis, 168
Snyder, D. D., 314, 316–17
Social status: of black legislators in South
  Carolina, 238–41
Société des Secours Mutuels des Artisans,
  166
Solomon, S. S., 347
Soulié, Bernard, 165, 166, 167
South Carolina: and black leaders, xv;
  black state legislators in, 223–46;
  Republican legislators, 1868, 227;
  membership of House of
  Representatives and Senate, 1868–76,
  228; General Assembly and blacks,
229; characteristics of black leaders
  in, 230–34; biographical summary of
  Negro legislators, 1868–76, 231;
  primary postwar occupations of
  Negro legislators, 1868–76, 232;
  education of black legislators in, 233;
  social status of black legislators in,
  238–41; black legislators and
  education, 241; and labor legislation,
  242; and Boseman, 339–62
South Carolina Phosphate and
  Phosphatic River Mining Company,
  347, 354
Southern States Negro Emigration
  Convention, 91
Speed, General James, 286
Spencer, Senator George, 80, 90, 261,
  264, 268
Stampp, Kenneth, xvii
Stanton, Edwin M., 286
Staples, Thomas S., xiii
State constitutional conventions,
  1867–69: black delegates to, 129–53;
  delegate breakdown, 132–36;
  characteristics of black delegates,
  137–40; issues at, 141–44
State Equal Rights Association: and
  Thompson, 264
State Register, 388
Steele, Charles, 85
Stevenson, Louis W., 382, 383, 384
Stewart, Representative, 259
Still, William, 53
Stringer, Thomas W., 3, 9, 139
Strobach, Paul, 85, 261, 262, 264, 268
Suffrage: and New Orleans black leaders,
  170–73
Sumner, Charles, 171; civil rights bill,
  70–71; civil rights bill and Rapier, 85
Sutton, Benjamin, 106
Swails, Stephen A., 289, 342

Talbert, T. N., 237–38
Tallahassee *Sentinel*, 73
Tate, James, 312, 314, 323–24, 327
Taylor, Alrutheus Ambush, xv
Taylor, William H., 249
Teamoh, George, 131, 139
Tebault, Dr. C. H., 156
Tennessee Negro Suffrage Convention,
  79
Terrell, Robert H., 52
Texas: Ruby in, 364–87
Thomas, Henry K., 88

Thomas, James P., 88
Thomas, King Solomon, 297
Thomas, William H., 380
Thomas, William M., 234
Thompson, Augustus R., 139
Thompson, Benjamin A., 139
Thompson, Binah Yancey, 249, 266
Thompson, Charlotte, 266
Thompson, Frederick, 252
Thompson, Holland, 249–80; early life,
    249; and Baptist church, 250, 252–53,
    257, 267; and civil rights, 250; and
    land for freedmen, 250; political
    career of, 250–67; and city council,
    253–56; concern for blacks, 254–55;
    and blacks on police force, 255; and
    education, 255–56; in state House of
    Representatives, 257–60; and racial
    discrimination, 258–60; and Rapier,
    261, 263, 269; personal life of, 266–67
Thompson, Holland, Jr., 266
Thompson, Mildred C., xii
Thornton, Alfred L., 200, 202, 210
Throckmorton, James W., 367, 372
Tilghman, Colonel Benjamin, 60-62
Tillson, General Davis, 286–87, 288
Tomlinson, Reuben, 242, 344
Toomer, Jean, 163
Toomer, L. B., 298
Tourgée, Albion, 142
Tracy, James G., 375, 376, 384
The Tragic Era, xiii, 55
Treadwell, James, 329, 334
Trelease, Allen, 145
Trévigné, Paul, 166, 170
Trott, Stanley G., 352
Trotter, James M., 289
Troy, N.Y.: and Boseman, 335–36
Turner, Benjamin, 80
Turner, Henry M., 130, 137, 402
Turner, J. Milton, 398
Tuskegee Institute: and Bruce, 28

L'Union, 170
Union League, 40; and Thompson, 252;
    and Bradley, 293; and Ruby, 366,
    368, 379
Union Radical Association, 155
U.S. House of Representatives: and
    Lynch, 43–44, 45–47; Rapier in, 82–84
U.S. Senate: and Bruce, 11–22
University of South Carolina, 345

Valfroit, P. Francis, 140

Vance, Zebulon, 102
Vandervall, Nelson, 201, 202, 211
Van Eaton, Judge Henry S., 49
Vicksburg: Times, 12; violence in, 12, 13
Villére, Norbert, 164
Violence: and delegates to constitutional
    conventions, 146
Viriginia Constitutional Convention,
    1867–68, 191
Virginia Star, 212, 214
Voting rights: and black delegates to
    constitutional conventions, 141–42

Waddill, Judge Edmund, 205, 207, 215
Wade, Senator Benjamin, 288
Walker, Acton, 73–74
Walker, Governor David, 73
Wallace, George, 297
Wallace, John, 62
Walls, Ella Ferguson, 62
Walls, Josiah T., xvii, 59–78, 82, 139,
    393; early life, 59–62; and Civil War,
    60–62; political career, 62–75; and
    radicals, 64; and status of blacks, 67;
    wealth of, 68; and 1870 election,
    67–69; and 1872 election, 69–70; and
    human rights, 70–71; in Congress,
    70–72; and education, 71; criticism of,
    73–74; political decline of, 73–75
Walton Act, 1894, 216
Warner, Senator Willard, 80, 92, 93, 260
Warren, H. W., 42
Warren, Mortimer, A., 168
Warrenton Gazette, 104
Washington, Booker T., 28, 31, 33, 217,
    404
Washington Bee, 32
Washington New National Era, 72
Washington Post, 31, 32
Wealth: of black politicians in New
    Orleans, 166; of black councilmen in
    Richmond, 200–201; of black leaders
    in South Carolina, 232–33; and
    Thompson, 250; of Boseman, 348
Weldon News, 117
Wells, C. Wiley, 11
Westberry, John, 240
Wharton, Vernon Lane, xvi–xvii
Wheelock, Edwin M., 364–66, 375, 376
Whipper, William J., 229, 237, 341, 346,
    347, 350
Whitaker, Spier, 110, 111, 112, 113, 114
White, Alexander, 80, 96
White, George H., 102

White, James T., 139
White, Richard W., 281, 297, 298
White, Royal, 213
White Leaguers, 12, 14
Whites: and freedmen, 40–42; and Finch, 321, 329; and Boseman, 354; and Ruby, 380, 382; and black leaders, 396, 398
Why the Solid South? xii
Wilder, Charles M., 140
Wiley, Colonel A. P., 368
Williams, Emperor, 161, 165
Williams, George H., 86
Williams, Jeremiah N., 86
Williams, Latty, 254, 261, 264, 265
Williams, P. M., 168
Williamson, Joel, xvii
Wilson, David, 140
Wilson, Peter M., 102

Wilson, Woodrow, xii
Wimbush, C. C., 328–29
Windom, Senator William, 91
Wise, George D., 215
Wise, Governor Henry A., 130
Wood, Robert H., 44
Woodward, C. Vann, 197
Woody, Robert H., xvi, 223–24, 226
Wooster, Ralph A., 138
Work, Monroe, xiv
Wright, Jonathan J., xvi, 229, 340, 342, 350
Wright, Richard R., 53
Wynne, Thomas Hicks, 210

Yancey, William Lowndes, 249
Young, Edward, 73
Young, Robert E., 121
Young, Winfield F., 124

BOOKS IN THE SERIES:

Before the Ghetto: Black Detroit in the Nineteenth Century   *David M. Katzman*

Black Business in the New South: A Social History of the North Carolina Mutual Life Insurance Company   *Walter B. Weare*

The Search for a Black Nationality: Black Colonization and Emigration, 1787–1863   *Floyd J. Miller*

Black Americans and the White Man's Burden, 1898–1903   *Willard B. Gatewood, Jr.*

Slavery and the Numbers Game: A Critique of *Time on the Cross*   *Herbert G. Gutman*

A Ghetto Takes Shape: Black Cleveland, 1870–1930   *Kenneth L. Kusmer*

Freedmen, Philanthropy, and Fraud: A History of the Freedman's Savings Bank   *Carl R. Osthaus*

The Democratic Party and the Negro: Northern and National Politics, 1868–92   *Lawrence Grossman*

Black Ohio and the Color Line, 1860–1915   *David A. Gerber*

Along the Color Line: Explorations in the Black Experience   *August Meier and Elliott Rudwick*

Black over White: Negro Political Leadership in South Carolina during Reconstruction   *Thomas Holt*

Keeping the Faith: A. Philip Randolph, Milton P. Webster, and the Brotherhood of Sleeping Car Porters, 1925–37   *William H. Harris*

Abolitionism: The Brazilian Antislavery Struggle   *Joaquim Nabuco, translated and edited by Robert Conrad*

Black Georgia in the Progressive Era, 1900–1920   *John Dittmer*

Medicine and Slavery: Health Care of Blacks in Antebellum Virginia   *Todd L. Savitt*

Alley Life in Washington: Family, Community, Religion, and Folklife in the City, 1850–1970   *James Borchert*

Human Cargoes: The British Slave Trade to Spanish America, 1700–1739   *Colin A. Palmer*

Southern Black Leaders of the Reconstruction Era   *Edited by Howard N. Rabinowitz*

Black Leaders of the Twentieth Century   *Edited by John Hope Franklin and August Meier*

REPRINT EDITIONS

King: A Biography   *David Levering Lewis*   Second edition

The Death and Life of Malcolm X   *Peter Goldman*   Second edition

Race Relations in the Urban South, 1865–1890   *Howard N. Rabinowitz, with a foreword by C. Vann Woodward*

Race Riot at East St. Louis, July 2, 1971   *Elliott Rudwick*

W. E. B. Du Bois: A Study in Minority Group Leadership   *Elliott Rudwick*

DATE DUE
